THE BLOOMSBURY HANDBOOK OF JAPANESE RELIGIONS

Also Available from Bloomsbury

The Bloomsbury Handbook of the Cultural and Cognitive Aesthetics of Religion, edited by Anne Koch and Katharina Wilkens

The Bloomsbury Handbook of Religion and Nature, edited by Laura Hobgood and Whitney Bauman

The Bloomsbury Handbook of Religion and Popular Music, edited by Christopher Partridge and Marcus Moberg

The Bloomsbury Handbook to Studying Christians, edited by George D. Chryssides and Stephen E. Gregg

THE BLOOMSBURY HANDBOOK OF JAPANESE RELIGIONS

Edited by

Erica Baffelli, Andrea Castiglioni, and Fabio Rambelli

BLOOMSBURY ACADEMIC
LONDON • NEW YORK • OXFORD • NEW DELHI • SYDNEY

BLOOMSBURY ACADEMIC
Bloomsbury Publishing Plc
50 Bedford Square, London, WC1B 3DP, UK
1385 Broadway, New York, NY 10018, USA
29 Earlsfort Terrace, Dublin 2, Ireland

BLOOMSBURY, BLOOMSBURY ACADEMIC and the Diana logo are trademarks of
Bloomsbury Publishing Plc

First published in Great Britain 2021
Paperback edition published 2023

Copyright © Erica Baffelli, Andrea Castiglioni, Fabio Rambelli, and contributors, 2021

Erica Baffelli, Andrea Castiglioni, and Fabio Rambelli have asserted their right under the
Copyright, Designs and Patents Act, 1988, to be identified as Editor of this work.

For legal purposes the Acknowledgments on p. ix constitute an extension
of this copyright page.

Cover image © DigiPub/Getty Images

All rights reserved. No part of this publication may be reproduced or transmitted
in any form or by any means, electronic or mechanical, including photocopying,
recording, or any information storage or retrieval system, without prior permission
in writing from the publishers.

Bloomsbury Publishing Plc does not have any control over, or responsibility for, any
third-party websites referred to or in this book. All internet addresses given in this
book were correct at the time of going to press. The author and publisher regret any
inconvenience caused if addresses have changed or sites have ceased to exist, but can
accept no responsibility for any such changes.

A catalogue record for this book is available from the British Library.

Library of Congress Cataloging-in-Publication Data
Names: Baffelli, Erica, 1976– editor. | Rambelli, Fabio, editor. | Castiglio, Andrea, editor.
Title: The Bloomsbury handbook of Japanese religions /
edited by Erica Baffelli and Fabio Rambelli with Andrea Castiglio.
Description: London ; New York : Bloomsbury Academic, 2021. |
Includes bibliographical references and index.
Identifiers: LCCN 2020052961 (print) | LCCN 2020052962 (ebook) |
ISBN 9781350043732 (hardback) | ISBN 9781350043749 (ebook) |
ISBN 9781350043756 (pdf)
Subjects: LCSH: Japan–Religion. | Japan–Religious life and customs.
Classification: LCC BL2202.3 .B59 2021 (print) | LCC BL2202.3 (ebook) |
DDC 200.952–dc23
LC record available at https://lccn.loc.gov/2020052961
LC ebook record available at https://lccn.loc.gov/2020052962

ISBN: HB: 978-1-3500-4373-2
PB: 978-1-3502-2747-7
ePDF: 978-1-3500-4375-6
eBook: 978-1-3500-4374-9

Series: Bloomsbury Handbooks

Typeset by Newgen KnowledgeWorks Pvt. Ltd., Chennai, India

To find out more about our authors and books visit www.bloomsbury.com
and sign up for our newsletters

CONTENTS

List of Illustrations — viii
Acknowledgments — ix
Notes for the Reader — x

1 Introduction — 1
  Erica Baffelli, Andrea Castiglioni, and Fabio Rambelli

2 Chaplaincy and Spiritual Care — 13
  Kasai Kenta

3 Cultural Heritage — 19
  Lindsey E. DeWitt

4 Disasters — 27
  Levi McLaughlin

5 Economy and Spirituality — 35
  Ioannis Gaitanidis

6 Economy of Buddhism — 43
  Jørn Borup

  Case Study: Buddhist Temples of the Future — 51
  Paulina K. Kolata

7 Empire and Colonialism — 55
  Emily Anderson

  Case Study: Aesthetics of Buddhist Modernism — 61
  Paride Stortini

8 Environmentalism — 65
  Aike P. Rots

  Case Study: Grassroots Environmental Activities in Risshō Kōseikai — 73
  Aura di Febo

9 Folk Performing Arts — 77
  Suzuki Masataka

10 Food Offerings — 85
   Allan G. Grapard

11 Gender *Kawahashi Noriko*	93
12 Globalization *Richard K. Payne*	99
Case Study: Diaspora Buddhism *Jørn Borup*	107
13 Islam *Komura Akiko*	111
14 Law *Mark R. Mullins*	117
15 Materiality *Halle O'Neal*	129
16 Media and Technology *Kaitlyn Ugoretz and Erica Baffelli*	137
Case Study: World-Wide Shinto: The Globalization of "Japanese" Religion *Kaitlyn Ugoretz*	145
Case Study: Robots *Kimura Takeshi*	149
17 Medicine *Katja Triplett*	151
18 Minorities *Takahashi Norihito*	157
Case Study: *Daijō Islam* (Mahayāna Islam) *Komura Akiko*	165
19 "New Religions" *Kato Masato*	167
20 Pilgrimages and "Sacred" Geography *Ian Reader*	175
21 Politics *Ōmi Toshihiro*	185
Case Study: Religion, Socialism, and Secularization *James Mark Shields*	189
22 Premodern Traditions *Hayashi Makoto*	193

23 Sexuality *Or Porath*	201
24 Sound *Ōuchi Fumi*	209
Case Study: The *Matsuri* as Sonic Event *Andrea Giolai*	217
25 Space *Tatsuma Padoan*	221
26 Spiritualism and Occultism *Yoshinaga Shin'ichi*	229
27 Spirituality *Horie Norichika*	241
28 Tourism *Yamanaka Hiroshi*	251
29 Women *Emily B. Simpson*	257
Case Study: Mountain Worship and Women *Kobayashi Naoko*	267
BIBLIOGRAPHY	271
NOTES ON CONTRIBUTORS	319
INDEX	331

ILLUSTRATIONS

Figures

3.1.	World Heritage stone stele at Tōdaiji, Nara	20
9.1.	After performing ascetic practices on the mountain, a Shugendō practitioner (*yamabushi*) shows his powers making an apotropaic dance during the Daijō kagura. Tōhoku region, Iwate prefecture	83
9.2.	The Shirokami kagura dance for protecting life and human activities performed by hunters and slash-and-burn farmers in mountainous areas. Kyūshū region, Miyazaki prefecture	84
13.1.	Changes in the number of mosques and Islamic groups in Japan (1935–2018)	113
13.2.	Changes in the number of registered foreign nationals by states of residence	114
13.3.	The number of Malaysian and Indonesian visitors to Japan (2010–2018)	116

Tables

18.1.	Changes in populations of major foreign residents in Japan (1980–2015)	158
18.2.	Mahayāna Islam versus Hinayāna Islam by Abe Haruo	166

ACKNOWLEDGMENTS

Our first conversations about this book started in Summer 2015 in Erfurt, Germany, during the 36th IAHR World Congress. It has been a long journey and new collaborators joined us over the years. We would like to thank all the contributors for their help in shaping this *Handbook* and for their patience. At Bloomsbury we owe a debt to Lalle Pursglove for her early encouragement and for supporting this project over the years, and to Lucy Carroll and Lily McMahon who have worked with us through the development of this *Handbook*. We are grateful to Emily Simpson for the copyediting. All mistakes and shortcomings belong to the editors.

NOTES FOR THE READER

All Japanese names are in standard Japanese order of family name first, followed by given name.

Long vowels are indicated by macrons (ō, ū) except for words and names commonly used in English (e.g., Kyoto, Tokyo, Shinto).

CHAPTER 1

Introduction

Erica BAFFELLI, Andrea CASTIGLIONI, and Fabio RAMBELLI

This book is a collection of essays on critical terms and concepts for the study and understanding of Japanese religious history and practices. The project developed in silent conversation with existing handbooks and introductions to Japanese religions/religion in Japan, and with a critical awareness toward the field. In this introduction, we delineate the approach we used in selecting the entries in this *Bloomsbury Handbook of Japanese Religions* in order to explain how we think they will contribute to a broader and better understanding of religion in the Japanese context. The epilogue will further contextualize this project by placing the project in the context of the unusual situation in which it came to completion.

INTRODUCING JAPANESE RELIGIONS: APPROACHES AND PROBLEMATICS

This new *Handbook* joins an increasingly crowded field. Several books have been published in the past two decades, in Japanese and in English, which present overviews of religion in Japan and assess the state of the field (Reader and Tanabe 1998; Tanabe 1999; Kasahara 2001; Nakamaki 2003; Bowring 2005, 2017; Swanson and Chilson 2006; Ellwood 2008; Dolce 2011; Prohl and Nelson 2012; Ambros 2015; Ōtani, Kikuchi, and Nagaoka 2018). Most of these publications constitute attempts to overcome old-fashioned scholarship that was overly dependent upon sectarian histories, and they provide an excellent introduction to different religious traditions and key themes. For example, *Nanzan Guide to Japanese Religions* (Swanson and Chilson 2006) follows a standard structure, with a first part dedicated to various religious traditions (Shinto, Buddhism, Folk Religion, New Religions, and Japanese Christianity), a second section that provides a six-chapter historical overview (from the Jōmon to contemporary Japan), and a third one organized by broad thematic areas (ritual, literature, state and religion, pilgrimage, history of thought, and gender issues). Following the example of Japanese textbooks, it includes an extensive chronology at the end, and a section with information on resources for research (reference works and libraries, archives, and fieldwork). Another recent handbook, the Brill *Handbook of Contemporary Japanese Religions* (Prohl and Nelson 2012), discusses religious practices and changes in contemporary Japan by taking a thematic approach. The first section, *Orientations*, introduces the Japanese religious context and discusses issues related to data and definition of religion; the following sections discuss changes and transformations in Shinto and Buddhism, religious responses to social issues, and, finally, new practices related to spirituality and New Age.

In *Practically Religious: Worldly Benefits and the Common Religion of Japan* (1998) Ian Reader and George J. Tanabe rely on the concept of "this-worldly benefits" (*genze riyaku*) as a keyword with which to decode theories and practices in Japanese religions. This bold analytical strategy proves to be particularly successful for interpreting practical religious aspects, which have been traditionally neglected by most of the scholarship in English on Asian religions since its incipit in the nineteenth century.

Gregory Schopen criticized the fact that initially, European scholars tended to consider as "real" only those aspects of Buddhism that showed a textual linchpin (Schopen 1997). Unfortunately, the shadow of this predominance of the text within Buddhist studies partially affected the early phases of the scholarship on Japanese religions abroad as well as in Japan. For example, Kishimoto Hideo (1903–1964), one of the founders of the modern study of religion in Japan, together with Anesaki Mahasaru (1873–1949), was deeply influenced by this textual-based approach to the subject. During the 1970s, the academic field dedicated to Japanese religions was still characterized by a deep fracture between scholars who prioritized doctrinal studies (mostly Buddhologists) and those who focused on anthropological or sociological themes within religious discourses. The first group concentrated on translating and interpreting written sources with a focus on doctrinal and theoretical matters, while the second analyzed rituals, devotional practices, and patterns of behavior within specific religious contexts.

Another very successful text, *Religions of Japan in Practice*, edited by George Tanabe and included in the Princeton Readings in Religions series (1999), tries to overcome these disciplinary limitations by taking two key steps: (i) while still focusing on primary texts, it moves away from doctrinal sources and includes documents of various kind (histories, legends, ritual procedures, etc.), and (ii) it shifts attention from beliefs and ideas toward practices and institutions. In terms of general approach, Tanabe aims at presenting Japanese religions in their "complex diversity rather than as neatly ordered systems of thought" (1999: 3), also by emphasizing the different ways in which theory and practice affect each other (4). Still, the overwhelming emphasis lies on Buddhism, with other traditions barely represented: of the forty-five chapters, each based on the translation of a primary source, thirty-four belong to Buddhism, six to Shinto, one to Christianity, three to Confucianism, and one to folk religion. Furthermore, the entries on Buddhism represent standard sectarian divisions (Shingon, Tendai, Pure Land, Zen, etc.).

Tanabe's analytical focus on practices in Japanese religious traditions can also be detected in Barbara R. Ambros's handbook, *Women in Japanese Religions* (2015), which redirects stereotypical androcentric narratives about Japanese religions toward the numerous, and too often neglected, female protagonists. The relevance of women's agency, power, and authority within specific religious networks clearly emerges once the rhetoric of patriarchal systems is confronted and deactivated thanks to the performance of religious practices, which allow female actors to play active roles even within oppressive discourses.

In the introductory remarks of *Japanese Religions: The Critical Discourse on Japanese Religions* (2011), Lucia Dolce argues that in Japan, this extreme polarization and ultra-specialization in the methodological approaches toward Japanese religions still prevent the formation of an authentic dialogue between scholars and blocks the development of a positive hybridization between heterogeneous fields of scholarship. Considering the same issue, Robert Sharf points out that a possible cause for the split between theorists and socio-anthropologists is also due to a different emphasis on the construction of time. Theoretic and Buddhological sight is often retrospective and diachronic, with a tendency to devalue the present; on the contrary, socio-anthropologists emphasize the synchronic dimension of religious phenomena (Sharf 1995).

The combination of these antithetical methodologies has too often resulted in reciprocal exclusions among scholars whose respective expertise is activated or deactivated according to a preconceived framing of the religious themes based on their temporal, spatial, textual, or practical characteristics. In order to dismember these misleading academic and methodological dichotomies, the contributors of this *Handbook* favor transversal, multi-perspective, and inter-methodological approaches to embrace and exalt the hybrid and polyphonic nature of religion in Japan.

A recent handbook published in Japan, *Nihon shūkyōshi no kīwādo* (Ōtani, Kikuchi and Nagaoka 2018), is a valuable contribution for rethinking the nature and structure of the field as a whole. It comprises many entries divided into sections, including materiality (articulated into "icons, items, and topos"), practices, agents, governance (defined as the relations between authority and belief), and discourses (which reformulates the more traditional term "thought" [*shisō*]). Overall, the book covers well-known subjects and terms, and discusses their origin and limits; the general framework reflects current approaches in the field, in which doctrines (thought, intellectual history) are just one component of a more complex system involving objects and their uses by various agents within different fields of power.

The project of Ōtani, Kikuchi, and Nagaoka also underlines the necessity to decolonize recurrent terms such as "Japan/Japanese" and "religion/religions," the semantic fields of which have been strongly exposed to biased paradigms of modernity since the beginning of the twentieth century. For instance, Anesaki Masaharu's conceptualization of the word "religion" worked to emphasize the self-cultivation (*jinkakushugi*) of the individual in order to produce forms of national indoctrination and myths of a unique ethnic identity (Isomae 2014: 138–41).

DISCUSSING RELIGION IN JAPAN

The separation between traditions, histories, and themes, no matter how commonsensical, is always problematic, since it reproduces the old reifying attitude that sees religions as substances and themes as their attributes. Received historical periodizations (from the religiosity of the Jōmon people to contemporary "new" religions) are also questionable, if only because it obscures that fact that "new religions" are not entirely a modern phenomenon, as some were formed almost two centuries ago, prior to the Meiji era. It is also problematic to project back into the past present-day classifications such as Buddhism and Shinto—or even sectarian denominations such as Tendai, Shingon, or Jōdo Shinshū. Indeed, it is not clear how most people in the past saw religious affiliation in terms of their own identity—or, for that matter, if they considered religious affiliation at all. Monks, kami priests, and other religious specialists, whose social status (and personal training) depended directly upon their membership in certain lineages, may have understood such lineages and their sectarian affiliations differently than lay people. Even after the implementation of new and diffuse religious policies by the Tokugawa government, in which all Japanese were required to register at Buddhist temples, people became aware of their sect, but typically not of what it meant in terms of doctrines (and, to a certain extent, of practices as well). Again, it is questionable whether such forced affiliation determined a change in identity formation. Even today, Buddhist "sects" are normally not close-knit organizations and solid markers of social or individual identities but loose networks of temples, priests, lay associations, and patrons. The same can be said for "Shinto," and the category of "new religions" itself has also been questioned in recent work (Baffelli and Reader 2019).

Part of the difficulty in discussing Japanese religions as a field rather than a constellation of "sectarian" subsets is due to a number of underlying factors and implicit biases that have been reproduced over decades in different ways by both academia and the mass media. First, much of what is published in Japan and elsewhere about religion tends to be normative and prescriptive, rather than descriptive. This is the reason for the proliferation of Japanese books with titles such as "What do the Japanese believe?" and "What is the Japanese vision of the afterlife?" One could argue that, to the extent that the "Japanese" have to find out what their "religion" is in such books, what these books describe is not "Japanese religion" but, to a varying extent, something invented by the authors. Descriptive works, on the other hand, tend to explain their finding in terms of a more or less ahistorical set of Japanese values, thus producing a circular effect: the Japanese beliefs and practices today, they claim, are rooted in Japanese values from the past, which in turn conveniently reflect what contemporary authors want them to be from today's perspective.

A second underlying factor is the lack of a public discourse on religion in Japan; as such, there is no shared information and no common understanding about what religion is and what it does. Japanese school textbooks increasingly tend to emphasize "ethics" (*rinri*, that is, a rather commonsensical set of norms of standardized social behavior) and some sort of Japanese "spirit" or "mind" (*kokoro*), which are somewhat related to religious figures and traditions, but no sustained and systematic treatment of these traditions is ever provided to the youth. In an important sense, acculturation to Japanese society as it is promoted by the education system in Japan excludes anything religious.

Yet, it is important to note that the lack of a public discourse does not mean that "religion" and religious organizations are not actively engaged in politics and in framing specific policies, in ways that are ignored (in both senses: as unknown to, and neglected by) the general public. Aside from the well-known cases of Soka Gakkai, closely related to the Kōmeitō political party, and more recently Kōfuku no Kagaku's political activities through the Kōfuku Jitsugentō (which has resulted in two of their candidates being elected in the Japanese parliament), an influential group is the Shintō Seiji Renmei (rendered in English as Shinto Association of Spiritual Leadership). Established in 1969, it has consistently promoted policies based "on the spirit of Shinto," which involve the protection of traditional Japanese culture, the creation of an orderly society, and a number of other conservative (if not clearly reactionary) issues, including changes to the constitution to allow direct military intervention and the rejection of gender equality and LGBTQ+ rights (see the organization's website at http://www.sinseiren.org/). Many members of the Japanese parliament are affiliated with this organization, including several ministers in the recent governments. The political vision of Shintō Seiji Renmei is closely aligned with that of Jinja Honchō on the Shinto side and with the Liberal Democratic Party (Jimintō) and Nippon Kaigi, another right-wing organization, on the political side.

On the other hand, a third factor is the important role played by the media in making visible and promoting trends that are broadly related to religious practices. Some of them are portrayed in a positive light, especially when involving traveling to "power spots" or visiting and praying at famous temples and shrines. Practices involving "new religions" or minority religions, such as Islam, however, are often presented as unusual, suspicious, or even potentially dangerous. It is perhaps no accident that the religious trends shown more favorably are largely those connected with the so-called traditional Japanese religions of Shinto and Buddhism.

Moreover, as a fourth factor, the formation of the category of "religion" itself, as well as of the "secular" in modern Japan, has been at the center of several academic debates in recent years (Shimazono and Tsuruoka 2004; Josephson 2012; Isomae 2014; Maxey 2014; Rots and Teeuwen 2017; Thomas 2013; 2019). As some of these works discussed, the idea of the origin of "religion" in Japan as essentially a modern, Western construct tends to be misleading, and—as some postcolonial approaches have shown—both deprives the Japanese of agency and overemphasizes the role of Euro-American cultures and authors. Before modernization and the introduction of the neologism *shūkyō* (coined to translate the modern Western concept of "religion"—which, by the way, is by no means a clearly defined and univocal term) in the early 1870s, the Japanese had complex ideas about discourses and practices related to divine beings and their agencies, and formulated classifications of such systems. They were also aware of such discourses outside of Japan; in China and India since the classical period, and increasingly about the rest of the world from the late medieval period, not limited to Christianity. The role of these discourses (*kyō* or *oshie*, *kyōhō*, *hō*, *dō*, or sometimes simply *gaku*) for the development of personal or group identity, and more generally in the system of knowledge of premodern Japan, has never been explored in depth.

These factors combined make it challenging for scholars to study "Japanese religions," as their understanding of what religion is and does often does not match the understanding of most people living in Japan, who tend to consider religious beliefs and practices as "tradition," "cultural heritage," or "customs." This in turn poses the important question as to whether scholars are justified in calling and treating as "religion" phenomena that, for the people practicing or performing them, are "traditions" or even mere remnants from the past, on the same order of meaning as certain seasonal foods or family customs. At the same time, we should not forget that the understanding of something as "tradition" is related to specific ideological discourses. As is well known, Shinto has long been defined, since the inception of modernity, as not being a "religion" but as the center of Japanese "tradition."

For these and other reasons, we have avoided a discussion on definitions. Accordingly, we have not divided the *Handbook* into parts but decided to focus instead on topics and issues, which are often trans-sectarian and multireligious. In this sense, this *Handbook* should perhaps be considered as closer to books highlighting "keywords" in a given discipline, with the crucial difference that in many cases, the entries in this volume have not yet attained the status of keywords (or are too broad to be reduced to a single keyword). They are simply themes that have not been studied enough, or could be studied in different ways, or in which we have noticed a growing interest.

In terms of scholarship on Japanese religions at large, the field has been moving steadily away from textual study and focus on rituals (including *matsuri*) toward more comprehensive approaches. Thus, we can observe shifts from texts to icons and from there to visual culture and materiality more broadly; from pilgrimage to tourism and from there to cultural heritage; and from festivals to performing arts. Several scholars have also tried to go beyond the confines of the modern nation-state to encompass larger, transnational, and global perspectives—after all, Japanese religions cannot be studied by referring exclusively to autochthonous factors. There has been a recent focus on agents and actors of Japanese religiosity—the individuals, groups, and organizations involved in creating, preserving, and destroying ideas, objects, and practices. Thus, the field is now very different from only a few decades ago, when a large section of scholarship was dedicated to "founders" or "patriarchs" and their writings. These figures still attract a significant amount of academic attention, but more interest is developing in other figures and groups (agents) who were also influential or worth studying.

THIS HANDBOOK (AND BEYOND)

This brings us to what makes this *Handbook* original and different from all other similar publications. Rather than presenting an introduction to the main religious traditions in Japan or a guide to the state of the field—something that has already been covered successfully by previous publications mentioned above—this *Handbook* offers a map of the field by highlighting the uncharted areas, the black spots, the "hic sunt leones" areas in the study Japanese religions. We have included themes and topics that are crucial to the study of religion in Japan but have been overlooked or not yet fully investigated, that correspond to new trends in research, and that we believe will attract the attention of scholars in the next several years. In order to do so, we aimed to include a broad range of perspectives from scholars in different academic contexts from several countries. In particular, we have also included in the conversation many Japanese authors, who sometimes tend to be excluded from editorial projects of this kind dedicated to an international, English-based audience. For some topics we have asked contributors to write shorter case studies to highlight emerging practices and less known topics, or to illustrate the discussion provided in the main entry with a concrete example.

We hope that in this way, this *Handbook* will become a resource for students and scholars to discover what has not been fully researched yet and what are possible new areas of research with regards to a number of topics. Graduate students at different levels of advancement are the ideal readers of this *Handbook*, but we are also hoping that undergraduate students from different disciplines would find this useful as a source of ideas for course research papers. For instance, instead of writing yet another paper on Zen meditation, Shinto love for nature, and Esoteric Buddhist rituals, perhaps students can put their efforts toward more original and little charted endeavors, and thus contribute to the growth of the discipline by outsourcing innovative (albeit tentative) new research to a diffuse and potentially unlimited network of agents, rather than limiting it to established research institutions, with their agendas and traditions.

Of course, when embarking in such an ambitious project, one has to accept that the final product will never be perfect, as it is impossible to cover all dark areas, blind spots, and missing links—if only because they are not clearly visible. There are some possible "future directions" and topics that we could not include, not because of lack of sustained scholarship, but simply because of lack of space. We would like to highlight a few of them.

Religion and science: Admittedly, this may sound like an obsolete topic, a revenant from discussions that took place more than a century ago. However, the topic has not lost its relevance: the ways in which religious specialists, institutions, and practitioners respond, adopt, co-opt, and reject scientific theories and methods is still an important subject today, particularly in light of fundamentalist movements that articulate anti-scientific positions without necessarily rejecting most aspects of technology. A sustained look at Japanese religious attitudes toward scientific paradigms, in both the past and the present day, would certainly contribute to the broader field of religious studies.

Religion on the periphery: Much of the history of Japanese religions is written from the perspective of the political centers: the Kyoto-Nara region on the one hand and Edo-Tokyo on the other. This seems to be extremely problematic especially in premodern Japan, when political and religious centers did not have a solid hegemony on religious discourses and practices. When "Japan" was not a unified or homogeneous country, does it make sense to talk about "Japanese" religions? Is there a way to account for regional differences, especially in those many locales where the influence from the main temples and shrines located in the capital cities was tenuous at best? How would a multicentered and poly-vocal history of religiosities in the Japanese archipelago look like? And what was/is the role of peripheries in shaping the religious identity of the centers?

Multilingual aspects of Japanese religions: This is often taken for granted, but historically, Japanese religions have emerged out of a multilingual environment. This includes not only visitors and immigrants from ancient Korea and China, but also texts written in Chinese, vernacular Japanese, and *shittan* script—and, later, various European languages. Japanese authors, of course, were conversant with several of these languages, but also with their own "dialects" and *argots*. This is all the more striking when we think of it today, when Japanese academia is very much monolingual. The impact of plurilingualism in the formation and development of discourses about Japanese religions and intellectual traditions, also in relation with local specificities, still needs to be studied.

Geo-spatiality of religion: In terms of the place of Japanese religiosity, scholarship traditionally focuses on agricultural lands (especially rice-growing areas) and sacred mountains. Strangely enough, the sea as a religious locus has received little sustained and in-depth attention (Rambelli 2018). One wonders about the nature of sea deities and their relation with more established gods; the ritual cycle of fishing communities (as opposed to agricultural villages); the cosmology of sea-based religiosity; the connections between the sea, the land, and the mountains (and, perhaps, the sky); and the symbolic status of fish and fishing.

Religion and sport: A topic that is rarely studied is the connection between religiosity and sports. While "sport" is a modern phenomenon, and its ties with religious sites and activities in the modern period until today are worthy of analysis, agonistic activities involving altered uses of the body in various ritual and performing settings were common in the past (examples include extreme types of *matsuri* such as the Onbashira at Suwa, *sumō* performed at temple and shrine festivals, *yabusame* archery rituals, and many more); these also deserve sustained research.

Religion, animals, and animality: The intersections between religion and animality constitute another theme, which deserves to be further explored in future studies. Not only do religious discourses tend to organize the space, role, and interpretative meanings associated with animals, but they also exploit animality to rethink, expand, and, in some cases, even reduce the limits of human life. Taking into consideration the multilateral interactions between religion and animality, it is possible to describe zones of discursive hybridity, where apparently separated agencies such as humans, animals, and gods meet together to produce a variety of new theories and practices. Previous study (Ambros 2012) and current research projects, such as the ERC-funded project "Whales of Power: Aquatic Mammals, Devotional Practices, and Environmental Change in Maritime East Asia," led by Aike Rots at the University of Oslo, have started developing a discussion on these themes that deserve further enquiry.

Religion, senses, and emotions: A promising emerging new field, with its specific methodologies emerging from the so-called affective turn in several disciplines and the development of the history of emotions, is related to the study of senses and emotions. These approaches go beyond visual culture and the study of materiality, focusing on different sensory responses to religious phenomena: smell, taste, touch, sound, in addition to vision (which has been studied extensively), as well as on the study of emotions and affects (Baffelli forthcoming; Baffelli et al. forthcoming). All these phenomena are deeply rooted in material and bodily aspects, but they are also connected to important theoretical elaborations.

AN EPILOGUE: RELIGION AND RELIGIOUS STUDIES IN TIMES OF THE COVID-19 PANDEMIC

A text is always affected by the historical contingencies in which it is produced. In the case of this *Handbook*, we found ourselves finalizing the entries and the introduction in the spring and summer of 2020, during the Covid-19 pandemic. Prior to that, because the editors live in three different countries, our collaboration for this project has mainly been done remotely and online, except for a few face-to-face meetings at conferences or in Japan. Nonetheless, the virus, a nonhuman agent, has had a significant impact on our lives, as well as the lives of contributors, editors, and publishers. This unprecedented situation also provides a chance to reflect on the relationships between religious studies and history, on how (Japanese) religions react to crisis and disasters, and future modalities of teaching and researching in this academic field.

First of all, it should be noted that the historical or contemporary phenomena that are the focus of research in religious studies are always embedded in unique spatial and temporal circumstances. This necessarily informs the act of researching per se. In this *Handbook* contributors consciously avoided a mere indexation of crucial moments in the formative processes of Japanese religious traditions, which could provide the comfortable but misleading impression of a linear and uniform development of religious practices and theories. As a result, entries and case studies embrace, to use Harry Harootunian's words, "mixed and uneven temporalities" (2019: 2). Each section of the *Handbook* emphasizes the modalities through which Japanese religions—and at times the study of Japanese religions—prioritize a randomized, fragmented, and discretional use of the past to create temporary visions of a meaningful present.

The contemporary angle, which characterizes many of the entries in this volume, is based on the recognition of traces and fragments of the past that are continuously and creatively shuffled and recycled to fit specific needs of the present, such as, for example, issues concerning nature, politics, economics, or food. Therefore, the contemporary aspects of Japanese religions, as envisioned in this book, are generated by the confluence of two oppositional streams of time. On the one hand, Japanese religions are plunged into a diachronic time, the linearity of which is demanded for historical narratives. On the other hand, Japanese religions are embedded in a synchronic time, the curvilinear structure of which is regulated by unpredictable interweavings of human and nonhuman agents such as Covid-19, just to mention one among infinite others. The twilight zone, which emerges from the conflict and mutual coproduction between these two models of perceiving time, is the arena where contributors presented their analysis.

The outbreak of Covid-19 and its impact on our ordinary lives compels us to make a second consideration on the impossibility to control or explain the present by merely comparing it to the past. This is a recurrent theme also in Walter Benjamin's work, where the past never transmits any specific teaching to the present but produces instead a shapeless multiplicity of events, some of which can be ostensibly selected to give a sense to certain contemporary phenomena (2001: 437). This is the moment in which Japanese religions play the role of mediators between a (not always) silent past and an anxiety-inducing present. For instance, the Japanese government has recently chosen *Amabie*, an aquatic hybrid creature with a bird face, a long mane, a scaly torso, and a tripartite tail, as official symbol for its biopolitical interventions to prevent the spread of Covid-19 (see also Chapter 16 by Ugoretz and Baffelli in this volume).

This iconographic selection had two immediate effects. On the one hand, this campaign evokes the apotropaic and curative power of the *Amabie*, which was a relatively common subject in prints that were sold as cheap reading materials and as paper talismans against epidemics around the mid-nineteenth century. *Amabie* is an oracular marine creature, which warns humans against the outbreak of a six-year-long epidemic; those who pay attention to *Amabie*'s prophecy are able to save their lives. On the other hand, this visual reference to the *Amabie* allows the Japanese government to use a peripheral element in discourses of healing from the past for deactivating the novelty of the present Covid-19 pandemic, linking it back to the epidemics in the Edo period. The contemporary *Amabie* represents a guiding teaching of the past, which is never actually delivered. Nevertheless, humans are constantly looking for, longing for, and manufacturing this past by accessing, for instance, the enormous visual and conceptual database of religions.

The philosophers Divya Dwivedi and Shaj Mohan underline that the notion of sovereignty is coincidently embedded in the popular name of Covid-19, that is, "coronavirus," where the molecular "crown" of this nonhuman agent implicitly recalls the concept of authority (Dwivedi and Mohan 2020). Moving along these interpretative lines, it is possible to describe two contrasting impacts of Covid-19's sovereignty on religious activities in Japan. First of all, the cancellation of many religious rituals in the name of biomedical injunctions, which discourage any form of crowd gathering to prevent spreading contagion. For example, the July 2020 edition of the Gion festival in Kyoto—which, incidentally, is centered on the worship of an anti-epidemic deity—has been cancelled due to public health concerns. Between mid-February and early March 2020, numerous new religions such as Soka Gakkai, Shinnyo-en, Risshō Kōsekai, and Seichō no ie rushed to close their centers for the same motivations. Levi McLaughlin points out that in the case of new religions, the fear of experiencing a public backlash by the media was probably one of the major triggers for their rapid embracing of the new social-distancing restrictions (2020a: 5–6). The second impact of Covid-19 is the reconfiguration of religious practices and ritual procedures within virtual spaces. Not all religious specialists have suspended their activities but instead perform them in isolation or following regulations about social distancing. Websites, chats, or Facebook groups allow devotees to follow religious ceremonies in real time while keeping themselves safe.

However, although this allows for religious practices to be performed, interactions with spaces and people, the copresence of the bodies of performers and onlookers and the synchronicity of being all together in the same place at the same time are missing. Examples of this virtual displacement of religious activities are detectable in the proliferation of YouTube streamings of *kagura* dances, which are performed only by the dancers without real spectators close by. In a similar way, Shugendō practitioners affiliated with Daigoji, Kinpusenji, and Ōminesanji made available online outdoor fire rituals (*saitō goma*) for generating worldly benefits for their physically removed communities of lay devotees, who can now follow the liturgy from their private screens. Further study will shed light on the impact of these new ways of performing religious rituals on practitioners and on their perceptions of mediated rituals.

In recent years, the commercialization of amulets has already seen a successful shift toward the internet, but the outbreak of Covid-19 could easily accelerate this tendency. For instance, since the end of March 2020, requests for home delivery of sutra copying materials for healing purposes at Buddhist temple Yakushiji in Nara went up by 30 percent compared to the same period in the past years. More creatively, the website of Katagiriya, a well-known shop of clothing and supplies for religious festivals in the city of Iida in Nagano prefecture, commercializes a special type of protective mask with printing of *Heart Sutra* scripts, which have always been revered for their protective power.

Many commentators (e.g., Benvenuto 2020) have pointed out that one of the most durable effects produced by Covid-19 will likely be on in the field of education and research. The teaching and research in religious studies is no exception. When courses and seminars had to be moved quickly online in several universities around the world, the lack of online open source material on religion in Japan quickly became evident. There are notable exceptions. Some of the major journals in our field, such as the *Japanese Journal of Religious Studies, Asian Ethnology*, and *Japan Review*, as well as the open-access publications and databases made available by the Nanzan Institute for Religion and Culture (https://nirc.nanzan-u.ac.jp/en/publications/) are all freely available online, but gaining access to archives and other material is far more difficult. Compared to a few years ago, many books are also now available in e-book format, but digital access to sources in Japanese is still very limited. Therefore, the new situation of largely virtual education may foster the creation of more material available online to be used by students and researchers, but it also presents significant new challenges for researchers in accessing primary sources, including direct access to the field itself. On the positive side, this situation might encourage scholars to focus on the digital archives of primary sources that are available, thus promoting new research on little-studied materials and phenomena.

As a consequence, researchers are now asking themselves whether and to what degree the Covid-19 pandemic represents a crisis for Japanese religions and the study of religion in Japan. It is worth noting that crisis derives from the Greek verb *kríno* ("to discern"), which indicates a spatial separation between two parts of the same unit and a temporal division between a preceding event and a following one. In 1995, the sarin attack perpetrated by members of Aum Shinrikyō marked a turning point for religion in Japan. Both "established" and "new" groups were pressured to adjust their practices and teachings to navigate an increasingly negative perception of religion (Baffelli and Reader 2012). At the same time, scholarship on religion in Japan also shifted its focus, and new topics, such as the relationship between religion and violence, attracted more attention.

Similarly, in the aftermath of the March 2011 Great East Japan Earthquake (also known as 3.11 triple disaster), religious groups were very active in mobilizing their members to bring help to the affected areas and in raising donations (McLaughlin 2016b). As a consequence, the last decade also saw the emergence of new scholarship on religious responses to disasters and on religiously motivated activism (see Chapter 2 by Kasai and Chapter 4 by McLaughlin in this volume). Will Covid-19 produce similar effects on Japanese religions and related academic fields? Will Covid-19 generate more dimmed metaphors of crisis, which foster ambiguities, conflicts, and transformations in Japanese religions without manifesting clear-cut fractures as in 1995? These may constitute some of the open questions to which future studies would do well to formulate answers.

Experts on climate change are suggesting that Covid-19 is just one example of what will happen in the near future with higher temperatures and more general weather disruptions. If this is correct, we should take this pandemic not as a mere exception but as a glimpse to the upcoming "new normal." As such, it should prompt us to rethink not only our everyday lifestyle and way of carrying out scholarship, as has been happening, but also to tackle more fundamental questions—of a more "religious" nature, as it were.

Many authors, academic or otherwise, have already been dedicating increased attention in the past few years to outlining visions for the future, inspired by ideas of the anthropocene and the growing effects of climate change. These visions are often characterized by religious metaphors related to eschatology, such as the apocalypse and the end of the world. Two underlying themes emerge. One is the human incapacity to protect themselves and their environment, often because of greed and ignorance—thus, a moral failure that brings about some kind of cosmic/natural retribution. The other theme is the fundamental vulnerability and frailty of humans, which demands a different approach to many aspects of culture and society. This may be a new ontology no longer based on images of ideal perfection, but one that includes as constitutive elements illness, decay, mistakes, and imperfections; a new politics, based on mutual aid rather than on rewarding success due to random and unpredictable factors; a new economy focused on sustainability, limitation and preciousness of resources, and care; and perhaps new ideas and practices about the sacred.

The latter might involve a rediscovery and reevaluation of a central element of religions, namely, their offering representations of the End—of individuals, communities, and the entire world. The End has been removed from private and public discourses as a remnant from a superstitious and non-technological past, but of course the end (some end) is always present in all our lives. The study of Japanese religions, in all of their multiplicity, transformations, demises, and continuities across many centuries, could offer some important contributions to a general record of human imagination about vulnerability, dissolution, and resilience.

CHAPTER 2

Chaplaincy and Spiritual Care

KASAI Kenta

A chaplain is a religious professional whose job is to perform rituals and listen to people's narratives in specific institutions, such as companies, universities, prisons, courts, hospitals, and or the military. In the recent film *Chaplains*, we also find chaplains who work in other places dealing with people's difficulties, including a police department, a food company, a car race, and the US Congress (Doblmeier 2016). However, what do chaplains do in Japan?

In Japanese history, the oldest historical record of a figure comparable to a chaplain refers to itinerant priests who practiced *nenbutsu* (chanting the name of the Buddha Amida) and followed samurai warriors in their campaigns (Thornton 2015: 441). In modern Japan, because of the principle of the separation of state and religion and of freedom of religion, sanctioned in the Constitution of Japan of 1947, people generally avoid performing religious practices in national "public" spaces or public facilities. There are some universities that are supported by religious organizations, and they provide facilities for training priest as attentive listeners. There are no chaplains in the Japanese Police Department or in the Self-Defense Forces, both of which are responsible for the security of Japan. No national or public hospital has hired a chaplain; it is often nurses who listen to the patients' life-and-death concerns.

However, people have begun to develop interest in the religious professional figure of the chaplain because Japan has become one of the fastest aging societies in the world. In particular, some people expect chaplains to guide patients in the terminal stages of life to a "better" acceptance of death, and after national-scale disasters and accidents, also to support the survivors in their grief (McLaughlin 2013; Kasai 2016).

WHERE CHAPLAINS WORK IN JAPAN: THE PRISON AND THE HOSPITAL

In Japan, the chaplains' typical working environments are prisons and hospitals.

A *kyōkaishi* 教誨師 or prison chaplain is a religious professional who is expected to have conversations with prisoners and even with criminals in death row. Before 1945, under the Meiji Imperial Constitution and the Prison Law, prisoners were not granted freedom to practice their religion. The available chaplains taught their own religion to comfort them; in addition, prisons offered elementary education such as reading, writing, and arithmetic for the rehabilitation of prisoners (Kanazawa and Manako 2013: 49–52). These prisoners were categorized as "unqualified" for full citizenship in Japan because they had disrupted the social order. They were thought to be people with no religious grounding who should be taught some, even if it was the chaplain's own religion (The Prison Law 監獄法 1908: Article 29; Kanazawa and Manako 2013: 49–52).

In 1947, the new Constitution of Japan declared the principles of the freedom of religion and the division of state and religion, which extended to prisoners (Article 20.2–3). Because of the division of state and religion, in prisons, which are in most cases national institutions, officers are public servants who are prohibited from practicing any religious activities in the workplace. Budgets appropriated for religious activities are strictly regulated. Accordingly, prison chaplains in Japan today cannot be hired by the government or be considered public servants but voluntary religious professionals who offer *kyōkai* 教誨, religious services under rigid surveillance, either at their own expense or with financial support from the religious organizations they belong to.

This Prison Law was abolished in 2005; instead, the new Act on Penal Detention Facilities and the Treatment of Inmates and Detainees was enforced. This new law bans the arbitrary limitation of prisoners' personal religious activities and freedom of religion. It also enables chaplains to offer both religious consultation and ritual guidance to prisoners (Act on Penal Detention Facilities 2005: Articles 67–68). Currently there are 1,864 active prison chaplains (Zenkoku kyōkaishi renmei 2017).

Because prison chaplains in Japan are the only third-party personnel who are permitted to attend the execution of the death penalty in order to bring comfort to the prisoners, and because the death penalty has long been a controversial issue, the Ministry of Justice prohibits chaplains from publicizing their experiences outside the prison. It is therefore difficult to find young successors for prison chaplains who retire, because (1) this position requires financial resources outside their chaplain activities, and (2) it is challenging to recruit and put out public advertisements for prison chaplains under such restrictions. Recent juridical and prison administration reforms promise to bring improvements, including the creation of a prison chaplain administration (Prison Reformation Conference 2003: 13–17; Kanazawa and Manako 2013: 63–4).

In contrast, the hospital chaplain activities have been inspired by the World Health Organization's definition of palliative care, referred to as "spiritual" care since 1990s. The revised 2002 definition elaborates the roles of the caregiver and the chaplain in detail as a team approach that may begin as early as the onset of illness, and serves as a model of palliative care units in Japan:

> Palliative care is an approach that improves the quality of life of patients and their families facing the problems associated with life-threatening illness, through the prevention and relief of suffering by means of early identification and impeccable assessment and treatment of pain and other problems, physical, psychosocial and *spiritual* … Palliative care … *integrates the psychological and spiritual aspects of patient care*; [it] *uses a team approach* to address the needs of patients and their families, including bereavement counselling, if indicated; [it] is applicable *early in the course of illness*, in conjunction with other therapies that are intended to prolong life. (World Health Organization 2002, emphasis and alteration added)

Takashi Yamamoto, a member of the House of the Councillors (the upper house of the National Diet of Japan), and also a thymus cancer patient, confessed his illness in the House and appealed for the enactment of the Basic Acts for Cancer Treatment. These

Basic Acts came into force in 2006 and encouraged medical staff to learn about palliative care. As of November 2019, hospice wards number 431 with a total of 8,808 beds in Japan (Hospice Palliative Care Japan 2019), but the number of chaplains or "spiritual" care professionals is far less than that of these wards; many of them are unpaid "volunteer" caregivers in temporary positions.

The national health insurance system, enrollment in which is mandatory for all citizens and residents of Japan, defines which treatments can be covered. This does not include any budget for chaplaincy. Therefore, hospitals have to pay their chaplains' salary outside the insurance system by interpreting their work variously as hospital advisors or counsellors, or as teachers or officers of the umbrella organization overseeing the hospital, such as a university or Christian mission. In the case of university-affiliated or local government-affiliated hospitals, hiring chaplains is not acceptable, as it is considered to be against the principles of freedom of religion and the separation of the state and religion. When Buddhist monks visit patients wearing priestly robes, they are criticized because that reminds other patients of a funeral. Religious solicitation and proselytization in a hospital setting is often met with disapproval, as people suspect it is merely a way of taking advantage of a patient's illness. However, medical staff often question whether their medical care for terminal patients is satisfactory or not. Furthermore, the staff themselves experience many cases of insufficient spiritual care and also suffer from grief and guilt in their work. Some of them are interested in chaplain's work, and nurses sometimes join chaplaincy seminars.

The first hospice in Japan was established in 1981 at Seirei Mikatahara Hospital. It was followed in 1984 by the hospice at Yodogawa Christian Hospital, which adopted the team approach and became a model for other domestic palliative care units. The pioneer chaplains who learned Clinical Pastoral Education (CPE) for chaplaincy in the United States were at pains to establish chaplaincy in these hospitals and also to carry out its education programs in Japan. One example of such efforts was Catholic Rev. Fr. Waldemar Kippes's Clinical Pastoral Education and Research Center Japan, which trains and contributes chaplains and caregiver volunteers for these hospitals. Soon after, Jōdo Shinshū priest and professor Tamiya Masashi questioned the fact that there was no Buddhist hospice available for Buddhists even though Buddhism has developed a wealth of spiritual resources for approaches to terminal care. Tamiya founded a hospice unit at Nagaoka-nishi Hospital in 1985 and named it Vihāra ビハーラ, a Sanskrit term which means "place of rest" (and which was used to refer to Buddhist temples). From his project, Buddhist hospices are now often called Vihara, and Buddhist chaplains for hospital are called Vihara priests in Japan (Taniyama 2012: 1237–65).

How does Japanese medical staff manage the patients' and their families' concerns beyond physical pain? A philosopher of attentive listening, Murata Hisayuki, analyzed one's spiritual pain for medical staff in order to avoid minimizing or masking the suffering of terminal-stage cancer patients. Murata classified spiritual pain in three existential dimensions. His model aims at the medical staff's predicament and intends to establish a common existential language of the heart without any shared religious values between the cared-for and the caregiver.

Murata sought to clarify and assess the structure of spiritual pain for the spiritual care of patients with terminal cancer, because he questioned the fact that medical staff working in palliative care units kept themselves away from patients in serious despair. He defined spiritual pain as "pain caused by the extinction of one's being and the meaning of the self." The human being is analyzed in three dimensions: a being founded on temporality, a being in relationship with others, and a being with autonomy. Then, spiritual pain in each dimension of those patients could be described as a sense of meaninglessness of life without a future, the loss of others, and the loss of self-made ability or autonomy of a dying individual. Murata suggested that medical staff in palliative care units focus on covering those three dimensions and listen carefully to the patients (Murata 2003: 15–21).

We should be reminded that the "religions" of the patients and their families might not necessarily be systematically organized religious systems but rather some syncretic blend that reflects their life experiences and environments, even when they mention their affiliation with a particular religious group or school. Murata's existentialist approach might be suitable for the medical staff's initial approach to the patients with unclear religious background in Japan. Though Murata's analysis of spiritual pain has been criticized for avoiding matters beyond relieving those spiritual pains, it has been broadly accepted among medical staff who are required to work in secular hospital settings. Murata's approach depends largely on verbal communication. Some chaplains also suggest offering other approaches, such as compassionate presence, when they cannot do anything for the patient. This constitutes a ministry of presence, to encourage the patients to develop and express more spontaneous attitudes than simply the relief from pain. They question Murata's approach, which seems to focus on alleviation of the medical staff's guilt for the patient rather than the actual pain of the patients.

JAPANESE CHAPLAINS AND TRAUMATIC EVENTS AND DISASTERS

For Japanese without impending health concerns or existential questions, spiritual care is a subject distant from their immediate experience. However, accidents and disasters, particularly those on a national scale, remind people to think about the death of others and their own.

Two big earthquakes, first in Kobe in 1995 and more recently in the coastal regions of Northeastern Japan followed by tsunami waves in 2011, forced many Japanese to reflect on the meaning of their own lives and the people close to them. Suzuki Iwayumi, a professor of religious studies at Tohoku University, and Okabe Takeshi, a doctor of in-home palliative care, both experienced the great earthquake of 2011. They have invited local religious specialists to preside over funeral services and to listen to the narratives of survivors who lost family members and friends to the tsunami and seismic waves. Those gatherings of religious specialists later resulted in the creation of a graduate program for "interfaith" chaplains (*rinshō shūkyōshi* 臨床宗教師) at Tohoku University (Okabe 2012: 1–4). Considering the importance of the separation of religion and state and freedom of religious practice, it is significant for a Japanese national university to have established a course for chaplaincy activities beyond secular religious studies or comparative religions courses.

Similarly, a serious train accident in Osaka in 2004 that killed more than one hundred people has also made people aware of the need of grief-care for survivors and the families and friends of the victims in such accidents. A Catholic nun and university professor, Takaki Yoshiko, offered peer support with individual counseling for families, friends, and even the railway company workers, who suffered both from guilt and blame from society. The railway company provided funds to establish the Japanese Institute of Grief Care, first at St. Thomas University in Osaka in 2010 and later at Sophia University in Tokyo in

2014, for Takaki's project to educate grief-care attentive listeners and nondenominational chaplains in Japan (Takaki 2013: 3–10).

TRAINING AT THE INSTITUTE OF GRIEF CARE, SOPHIA UNIVERSITY

The two university projects above are based on an interfaith chaplaincy education program incorporating nonreligious caregivers, called Professional Association for Spiritual Care and Health (PASCH). PASCH was established by two CPE supervisors, Kubotera Toshiyuki of the Free Methodist Church and Itō Takaaki of the Anglican Church, and a Jōdo Shinshū Buddhist priest and Vihara supervisor, Taniyama Yōzō. Although its training program originated from the CPE in Christian seminaries and health care institutions, it offers a training environment for people who are not affiliated with any religious group or are nonreligious.

Because Taniyama now teaches at Tohoku University and Itō at Sophia University, both universities provide the same CPE-style education system. A remarkable difference is that while the Tohoku interfaith chaplaincy program (at a public university) requires the applicants to be religion specialists endorsed by a religious group in the local community, the Sophia program (at a Jesuit university), is open to both non-Christians and the nonreligious. Though the latter requires three years of training, the former offers intensive training. About half of the Sophia program trainees are nurses. This number shows that some medical professionals are eager to provide something beyond the physical and psychological treatment currently available at hospitals.

It is then necessary to ensure continuity in the training system for chaplains to enable them to build interfaith cooperation, improve their work quality, share ethical codes for professionals, and guide the next generation. The pioneering chaplains and supervisors of the training programs at seminaries or colleges created a partnership in order to launch the Japan Society of Spiritual Care in 2007 for the certification of spiritual caregivers, supervisors, and researchers, and to provide training courses for them. Buddhist universities such as Ryūkoku and its Institute for Engaged Buddhism (*Rinshō bukkyō kenkyūjo*) also are developing interfaith or Buddhist chaplaincy programs and have organized the Society for Interfaith Chaplaincy in Japan.

THE INSTITUTIONAL CHALLENGES FOR CHAPLAINS IN JAPAN

As noted above, neither prison chaplains nor most hospital chaplains are permanent paid professionals. Religious support for patients is often disregarded, or sometimes undertaken by medical personnel such as nurses, who are expected to pride emotional support in addition to their other duties. Patients and families are thus dependent on the staff's additional goodwill, and staff have to fill multiple roles. A systematic study of the efficacy of chaplain activities for treatment is necessary. A qualified chaplain should be paid properly.

Many large hospitals in Japan are striving to be recognized as excellent facilities for medical tourism. For instance, the Joint Commission International (JCI), a hospital-grading organization in the United States, requires religious support for patients of diverse religious and cultural backgrounds—a chaplain—in order to be certified. There are thirty-one organizations in Japan certified by JCI as of December 2020 (Joint Commission International 2020). In addition to the hospitals' desire to receive certification, the strengths and weaknesses of such programs should be seriously discussed in order for chaplaincy to be included in the Japanese medical health insurance system.

There are differences among religious organizations in their commitment to nurturing and supporting chaplains. It is vital to have more interreligious dialogues among Christian chaplaincy traditions and interfaith chaplain groups (currently mostly Buddhists, with some priests from Shinto organizations and some from new religious groups), as well as including unorganized nonbelievers and nonaffiliated peoples. Some scholars are trying to establish Japanese standards for the proper chaplain who is both ethical and skillful.

Now many young urban residents are not sure of their own family's Buddhist temple affiliation. Some of them may decide to learn Buddhist meditation at some point. Other people simply think of religion as an affirmation of life after death, so that they can die in peace. Others yet presume that a priest has supernatural powers to lead them to a good death. Can Japanese people accept existing religious traditions broadly enough to enable proper connections and encourage religious literacy through chaplaincy?

See also Chapter 4, "Disasters."

CHAPTER 3

Cultural Heritage

Lindsey E. DEWITT

For the millions of people visiting Japan's temples and shrines or attending its festivals and traditional performing arts each year, cultural and religious phenomena—and hence culture and religion—are typically encountered in tandem, as a pair. Eye-catching signposts stand at the entrance to most famous sacred sites proclaiming "World Heritage" on inscribed stone stele (Figure 3.1). The words "National Treasure" (*kokuhō*) and "Important Cultural Property" (*jūyō bunkazai*) label thousands of religious icons and furnishings in museums and temples. In these ways, and others more subtle, we observe a normalization of this particular pairing within Japan's contemporary cultural landscape.

A combined consideration of cultural heritage and religion in Japan for this *Handbook* does not unfold with such ease, however. A pairing of cultural heritage and religion forces an unnatural alliance between two complex fields of inquiry in Japan, one very new (cultural heritage) and one more established (religion)—although the latter, as an academic discipline, is still relatively young. Terminological considerations alone could fill an entire volume, given the burdensome karma of "cultural heritage" (*bunka isan*) and "religion" (*shūkyō*), two neologisms adopted by Japan's government in the late twentieth and late nineteenth centuries, respectively, to translate English words.[1] The expression *bunka isan* effloresced following a shift in Japan's foreign cultural policy in 1988 and the nation's 1992 ratification of the UNESCO World Heritage Convention. *Bunka* in the Japanese context concerns social (and national) development or progress. Article 1 of the 1950 Law for the Protection of Cultural Properties, for example, defines its purpose in terms of "cultural improvement" (*kōjō*).[2] The characters for *isan* 遺産 concern forward movement as well, although in the different sense of leaving behind (*i*) and bearing or producing (*san*).[3] *Shūkyō*, as many fine publications carefully detail and debate, denotes the conceptual overhaul of a Buddhist term in the late nineteenth century.[4]

The real awkwardness of these bedfellows, however, derives from the constitutional and attendant social bifurcation of culture and religion in Japan, one complemented by the liberal, secular parameters of UNESCO. To be sure, UNESCO did not invent cultural heritage, but it certainly propelled its epistemological status and provided a global framework for its formal recognition. Japan's 1947 Constitution stipulates that

---

[1] My use of "karma" here draws on Morris-Suzuki's apt description of culture/*bunka* as "burdened by the karma of previous incarnations" (1998: 63).
[2] https://elaws.e-gov.go.jp/search/elawsSearch/elaws_search/lsg0500/detail?lawId=325AC1000000214#A.
[3] Koga (2016) glosses the compound as "inheritance of loss."
[4] Recent contributions (in English) on *shūkyō* include Josephson (2012), Klautau (2012), Thomas (2013), Pye (2013), Lowe (2014), and Maxey (2014).

FIGURE 3.1: World Heritage stone stele at Tōdaiji, Nara. ©crystaltmc/123RF.COM.

"no religious organization shall receive any privileges from the State, nor exercise any political authority" (Article 20) and that "no public money or other property shall be expended or appropriated for the use, benefit or maintenance of any religious institution or association" (Article 89).[5] And yet, the allure of heritage designation encourages and normalizes precisely the opposite, even if the "grammar" of cultural heritage that flourishes today in the domestic and international "heritage-making" arenas consciously excludes religion.[6] State instruments support and manage cultural heritage resources; thus, the "heritagization of the sacred" (Meyer and de Witte 2013) requires a secular refashioning, a separation and an additional layer of "sacralization" but devoid of the overt trappings or signs of religion. Words squarely in the domain of the religious, for instance, "shrine," "temple," "deities" (*kami*), and "worship" (*shinkō*), appear frequently in official heritage documentation; "religion" (*shūkyō*) does not.[7] The official absence of religion underscores the history of political and cultural struggles around its definition, legality, and function in Japan.[8] Caveats and taboos aside, the frame of "cultural heritage

---

[5] http://japan.kantei.go.jp/constitution_and_government_of_japan/constitution_e.html.
[6] By "grammar" I mean to recall Noam Chomsky's theory of "universal grammar" and the diverse body of works it inspired. See Maxey (2014) on the Meiji government's "grammar of religion." Weiss (2007) discusses heritage, and "heritage-making," in terms of an insidious politics of recognition; alternatively, Brumann and Cox, writing on Japan, read heritage as "self-conscious tradition" (2010: 3–4) and direct attention to the agents involved and their wide-ranging intentions.
[7] See Teeuwen (2020) on the efforts to excise, on paper at least, all traces of religion from Kyoto's Gion festival in order to designate it an Important Intangible Folk Cultural Property in 1979.
[8] On "formations" of religion and the secular in modern Japan, two dynamic categories that are continuously renegotiated, see Rots and Teeuwen (2017).

and religion" provides us an excellent vehicle for probing the coexistence and mutual constitution of the two in Japan today, and for calling attention to the historical and social agencies behind and beneath them.

RELIGIOUS CULTURAL HERITAGE

Despite careful efforts to avoid the stigma-laden category of religion, a process Rots (2017) has termed "discursive secularization," myriad things religious—from enduring monuments and texts, to moveable artifacts and intangible traditions—receive special governmental protection and distinction. Any attempt to definitively distinguish heritage from non-heritage and religious from secular would be riddled with problems. Would swords, for example, weapons classified as Crafts (*kōgeihin*), qualify as religious cultural heritage? What if they had been passed down in the holdings of temples and shrines, for example, two National Treasure blades held at Shitennōji Temple in Osaka, and attributed to the semi-legendary Buddhist exponent Shōtoku Taishi (traditionally 574–622)? What about National Treasure swords used by Buddhist warrior monks (*sōhei*) during the Kamakura period (1185–1333)? Must an object or practice bear an official heritage designation to be considered as heritage, in which case anything administered by the Imperial Household Agency, such as tumuli viewed as imperial mausolea (some designated as World Cultural Heritage in 2019), would be excluded? Conversely, must something be legally classified as "religion" to be considered religious?

Interpretive challenges notwithstanding, a brief survey of Japan's "World Cultural Heritage" (*sekai bunka isan*) sites, "cultural properties" (*bunkazai*), and Japan Heritage Stories (*Nihon isan sutōri*) offers some indication of the weightiness of religion in the current corpus of cultural heritage. Twelve of Japan's nineteen cultural World Heritage designations are in whole or part religious sites; compare this 63 percent religious portion to the roughly 20 percent of all World Heritage Sites UNESCO agencies consider as "heritage of religious interest" (the single-largest category of the List).[9] Of Japan's twenty-one items inscribed as Intangible Cultural Heritage of Humanity on UNESCO's Representative List, more than half embody or incorporate religious elements: sacred performance traditions (*gagaku*, *kagura*, Dainichidō Bugaku, and Nachi no Dengaku), float festivals such as Kyoto's Gion festival, agricultural rituals (Akiu no Taue Odori, Okunoto no Aenokoto, Mibu no hana Taue), and a grouping of nine "visiting-god" (*raihōshin*) rituals.

Religion plays a similarly influential role in the domestic body of cultural properties designated by the Agency for Cultural Affairs (Bunkachō, hereafter ACA). The single-largest category of National Treasures and Important Cultural Properties, sculptures (*chōkoku*), numbering 2,723, is populated almost exclusively by religious works, mostly representations of Buddhist and Shinto deities or Buddhist priests.[10] Not a single secular or post-Edo-period statue has been designated as a National Treasure, however. Only six nonreligious sculptures have been designated as Important Cultural Properties, as

---

[9] As estimated by the *UNESCO Initiative on Heritage of Religious Interest*, an effort of the World Heritage Centre and its Advisory Bodies: http://whc.unesco.org/en/religious-sacred-heritage/.

[10] Figures drawn from http://www.bunka.go.jp/seisaku/bunkazai/shokai/shitei.html and https://kunishitei.bunka.go.jp. Guth (2004: 152) locates the first use of the term "sculpture" in Japan in an 1876 description of training in the Western plastic arts to be offered by Italian sculptor Vincenzo Ragusa at the new Technical Art School in Tokyo.

have two secular portrait sculptures from the Edo period, both of which are held in the possession of Buddhist temples. To further underline the significance of religion in the category of sculpture (2,723), we can compare it to the 2,037 paintings designated as National Treasures or Important Cultural Properties, a figure that includes both secular and religious works. Buildings on premodern Buddhist and Shinto sites comprise more than 60 percent of the total number of physical structures designated as National Treasures or Important Cultural Properties (Bunkachō 2018: 48). To this tally we add Buddhist- and Shinto-themed paintings, Christian historical materials,[11] Daoist and Confucian manuscripts, sutra transcriptions from China, Korean temple bells, Buddhist ritual goods, and other "religious" items recognized as Tangible Cultural Properties.

"Things used in relation to worship" (*shinkō ni mochiirareru mono*) constitutes the second-largest category of Important Tangible Folk Cultural Properties (*jūyō yūkei minzoku bunkazai*): ritual implements, dedicatory wooden plaques at shrines (*ema*), miniature stupas, amulets and costumes of mountain worship traditions, festival floats (and entire festivals), votive offerings, instruments, lanterns and banners, and more. "Festivals (worship)," in Japanese *sairei* (*shinkō*), comprises by far the largest grouping of Important Intangible Folk Cultural Properties (*jūyō mukei minzoku bunkazai*), a category added in 1975 that currently comprises 318 items. "Festivals (worship)" includes all but one of the thirty-three float festivals designated at the UNESCO level, along with diverse other ritual performances held for the purpose of propitiating deities or expelling demons. Thirty-eight *kagura* and twenty-five *dengaku* also receive distinction.[12] The ACA considers many more (109 to be exact) "Festivals (worship)" worthy of protection and preservation under the title of "Intangible Folk Cultural Properties that need measures such as making records" (Kiroku sakuseitō no sochi o kōzubeki mukei no minzoku bunkazai), a figure trumped only by traditional folk dances (*furyū*), a grouping that itself contains religious examples, such as music and dance performances held during the annual Buddhist event of Obon. Turning to Important Intangible Cultural Properties (*jūyō mukei bunkazai*), a category created in 1954 for "artistically sophisticated classical performances preserved by experts" (Ōshima 2007: 19), we find *gagaku* (imperial court music often featured in Shinto and, to a lesser extent, Buddhist ceremonies), the performance traditions Noh and Kabuki, which often incorporate religious themes or are (in the case of Noh) performed in religious settings, and textile, ceramic, and metalworking techniques used to produce religious implements.

Finally, the domestic level of designation includes a new scheme, "Japan Heritage" (*Nihon isan*), which at the time of writing (December 2020) consisted of 104 "Stories." Those with knowledge of Japanese history and religion will catch the scent of highly romanticized presentations of religious sites, figures, and practices that often serve as the cornerstone of these narratives. As an example, "The Dawn of Japan: Women in the Asuka Period" features sites associated with five women who played formative roles in the political and religious context of their day. The narrative describes Empress Saimei (r. 655–661), the same woman who ruled earlier under the name Kōgyoku (r. 642–645), as a "mysterious empress who performed rain-making rituals" (Asuka Heritage Promotion Committee 2016).

---

[11]These materials include a portrait of Pope Paul V, a portrait of the Christian daimyō Hasekura Tsunenaga (1571–1622) in prayer following his conversion in Madrid, and nineteen religious paintings held by Sendai City Museum.

[12]On Important Intangible Folk Cultural Properties, see Thornbury (1997).

Given the visibility of sacred (or at least sacralized) sites, objects, and actions in Japan's World Heritage inscriptions and domestic designations, we should be attentive to—and question—the relationship between cultural heritage and religion.

RESEARCH AND METHODOLOGIES

Let us first situate cultural heritage and religion within the vast body of English-language literature on "tradition" (*dentō*) and Japan's experience of modernity (e.g., Ivy 1995; Morris-Suzuki 1998; Vlastos 1998; Isomae 2015). Works on cultural policies and practices in the Meiji period (e.g., Guth 1996; McDermott 2006; Pai 2013) and after the Second World War (e.g., Russell 2011; Kakiuchi 2014; Akagawa 2014, 2015, 2016a) bring many additional historical and art historical contours into relief. We can also avail of a substantial crop of case studies that articulate the "second life" (Kirshenblatt-Gimblett 1998) of religious sites and practices as cultural heritage objects (e.g., Law 2010; Yasuda 2010; Blair 2011; Foster 2011, 2015; McGuire 2013; Reader 2014; Akagawa 2016b; Rots 2019a; DeWitt 2020). More case studies, accompanied by a helpful introduction, appear in a volume edited by Rots and Teeuwen (which, to my knowledge, marks the first book-length study in English on the paired topics of cultural heritage and religion; Rots and Teeuwen 2020).

Japanese publications on religious cultural heritage, albeit rarely under that name, are abundant and may be divided into three distinct categories. First, we have academic works, which fall into two types. Scholarship specific to the disciplines of archaeology, architecture, art history, geography, tourism, and local history, among others—research that is empirical, technical, and descriptive in nature—provide us with focused studies of particular sites, structures, and remains. Scholarship focused on intangible cultural elements like festivals and other ritual practices, worship cults, and performance arts come primarily from folklorists, anthropologists, and sometimes literature specialists. The second category includes publications from Japan's public sector (government and nongovernmental agencies), emic works representing what heritage scholar Laurajane Smith has termed the "authorized heritage discourse" (2006: 299). These publications reflect the combined voices of local governments, the ACA, and the culture industries; as such, they reveal expectations and constructed histories for sites and practices. The third type of Japanese publications circulate in the popular media and are written for general audiences and often in support of tourism. Although these works tend to essentialize and romanticize "Japan," "Japanese culture," and "heritage," a very small number of them engage rigorously with critical concerns in global heritage research, such as the politicization of heritage designations, site selection, and competing versions of history (e.g., Sataki 2009; Noguchi 2014; Kiso 2015).

As it stands, the lion's share of Japanese publications demonstrates little awareness of the larger body of global research on the complexities and "metacultural" (Kirshenblatt-Gimblett 2006) aspects of cultural heritage.[13] This shortcoming stems in part from the reality noted above: most of the Japanese discourse on cultural heritage does not employ—and thus does not conceptually engage with—the term "cultural heritage"/*bunka isan* (or

---

[13] A metacultural perspective of heritage recognizes it as a mode of cultural production through which governmental agents resituate—and, hence, reproduce—local and national cultural goods within an imagined cultural commons, one premised upon a particular (i.e., modern, Western, liberal) vision of humanity.

the term "religion"/*shūkyō*).¹⁴ Critical and theoretically aware research coming out of the fields of ethnology and folklore (e.g., Ōshima 2007; Iwamoto 2013; Kikuchi 2020), history and archaeology (e.g., Suzuki and Takagi 2002; Imao and Takagi 2017), tourism (e.g., Hirayama 2015; Kadota 2017), and geography (e.g., Matsui 2018; Fujimura 2019) hopefully signals a changing tide.¹⁵

On the other hand, in global scholarship on cultural heritage, we observe a reluctance to probe the interplay between cultural heritage and religion, even though religious sites and practices often serve as the setting for cultural heritage research. The global rush to stake out and refashion places, objects, practices, and even living people through the lens of cultural heritage invites fresh consideration of inquiries that have long been regarded as fundamental in the study of religion. What becomes regarded as sacred and why (and how and by whom)? Does sacredness manifest of its own accord, or does human activity and interpretive labor conjure it up?¹⁶ How does sacrality operate and how does it change over time? It may come as a surprise, as it did to the present author, to learn that these and other questions at the heart of religious studies occupy only a tiny space in today's mass of monographs, articles, handbooks, journals, and even degree programs dedicated to cultural heritage.¹⁷ Solid, if disparate, studies excavate the meanings of heritage (e.g., Harvey 2001; Winter 2014), the contested dimensions of heritage (e.g., Silverman 2011; Meskell 2015; Brumann and Berliner 2016), and the World Heritage realm (e.g., Cleere 2001; Jokilehto 2006; Brumann 2012, 2014a; Labadi 2013). A number of recent works on Asia help to counter the long-standing Eurocentrism of heritage studies, but they contain scant discussion of religion specifically (e.g., Brumann and Cox 2010; Daly and Winter 2012; Silva and Chapagain 2013; Akagawa 2014; Matsuda and Mengoni 2016; and Hsiao, Hui, and Peycam 2017).

Historian David Lowenthal, one of the earliest to articulate the contemporary heritage boom, described it in terms of "cult," "creed," and "faith" (1998: 1–2). More recently, anthropologist Christoph Brumann critiqued the presence of heritage "belief" and "theology" within academia and called for "agnosticism" in its study (2014b: 173–4). Religious analogies like these circulate in the realm of heritage publications, but the analytic potential of religious studies methodologies has not been fully engaged. Four exceptions warrant mention that might stimulate comparative insights if applied to Japan. Essays collected in Hall (2011) draw out the close association between religion and the modern preservation movement. Second, a special issue of *Material Religion* edited by

---

¹⁴The reflexive shift in Japanese religious studies from the turn of the millennium, exemplified by the works of scholars like Shimazono Susumu and Isomae Jun'ichi, seems pertinent to mention here.

¹⁵I wish also to acknowledge a statement issued in September 2018 by a group of thirteen academic associations concerned regarding the then-impending World Heritage status of "Mozu-Furuichi Kofun Group: Mounded Tombs of Ancient Japan" (designated in 2019). The statement sharply criticizes the Imperial Household Agency for restricting access to so-called imperial tombs and calls for "proper" conservation and a system of naming "based on academic reasoning." The full text of the statement (in both Japanese and English) can be found at http://www.nihonshiken.jp/百舌鳥・古市古墳群の世界文化遺産推薦に関する/. For more on the refashioning of these tumuli as heritage, see Loo (2020).

¹⁶Mircea Eliade, Rudolf Otto, and Gerard van der Leeuw represent the former view, and Émile Durkheim, Henri Lefebvre, and J. Z. Smith typify the latter position.

¹⁷The roughly contemporaneous publication of Anderson (1983), Hobsbawm and Ranger (1983), and Lowenthal (1985) marked the beginning of focused academic attention on heritage (and tradition), at least in the Anglophone world. These works did not "invent" the deconstructive study of tradition, heritage, and community/nationhood, but they did help to establish new paradigms of academic inquiry. For an earlier inquiry, one that reflects on Japan specifically, see Chamberlain (1912).

cultural anthropologists Birgit Meyer and Marleen de Witte probes the "heritagization of the sacred," mentioned above, and its counterpart "the sacralization of heritage" (2013: 277). The refashioning of religious space as cultural heritage forms the focal point of a special issue of *Religions* (Wetterberg and Löfgren 2019). Finally, Isnart and Cerezales (2020) examine the interaction between (Western) religious institutions and heritage-making practices, which they term "the religious heritage complex."

Looking back on the whole of previous publications, a certain dissatisfaction lingers because most of them take the form of collected essays. Introductions to these volumes can and do break new ground, but the time seems ripe for scholars interested in cultural heritage and religion and/or religious cultural heritage in Japan to consolidate and systematize the vast corpus of site- and case-specific studies, inquire into patterns and structures, and begin to propose theoretically useful frameworks. For starters, future research will need to confront questions concerning the co-constitution (and likely conflation) of tradition, culture, heritage, and religion in Japan, and examine the historical roots of their framings and juxtapositions vis-à-vis the state.[18] Works that manage to bring the disparate pieces of the puzzle together, the poetic and the political, will reap their combined virtues and situate the field of Japanese religions in new and fertile ground.

See also Chapter 10, "Folk Performing Arts," and Chapter 28, "Tourism."

---

[18] To give one example, Meiji-period modernists enacted systematic legislation to document and protect religious objects and sites, yet also promulgated policies that led to the destruction of a great number of precious heritage objects. The 1868 legal separation of gods and buddhas (*shinbutsu bunri*) and the subsequent government confiscation of lands owned by Buddhist temples precipitated one of the darkest moments of Japan's religious history, the anti-Buddhist movement known as *haibutsu kishaku* (lit. "abolish Buddhism, destroy Śākyamuni"). Many surviving religious artworks were hidden or sold to foreign collectors, and many surviving temples and shrines succumbed to neglect and decay. The image of cultural heritage and religion that emerges in this respect is far less sanguine than the one we encounter today. On *shinbutsu bunri* and *haibutsu kishaku*, see, e.g., Grapard (1984) and Sekimori (2005).

CHAPTER 4

Disasters

Levi MCLAUGHLIN

10:15 a.m., June 25, 2014: Morning light pours through an open temple window onto a circle of eight priests, six men and two women. They crowd together, close enough to hear one other's soft-spoken exchange. A circle of students and researchers surround them, scribbling notes, their digital recorders on. We are in Natori, a city in Miyagi Prefecture, on the northeast coast of Honshū, Japan's largest island. The session falls on the second of two days of intensive instruction at Renkōji, a Pure Land Buddhist (Jōdoshū) temple. We may be in a temple, but the priests do not speak of Buddhism, and not all of them are Buddhists. They are halfway through an intensive three-day workshop, a required component in their training as *rinshō shūkyōshi*, a professional certification that can be translated literally as "clinical religious instructor" but is rendered into English by its advocates as "interfaith chaplain."

This is certainly an interfaith gathering. A bespectacled True Pure Land (Jōdo Shinshū) sect priest smiles wryly as he describes his field placement at a retirement home in Niigata Prefecture, where he attempted to provide solace to one elderly male resident, only to be rebuffed. He receives feedback from the principal instructor, a Sōtō Zen priest, and also from a minister from the United Church of Christ in Japan, who reflects on her own recent work with residents of temporary housing units in the disaster region, which includes the area around this temple. "You should think of ways to adapt to the point of view of your care recipient," they urge. They go so far as to analyze the old man's specific word choices—a tough mix of local dialect and gruff dismissals—and the priest's word-for-word responses, carrying out a discourse analysis indebted to a technique called *keichō*, or "active listening," an approach adopted largely from American treatments for post-traumatic stress disorder (PTSD). The others in the circle are male Buddhist priests from other denominations and one woman from the new religion Tenrikyō. They duly share their own reconstructed dialogues from their field placements, which have included treating alcoholics, operating a suicide hotline, and providing palliative care in hospital wards.

This range of practitioners is being trained by faculty from the Department of Practical Religious Studies at Tohoku University in Sendai, the largest city near the epicenter of the March 11, 2011, earthquake that triggered a massive tsunami and meltdown at the Fukushima Daiichi nuclear plants—compound cataclysms that have come to be known as "3.11."[1] Upward of 18,800 people were killed or remain unaccounted for after the 3.11

---

[1] Information on Practical Religious Studies at Tohoku University is available at https://www2.sal.tohoku.ac.jp/p-religion/2017/index.html. See also Berman (2018) for an analysis of the program, particularly the training of interfaith chaplains, and the place of post-3.11 religious initiatives in contemporary Japan.

disasters. Many thousands more were traumatized by their physical and psychological injuries; hundreds of communities were destroyed, mostly by the tsunami; and hundreds of thousands of people were displaced by the disaster, many never to return.[2]

As the morning session progresses, we observe religion theory-making that the chaplains in training elaborate before us in real time. Earlier this morning, they took in a lecture from a Tohoku University professor, who expounded on concepts they were encouraged to apply during their caregiving placements: the danger of *ikigire*, or "running out of breath," running out of energy to either provide or receive aid; *konton*, or "chaos," the frustrating social and psychological disarray that persists years after the initial catastrophe; and *jikansa*, or "time gap," a term that addresses the mindset gap that yawns between those who suffer and those who did not. For sufferers—3.11 survivors in this context, but potentially anyone who experienced a traumatic event—disaster persists as an immanent state. It is ongoing, a ripping apart of linear time. Survivors continue to inhabit the disaster, while others treat it as one in a series of events that grows progressively distant. Aid providers must bridge this ever-growing time gap to address survivors' needs.

The caregivers in this circle begin applying these concepts to their care practices. They consult with one another on suitable means of carefully introducing memorial ritual, prayer, or doctrinal interpretations, at times commiserating about the difficulties of forging a connection with recipients to allow for these types of religious care to proceed. The budding interfaith chaplains are constantly reminded to overcome their individual sectarian commitments, to be ready to provide any type of religious service a recipient may require. A Buddhist priest should be ready to join in a Christian prayer, and a Protestant minister should be prepared to chant a *sūtra*, if necessary.[3]

JAPANESE RELIGION AS RELIGION OF DISASTER

There is nothing new about religion in Japan being redefined by disaster. Japanese history can in fact be summarized as a history of cataclysms and religious responses. Japan is, after all, an archipelago that has and continues to erupt at the meeting point of tectonic plates, so its social history is necessarily formed by seismic activity and its aftermath. From early in Japan's historical record, disasters have been attributed to the actions of the kami, buddhas, and other divine powers that are understood to populate every portion of the country and respond to human activity. Earthquakes, tsunamis, fires, tornados, droughts, famines, and wars merge in accounts of Japan's past, just as they have across Asia, and the line between natural and human-created disasters has always blurred in records of calamities as punishments meted out by transhuman forces for human shortcomings (Kern 2000; Janku 2009; Fountain and McLaughlin 2016).

Popular Japanese medieval tale collections, Buddhist morality stories, officially sponsored chronicles, and other sources indicate that it has been the responsibility of

---

[2] 3.11 data is maintained by the Disaster Management Office at Cabinet Office Japan (http://www.bousai.go.jp/kaigirep/hakusho/h24/bousai2012/html/honbun/1b_1h_1s_01_00.htm) and information on post-disaster reconstruction is publicized by Japan's Reconstruction Agency (http://www.reconstruction.go.jp/). For a vivid journalistic account of 3.11 and its aftermath, see Parry (2017).

[3] See a translation of Taniyama Yōzō's guidance for interfaith chaplains in McLaughlin (2019a) for examples of how religious professionals are taught to navigate around their religious identities. See also Benedict (2018) for analysis of religious hospice care in Japan.

ritual specialists to mitigate disaster through their interactions with divinities (Marra 1991; Pandey 1998; Watson 2013). Human mismanagement *is* a disaster: Kamo no Chōmei, a courtier who took Buddhist vows before penning the *Hōjōki* (An Account of My Hut) in 1212, counted the move of the imperial capital in 1180 among five *fushigi*, or "inexplicable phenomena," that brought about ruin (Wakabayashi 2015). But humans also possess the resources to prevail through disaster: Japanese commentators have drawn on Buddhist and other resources to explain the causes of calamity to a distraught populace, and religious communities have consistently contributed in significant ways to post-disaster reconstruction (Rambelli 2014).

Numerous important religious institutions were founded in the wake of catastrophe. The worship site that came to be known as Gion in Kyoto traces its origins to the Nara era (710–794). It is centered on reverence for "disease-divinities" (*ekijin*), which are understood to cause not only pestilence but also earthquakes and other calamities. Kyoto's spectacular annual Gion festival began as one of many medieval rituals performed to quell the anger of these deities, which emerged as *goryō*, powerful spirits of deceased rulers whose anger at political events was credited as the cause of worldly misfortune (McMullin 1988). The Buddhist reformer Nichiren (1222–1282), marginal during his lifetime, but posthumously of great renown, gained notoriety for his 1260 petition *Risshō ankokuron* (On the Establishment of the True [Teaching] for the Peace of the Country), in which he rebuked Japan's governmental authorities for bringing about earthquakes, wind storms, famine, and disease through their failure to reject all teachings save exclusive embrace of the *Lotus Sūtra* (Deal 1999; Stone 1999). The *Heike monogatari* (Tale of the Heike), compiled before 1330, contributed to a widespread understanding that the 1185 earthquake that shook Kyoto was caused by defeated Taira clan warriors who died in the sea battle at Dan no Ura and transformed beneath the waves into dragons that signaled their enmity to subsequent regimes by sending up tremors. This was part of a long-lasting Japanese belief that earthquakes and their accompanying destructive events were caused by mythological creatures—dragons (*nāgas*), but also the Indian deities Agni, Indra, and the great bird Garuda—which, in most cases, entered Japanese folklore from continental sources (Rambelli 2014).

Explanations that credited powerful divinities as agents of destruction dominated late into the modern era. The 1855 Ansei earthquake that wreaked havoc in Edo (present-day Tokyo), for example, inspired a popular trade in *namazue*, woodblock "catfish prints" that depicted the kami Kashima Daimyōjin pressing either the Kashima shrine's foundation stone or a great gourd onto the head of a giant catfish, an adaptation from Chinese Daoist legends of immortals from the island Penglai riding great beasts and suppressing their volatile strength (Smits 2012; Miura 2019). Even after Japan transformed into an industrialized nation-state, the catfish continued to swim into seismological inquiry. A Tohoku University professor in 1932, for example, was reported in the newspaper *Yomiuri shinbun* as being able to predict earthquakes by observing catfish swimming patterns, advancing laboratory investigations on catfish and earthquakes that began after the Great Kantō Earthquake of 1923 (Smits 2012). This investigation exemplifies the shift from popular reliance on religiously guided explanations to a rationalized scientific episteme, as Japan transformed into first an expansionist empire and then a postwar economic powerhouse.[4]

---

[4] See Weisenfeld (2012) for an examination of how image production in art, religion, and science following the 1923 Kantō earthquake propelled Japan's transformation into a modern nation-state.

Over the course of Japan's postwar development, as responsibility for explaining natural phenomena shifted decidedly to science, the number of people who readily self-identified as religious dropped. Just after the 3.11 disasters, the Japanese people were among the world's least likely to identify as religious; in a 2012 WIN-Gallup poll, only 16 percent of respondents claimed religious faith and 31 percent said they were atheists (cited in Chilson 2017). This decline accelerated precipitously after 1995, a year in which two calamitous events combined to destroy religion's public image. The most grievous blow to religion in Japan was struck on March 20, 1995, when members of the apocalyptic sect Aum Shinrikyō released sarin gas on the Tokyo subways. Religion's public image had already been compromised immediately before this through negative public reactions to aid offered by religious activists in the aftermath of the January 17, 1995, Great Hanshin Earthquake, which killed approximately 6,400 people, mostly in the city of Kobe. Even though Kobe-area Buddhist temples, Shinto shrines, Christian churches, and other religious facilities opened their doors to refugees, in some cases for months at a time, a negative media narrative took shape in which religious aid providers were accused of using disaster relief as a means of proselytizing or prioritizing their own followers over other victims. Their efforts were then devastated by the Aum attacks, which triggered a media-driven moral panic during which even a humble local Buddhist priest ran the risk of associating himself with social danger if he offered disaster relief dressed in his ceremonial garb (Hardacre 2007). Meanwhile, religious scholars after the Hanshin quake sabotaged the efforts of post-disaster clerical volunteer work by questioning the qualifications of priests who offered aid. Most famously, Yamaori Tetsuo, a professor of religious studies who is a widely published public intellectual, decried religious volunteerism as inappropriate and urged Buddhist clerics to focus on their traditional ritual duties and leave material aid to credentialed experts.[5]

A NEW RELIGION NARRATIVE AFTER 3.11

Religious responses to the 3.11 disaster made clear that activists had applied the harsh lessons of 1995 to prepare disaster mobilizations that presented religion in a positive light. They were aided by changes in legislation and popular Japanese sentiment from the late 1990s that saw a growth in Japan's religious NGOs and efforts to train clergy in counseling and related skills (Kawanami 2013). By the early 2000s, Christian and Buddhist hospice care had been established as a small-scale yet dependable service in a number of regions, and training was available in religious universities across Japan for practitioners who sought work in social welfare (Kasai 2016).

These programs fed into more robust post-3.11 efforts. Immediately following the earthquake, tsunami, and nuclear meltdown at Fukushima on March 11, 2011, hundreds of Japan's religious organizations sprang into action. Within minutes of hearing news of the earthquake, volunteers at headquarters for Buddhist, Shinto, Christian, and new religious organizations began loading trucks with supplies and driving on ruined roads to deliver aid to refugees housed in temples, churches, and other facilities, while teams dispatched from religious groups searched the rubble for survivors and bodies. In the months after 3.11, thousands of volunteers delivered billions of yen's worth of aid and

---

[5]See McLaughlin (2016a) for an overview of religious responses to the Hanshin disaster.

provided countless hours of service, and tens of thousands of refugees were cared for by religious institutions (McLaughlin 2016b).

As religions provided aid, they also took advantage of print and electronic outlets to mobilize carefully chosen images of their aid efforts. Clearinghouses of reports on religious aid, organized for the most part by scholars of Japanese religion, began receiving attention from reporters. The most influential was the Faith-Based Network for Earthquake Relief in Japan, a Facebook-based source that, once in place after 3.11, continued to provide links to reports on religious aid efforts after subsequent disasters, including rescue and relief offered after the great floods of July 2018 in western Japan.[6] The Faith-Based Network is linked to the Japan Religion Coordinating Project for Disaster Relief (JRPD), which is headed by Shimazono Susumu, professor emeritus in religious studies at the University of Tokyo, who now heads the Institute of Grief Care at Sophia University in Tokyo.[7] From April 2011, the JRPD organized information exchange meetings at the University of Tokyo's Young Buddhist association at which academics, representatives of religious NGOs, and activists from a range of religions gave reports on their relief initiatives. The JRPD was one of several meeting points for academics and religious professionals that guided the creation of a new post-disaster religion narrative, one in which the category "religion" was disaggregated from sectarian identities and associated with care providers who "overcome religious boundaries" (*shūkyōtekina waku o koe*) or "overcome sectarian divides" (*shūha o koe*) to dispatch relief to those in need, regardless of their religious beliefs.[8]

The efforts that received the greatest amount of media approbation were those that downplayed sectarian identity in favor of attention to the efforts of religious people. This shift from the institutional to the individual coheres with a global secular shift, also at work in Japan, that has seen religion relegated to the interior realm, a personal dimension increasingly apt to be defined as a distinctive "spirituality" rather than as practices and dispositions informed by religious traditions.[9] The post-disaster efforts deemed most palatable for public consumption have been those by religious individuals who distinguish themselves as personally relatable contributors to social reconstruction; in other words, practitioners whose efforts typically contribute to the field of "spiritual care."[10]

POST-DISASTER RELIGION AS RELIGIOUS CARE

Activists affiliated with the programs coordinated by Tohoku University's Department of Practical Religious Studies are the primary exponents of religion as a clinical treatment. These programs grew out of post-3.11 clerical responses in Sendai. As bodies from the tsunami arrived at municipal funeral homes and police stations, clergy with links to the Sendai Buddhist Association, the Sendai Christian Alliance, and the Miyagi Prefecture Association of Religious Juridical Persons sought permission from city- and prefecture-level authorities to perform volunteer prayers for the mass dead—something that required

---

[6] Available at https://www.facebook.com/FBNERJ/.
[7] See https://sites.google.com/site/syuenrenindex/.
[8] Examples of these linguistic uses are cited in McLaughlin (2016a) and Berman (2018).
[9] For discussions of ways "spirituality" is developing in Japan today, see Carter (2018) and Chapter 27 by Horie in this volume.
[10] For analysis of ways "spiritual care" developed in Japan and how it is applied in clinical treatments, see Benedict (2018).

careful negotiation around separations between religion and government guaranteed by Japan's 1947 constitution. They simultaneously offered help to the living on the second floor of a crematorium in Aoba Ward, Sendai, where priests sat at tables counseling bereaved family members. By April 2011, the priests replaced in-person consultation with an anonymous telephone counseling service, with help from Sendai Inochi no Denwa, the city's suicide prevention helpline.

In May 2011, these activists founded the Kokoro no Sōdanshitsu, the "Counseling Room of the Heart" (hereafter KSS). The KSS began as a truly ecumenical effort that distinguished itself by reaching far beyond religion to engage clergy with specialists in medicine, education, and social services. It was headed by the physician and palliative care specialist Okabe Ken and was subsequently administered by Reverend Kawakami Naoya, pastor at Sendai Citizen Church, and Suzuki Iwayumi, professor of religious studies at Tohoku University. It began with funding from a wide range of religious associations and now falls under the auspices of Tohoku University's Department of Practical Religious Studies, which was endowed in April 2012. The KSS is maintained as one of several related initiatives that maintain links to this university department, including the Café de Monk, a mobile counseling service and radio broadcast begun by the Sōtō Zen priest Kaneta Taiō, and the interfaith chaplaincy training program (Graf 2016).

Notably, Practical Religious Studies has staked out new territory by situating training activities for religious professionals in a Japanese public university, ordinarily something that is prevented by constitutional separations of religion and government (Berman 2018). Competition to enter the Tohoku program to qualify as an interfaith chaplain remained strong after 3.11. It inspired six Buddhist universities across Japan and the Jesuit Sophia University in Tokyo to begin their own interfaith chaplaincy modules. The program originators also determined that a nationally recognized accreditation process was required to create a stable institutional presence, something that would establish interfaith chaplaincy as a viable professional track. In February 2016, the Society for Interfaith Chaplaincy in Japan (Nihon Rinshō Shūkyōshikai, or SICJ) was inaugurated at the Kyoto temple Kiyomizudera.[11]

In March 2018, the SICJ held its first board of governors meeting, marking the official start of a nationally recognized certification for interfaith chaplains to be granted via two tracks: (1) lecture courses at a university that offers interfaith chaplaincy courses, field experience, and follow-up training. These chaplains are designated as "course completers" (*shūryōsha*); (2) chaplains who have already completed in excess of 300 hours of clinical work experience in the public sphere, practitioners who are designated as "pioneers" (*senkusha*).

CONCLUSION: DISASTER AS DEFINITION

Just as understandings of particular teachings and practices sharpened in the wake of calamities throughout Japanese history, so too will the category "religion" continue to be redefined in Japan after disasters in the future. The influence of post-disaster redefinitions of religion is evident in ways the category has been shaped in popular discourse since 2011. The number of interfaith chaplains in Japan is small, and even with the growth of the training programs, they remain a tiny percentage of Japan's religious practitioners.

---

[11] The SICJ site is at http://sicj.or.jp/.

Nonetheless, this program has exerted a disproportionate influence on popular understandings of religion in post-3.11 Japan. Paradoxes abound as tonsured Buddhist priests and ordained Christian clergy rely on sectarian resources to "overcome religion" to provide aid. However, no matter the disconnect between ways these individuals are profiled and the institutions to which they remain beholden, no matter the comparatively small number of practitioners who train as purveyors of religious care, and no matter the difficulties interfaith chaplains may encounter in their efforts to offer aid to a Japanese population that remains leery of religion, the clinic-oriented definition that took shape in the years after 3.11 will continue to influence how religion is understood in Japan. It remains to be seen what new definitions will emerge following future disasters.

See also Chapter 2, "Chaplaincy and Spiritual Care."

CHAPTER 5

Economy and Spirituality

Ioannis GAITANIDIS

It is perhaps no surprise that the subject of economy and spirituality does not figure prominently in introductory textbooks on spirituality in the contemporary world. A case in point is the *Spirituality* volume from the Short Introductions series published by Oxford University Press. Written in 2012 by Philip Sheldrake, a theologian of Christianity, the book contains only five paragraphs on the topic of "Spirituality and Economics" and these mostly summarize the activities of SPES, a European-centered international forum for "Spirituality in Economics and Society," which conceives of spirituality as "a public value with social and public effects" (Sheldrake 2012: 89). This scant treatment does little justice to what is perhaps a fundamental aspect of "spirituality" today, but I argue that such minimal consideration reflects two significant issues associated with these two terms.

One, which has already been discussed in this volume,[1] has to do with the cumbersomeness of "spirituality" as an analytic concept.[2] Indeed, most definitions of the term do little more than generalize vernacular understandings, often originating in essentially Christian settings, and/or rehash phenomena previously described by terms such as "religiosity," "religious character," and so on. As I will discuss below, the issue seems to be related to the ways in which the term "spirituality" has been deployed both in popular and academic circles to cover a wide variety of interests, activities, and ideas, ranging from "traditional" religious practices reframed under new consumer labels, to formerly "secular" topics that have invited the scrutiny of religious studies researchers interested in the psychological aspects of "(hyper-)consumer cultures."

The second issue, which I shall discuss in detail hereafter, is more specific to how the relationship between spirituality and economics has until recently been the object of polarization of academic discourses. One cannot start thinking about this topic without first overcoming this otherwise simple trap, which in effect produces the illusion of (contemporary) spirituality and economics being two completely separate entities. In the following section, I examine this controversy and locate it within more general debates in post-Aum Japanese academia.

---

[1] See Chapter 27 by Horie in this volume.
[2] A look at the programs of the annual conferences of the Japanese Association for Religious Studies reveals that, in the last decade, the use of the concept has become associated with certain specific fields of interest (such as "spiritual care") and limited to research conducted by a few specific scholars.

Good Spirituality and Bad Economics or Bad Spirituality… and (still) Bad Economics

Today, perhaps more than ever, criticizing our own consumption habits has become a habit too, one that often survives on Facebook posts and tweets that perpetrate pastiche-like messages encouraging inner knowledge over futile materialism, such as a yoga lesson over the purchase of a new smartphone. Critics of such "spiritual" narratives have not failed to warn us that late capitalism feeds on the ideology of individualism because it allows individual consumers to believe that their behavior is not dictated by the market but by their inner self. Hence, whatever issue they may experience, this should not and cannot interfere with the processes of capitalist production and consumption (see, e.g., Illouz 2008, Martin 2014). Another group of scholars, however, claim the contrary: they argue that this individual spirituality is a reaction to capitalism and an expression of individual agency that allows us to cope with the alienating and rapid changes of late modernity (see, e.g., Heelas 2008, Aupers and Houtman 2010).

This chicken-or-egg causality rhetoric has not failed to draw attention, and as Teemu Taira (2009) already noted more than a decade ago, it has created a bifurcation between studies that consider spirituality as a progressive and anti-capitalist ideology (see, e.g., Lynch 2007) and studies that treat spirituality as a neoliberal ideology (see, e.g., Lau 2000, Carrette and King 2005). Koike Yasushi has called the first camp of scholars "the romantics" and the second camp "the popular culture critics" (2013: 216). However, Koike does not necessarily refer to local, Japanese scholarship in his analysis. The reason for this lies, I argue, in the somewhat different polarization of Japanese scholarship on the topic of economy and spirituality, and on the ensuing lack of serious theorization of case studies from Japan. Indeed, scholarship on this subject in Japan has been significantly influenced and remains essentially dependent on research about New Religious Movements (hereafter NRMs), for which Japan arguably offers a rich ground. It is therefore necessary, when talking about spirituality and economy in Japan, to be aware of the post-Aum climate of research on NRMs in Japan.

In his survey of scholarly reactions to the Aum affair, Ben Dorman (2012a) observed a certain division between those who reacted negatively to the affair, and, as a result, intensified their criticism of the so-called cults and the spiritual sales on which many of these groups survive (see Fujita 2016 [1996] for an early account); and those who decided to focus on the New Age Movement and alternative spiritualities, an area that attracted significant attention, particularly in the first decade of the new millennium. In this divide, the first camp of scholars tend therefore to resemble Koike's popular culture critics and typically place the blame both on the charlatanism of healing salons and on the lack of rational thinking on the part of the new generations of Japanese consumers. Meanwhile, the second camp of scholars tend to duplicate romantic arguments about "new" forms of religious engagement in increasingly uncertain and unstable social settings. On the surface, therefore, the situation in Japan perhaps resembles European trends, but I argue here that there are important differences.

The first difference is that, despite appearances, there is an overall lack of serious theoretical critique. Indeed, Sakurai Yoshihide, a staunch critic of "spiritual sales" in and outside organized religion, concludes his analysis of the "spiritual business" by blaming the popularity of holistic spiritualities on the lack of socioeconomic stability and vision for a future, which, coupled with the loosening of human relationships, drive young individuals to seek solutions to their problems and to their crisis of identity in new forms of community, such as healing networks and "cults" whose value they judge based on their feelings rather than on rational knowledge (2009: 241–2). In a more recent study of color therapy in Japan, Katō Yukiko categorizes a large variety of self-development, spirituality, and New Age activities under a single term: "kitsch culture of a hyperconsumer society" (2015: 20). One cannot but sense that such surveys reflect certain ideals regarding what the "appropriate way" of "doing religion" is, in addition to romanticizing "traditional" communities and their values, with which the authors seem to nostalgically associate "proper" religious practice.

The second difference is the lack of response from the other side of the debate. In other words, none of the "romantics" has attempted to deal with the economic aspects of spirituality in Japan, beyond the classic argument that narratives of spirituality have helped young generations to cope (see, e.g., Hashisako 2014) with the same problems (lack of relationships, "liquid" identity, etc.) that Sakurai identifies as the reasons for these same youth falling victims of religious scams. In 2017, in a panel on "Religion, Spirituality and Consumption" at the annual conference of the Japanese Association for the Study of Religion and Society (JASRS), and in a subsequent special issue of the *Journal of the Japanese Association for Religious Studies* (volume 91, issue 2), an attempt was made to engage with the field of religion and economics more theoretically. However, the only paper explicitly discussing spirituality is essentially a review of the English literature (Horie 2017b),[3] in which the author tends to lean toward Aupers and Houtman's argument for studying the increasingly public display of spirituality, especially at the workplace.

There is still, no actual discussion between the two camps and no new research coming out of Japan that could perhaps join Euro-American theoretical developments that have recently attempted to overcome the aforementioned polarization.[4] For example, one approach looks at neoliberalism as a form of religious occupation of the economy: "a way of seeing the self in the world as a calculating sovereign person enfolded in systems of power, class, and experience through the selection of particular goods and services" (Lofton 2017: 9).

Indeed, regardless of the personal convictions of scholars, the spiritual market in Japan is, to use an expression especially popular in Japanese media, "booming," and also constantly adapting not only to new concerns of the Japanese society but also to new technological trends. In the following section, I offer a few representative and recent examples of how spirituality and economy can be observed in Japan today.

CASE STUDIES FROM JAPAN

There are several ways of conceptualizing a juxtaposition between economy and spirituality. One is to simply consider the influence of the economic situation in Japan on spirituality among the Japanese and, if necessary, vice-versa. A second, more widespread

---

[3]A review by Horie Norichika presented at the JASRS panel included only the following literature on this topic in Japan (and/or written in Japanese), with merely four academic studies espousing a religious studies perspective, one nonacademic market research, and two monographs from other disciplinary fields (sociology of health, and marketing): Hashisako (2008), Sakurai (2009), Gaitanidis (2010, 2011), Arimoto (2011), Matsui (2013), and Fujioka (2015). By contrast, the review included at least thirty-two non-Japanese references on spirituality and economy.

[4]In a very fortunate turn of events, since the writing of this chapter, four religious studies scholars have published an extremely important manifesto that employs case studies from Japan to argue for the importance of studying the corporate form (McLaughlin et al. 2020).

conceptualization describes the characteristic features of the economic aspects of spirituality in Japan today, including how individuals involved in the spiritual business establish monetary transactions in their provision of spiritual services. Yet, a third way would consist of identifying the theoretical underpinnings of this juxtaposition, *spirituality and economy*, and consider how these may be informed by Japanese case studies. This section will treat with the first and second approaches. I will leave the third theoretical approach for the last section.

In Japan, researchers frequently link the rise of what Shimazono Susumu, the most prominent researcher in the field of contemporary spirituality in Japan, has termed the "new spirituality culture" (Shimazono 1996; 2007a for an early and thorough account) to Japan's bubble economy of the late 1980s and its subsequent collapse in the early 1990s. Indeed, as early as the mid-1990s, a special issue called "The New Age in Japan" in the *Japanese Journal of Religious Studies* noted, for example, the connection between the affluence of the bubble economy years and the corresponding increase of the number of self-development seminars (Haga 1995: 288), as well as the rise of a healing fad following the disillusionment with material wealth provoked by the burst of the bubble in the 1990s (Yumiyama 1995: 279). Yumiyama later repeated his argument by emphasizing that the economic downturn has resulted in the individualization and relativization of the sense of values of the Japanese, leading them to espouse more eclectic strategies when looking for answers to existential issues in their everyday life (Yumiyama 2004: 263). This argument allows us to make a comparison with the United States, a cradle of the New Age movement, where Ronald Reagan's neoliberal policies of the 1980s worsened the economic situation and led, by an interesting turn of events, to the popularization of various New Age ideologies. As Ahlin argues, "one goal of the movement had been to free human beings from the constraints placed upon them by society, thereby making it possible for individuals to evolve according to intrinsic conditions" (Ahlin 2013: 186).

For both Shimazono and Yumiyama, as well as for others (see, e.g., Itō 2003), the so-called lost decade of the late 1990s and early 2000s witnessed the spread of the minority culture of spirituality into the majority culture, a phenomenon that scholars have called "minoritization" and one that is intensified by the prevalence of global capitalism (Burity 2013: 23). Here, therefore, it is important not only to look for the popularization of alternative spiritualities in Japan in the Japanese "psychological" reaction to the economic downturn but also to consider developments in the wider consumer market, such as the brief boom of the publication market (especially the market of popular weekly/monthly magazines) in the mid-1990s, or the universalization of access to internet technology from that period onward.

Undoubtedly the market of religious/spiritual services seems to have increased overall in the last thirty years, but again, one needs to be careful when reading the scarce statistics that are currently available. For instance, the annual reports published by the Statistics Bureau of the Japanese Ministry of Internal Affairs and Communications show that average "religious contributions" per household have barely changed over the last twenty years, even showing a decline from 18,257 yen in 2000 to 12,250 yen in 2018. Again, as is common with statistics on religion in Japan, the term used by the Bureau's Family Income and Expenditure Survey[5] is "religious contribution," the official translation

---

[5]The data can be accessed at the website of the Statistics Bureau of the Japanese Ministry of Internal Affairs and Communications: http://www.stat.go.jp/data/kakei/npsf.htm (accessed May 15, 2017).

of *shinkō/saishihi* 信仰・祭祀費, which includes membership fees to parishioners' associations, donations and offerings to temples and shrines, and the purchase of amulets and charms. Yet, it does not include funeral or wedding fees, the purchase of family altars and gravestones, or other ceremonial fees, all of which are categorized separately. Thus, the term likely does not reflect the breadth of consumer behavior seen, for example, in the purchase of a reiki massage, or of a monthly membership at a telephone fortune-telling service.

In fact, in 2011, based on a sample of sixty-eight spiritual therapists providing in total over a hundred different types of sessions, from spiritual counseling, hypnotherapy, and reiki to oracle card reading and herbal massages, I calculated that the average price of a single session was approximately 16,000 yen (Gaitanidis 2011). Yumiko Arimoto, who has published the only (nonacademic) survey of the spiritual market in Japan to this day, estimates, based on a sample of 3,011 users, that a light user (i.e., someone who only accesses web-based or phone-based fortune-telling services) spends 130,000 yen per year, whereas a heavy user (i.e., someone who attends New Age fairs and pays for individual sessions at a therapist's salon on a regular basis) annually spends 620,000 yen (Arimoto 2011: 53). It is therefore probable that these types of expenses are recorded under different categories in official statistics, such as the purchase of "personal effects" (*mi no mawari no yōhin*), money gifts (*zōyokin*), recreational services (*kyōyō goraku sābisu*), or personal care services (*ribiyō sābisu*).

For example, the White Paper on Leisure, published annually by the Japan Productivity Center, added yoga and pilates among its survey items in 2016 in order to respond to the rising percentage of consumers who would like to try those activities (Nihon Seisansei Honbu Yoka Sōken 2017: 32–3). It is important to note here, however, that these particular tendencies seem to reflect a commoditization of health and healthcare (as was observed in the 1990s) rather than a genuine rise of health consciousness among the Japanese population (Fujioka 2015). Yet, some researchers are inclined to interpret these market activities as demonstrating the continuing spread of contemporary spirituality in the public sphere. In a similar turn of events, the media and related tourist fad of "power spots" (Suga 2010, Carter 2018), particular locations within (most frequently) Shinto shrines and/or natural sceneries that are accorded certain spiritual value in the sense of being "soothing" to the visitor's eye and "healing" to the visitor, being full of natural "power" or "energy," have recently given birth to new business opportunities. For example, the Association of Design about Strategy for Zone Industry and Zone Brand (*Chiiki Dezain Gakkai*) has published a study of strategies for creating regional value by designing "spirituality zones" that are meant to help depopulated or isolated areas to attract more visitors (Harada, Tachikawa, and Nishida 2017).

Technology also seems to have recreated many of the services that used to require face-to-face interactions and human contact, and for a cheaper price. Now that the majority of the population holds a small computer in the form of a smartphone in their hands, they have become potential customers of a multitude of online businesses. E-books of famous self-spirituality manuals or of private publications by popular spiritual therapists and Facebook communities that often form temporarily around a healing fair or charismatic healer have become the norm. Skype sessions are now almost a must for Japanese spiritual therapists, who go to great lengths in order to offer online the same services they offer in their salon, even sessions such as reiki, which traditionally required the practitioner's physical presence. Smartphone applications are also on the rise, with some therapists launching, for example, their own meditation software or companies selling their own applications allegedly capable of capturing the aura of users on screen (Gaitanidis 2019). As with other online services, customers are able to gain credits or transfer those credits to other online services, rendering such exchanges seamless in the unlimited net of possibilities that the online market has to offer. Despite existing research on the internet and organized religion in Japan, however, this area of the online market and spirituality has not yet been explored.

Today, typical face-to-face spiritual counseling or therapy sessions happen in small-scale events rather than large-size fairs such as the *Iyashi* (healing) *Fair*, which used to attract large numbers of consumers a decade ago. In the case of *Iyashi Fair*, the type of services promoted have also significantly expanded beyond what the word "spiritual" was originally associated with in the early years of the twenty-first century. Indeed, today someone visiting the *Iyashi Fair* should not be surprised to see booths offering sightseeing tour packages or organic products next to someone claiming to be channeling the spirit of a dolphin.

One could see these developments as an expansion of contemporary spirituality into other market domains, as the panelists of the 2017 conference of the JASRS tended to claim. But if we agree with Dawson that "modern society is *in toto* a consumer culture, and not just in its specifically consuming activities" (Dawson 2013: 136), then what we identify as "spirituality" in the current capitalist market seems to merely be the adoption of a concept employed by prosumers of a specific cultural section of this market to describe the rest of the market. This, therefore, would be a categorical fallacy.[6]

FUTURE DIRECTIONS

For new directions on research on economy and spirituality, one must look at the wider field of religion, economics, and consumer society. Here, recent scholarship has emphasized that "the question therefore is not whether economics have become religious or if religion has become an economic product like any other: there is a religious dimension to consumption at the same time that religion has been commoditised" (Gauthier, Martikainen, and Woodhead 2013: 18). From this point of view, Aupers and Houtman's call for more research on the introduction and subsequent significance of spirituality into the workplace (2006: 219), which some researchers in Japan have called for as well, is missing the mark because it still considers the two concepts, (self-) spirituality and economics, as two separate entities. In this case, Japan could provide a rich ground for counterarguments to show that contemporary manifestations of the religious dimensions of capitalism are not new phenomena but alternative or evolved manifestations expressing a mixture of local and global trends.

To prove my point about the degree to which an examination of spirituality and economics in Japan could help us revise and historicize our understanding of the term "spirituality" and of its relationship with modern processes of production and consumption, I would like to finish with an anecdotal yet illustrative example from my university teaching. In 2011, Mark Mullins suggested I watch *The Long Search*, a 1977 BBC documentary series that surveyed major religious traditions around the world, as

---

[6]This category fallacy is certainly linked to the more general tendency in sociological studies of contemporary religion to contrasting "religion" to "spirituality' and to taking accounts of social actors at face value, which tells us more about academics than the social world they intend to describe (Altglas 2016: 424).

potential teaching material for a class on religion in Japan. The ninth episode of the series, titled "The Land of the Disappearing Buddha," concerned Buddhism in Japan and found the presenter, Ronald Eyre, walking around Tokyo in search of "religion." To his "disappointment," however, the first man that he comes across is a businessman in his eighties, who requires his four hundred employees to practice *zazen* (sitting meditation) once per month in addition to occasional weekend retreats. After having observed one of these sessions (held in a room with "no images, no chanting, no scripture … nothing a Westerner can nod to and say 'ah yes, religion!' "), Eyre asks one of the employees who had been hit by the *keisaku* (the flat stick used to help those mediating to keep their concentration) how people outside reacted to her doing *zazen* at work, to which she replies that although surprised at the beginning, they now see a change in her: she seems gentler (and, presumably, a better worker).

Putting aside for a moment the (self-)orientalism that often plagues studies of religion in Japan, especially those which try to connect Japanese religious behavior to so-called Japanese or Asian values, excerpts of lived religion, such as the one above, clearly demonstrate that religion and economy have never been "happening" on separate fields and that "spirituality at the workplace," for example, is clearly not a new, twenty-first-century phenomenon that has appeared *as a result of* something like economic instability or new approaches to labor. Although contemporary popular discourse may be using a novel-sounding concept such as *supirichuariti* to present yoga retreats organized by Japanese companies, for example, as the new fad, there is absolutely no reason to consider this a "rise of spirituality" in market economies (see Shimazono 2007b). This is because such an approach would basically reify assumptions (now long-negated) about the secular essence of capitalism and about the possible existence of a capitalism-free religion. In contrast, Japan presents an opportunity to expand the overwhelming tendency of studies of economy and religion/spirituality to focus on Christianity (Bartel and Hulsether 2019: 586) and to historicize the process by which a multitude of religious practices that have been (re)interpreted and adapted out of their original contexts (which is what the term "spirituality" often refers to; see also Yoshinaga's entry in this volume) have always been intrinsically connected to, ideologically supporting, and also enhancing global market societies.

See also Chapter 19, "'New Religions'," Chapter 26, "Spiritualism and Occultism," Chapter 27, "Spirituality," and Chapter 28, "Tourism."

CHAPTER 6

Economy of Buddhism

Jørn BORUP

The financial aspects associated with Japanese new religious movements have always been inaccessible to observers, but there is no doubt that such movements are in general extremely wealthy. Though shielded from the investigative principles of transparency, the physical evidence of their sumptuous buildings and ambitious institutions leaves no doubt that they are truly rich and prosperous. But this is nothing new; throughout Japanese history traditional temple Buddhism has also had its natural share of wealth. From the early Heian period until the present day, money has always made religion go around. This chapter provides an introduction to the relationship between the economy and religion in the Japanese context, with a focus on Buddhism as a lived religion.

FROM DOCTRINE TO PRACTICE, MATERIALITY AND THE ECONOMY

The early study of Japanese religion was largely inspired by the general understanding of religion through the perspective of (mainly Protestant) Christian ideas and concepts. The so-called Sacred Books of The East were seen as the canonical counterparts to the Christian Bible, and the selective reading of the Buddhist Pali canon was taken to represent an Orientalized idealization of a Protestantized Buddhism with no rituals, no lived religion, and no materiality. Similarly, Japanese Buddhism was placed within this evolutionary kaleidoscope, measured through doctrinal and institutional developments. Buddhist theology was (and often still is) the dominant field of study, leaving materiality and folk religion to anthropological case studies. The approach of D. T. Suzuki to the study of Zen Buddhism as a nonmaterialistic and noneconomic form of Buddhism was characteristic of this tendency, influencing generations of Western scholars and practitioners and reducing (Zen) Buddhism to spirituality and meditation, with all issues related to the economy and materiality being regarded as irrelevant.

The "practice turn" in the 1990s not only supplemented doctrinal studies with ritual studies but also paved the way for counterbalancing *believing* and *understanding* with *doing* and *being* as important expressions of religiosity. Ian Reader and George Tanabe's *Practically Religious* (1998) was significant for this important development, following general deconstructions of theologizing tendencies in the study of (Japanese) religion. The "material turn" of the 2000s took this one step further, underlining the essential importance of objects as central to religion, with ritual paraphernalia, architecture, technology, and less tangible aspects such as sound, smell, and visions being regarded as representing, generating, and mediating religion as a human and cultural practice. Fabio

Rambelli's *Buddhist Materiality* (2007) was a quintessential contribution to this field in the study of Japanese religion.[1]

Economic aspects have often been ignored in the study of Buddhism (Brox and Williams-Oerberg 2019), which is generally regarded, particularly in popular literature, as a kind of "non-economic spirituality" (Obadia 2011). However, Max Weber's classical study of the Protestant ethic and the causal relations between religion and economic development have influenced other scholars of religion and Japanese culture, including Robert Bellah (1957), S. N. Eisenstadt (1996), W. Davis (1992, esp. ch. 4) and Randall Collins (1997), with Collins concluding that the medieval monastic system contributed to a "Buddhist capitalism." Other Western scholars have included economic aspects in their analyses of Japanese Buddhism, including Martin Collcutt (1981, ch. 7) on Zen in the Kamakura period, Neil McMullin (1984) on Buddhism in the sixteenth century, and Stephen G. Covell (2005, ch. 7, and 2012b) on contemporary temple Buddhism and the economy.[2] In the Japanese context, a "new paradigm of 'economics of religion'" (Obadia and Wood 2011) is a relevant prism to understand Buddhism, and if the term "economics" is further extended to apply to a broader field of values and different kinds of capital (social, cultural, symbolic, religious), exchange patterns will reveal additional intersections between material and immaterial values, ideas and practices relevant for the general study of religion.[3]

THE COST OF JAPANESE BUDDHISM

Today, the 85,000 Buddhist institutions with 344,000 priests serving its 89 million adherents[4] contribute significantly to the Japanese economy by circulating economic transactions between individuals, temples, organizations, external stakeholders, and the state. As "religious juridical persons" (*shūkyō hōjin* 宗教法人), each temple must live up to its tax-exempt status by offering transparent information on finances, and the larger "comprehensive religious juridical persons" (*hōkatsu shūkyō hōjin* 包括宗教法人) have financial departments administering such accounts.

Looking at reports from representative groups, the economic proportions reveal differences according to size and number of affiliated parishes (*danka*). For instance, Shinshū Ōtani-ha has an annual expenditure of 8.5 billion yen (a decrease from 11.7 billion yen the year before), while the figure for Tendaishū is 1.1 billion yen, the proportion of individual labor (*jinkenhi*), administration (*kanrihi*), and education being substantial.[5] Each temple sends a fee (賦課金 *fukakin*) to the main organization, the share of the temple's total income varying from 9 percent (Shinshū Ōtani-ha) to 88 percent (Sōtōshū),

---

[1] Special issues of *Japanese Religions* (Borup and Rambelli 2019) as well as *Japanese Journal of Religious Studies* (Hirasawa and Lomi 2018) and *Asian Ethnology* (Baffelli and Caple 2019) are examples of such efforts to understand Japanese religions through the lens of materiality.
[2] See also Nagamura 2018 on temple monks and estate management in medieval Japan.
[3] The subtitle "from doctrines … to economy" is not meant to signal a necessary teleological evolution of theoretical approaches, but rather the historical development of theoretical phases, each of which is accumulated in a broad container of relevant theories.
[4] Statistics Bureau (2018). This is not the place to discuss the ambiguities of statistical data on religion; suffice it to say that the data can be used to demonstrate the existence of a rather large Buddhist contingent in Japan.
[5] Jōdo Shinshū Honganji-ha spends 36 percent on individual labor, 12 percent on administration, and 44 percent on education, while the corresponding figures for Nichirenshū are 19 percent, 4 percent, and 30 percent (*Gekkan jūshoku* February 2017: 24–5). Apart from these, there are expenses for assemblies for the organization and disaster prevention.

and the contributions made by *dankas* at local temples to the ten largest Buddhist organizations (*shūmon jiin*) make up more than three hundred billion yen annually.[6] This figure does not include donations for ritual services, which constitute just one part of the overall annual funeral business, estimated at almost 1.8 trillion yen.[7]

Buddhism was also an active part of economic development in earlier history. Temples and shrines in late classical and medieval Japan were among the greatest landholders, "easily rivaling the extent of church and monastic land in medieval Europe" (Garrett 2018: 378). In the Nara and Heian periods, temple income came from the imperial court, and court nobles had a political interest in being financial patrons. Temples became financial power centers, especially in the Kamakura period, when Zen, Nichiren, and Pure Land schools "constituted the leading sector of economic growth" (Collins 1997: 852). The effective organization and estate management of large land possessions, combined with foreign trade, moneylending, specific markets (even including *sake* breweries), and cash donations from warriors, nobles, and emperors made Zen monasteries particularly wealthy in medieval Japan (Collcutt 1981: 289).

Meiji reforms reduced the financial authority of the Buddhist temples by restructuring the power system. Buddhists were suppressed, priests were forcefully laicized, temples destroyed, and state support withdrawn, and the traditional "household affiliated system" (*danka seido*), the financial guarantor of individual temples, was officially abolished. Later postwar reforms did not make life easier for the previously wealthy Buddhist temple complexes. Land reforms, in which the government bought or simply confiscated land from the temples, meant less income from property and forced temples to rely more on potential income from the parishioners. After the Second World War, the system was no longer secure and controlled by the government, forcing the Buddhist temples to rely increasingly on "revenue from temple graves, funerals, and memorial rites" (Rowe 2011: 29), and generally on free-market capitalism with individual rights of property. Many temples still own land and rent out property for commercial use. In cities this can generate considerable amounts of money, no matter whether the leaseholders use such land and property for parking lots, shops, restaurants, golf courses, teahouses, or kindergartens. Apart from the property owned by individual temples, Buddhist organizations are important players in the public sector, owning 241 universities and schools as well as hospitals, hotels, museums, kindergartens, and retirement homes.[8]

The main source of income for the individual temple, and thus the individual priest, is donations for ritual services based on the officially abolished but still existing family temple system, under which families are part of a symbiotic relationship with a local temple. The priest needs income to pay for ritual supplies, maintenance of property, administration, liability, insurance, utility bills, his own salary, and other expenses necessary for a priest and a modern family. A survey among Jōdo Shinshū priests showed that their average annual income was between three and six million yen, with almost one-fifth earning less than one million and almost one-fifth earning more than ten million yen (Jōdo shinshū 2011: 80). As donations to temples are tax-exempt, fees (to enter temple buildings in some of the more touristic temples), prices (for *omamori*, books, etc.)

---

[6]The figures are from *Gekkan jūshoku* February 2017: 15–24.
[7]The figure is from a Yano Research report: https://www.yano.co.jp/press-release/show/press_id/1765 (accessed September 10, 2018).
[8]According to a survey from 1965, in Tokyo alone Buddhist temples ran 1,598 parking lots, 135 kindergartens, 40 preschools, 40 apartments, 13 rental properties, and 8 medical clinics (Rowe 2011: 28).

and ritual services are categorized as "donations," being thus legitimate under both the traditional standards of the Buddhist gift (see below) and the tax system. While what has been referred to pejoratively as "funeral Buddhism" (*sōshiki bukkyō*) is constantly being criticized, sometimes by Buddhist organizations themselves, it is a fact that the temples depend on the donations paid for funerals and memorial services as their main source of income.[9] There are typically no set prices for services related to these rituals, which vary according to the sect and even the individual temple in question. Therefore, the size of donations made to priests is also a topic of consideration, and sometimes confusion, being discussed in online discussion forums or homepages by companies giving information about average or suggested donation amounts.

By 2040, the mortality rate in Japan is expected to be 1.67 million per annum.[10] This will be a peak not only for the individual temples but also for the entire supply market that is part of the funeral industry: companies producing and selling ritual paraphernalia, Buddhist altars (*butsudan*) and gravestones (*haka*), the undertaking business, and the funeral companies taking care of the whole package—some of which do not even include Buddhist priests.[11] Commercial death fairs showing the latest post-death trends and possibilities have become part of the industry, as have new suppliers of funeral services such as Aeon Co., Yahoo Japan Corp, and Amazon.com.[12] At industrial fairs in Tokyo and Osaka, equipment and modern technology for shrines and temples are shown and sold by hundreds of exhibitors for the tens of thousands of visitors (the 2017 fair featured the robot Pepper performing Buddhist rituals), and each year the funeral industry sells more products to an increasing audience.[13]

Beyond the funeral industry, other nonreligious businesses are also closely involved in the generation of financing related to Buddhism. Producers and suppliers of religious goods, artifacts, and paraphernalia provide customers with images, figures, statues, altars, amulets, books, incense, and rosaries. The 88 Temple Pilgrimage on Shikoku continues to attract millions of pilgrims (Reader 2014), creating an industry for the temples on the island as well as for travel companies, hotels, restaurants, manufacturers of religious goods, and publishers of religious guidebooks. The use of Buddhist temples as refuges for meditation or tourist experiences, including lodging (*shukubō* 宿坊), seems to be increasingly popular. Zen Buddhist temples have a tradition of being centers for company courses and the training of new employees. In recent years, tourist organizations have marketed Buddhist temples as authentic places for experiencing Japanese spirituality and

---

[9]In the Sōtō sect, 90 percent of the temples depend on the income generated from funeral rites (Rowe 2011, 368). See Covell (2005: 145) for examples of funeral expenses.
[10]This prediction is made by the National Institute of Population and Social Security Research http://www.ipss.go.jp/pp-newest/e/ppfj02/ppfj02.pdf (accessed September 10, 2018).
[11]One company promises a one-third reduction from 1.8 million yen to 600,000 yen (http://www.funeral.co.jp) (accessed September 10, 2018).
[12]http://www.bloomberg.com/news/articles/2015-12-15/try-a-coffin-for-size-the-death-business-is-thriving-in-japan (accessed September 10, 2018).
[13]At Ceremony Japan 2018 in Osaka, there was a temple and shrine industry show with "facilities, equipment, service specialty exhibition for Shinto shrine and temples," a funeral and cemetery show with "equipment, machines and services for the funeral and cemetery industry," and a wedding and party industry show with "equipment, machines and services for the wedding and party industry." In 2021, the number of exhibitors is expected to be 750 and the number of visitors 40,000 (http://ceremonyjapan.jp/en/, accessed September 10, 2018).

culture—and this marketing also targets the increasing number of foreign tourists.[14] In Tokyo and Kyoto in particular, the major "tourist temples" (*kankōdera*) benefit a great deal from the tourism industry. Millions of visitors buy entrance tickets (or pay an entrance "donation"), and many also buy amulets, talismans, fortune papers, pictures, books, figures, or postcards, the accumulated value of which contributes financially to the temples in question.

SYSTEMS OF EXCHANGE

In the heyday of Buddhism, money was donated to the monasteries in exchange for protective rituals and to confirm the legitimacy of state power. Property was invested, and finances could potentially accumulate through a network of temple systems dominating major towns and vast areas of land. Both then and now, the traditional system of exchange between the individual Buddhist donor and priest has always been dominant. The Buddhist gift (*dāna*, Japanese *fuse*) represents the material object communicating transactions between the clergy and the laity, supporting the former with religious donations (*kishin*) or offerings (*orei*). The gift brings merit, and the ritual space is the field of merit generating and consecrating the ritual meritocracy. The gift exchange was and is most explicitly performed when the laity gives material objects (nowadays mainly money, previously also food) to the ascetics in monastic Buddhism in exchange for religious returns (teachings, this-worldly benefits, or even hopes of future enlightenment). But donations are also the material and symbolic object of gift exchange in non-monastic Pure Land Buddhism. Donations can also be given for the upkeep and restoration of individual temples, or as part of national campaigns such as relief aid to the victims of the tsunami catastrophe in 2011, extending the contractual relations beyond the individual level to serve social or even national purposes.

In one sense, the lower part of the exchange (the laity) will always be kept in an inferior position, supporting the superior part in the hierarchy (the clergy), since the former will always be indebted to the latter as proximate material gifts will never equal the eternal gifts of salvation. Monasteries and temples provide frameworks for ascetic efforts and ritual efficiency, but rather than being concrete payments for concrete output, donations are mainly to be seen as general investments with immeasurable outcome. The exchange is, however, not necessarily hierarchically unidirectional, being potentially circular (or reverse hierarchical). It creates institutional and social bonding, and as a "culture religion," traditional temple Buddhism carries a brand value generating social capital (*shakai kankei shihon*), which is also convertible beyond the religious community (Borup 2016). But the balance is dynamic. The donors (laity) can choose to opt out, adding to the challenges of secularization and the occasional critique of a commercialized religious industry whose glory days will eventually come to an end.[15]

As an actor on the market, the traditional *danka* may also choose alternative ways of being religious. Lay-oriented new religious movements with a Buddhist flavor have long been on the market, and some of them rely on different value exchange systems.

---

[14] In joint ventures with hotels and Buddhist Zen temples, the Nippon Foundation makes efforts to attract both Japanese and foreign tourists to "experience the soul of Japan" (https://www.nippon-foundation.or.jp/en/what/projects/culture_support/iroha-nihon/).

[15] One Jōdō Shinshū Buddhist priest and author suggests that 30–40 percent of all Japanese Buddhist temples may have closed by 2040 (Ukai 2015a: 266).

As opposed to the tradition-based temple affiliation as a *danka*, several (especially postwar) new religious movements have proposed prospects for economic progress for the individual urbanites. Born-again Buddhists can access the religion through material commodities and services that are often not found in traditional temples, with instrumental rituals leading to concrete rewards and a sectarian exclusivism based on membership fees and a system of widespread voluntarism.[16] Unlike the family-based religious communities, donations of property and money (fees, tuition fees, subscriptions) are part of a commodity exchange between producers and consumers for exclusive religious communities (Shimazono 1998: 187). Such "prosperity Buddhism" is typical of contemporary Happy Science and Soka Gakkai in its earlier phases, both groups having their wealth represented by successful business leaders, ostentatious buildings, and rather substantial properties.[17] Following Japan's general economic development, Soka Gakkai's members have become more affluent. The previous focus on materialistic and economic capital has been supplemented by rituals, activities, ideologies, and buildings signifying social and cultural capital as well, although the religious capital invested still does not have transferable value beyond sectarian, religious cultures (Borup 2018).[18]

CONCLUSION

Rather than being seen as merely epiphenomena, economic factors and materiality should be regarded as core components of the field analytically termed "religion." Economic factors and Buddhism have always had a close relationship, particularly in Japan. Monastic and non-monastic communities and religious organizations have been engaged with the surrounding state and society in mutually interdependent bonds based in part on economics and value transactions, the significance and effects of which are historically comparable to the monastery-society relations in Europe, which were co-constitutive factors behind modern capitalism. Modern Japanese Buddhism is part of a large, economically profitable funeral industry, and individual religious organizations are generally wealthy—although there are also huge variations between individual temples and priests, whose income is still mainly based on donations from temple-affiliated *danka*. Several Buddhist new religious movements have become successful, basing their finances on membership among devoted urbanites looking for meaning and prospects of prosperity, although the general economic development in Japan has also made a group like Soka Gakkai change focus from ideals of material gain to broader and alternative kinds of (social, cultural, and spiritual) capital.

---

[16]Shimazono Susumu calls this a "congregation-bureaucracy linkage model" characterized by "strong constraints and heavy financial burdens on its local members" (Shimazono 1998: 195).

[17]Soka Gakkai is probably one of the wealthiest organizations in Japan, owning more than 1,200 community centers as well as large building complexes, museums, culture centers, schools, a university, Japan's third-largest daily newspaper, thirteen cemeteries (themselves contributing annual taxation of several hundred billion yen), and an estimated value of properties of nine trillion yen. Happy Science is smaller, but more explicitly a business-oriented kind of prosperity religion (Borup 2018). See McLaughlin (2012b, 2019) for a thorough analysis of Soka Gakkai in general, and Sakurai (2011) and Yamada (2010, 2012) on Japanese new religious movements and the economy.

[18]If community-based temple Buddhism is characterized by exchange between clergy and laity, and new religious movements by exchange between organizations and members, the Japanese New Age (or new spirituality), with its individual enterprises and networks of spiritual providers, is typical of service-based payments for concrete services or products—often not identifying themselves with labels such as "Buddhism." On Japanese New Age and the economy, see Gaitanidis (2010).

It remains to be seen whether the Buddhist new religious movements in the future will become more mainstream and domesticated, and whether traditional temple Buddhism will correspondingly adapt to the challenges of the market and new business models used primarily by new religious movements so far. In general, the relationship between religion and the economy in Japan seems to be a field that is still open for investigation. More analyses of individual and institutional levels, impacts of and on society, historical developments, in-depth empirical case studies, and informed theoretical approaches will undoubtedly be seen (and welcomed) in the near future.

See also Chapter 5, "Economy and Spirituality," Chapter 15, "Materiality," Chapter 16, "Media and Technology," and Chapter 27, "Spirituality."

CASE STUDY

Buddhist Temples of the Future

Paulina K. KOLATA

The mechanics of Japanese Buddhist temple management have long constituted an important topic of public and scholarly debate in Japan, particularly in the postwar period, when the legal transformations relating to the temples' legal status and their incorporation under the Religious Juridical Person Law (*Shūkyō hōjin hō*) solidified the inherited model of temple ownership and forced Buddhist priests to pay closer attention to earning a living. Already in the 1920s, Morita Torao (1925) declared an economic crisis of Buddhist temples and pushed for a debate on the impact of modernization, urbanization, and rural-to-urban migration, among other issues, on the secular management of temples. The language of crisis and economic fragility of Buddhist institutions became a new status quo for Buddhist temples in the postwar period (Imon 1972; Chiba 2001; Nakajima 2005), particularly in rural areas over the past couple of decades (Tamamuro 1999; Covell 2005, 2012a; Reader 2011; Rowe 2011; Ukai 2015b).

The decentralized institutional model of traditional Buddhist temples also means that there are no overarching support programs for economically struggling temples across any of the seven major Buddhist sects. This has created an opening for the emergence of alternative commercial initiatives providing Buddhist priests with guidance and advice regarding temple management and tackling economic difficulties. One such initiative is *Otera no mirai* ("Japan Fellowship of Buddhists" or literally "future of Buddhist temples"), a management consultancy that offers strategic planning and a management-training program for Buddhist temple custodians seeking to boost their economic prospects.

Otera no mirai was set up in 2013 by Matsumoto Shōkei, an ordained priest in the Jōdo Shinshū school of Japanese Buddhism. When I met with Matsumoto in October 2016, he explained that his aim was to transform temples into "agents of change" that would act as a catalyst for change, allowing people visiting them to achieve spiritual awakening. Buddhist priests implementing this vision are to provide impetus for broader institutional changes that would ultimately make Buddhist temples more relevant to the contemporary Japanese society, enabling people to connect with each other through Buddhist values and, in turn, addressing Buddhist temples' financial difficulties. This message has attracted Buddhist professionals from across the seven major Buddhist sects in Japan today. Despite doctrinal differences, socioeconomic changes from the postwar era to recent years have affected all Buddhist temples in largely similar ways. As such, Buddhist priests and staff from any school are welcome to use the services of *Otera no mirai*.

On the consultancy's website, such services are categorized as "free" and "paid." Free services include a magazine subscription that features opinion pieces regarding recent news and grassroots level initiatives related to Buddhism and temples in general. Paid services are related to temple management and include online web design (80,000 yen), designing promotional pamphlets and other merchandise promoting the temple (150,000–300,000 yen), and an integrated service package that combines online and offline marketing campaign design (200,000–360,000 yen).[1]

Matsumoto's management consulting service, patented as *Otera 360 do shindan* ("360-degree diagnostics of the temple"), is another paid service offered as part of the organization's management consulting portfolio. It involves designing and conducting surveys on behalf of a local temple with the temple's lay membership and other potential stakeholders. The basic fee for the service is 35,000 yen, with additional charges per person depending on the form of data collection, that is, paper surveys cost 1,000 yen per person, while administering a web survey costs 4,000 yen per person. Matsumoto also developed an affiliated free guide for Buddhist priests to conduct a preliminary evaluation of one's own temple in accordance with the set principles of creating a temple "where people can find peace of mind" (*anshin otera*) that is relevant for individuals and society as a whole (Ide 2017). According to the *Otera no mirai* website, transforming into such a "temple of a future" is thus grounded in extensive research and quantitative and qualitative data collated by Matsumoto and priests themselves.

The free guide offers a preview of what a full-service package could deliver and is designed to reflect values that Matsumoto's approach offers to his clients, such as focus on anticipating the stakeholders' expectations, awareness of social change, and on promoting the original function of the temple. *Otera no mirai* endorses a framework of institutional engagement based on people's subjective sense of belonging to a temple, which they could associate with as *maitera* (meaning "my temple"). *Mytera* is also an online platform within the *Otera no mirai* website that provides a catalog of Japanese Buddhist temples in different parts of the country where, as the website claims, people can find "peace of mind." Linked to the idea of *maitera* are activities that Matsumoto frames as *otera-zukuri* ("creating a temple") efforts, which is a flagship slogan of his consultancy. It represents the idea of developing a community centered on a Buddhist temple as a place of belonging. However, this belonging and the sense of personal affiliation, as epitomized through the "my temple" narrative, relates strongly to the importance of agency and leadership among priests, which could bring tangible economic benefits for individual local temples.

The consultancy aims to engender such agency and leadership among Buddhist priests through the *Mirai no jūshoku juku* training program offered by his company NPO (nonprofit organization). The training program is a six-month "MBA" in strategic planning and leadership for Buddhist monks. The program is offered once a year and runs from April until January and consists of six sessions, each dedicated to a different topic, where participating Buddhist priests conduct a strategic planning program of their own temple. The goal of the course is to develop a tangible and achievable management implementation plan for each temple. Individual sessions focus on: (1) the basics of temple management, including who the temple is for; (2) using SWOT (Strengths, Weaknesses, Opportunities, and Threats) analysis to develop a strategy for a temple; (3) marketing strategies employing the previously mentioned 360-degree evaluation tool; (4) learning

---

[1] As of October 2019.

about leadership through case studies; and, finally, (5) developing an individualized strategy through peer-coaching in preparation for (6) the final presentations during the last session. The course is offered in twelve different geographical locations across Japan (eighteen participants per group), which allows participants to develop cross-sectarian support networks in their region. The program is in its eighth year of running with an average of two hundred graduates each year, with some people choosing to repeat the program. The cost of this six-month course is 148,000 yen (plus tax) per person (approx. $1,400).

The vision of leadership marketed through the program's commercial consultancy model endorses an understanding that a Buddhist priest, through his work at the temple, should also be an example for a Buddhist way of life. Thus, the priest's job is to promote Buddhist values and teachings focused on the growth of individual members of the temple. As such, Matsumoto insists that this ideal ought to be embodied through priests' appearance, including a traditional shaved head and wearing of the priestly working robes even when not conducting rituals. He sees it as a symbolic way of reclaiming, visually, the identity of a Buddhist monk that is visible and active in the society. He refers to the graduates of his course as *sangha*, the traditional word for the Buddhist community, and sees them as part of the process of building a temple community that transcends individual temples. He keeps his clients (= graduates) engaged with the project and with each other through a number of follow-up one-day seminars, the online *Mytera* community, and by involving past participants to deliver presentations as case studies, which become part of the program's curriculum.

The *Mytera* platform supports Buddhist priests in attracting to their temple community people who lost or do not maintain connections with their family temple. The objective is to establish traditional connections with people through Buddhist rituals, funerary and memorialization practices, and spiritual guidance and community building. On the surface, the model offered through the site is no different from a traditional temple community setup, but the site is an outlet for showcasing the social impact of activities that serve to establish and nurture such links with individuals. Examples include organizing crowdfunding campaigns for end-of-life support for the elderly, temple cleaning events aimed at young adults to support their mental well-being, organizing yoga classes, and running cafeterias for children living in poverty (Mytera n.d.).

One of the most successful initiatives facilitated through the network is *Otera oyatsu kurabu* ("temple snack club") initiated by Matsushima Seirō, a Buddhist priest from Osaka. When we met in June 2017, Matsushima explained that he created a community of temples around the country to facilitate the distribution of offerings to economically struggling families in collaboration with other organizations.[2] His vision was clear: such initiatives create connections between temple membership and the social support networks that it helps to sustain. As such, the site is designed to guide people in making informed choices about their temple membership through learning about individual profiles of priests, their social engagement and temple communities that they represent. Such initiatives also serve as examples for participants in Matsumoto's program.

Matsumoto, who has no temple of his own and has never had to face the struggles that many of his clients do, has been successful in gathering quite a following for his vision of temple Buddhism and in developing a significant position of authority in

---

[2] As of December 2020, the number of temples involved in the network was 1,545 (Otera Oyatsu Club n.d.).

relation to tackling issues such as depopulation, fragmentation of the family system, and secularization. By applying a business model of management consulting and utilizing his MBA knowledge, he focuses on agency and manages to attract people to his vision and method of approaching the contemporary struggles of Buddhist temples.

Matsumoto's initiative presents a fascinating case of capitalizing on the economic and religious anxiety of Buddhist priests concerned with the survival of their temples. However, it also endorses an alternative solution—and, for many, an exciting prospect—of asserting Buddhism's relevance by tapping into an economically rich consumer culture. The consultancy model for temple management promoted in *Otera no mirai* constitutes a potential shift toward a commercially and socially conscious framework for religious belonging.

While the "experimentalism" of Matsumoto's approach to revitalizing Buddhism is not novel (Nelson 2013; Ueda 2004), the scope of his agenda in tackling Buddhist temples economic crisis is noteworthy. Matsumoto's activities do not represent a survivalist effort of an individual priest in a specific geographical location. Although many participants come from regional temples, the program attracts people from both urban and rural settings with a fairly even spread across all prefectures. Thus, Matsumoto's consultancy program mobilizes groups of priests and their family members across geographical, sectarian, and socioeconomic lines.

CHAPTER 7

Empire and Colonialism

Emily ANDERSON

The phrase "religion and the Japanese empire" may bring to mind images of rows of obedient schoolchildren worshipping at Yasukuni Shrine, or even a Shinto shrine in colonial Korea, or a similarly iconic image featuring the worship of the Japanese emperor based on the convoluted and dubious assertions of the non-religion religion of State Shinto. These images are, of course, not wrong, and the state's unforgiving demand that all subjects of the empire be united in their reverence for the emperor was certainly employed to drive the nation into a destructive and cataclysmic war.

However, to project back onto the entirety of the history of the empire this image that dominated its end is to efface the dynamic and diverse expressions and aspirations of adherents to a myriad of religions. The Japanese empire was not simply populated by emperor-worshipping subjects, nor by colonial subjects forced into at least superficially showing similar reverence. It was, in fact, an empire of many religions, and the government officials tasked with gaining the single-minded and unwavering loyalty of its subjects were, from the beginning, troubled with how to confront the challenge religious belief and adherence posed to a modern empire.

As scholars of Japan have taken up the work of examining the empire—not just the nation—of Japan, using religion as an organizing framework promises new possibilities that can move scholarly inquiry beyond the limiting demands of the nation and the imperial (and colonial) subject. Furthermore, given the dynamic history of the relationship between the state and "religion," broadly defined, or the tension between orthodoxy and heterodoxy throughout the region, focusing on the intersections of religion with colonialism in the Japanese empire enables an investigation of continuities before, during, and even after Japan's colonial expansion.

The notion that religion as a category posed a particular challenge to colonial governance is not a new one—scholars of British empire have argued that the British confrontation with ruling different, and often competing, faiths compelled it to adopt a nominally secular form of governance (Viswanathan 1998; van der Beer 2001; Fitzgerald 2007). This extended back to the colonial metropole, where colonial practicalities prompted the passage of legislation that extended rights to British subjects who were also religious minorities. The establishment of far-flung empires forced Europeans to adopt systems beyond what had been imposed in the metropole, and competition among Christian sects and denominations were replaced with an awareness—if not tolerance—of religions besides Christianity.

Japan's exposure to the rest of the world occurred just as Western powers were coming to terms with the complications presented by multireligious empires, and informed the development of the constitution itself. Ever diligent in their study of the other powers in an attempt to avoid potential pitfalls, as Trent Maxey has observed, Japanese leaders from the early Meiji period designed the Japanese state's relationship to the category of religion in an effort to both assert the state's modernity and to dilute the potency of religions to challenge the state's legitimacy (Maxey 2014).

The challenge that religions posed to state legitimacy and authority multiplied with Japan's imposition of colonial rule.[1] Recent scholarship on modern Japan has seen a boom in approaching Japan as an empire, in a departure from earlier scholarship that viewed Japan as the *naichi*, or home islands, alone, and colonies, or *gaichi*, as part of its foreign relations history (Schmid 2000). This recognizes that even for those Japanese whose daily lives were physically circumscribed by the limited space of their villages and regions, their virtual lives were not. Empire—whether in the form of actual colonies, products, or the governing ideology—touched everyone somehow, and this recognition has greatly enriched the study of modern Japan, even as it has complicated it. However, this explosion of new approaches to scholarship is just beginning to influence approaches to studying religions in Japan and its empire.

What changes when we examine the activities of Japanese Buddhist priests in Korea, not simply as agents of the state, but as religionists concerned with rehabilitating the vitality of Buddhism and wary of the threat of Christian evangelism? Or the activities of Shinto shrine supporters in colonial Seoul, who were more than likely convinced of their relative superiority compared to their Korean neighbors but were also concerned with the colonial government's cooption of their shrine for state interests? What do we make of the Japanese Christians, who asserted their devotion to both God and Japan, and went so far as going to Korea as missionaries to facilitate so-called Japanese-Korean unification? To limit any of these and myriad others like them to their affiliation to nation alone is to discount the messy relationship between subjects and empire, and the unexpected ways that religious belief and practice can shape and alter the contours of colonial rule (Makdisi 2008).

This is not to say that Japanese in the colonies did not benefit from a profoundly unequal relationship, or that this different approach somehow lessens the inherently problematic and oppressive nature of colonialism. But focusing on religions and their adherents as active and interactive participants in Japan's colonial empire is a particularly productive way of exposing issues, networks, and dynamics that remain concealed otherwise.

EMPIRE AS PLACE, EMPIRE AS IDEA

The empire was not simply a geographic space but was also a governing ideology. In this sense, it is important to consider two bodies of work that, while generally distinct, are not exclusively so: work that explores how imperial ideology—or *tennōsei/teikoku shugi*—intersected and was in turn shaped by the category of religion and the practitioners of different religion, and work that examines actual religious activities in the Japanese empire.

---

[1] Starting with the island of Hokkaido and the Ryukyu archipelago, modern Japan embarked on an endless quest for global acceptance and competitiveness through the acquisition of territories. Hokkaido and the Ryukyus, now Okinawa, were incorporated into the home islands, or *naichi*, but by the 1920s, Japan's colonies, or *gaichi*, included Taiwan, Korea, southern Sakhalin, and the Nanyō (South Sea Islands). Japan also had concessions or other forms of informal colonial power in areas of China, including the Kwantung Leased Territory in southern Manchuria and in cities like Shanghai.

The role of State Shinto in the validation and perpetuation of the emperor system can frustrate any scholar of religion. Presented as civil ritual and a system of observances, and most emphatically not a religion, State Shinto was imposed on all imperial subjects with the insistence that it did not violate anyone's right to practice their religion. The slippery boundaries around State Shinto, and the difficulty pinning down the actual line between state and church under the Meiji constitution, seem to justify the argument that Japan, unlike other empires, deployed and relied on a religious framework to demand unyielding and singular loyalty from its subjects. Whereas Western empires, so this line of reasoning goes, operated according to modern and secular governance, the Japanese empire was not quite modern, relying instead on a religious devotion to its sovereign and only allowing limited religious freedom. If this train of thought is followed further, there is also an assumption that such single-minded adoration and reverence for the emperor came naturally for Japanese imperial subjects, and its imposition on colonial subjects revealed the fundamentally oppressive and backwards nature of Japanese colonial rule.

The folly in such an assertion is the assumption, of course, that Western empires were fully secular and that they promised and practiced full religious freedom. Similarly, the assumption that Japanese all happily and eagerly accepted imperial ideology is problematic. In *The Greatest Problem: Religion and State Formation in Meiji Japan*, Trent Maxey traces how the early Meiji state gradually came to terms with the category of religion as they laid the ideological foundation for the Japanese empire (Maxey 2014). As he demonstrates, State Shinto was the governing ideology, the framework employed to unite imperial subjects with their emperor—and later, colonial subjects as well—in singular purpose. What is crucial, as Maxey lays out, is that State Shinto was developed and constructed as the antidote to religion and the problems religion would pose to transforming a fragmented and diverse population into a united (and docile) set of subjects. State Shinto was not an organic constellation of practices familiar and "natural" for all Japanese but was instead the nonreligious, religious answer to the problem of how to exact unquestioning loyalty from a rather willful and unruly bunch of people across the archipelago. This point deserves our full attention because the slippery nature of State Shinto was in response to the difficulties identified under the failed Great Promulgation Campaign of exacting unwavering loyalty as defined by the state (Maxey 2014: 32–53). In other words, from its emergence, the Japanese empire was wary of religion and recognized its potential power to compete for the hearts and minds of subjects.

The complex relationship between colonialism and religion rests partly on how State Shinto was deployed to motivate and sanction colonial aggression, and to sacralize it at home. Takahashi Tetsuya's powerful metaphor of spiritual alchemy captures the process by which Japanese soldiers killed in all of the empire's wars of aggression—even before the Pacific War—were transformed into gods worshipped by the emperor himself, making colonial expansion a spiritual mission (Takahashi 2005). Thus, the very emergence of modern Japan as the Japanese empire was predicated on an uneasy relationship with the category of religion and was imposed through the apparatus of the nonreligious, yet religious construct of State Shinto. Colonialism was fueled by this framework, and soldiers were exhorted to lay down their lives according to this so they supposedly would be enshrined for all eternity.

RELIGIONS IN THE COLONIES

The Japanese empire was, of course, not simply a concept or abstraction imagined in the home islands but began and was perpetuated by territorial aggression and expansion. The temptation to equate the imposition of State Shinto with religion in the Japanese empire has concealed and elided a particularly rich and messy religious landscape. In turn, investigating religion and colonialism in the Japanese empire offers new possibilities that overcome the overdetermined and limiting demands of nationalism. Regulating and policing religions in the empire was just as important as it was in the home islands, and required the implementation of laws and ordinances, and the work of colonial officials who policed the lives of colonial subjects and Japanese settlers alike.

There is a rich body of scholarship that examines the establishment of Japanese laws and ordinances created to govern and regulate religions. The laws put in place by the Government-General of Korea, for example, offer an interesting comparison, but these are often mostly mentioned in the context of state-imposed Shinto shrine worship and how this infringed on the religious freedom, especially of Korea's Christian population (Kawase 2017: 19–37). Did the Government-General's experiences with Taiwan, Korea, or other areas influence amendments and revisions to law in the metropole? Did colonial subjects study the ways imperial subjects attempted to circumvent these religious laws? What about vice versa? A thorough examination of laws directed at religious beliefs and institutions across the empire can offer new perspectives on both religion and imperial rule.

In existing scholarship, the vast majority of work addressing religion in the Japanese empire focuses on Korea. When Japan first imposed the Treaty of Ganghwa on Korea with its use of gunboat diplomacy in 1876, it was not entering a religious vacuum. The religious landscape of Joseon Korea was complex: the Neo-Confucian court had marginalized Buddhism for centuries, new religions like Tonghak were challenging the social and political order, and the introduction of first Roman Catholicism and then Protestant Christianity—despite opposition and persecution under the Taewongun—added yet another complex layer and a source of anxiety (Kim 2012: 25–50; Rausch 2014; Young 2014; Oak 2015; Baker and Rausch 2017). These were two worlds colliding in the midst of an uncertain and rapidly shifting landscape.

So often, the narrative of Japan's intrusion into and eventual colonization of Joseon Korea focuses on two monolithic subjects—the nations (or in religious terms, State Shinto and Christianity)—without considering horizontal relationships among these two groups (Henry 2014). The challenge for scholars has been that the accusation of being pro-Japanese, a collaborator, is quick in coming if a Korean religionist of any kind does not appear to put nation over all else. But such is not the way of men and women in reality. Without dismissing the stakes of how the history of colonial Korea has been studied and presented, focusing on religion instead of nation helps create new possibilities. Hwansoo Kim's research has helped to elucidate the ways in which Korean and Japanese Buddhists briefly found common cause in promoting and seeking a pan-Asian Buddhism because they saw Christianity, not Japan, as the greatest existential threat (Kim 2012, 2018). Their attempts at forging institutional and communal relationships was struck down, not by the Korean government, but by the Japanese Government-General, which arrogated to itself the authority to establish head priests and successors in Korean temples, and viewed Japanese Buddhist missionaries' efforts in Korea as a potential threat to their power. Kim does not deny or negate the inherently unequal relationship between Korean and Japanese

Buddhists, but by complicating the picture, he demonstrates the potential presented by extending the scholarly gaze beyond the overdetermined focus on the nation.

Reframing the perspective is equally dynamic when exploring Christianity in Korea. The conventional narrative is that because the missionaries who introduced Christianity to Korea did not come from the same country that colonized it, Christianity was free of the imperialist taint it suffered elsewhere and not only offered Koreans advocates in the missionaries among them but also provided a narrative of liberation and salvation from Japanese imperial oppression (Lee 2000; Park 2003; Min 2005; Choi 2009). More recently, scholarship has emerged that interrogates these long-held assumptions. Matsutani Motokazu, for example, argues that in fact, Korean Christians were quite sensitive to the hegemony of white imperialism and the considerable wealth that fueled American missions (Matsutani 2012). Far from viewing American missionaries as benevolent but impotent allies, Matsutani points to the extreme disparities in wealth between missionaries and Korean members, the reluctance of missionaries to allow Korean members to make decisions about their own congregations, and how missionaries discouraged political activism and dissent. Far from being havens for anti-Japanese political activity, most churches stayed out of politics, and those Christians who actively engaged in opposing Japanese rule were marginal—or marginalized—by mainstream Christian communities.

Furthermore, while a much smaller group, there were Korean Christians who found common cause with Japanese Christians because they objected to the control of American missions. In other words, Americans were not viewed as somehow neutral or un-imperial, even under Japanese rule. At the same time, the Japanese Christians who established a mission in Korea failed to recognize the significance of colonialism; expecting to be embraced by Koreans as civilizers, they were shocked to be rebuffed. In a world of overlapping imperialisms and religious affiliations, identity and association was not simple or static (Anderson 2014).

Japanese colonialism extended beyond the boundaries of the formal empire, of course, into areas like pre-Manchukuo Manchuria, or the treaty port of Shanghai. In these spaces, the efforts of Japanese missionaries to promote Japanese imperial interests and facilitate the gradual occupation of new territories presents even more interesting avenues for research. Of course, in these places Japanese were not the only missionaries, and they interacted with international mission agencies and para-church organizations like the YMCA. Some Japanese missionaries knew their American counterparts, for example, from their schooling in the United States. The transnational nature of religious affiliation overlapped with the confounding and conflicting boundaries of border communities and the vagaries of extraterritoriality. Where jurisdictions were porous or difficult to reinforce, religious actors, political refugees, immigrants, colonial settlers, and diplomats made strange bedfellows, sometimes with unexpected results. These transnational spaces made inadvertently possible by imperialism and colonialism offer immense possibilities, and tracing the activities of the religious actors offers a new perspective on the colonial worlds in Asia (DuBois 2016).

NEW RELIGIONS IN THE JAPANESE EMPIRE

The large, well-established religious organizations were not the only ones who engaged with the idea of imperialism or threw themselves into establishing their own foothold in the colonies. For some of Japan's new religions, the colonies presented potential for freedom and success obstructed in the metropole. Tenrikyō offers an excellent example. Founded in the mid-1800s by the charismatic Nakayama Miki (1798–1887), Tenrikyō's popularity among the poor and its reliance on a syncretic mythology made it potentially subversive and threatening to the Meiji state. As the scholarship of Yamakura Akihiro demonstrates, Tenrikyō missionaries were not only drawn to colonial Korea for the opportunities it provided, but they also sought to develop linguistic and cultural literacy as part of their preparation for evangelism there (Yamakura 2017: 153–76). This policy directly contradicted the official government policy of assimilation. Furthermore, due to frequent crackdowns on leadership at home, expansion to the colonies—as well as among diasporic communities around the Pacific—seemed to offer respite from political oppression.

Tenrikyō missionaries entered a Korea that itself was site to multiple new religions that had presented adherents alternative with visions to that offered by the Joseon court, then Japanese colonial government. Given that adherents of different so-called new religions were aware of each other's existence—and the ways they were similarly persecuted by the Japanese state—another interesting future focus of research would be a comparative study of these religions, as well as an investigation of the degree to which they studied each other as they attempted to negotiate hostile authorities (Jorgensen 2017: 190).

FINAL STAGES OF RELIGIOUS EMBRACE WITH JAPANESE COLONIALISM

As with all things in the Japanese empire, what still remained possible—or, however improbable, imaginable—came to a screeching halt by the early 1930s. The creeping imposition of more restrictive censorship laws, more consistent enforcement of such laws, an increasingly hostile and reactionary public, and the threat of violence against detractors from imperial ideology made alternatives unspeakable, including religious ones. This did not mean, of course, that religious activity in the colonies ceased, or that they were mere puppets of the various administrations under which they existed. Even with the limitations placed on sources due to censorship, there are plenty of interesting avenues for exploring these efforts, as well as other initiatives spearheaded by religious organizations in service of the empire.

One especially interesting issue that deserves further attention is the transnational interest in agrarian settlements—especially in emulation of a Danish model—that emerged in the 1920s. In Japan itself, this was epitomized by the labor movement of Kagawa Toyohiko (1888–1960), but there were other more localized efforts, including a Shinto-influenced one that Miyazawa Kenji (1896–1933) was involved in (Long 2012). Similar efforts emerged in colonial Korea as well, as Albert Park has demonstrated (Park 2015). In the Japanese case, these efforts eventually were linked to the great state-sponsored attempt to "settle" Manchukuo through a massive campaign of agrarian settlement. Not only did Japanese Christians, under Kagawa Toyohiko's leadership, attempt to create their own Christian agrarian settlement near Harbin, but also other settlements affiliated with religious institutions began to dot the Manchurian landscape (Anderson 2014: 217–37). Were these efforts motivated by similar factors? Did they communicate with each other and study each other? Were any successful (e.g., the Christian one most certainly was not)? The alluring promise of pan-Asian utopia in Manchukuo was as enticing to different religious groups as it was to others, and resulted in similarly devastating results.

See also Chapter 12, "Globalization," Chapter 18, "Minorities," Chapter 19, "'New Religions'," and Chapter 28, "Tourism."

CASE STUDY

Aesthetics of Buddhist Modernism

Paride STORTINI

In an article that explains the particularities of Buddhist marriage ceremonies, less common in Japan than Shinto weddings, the closing photo shows a bride climbing the front steps of Tsukiji Honganji temple in Tokyo. The caption beneath the image says: "Both Western and Japanese dress suit the Indian style of the Main Hall" ("Butsuzen" 2010). "Western" here refers to the white wedding gown the bride is wearing, while "Indian" marks the article's interpretation of the unusual architecture of the temple. Why was such an exotic style chosen for a temple belonging to a traditional Japanese Buddhist sect? How can this style ease the feeling of being out of place potentially produced by a Western-fashioned wedding dress worn in a Buddhist temple? The aesthetic choice for Tsukiji Honganji provides an exemplary case to discuss how ideas and images about ancient India and Indian Buddhism became part of the way Japanese Buddhists navigated modernity, confronted ideas from both Europe and America, and defined their own role in the construction of the modern nation-state since the second half of the nineteenth century.

Tsukiji Honganji belongs to the Nishi Honganji sect of Jōdo Shinshū Buddhism. It was originally built in 1617 as the headquarters of the sect in the new shogunal capital of Edo, and it was moved to its current area, near the former site of the famous Tsukiji fish market, after the great fire of 1657. The current structure dates to the early 1930s, when the temple was rebuilt after the Great Kantō Earthquake of 1923. It is at this time that the "Indian style" was chosen for the new building by its architect, Itō Chūta (1867–1954), in agreement with the Nishi Honganji sect. The temple materialized the encounter of two ongoing processes of modern identity formation: on one side, that of creating "modern" Japanese architecture, of which Itō was a pioneer, and on the other, of Japanese Buddhist institutions, among which the Nishi Honganji sect was particularly active in reshaping its image through both collaboration with the Meiji government and across international networks.

What makes Tsujiki Honganji's style "Indian?" The semicircular decoration above the main entrance and the vaulted roof are modeled on an ancient Buddhist cave in Ajanta, in today's Maharashtra State. Moreover, two structures framing the extremities of the building recall the hemispherical shape of a stupa, traditionally used in South Asian Buddhism to enshrine relics. However, rather than an accurate reproduction of ancient Indian temples, the style must be interpreted as an eclectic and modernist product of Itō's many travels across Europe and Asia in the early years of the twentieth century (Wendelken 2000). In addition, the temple is part of a broader series of buildings in which the architect blends together various sources, ranging from European neoclassical architecture to Mughal art and Buddhist archaeological sites (Jaffe 2006). It even includes elements more typical of Christian churches, such as pews, stained glass windows, and a pipe organ that was donated after the Second World War by the Buddhist philanthropist and businessman Numata Yehan (1897–1994). Following Itō's journey, the construction of a modern identity for Japanese architecture passed through a confrontation and appropriation of Western ideas at the same time that it (re-)discovered a link with Asia, exemplified by the eastward spread of Buddhism from India.

A similar process of self-definition explains the interest in the Indian origins of Buddhism that characterizes the intellectual history of Japanese Buddhism in the Meiji (1868–1912) and Taishō (1912–26) periods. Since the 1870s, a number of Japanese Buddhist priests and scholars traveled many of the same routes that Itō would later travel, both physically and metaphorically, not only exploring the collections of Sanskrit and Pali Buddhist texts at European universities but also visiting archaeological Buddhist sites in Central and Southern Asia and establishing networks with local intellectuals and reformers (Jaffe 2004, 2019; Ogawara 2010; Okuyama 2016). While traveling in China, Itō himself met one of these Buddhist travelers, Ōtani Kōzui (1876–1948), who would soon after become head of the Nishi Honganji sect. At that time (1902), Ōtani was leading the first of a number of Nishi Honganji-organized expeditions to explore ancient Buddhist sites in Central Asia (Tankha 2017).

The excursion into ancient sources of Buddhism, through the study of texts in Indic languages and archaeological exploration, was a way for Japanese Buddhist institutions to respond to the intellectual challenge of Euro-American scholars. The latter, guided by a romantic quest for the original text, prioritized Sanskrit and Pali sources and discredited East Asian Buddhist traditions that were based on the Chinese canon—which was considered to be flawed with mistranslations and apocrypha. In Japan, the new tools of Indology and Buddhist studies coming from Europe revived long-standing criticism against Mahāyāna Buddhism for not being the word of the historical Buddha (this criticism is called in Japanese *Daijō hi-bussetsu ron*) and were likewise appropriated by Christian missionaries in anti-Buddhist polemics. By reestablishing a cultural connection with the Indian sources of Buddhism through philology, archaeology, and art history, Buddhist priest-scholars and intellectuals claimed a purportedly scientific approach to their faith as they responded to the criticism of Euro-American Orientalists and Christian apologists. In addition, the redefinition of Buddhism as a spiritual connection among Asian peoples, and in opposition to the nihilism and materialism of modern Western societies, became an ideological tool to justify pan-Asian views, ultimately supporting Japanese imperialism in East and Southeast Asia (see special issues edited by Jaffe 2010 and Klautau 2014, respectively, and the article by Stone 2014).

The "Indian" style of Tsukiji Honganji is one among many visual forms that this interest in the ancient sources of Buddhism took in modern Japan. In fact, its architect Itō was not the first to be inspired after a visit to the Ajanta caves, which, in the early decades of the twentieth century, became an almost mandatory stop for Japanese Buddhist pilgrims and scholars. In India, these pilgrims met and established connections with artists, religious reformers, and intellectuals from Europe and India (Inaga 2009; Fukuyama 2010). This connection between religious and artistic milieux expanded the transnational network centering on the Japanese thinker Okakura Kakuzō (1862–1913) and the Indian poet Rabindranath Tagore (1861–1941). The artistic products of these interactions were hybrid reimaginations of India that combined elements of the traditional Japanese nihonga style, influences from Western art, and quotations from both contemporary and ancient India (Wattles 1996).

In the 1930s, a Japanese painter in this cosmopolitan milieu, Nōsu Kōsetsu (1885–1973, also romanized as Nosu Kosetsu), was commissioned to paint frescoes of the life of Shakyamuni in the newly built temple in Sarnath of the Maha-Bodhi Society (Nosu 1939), an organization still in existence today whose aim is the support of Buddhism in India. The style of Nōsu's wall paintings was deeply influenced by his previous research at the Ajanta caves. Later, reproductions of Nōsu's images appeared in a 1975 children's picture book on the life of the Buddha written by the renowned scholar Nakamura Hajime (1912–1999), who chose them because both their style and the history of their making stress the international dimension of Buddhism as a world religion (Nakamura 1975).

On the cover of another picture book from around this same time (Takahashi 1960), the child Shakyamuni stands in front of a series of buildings that mix elements likely inspired by Islamic art with two vaulted roofs resembling those of Tsukiji Honganji. As in the caption of the photo that we quoted at the beginning of this case study, the Indian style of these images and buildings incorporates hybrid elements of transnational Buddhist modernism and stresses the international dimension of Buddhism as a world religion. In this sense, the Indian-ness of Buddhism, reimagined through modernism, creates a cultural bridge between Japan and the outside world, both Asia and the West, suiting "both Western and Japanese dress."

But what is left outside of these pictures? To suggest an answer to this question, I will use another image involving children, this time coming from an immediately postwar film: "Record of a Tenement Gentleman" (*Nagaya Shinshiroku*, 1947) by Ozu Yasujirō (1903–1963). The film portrays a lower-class widow who reluctantly takes care of a homeless boy, eventually becoming fond of him and deciding to adopt an orphan after the boy returns to his father. Film critics are divided between those who stress the utopian representation of postwar poverty and those who instead point out the central role occupied by homeless children and ruins in its scenes. Tsukiji Honganji, which survived the Second World War bombings, appears in two moments in the film, towering over the poor row houses and also in the background of a shot of children fishing in the river.

While it is difficult to determine why Ozu focused the camera on Tsukiji Honganji, perhaps we can see it as a reflection on the juxtaposition of the temple to the postwar city and human landscape. Tsukiji Honganji looming over the ruins of the conflict can be interpreted as a reminder of the consequences of Japanese imperialism, which the intersection of pan-Asianist and Buddhist modernist discourses helped justify. At the same time though, as an image of Buddhist cosmopolitanism, it can also represent a call for reconstruction and an invitation to rethink the place of Japan after the conflict as a promoter of international collaboration and cultural contact. The Indian style of Tsukiji Honganji, and more generally ideas and imagery about ancient India and Indian Buddhism that developed in the intellectual and artistic milieu of modern Japan, provided a cultural connection and response to Western Orientalism, but also ended up supporting the pan-Asian views of Japanese imperialism. While the postwar reimagining of the Indian-ness of Buddhism stressed again the cosmopolitan role of Buddhism as a cultural bridge, this image is complicated when we bear in mind the ideological use of Buddhism as a universal world religion in prewar Japan.

CHAPTER 8

Environmentalism

Aike P. ROTS

In recent decades, religious traditions worldwide have been reinterpreted in light of environmental concerns. Various scholars and religious actors have described Asian worship traditions such as Buddhism, Confucianism, Daoism, and Hinduism as vestiges of "holistic ecological wisdom" and "ancient sustainability," in contrast to Abrahamic religions, which are often said to legitimize or even encourage exploitation of the natural environment (see White 1967). They have suggested that Asian traditions contain important resources—philosophical, practical, and physical—for overcoming today's global environmental crisis (e.g., Smith 1972; Tucker and Williams 1997; Tucker and Berthrong 1998; Duara 2015). As some critics have pointed out, such interpretations are often anachronistic and orientalist, and may be employed to support nationalist or other ideological agendas (Pedersen 1995; Kalland 2002). Although this critique is justified, there is no denying the fact that environmental concerns have contributed to the actual transformation of religious identities and practices. Today, religious leaders and laypeople throughout the world are expressing concerns with environmental issues. Some of them are making serious attempts to put these ideas into practice, ranging from mosque and church communities investing in alternative energy to temple and shrine communities actively resisting the destruction of local environments (e.g., Darlington 2012; Kent 2013).

These global trends have exercised considerable impact upon Japanese religious organizations. Scholars and religious leaders in Japan have combined contemporary notions of Asian religions as "holistic" and "sustainable" with earlier modern ideas of Japan as a nation characterized by a unique attitude to nature. In popular discourse and nationalist scholarship, this spirit of "harmonious coexistence with nature" is typically presented as a defining feature of "the Japanese people" since times immemorial, which is said to have had a strong impact on aesthetic and religious traditions. In reality, this famous Japanese "love of nature" is largely the product of Meiji-period nationalist mythmaking and therefore not nearly as ancient or traditional as it is commonly imagined (see Kalland and Asquith 1997; Morris-Suzuki 1998: 35–59; Rots 2017b: 47–63). Moreover, the popularization of these ideas in Japan and abroad paradoxically coincided with the emergence of large-scale industrial pollution and environmental exploitation by Japanese state and corporate actors, domestically as well as abroad (Dauvergne 1997; Walker 2010).

Nevertheless, although demonstrably at odds with reality, the perception of Japan as a "green archipelago" possessing outstanding natural beauty, preserved throughout the centuries because of the Japanese people's unique love of nature, remains widespread. In recent decades, numerous scholars and religious leaders in Japan have drawn upon such modern nationalist imagery, combining it with newly conceived ideas about Asian traditions as resources of "ecological knowledge" said to be diametrically opposed to Abrahamic (i.e., Western) religions. As a result, Japanese religious traditions have been reimagined as "ecological" traditions that offer suggestions for living sustainably today, and there is a large body of literature discussing the green credentials of Japanese worship traditions.

In this chapter, I discuss some of the ways in which (Zen) Buddhism, Shinto, and other religious traditions have been reinterpreted in the light of contemporary environmental concerns. In the first section, I begin by giving a brief sketch of the discourse on Japanese religion as ecological and sustainable, as it has developed in the past decades. My focus will be on the two traditions that have received the most attention and are associated most often with "nature" and environmental issues: Zen Buddhism and Shinto. In addition, I briefly discuss some of the main postwar Japanese theories on religion and nature. These claims center on the notion of "animism," which has become a core trope not only in nationalist ideology but also in academic debates. Having discussed some of the main theories, in the second part I focus on actual practices. I give some examples of environment-related initiatives undertaken by Japanese shrines, temples, and popular lay religious movements ("new religions"). As I will show, there is a widespread concern with forest preservation and reforestation on the part of Japanese religious actors. Other than that, however, cases of environmental activism are few and far between, and the impact of Japanese religions on environmental policy-making has been limited.

GREEN ZEN, GREEN SHINTO

The association of Zen with the natural environment goes back to the 1960s, when the beatnik generation in the United States discovered the texts of D. T. Suzuki and started producing their own hybrid popularizations of the tradition (e.g., Borup 2004). Drawing on preexisting nationalist myths, Suzuki promoted Zen as the essence of Japanese culture, characterized by harmony with nature, in contrast to the supposedly Western mentality of conquering nature (Suzuki 1959: 331–95). Historian Lynn White Jr. was clearly informed by this discourse when he wrote his influential article in *Science*, "The Historical Roots of Our Ecologic Crisis" (White 1967). In this article, White famously argued that modern environmental degradation is grounded in the Judeo-Christian view of nature as subordinate to man, which is used to legitimize the exploitation of natural resources. By contrast, he argued, Zen conceives of "the man-nature relationship as nearly the mirror image of the Christian view" (1967: 1206). This argument was copied by subsequent authors, who asserted that Zen—reimagined as the quintessential expression of the Japanese spiritual tradition and its attitude to nature—could serve as the basis for a new environmental ethics (e.g., Earhart 1970; Watanabe 1974; Shaner 1989). Similar arguments have been made repeatedly since, by numerous Zen philosophers and practitioners, in Japan as well as abroad (e.g., Habito 1997; James 2004). Many of them have pointed to Dōgen's statements that physical objects have Buddha nature, which they see as an example of Zen's eco-centric worldview (e.g., Parkes 2010).

The association between Zen and nature is not merely philosophical: it has been made so often that it has become a recurring theme in popular texts on "Zen" gardening, cooking, interior design, and so on. One of the problems of such representations of Zen, whether popular or philosophical, is that they are far removed from the daily reality of actual temple practices and do not necessarily translate into environmentally sustainable behavior. In Japan, Zen temples are similar to those of other Buddhist denominations; most of them are primarily concerned with funeral practices, as this constitutes their main source of income, and in some cases with tourism. Environmental activism is not high on most temples' agendas, if at all.

That said, it is worth mentioning that the Sōtō Zen sect has developed a "Green Plan," which encourages temples and their members to consume less, reduce energy use, and pick up litter (Williams 2012: 376–9). Furthermore, there are some noteworthy examples of temples developing local initiatives for environmental conservation. For instance, Sébastien Boret has studied an interesting case of a Zen temple in Tohoku that has been a pioneer in the development of "nature funerals," investing in tree planting and landscape conservation (Boret 2014). This is a rather unique grassroots project, however, which is not necessarily representative for Zen as a whole. Despite the existence of initiatives such as the "Green Plan," there is little evidence suggesting that Zen priests are more concerned with the environment than, say, those belonging to other denominations. Zen's green credentials are primarily due to the association with natural aesthetics and simplicity, but this does not necessarily translate into environmentally sustainable behavior, let alone activism.

A similar argument can be made for Shinto. The association between Shinto kami and natural phenomena is made often, and the claim that Shinto is a "nature religion" and *ipso facto* concerned with environmental issues has become commonplace in popular discourse on the topic. However, the fact that certain designated natural elements (e.g., particular trees, rocks, and rivers) are seen as the embodiment of divine beings does not necessarily imply that Shinto practitioners are concerned with the protection of the environment *as a whole*. The idea that Shinto might have some significance for contemporary environmental issues was first put forward by the American scholar of religion H. Byron Earhart in 1970 (Earhart 1970) but did not gain currency in Japan until the late 1990s. Of particular significance in this respect was the organization of the international "Shinto and Ecology" conference at Harvard University in 1997, which was one in a series of large conferences on "Religions of the World and Ecology." Whether the conference was a success or not may be subject to debate—reportedly, there was little interaction between representatives of Shinto and foreign scholars, and the conference proceedings never made it into a book, unlike the other conferences in the series.[1]

However, the event did teach the Japanese participants one important lesson: environmental issues constitute an important concern for religious organizations worldwide these days, and associating one's tradition with these issues can be an effective strategy for asserting its ongoing significance and for acquiring positive publicity abroad. It is no coincidence that several of the participants at this conference would move on to become leading figures in Shinto and contribute to the popularization of the notion of Shinto as an "ancient nature religion" that contains important lessons for living sustainably today (e.g., Sonoda 2000). Today, this view has achieved paradigmatic status even within conservative circles, to the point that the former president of the Association of Shinto Shrines (Jinja Honchō), Tanaka Tsunekiyo—significantly, one of the participants in the 1997 Harvard conference—asserted that the foundation of Shinto is "nature worship" in "sacred forests" (*chinju no mori*) (Tanaka 2011). Thus, the Shinto environmentalist

---

[1] The Association of Shinto Shrines (Jinja Honchō) did publish a report, which contains summaries of most of the conference papers in Japanese (Jinja Honchō 2000), but this report is not endorsed by the conference organizers and was not distributed widely.

paradigm, as I call it, has now achieved mainstream status, as even the shrine establishment endorses it (Rots 2015, 2017a, 2017b).

The popularization of notions of Zen and Shinto as "nature religions" with green credentials is clearly related to the global trend to associate religion with environmental issues. However, within Japan, such ideas are also influenced by domestic scholarship and ideology. Of particular significance in this context are the writings of a diffuse group of scholars, collectively referred to as "spiritual intellectuals" (Shimazono 2004: 274–92), who have made attempts to define the "spirit" or underlying "religiosity" of the Japanese nation. Authors such as Iwata Keiji, Kamata Tōji, Nakazawa Shin'ichi, Umehara Takeshi, Yamaori Tetsuo, and Yasuda Yoshinori have all argued that the foundational value orientation of the Japanese people lies in their intuitive appreciation of nature as sacred—or, put differently, in the "spirit of animism" that supposedly goes back to the "forest civilization" of the prehistoric Jōmon period and has survived until today. This animism, scholars such as Umehara and Yasuda have argued, constitutes the foundation of Shinto and Japanese Buddhism (including Zen); it has been largely forgotten as a result of the twin evils of modernization and Westernization, but a return to these values would lead to the rediscovery of the spirit of sustainability that supposedly characterized ancient Japan and help us overcome today's environmental problems (e.g., Umehara 1995 [1991]).

In this narrative, ecological decline goes hand in hand with moral decline, and the solution to the global environmental crisis is found in a return to "traditional Japanese culture." The term "animism," then, serves as a marker of difference and is used to distinguish between an essentialized Japan and "the West" (or, alternatively, "monotheism"), which is seen as morally degraded and responsible for environmental destruction worldwide (Rots 2017b: 107–20). These ideas have been taken over by leading Shinto priests and constitute an important foundation for the Shinto environmentalist paradigm.

Critics of the narrative have pointed out that notions of nature as "sacred" could not prevent the depletion of resources, neither in the past nor the present, and that Japan has a poor track record when it comes to environmental protection (e.g., Reader 1990; see also Totman 1989). Nevertheless, notions of Japan as a nation characterized by some sort of unique "animism"—today expressed in robot technology and popular culture, according to some—that may offer alternative ways for conceptualizing human-nature relations continue to fascinate, and the association has been endorsed by leading anthropologists (Allison 2006; Robertson 2007). In fact, there are several methodological and ideological problems associated with the term "animism", not least in the Japanese context (Wilkinson 2017; Thomas 2019c; see also Rambelli 2019). But even if we do accept the controversial premise that Shinto and Japanese Buddhism have some sort of underlying animistic worldview, the question still remains: how does such a worldview translate into concrete practices, and how do such practices contribute to solving environmental problems?

ENVIRONMENTAL PRACTICES

Despite all the rhetoric on the "animistic" orientation of Japanese religion and its alleged tradition of sustainability, the number of religious actors that are actively engaged with environmental issues is small. Shrines and temples are competitors in a crowded, shrinking religious market; most priests are primarily concerned with performing rituals and maintaining relations with their sponsors and parishioners. Few of them are inclined to engage in environmental activism, which could jeopardize such relations. As Duncan

Williams has observed, "much of mainstream Buddhism [is] aligned politically with the right-wing conservatives and big business" (2012: 384). Similarly, Shinto is a corporate religion, which is highly dependent upon sponsorship from business enterprises (Rots 2017b: 132; see also McLaughlin et al. 2020). Priests are generally interested in preserving shrine and temple grounds, but most of them are reluctant to engage in protests that challenge the sociopolitical status quo. There are a few noteworthy examples of priests who have become active in local environmentalist movements; for instance, some Shinto and Buddhist priests have protested the destruction of sacred forests in order to make way for highways, dams, or nuclear power plants (Breen and Teeuwen 2010: 207–8; Williams 2012: 373–5, 384–6; Rots 2017b: 135–6). These are exceptions, however; generally speaking, religious actors in Japan refrain from protesting infrastructural or industrial projects, even if these developments move forward at the expense of sacred land (Rots 2017b: 133–5).

Much more common is the development of initiatives focusing on forest conservation, environmental education, and cultural activities, taking place at local shrine or temple forests. Williams characterizes Buddhist attitudes to nature as "conservative conservationism" (2012: 376), and this term arguably applies to Shinto as well. In recent decades, sacred shrine forests (*chinju no mori*) have become the core symbol of the Shinto environmentalist paradigm (Rots 2015). The preservation of these ancient forests, present-day Shinto scholars argue, is a result of the Japanese tradition of worshipping "nature" as sacred, which should serve as a model for present-day environmental ethics (e.g., Sonoda 2000; Ueda 2013). Although their historical narrative may be challenged—many shrine and temple forests were planted in the modern or early modern periods, and even "sacred" lands were subject to periodical deforestation and resource depletion (Domenig 1997; Rambelli 2001, 2007: 129–71)—it is true that many shrines have small forests around them, as do some Buddhist temples. Some of them have created projects focused on preserving these forests, improving species diversity, and engaging local citizens with the shrine (or temple). For instance, at Shimogamo Jinja, a World Heritage-listed shrine in Kyoto, forestry scientists and priests have developed a project to improve the ecosystem of the historic shrine forest, Tadasu no Mori (Rots 2017b: 120–9). Likewise, at Meiji Jingū, a modern shrine surrounded by a large forest in central Tokyo, a nonprofit organization has been set up, members of which are active in collecting and planting acorns that are used for reforestation projects elsewhere, giving guided forest tours, and growing rice on a small urban paddy (Rots 2017b: 171–81).

The focus on "forests" as the main symbol of Japanese religious sustainability—or even, in Umehara's terminology, as the essence of Japanese civilization—is not limited to Shinto but can also be observed in Buddhist initiatives. For instance, the Jōdo Shinshū sect has set up the Honganji Forest Network, "which intends to foster respect for the environment through a national database of forests and trees" (Dessì 2017: 71). There are various local Buddhist forestry initiatives as well: for example, the abbot of Hōnen-in, a Jōdo Shū temple in Kyoto, has set up a "forest center" for environmental education purposes (Singer 2012), while his colleague at Rinnōji, a Sōtō Zen temple in Sendai, organized an ambitious reforestation project after the previous temple forest was demolished and has been involved in post-tsunami tree-planting initiatives (Rots 2019). In sum, forest conservation has emerged as an area in which religious actors can become active, contribute to local environments, and gain social capital, without challenging existing economic or political structures.

One organization that is worth mentioning in this context is Shasō Gakkai (Sacred Forest Research Association). Founded in 2002 by a group of scientists and Shinto priests, the association is devoted to preserving sacred forests nationwide and to promoting "sacred forest studies" (*shasōgaku*) as an interdisciplinary research field (Rots 2017b: 101–5). Through its annual journal, book publications (e.g., Ueda 2004), documentaries, conferences, and forest conservation courses, Shasō Gakkai has contributed to the establishment of social relations between religious actors (mostly Shinto priests, but some Buddhist members as well), forest scientists, and environmental activists, providing them with an opportunity to share experiences from different local forest conservation and environmental education projects.

Jinja Honchō has likewise expressed an interest in forest conservation. It is actively involved with the Alliance of Religions and Conservation (ARC), a UK-based nonprofit organization that defines itself as "a secular body that helps the major religions of the world to develop their own environmental programs, based on their own core teachings, beliefs and practices" (ARC n.d.-a). In 2000, Jinja Honchō staff made the "pledge" that all shrine forests in Japan would be managed sustainably, and they have been active in developing an international "religious forestry standard" (ARC n.d.-b). In 2014, Jinja Honchō and the ARC co-organized a large interreligious conference at the shrines of Ise on the topic of religion and sustainability, in which representatives from various religious traditions worldwide took part (Kōshitsu henshūbu 2014; Rots 2015, 2017b). This conference is illustrative of the fact that Jinja Honchō has become more concerned with international cooperation and publicity, and has discovered the legitimacy provided by a positive association with environmental sustainability. It is no coincidence that the conference took place at Ise—Shinto's sacred center, according to many—for Ise has recently been promoted actively as a place with unique natural beauty, characterized by centuries-old "sustainable" traditions (Rots 2017b: 183–97).

Forest preservation and reforestation have also been high on the agenda of a number of Japan's lay religious movements. Several of them have developed tree-planting projects, both in Japan and abroad, directly or through associated nonprofit organizations. This applies to Ōmoto-derived religious groups such as Ananaikyō and Worldmate as well as Lotus Sutra groups such as Risshō Kōseikai and Soka Gakkai. Ananaikyō, for instance, is relatively small in terms of membership, but the affiliated "nonreligious" development organization OISCA is influential throughout the Asia-Pacific region, where it seeks to spread the Japanese spirit of "harmony with nature" through reforestation projects and organic farming training centers (Watanabe 2019). Some of these movements have gone so far as to embrace environmentalism as a core aspect of their institutional identity, expressing an interest not only in forest conservation but also in alternative energy and organic agriculture. Seichō no Ie, for instance, is known for its ultranationalist ideology and involvement with Nippon Kaigi (Mizohata 2016), but it has turned green and now places great emphasis on environmental issues. It has recently completed its new, carbon-neutral and sustainable headquarters, the "office in the forest" (*mori no naka no ofisu*) in Yamanashi Prefecture, from where it seeks to contribute to building a society in which humans and nature live in balance (Taniguchi and Taniguchi 2010; Lian 2019). Another large Ōmoto-derived religion, Sekai Kyūseikyō Izunome Kyōdan (Church of World Messianity), likewise expresses an interest in nature and environmental issues. It is especially known for its emphasis on organic farming, and it has been involved with the development of "effective microorganisms" (EM), which are said to purify polluted soil and water (Sekai Kyusei Kyo Izunome 2008).

Thus, generally speaking, Japanese religious organizations have shown an interest in relatively apolitical topics such as forest conservation and organic farming, which are compatible with conservative, nationalist, and corporate ideologies, but refrain from engaging with more controversial issues. There has been a strong interest in forests and tree planting, but more pressing environmental problems, such as climate change and industrial pollution, have received considerably less attention. Until very recently, few (if any) Japanese religious organizations were concerned with maritime environmental issues such as overfishing, toxic pollution, or plastic waste. In 2019, however, the problem of plastic pollution was discussed at the G20 summit in Osaka, leading to more awareness of the issue in Japan. In response, an editorial in *Jinja Shinpō* (the Jinja Honchō newspaper) called for shrine priests and practitioners to recognize the importance of the ocean and consume less plastic (*Jinja Shinpō* 2019). This was not the first time the newspaper stated that Shinto should be concerned with environmental issues, but unlike previous editorials, this time the focus was not on shrine forests and moral education but on marine pollution. As usual, however, suggestions for concrete environmental actions were lacking.

Recent years have also seen an emerging interest in energy issues on the part of some religious actors and organizations. After the Fukushima crisis in 2011, various Buddhist organizations and new religions have spoken out against nuclear power and argued for a nationwide transition to alternative energy (Dessì 2017: 74–82). Konkōkyō, Seichō no Ie, Risshō Kōseikai, and two Buddhist temples have set up "the Religious and Scholarly Eco Initiative (RSE) and the Religious Based Solar Power Generators Association," pleading for the installation of solar panels at temples, churches, and shrines that can provide energy to surrounding communities (JNEB n.d.; Watts 2013). Similarly, some scholars and priests have argued that Shinto shrines could take the lead in producing solar power (Rots 2017b: 138). Thus far, however, such initiatives have had a limited impact, and have not (yet?) resulted in the widespread installation of solar panels at shrines and temples. After all, most religious denominations in Japan employ environmentalist rhetoric, but few of them seriously challenge existing economic structures and consumption patterns.

The main exception to this rule is Okinawa, which suffers from serious environmental problems ranging from toxic pollution to rapid biodiversity loss, partly caused by the large US military presence on the island. In recent years, a sizable coalition of citizens' groups has tried to prevent further military expansion, in particular the construction of a new base at Henoko Bay. Among the regular protesters are members of a small Lotus Sutra movement, Nipponzan-Myōhōji, a radical pacifist organization that is known for its peace pagodas, peace walks, and antinuclear stance (see Kisala 1999). Furthermore, some of the most prominent Henoko protest leaders are Protestant Christian ministers and Buddhist (Shingon and Jōdo Shinshū) priests. The protest movement also includes some vocal Okinawan *kaminchu* (ritual specialists). Thus, in Okinawa, a shared pacifist and environmentalist agenda has provided different religious actors with an opportunity to establish new interfaith relations. Yet even here, they constitute a minority; the majority of religious specialists are reluctant to join such explicitly political movements, even if they support them in private.

CONCLUSION

Religious actors in Japan are predominantly conservative. Most Shinto, Buddhist, and new religious organizations see it as their task to preserve Japanese traditional culture and corresponding social structures, not challenge them. They are eager to employ nationalist myths about the unique Japanese love of nature and perceive today's environmental problems as symptoms of the moral degradation that comes with individualization and a decline in "traditional values" such as patriotism and respect for nature. A return to these values, many of them believe, will automatically result in more sustainable behavior.

By contrast, the economic, ideological, and technological reasons that lie behind the widespread environmental pollution, climate change, rapid species loss, and large-scale waste problems facing today's world are not widely recognized. There is no doubt that some Japanese religious actors have played a positive role in the preservation of local (forest) environments. Few of them, however, have joined forces with other environmental groups in Japan, or used their influence to change policies. For instance, although Jinja Honchō and several new religious and Buddhist groups are prominent members of the powerful nationalist lobby organization Nippon Kaigi (Mizohata 2016; Guthmann 2017), they have made no attempts to push for greener national policies. Despite the development of some interesting projects for local nature conservation and the promotion of alternative energy, therefore, thus far the environmental engagement of Japanese religions has been limited.

See also Chapter 12, "Globalization," Chapter 20, "Pilgrimages and 'Sacred' Geography," Chapter 27, "Spirituality," and Chapter 28, "Tourism."

CASE STUDY

Grassroots Environmental Activities in Risshō Kōseikai

Aura DI FEBO

At dawn's early light on a Sunday morning of November 2016, I joined a group of young Japanese women and men headed to a major train station in central Tokyo.[1] They belonged to a nearby congregation of the lay Buddhist organization Risshō Kōseikai, a new religious movement (*shinshūkyō*) originally developed within the Nichiren Buddhist tradition. The group was founded in 1938 by Niwano Nikkyō and Naganuma Myōkō, who jointly led the organization until Naganuma's death in 1957. Her demise was followed by a series of radical reforms that substantially reshaped the movement's doctrine and organizational structure. These changes also brought about a progressive expansion of Kōseikai's missionary focus, together with its social activities. From the 1960s, the organization became earnestly involved in interfaith dialogue, peace work, and humanitarian activities on an international scale, as well as social welfare provision at the local level.

Among the various forms of service to the community promoted by the group—in particular, through its Youth Division and the Movement for a Brighter Society (Akarui Shakai-zukuri undō, Meisha for short)—environmental activities such as cleaning campaigns, beautification, and greening initiatives were among the most common. These activities were extensively reported in the movement's publications of the time, such as *Kōsei shinbun* and *Kōsei*. Although Kōseikai has a long history of environmental commitment, in recent years, the movement has shown a renewed interest in ecology and the global environmental crisis at the institutional level, as demonstrated by the Environmental Policy issued by the headquarters in 2009 (Dessì 2014). These concerns are also reflected in an ongoing engagement in environmental activities on a local scale, such as the one that I was about to observe that November day.

The initiative, labeled "CleanPeace", took place approximately once a month and brought together young members of the congregation and representatives of Meisha such as Miura,[2] the elderly lady in charge of the local branch. When we reached our destination, the participants and I met with a few more people carrying brooms, buckets, and dustpans. Makoto, one of the leaders of the Youth Division, distributed gloves and bibs reciting the slogan "Let's stop littering!" (*Poi sute yameyō*). The participants then

---

[1] This piece is based on data collected during a twelve-month fieldwork stay in Japan, from September 2016 to August 2017, when I conducted participant observation of social activities promoted by Risshō Kōseikai and in-depth interviews with the members involved.
[2] All the names used are pseudonyms.

started to clean the surroundings, collecting rubbish and picking up cigarette butts, cans, and litter. After about half an hour, we moved to a nearby Shinto shrine and began cleaning its premises. As explained by Makoto, the initiative was conceived as a form of service to the local community, but also as a means to promote interfaith dialogue and cooperation, primarily through engagement with the shrine. More generally, Makoto highlighted how members saw cleaning activities as a tool to foster mutual understanding and peace.

This episode was representative of Kōseikai's environmental activities, which were articulated at the grassroots level in markedly relational terms, as a means to both offer a contribution to society and to strengthen cooperative ties within local communities. These ideas stem from a general conception of social engagement as missionary practice, both narrowly and broadly defined. For Kōseikai members, serving community members and helping create a better and "brighter" society possessed inherent value as a salvific tool, based on a this-worldly conception of salvation, which is understood as liberation from suffering on both material and emotional or spiritual levels. As common to many other new religious organizations (Reader 1991; Shimazono 2004), Kōseikai conceives salvation as the realization of a state of happiness and fullness that results from a harmonious relation with the cosmos and is to be achieved in this life. Alongside their missionary value, however, environmental activities represent an opportunity to cultivate personal relationships beyond the congregation and strengthen social ties.

More broadly, in the founder's understanding, all activities directed at preserving the natural environment were closely related to the principles of interconnectedness and interdependence of all existence informing Kōseikai's cosmological and soteriological framework. In Risshō Kōseikai, the cosmos is conceived as an interrelated whole permeated by a universal life force identified with the Eternal Buddha. Within such a "vitalistic" worldview, which is not exclusive to Kōseikai but rather common to most early new religions (Tsushima et al. 1979; Hardacre 1986; Kisala 1999), all living beings are believed to exist in a state of interconnectedness within this single vital principle. As stressed by the founder Niwano: "All things in this world, with no exception, are related to one another … We all exist through being permeated by the same life-energy" (1976: 30–1). In Kōseikai's publications, communing with nature is often presented as a means to increase one's awareness of such interconnectedness (e.g., *Kōsei* 11, 2016: 5–8). These notions are also combined with karmic beliefs: the fundamental interdependence of all phenomena is explained in relation to the law of dependent origination, which states that everything in the universe changes based on a fundamental relation of causation.

These principles are strongly felt at the grassroots, as demonstrated by a speech given by the head minister of one the congregations visited during fieldwork. She stated that, based on the principle of dependent origination, climate change and environmental problems resulted from the combined effect of each individual action. Everyone, thus, should feel responsible for these issues and take measures to address them. She encouraged members to rethink their daily habits, try to reduce their energy consumption, and recycle. Asking oneself how to contribute to the common good, she added, is essential to the creation of a more peaceful society. These ideas echoed in many interviews. Representatives of Meisha in particular highlighted the importance of environmentalism as a practice of "community-building" (*machi-zukuri*). An overview of activities published by Meisha's national administration reflects this well: greening campaigns, garbage collection, and cleaning activities emerge as the most popular form of engagement on the local level.

A further example in this respect was offered by a Meisha branch located in Saitama prefecture, which had launched a reforestation (*mori-zukuri*) campaign in the surrounding urban area. The initiative was supported by a network of local actors, including entrepreneurs, and neighborly associations, and benefitted of the support of the city office. Similarly to other cases encountered in the field, for this particular branch, environmental activities had opened a space for cooperation with local authorities and institutions. Miura spoke of this cooperation as a crucial aspect of the "locality" (*chiikisei*) of Meisha activities. More generally, participants tended to articulate these activities in terms of contribution to the community and opportunities to strengthen social ties.

These principles also informed Kōseikai's response to natural disasters, most notably the relief activities following the earthquake, tsunami, and nuclear disasters that hit Tohoku in March 2011. In the wake of the disaster, Kōseikai's headquarters and local branches mobilized people and resources as part of a nationwide campaign labeled "Together in One Hearth" (*Kokoro hitotsu ni*), still ongoing. Alongside activities catering to the pressing needs of the refugees and the commitment to restore disrupted social networks emerged as the leitmotif of Kōseikai initiatives, as demonstrated by practitioners' earnest engagement in "emotional care" (*kokoro no kea*) services and community-building projects. These initiatives stand as further evidence of the centrality of interpersonal relationships within Kōseikai, which also informs their environmentalism. This stems from its doctrinal background, but also from notions of mutual dependency and communal support well rooted in Japanese culture. Drawing from these premises, Risshō Kōseikai fosters an understanding of "environment" (or "nature") that is strongly imbued with a sense of place and locality, and tightly bound to the lives of the human and nonhuman beings who inhabit it.

CHAPTER 9

Folk Performing Arts

SUZUKI Masataka

Folk performing arts (*minzoku geinō*) are annual ceremonies (*nenchū gyōji*) involving dances, songs, performances, and plays, which are based on local communities and take place during rituals and religious festivals (*matsuri*) during particular seasons. The purpose of these folk performing arts can be the abundance of new crops, fishing prosperity, health protection, business success, spiritual support, and the regeneration of vital forces. Different from standard annual ceremonies, certain folk performing arts can also take place as rites of passage to mark crucial moments in a person's life. In the past, various folk performing arts dealing with rituals for rainmaking, rain stopping, and against contagious diseases were also performed to deal with unexpected events such as famines, droughts, epidemics, and other threats to human life. Originally, folk performing arts developed in conjunction with a great variety of human activities such as agriculture, fishing, forestry, and commerce, and followed the lunar calendar. With their progressive alienation from the occupational sphere, however, folk performing arts started to be perceived as amusements and, in certain cases, fundamental elements for rebuilding social ties. Although the term *minzoku geinō* can be translated in English as "folk performing arts" or "folk performances," it is substantially different from the Euro-American concept of "artistic activity" (Thornbury 1997; Lancashire 2011) because of its strong connection with religious traditions.

The fundamental structure of religious festivals centers on the summoning of divine spirits (*shinrei*) to the ceremonial stage in order to express gratitude to them through songs, dances, and music. After a period of general excitement, the divine spirits are sent back to their customary place of residence. Songs and dances are often presented to local gods and buddhas to propitiate the realization of vows and prayers. This aspect shows the deep correlations between folk performing arts and ancestor spirits, local gods, and buddhas. Liminal natural areas such as forests, trees, springs, riverbanks, beaches, and capes are considered particularly suitable to host religious festivals. In certain areas, agricultural, fishing, and mountain villages; urban temples; shrines; little chapels and especially designated village houses, known as *tōya*, can serve the same purpose.

The setting of the stage marks the beginning not only of entertaining activities but also of ritual music and dancing (*kagura*), which are often followed by kabuki and nō plays. Performers are nonprofessional common people who belong to the local community. In the past there were also itinerant professional performers who visited houses making auspicious comedies (*manzai*) and lion dances (*shishi mai*) for propitiating good fortune and expelling impurity during the new year period. Even now the Ise daikagura performers pay annual visits to various regions of the archipelago to practice purificatory prayers, and in Shikoku there are farmers who at the end of the harvest season go door-to-door performing the Awa ningyō puppet theater. In the past, performers visiting from outside the village were perceived as ambivalent presences—mendicants who could be, at the same time, emissaries of the deities.

Before the Second World War, folk performing arts were defined as "local dances" (*kyōdo buyō*) because of their considerable influence on local societies, and scholars tried to understand them within the intellectual frame of "folk arts" (*minzoku geijutsu*). The term "folk performing arts" (*minzoku geinō*) started to be used in the fifties and became a common expression in 1952 with the creation of the Association for the Folk Performing Arts (*Minzoku geinō no kai*) and the systematization of the criteria for designating intangible cultural heritage. The concept behind the definition of "local dances" had strong overtones that tended to limit the characteristics of folk performing arts within the boundaries of small local societies. In contrast, the idea of "folk performing arts" attempts to clarify the history of common people as based on a substratum of folkloric culture (*minzoku bunka*), embracing not only written sources but also songs, dances, and musical compositions.

There are multiple theories and methodologies associated with the study of folk performing arts. Environmental theories take into account performing arts as historical sources with a relevant place within the history of common people. Functional theories interpret performing arts as human attempts to maintain, consolidate, or oppose social structures. Artistic theories analyze the changes of the movements, which refer to bodily techniques in dance and acting in the ritual arena. Semantic theories try to understand world and cosmic constructs through the relationships between gods, performing arts, and local societies.

TRANSFORMATIONS IN FOLK PERFORMING ARTS

Folk performing arts change according to social, economic, and political situations in specific historical periods. A great turning point for folk performing arts was the economic development that occurred in urban areas during the Tokugawa period (1600–1868). Unlike agricultural and fishing villages, in which religious festivals were administered by the community, cities hosting religious festivals included spectators who attended them without actively organizing them. Therefore, festival sites, ritual tools, and decorations were often selected and displayed for mere aesthetic purposes. This type of à la mode religious festival was called *fūryū* and focused on the parade of lavishly decorated floats (*dashi*) and concentrations of entertainment booths (*yatai*) for the visitors. For instance, the Gion matsuri in Kyoto originally took place in a densely populated area, which was often stricken by epidemics during the summer. For this reason, the main deity of the Gion matsuri was Gozu Tennō, the bull-head god of epidemics, who was cheered and entertained by beautiful decorations before being accompanied toward the river and sent back to his realm. The Gion matsuri developed into a great festival in which gorgeous floats mounted with long halberds were pulled along the streets swinging to the rhythm of bells' jingling, steamed rice cakes were thrown around to dispel contagious diseases and pacify epidemic gods, and crowds of onlookers were entertained with roadshows (*misemono*). The splendor of floats and halberds were amplified with tapestry made of not only Japanese Nishijin brocades but also French Gobelin brocades and Persian carpets, which displayed the refined taste of the urban population.

In his analysis of the aesthetic changes of *fūryū*, the ethnologist Yanagita Kunio (1865–1962) pointed out a transition "from religious festivals to religious events (*sairei*)," in which most of the spectators were not residents of the city. Yanagita also underlined how the community of nonresident spectators fostered the development of a threefold structure based on the activities of looking (*miru*), showing (*miseru*), and being seen (*mirareru*), which characterized these types of religious events. In so doing, Yanagita was able to describe the correlations between the changes occurring within specific religious festivals and society in general (Yanagita 1998 [1942]). The originality and creativity of the urban population had a huge transformative impact not only on the structure of religious festivals held in cities but also on those held in rural villages.

Nowadays, the survival of folk performing arts is threatened by industrial and social transformations, the performers' old age, and a decreasing younger population, and thus, a scarcity of inheritors (Suzuki 2014). On the other hand, the assembling techniques for floats and decorations continue to constantly improve, augmenting the overall aesthetic impact of the performances (Fukuhara 1995; Ueki 2001)—so much so that in 2016 the United Nations Educational, Scientific and Cultural Organization (UNESCO) defined floats, decorations, and booths as cultural patrimony, and included them in the list of intangible cultural heritage. Folk performing arts provide a unique view of the relationships between materiality such as architecture, sculpture, painting, craft, and cultural heritage politics and even tourism.

Politics and cultural heritage administrative choices also triggered relevant changes in folk performing arts. In 1950 the Law for the Preservation of Cultural Heritage defined the category of intangible cultural properties; the system for appointing intangible cultural assets was established in 1954. In 1975 the system for appointing nationally important intangible folk cultural properties was enforced, and various elements that had a value from a historical and folkloric perspective were selected among the folk performing arts in each region of the country. The state organized various preservation activities, including examinations, classifications, conservations, and transmissions of intangible folk cultural assets. However, the transformation into cultural heritage of folk performing arts opened the way to new problems. For instance, local communities were caught by a fervor for preserving traditions, which led to a complete renewal of traditional costumes and other forms of extreme restoration. At the same time, there was also a tendency toward an "invention of tradition" based on a self-conscious process of fictive resurrection of the past. Present folk performing arts are often used as cultural resources for events, which aim to exploit their aesthetic characteristics for revitalizing local communities or tourism.

In addition, the filming of folk performing arts has generated a great number of unique visual productions, while the integration of folk performing arts within certain theatrical experiences also gave birth to new challenging forms of hybridity. Downplaying the aspects concerning the invocations to kami and buddhas, contemporary folk performing arts have begun a strong process of objectivization. Today, information on folk performing arts can be immediately obtained on the internet, and it is easy to approach them thanks to the diffusion of videos and animation. People, performers, and local communities keep transforming themselves, adding complexity to the multi-directionality of their social relationships.

In recent years, the effects of globalization can be summed up by way of UNESCO's activities. In 2001 UNESCO issued the Declaration of Masterpieces in Oral Traditions and Intangible Heritage of Humanity (hereafter Declaration) due to a growing consciousness of heritage theories and cultural diversity. Nevertheless, in so doing, UNESCO further expanded the framework of intangible cultural heritage, and in 2003 it proposed the Treaty on Intangible Cultural Heritage. Japan ratified this treaty in 2004 and it went into effect in 2006. In 2008 nō dances, *jōruri* puppet theater, and kabuki plays, which were mentioned in the Declaration (2001, 2003, 2005), were included in the list of intangible cultural properties. In 2009 every country had to base its application for inclusion of new items in the list on a new system, which caused the number of inscriptions to the

UNESCO's list of intangible cultural properties to skyrocket. Hayachine kagura, a group of folk performances with strong Shugendō influences based in Tōhoku, was registered in 2009. In 2018 *raihōshin*, representations of visiting deities in masks and costumes, were also nominated as intangible cultural heritage, further widening the category. On the other hand, there have been problems due to the drastic changes introduced to popular cultural assets after UNESCO's recognition. For example, certain dances went so far as to hire producers who increased the presence of gorgeous decorations, leading to these "traditions" being kept alive on the basis of show-business logic.

In 2011 lion-dances and kagura played a pivotal role in the social reconstruction of the Tōhoku region after the destruction due to the Great East Japan Earthquake and tsunami. Folk performing arts helped maintain cohesion between local communities, reestablishing social ties among people in spite of the terrible damage to the region and its people. Yet again, folk performing arts returned to be perceived as the cornerstone of local communities. Folk performing arts also benefitted from being defined as "social capital." There is a new consciousness according to which folk performing arts do not belong to the past but deserve to be kept alive even in the future and to be promoted as living examples of intangible popular cultural heritage.

FROM FOLK ARTS TO FOLK PERFORMING ARTS

Field work and research on folk performing arts began systematically on the occasion of a performance that took place at the conference of the Association for Local Dances and Folk Songs (*Kyōdō buyō to min'yō no kai*) as the inaugural event of the Nippon Seinenkan in Tokyo in 1925. The Nippon Seinenkan, one of the main stages for folk performing arts, was built in 1920 near Meiji shrine as a training place for the young devotees of the shrine, who were supposed to learn folk performing arts to sustain the state. Therefore, folk performing arts were also exploited for sponsoring nationalistic political discourses. In 1925 the scholar of folk dances Kodera Yūkichi organized a performance of local dances and songs from various regions. After 1925, a similar event took place every year at the anniversary of the building's opening. This operation had pros and cons: dance movements and costumes changed to fit the needs of the new urban stage, performers gained a certain fame, and there were processes of hybridization with different performing arts.

In 1927 Yanagita Kunio, Orikuchi Shinobu, Kodera Yūkichi, and Nagata Kōkichi founded the Association for Folk Arts (*Minzoku geijutsu no kai*), and in 1928 the Association's journal, *Minzoku geijutsu*, began publishing research reports and articles, which testified to the great progress in the field. The opening article of the first issue was "The genesis of okina" written by ethnologist Orikuchi Shinobu (1887–1953), with an introduction by Yanagita Kunio in which the author tried to reframe folk dances and songs using American and European art theories. The Association for Folk Arts interpreted local religious festivals and performing arts as examples of folk culture based on extraordinary ancient customs diffused in remote and isolated areas of the archipelago. This model of ethnic culture brought about a reevaluation of folk performing arts as living historical documents (Suzuki 2015a). Thanks to these research activities in various locales, folk arts performers themselves became aware of the crucial importance of transmitting their knowledge to future generations.

A good example of this prewar research phase is the book *Hana matsuri* (1930) by Hayakawa Kōtarō (1889–1956) on the Shimotsuki kagura in the Oku-mikawa region (Aichi prefecture), which considers the concepts of "rebirth and purification" as the two central themes in kagura performances (Hayakawa 1971 [1930]). In *Geijutsu to shite no kagura no kenkyū*, Kodera Yūichi (1895–1945) clarifies the aesthetic sensibilities of folk communities by an analysis of dances and local performances as bodily techniques and by interpreting kagura from theatrical and artistic perspectives (Kodera 1929). In *Kodai kenkyū* (1929–1930), Orikuchi Shinobu focuses on the relationships between the human body and spirits by interpreting the birth of performing arts in conjunction with the unrestrained movements of invisible presences during rituals for summoning back and stabilizing the spirit (*tama*) (Orikuchi 1995 [1929–30]).

During the Second World War, the Association for Folk Dances and Songs, which became the main stage for showing folk performing arts, held no conferences. In 1947 a group of young performers reorganized the event to contribute to national reconstruction after the end of the war. In 1950 Honda Yasuji (1906–2001) changed the name of the Association to National Assembly for Local Performing Arts (*Zenkoku kyōdo geinō taikai*), which had been sponsored by the Executive Board for the Arts of the Ministry of Education since the second meeting at the Nippon Seinenkan, and continued its activities until 1958. In 1959 the name was changed again to National Assembly for Folk Performing Arts (*Zenkoku minzoku geinō taikai*), which it remains today.

After the Second World War, there was a decline in folk performing arts, but the vitality of research in this field contributed significantly to their preservation. Moreover, since 1954 folk performing arts have been included in the national plan for protecting cultural heritage, and since 1975 they have also been preserved according to the policy for maintaining important intangible folk cultural assets. In 1984 scholars of folk performing arts founded the Association of Folk Performing Arts (*Minzoku geinō gakkai*) to present and share the most recent achievements in research and fieldwork activities. Today every prefecture has its intangible folk cultural properties, which are preserved and transmitted by local administrations. Although the history of folk performing arts has always developed in symbiosis with "spectacularization," it is necessary to pay attention to the positive as well as negative aspects of this phenomenon.

CLASSIFICATION OF FOLK PERFORMING ARTS AND FUTURE ISSUES

It is difficult to classify Japanese folk performing arts due to their great variety. Honda Yasuji divided folk performing arts into five groups according to their style, religious contents, and historical background: (1) ritual music and dance (*kagura*); (2) "field music and performances" (*dengaku*); (3) group dances (*furyū*);(4) propitiatory performances (*shukufuku gei*); and (5) dances originating overseas (*gairai myaku*). It is important to keep in mind that from the point of view of performing art history, these five groups always share a certain degree of commonality (Honda 1960).

Kagura (Honda's first group) are sacred performances constituted by songs and dances dedicated to kami and buddhas, which were principally performed by female shamans (*miko*); they used *sasaki* branches or fans as ritual tools (*torimono*) for summoning the kami and offered them the boiling water of a ritual caldron placed in the middle of the arena. This type of *kagura* is known as Ise-style kagura or Yudate kagura and differs from Lion-dance kagura (*shishi kagura*), in which the dancers use the wooden mask of a lion head (*shishigashira*) as a temporary vessel for hosting the kami (*Yamabushi-kagura*, *bangaku*, and *Dai kagura* are also included in this category).

Dengaku (second group) consists of ritual music and dances performed in association with rice planting for propitiating a good harvest. *Dengaku* dances reproduce the gestures typical of agricultural activities and are performed as fertility rituals (*ta asobi*) in the new rice-growing season or in correspondence of rice planting festivals (*taue matsuri*) at the beginning of the rice-transplantation period (this group also includes *otaue matsuri, taue odori, hana-daue,* and *dengaku odori*).

Next, *fūryū* dances (third group), served to dispel epidemics and vengeful sprits while praying for abundance of crops. *Fūryū* also included danced recitations of the Buddha's name (*nenbutsu odori*), dances for entertaining the dead (*bon odori*), dances accompanied by large drums (*taiko odori*), and lion-dances for rain rituals, abundant crops, and elimination of contagious diseases. The same category also includes short dances and songs accompanied by musical instruments such as shamisen or flutes (*kouta odori*), baton dances (*aya odori*), ornamental floats and carts (*tsukurimono fūryū*), fancy dress parade dances (*kasō fūryū*), and walking parades (*neri fūryū*).

The fourth group refers to propitiatory dances with masks and costumes to celebrate the visiting deities during the new year period (*shinnen no raihōshin*), auspicious comedies for the first month of the year (*shōgatsu no manzai*), spring colt comic monologue (*harukoma*), and epic recitative of local legends (*katarimono*). Finally, the fifth group describes performing arts such as the lion-dance, which originated from abroad and became part of Japanese culture. This group also includes dances for the prosperity of the country that were performed at the end of Buddhist services, such as the ceremony for the descent of the twenty-five bodhisattvas (*nijūgo bosatsu raigō-e*) as well as demon dances (*oni mai*) and buddha dances (*hotoke no mai*).

All together, these five groups embrace the entire panorama of the Japanese folk performing arts and are useful for a comparative analysis of their development, transmission, and transformations. On the other hand, it is important to consider that folk performing arts of Okinawa prefecture differ from those of the Japanese mainland and require a different set of interpretative categories to be properly analyzed.

Moreover, there is room to rethink Honda's definitions and categorizations. For example, his taxonomy does not take into account the fact that classificatory standards can change according to the goals of the performance (*kagura*), the temporal and spatial circumstances for its enactment (*dengaku*), and expressive means (*fūryū*). In addition, these five groups disregard reciprocal influences due to changes in bodily techniques, differences between inheritors, and an overly clear-cut distinction between indigenous and foreign origins. Moreover, Honda emphasized the shared aspects between various performing arts but neglected their local differences. For a long time, Honda Yasuji held a seat in the council for the protection of national cultural properties and exerted a great influence on administrative processes for their designation. Therefore, Honda's five groups became the standard taxonomy for categorizing folk performing arts and recognizing them as cultural properties. For the future of folk performing arts, it is necessary to create new categories, in tune with the changes brought about by new research developments. For example, if a folk performing art such as *kagura* is studied from different interpretative perspectives, the result would be a plurality of provisional definitions such as "an exchange between humans, buddhas, and kami based on songs, dances, and music"; "a set of theatrical dances with masks and costumes for amusing the gods"; "an ecstatic séance (*kamigakari*)"; "a pacification ritual for the spirits of the dead," or "an apotropaic ritual against demons" (Suzuki 2018b). Future research on kagura should also analyze the complexity of Japanese cosmological discourses as expressed in invocatory formulae (*saimon*) and rituals that are related to this type of performance (Iwata 1983; Ushio 1985; Yamamoto 1993; Suzuki 2001) (Figures 9.1 and 9.2).

FIGURE 9.1: After performing ascetic practices on the mountain, a Shugendō practitioner (*yamabushi*) shows his powers making an apotropaic dance during the Daijō kagura. Tōhoku region, Iwate prefecture.

Source: Photo by the author.

FIGURE 9.2: The Shirokami kagura dance for protecting life and human activities performed by hunters and slash-and-burn farmers in mountainous areas. Kyūshū region, Miyazaki prefecture.
Source: Photo by the author.

There are many open issues in the research field of folk performing arts. For instance, very few studies focus on the "social liminality" of people who work in performing arts. Future scholarship should take into account the nomadic nature, the discriminatory discourses, and the ambivalences that have characterized the social status of these performers. The techniques for creating entertaining, aesthetic, and humorous expressions, which are adopted by folk arts performers when moving and speaking, should also be given more attention. Another issue concerns the study of beauty, which is reified through gestures and art forms that originate from "those territories of individuality where aesthetic values keep overflowing" (Hashimoto 2006).

Further research on folk performing arts can also help to reconsider individual problems vis-à-vis with groups and local societies. Currently, folk performing arts are interpreted in close connection with the ethnic culture of Japan, emphasizing their enactment within the borders of the Japanese state and rarely making comparisons with other folk performing arts overseas. Nevertheless, it is fundamental to consider that Japanese folk performing arts spread all over the world as examples of folk music and dances. Therefore, the future analytical developments should try to make connections and comparisons with similar research done abroad.

See also Chapter 3, "Cultural Heritage," Chapter 15, "Materiality," and Chapter 24, "Sound."

CHAPTER 10

Food Offerings

Allan G. GRAPARD

Apart from the many Japanese scholarly works on the topic, very little scholarship from outside Japan does justice to the fact that food offerings in Shinto shrines and Buddhist temples form a central component of Japan's cultic and cultural systems. In the following pages, I intend to present basic data and then shift to interpretive questions and suggestions for future research.

The oldest extant records, as well as an astonishingly large body of subsequent literature, provide unassailable evidence that life in Japan was (and in some significant ways still is) characterized by the observance of a plethora of rites. And yet, few scholars outside Japan have paid sustained attention to ritual and ceremonial life in any period of Japanese history, and it can be said that even fewer have ever mentioned or studied the exceptional importance of food in ceremonial and ritual life, be it in the context of major religious observances or of daily practices.

In this chapter, I propose to partly fill this lacuna by bringing our attention to three types of ritual domains. First, no ritual can take place in Shinto shrines if food is not offered; some of these offerings are elaborate, determined by rules or tradition, and, ideally, prepared by shrine officiants. Second, food is also offered in Buddhist temples, where monastic repasts tend to be highly ritualized; the dead are offered food; and Buddhism has developed specific dietetic regimens as well as a number of rites and doctrinal propositions concerning food. Third, many people in contemporary Japan observe a fairly large number of rituals and ceremonies of either public or private character that involve food preparation, sharing, or offering (the world of *nenjū gyōji*, *omiyage*, *shikitari*, and *shitsurai*). These three domains should not be thought of as separated by absolute boundaries, for Shinto and Buddhism have interacted on many levels for most of their history, and the third category is, in many ways, the result of such interactions. Provisional distinctions, however, facilitate the analysis.

THE MODERN PERIOD

The first "modern" study of food offerings was written by Terumoto Yutaka in May 1932, probably for didactic purposes and in response to the need to standardize rituals after Shinto shrines were placed under rigid government control after the Meiji "Restoration" of 1868. Terumoto begins his study with a statement to the effect that the kami do in fact eat what is offered to them; he then goes on to elaborate on the ancient terms used for what is called today *shinsen* 神饌, literally "kami viands." Two of these ancient terms stand out: *mi-ae* 御饗 and *mi-nie* 御贄. The former may be translated as "gracious regale" and the latter as "respectful offering." According to etymological dictionaries, the term *ae* (regale) sometimes referred to a banquet, that is, any festive gathering during which food is shared. Second, it also referred to various banquets that take place at the end of a ritual performance and are known as *naorai* 直会 indicating a "communal repast, return to everyday life." Third, the term *ae* referred to foodstuffs that are offered to divine beings. Fourth and last, it referred to those divine beings' acceptance of the offering. In contrast, the graph pronounced *nie* in Japanese has long been used, both in China and Japan, to refer to the "gift" (very often consisting of foodstuffs) one makes when introduced to someone of higher social standing, and only then.

In other words, the first term seems to refer to a group activity, while the second indicates a form of barter—an offering made in the expectation of a lasting bond between two people of different status. Both types of meanings undergird many of the gift practices (*o-miyage*) one sees in contemporary Japan, where eating is often done in order to acknowledge, reinforce, or re-enforce social relations, and where gift-giving and exchanges routinely take place in a wide variety of contexts. Group dining is ubiquitous, particularly at the events related to various ritual calendars; so is gift-giving to an individual on special occasions, with a stress on first-time meetings or critical moments. It should be noted that both entail a quasi-hidden emphasis on social power relations: none of these activities are equal-to-equal transactions, and one may therefore speak of an economy of power relations in "gift-giving societies."

Let us return to Terumoto's study. The technical term for "food offerings in Shinto shrines" is *mike* 神饌, today normally read *shinsen*, a compound in which the first graph means kami, and the second graph means either "surplus" or "remnant." This term's usage is, like many rituals and their terminologies today, a Meiji creation; prior to Meiji, other terms were used, but that list is too long for this short chapter. The first important distinction made by Terumoto is in types of food offerings: raw (*seisen* 生饌) and cooked (*jukusen* 熟饌), both of which are normally used today. Seisen refers to any raw foodstuff, such as sacrificed animals ("of soft and coarse fur, of wide fin and narrow fin from rivers or seas"), crustaceans and fowl of all kinds, live animals (usually, but not limited to, horses or birds), and to cereals, vegetables, and fruit. When vegetables, cereals, or fruit are emphasized separately from "raw" animals, they then receive the name *sosen* 素饌 (unaltered natural foods), also referred to as *marumono* 丸物 (simple food—not "things"): indeed, the term *mono* or *o-mono* was often used prior to the Meiji period to refer to food offerings in general. The term *jukusen* ("cooked offerings") may be used to qualify any of the foodstuff mentioned above that is submitted to heat, but it does not specify whether the cooking is achieved through steaming, boiling, stewing, grilling, frying, deep-frying, baking, or roasting (each of which may carry its own signification). Regrettably, Terumoto also makes no distinction between the raw/cooked dualism and other modes of food preparation, such as sun-drying, smoking, salting, or brewing, even though these matters are of no little importance.

The terms *seisen* and *jukusen* are standard in contemporary Shinto usage; they reflect the standardizing efforts that marked the late-nineteenth-century transformation of Shinto by the modern nation-state, but they fail to shed light on the complex symbolism of food as a cultic and cultural system. They equally fail to shed light on the origins of table manners, or on the aesthetics of food presentation, all of which are of the essence when considering the matter at hand. Last but not least, they fail miserably in that, contrary to a historical consciousness hidden behind the term "tradition," they display an aberrant consciousness of the past: at the all-important Ise Shrines, for examples, raw food was not offered prior to Meiji, with a few seasonal exceptions for soup (*atsumono* 羹), gruel (*kayu* 粥), and pounded rice (*mochi* 餅). What this example tells us is that we should worry a great deal about statements, oral and written, concerning history and traditions, and not just on the topic of food offerings. In closing, Terumoto assesses the goals and functions of food offerings, of which he distinguishes four major types: request, gratitude, fear, and magic. I believe this list will need be considerably enlarged in the future.

A BUDDHIST EXAMPLE: THE *SHŌRYŌ-E* AT HŌRYŪJI

Let us now look at one example of Buddhist food offerings. The *Shōryō-e* (august spirit ritual assembly) is a series of rites performed once every fifty years at the Hōryūji Temple in Nara Prefecture on March 22–24 (originally on the twenty-second day of the second lunar month), the day when the imperial prince today known as Shōtoku Taishi (574–622) is believed to have died. The prince is said to have played a central role in the acceptance of Buddhism by the court, and almost immediately after his death, he became the object of popular cults, miraculous stories, and painted as well as written hagiographies. Substantial commemorative rites are held for the prince's spirit at Hōryūji every year, but a special rite takes place once every fifty years. These rites are also held at Shitennōji (established by Shōtoku Taishi) in Osaka on April 22, at Kōryūji in Kyoto on August 22, at other temples connected to him around the country, and at his tomb in Shinaga, south of the Hōryūji. The Hōryūji commemorative rites are distinguished by the fact that they are held in front of highly elaborate food offerings said to reflect key features of classical and medieval high society ritual repasts. They are also comparable to commemorative rites dedicated to a variety of many other illustrious historical figures.

The offerings are positioned in three different areas of the mausoleum dedicated to Shōtoku Taishi's spirit in the Hōryūji temple complex. First, a small table is placed right in front of the alcove where a statue of the prince presides. Second, a few meters in front of this table, there is a large, three-tiered platform in front of which the raised seat of the lead officiant is located. Finally, closer still to the entrance of the sanctuary, there is a table where food offered by commoners is displayed.

On the small table immediately facing Shōtoku Taishi's statue, we find a black lacquered stand that supports a red lacquer plate, on which rests a clay bowl filled with a pile of white sugary confections embossed with the emblem of the prince, and another stand holding *konnyaku*, waterlily buds made of rice paste, and other vegetables. Then there is a cup of tea and a lacquered plate covered with folded white paper, on which rest five sweet confections, white on the outside, red at the center. The offerings on this table seem to suggest that they are mere hors-d'oeuvres, to be followed by the main courses laid out on the central table, but they are representative of Buddhist food offerings around the country in temples large and small, independently of sectarian affiliation: sweets, vegetables, flowers, and fruit.

The main display at the center of the hall consists of a three-tiered platform placed in the back of a ritual platform, all covered with a single, highly ornate gold and red brocade. The highest tier in the back holds, on the left, a pile of three large moon-shaped rice dumplings that have been dyed yellow at the top, white at the middle, and light-green at the bottom. To the right is a large, cone-shaped pile of rice cooked at dawn on the day of the rite; it is held together by a "belt" made of kelp (*konbu*), and by an X-shaped arrangement of dried kelp, to stabilize it in the front.

The second lower tier consists, from the right, of a pile of white round rice dumpling layers separated by what appears to be Japanese cypress branches, topped with a large rice dumpling, all contained within a square crown made of paper and brocade, itself set on a paulownia stand; a large, elaborate display, on the same crown and stand, of what is called *mimizukuri* ("ear style"). This large cone-shaped structure is made of hundreds of layered wheat dough objects looking like cat's ears, each attached to a central invisible pillar. To the left of this construct is a wooden pillar, from the top of which strands of wheat vermicelli (*sōmen*, also pronounced *sakumen*) stream downward. To the left, the last pile reflects the first pile of rice dumplings, but in this case, the dumplings are yellow.

The third lower tier consists of several towerlike structures: from the right, a tower of staggered, octagonal dried rice dumplings resting on a paulownia receptacle; a tower of kumquats (*kinkan*, *Citrus japonicus*) held together by pins glued to a central, invisible tube; a tower of dried (white) soybeans, arranged in the same manner; a tower of ground cherries, also known as winter cherries or strawberry tomatoes (*hōzuki*, *Physalis alkekengi*); a tower of black (fermented) soybeans; a tower of arrowhead bulbs (*kuwai*, *Sagittaria sagittifolia* or *trifolia, var. edulis*). Then comes a tower of sweetened jelly cubes dyed red and white; the sweetened jelly called *kanten* is agar-agar, which is made from a red seaweed (*tengusa*) known as Bengal or Japanese isinglass and Ceylon moss. *Kanten* was (and still is) widely used in sweet confections (such as *yōkan*), as well as in Buddhist temple food. The next tower is made of gingko nuts (*ginnan*); then a tower of dried persimmons; next is a tower of "cat ears"; then follows a tower of kaya nuts (*Torreya rucifera*). The last tower consists of green soy beans (*edamame*).

The masterpiece, however, consists of two identical displays, on each side of the table and placed toward its back; they frame the three tiers and dominate them by their sheer height, which almost reaches the ceiling of the sanctuary. It is said that they are symbolic representations of the Buddhist cosmic mountain Meru (Jap. *Shumisen*) or of the Island of the Taoist Immortals (Ch. *Penglai*, Jap. *Hōrai*). These elegant structures are supported by horizontal layers of white rice dumplings separated by Japanese cypress branches, above which rises another set of vertical layers of white rice dumplings, superimposed "belts" made of multicolored ropes, mandarins, and dried persimmons from which emerge bunches of daffodils made of rice paste. Projecting in all directions and upwards of this construct are tall bamboo branches forming an exuberant display; to these branches are attached phoenixes, swallows, and cranes, all made with rice paste and dyed in various colors. This type of offering, characterized by various foodstuffs attached to branches, is paradigmatic of the "Small New Year" offerings in many parts of Japan.

SHINTO FOOD OFFERINGS

The *norito* (ritual chants) contained in Book Eight of the Procedures of the Engi Era (early tenth century) codified the general process of ritual performance in shrines sponsored by the state at the time (Bock 1970). After the erection of a shrine came the intonation of words of praise; then, food and other types of offerings, followed by an entreaty. Finally, the proclamation of auspicious and/or laudatory words. One cannot but be stunned by the variety and quantity of offerings. Both food offerings and the man-made objects used to serve them required much work: the entire growing year for cereals and vegetables; the gathering of herbs, flowers, fruit and mushrooms in mountains and moors; both hunting and fishing expeditions; the all-important sake-brewing techniques; the lengthy cloth-making and dyeing processes; and the industrial preparation of dishes, tables, jewels, weapons, and other types of regalia. All this required power over producers who were expected to provide these offerings as tributes, but it also required coordination of transportation means and schedules, and a prodigious outlay of special clothes and refinery for all participants. In other words, as soon as one thinks about the connections between food and ritual, one detects the presence and structure of what must be termed a ritual economy of power. One brief example will suffice: The Ise Outer Shrine's Twice-Daily Food Offerings.

The Inner and Outer shrines of Ise may be symbolized, in my view, by the industrial amounts of food offerings prepared for their deities. These offerings used to be hidden from view for commoners prior to 1868. As is well known, the Inner Shrine is dedicated to Amaterasu Ōmikami, the ancestral spirit of the Imperial house, while the Outer Shrine is dedicated to Toyouke Ōmikami, the kami of food.

At the Outer Shrine, food is offered twice daily: in summer, at 8:00 a.m. and 4:00 p.m.; in winter, at 9:00 a.m. and 3:00 p.m. The day before the offerings are presented to the gods, they are prepared in the Ritual Office (Saikan 祭館) by high-ranked priests who purify themselves with salt, prepare sanctified fire by rubbing sticks in the building called Observance Fire Hall (Imibiyaden 忌火屋殿), and sleep in the ritual office. At 3:30 p.m., the vice-head officiant (*gon-negi* 権禰宜), followed by two priests, go to the Observance Fire Hall, where they pick up a large box containing six layers of food offerings, one for each of the six kami enshrined there. At 4:00 p.m. they cross over to the Outer Shrine, open the wooden doors of the Eating Hall of the kami (Mikeden 御饌殿), and present the offerings to the gods, starting with Amaterasu. They then wait and remove the offerings (with Amaterasu's as the last to be taken away), and carry them back to the Imibiya; they then return to the ritual office. The offerings will be shared among the officiants, who add some of them to their daily fare.

All this takes place under a strict veil of secrecy: except for the crossing point between the two paths, where people are allowed to stand and see the three officiants go from the ritual office to the Imibiya, and from which they can faintly see the officiants carry on their shoulders a large box containing the offerings from the Imibiya to the Outer Shrine and back, nothing can be seen. Silence must be observed; it is broken only by the slow screeching sound made while opening the large doors of the eating hall, the recitation of a *norito*, and hand clapping by the officiants. The food offerings themselves may not be touched by the eyes, and are described by guides only in the vaguest terms; prior to Meiji, they included only water, rice, and salt.

Two famous chefs, however, Tsuji Kaichi and Takahashi Tadayuki, were invited in 1985 to write a book on food at Ise, and they describe the current offerings in some detail; what follows is based on their account (Tsuji and Takahashi 1985). There are six layers of offerings, one each for the main kami (Amaterasu and Toyouke), and one for each of four gods worshiped at separate shrines (*betsugū*). Each god receives roughly the same offerings: three servings of pure *o-miki* (sacred sake), three dishes of cooked rice, one dish of baked salt, one dish of water taken from the shrine's sacred spring, one whole raw fish (between April and October, dried fish), one filet of dried bonito (*katsuo*), one dish of seaweed, one dish of fresh vegetable, and one dish of fruit. Many foods are grown, fished, or caught in the Ise region, and salt (in huge amounts) is prepared near the shore and then baked at the shrines. To describe all shrines and their offerings—some of which are extravagant—is simply impossible in the present context, but it is clear from the case of Ise alone that we are dealing with a central aspect of the Japanese cultic-cultural systems.

RESEARCH PERSPECTIVES

Toyouke Ōmikami, the central deity of the Outer Shrine complex of Ise, is also known as Toyouke himegami. Seen early on as a deity presiding over food production, she is also known under different names, probably as the result of accretions with other food-related entities or of mergers that often occur in myths. We are also told that she served Amaterasu under the name Miketsugami, which means "kami of food," and that this is the name under which she became the object of a cult in the Watarai area, the site of the Ise Outer Shrine, upon reception of an oracle ordering her to attend to Amaterasu. The mythology related to this kami of food describes terrifying scenes of life and death, growth and decay, ingestion, digestion, and excretion, anger and violence. Indeed, there is simply no food without some sort of violence, even if it is claimed that food-sharing lubricates human relationships. All humans are world-eaters, consumers of somebody else's work, and they have to assign meanings to everything they touch, to all elements they ingurgitate.

Claude Lévi-Strauss has written memorable pages on beans in America and Japan (1983: 263–75), and I wish that his deep love for Japan had driven him to write about offerings, these poisonous gifts (as Jacques Derrida's knowledge of German would have it).[1] In addition, questions must be raised concerning why such displays and arrangements of food are accompanied by court music and ancient dances: the kami eat with their eyes. This needs to be studied in depth, if only because there are ocular taboos and because food has been treated mostly from the point of view of taste. Indeed, most Western books on food have fallen into the same trap! The word "gift," ever since Marcel Mauss (1990), has become a cornerstone of anthropology and indeed has been applied to food offerings. But is it really the case that we are looking at gifts? That we simply offer fine dishes while proffering beautiful words of praise? Are we saying "thank you" or "please," depending on the time of the year? Is an exchange taking place between interested individuals who can see what they give but cannot see the divine beings they thus engage, while the beings in question are offered spectacles they are supposed to appreciate?

Asking different questions may prove useful. What about the nature of sacrifice, which has been the focus of so many historians of religions? Violence it definitely is. A mere forty-give years ago, most Japanese would have us believe that there was no such thing as sacrifice in their culture; that is, until interesting books on the subject began to appear and it became common knowledge that food offerings at shrines such as Suwa in central Japan, Hiromi in Miyazaki, Katori, and Kamo, among many others across the country, involved a lot of bloody sacrifice. So, the question remains: why so much violence? It is not merely a matter of atonement such as is seen in the Buddhist context of Hōjō-e ritual assemblies taking place in what is today Shinto shrines, such as Usa Hachimangū and Kamakura's Tsurugaoka Hachimangū, in which birds and fish are released back into the wild. It may be a tad too violent to be explained away as a gesture of gratitude or of hope for good crops. Perhaps, then, it is a matter of debt that needs to be repaid in kind—even though it can never be fully repaid, to be sure. Perhaps one is not repenting or atoning for the death of founders of religions, or of Zen masters who created major temples, or atoning for one's transgressions as I am sure is often the case.

---

[1] In German, the noun "Gift" means poison and is thus obviously not a cognate of the English term.

One must repay the existential debt: the fact that humans have been given life still causes an indelible debt, but we must push the hypothesis further. A good reason why work was held to be sacred is that it was precisely what made surplus production possible, and it is the surplus that is offered and, eventually, shared, or, as is often enough the case, thrown away, interred, or burnt. Furthermore, one should not forget the instances in which elaborate food offerings are made to young girls, but not eaten by anyone, as is the case, say, of the Sumiyoshi shrine's Taue rites in Sakai. There is a debt to be repaid all right, but not everybody could, unless forced to do so: that is why special taxes were levied to provide food, cloth, silk, gold, and other riches for shrines and temples ritual festivities around the country. Rituals were *shiki* 式, that is, they were based on the ancient equivalent of laws and norms, presented in great detail in the Ritual Procedures of the Engi Era and many other ritual rule books thereafter, all of which prove that food offerings are an economic fact.

While I cannot emphasize enough this legal/economic feature, I do not wish to overplay my hand while obfuscating the aesthetics that make these quasi-orgies palatable to reason. There is a world of difference between a village where only one fish is offered, only to be grilled a few instants later and shared by a hungry community with the help of a lot of sake, and the elegant, classy world of the court, where aesthetics ruled supreme, such as *hōchō[shiki]* 包丁[式], the cutting of fish or poultry by specialists who have transmitted their knowledge and techniques for generations, like the members of the Shijō school and its sub-branch, the Ikama-ryū 生間流, who are still active today. It is regrettable that someone belittled this practice by reducing it to "stunt cuisine," but in a fascinating book, Eric Rath (2010) offers a discussion of Shijō-school techniques and of the Esoteric Buddhist procedures of "knife" ceremonies.

A study of ritual food offerings requires lengthy analyses steeped in research "on the ground." Then, one should open the discussion by way of problematizing the context within which food is offered after laudatory words are proffered. Then, one must proceed from types of realities to types of conceptualization—from the tangible through the visual, and then move on to consider the inescapable philosophical, ethical, social, and economic dimensions. There is more to food offerings than meets the eye alone: what one sees is esthetically pleasing ("le beau"), which naturally generates moral and philosophical considerations ("le bon"). One is therefore invited to think food, a practice that inevitably suggests that what is visible must be treated as legible.

Furthermore, the production of surplus food inevitably opens questions concerning the ritual economy of power. The complex of all sorts of laws and social norms lends itself to a consideration of food offerings as a central part of the conceptions and practices that together form a large part of the cultic and cultural systems of Japan: even a cursory reading of an encyclopedia of etiquette and protocols (*yūsoku kojitsu* 有識故実) should justify my use of the compound term "cultic and cultural system," by clarifying the need to dive into the mesmerizing world of a highly ritualized universe—even if only in its modern echoes. This world includes the aesthetic dimension (food displays, music, dance, clothing, shrine and temple architecture, etc.), philosophical dimensions (how offerings encourage reflection), the spiritual materialities and esoteric rituals, the semantic dimension ("reading food" questions how meanings are constituted and transmitted), and the moral dimensions that open onto an understanding of gratitude (or vice-versa): the discovery that gratitude for life does enlarge the mind and reveals the conditions for, and the rewards of, becoming a member of society. In *The Enigma of the Gift*, Maurice Godelier probed the question of whether a gift is ultimately an exchange and reached the following conclusion: "the gift of life on the part of these gods etc., must be compared to the gifts humanity makes to them." And he argues, correctly I think, that "nothing can be returned: humans are condemned to give forever, they are enslaved to the debt that can never be fully repaid, for no gift to any object of cult can pretend to match the value of the original gift of life" (Godelier 1999: XXX).

Most importantly, at the present we must tread beyond the narrow limits of academic specializations and enlarge our field of vision through fieldwork. Lake Biwa serves as an example of work that both needs urgent attention and also promises to be rewarding. There are two small but fascinating books on rituals and food offerings surrounding the lunar new year all around Lake Biwa: one on food offerings at one hundred shrines and temples (Nakajima and Uno 1999), and the other on eight shrines and one temple, but in more detail (Nakajima et al. 2008); each shrine and temple has different food offerings. Or take the example of the Kakitsusai ritual dedicated to Sugawara no Michizane at the Kitano Tenmangū Shrine in Kyoto, in which the portable shrines are made of nothing but vegetables and fruit.

In conclusion: we are dealing with more than recipes, violence, gratitude, hope, economics, aesthetics in various forms and settings, or markings of the inexorable movement of time and the constitution of space. Maybe we are standing right in the middle of what ritual is, in the nexus where all these cultural matters fuse to produce, almost alchemically, what we call value. This term is neutral but strong enough and prods one to think economics, ethics, aesthetics, politics, history, and culture—all at once in their human dimension. Along these lines of thought, one may wish to also consider the psychological aspects of expectations (which often lead to insecurity, divination, oracles, etc.); these characteristics too are obvious in a variety of ritual contexts involving food. One thing is certain: the kami and the buddhas must be satisfied, and this can happen only if they are regularly sated.

It is small wonder that the enthronement of Japanese emperors is predominantly a matter of cultivation and sharing the first fruit. For it is, after all, a matter of production of food, of the actualization of desires, and of the imagination of society.

See also Chapter 15, "Materiality," and Chapter 22, "Premodern Traditions."

CHAPTER 11

Gender

KAWAHASHI Noriko

Religions act through belief, ritual, symbol, and other such elements, and in doing so have come to shape gender, to sanction the shape it has been given, and to legitimize that shape as a norm. To phrase this differently, one of the functions that religions perform is to prescriptively define the "unchanging essence" of man and woman. This is why religion becomes subject to criticism for complicity in establishing a hierarchical disparity between men and women, in giving rise to discrimination, and in maintaining the status quo. There is no doubt that many religious traditions, both within and outside Japan, have considered women to be inferiors that nonetheless threaten the sanctity of men and have therefore placed restrictions on the possibilities for women's participation in both ritual and organizational roles. Women have thus been placed in the positions and functions prescribed for them without consideration for their religious qualifications as individuals.

RELIGIOUS STUDIES' RESISTANCE TO GENDER

Gender and feminist studies have slighted the topic of religion because in so many cases religion has, at both conceptual and institutional levels, appeared to repress and suppress women. Just as so much of gender research has shown an aversion to religion, so have religious studies also shown strong resistance to gender research. The feminist scholar of religion Ursula King has used the term "double blindness" to describe how, just as most gender studies are excessively uninterested in religion, to the point of keeping eyes closed to the subject, so too do most religious studies leave gender out of consideration, not recognizing the importance of the subject (King 2004: 1–2). This is because religious institutions tend to perceive the gender perspective as denying the authority of Buddha and deity (and institution) and fear it will overturn traditional ethical canons that religions continue to uphold.[1]

The fact that gender perspectives have been so disparaged in studies of religion is not unrelated to the norms of objectivity and value neutrality advocated in religious studies. The religious studies academy in Japan, in particular, has a history of criticizing scholarly approaches from gender perspectives as politically biased and lacking in scholarly neutrality, and therefore of excluding such approaches (Kawahashi, Komatsu, and Kuroki 2013). To position the gender viewpoint and the study of religion as mutually exclusive, however, is to relegate religion to the bastion of androcentrism and to drain it of any appeal whatsoever.

---

[1] For further insight into Ursula King's achievement, see Corrywright and Schmidt (2018). This collection can be read online at the *Journal of the British Association for the Study of Religions* as Volume 19 (2017).

CONFLICTING INTERPRETATIONS

For women, religion has had an ambivalent significance in that it encompasses both liberation and bondage. On the one hand, religion excludes women, and on the other, religion seeks to bring women in. There are cultures that have goddess faiths, for example, but it would be overly naive to conclude that simply because a religious culture possesses symbols that positively value feminine elements, that same culture therefore places women in high positions and supports gender equality. A look at how Shinto in Japan today is struggling with gender backlash movements makes this highly apparent (Kawahashi 2016a). There are risks in an interpretation that arbitrarily picks and chooses essential elements from religions to suit its own purposes.

Furthermore, the issue is not only that religions present ambivalent aspects to women but also, at the same time, that the interpretations involved in assigning the position and the significance of women in a religion commonly involve a polarization between opposites. Faure, for example, has pointed out that women's gender in Buddhist history has more often than not been polarized between either extolling the achievements of privileged women or recording the history of hardships undergone by abused women (Faure 2003: 6).

Much the same can be said about how women and Japan's new religions (*shinshūkyō*) have been construed. The women followers of new religions are painted, on the one hand, as mute victims of exploitation by patriarchal religion (and who are therefore unable to comprehend feminism) or, on the other, as fortunate women who have been rescued from their predicament (and who therefore have no need for feminism). This means, in other words, that scholars' constructions of extant religious groups and of traditions fall either on the side of praise for bringing salvation to women or of censure for oppressing women. There is also the situation of studies on women and folk religion that are predicated on the existence of a spiritual power that is unique to women. The result, it has been pointed out, is that such studies have taken women's positive role in religion to be self-evident and have directed little criticism toward the patriarchal order and thought that exclude women (Kawahashi 2005).

Even worse, there is also a common tendency to believe unquestioningly that any research taking women as a topic, and all research that is conducted by women, is research from a gender perspective. The word "gender" is not a synonym for "woman," but the alarming reality is that "the woman's perspective" and "the gender perspective" are nevertheless being uncritically conflated (Kawahashi and Kobayashi 2017).[2] We need to pay attention to the fact that women's experiences are not unitary, and that consequently, not all women possess a gender critical awareness. Meanwhile, men who are perceived to diverge from heteronormative imperatives also experience gender discrimination and oppression.

THE TURN TO THE SUBJECT—OR THE TURN BACK

There is a key issue in gender studies that requires clarification. It has to do with the accounts of women as active agents in religious history, which often represent those women in an overly romanticized manner. The point to be made here is that such

---

[2] The special issue of the *Japanese Journal of Religious Studies* on gender and religion guest-edited by Kawahashi and Kobayashi in 2017 is a survey of the latest studies that examine issues of religion and gender in present-day Japan, in theoretical terms and with a foundation in specific cases.

representations are ineffective. Religion is often construed as a symbol of discrimination against women, and religious salvation is interpreted as ingeniously camouflaged oppression, because there is doubt as to whether women can even become agents of action in the religious sphere. That doubt arises because religions are perceived as blocking women from autonomy and self-liberation, in effect making women subordinate to the authority of men.

What has been complicating the matter in recent years, however, is a trend in research that has emerged somewhat in opposition to previous studies that presented religion as a means for the oppression of women. This research pays attention rather to the agency of Japanese women as religious practitioners, claiming that Japanese women have exercised that agency from within the ideology of the patriarchal system and have benefited thereby.[3] Accounts seeking to revise previous histories of religion in this way will end up having the same effect as previous accounts, claiming that the new religions brought salvation to women who were relegated to a very low level, or claiming that Buddhism transcends gender discrimination, or making some other such androcentric claim. That is, they will no doubt make the ways in which patriarchal religion oppresses and exploits women invisible.

For example, there is the matter of the self-perception of Buddhist nuns in present-day Japan. Women priests are subordinated to male priests in terms of their position and their role in the ritual context, but the recognition that women as religionists perform a function unique to women has gained a certain currency even among Western scholars of Japanese religion.[4] There is a notion that gender roles performed on the basis of an internalized patriarchy can also serve women as a strategy of self-affirmation. In this understanding, therefore, some advantage is actually to be gained for women by performing in their gender roles, but this understanding still needs to be substantiated by a sampling of more specific cases. There is some question as to the extent to which this strategy, with its limitations, has enabled women to voice objections that were not previously allowed. There are also some questions as to the extent to which or the way in which men's awareness of women's self-understanding and self-realization can influence men or foster their consciousness of change. Further clarification is called for.

There are also issues regarding the attitude shown by some scholars who take the agency of Japanese women under their protection, as though they are acting as patrons to those women. There is a distinct danger that attitudes of this kind may in effect be complicit in maintaining patriarchal religious structures. Moreover, as Alison Boden has observed, women who practice religion and are at the same time respected for their worth as women are to be found in every religious culture. What this means is that the issues of women's rights and religious commitment are not mutually contradictory. Many women do not want to renounce and repudiate religion but rather to dismantle the oppression and unfairness that occur in religion due to androcentrism. These are two different things, and it should go without saying that they must be strictly distinguished one from the other (Boden 2007: xi).

---

[3] One example is the recent textbook by Barbara Ambros that presents a historical survey (Ambros 2015). The criticism of Ambros's book is detailed in Kawahashi (2016b).
[4] Arai (1999) is one text that can be cited as representative of this interpretation.

DISCOURSES OF THIRD-WORLD FEMINISMS SUBJECTED TO APPROPRIATION

There are discourses according to which non-Western women are passive victims of entrenched patriarchal systems and thus are at the opposite pole from Western women. These discourses belong to the so-called colonial feminisms of Europe and America, and over three decades have now passed since theoretical rebuttals by third-world women and women of color began emerging in opposition to them.[5] In short, third-world feminist accounts and postcolonial feminisms contest the characterizations by white women's feminism that deny women of color their own creative and active agency.

Considering the circulation given to accounts of the kind noted earlier, however, there is a discomfiting incongruity in this situation. Third-world feminism and the discourses by feminists of color have in a sense overtaken those colonial discourses, advancing ahead of them by a whole circuit or more, and they are being appropriated by European and American feminists, who are actually positioned far behind in this discursive arena. The reason for this is that non-Western women are subject to being read in essentializing, othering ways that attribute to them an agency that, unlike that of Western women, is said not to resist patriarchy, and this putative lack is taken to characterize the "agency" of non-Western women.

Ironically, the view that non-Western women have voluntarily internalized patriarchal religious norms falls into alignment with the traditional androcentric position that women who believe in religion have also chosen to endorse their gender roles and are content with the status quo. In other words, these two discourses, each with its time difference relative to the discourses by feminists of color, appear to be forming a relationship of mutual complicity. In a recent compilation they edited, Chia Longman and Tamsin Bradley present critical examinations of child marriage, honor killing, female circumcision (FGM), dowry murder, and other such cultural practices that are harmful to women, and they sound an alarm regarding a turn to agency so overemphasized that it views all those practices as choices that women make of their own free will. Longman and Bradley are critical of accounts that depreciate the violence and pain experienced by women when they are constrained and coerced, and that discuss these rather as issues of agency. They therefore argue the necessity for feminist perspectives that place the focus on the bodies of women who are under an oppressive patriarchy (Longman and Bradley 2015: 21–6).

In a recent compilation on gender, agency, and coercion, Sumi Madhok, Anne Phillips, and Kalpana Wilson argue similarly to Longman and Bradley that researchers should not suspend their judgment as feminists but rather should take responsibility for facing up to the structures of exploitation and the unbalanced power relationships that are involved in matters of agency. Questions of agency cannot be uncoupled from the politics of being feminist (Madhok, Phillips, and Wilson 2013: 11–12).

A further consideration is the problem that the feminist scholar of religion Morny Joy perceives in the backlash against women's human rights carried out by religions in the name of traditional culture. She points out the risk inherent in a stance that gives the superficial appearance of respecting the cultural identities of women of different cultures (Joy 2008: 188–94). In order to fully engage with gender issues in the present era,

---

[5] Some characteristic arguments along these lines have been made, e.g., by Kwok Pui-lan, Rey Chow, Chandra T. Mohanty, and Uma Narayan.

religious studies will have to correctly perceive and explicate the complex interactions between religions and the human rights of women as these issues surface in different locations. The same also applies to religion and gender studies in Japan.

CONCLUSION

To sum up, it will be necessary to eliminate those approaches that depict women as pitiful victims of patriarchy who depend upon their religion for relief. In eliminating them, however, priority must also be given to critical analysis of the various hierarchies of authority and discrimination that oppress women, and to accomplish this without romanticizing the agency of women. At the same time, it will be important to provide in-depth accounts of women's initiatives for reform or resistance, which they seek to enact in their own real-world contexts.

One final point to emphasize in closing has to do with the tendency, found also in Japan, to view the complex of gender-related issues in religious studies as being merely a remnant of the past. What is actually inappropriate, however, is for studies in religion to utterly lack gender perspectives. In a study relating to women's rights and religion, the previously cited Boden states that religions are a repository of moral power and influence, and concludes that religions have an active, crucial role to play in assuring global gender justice (Boden 2007: 171–2). It is because religions have such symbolic force and immense organizational power that they must be transformed or rebuilt to be sensitive to gender equality. Religious studies with gender perspectives open up the ways in which women have been—and remain—marginalized and made invisible in religion. This would serve both to make religions and their views available for critical examination, and can also supply critical viewpoints that cast doubt on the interpretations and values brought forth by androcentrism.

Only recently has the Japanese Association for Religious Studies (JARS) done as the American Academy of Religion (AAR) did and establish a working group (of which I am a member) to advance gender equality and support younger scholars. More recently, the JARS journal *Shūkyō kenkyū* (Studies on Religion) published a special issue on gender and sexuality (September 2019, vol. 93, no. 395) containing articles that take issue with androcentrism, heteronormativity, and misogyny in religious studies. The matter of how religious studies that adopt critical perspectives in terms of gender will develop in the studies of Japanese religion, pursued in Japan and other countries, is a matter for future consideration and eager anticipation.

(Translated by Richard Peterson)

See also Chapter 23, "Sexuality," and Chapter 29, "Women."

CHAPTER 12

Globalization

Richard K. PAYNE

Globalization has become a key conceptual tool in understanding late modernity and postmodernity. Theorizing globalization as a unique characteristic of this era, however, runs the risk of deploying the rhetoric of rupture—the tendency to think that time is divided by some unique event. And more specifically, it suggests that our own time is in some way fundamentally different from what went before.

Rupture, however, is not an empirical entity that can be identified, described, measured, or observed. It is instead a narrative entity that is constructed, a socially defined creation. Fundamentally, it is a religious construction of time— "this revelation changes everything, nothing will ever be the same again." It is no doubt easier to ignore everything that went before as irrelevant in the face of some single, dramatic transformation of the human condition than to attempt to identify the small, cumulative changes that produce the real differences between how things were then and how they are now.

The rhetoric of rupture often also implicates the idea of a unilinear developmental process, a progressive sequence that moves forward through time in one set of universal stages. Whether conceptualized in Marxist terms, or in terms of the inevitable conversion of economies to consumer capitalist ones, the idea that such a single sequence applies everywhere, to all peoples, gives changes being made or imposed the valence of inevitability.

A rupture establishes a center in relation to which everything else is periphery, adding a third metaphor to an increasingly potent historiographic *imaginaire*. Centers are not purely narrative constructions, but they are also not fixed. In addition to being temporary, and dependent on a particular set of values that promote some one place as center, an exclusive focus on centers obscures the necessity—both conceptual and practical—of the center's relation with periphery.

Naturalizing this threefold construct—that is, treating it as simply the natural way in which history proceeds—strengthens the sense of inevitability. Such a sensibility enables the disregard of moral considerations in acts of Sartrean bad faith, avoiding responsibility by pointing to inevitable historical forces. In addition, as the effects of the initial rupture spread out in time and space, there is an inevitable diminution or decay of the effect—the rhetoric of decadence.

The conflation of these metaphors as ways of thinking about history may be called "pebble in the pond" historiography. Like a pebble hitting the surface of a pond, the cumulative metaphoric entailments construct an understanding of history in which rupture induces a regular sequence of changes that spreads out from the center to the periphery in a natural and inevitable fashion, with the effect diminishing over time and distance. All of which is not to say that globalization is not taking place, or that the changes identified are not real. It is, instead, a critique directed against the presumption that it is unprecedented and makes our own time unique.

Globalization is not an autonomous force that came into existence at some particular point in history, but rather the gradual accumulation of the effects of many local events in an always and already global network. In other words, globalization is a descriptive category and not an explanatory one.

ALWAYS AND ALREADY GLOBAL

As Mark Juergensmeyer has said, "Religion has always been global, in the sense that religious communities and traditions have always maintained permeable boundaries. They have moved, shifted, and interacted with one another around the globe" (2006: 3). This is the case for the religions of Japan, which from the earliest records is revealed as the religions of immigrants. Furthermore, people living on the islands of the archipelago have always lived in connection with the wider world—networks of trade and conquest that stretched across Asia to Europe, and to the Indian subcontinent (Beckwith 2009). Early clans (*uji*) brought with them their own fictive ancestral gods (kami).

Kami cults seem to have originally been local, whether linked to a specific place or a specific tree or rock, but also included ancestral cults, and kami were "conceptualized in terms of their actions and effects on the environment and humankind" (Andreeva 2017b: 16). By the second half of the sixth century, ancestral deities of already established clans were being joined by those of immigrant clans arriving via the Korean peninsula (Lewin 1994; Bowring 2005).

Immigrant clans were welcomed, or encouraged to immigrate, for the technological skills they held, and clan identity and technological skill sets were jointly embodied in the clan's deities. As the Yamato clan centralized authority, "the veneration of local divinities included many continental gods that continued to 'cross over the seas' and that were becoming steadily localized" (Andreeva 2017b: 17).

The introduction of Daoist influences (Richey 2015), such as yin-yang and five elements theories, were under the control of the state department of Onmyōdō, while Confucian thought and practice was the responsibility of a different department, and Buddhism was under the administrative control of yet a third bureau. In other words, although we categorize these jointly as religion, at the time they were conceptualized as distinct (see Josephson 2011, 2012: 256–7).

Such Indo-Sinitic influences on Japan's religious culture were profound. From the Heian throughout the medieval period, the effects of Esoteric Buddhism, both Shingon Tōmitsu and Tendai Taimitsu, were pervasive and created a broad range of what can be called the tantric penumbra, even in traditions not normally identified as tantric. For example, Ryūichi Abe describes the figure Kūkai as

> a major cultural icon illustrative of the deep cultural assimilation in which Buddhism constituted, almost transparently, the nucleus of Japanese society. That assimilation would have been impossible without Esoteric Buddhist ritual for communicating with and manipulating Buddhist and Shintō deities and the ritual language of mantra, whose phoneticism (in contrast to the hieroglyphism of Chinese characters) encouraged the development of the native syllabary. (Abe 1999: 3)

In other words, although Esoteric Buddhist praxis was filtered through China and adapted to Japanese applications, the ritual, conceptual, and linguistic influences originate in India.

Such influential imports continued up to the modern period, including both additional resources for existing traditions, such as Zen, and Chinese intellectual resources, such as Neo-Confucianism. Indeed, Ōbaku Zen masters introduced Ming dynasty culture, in addition to setting the groundwork for the adoption and adaptation of Neo-Confucian thought by Japanese nativists at the end of the Tokugawa era (1600–1868).

IMPERIAL AND COLONIAL

In the nineteenth century, the earlier feudal society was transformed by the modern conception of the "nation-state" and the violent shift to the Meiji regime, an imperial system including colonialism that deployed religion in its support. These changes created economic upheavals, leading to out-migration. Nakajima Michio succinctly describes the close relation between governance and religion: "In order to establish a unified nation-state, the Meiji government brought the divine image of the emperor to the foreground" (Nakajima 2010: 22). By the early twentieth century, this conjunction of governance and religion extended to include Buddhism in ways demonstrably contrary to the generalization that "globalization provides a means for Buddhism ... to penetrate our world in somewhat limited ways but without the shadow of colonialism" (Obeysekere 2006: 70).

ASSIMILATION, OR LACK THEREOF

The establishment of colonies in Korea (Kim 2010: 287–99), Taiwan, and Manchuria led to attempts to assimilate the colonized populations. In part, this meant instilling the proper attitudes toward the Emperor and the Imperial system expected of Japanese subjects through extending the Imperial Shinto system (Jaffe 2010: 4). In some cases, such as Hawai'i, the project led to Imperial authorities attempting to co-opt the religious institutions of immigrant communities. In other cases, religious institutions were implanted in colonial settings as part of an effort to socialize colonized peoples into the Japanese empire. At the same time, preserving the Japanese identity of those who had immigrated was also recognized as a desideratum. These two complementary understandings of the function of Shinto outside of Japan were formulated by Ogasawara Shōzō (1892–1970) in his attempts to promote Shinto internationally. One function was to resist the assimilation of ethnic Japanese immigrants to the cultures in which they were now located. The other function was to assimilate colonized peoples into the Japanese culture (Suga 2010: 62).

In pursuit of these complementary goals, Ogasawara attempted to reformulate Shinto as a universal religion—a goal that appeared possible given the flexibility of the concept of kami, seen from the earliest history of Japanese religion. That is, new deities who provided an integrative function could be recognized in countries with immigrant populations. This goal of universalizing Shinto could only have been conceived in the intellectual and cultural context of a nineteenth-century global society, which was now exposed to a much wider diversity of religious traditions than ever before. Responses to this diversity included the various rhetorics of "world religions" which deployed the distinction between universal and ethnic religions (Fitzgerald 2000; Masuzawa 2005).

Initially in Taiwan, this assimilationist project attempted to proceed by accommodating the religious culture of the colonized people. The official policy was the preservation of local customs, including religious ones. However, Suga Kōji has noted a distinct shift in imperial policy in 1936, when a more "fundamentalist" understanding was codified as the "Clarification of the National Polity" (Suga 2010: 51). This led to compulsory assimilation, including such activities as mandatory worship at Shinto shrines and the erection of household "god shelves" (*kamidana*).

OUTMIGRATION: THE EXAMPLE OF PAIA, MAUI

From the 1860s onwards, the end of the feudal system and contact with European and American powers created both the economic disturbances that motivated outmigration and opportunities to emigrate to various parts of the globe, including Hawai'i, California, Peru, and Brazil.

Migration from Japan to Hawai'i began with a labor program that brought almost thirty thousand workers to the islands between 1885 and 1894. Migration continued thereafter, bringing almost a quarter of a million Japanese by the mid-1920s (Borup 2013: 24). Jørn Borup has examined two Zen temples in Paia, Maui, the Paia Mantokuji Soto Zen Mission (est. 1906) and the Rinzai Zen Mission (est. 1935) (Borup 2013: 25), both of which originate from plantation life in the early part of the twentieth century. While Paia was almost entirely a Japanese community at the beginning of the twentieth century, global events—the Second World War, the 1945 sugar strike, and the relocation of sugar growing to less costly locations—all led to a decline of the Japanese population and an increasing mixture of ethnicities in Paia. Borup identifies four factors that contributed to the decline of Zen Buddhism in Paia, factors that can *mutatis mutandis* be found in other immigrant temples in late modernity.

First, the decreasing importance of ethnic religiosity. Temples originally served as community centers, providing venues for community activities and maintaining cultural practices (Borup 2013: 33). Second, "re-ethnicization," with authorities in Japan insisting that priests be trained in Japan and conduct services in accord with Japanese custom. As a consequence, "temple communities are more ethnically bonding than trans-ethnically bridging" (Borup 2013: 34). Third, individualization tended to undermine the cohesion of religious groups and at the same time emphasized individual choice (Borup 2013: 34). And finally, increasing plurality combined with the idea of individual choice to create an inner-oriented spiritual marketplace (Roof 2001; Borup 2013: 36–7).

"GLOBAL BUDDHISM?"

Martin Baumann has suggested that there has been a shift in the forms that Buddhism takes, reflecting the broader cultural shift from modern to postmodern, which he terms "global." "To my mind, there are good reasons to argue that, at least in Western industrial countries, Buddhism has acquired a new post-modern shape" (Baumann 2001: 4). One of his conclusions is that changes in the Asian countries of origin are as important for understanding global Buddhism as are changes taking place within the countries to which Buddhism has been introduced in the modern era. Earlier scholarship tended to see Japanese Buddhism in North America, for example, as merely "reactionary," that is, simply adopting cultural forms from the Christian religious culture. For example, "Immediately upon introduction into the Canadian cultural context, the ritual structure of Jodo Shinshu was adapted to aspects of the normative model set by Christian churches" (Goa and Coward 1983: 363).

This is one of the essential points of Ama Michihiro's work on Shin Buddhism as a trans-Pacific phenomenon. Many of the adaptations taking place in the Buddhist Mission of North America (BMNA, later Buddhist Churches of America, BCA) were all-too-easily theorized as entirely reactions to the Protestant culture of the United States—adaptations intended to allow immigrant communities to blend into the religious landscape of what was increasingly understood to be their home. Contrary to this image, Ama's study shows that modernizing trends were being initiated in Kyoto and exported to the BMNA, and that the process was bidirectional—going both from Japan to the United States and from the United States to Japan.

MODERN: INDIVIDUALISM VERSUS CLASS

Baumann's claim regarding "global Buddhism" is that it is "neither monolithic nor standardized" (2001: 32). What unifies the category is that "they strive to adapt to the pluralistic settings, globalized contexts, and post-modern, individualized times in which they are placed" (Baumann 2001: 31). While the reified character of this description is problematic, Baumann has identified several characteristics of "Buddhisms" in the present day. One of these is the dominance of the discourse[1] of individual identity formation that we saw above in the changes in Paia. For example, Christina Rocha argues that in the contemporary world, religious practice is a private choice. In a process of *bricolage*, the practitioner chooses characteristics from different practices to condense them into a spiritual quest. Thus, each practitioner constructs his or her religion as a unique praxis that is different from all the others, mixing various traditions in order to build a new contemporary spirituality (Rocha 2000: 48).

This discourse of individualism, however, cloaks the social dynamics of class. Some Buddhist traditions, such as Zen in Brazil, have become markers of upper-middle-class status, in which the person has the individual freedom to adopt foreign practices and life styles. Having the free time to engage in a regular meditation practice, or spend weekends or weeks at a meditation retreat, constitutes gestures of status and the social and economic freedom to determine one's own individual religious identity. John Nelson has emphasized this, saying: "Especially for better-educated individuals able to take advantage of an intellectual approach to Buddhism and the lifestyle it promotes, their affiliation reinforces class distinctions in a nation where this type of status has a major influence on cultural and personal identity" (Nelson 2017: 390). Although referring to Rocha's work on Zen Buddhism in Brazil, Nelson's summary applies equally well to the United States and to China (2017:391).

Perhaps the most successful of Buddhisms at globalizing has been Soka Gakkai, though seemingly at the cost of losing its connection to the traditional, monastic forms of Nichiren-shū (Ōkubo 1991; Pereira 2008; Métraux 2013). The success of some Japanese forms of Buddhism in the modern period has, however, institutionalized them in ways that inhibit globalization. Shin Buddhism in the United States has largely adapted as a federation of churches, a structure that has sometimes actively impeded even national efforts of propagation, much less international. Some members seem to respond to globalizing efforts originating in Kyoto with the (perhaps silent, but rhetorical) question, "How would this benefit my local temple?"

---

[1] "Discourse" pointing here to both how people are understood to engage the present variety of religio-cultural traditions available to them and how they come to think of themselves. Discourse is then, in this sense, a hermeneutic circle: people learn to think about themselves in a particular way and then act accordingly, making that understanding the appropriate interpretation for their behavior.

IMMIGRANTS AND INTELLECTUALS

As varied as the conditions have been for different countries in the modern era, a consistent pattern has been the role of two different groups in the introduction of Buddhist ideas and practices: immigrants and intellectuals. Attempts to categorize different forms of Buddhism in modernity has been questioned and problematized, particularly such connotatively loaded categories as ethnic and convert (Hickey 2015). The categories of immigrant and intellectual are not meant to covertly replicate the ethnic/convert dichotomy in new terminology but to highlight motivations for affiliation with Buddhisms. The categories work as well for the history of the introduction of Buddhism into China and Japan but are only intended as heuristic in nature.

That said, many of the forms, dynamics, and contestations surrounding present-day Buddhism can be understood as having their origins in the different interests and motivations of these two groups. These motivations may be described as orthogonal: coming close to one another but never quite meeting. This pattern has been noted by Rocha in Brazil. While the Japanese immigrant community helped to introduce Sōtō Zen, the Sōtō Zen priests (*kaikyōshi*) themselves may have brought a Buddhist modernist understanding of Zen largely associated with the figure of D. T. Suzuki emphasizing sitting meditation (*zazen*) as the essence of Zen, but encountered communities more committed to devotional practices. These two understandings of Zen were not only orthogonal but at times came into conflict with one another (Rocha 2004, 2008).

A particularly revealing instance of the orthogonal relation between the motivations of immigrants and intellectuals is the figure of Sunya Gladys Pratt (Ama 2015). Today the media has a consistent tendency to focus more on the supposed exoticism of Anglo-American converts to Buddhism and to marginalize immigrant Buddhist communities. Despite the fact that Pratt not only received media attention at the time of her ordination (exemplifying the exoticism of Anglo-American convert) but was also awarded the Sixth Class of the Order of the Precious Crown from the Japanese government in 1986, and was an important figure in the modern history of female ordination, she is today almost unknown outside the Tacoma Temple.[2]

Ama locates Pratt at the interface of three different rhethorics about Buddhism that were operative in the early twentieth century: Theravāda, Shin, and "Universal." Theravāda had been the focus of scholarly attention from the nineteenth century, and consequently more information was available about it than for other Buddhist traditions. Especially prominent was the rational and atheistic interpretations promoted by apologists, which made it amenable to American intellectuals seeking an alternative to Christianity. Despite an early orientation toward modernist Theravāda, Pratt and others became affiliated with the BMNA, itself based in the Shin tradition of Pure Land Buddhism. Ama explains that this affiliation resulted in part from the fact that at the time, the BMNA presented itself as a form of Buddhism lacking "both sectarian and national identity" (2015: 66). This was an attempt to participate in the "Universal Buddhism movement" for which "Theravadin elements were deemed indispensable" (Ama 2015: 66). Indeed, the BMNA "shifted the orientation of its propagation from Shinran to Śākyamuni" (Ama 2015: 66), and even the ordination ceremony created for Pratt and others was modeled not on Japanese ritual forms but instead on Sri Lankan forms of Theravādin ritual.

---

[2] I myself only became aware of Rev. Pratt and her history with the Tacoma Temple when I was invited to give a lecture sponsored by the "Reverend Pratt Fund," established for Buddhist education.

It is, therefore, not particularly surprising that all of the Caucasian ministers ordained by BMNA in the 1930s eventually broke off their affiliation—with the noteworthy exception of Pratt. She continued to serve the Tacoma temple community through the difficult years of wartime internment until her death in 1986. Intellectuals, such as Pratt and others in her cohort of ordinands, had an orientation toward Buddhism as a universal religion, an orientation that was not congruent with the sectarian orientation of BMNA as an immigrant institution rooted in Japanese Shin Buddhism.

GLOBALIZATION, OR NEOCOLONIALISM?

Shimazono Susumu has highlighted the relationship between the international expansion of Japanese economics in the last part of the twentieth century and the expansion of Japanese new religions into international venues. Writing in 1991, Shimazono notes that the "success of Sekai Kyūseikyō and Soka Gakkai in Thailand, for example, cannot be fully comprehended unless one takes into account the huge economic influence wielded by Japanese businesses in the country and the financial and spiritual help liberally poured into Thailand from Japan for the sake of propagation" (Shimazono 1991: 127). He further suggests:

> At present, it appears that in most of the groups, the authority of Japanese propagators is preserved, but it is only a matter of time before local propagators will have more say. In the future, financial aid coming from headquarters will undoubtedly decrease when Japan's status as an economic super-power begins to decline. When that happens, the question will surely arise: how will the central body in Japan be able to maintain control over religious bodies overseas? (Shimazono 1991: 126)

Thus, in the recent past, a pattern similar to that of the colonial nineteenth century appears to be repeated—a link between Japanese religious presence outside Japan and the expansion in this case of an economic empire.

CONCLUSION

While globalization has been taken by some to mean a hegemonic uniformity created by the extension of Western culture to the rest of the world, Saskia Sassen has pointed out that "the global does not (yet) fully encompass the lived experience of actors or the domain of institutional orders and cultural formations; it persists as a partial condition" (Sassen 2001: 260). Nor is there any uniform direction of globalization, leading some scholars such as Natalie Quli to talk about "multiple Buddhist modernisms" (2008).[3] Similarly, Rafael Shoji suggests that the reception of Buddhism in Brazil is markedly different from the way it has been received in Europe or the United States (2003: 71). He describes the latter as often "reducing Buddhist beliefs and devotional aspects to a minimum, in a practice that often emphasizes a psychological approach or social engagement and transformation" (2003: 71).

Scott Mitchell explains that "global culture flows in multiple directions and between multiple cultural centers and actors" (Mitchell 2016: 243). The uneven nature of globalization points to networks as the appropriate analytic concept for understanding

---

[3] A case in point is the flow of Buddhist praxis from the United States to Korea. See Joo (2011).

the process by which Buddhist teachings have been taken up in various locales. Indeed, in the view of some scholars, globalization is better understood as an "apparatus" that enables the spread of existing forms of Buddhism rather than as a particular form of Buddhist praxis. In the case of the United States, for example, Mitchell has argued that "U.S. Buddhism is the result of modernist discourses being made possible through the apparatus of globalization" (2016: 245).

The gradual establishment and uneven character of networks linking different global locales in different ways, and creating religious flows moving in multiple directions, undermines the image of globalization as an inevitable process created by the rhetoric of rupture, as unilinear progress, and as a question of center/periphery.

See also Chapter 5, "Economy and Spirituality," Chapter 6, "Economy of Buddhism," Chapter 7, "Empire and Colonialism," and Chapter 18, "Minorities."

CASE STUDY

Diaspora Buddhism

Jørn BORUP

The reform Buddhism of the postcolonial late nineteenth century also influenced and became intertwined with Japanese Buddhsm. The Meiji restoration forced individual priests and organizations to respond to the criticism and persecution of Buddhism, and a modernist "New Buddhism" movement emerged to proactively counteract such political and discursive challenges (see Shields's case study in this volume). One of the ways Buddhism reinvented itself was to develop international networks and alliances with contemporary representatives from Asian reform Buddhists and their Western allies. The legacy of D. T. Suzuki as an intercultural interpreter who made an enormous impact on Zen in the West has been firmly established,[1] and later Sōtō and Rinzai Zen Buddhist missionaries have also achieved enduring success by establishing Zen centers that primarily address Euro-American meditation practitioners. "Suzuki Zen," with its underlying assumptions of a spiritually universal rationale, was "imported" to suit the needs of mainly intellectual individuals with an interest in Eastern religion, and it was institutionally "exported" through missionaries propagating Japanese Buddhism to non-Japanese Buddhists, the internationalization process itself being a strategic device for national legitimation.

While some of these individual priests and missionaries participated in various diaspora networks and activities on the West coast from the 1950s, the earlier Japanese "diaspora Buddhism"[2] was disseminated rather differently; it included different segments of people with different interests, ascribing different meanings and functions to the religion. In the years following the Meiji restoration, a number of Japanese took advantage of the newly given freedom allowing them to travel abroad. America was the main destination for most emigrants, many of whom were poor workers looking for jobs in the sugar plantations in Hawai'i through the Hawai'i labor program (1885–94). To secure stable settlements, the workers were allowed to invite women, and, as the number of families with children grew, the immigrant communities reinvented local forms of civilization, culture, and religion. Schools, stores, hospitals, markets, and movie theaters were part of daily life for many of the Japanese in the following decades, where the second-generation comprised almost half of the Japanese immigrant population (Odo 2004: 37).

The arrival of Buddhist missionaries in the late 1880s succeeded in keeping Japanese Buddhism alive abroad. The emerging Zen, Pure Land, Shingon, and Tendai temples were physical and spiritual manifestations of a true transnational, migrant diaspora Buddhism,

---

[1] On D. T. Suzuki, see Jaffe (2015) and Wilson and Moriya (2016).
[2] On Japanese Buddhism in diaspora, see Porcu (2018).

often with a clear sectarian identity. The priests did not make missionary efforts to convert but were instead there to propagate within the group, to secure and keep the proper Japanese culture, and to "preserve a religion for Japanese family ancestry" (Tanabe 2005: 94). The Japanese settlers came to the Buddhist temples to hear the priest chant sutras and to see him conduct rituals for the ancestors in front of the altars decorated with classical Japanese Buddhist paraphernalia. They came to make offerings to Buddha and the Buddhist deities, and they came to participate in traditional festivals such as *obon* and *hanamatsuri* in temple environments with clear architectural and symbolic reference to their country of origin.

The temples also functioned as communal culture centers. Language schools helped the younger generations keep their heritage language alive, and women's groups were engaged in perpetuating the proper cultural codes by making Japanese food, singing Japanese songs, or reading Japanese books. The diaspora communities generated social capital to strengthen bonds both internally and externally as a smooth device of adapting to the surrounding society. They undoubtedly also shared the diasporic ideal of one day returning to their homeland, or they at least maintained a transnational, symbolic lifeline to Japan, the concrete contours of which eventually faded throughout the generations.

Parallel attempts to appropriate and domesticate Japanese Buddhism to a local, American linguistic, cultural, and religious context were also part of the early phases of integration for Japanese settlers in America. Together with the British convert Buddhist priest Ernest Shinkaku Hunt (1876–1967), the first Honpa Hongwanji missionary to Hawai'i, Imamura Emyō (1867–1932), established Sunday schools and Young Men's/Women's Buddhist Associations, authored Buddhist hymns and books in English and designed Buddhist services with sermons, organ music, pulpits, and pews, contributing to a general nonsectarian protestantization of Buddhism in Hawai'i with Christian standards for activities, rituals, and organizational structures, including "congregationalization" in the Buddhist "church."[3]

With the onset of the Second World War (and especially the attack on Pearl Harbor), the Japanese were seen as enemies and Buddhism became de facto criminalized. Large numbers of priests and community representatives were sent to internment camps.[4] The natural process of generational de-ethnification became part of a general strategy of assimilation; it was simply not popular to flaunt too much "Japaneseness." Converting to Christianity as well as abandoning characteristics of Japanese identity through language and culture became a way in which to secure the cultural label of Americanization.

Postwar individualization and secularization have further threatened the existence of the original diaspora Buddhist groups. In Hawai'i, the religious market has increasingly been dominated by Christian evangelical churches, a plethora of new religious movements (including those of Japanese origins), and Euro-American New Age spirituality, leaving the remnants of a predominantly mono-ethnic Japanese "heritage Buddhism" as a diminishing tradition, which, according to George Tanabe, is "suffering a slow but certain death" (2005: 96), not least due to continued insistence on sectarian exclusivism defined by the headquarters in Japan.[5] Descendants of the first Japanese immigrants only have a limited

---

[3]On Imamura, see Moriya (2000).
[4]On Japanese American Buddhists and internment camps, see Williams (2002, 2019) and Odo (2004).
[5]On Japanese Buddhism in Hawai'i, see Borup (2013), Tanabe and Tanabe (2012), and Porcu (2018).

identity as Japanese, and it is conceptually problematic to talk of a surviving (religious) diaspora consciousness. Lives, identities, and religiosities have changed throughout the generations, yet the remaining temples and occasional ritual performances ensure that the story of an important part of Japanese Buddhist history continues to be told and symbolically celebrated.

CHAPTER 13

Islam

KOMURA Akiko

Islam in Japan has a relatively long history. This chapter will focus on how Islam entered Japan and how it was interpreted and discussed in the Japanese context, starting from the Meiji era.

STUDY OF ISLAM IN JAPAN BEFORE AND DURING THE SECOND WORLD WAR

The first Japanese Muslim appeared in the Meiji period. His name was Noda Shōtarō, a journalist with a Japanese newspaper. In 1890, a military ship of the Ottoman Empire was shipwrecked near Wakayama prefecture due to a typhoon. Sixty-nine people survived and were brought back to Turkey on two Japanese military ships, the *Hiei* and and the *Kongo*.[1] Noda was on board of the *Hiei* carrying a monetary donation to Turkey collected by his employer after this accident. He remained in Turkey for about two years and converted to Islam in 1891. His conversion, however, was only a formality.

Later, Japan needed expertise on Islam during the expansion of its colonies in areas with Muslim communities such as Manchuria, Northwest China, and Southeast Asia. The Japanese government made the study of Islam into a state policy, the so-called Islam Policy (*kaikyō seisaku*).[2]

At the time, Islam was a new religion totally unknown to Japan, and scholars initially tried to understand Islam by comparing it with familiar religions such as Buddhism and Shinto. For example, some of them regarded the Five Pillars of Islam (profession of faith, prayer, almsgiving, fasting, and pilgrimage) as a form of ascetic training similar to Buddhist practices (*shugyō*). Yet in this interpretation, it proved difficult to include Shahāda (the profession of faith) as one of the pillars, because it was a declaration of creed or faith, not a practice. As a result, at times only Four Pillars of Islam were discussed, excluding Shahāda (Suda 1936).

The work of Suda Masatsugu (1936) is an example of this trend. Suda (1893–1964) was an important figure in the early history of Islam in Japan. He was initially an expert on Russian Muslims (Tatar Muslims), and in the postwar period, he provided a platform for cross-cultural exchange between Japanese and Muslims. He also supported building the first Islamic cemetery in Japan. His knowledge of Islam was highly respected by the Japanese Ministry of Foreign Affairs, but his understanding of the tradition was based on

---

[1] This shipwreck and its aftermath was recently the subject of the 2015 film *125 Years Memory*, a joint Turkish-Japanese production.
[2] *Kaikyō* 回教 was the Japanese term used for Islam at that time.

Buddhism. He claimed that the essence of Islam was "the Six Articles of Faith and the Four Pillars of Islam" (*rokushin yongyō*). As a translation of the word Pillar, Suda used the Chinese characters *gyō* 業 (studying and learning, or deed) rather than *gyō* 行 ("religious practice" in Buddhism).

Suda had a distinctive opinion on religious training. He believed that everyone should be as serious as Muslim practitioners in their teachings and practices, such as the five daily prayers. He also claimed that all religions do ascetic practices (Suda 1936: 57). For example, in the article *Kaikyō mondai (Kan)* ("Islamic Issues (The Last Volume)"), Suda mentioned that although the attitude of the Japanese is to look for an "easy religious practice," "genuine religious faith should be born out of constant ascetic practices" (1936: 57). In the same work, he claimed that "any religion demands that its followers be engaged in considerable ascetic practices involving soul and body to reach an advanced religious state of emotions" (1936: 57).

Similarly, Segawa Hisashi (1918) presented the essence of Islam by discussing the Five Pillars, including Shahāda, but he also regarded them as an ascetic training akin to Buddhist *shugyō* and explained that Shahāda was "a theoretical aspect of Islamic doctrine, so-called faith [امن Īmān in Arabic]." He explained the other four pillars as "practical aspects of Islamic doctrine, so-called religious training [دين Dīn in Arabic]"(1918: 139).

Finally, Ōkawa Shūmei (1886–1957) was a distinguished scholar of religion and Islam in Japan. He clearly recognized that Shahāda is a declaration of faith and belongs to "creed (*shin* 信), *Īmān* امن in Arabic," not to "ascetic training (*gyō* 行), *Dīn* دين in Arabic" (Ōkawa 1942). He repeatedly mentioned this understanding of the Five Pillars of Islam in his work. He insisted that Shahāda should be eliminated from the five pillars and replaced by purification (*seijō* 清浄), طهارة *ṭahāra* in Arabic.

As we can see, early Japanese scholars of Islam thought that religion should include ascetic training and tried to understand Islam from the point of view of traditional Japanese religions.

ISLAM IN JAPAN AFTER THE SECOND WORLD WAR

From the postwar period through the 1970s, there were only a small number of Muslims living in Japan (thirty thousand in 1979). They lived in small communities where people tended to know each other.

By the mid-1970s there were a few mosques and Islamic group offices in Japan, such as the Tokyo Mosque and the Islamic Center Japan, established in Tokyo in 1938 and 1968, respectively, and the Kobe Mosque, opened in 1935. The Tokyo Mosque was closed in 1984 due to building deterioration. After that, Muslims tended to gather in hotel halls or public parks for collective prayers during religious festivals such as *'īd*, the festival marking the end of Ramadan (the month of fasting). During the 1980s and through the 1990s, some new mosques and Islamic centers were built in large cities; communication with local governments also improved over time (see Figure 13.1). There are now over one hundred mosques and Islamic centers all over Japan.

FROM THE MID-1970S THROUGH THE 1980S

In December 1974, four Japanese converted to Islam and established an organization called Japan Islamic Congress (Nihon Isuramu Kyōdan). Their representative was Futaki

ISLAM

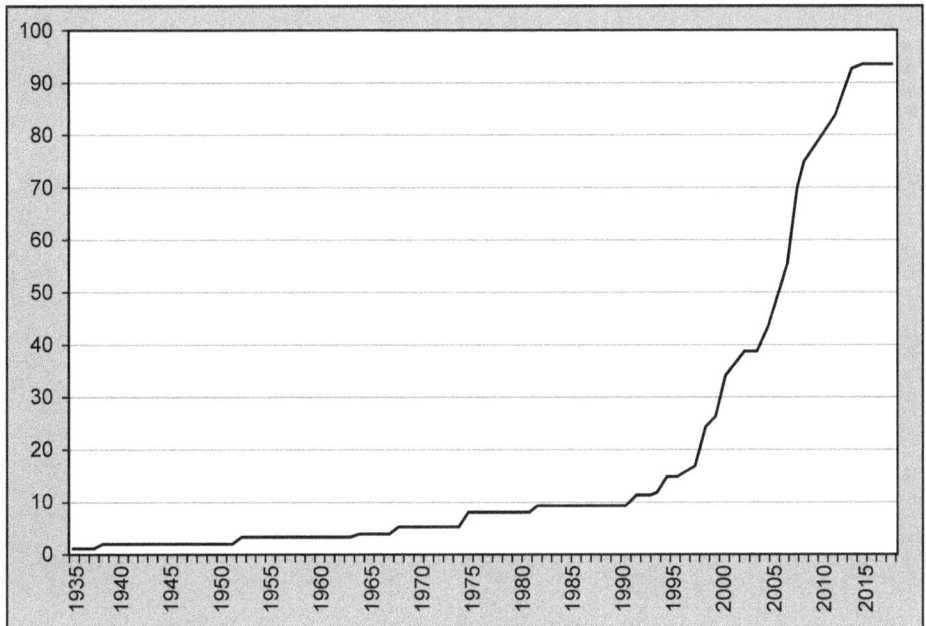

FIGURE 13.1: Changes in the number of mosques and Islamic groups in Japan (1935–2018).
Source: Komura (2019): 65.

Hideo (1908–1992), a doctor who was seen as a controversial figure. The organization was very active and their proselytizing efforts resulted in several conversions.

Futaki taught a modified version of Islam geared toward Japanese people. In trying to teach his patients the essence of Islam he frequently said, "O (Zero) is existence." This could be interpreted that human existence is nothing, so small when compared to the almighty Allah. He also often said, "Let Japanese Islam follow the Japanese way." These ideas were actually put into practice in his organization's activities. His words must have been easy to understand and effective for his patients. He did his best to make Islam fit into the daily lifestyle of the Japanese and their way of thinking. These efforts were later developed into Daijō Islam (Mahayāna Islam), which was theorized and publicized by Abe Haruo, an executive director of the Japan Islamic Congress. (See Case Study "*Daijō Islam (Mahayāna Islam)*" for details.)

FROM THE LATE 1980S TO THE PRESENT

Until the mid-1980s, Muslims in Japan were an extremely small minority. This situation changed when the number of Muslim foreign workers increased dramatically in Japan. The Bubble Economy of the late 1980s demanded a new labor force, and this caused large numbers of workers to come to Japan from other countries. They worked in low-wage, physically demanding jobs such as assembly lines in factories or at construction sites.

Foreign workers brought their cultures to Japan. When the local communities encountered people with different cultural backgrounds, unavoidable problems often occurred. In particular, debates arose regarding Muslims' unfamiliar religious activities, such as the five daily prayers, fasting, حرام Harām and حلال Halāl food and drinks, as well as the construction of mosques.

Most Muslim workers in Japan were males and came from Asian countries, in particular Iran, Pakistan, and Bangladesh (see Figure 13.2).

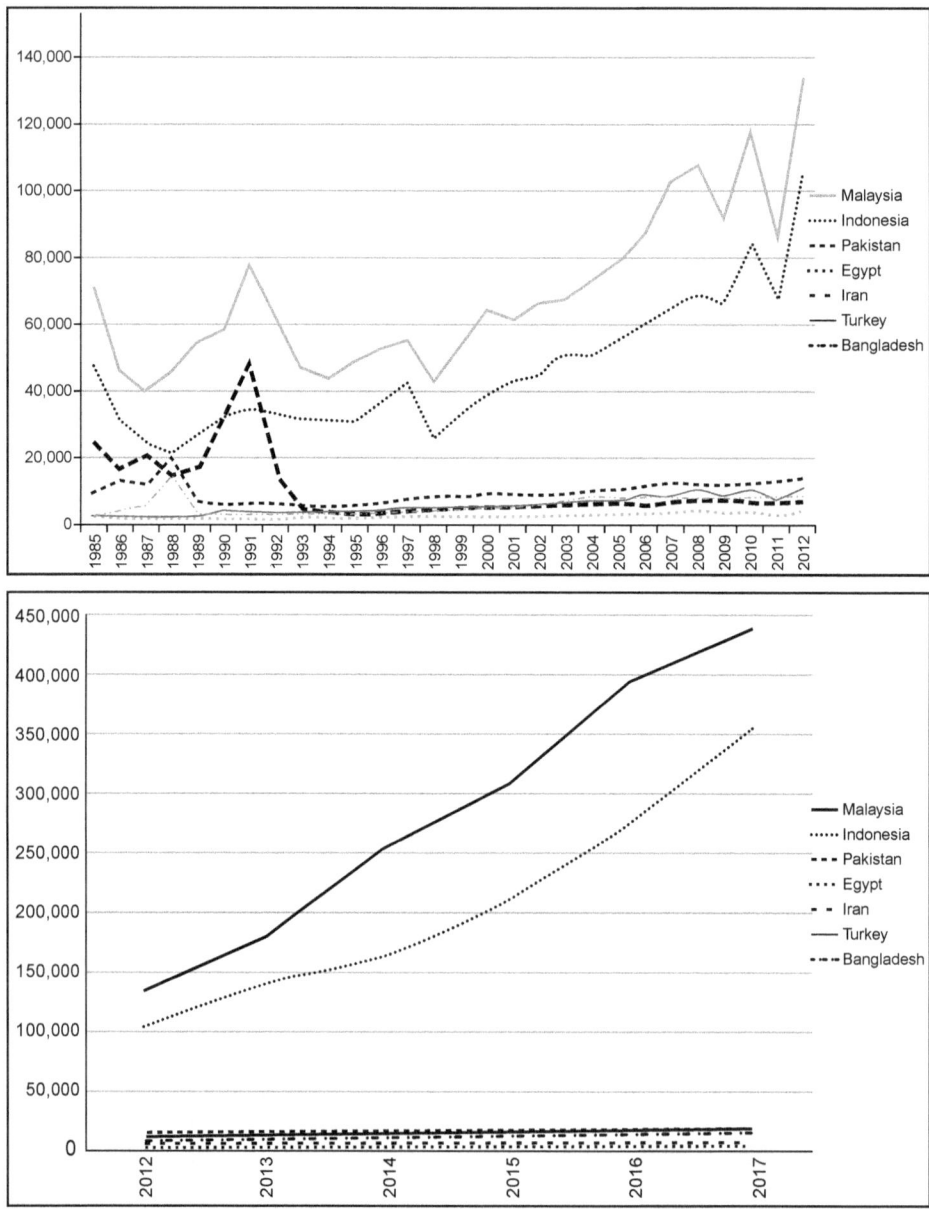

FIGURE 13.2: Changes in the number of registered foreign nationals by states of residence (1987–2012 and 2012–2018).
Source: Komura (2019): 57.

Some of these workers married Japanese women, who then converted to Islam and attended mosques to learn about the religion. However, their husbands were from different countries and therefore belonged to different Islamic schools. For instance, Sunni Islam has four schools; al-Ḥanafī, al-Mālikī, al-Shāfiʿī, and al-Ḥanbalī. While many Pakistani Muslims belong to al-Ḥanafī, Malaysian Muslims generally belong to al-Shāfiʿī. This caused confusion among the Japanese converts as to what exact tenets of Islam they should follow.

Japanese wives also tried to do their best to meet their husband's expectations, but this also posed challenges. In particular, they wore a veil on their head whenever they went out, but this at times caused problems when working at Japanese companies, where they became targets of discrimination (Komura 2015: 109–10).

Problems also emerged for second-generation Muslims, especially regarding Islamic education, which is provided at only a few mosques in Japan and usually takes the form of weekend classes or after-school lessons. Even today there is no Islamic school officially recognized by the Japanese government, which is very different from the situation in the UK, France, or the United States. The Muslim population in Japan is very small, about 120,000~140,000 people (Pew Research Center 2009: 28),[3] representing only 0.1 percent of the population. The number of Japanese Muslim converts is about ten thousand (Komura 2019: 81–5). Most of them are converts following marriage, and women tend to leave Islam when they divorce (Komura 2015: 114–59). Still now, Japanese Muslims are a small minority group in Japan.

Aside from Muslim families living in Japan, the Japanese government has actively promoted international tourism in the last few years, and tourists from countries such as Indonesia and Malaysia have increased steadily (See Figure 13.3). This has given rise to a growing interest in obtaining Halāl certification in food production and import/export businesses.

However, the rise in Halāl certification has not always been an absolute success. For instance, the Japanese news media have occasionally reported about food fraud cases in which Halāl materials were replaced by Harām (forbidden) products. Two Halāl-related cases in particular were widely reported. One concerns Ajinomoto-Indonesia, in which the Japanese company obtained Halāl accreditation for their artificial seasoning by LPPOM MUI Majelis Ulama Indonesia (Indonesian Council of Ulama) but failed to inform the council that the ingredients had been changed in 2001. The other case occurred in 2008, when a local government officer in Japan took Japanese beef to the United Arab Emirates without checking whether it met Halāl rules.

In general, Japanese business people are aware of Islamic religious rules. They also tend to have considerable knowledge about Islam (in particular, Halāl food), sometimes even more than newly converted Japanese Muslims. However, Japanese business people tend to think of Halāl as only food culture, not as part of Islamic tenets (Komura 2019: 183–8) encompassing many aspects of a Muslim's lifestyle. In other words, they understand Islam only as a culture and not as a religion, because their immediate goal is to do business successfully; they seem to think that understanding Islam as a religion is not necessary at all (Komura 2015: 109). Some Japanese Muslims understand and accept this current situation of Halāl in Japan, but some refuse to buy Halāl products sold by Japanese companies. A few say that they only buy Halāl products imported from Islamic countries.

---

[3] According to Pew Research Center, Muslim population in Japan was estimated about 183,000 people in 2005.

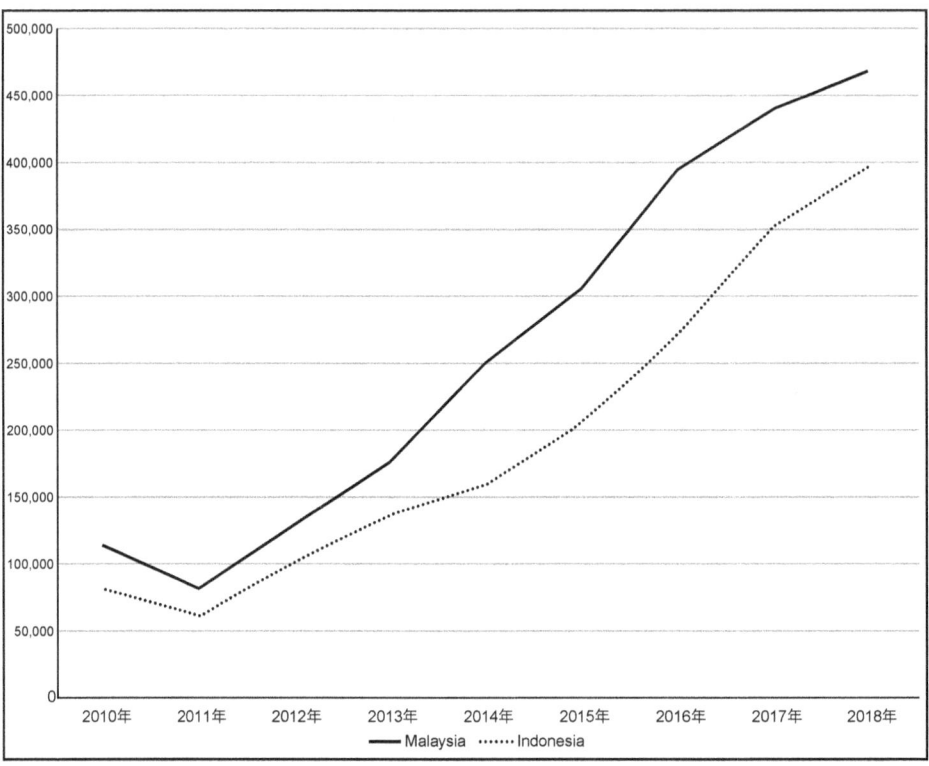

FIGURE 13.3: The number of Malaysian and Indonesian visitors to Japan (2010–2018).
Source: Komura (2019): 138.

CONCLUSION

The history of the study and understanding of Islam in Japan has seen three main waves. The first wave was encouraged by the necessity of acquiring knowledge about Islam for use in Japanese foreign policy. The second wave was brought by Muslim workers who were staying in Japan. This wave led to a significant increase in the number of Muslims in Japan, including new Japanese Muslim converts. The third wave is currently developing, driven by economic reasons such as Halāl food.

These three waves suggest that necessity and experience constitute the first step to understanding Islam, and that having proper knowledge and understanding of Islamic tenets is the second, important step toward building a harmonious relationship with this religion. In addition, it may also be noted that many people in Japan have tried to understand Islam in such a way as to incorporate it into their Japanese life, for example, by finding similarities with Buddhism or Shinto or by modifying Islamic tenets according to the needs of ordinary people living in Japan.

See also Chapter 12, "Globalization," and Chapter 18, "Minorities."

CHAPTER 14

Law

Mark R. MULLINS

The topic of law and religion encompasses a range of complicated issues, including the relationship between political authority and religious institutions, the edicts and laws governments issue that define and limit the role of religion in society, and the monitoring of the population by "enforcers," that is, police agencies, whose responsibility is to ensure that the behavior of individuals and groups conform with the established laws and norms. Over the course of Japanese history, these norms and expectations have changed a number of times, and the state patronage of religion has shifted from one religion to another in response to new challenges and the interests of those holding political power.

In order to understand the contemporary situation, it is necessary to first highlight some of the ways in which religion has been promoted, regulated, and proscribed by political authorities in earlier times, which have established particular cultural expectations with regard to the appropriate relationship between the government, law, and religion in modern Japan. As we will see, the legal structures that shaped religion in both premodern and Meiji Japan were designed for social control and support for the political authority. The protection of religious freedom for individuals and institutions—even under the Meiji Constitution—remained secondary to this larger purpose.

BACKGROUND: PREMODERN DEVELOPMENTS

At the outset, it is important to note that the relationship between law and religion in Japan has been forged in reaction to foreign influences and political challenges as the country's international relations developed over the centuries. Foreign imports and political challenges from both China and the West have shaped the shifting legal and administrative structures regulating religion across the centuries. Here, I highlight two formative encounters that shaped Japanese thought and policies in the premodern period.

First was the impact of continental culture from China, which was transmitted via the Korean Peninsula from the sixth to eighth centuries. During this period, the Japanese court sponsored numerous imperial envoys, whose missions brought back the Chinese writing system, models of government and administration, and a wide range of cultural, intellectual, and religious traditions. Shōtoku Taishi's (573–621) Seventeen Article Constitution is one manifestation of the early foreign influence on Japan's development, which led to the adoption and adaptation of Confucian-Buddhist ideals and principles for Japanese life and institutions.[1]

---

[1] Although commonly referred to as a "Constitution," Steenstrup explains it was "no Constitution," in fact, "for it did not restrict any extant legislature. It was not even a statute, for nothing could be effected or changed

The close association between political authority and religious institutions continued to develop in the Nara period (710–794). During this time, the imperial court adapted Chinese legal codes (*ritsuryō*) to the Japanese context and established the Jingikan (Council of Divinities), which eventually organized, mandated, and monitored the proper performance of annual rites, offerings, and ceremonies related to the kami enshrined in imperial and national shrines throughout the provinces (Hardacre 2017: 29–40). These early developments reveal a symbiotic relationship between political authority and religious institutions, one that defined religion-state relations in terms of "the unity of rites and government" (*saisei itchi*), which became the normative framework shaping how political elites usually dealt with issues surrounding law and religion in Japan.

The institutionalization of native traditions did not prevent the simultaneous adoption and patronage of Buddhism. This is particularly apparent in the policies instituted during the reign of Emperor Shōmu (724–749), such as the establishment of temples in each province (*kokubunji*) and the building of Tōdaiji, a large temple complex, which represented the *kokubunji* of Nara, the capital. Such official sponsorship and financial support of Buddhist institutions has led some scholars to adopt the term "state Buddhism" (*kokka bukkyō*) to characterize this period.[2]

The mid-sixteenth century marks the beginning of another formative period for the shaping of religion-state relations and legal codes dealing with religious institutions, this time formulated in response to the threat represented by European colonialism and their efforts to expand empires and religious territories. The arrival of Jesuit missionaries in 1549 marked the launch of the Roman Catholic mission in Japan. The arrival of this foreign-born religion followed many years of civil war and military conflict. The fact that Japan was a politically divided nation is what initially allowed some of the great lords (*daimyō*) to permit the Catholic missionaries to work in their domains, which facilitated both mass conversions and the rapid growth of the Catholic mission in what has been referred to as the "Christian century." This ended rather abruptly with the unification of the country by Oda Nobunaga and the adoption of strict policies that prohibited Christianity as an evil teaching (*jakyō*). In 1587 Hideyoshi Toyotomi issued an edict ordering the expulsion of all foreign missionaries and offered the rationale that "Japan is a country of the Kami [Gods] and for the padres to come hither and preach a devilish law, is a most reprehensible and evil thing" (Boxer 1951: 148). A nationwide ban on the Kirishitan religion was issued in 1614, which eventually brought the Catholic mission to an end.

While Japan had been identified as a "land of the kami," it was Buddhist institutions that the Tokugawa authorities mobilized to monitor the population and enforce their anti-Christian policies. In 1635, the government issued a decree—the *Sakoku rei*—to inaugurate a policy of nation isolation and established a temple registration system (*danka seido*) for the entire country in an effort to eradicate the threat of the foreign religion. All residents of a given area were required to register their household with a local temple and record births, marriages, and deaths. Buddhist priests were employed to issue certificates (*tera-uke*) to individuals each year attesting that the person in question

---

without the will of the Soga … The contents are moral maxims, inculcating *Buddhist* piety, *Confucian* probity, and *Legalistic* obedience to the ruler. . ." (1996: 17).
[2]See Bryan D. Lowe (2014) for a critical review of Japanese scholarship on the category of "state Buddhism" applied to the Nara period.

was not a Kirishitan.³ This was sometimes ascertained through the act of *e-fumi*, a ritual that required individuals to step on a picture of Christ or the Holy Mother to publicly deny having Christian faith.

The implementation of this registration system required the government to build temples throughout towns and villages across Japan. As a result, the number of temples increased from 13,037 in the Kamakura period to some 469,934 by the end of the Tokugawa period (Kitagawa 1966: 164). Many of these temples remained Shinto-Buddhist complexes and were recognized as politically and financially important, which is why the Tokugawa authorities appointed a Temple-and-Shrine Commissioner (*fudai daimyō*) to monitor and oversee them.⁴ While these policies were enacted to eliminate the threat of a foreign power and religion, their larger impact was to transform the entire population into Buddhist parishioners whose familial identity would remain inextricably tied to the *danka* temple well into the twentieth century.

THE MEIJI RESTORATION, CONSTITUTION, AND LEGAL TREATMENT OF RELIGION

The perceived threat from the West shaped both the policies of the Tokugawa authorities from the late sixteenth century and the Meiji government's evolving policies toward religion in the late nineteenth to early twentieth centuries. After two and a half centuries of national isolation, Japan faced intense pressure from Western powers to reopen its ports and establish diplomatic relations. In 1858, five years after Commodore Perry sailed into the Tokyo harbor, Japan signed the Treaty of Amity and Commerce with the United States. These developments occurred as the Tokugawa feudal order was disintegrating; with the ensuing internal political realignments and civil wars, a new political system emerged under the "restored" Emperor.

The *kokugaku* movement, especially the views of Hirata Atsutane (1776–1843), greatly influenced the leadership and policies of the early Meiji government. In 1868, the new government indicated its intention to "restore" the *saisei itchi* tradition ("the unity of government and rites"), which involved the promotion of Shinto as the foundation for the new Emperor-centric social order through the reestablished Council of Divinities. This brought an end to the state patronage Buddhism received during the Tokugawa period and marked the beginning of a difficult period for Buddhist priests and institutions.

On March 28, 1868, the new government issued a decree to separate the "gods and the buddhas" (*shinbutsu bunri rei*), which was a policy aimed at purifying the indigenous Japanese tradition from foreign influences and the centuries-old Shinto-Buddhist amalgam. This unleashed a movement that targeted Buddhist institutions for suppression and destruction under the slogan "abolish Buddhism, destroy Buddhist images" (*haibutsu kishaku*). As a result of this anti-Buddhist activity, at least eighteen thousand temples were demolished between 1872 and 1874, and an untold number of sacred objects were destroyed.⁵ The government also confiscated many temple estates, which weakened the

---

³For a comprehensive treatment of the development and implementation of the *danka* system in the Tokugawa period, see Hur (2007).
⁴As Steenstrup notes, the Commissioner's role was "to see to it that the *bakufu's* stringent laws against taxpayers's siphoning off into monastic tax-havens were obeyed; and to decide the clergymen's internal quarrels over ranking" (1996: 115).
⁵See Grapard (1984), Ketelaar (1990), and Breen and Teeuwen (2000) for detailed treatment of the Meiji government's policies and their impact on Buddhist institutions and the priesthood.

support base of Buddhist institutions, and even tried—unsuccessfully—to establish a compulsory shrine registration system (*ujiko shirabe*) to replace the *danka seido*, which the Tokugawa authorities had used as a method of social control. Popular reaction to these extreme measures soon led the government to moderate their policies, but the precarious status of Buddhist institutions lingered.

The situation and legal status of Japan's other foreign-born religion, Christianity, also changed rapidly during the early Meiji period. This was due to multiple factors, including pressure exerted by Western governments, the return of foreign missionaries from 1859, and the unexpected survival and reappearance of over thirty-five thousand or more "hidden Christians" (*Kakure Kirishitan*) after two centuries of underground existence. The new and growing missionary presence was not just Roman Catholic this time but also included a diverse array of representatives from a variety of Protestant denominations, as well as the Russian Orthodox Church. Christianity remained an illegal religion in the early Meiji period, but diplomatic efforts finally persuaded the Japanese authorities to remove the public notice boards proscribing Christianity in 1873, which changed the legal status of Christianity from one of "prohibition" to "toleration."

Foreign diplomatic pressure upon the government led the Meiji leaders to draft and include an article on religion in the 1889 Constitution, which reads as follows: "Japanese subjects shall, within limits not prejudicial to the peace and order, and not antagonistic to their duties as subjects, enjoy freedom of religious belief" (Article 28). As this new legal code was interpreted and applied, it separated and treated Shinto differently than other organized religions. Shinto institutions were overseen and managed by the Bureau of Shrines (*Jinja kyoku*), which was established in the Ministry of Home Affairs in 1900. Buddhist temples, Christian churches, and New Religions, on the other hand, were all under the administration of the Bureau of Religion (*Shūkyō kyoku*). Within this regulatory system, Shinto was defined as "nonreligious" and shrines became the carrier of a system of national morality and rites, which soon constituted the duties of all imperial subjects. Freedom of religious belief was allowed in the "private sphere" for Buddhists, Christians, and members of New Religions, as long as these duties were performed and their teachings did not undermine "peace and order."

This framework for understanding religion was diffused through public education, military training, and the adoption of various ritual practices in government offices. The public school system became the primary vehicle for nurturing a range of ritual practices that were a part of nonreligious Shinto, including shrine visits, the installment and special ritual care of the Imperial portrait (*goshinei*), and the public reading of the Imperial Rescript on Education, all of which became the normative and customary practice in all public schools by the Taishō period. These rituals not only nurtured loyalty to emperor and nation but also disseminated the idea that these Shinto shrine-related social rituals were separate from those associated with religions (i.e., Buddhism, Christianity, and New Religions).[6]

The term "State Shinto" has been used to refer to the administration of shrines from the Meiji era until 1945, but the extent of government control and actual financial support varied widely over the decades. At the very least, we must acknowledge that the kind of patronage Buddhist institutions received from the Tokugawa authorities

---

[6]See Yamamoto and Imano (1973; 1976) for extensive documentation and analysis of the spread of these "nonreligious" social and national rituals (*kokkateki gyōji ni kansuru gishiki*) in the public schools and other public offices.

was deliberately shifted to Shinto during the period under consideration. While most local shrines continued to operate as local *ujigami* communities that depended upon the support of parishioners, the government was involved in providing some form of financial support for the Imperial (*kanpeisha*), National (*kokuheisha*), and Special shrines (*bekkakusha*), according to the ranking system imposed in 1871 (Hardacre 2017: 374–5). The government also sponsored the building of new shrines, including Yasukuni Shrine (1869), the first of the "nation-protecting shrines" (*gokoku jinja*), and Meiji Shrine (1920). Many more *gokoku* shrines were built in the capitals of each prefecture after 1939 as the number of war dead increased substantially and wartime conditions made it increasingly difficult for family representatives outside of the Kanto region to travel to Yasukuni Shrine in the capital. In addition, over six hundred shrines were built outside of Japan proper (*gaichi*) in the expanding Japanese Empire (Suga 2010: 48).

The treatment of New Religions and Christian churches in the last decade before the end of the Pacific War reveals the limited and precarious nature of religious freedom and its protection under the Meiji Constitution. In order to deal with groups deemed problematic—New Religions and sectarian Christian groups in particular—the Diet passed the Religious Organizations Law (*Shūkyō dantai hō*) in 1939. Enacted the following year, it authorized the State to disband any religious organization known for propagating "dangerous" thoughts (*kiken shisō*), that is, teachings in conflict with the "Imperial Way."

In addition, the 1925 Peace Preservation Law—designed initially to control radical socialism and the communist movement—was revised in 1941 to address the subversive potential of various religious groups (Mitchell 1976: 167). The Japanese Special Higher Police (*Tokubetsu kōtō keisatsu*), usually referred to as Tokkō, were mobilized to investigate suspect religious groups under the new law. Until the 1930s, the Tokkō were largely occupied dealing with political subversives, but they shifted their concerns to religious deviants by the end of the decade. They were responsible for investigating and documenting any religious group advocating "subversive teaching" or refusing to participate in the "rituals of citizenship" (*kokumin no girei*) such as bowing in the direction of the Imperial Palace and singing the national anthem "Kimi ga yo." While Japanese were allowed to embrace religious beliefs in private, their freedom did not include the right to avoid participation in public patriotic rites, even if they found these to be in tension with their personal faith.

As enforcers of the state-defined orthodoxy, the Tokkō investigated and arrested leaders and members of seventeen different groups before the end of the war. Ōmotokyō, Hitonomichi, and Tenri Honmichi were some of the targeted New Religions that were accused of holding heretical beliefs about the Emperor or promoting the elimination of his sovereignty and the national polity (*kokutai*) by advocating the "rebuilding and renewal of the world" (*yo no tatekae, tatenaoshi*). Some Christian groups—notably the Jehovah's Witnesses, Plymouth Brethren, Seventh-Day Adventists, and the Holiness groups of churches with the Nihon Kirisuto Kyōdan—were the next to attract the attention of the investigators for a range of problematic beliefs and behaviors, including pacifism, refusal to participate in shrine visits, and apocalyptic beliefs about the Second Coming of Christ and judgment of all humanity, including the Emperor. Leaders were arrested and churches closed until the end of the war.[7] Given the treatment of religious minorities during this

---

[7] See the volumes edited by Akashi and Matsuura (1975) for rich documentation of the Tokkō investigations during this period.

period, it is widely recognized by legal scholars that "religious freedom was insufficiently guaranteed by the Meiji Constitution" (Abe 1968: 282).

THE ALLIED OCCUPATION OF JAPAN AND POSTWAR CONSTITUTION

Japan's defeat and surrender on August 15, 1945, marked the end of the hostilities of the Second World War and the beginning of the Allied Occupation (1945–52), which would fundamentally alter the legal framework and official understanding of what constituted religion and its relationship with the state. The "unity of rites and government" (*saisei itchi*) tradition, which had dominated religion-state relations over many centuries, would be quickly replaced by the strict application of the separation of religion from the state (*seikyō bunri*).[8] In the first few weeks of the Occupation, the Supreme Commander of Allied Powers (SCAP) announced that a range of democratic freedoms—freedom of thought, freedom of expression, and freedom of religion—were to characterize the new social order, but these freedoms were quickly regulated and limited by censorship and the monitoring of individuals and groups that expressed views incompatible with SCAP's policies.

The Religions Division, which was a part of SCAP'S Civil Information & Education Section, was responsible for implementing policies to establish religious freedom and the separation of religion and state. Several changes were quickly initiated in an effort to achieve these objectives. After several months of consultation with Japanese scholars and government officials, W. K. Bunce drafted the "Shinto Directive Staff Study" on the problem of State Shinto (December 3, 1945). This document provided the basis for the "Directive for the Disestablishment of State Shinto," which was issued by SCAP on December 15, 1945.[9] This required that the government end any financial support for Shinto institutions and the administration of shrines separate from other religions; it essentially reduced Shinto to the status of a private voluntary organization. The Directive also instructed the Japanese government to remove Shinto elements from all public institutions, which included taking *kamidana* (offertory shelves) out of schools and public offices, and ended forced shrine visits (*sanpai*) on the part of students, teachers, and government officials.

The Occupation authorities redefined as "religious" the various ritual practices that the government had for decades designated as "nonreligious," and policies were initiated to restrict public officials from engaging in Shinto-related practices. The Occupation archives provide extensive evidence of tension and disagreement between SCAP's Religions Division and the Japanese Government's Religious Affairs Office (*Shūmuka*) over this redefinition of Shinto practices as "religious." In 1946, the Religious Organizations Law (*shūkyō dantai hō*, 1939) was replaced by a new Religious Corporation Ordinance (*shūkyō hōjin rei*), which required Shinto shrines—like Buddhist temples, Christian churches, and New Religions—to register with the government as religious bodies. Shinto institutions—including both shrines that became a part of Jinja Honchō (the Association of Shinto Shrines) in 1946, as well as independent religious corporations, including Yasukuni Shrine

---

[8]See Yanagawa and Reid (1979) for a helpful overview of the *saisei itchi* and *seikyō bunri* traditions, which examines their significance for understanding postwar lawsuits and legal disputes over religion-state separation.
[9]These documents may be found in the Appendices of Woodard (1972).

and Meiji Shrine—all survived the Occupation period by embracing a "religious" identity, registering as religious corporations (*shūkyō hōjin*) and, in some cases, by suppressing their views that Shinto shrines should still have a "public" role and special status as carriers of authentic Japanese tradition. The Religious Corporation Ordinance was replaced by the Religious Corporation Law (*Shūkyō hōjin hō* 宗教法人法) in 1952, which has defined officially registered religious bodies as a part of the larger category of "public service corporations" (*kōeki hōjin*), a designation that qualifies them for favorable tax treatment.

The strict separation of religion and state required by the Shinto Directive was also incorporated into the postwar Constitution (1947) in Articles 20 and 89, and these have provided the legal framework for the debates surrounding religious freedom and religion-state separation for the past seventy years.[10]

> **Article 20.** Freedom of religion is guaranteed to all. No religious organization shall receive any privileges from the State, nor exercise any political authority. No person shall be compelled to take part in any religious act, celebration, rite or practice. The State and its organs shall refrain from religious education or any other religious activity.
> **Article 89.** No public money or other property shall be expended or appropriated for the use, benefit or maintenance of any religious institution or association, or for any charitable, educational or benevolent enterprises not under the control of public authority.

While SCAP proclaimed "religious freedom" and ended the government's intervention and persecution of religious bodies by the Tokkō, the Occupation authorities began to monitor Shinto institutions and public officials for any violations of the Shinto Directive and their strict interpretation as well as the application of Articles 20 and 89. This special focus on issues related to Shinto is apparent in the "Instructions to agencies of the Occupation Forces in the field of Japanese religions," issued on March 25, 1946. This document states that

> surveillance should be exercised to detect and remedy" a number of possible violations, including "pressure brought by officials of neighborhood associations (*tonari gumi*), district associations (*chōkai*), villages, towns, or cities upon any person (1) To declare himself an adherent (*ujiko*) of any shrine or tutelary deity or (2) To buy or receive any talisman, charm, calendar, or other object sold or distributed by or for the benefit of any Shinto shrine or any other religious group.

Agencies were also instructed to watch out for "official visits to shrines by government officials" and the misuse of Occupation personnel and facilities in support of the "propagation of Christianity" and efforts to "further the cause of Christianity over other Japanese religions."[11]

SCAP's Religions Division was critical of the Japanese government's Religious Affairs Office (*Shūmuka*) in its implementation of the Shinto Directive, especially for its failure to provide clear instructions to public officials and government offices that Shinto-related

---

[10]Readers should consult Zachmann (2012) for a more in-depth treatment of the 1947 Constitution and a review of legal conflict surrounding religion-state separation in the postwar period.

[11]"Instructions to agencies of the Occupation Forces in the field of Japanese religions" (March 25, 1946, General Headquarters, Supreme Commander for the Allied Powers, Civil Information and Education Section, Religions Division), 3–4; preserved in the William Woodard Special Collection (153), Box 15, Folder 5. Special Collections and University Archives, University of Oregon Libraries.

rituals could no longer be promoted or paid for by those in political office. At the same time, the Religions Division issued a Memo in 1948 that identified a number of other problems with the performance of the *Shūmuka,* including "a tendency to violate the freedoms of religious groups by unnecessary inquisitions into their organization, doctrines, finances, and activities," "an interest in maintaining the status quo in the Japanese religious world," and "an inclination to 'whitewash' all alleged violations of occupation directives in the religious field." The problems were such that the Memo recommended that "the Religious Affairs Section of the Secretariat, Ministry of Education, and the religions officials on the prefectural level be liquidated as of 1 April 1948 and that their functions be abolished."[12] This recommendation was never acted upon, but it did seem to favor a hands-off approach to religious organizations that also characterized the government's orientation in the post-Occupation period.

While the monitoring of Shinto institutions—particularly the controversial Yasukuni Shrine and other *gokoku* shrines—continued into the last year of the Occupation, General Douglas MacArthur completely undermined the Religions Division's instructions by promoting Christianity as the "quasi-official" religion of the Occupation based on his conviction that "democratization" would require "Christianization." With the Supreme Commander's endorsement, the resources of the Occupation were often used to support the Christian enterprise by providing temporary housing, contributing to fundraising efforts for the rebuilding of Christian churches and schools, and by assisting with transportation and shipment of personal baggage, Christian literature, and Bibles.[13]

RELIGION AND THE LAW IN THE POST-OCCUPATION PERIOD

The postwar Constitution (1947) guarantees religious freedom, protects individual rights, and clearly separates the state from religion (*seikyō bunri*). These distinctive features were first introduced and "imposed" during the Occupation period, which means they have only shaped the Japanese understanding of the legal status of religion for just over seven decades. Although the separation of religion and state had been promoted by some Japanese intellectuals, Communists, and Christians before this time, "the fact remains that its institutionalization in the structure of Japanese law began as something imposed from without" (Yanagawa and Reid 1979: 502). The fact that current laws pertaining to religion were largely put in place by "foreign imposition" is the source of lingering resentment, and thus calls for the revision of the Constitution began soon after Japan regained its sovereignty in 1952.

Since the end of the Occupation, the policy of officially monitoring religious organizations by government agencies had been largely discontinued. This all changed in response to the sarin gas attack on the Tokyo subway by members of the new religion Aum Shinrikyō on March 20, 1995. Over two thousand police officers were mobilized

---

[12]"MEMO to Chief, R & CR Division; Subject: Religious Affairs Section," January 21, 1948: 2. The Memo also explains that "a strong governmental agency with administrative supervision over religions supplemented by religions officers on the prefectural level has existed in Japan since the Meiji Restoration. Japanese, accordingly, do not find it easy to conceive of religions without governmental control and supervision. Japanese religionists are conditioned to such control; Japanese officialdom takes it for granted" (1–2).

[13]For more details on the various ways Christianity was promoted and supported by General MacArthur and by the Occupation, see Wittner (1971), Moore (2011), Okazaki (2012), and Mullins (2017).

for a nationwide investigation of Aum Shinrikyō centers, which resulted in over arrests of over two hundred Aum members. Aum's legal status as a tax-exempt religious body was quickly dissolved and those arrested began the long process of trial proceedings. After months of investigation, the founder—Asahara Shōkō—and over one hundred followers, were indicted on a range of charges, including the sarin gas attack on the subway, other kidnapping and murders, as well as illegal production of various drugs. After over two decades of trials and appeals, Asahara and twelve of his followers were convicted and received the death penalty. These executions were carried out in July 2018.

In addition to conducting these criminal cases, the government acted quickly to pass legislation to address the pervasive sense of social crisis across the nation. On December 8, 1995, the Diet hurriedly approved changes in the religious corporation law (*shūkyō hōjin hō*), which gave new power to the authorities to investigate religious groups and required more transparent reporting of assets and activities, including the submission of an annual report of financial assets and properties. New legislation was also passed that allowed the authorities to monitor Aum and its successor groups more closely. Although there was serious debate about applying the Anti-Subversive Activities Law (*hakai katsudō bōshihō*) to this particular situation, in the end the national government passed two bills in December 1999 that gave the Public Security Investigation Agency the authority to monitor and investigate Aum for an initial three-year period.

This law required Aum—and eventually the successor groups, Aleph and Hikari no Wa—to provide a list of members and business activities every three months and allowed the authorities to enter the religious groups' facilities to conduct additional inspections as deemed necessary. In January 2018, the Public Security Investigation Commission announced that surveillance of these two successor groups would be continued for another three-year period until January 31, 2021, which is the sixth extension since surveillance was first initiated.[14] Placing these legal developments and responses to Aum in historical perspective, Helen Hardacre has suggested this may eventually be seen as a watershed moment: "Future researchers may come to regard the liberal period of 1945 to 1995 as a brief, foreign-dictated abnormality in Japan's long history of state monitoring of religion" (2003: 152).

Apart from the government's response to Aum, religious groups have largely avoided the watchful eye and intervention by the authorities during the post-Occupation decades. A number of concerned citizens and religious minorities, however, have regularly drawn attention to potential violations of religion-state separation, particularly in relation to Shinto institutions. Over the years, public criticism and a number of lawsuits have been launched against the Japanese government—at both the national and municipal levels—for public funding of ritual events conducted by Shinto priests, such as the *jichinsai* (a grounds purification ceremony) and the *Daijōsai*, the rites of imperial succession last conducted in 1989.[15] Legal action has also been taken against prime ministers and cabinet members for their official shrine visits (*kōshiki sanpai*) and offerings to Yasukuni Shrine.

---

[14]Here I am drawing on Mullins (2001), which provides a more detailed overview of the initial legal and political response to the Aum affair. Information on the latest extension of surveillance of the two post-Aum groups, Aleph and Hikari-no-Wa, is in the Public Security Intelligence Agency report *Review and Prospects of Internal and External Situations* (January 2020: 58), which is available online: http://www.moj.go.jp/content/001255171.pdf (accessed December 4, 2020).

[15]For a discussion on the *Daijōsai* again in 2019 with the abdication of Emperor Akihito and enthronement of Crown Prince Naruhito, see Breen (2019).

Yasukuni Shrine has also been the focus of lawsuits related to the continued enshrinement of the war dead in the postwar period without the permission of the bereaved families concerned, which includes Japanese Buddhists and Christians, as well as some foreigners (citizens of Taiwan and South Korea). Their personal appeals to Yasukuni Shrine for the names of their family dead to be removed from the shrine register (*gōshi torikeshi*) have been unsuccessful, and the courts have concluded that to intervene in these cases would violate the religious freedom of the shrine.

By way of conclusion, it needs to be noted that in 2005 the Liberal Democratic Party (LDP) made public its proposed revisions to the postwar Constitution and issued a slightly revised version in 2012. The proposed changes to Articles 20 and 89 in the LDP draft are clearly designed to eliminate at least some of the controversies and lawsuits surrounding religion-state separation. Given that constitutional revision is a key agenda of the current prime minister, Abe Shinzō, it is important to briefly examine what changes are proposed for the articles that have provided the legal framework for religion-state separation and guarantee of religious freedom for the past seventy years.

The LDP made public its proposed revisions to the postwar Constitution in 2005 and issued a slightly revised version in 2012. The key change is the addition to clause 3 in Article 20, which is also incorporated into Article 89 (the amendments are in italics below):

> **Article 20.** Freedom of religion is guaranteed to all. The State shall not grant privileges to any religious organization [*Omitted: "No religious organization shall exercise any political authority"*].
>
> No person shall be compelled to take part in any religious act, celebration, rite or practice.
>
> The State, local governments and other public entities shall refrain from particular religious education and other religious activities. *However, this provision shall not apply to activities that do not exceed the scope of social rituals or customary practices.* [ただし、社会的儀礼又は習俗的行為の範囲を超えないものについては、この限りでない].
>
> **Article 89.** No public money or other property shall be expended or appropriated for the use, benefit or maintenance of *religious activities conducted by any institution or association, except for cases set forth in the proviso of the third paragraph of Article 20.*[16]

The important terminology and phrases in the amended portions here are "social rituals" (*shakaiteki girei* 社会的儀礼), "customary practices" (*shūzokuteki kōi* 習俗的行為), and "this provision shall not apply to" (*kono kagiri de nai* この限りでない). The proposed revisions are based on the assumption that one can identify certain actions as nonreligious "social rituals" or "customary practices," which should then be regarded as outside the scope of the strict application of religion-state separation. This language is clearly reminiscent of the framework and categories that were created to regulate religion and Shinto following the Meiji Restoration until the end of the Second World War and also resembles the language used in some postwar Supreme Court decisions surrounding lawsuits related to Shinto rituals and alleged violation of religion-state separation.

---

[16] The draft English translation of the LDP's 2012 proposed revision is available online: https://www.voyce-jpn.com/ldp-draft-constitution (for the original Japanese, see: http://constitution.jimin.jp/draft/) (accessed December 11, 2020).

The Supreme Court decision in the Tsu City case provides one helpful illustration of what appears to be a taken-for-granted distinction between "religious" and "nonreligious" observances, which has found its way into the proposed revisions of Articles 20 and 89. This case began in 1965 as a result of a lawsuit launched against the city by Sekiguchi Seiichi, a local citizen, for violating the constitutional separation of religion and state by using public funds to pay Shinto priests to conduct a *jichinsai* (grounds purification ceremony), prior to the construction of a municipal gym. The Tsu District Court ruling in 1967 concluded that the city's compensation of the priests did not violate the Constitution, regarding the ceremony as merely a "folkway" or social custom, which was not aimed at propagating Shinto. Sekiguchi appealed this decision to the Nagoya High Court, which reversed the District Court's ruling, and concluded that it had violated the constitutional separation of religion and state, a principle that needed to be enforced given the earlier history of state-sponsored Shinto under the Meiji Constitution. The mayor of Tsu City then challenged the 1971 Nagoya High Court decision and appealed to the Supreme Court.

The Supreme Court's final decision in 1977 overturned the Nagoya High Court's decision and ruled that if the purpose of the activity (*kōi no mokuteki*) was not religious, and the action did not aim to support or promote one particular religion (*shūkyō ni taisuru enjo, jochō, sokushin*) or involve coercion or interference (*appaku, kanshō nado*) in the free practice of another religion, then the activity would not constitute a violation of Article 20.[17] Although a religious ceremony was conducted by a Shinto priest, the grounds purification ceremony was "probably not understood by the general public as a religious activity and was therefore constitutionally permissible" (O'Brien 1996: 92). If religious practices are regarded as nonreligious or secular folkways, the path is opened for a closer government support of Shinto-related practices, such as official visits (*kōshiki sanpai*) to Yasukuni and other shrines, without concern over violation of the Constitution. "By defining the ceremony as non-religious," Yamagishi explains, "the Court moved a step toward increasing and broadening the scope of permissible ways in which religion and state may mix" (2008: 931).The proposed revisions to Articles 20 and 89 introduced above clearly incorporate the language and reasoning of the Supreme Court here in what one legal scholar refers to as the "Shinto as culture" case (Ravitch 2013: 510–11).[18]

This Supreme Court decision has been celebrated by groups in favor of constitutional revision, including the Association of Shinto Shrines, its political arm, Shinto Seiji Renmei, as well as the Association for the Rectification of the Relationship between Religion and State (Seikyō Kankei o Tadasu-kai). The latter association was formed in 1971 in response to the legal debate surrounding the Tsu City case and over concern about the Nagoya High Court decision, Since then, the association has been promoting a more flexible interpretation of religion-state separation to replace what it regards as the unfairly strict interpretation, which began when the Occupation authorities implemented the Shinto Directive.[19] Critics of the proposed revisions, particularly religious minorities, argue that

---

[17]For more on this case, see Ravitch (2013), O'Brien (1996: 84–97), and the English summary of the case, which is available online (http://www.courts.go.jp/app/hanrei_en/detail?id=51).

[18]It should be noted that the Supreme Court is sending out mixed messages. In 1997, two decades after this decision, it ruled that the use of public funds for offerings (*tamagushi ryō*) to Yasukuni Shrine and to the prefectural Gokoku Shrine by Ehime Prefecture's government officials was a clear violation of Article 20, since it could be perceived by the public as government support for a particular religion (Ravitch 2014: 720).

[19]See Seikyō Kankei o Tadasu-kai (2001; 2013) for a collection of short essays that provide their perspective on numerous court cases that deal with religion-state separation over the past few decades.

if the proposed amendments to Articles 20 and 89 are passed, it will clearly weaken the clear separation of the state from religion and allow for government support of ritual activity in public institutions redefined as a "customary practices" or "social rituals," which approximates the strategy used by the government in relation to shrine visits by teachers and students in the period of State Shinto until 1945. By reintroducing the notion of "nonreligious Shinto," these critics maintain that the LDP proposal is setting up a situation in which "coercion"—rather than freedom of conscience—could once again dominate public institutions.[20]

CONCLUSION

As we have seen, the practice of religion in everyday life has often been constrained or controlled by Japan's political authorities, and religious institutions have been allowed to exist to the extent that they serve the larger interests of the state. For much of Japanese history, in fact, religion was not conceived of as a separate domain with an independent source of authority but as the ritual and ceremonial aspect of government rule and administration. The free market religious economy that emerged following the Occupation has only shaped Japanese society for a relatively brief period of time. Recent court decisions and the proposed revisions to the Constitution promoted by the LDP indicate that a significant number of legal, political, and religious leaders and groups are still attached to the *saisei itchi* tradition that preceded the foreign imposition. The weight of these accumulated traditional expectations with regard to the place of religion must be recognized in order to understand and appreciate the fault lines of recent legal conflicts and public debate over the relationship between law and religion in contemporary Japan.

See also Chapter 21, "Politics."

---

[20]See Tani (2007) for a more detailed critical Catholic perspective on the proposed revisions and Hishiki (2007), which provides a response by a Jōdo Shinshū Buddhist scholar and activist.

CHAPTER 15

Materiality

Halle O'NEAL

Those of us who choose to study a culture and its religion through visual material often do so because we find objects the most compelling way to make sense of history. Buddhism, a religion that reveals the illusion of the phenomenological realm, nevertheless makes constant use of material objects and relies on metaphors that are gloriously visual and elaborately descriptive. Much like the metaphor of the inexhaustible jeweled net that sparkles and reflects *ad infinitum*, doctrine, ritual, and the spaces of Buddhism show consistent concern for the aesthetic. Buddhist objects, in the form of embodied icons, ritual implements, rolls of texts, mandalas, relics, censors, and all other manner of rich material culture, were central components of Buddhist experience throughout Japanese history. Some instantiated the Buddha, readied sacred space, manifested cosmological order, articulated the life of a revered priest, and described the auspicious origins of a religious institution, while others served as private devotional objects or tailored expressions of righteous authority and social cachet. And of course, objects were multivalent and expressed a richness of overlapping purposes.

Part of the enduring curiosity surrounding the materiality of Buddhism are the boundless varieties, functions, and afterlives of objects, from the beautiful to the ordinary, the functional to the decorative, and the marginal to the monumental. We are told repeatedly in all varieties of texts and records and by the extant objects themselves that visuality and materiality were at the heart of Buddhist life. And by pulling at the multifaceted threads emanating from artifacts, scholars of material culture uncover rich networks entangling things and people. These investigations center the materiality of Japanese religions in order to disclose the indispensability and interconnectedness of objects to the stories of historical figures and forgotten people, to the complexities and efficacy of ritual and doctrine, to the layers of literature and poetry, and to expressions of sociopolitical and soteriological power. Moreover, objects expose the important links between the internal world of the devotee, the external worlds of teachings, rituals, and texts, and the immaterial though nonetheless highly imaginative realms of the buddhas. This short chapter, heavily weighted toward premodern Buddhist objects, highlights just a few of the important past and current movements in cross-disciplinary scholarship on this subject and concludes with a few thoughts about future directions and questions.

Several friends and colleagues to whom I owe thanks helped shape this piece by commenting on meandering lists and chapter drafts: Mimi Chusid, Sherry Fowler, Hank Glassman, Gregory Levine, Max Moerman, and Morgan Pitelka. Andy Hom, as always, provided insightful critiques and humor. My sincere thanks as well to the editors of this volume for the invitation to contribute.

RECONSIDERING AUTHENTICITY AND ART

Asian art historical scholarship and connoisseurship for much of the nineteenth and twentieth centuries had become fixated on questions of style and authenticity for a narrow range of objects (Fenollosa 1912). And while these studies laid an important foundation for the understanding of formal and chronological qualities of (primarily) paintings and sculptures, clarion calls for change (notably Sharf 2001) spurred a fruitful reaction, resulting in contextual studies of artifacts. For at least the past twenty years, scholars have treated objects as aesthetic and religious works that embody the particular sociohistorical contexts of their production by grappling with not only issues of style and iconography but also of gender, sexuality, ritual function, economics, patronage, labor, belief systems, literary links, and sociopolitical implications.

One of the most important interventions in the broader field of Japanese studies has been the recovery of the lives and stories of premodern women and non-elites. This critical literature has brought to light the diverse roles and practices of women eclipsed by a patriarchal society as well as the complex daily lives of non-elites ignored by scholarship, which tended to focus on institutional histories and the tales of powerful men.[1] This focus on the recuperation of lost or neglected stories has also impacted scholarly discourse and activism on issues of representation within the field, spurring new initiatives such as the Women in the Study of Asian Religions, cofounded by Natasha Heller and Elena Valussi.[2]

Scholars likewise continued to interrogate methodological approaches to religious objects, such as the fundamental and critical question of the appropriateness of classifying Buddhist icons as art when all evidence points to the understanding that many were vivified and embodied, and that these icons, along with a great variety of Buddhist artifacts, were not art in any Eurocentric sense (Gell 1996; Marra 2002; Pfister 2008). Art is still widely used as the most convenient catchall, but it is usually done with the understanding of the term's limitations that must be countered within the body of the analysis. And even though the use of the term is no longer inextricably bound up with old value-laden assumptions and problematic methodologies, its continued, qualified application is nevertheless rooted in epistemological biases in art history that still govern our language and, if we are not careful, our analysis. Using art to describe premodern religious objects in our scholarship and in our teaching sends the reader and student signals as to what kind of things they can expect to encounter, namely, paintings and sculptures of various types. This, on its face, does little to dispute the hierarchical ordering of objects embedded within the term and its legacy, a subject I shall return to soon.

Within the world of museums, curators also confront this issue when considering the care and display of icons divorced from their religious context. With temples and shrines increasingly struggling for visitors and donors, more religious objects have entered the museum, gallery, and art market.[3] In this displaced stage of an icon's modern afterlife,

---

[1] E.g., see Nishiguchi (1987); Wakita (1992); Amino (1994); Nomura and Usui (1996); Tonomura (1997); Takano (2000); Gay (2001); Ruch (2002); Faure (2003); Meeks (2010); Laffin (2013); Ambros (2015); and Gerhart (2018).
[2] http://libblogs.luc.edu/wisar/.
[3] Temples are increasingly interfacing with technology and contemporary culture to drive tourism. See, e.g.: the sermon-delivering android Kannon "Mindar," also discussed by Kimura in this handbook, https://www.youtube.com/watch?time_continue=3&v=fKhgSCc6OAE&feature=emb_logo; paintings by contemporary artist, Kimura Ryōko, on the exterior walls of a Buddhist temple, http://www.asahi.com/ajw/articles/AJ201908010076.html; and an anime temple offering sexualized imagery of the deity Benzaiten, http://ryohoji.jp/20140918/4723/.

has it finally transitioned into art? The Museum of Fine Arts (MFA), Boston, established in 1909 the Japanese Buddhist Temple Room, modeled on the architecture of the famous temple Hōryūji, in awareness of the problem posed by the white gallery wall for the display of religious icons. In a dramatic contrast to the brightly lit presentations of the adjoining rooms, altar-like wooden platforms raise clusters of Buddhist deities interspersed with wooden columns in a darkened space illuminated overhead by lanterns. The ambience attempts to approximate the atmosphere of a Buddhist temple for a general public who might not have the opportunity to experience icons in a Japanese ritual space.[4]

VISUAL AND MATERIAL CULTURE

Visual culture as a term helped scholars of Buddhism to problematize art as the label for artistic productions meant for worship, offerings, sacred spaces, and other practical or functional uses because of its failure to capture the objects' religious dimension. But visual culture is itself not without issue due to its overreliance on the "image" and neglect of the materials, issues of materiality, and mechanics of making. One might wonder if we need visual culture if material culture is capable of encompassing the full diversity of *things* without hierarchical strictures, particularly if material studies also ensures investigations into the meanings encoded within an object's surface and visuality. Skilled craftsmanship and beauty do not equate to superficiality, so why should we turn away from studies of what is exquisitely and carefully made?

The Buddhist concept of *shōgon* (elaborate effort and beauty engendering karmic merit) accounts in part for the artistry and abundance we see in artistic projects, but we should also allow for these artifacts to operate on different registers. That is, artistic, even opulent, commissions in addition to their karmic merit and ritual function held other value, from the highly personal to the overtly public. Moreover, sculptures, paintings, sutras, and other religious artifacts were not always ritualistically functional, indicating that their value could and did lay elsewhere. And aside from their religious registers, countless artistic productions were also social objects, and tracking the crisscrossing vectors of an artifact's many lives is part of the joy of these investigations. Paying meticulous attention to the surface's visuality and aesthetics as well as the object's materials and mechanics of production is a complex and fecund source of information. Therefore, by analyzing religious material culture through both its visuality and materiality, we have the possibility of attaining the best of both analytical worlds. We need not lose sight of the meanings communicated by an object's crafted formal qualities and intervisual community, but we can also open up questions into the process of making, the importance of materials, and its thingness.

Just as it is important to recognize the meaning within the beautiful—allowing for the understanding that beauty is a mutable concept, particularly when dealing with premodern productions—it is also imperative to open up the range of artifacts we study to include ordinary or "modest" objects (Hirasawa and Lomi 2018). The material turn that has swept through scholarship since 2000 has fundamentally and positively changed the nature of object-based studies. Somewhat curiously—but also indicative of the field's past

---

[4] Another case is the careful consideration given to creating the most resonant ways of displaying icons, and even more trickily, the interior contents of those sculptures in the newly redesigned Harvard Art Museums. See Saunders (2019).

tendency toward established canonical material and questions—the focus on materiality and "thingness" did not originate in art history, a discipline grounded in the study of objects, but rather with anthropologists like Alfred Gell (1998), literary historians like Bill Brown (2001), and social scientists Bruno Latour (1993) and Jane Bennett (2010), to name but a few. One of the key impacts of material culture studies has been its challenge to the art historical canon. The previous divisions between low and high art that elevated painting and sculpture over all else are being jettisoned. Bells, talismans, relics, reliquaries, ordinary ceramics, letter sutras, maps, censors, bezoars, and countless other material things are increasingly coming under investigation, and this diversification takes us closer to *seeing* the richness of objects through which religious life was experienced, rather than material culture being relegated to footnotes or mistrusted as primary sources.[5]

Beyond expanding the range of objects we study, material studies also asks different questions of the artifact (Rosler et al. 2013). What does the object's material composition and tangibility reveal about its history and social lives? But as pertinent calls have also articulated, it is not enough to qualify material culture as simply objects of use because this erects a false dichotomy between objects valued for being purely aesthetic and those with either functional qualities or stained by their affordability, creating the potential to reinforce elitist hierarchies that privilege the wealthy (Yonan 2011). Indeed, it is an ill-fitting dichotomy for many other reasons, but most certainly because when dealing with premodern Buddhist artifacts, the visual, material, and functional are very often inextricable. Furthermore, the concept of the "embodied object" in material culture studies is augmented when treating Buddhist artifacts because of the ritual ability to invest ordinary materials with Buddha nature. As a result, questions posed about Buddhist objects have the potential to illicit an alternative understanding of "objecthood."

Another way of accessing the full spectrum of an object's biography (Kopytoff 1986; Hoskins 1998; Gosden and Marshall 1999) is through the prism of reuse and recycling. One of the benefits of this approach is that it theorizes the religious, social, political, and personal reasons underlying the different practices and manifestations of repurposing in order to foreground the significant role that material refashioning played in Japan.[6] By focusing on the alterations both materially and conceptually, the framework of repurposing reveals an object's biographical trajectory and inevitable shifts in meaning, function, ownership, and agency. It can also expose a premodern understanding of both the commoditization and the multiplicity of purposes encompassed by a single object. The topic of reuse and recycling draws a plethora of other important discussions from the background into the scholarly conversation, including larger issues of embodiment, fragmentation, materiality, and transference, all of which help uncover the many lives of Japanese religious artifacts after their creation. In other words, it is important to interrogate the assumptions around what it means for a religious object to be "extant" today.

Other queries might concern access to objects. Who might have touched it? Experienced its material dimensions? Materialist questions (Doy 1998) into who would be allowed to see an object are particularly complex in the history of Japanese religious institutions,

---

[5]An early example is Hanley (1997), who uses material culture to explain the economic history of early modern Japan. Fabio Rambelli's work on Buddhist materialities is extensive (2007, 2019). See also Matsuzaki (1996), Mrazek and Pitelka (2008), and Baffelli and Caple (2019).

[6]Increased interest in this issue is reflected in the most recent Getty Foundation fellowship call focusing on "fragments" and the forthcoming *Ars Orientalis* special issue, "Reuse and Recycling in Japanese Visual and Material Culture," ed. Halle O'Neal (2022).

many of which would have been inaccessible to most of the population, whether from lack of wealth that restricted their travel, lack of status that barred certain doors, or issues of gender and pollution that medieval and early modern women faced. Even today, access to objects can be incredibly complicated. Some involve a dizzying number of permissions through institutional and temple bureaucracies, years' long wait, and the right connections within the Japanese academy and museum world in order to gain direct access.

Digital innovations are providing a rewarding alternative for objects difficult to access, as museums, libraries, and religious institutions increasingly make available high-quality scans of objects and texts to the interested public.[7] While no replacement for direct study, digital humanities (DH) has opened up a wealth of inventive possibilities. With the ability to reveal and revel in exquisitely fine detail and to return time and again to digital renditions for continued study rather than rely exclusively on memory and lesser-quality photography, DH has changed the way we conduct research. DH projects make it possible to animate the process of production, to deconstruct the constitutive components in order to disclose their layered relationships, to demonstrate the use of the object by rendering it in motion, to uncover the meaning within the visuality of the object—all things that traditional scholarship does but with the communicative immediacy of digital engagement that brings the artifact to life before your eyes. They also allow for interactive intervisual analysis across a range of objects, such as Akiko Walley's fragmented calligraphy online exhibition and database, *Tekagami and Kyōgire: The University of Oregon Japanese Calligraphy Exhibition*.[8] Text mining and exciting advances in artificial intelligence (AI) are unlocking with inhuman rapidity information long embedded within and across texts as well as demystifying challenging calligraphic script.[9]

DH has also had profound implications for how museums communicate with their audiences. For instance, looking to the technical art historical[10] practices of the MFA Boston, the museum has recently introduced an "open conservation space" where visitors can witness first-hand the conservation of Buddhist sculptures, involving visible and ultraviolet light photography, X-Ray, and 3D modeling.[11] Indeed, with technological advances in computed tomography (CT) scanning in the museum and art market worlds, sculptures have transformed from lacquered icon to mummified monk with a miraculous splendor that recalls the astonishing feats of premodern icons.[12] Digital pedagogies have also made a major intervention in how we teach religious material, particularly for those instructors and students who lack direct access to Japanese objects.[13]

---

[7]The digitization of the *Taishō Shinshū Daizōkyō* (http://21dzk.l.u-tokyo.ac.jp/SAT/index.html) and the associated image database, *Taishō Shinshū Daizōkyō Zuzō* (https://dzkimgs.l.u-tokyo.ac.jp/SATi/images.php?alang=ja), were landmark moments in the contemporary study of Buddhism.
[8]https://glam.uoregon.edu/s/tekagami-kyogire/page/welcome (accessed December 4, 2020).
[9]For more on digital approaches to Buddhist material, see Veidlinger (2019).
[10]Caroline Fowler (2019) points out that multiple graduate school programs in the United States and a large initiative by the Andrew W. Mellon Foundation are bridging the application of technical art history, traditionally seen as the purview of museums and conservation labs, with traditional art historical scholarship and training.
[11]The museum created a segment to reach out to potential visitors about the project: https://www.youtube.com/watch?v=Qtlml5sE8o0.
[12]See Denise Patry Leidy's essay for the National Museum of Asian Art: https://asia.si.edu/essays/lacquer-relics-and-self-mummification/.
[13]Paula R. Curtis runs the very useful *Digital Resources and Projects on East Asia* (http://prcurtis.com/DH/resources/).

FUTURE DIRECTIONS

Future directions in the study of religious objects might take into greater account the haptic nature of artifacts (Sedgwick 2003). Paying attention to the sensual dimension of objects, the experience of their physicality, and the mechanics and performativity of use can reveal how their materiality was perceived by the senses, both then and now. Scholarly explorations into the thingness of objects, their tangibility and materiality, can reveal the sometimes-hidden ways in which they were designed to be handled or seen and what senses they were created to engage. For instance, one might imagine how it felt to hold an object, for the hand to experience its weight and texture, to consider the physical requirements of its performance for the handler and any viewers.

This strand is closely linked with the ever-growing study of performativity of religious rituals and objects. These types of questions unlock the possibility of understanding the lived experience around artifacts and deepen our conceptualization of the full range of an object's design, function, and materiality. There is, of course, the impossibility of knowing for certain how contemporary viewers experienced Buddhist objects, and any exploration into the tactile dimension of objects requires imaginative thinking. However, this should not cause us to swing too far to the extreme to the neglect of the obvious sensory information of artifacts, which can tell us more about why they look the way they do—a deceptively simple question that, in the answering, can draw out the experientiality of things. And while it might seem paradoxical, explorations into the materiality and haptic nature of objects could fruitfully lead to more future studies on the immaterial, ephemeral, and intentionally invisible dimensions of Buddhist material culture, a fecund ground for further study. In addition to material studies of the immaterial, developing areas on music, sound, orality, and movement will surely produce exciting new understandings on the performance of the impermanent.

Relatedly, *making* as methodology and pedagogy is another way to interrogate the thingness of objects and the intentionality of their design through the direct experience of making replicas. Making in the form of replication opens up questions into the selection and sourcing of materials, the visuality of their combination and design, and allows for us as modern scholars to approximate their sensual dimension. It helps us to understand the required bodily mechanics involved in the production process, thereby enlivening the role of the original maker. For students, it engages them in creative learning and somatically encodes the material in different and perhaps more profound and lasting ways. Facsimiles have long augmented classroom study, but taking it a step further and asking the student to make a replica or produce their own take on the object engenders a deeper engagement with the artifact.[14] For researchers, it sparks new questions based on the experience of making a version of the object and of handling it physically and considering its substance. In the process of making, renewed emphasis is placed on makers, context, and means of first production as well as the labor and transmission of knowledge and skills. Making as research methodology and pedagogy has historic links to the tradition of creating and

---

[14]For instance, I ask students to create their own relics and reliquaries (religious associations not required) in order to engage the process of creation, of encoding memory, and of concealment. Paula R. Curtis recreates wooden tablets (*mokkan*) for her students so that they can handle the slender strips of wood and contemplate the textuality of the inscriptions. Mindy Landeck mixes tea with her students to bring this fundamental cultural practice to the classroom. Charlotte Eubanks uses a cartographic exercise whereby students map the Heian imperial court in order to understand the relationship of individuals to the spaces in which they labour and live and to visualize the flow of movement and areas of interaction.

worshiping copies of Buddhist icons, fostering fascinating discourses on the nature of original, replica, authenticity, transference, and embodiment.

And while without a doubt many additional exciting avenues of innovative research and teaching are percolating, I will close with eco art history because of its crucial links to our own perilous position in the global climate crisis (Lee 2019). Within this newly developing area, both historic and modern/contemporary material culture is being critically reexamined in light of environmental shifts, political economies, structural inequalities, and accountability in the anthropocene. At its current trajectory, this area is also primed to confront issues of colonialism underlying the field. And by probing the relationship between the materiality of art and its environmental origin and impact, an entirely new perspective about materials, sourcing, and environmental care but also degradation in the creation, maintenance, and loss of Buddhist material culture opens up.

See also Chapter 16, "Media and Technology," Chapter 24, "Sound," and Chapter 29, "Women."

CHAPTER 16

Media and Technology

Kaitlyn UGORETZ and Erica BAFFELLI

Scholars have argued that religion can always be seen as a part of mediated practices (De Vries 2001; Plate 2003; Meyer and Moors 2005; Stolow 2005). However, advancements in technology, such as the invention of the printing press, satellite broadcasting, and the internet, often precipitate transformations in the mediation of religious discourses and practices. In particular, scholars have argued that in contemporary society, it is difficult to understand religious phenomena without considering their relationship with media and cultural practices (Lynch, Mitchell, and Strahan 2011). The term "mediatization" has been employed by scholars to indicate a process by which institutions and society are shaped by and dependent on media technologies and organizations (Hjarvard 2008). Other scholars have criticized this definition, arguing that mediatization is not necessarily a universal phenomenon (Hoover 2009), nor necessarily a new and contemporary one (Morgan 2011), and proposing instead the concept of "mediation of religion" to highlight that media and religion are interdependent.

In this chapter, we look at themes emerging in the study of media and religion in Japan and possible avenues for further development. Topics of particular concern to the field are media orientations toward and representations of religion, religious content in popular media such as manga and anime, and the mediation of religion via the Internet.

OBSERVING RELIGION AND RELIGIOUS OBSERVANCE

One of the central topics in the research about media and religion in Japan has been the role played by media in shaping the image of religion and its role in, or potential danger to, society. Sawada (2004) investigates how print media in the late nineteenth century assumed the role of "public moralist" and how such media played an important role in defining religious orthodoxy. Religious groups that were perceived as a potential threat to national ideals were attacked by media campaigns and condemned as "immoral heresy" (*inshi jakyō*). In particular, studies by Takeda (1991), Inoue (1992), Sawada (2004), Stalker (2008), and Gardner (2005) have discussed the defamatory campaigns run by newspapers toward emerging religious organizations such as Tenrikyō, established in 1838 by Nakayama Miki (1798–1887) and the short-lived organization Renmonkyō, established by Shimamura Mitsu (1831–1904) in 1883.

Religious organizations continued to be closely monitored by the media during the period up to the Second World War. Morioka (1994) argues that the press uncritically embraced the accusations made by authorities toward religious organizations that were considered suspicious, while Dorman (2005) highlights that, up to the mid-1930s, some journalists were more critical toward authorities and their claims. The conflictual relationship between media and religion, in particular "new" religions, has also been one of the central themes in the field (Inoue 1994; Dorman 2012; Baffelli 2016). Media reporting on these groups in the postwar period tended to be especially critical, and influential journalists such as Ōya Sōichi also played a role in shaping the image of new religions and their practices.

In some cases, tensions between the press and "new" religions resulted in acrimonious disputes and trials, such as the Yomiuri Affair (*yomiuri jiken*) between the Buddhist organization Risshō Kōseikai and the newspaper Yomiuri in the 1950s (Morioka 1994); the weekly tabloids campaign against Soka Gakkai, a large Buddhist organization, in the 1970s; and in the 1990s, the Kōdansha Friday Affair (*Kōdansha Furaidē Jiken*), the legal dispute involving the publisher Kōdansha and the religious organization Kōfuku no Kagaku (known in English as Happy Science). Later studies have also demonstrated the role played by media in drawing public attention to particular religious trends, or "booms" (Inoue 1992; Shimazono 1992; Haga and Kisala 1995; Ishii 2008), pointing out that although these "booms" tend to be difficult to quantify, media interest has played an important role in the consumption of religious information.

In the postwar period, there have been two watershed moments in the relationship between religion and society in Japan. In 1995, Aum Shinrikyō, a religious organization established in 1984, became notorious for releasing lethal sarin gas in the Tokyo Subway, which would soon be referred to in the media as the Aum Shinrikyō Affair (*Oumu Shinrikyō jiken*) (Kisala and Mullins 2001; Baffelli and Reader 2012). Being a relatively small organization, academic studies on Aum before 1995 were limited. Hardacre (2007) discusses how media became the primary source of information about the group and how they shaped public understanding of its dynamics. Yet, studies by Reader (2000), Gardner (2001), Dorman and Reader (2007), and Baffelli (2016) showed how the relationship between media and Aum was also ambiguous, as the group actively used the media for both promoting its activities and to respond to criticism.

After 1995, however, media representations of religion, and in particular of new religions, became even more critical, with media publicly exposing groups that they considered potentially dangerous (Dorman 2005 Dorman 2012a; Baffelli 2016). Research undertaken after the Great East Japan Earthquake disasters in March 2011 discussed changes in media discourse about religion, in particular religious activities (Fujiyama 2011a, 2011b; McLaughlin 2016a). As these studies show, media reporting about religion were generally more positive as compared to the post-1995 Great Hanshin/Awaji earthquake, when religious organizations were criticized for not being sufficiently active, or their support activities were largely ignored. However, positive representations largely focused on specific interdenominational activities and tended to exclude groups that are still seen as potentially controversial.

There are several possibilities for further study, and we would like to mention three potential areas here. First, economic aspects in the relationship between media and religion have been largely overlooked, and more research is needed on the impact of revenue from advertising and on the relationship between the services of communications agency and religious organizations. Second, ethnographic research on how media texts are produced and consumed inside the organizations would shed light on both the internal decision-making process and contents (Who runs the group's publishing company? Who decides the content of magazines? What kind of guidelines are put in place, if any, for members' own use of media, such as, for example, social media?), and on followers' reactions and resistance to the introduction of new ways of communication. Finally, more analysis is needed on the role of media not only in shaping images of religion, in particular minority religions, but also in defining what should be included or excluded in the category of "religion" itself.

ANIMATING RELIGION

As may be expected, considering how large manga and anime loom in Japanese media and popular culture, several scholars of Japanese religion have examined religious engagement with comic books, animated television series, and films. Yamanaka Hiroshi's work on the religious dimensions of manga is an early example (1996). Studies have tended to cluster around a few key topics: the films of Studio Ghibli animator Miyazaki Hayao, religious organizations' use of manga and anime to boost their message to younger generations, and anime pilgrimages. A few monographs demonstrate a recent movement in the field toward sustained research and theorization of the dynamic between religion, manga, and anime.

It is difficult to overstate the impact that manga illustrator and anime auteur Miyazaki has had on these media. For decades, his stories of brave heroines and strange yet familiar lands inhabited by spirits have caught the imagination of viewers around the world. Scholars have sought to explain the enigmatic source of Miyazaki's environmental ethics and mythical motifs (Yamanaka 2008; Reinders 2016), as the creator himself disavows any religious motivation. Several have been tempted to attribute the moral and visual foundations for Miyazaki's work in Shinto tradition (Boyd and Nishimura 2004; Wright and Clode 2005), though others—including Miyazaki himself—have argued against this interpretation (Miyazaki in Vincentelli 1999; Thomas 2012).

It is important to note, however, that viewers' potentially religious interpretations of anime are multifarious, personal, and highly contextual (Ugoretz 2019a). Jolyon Baraka Thomas (2012) and Eriko Ogihara-Schuck (2014) find a productive way past the issue of Miyazaki's ambiguous authorial intent by conducting audience reception studies. Thomas surveys Japanese fans and discussion threads on the Japanese social media platform MIXI, whereas Ogihara-Schuck compares American and German audiences' perceptions of religious content when presented with various translation strategies and visuals. Taken together, Thomas and Ogihara-Schuck convincingly illustrate that a range of interpretations of Miyazaki's spiritually charged media are possible, from tradition-affirming, to ambiguously spiritual, to simply entertaining. These studies offer scholars useful methodologies that could be applied to numerous anime which feature religious content or inspire religious responses.

Religious organizations are keenly aware of the popularity of manga and anime and their potential as a medium for their representation and messaging. Erica Baffelli (2016) has examined the media strategies of new religions in Japan, including Aum Shinrikyō and Kōfuku no Kagaku. Though new religious movements are often early adopters of new technology and media, traditional religious institutions have also dabbled in producing animated content. Ryōhōji, a Nichiren sect temple in a suburb of western Tokyo, has harnessed animated media as a skillful means to reach a wider audience and attract visitors by showing that they are in tune with "modern," popular culture (Porcu 2014; Thomas 2015). Establishing its own branding company, Hachifuku, Ryōhōji boasts manga-inspired *kawaii* (cute) and *moe* (sexy-cute) transformations of its enshrined deities, several animated music videos on YouTube, and a website featuring themed merchandise. Comparing cases like Ryōhōji with Buddhist temples' historical promotion of various visual and textual media challenges the notion that the "media mix," or transmedia franchise, is truly a modern Japanese marketing innovation, rather than the latest iteration of a much older tactic.

Bearing in mind that many forms of media have historically been employed to promote pilgrimages (Reader 2006), so-called anime pilgrimages have become a topic of interest as throngs of fans conspicuously visit shrines, temples, and other "sacred sites" that appear in anime (Okamoto 2015, 2018; Imai 2018; see also Chapter 20 by Reader in this volume). At Shinto shrines like Washinomiya Shrine in Saitama Prefecture (which appears in the wildly popular franchise "Lucky Star"), visitors may leave behind *ema* (votive tablets) that feature artwork and prayers dedicated to the anime's characters as often as the enshrined kami, melding traditional rituals and sensibilities with aesthetics and practices inspired by new media (Imai 2009; Andrews 2014). This phenomenon raises an intriguing question for scholars of media and religion alike: where do fandom and tourism end and religious devotion and pilgrimage begin (Imai 2018)?

To date, there are very few books that grapple with religion and anime by exploring a broad range of genres and titles in a comprehensive and theoretical fashion. Thomas (2012) combines media content analysis with sociological methods to consider the role of religion in both the production and consumption of manga and anime. He asserts through his concept of *shūkyō asobi* or "recreating religion" that religion and entertainment are bound together in recursive relationships. Katherine Buljan and Carole M. Cusack (2015) sketch the intersecting histories of the development of manga and anime from premodern precursors to modern innovations, the religious and supernatural wellsprings that Japanese media draw from and the influence that religious elements have on fan cultures in Japan as well as the West.

Thomas (2012) and Buljan and Cusack (2015) suggest several productive avenues for further research. There is much more to be learned about both the religious production and consumption of manga and anime. Longitudinal sociological studies of how particular communities engage with anime in a religious or spiritual mode are sorely needed to contextualize what it is about the medium that is so affecting. For example, Ugoretz has found that anime including Miyazaki's oeuvre, Shinkai Makoto's blockbuster film *Kimi no na wa* (Your Name), and other series that prominently feature kami function as "first encounters" with, and touchstones for, Japanese religiosity among transnational Shinto practitioners in digital communities (Ugoretz 2019b). Finally, the field would benefit from greater critical discussion of the supposed relationship between "animism," animation and anime (Castiglioni 2019; Thomas 2019c).

UPLOADING RELIGION

The study of digital religion has developed rapidly over the last thirty years, as scholars strive to keep pace with the evolution of the internet and individuals' creative uses thereof. The first wave of digital religion scholars in the 1990s was primarily concerned with identifying and describing religion on the Internet (Campbell 2017). Researchers predicted that the internet would radically transform religious practice, though they speculated as to whether this influence would ultimately save or threaten religious institutions (Campbell and Lövheim 2011).

The social media revolution known as Web 2.0 (or more popularly as the World Wide Web)—sparked the second wave of research in the early 2000s, this time focused on establishing a taxonomy of key themes and forms of digital religion (Cowan and Hadden 2000). Christopher Helland (2000) distinguished between "religion online" and "online religion," with the former referring to the expansion of offline religious traditions into cyberspace, while the latter covered what could be called "digitally native" online religious activity. In Japan, religious organizations and communities developed a significant online presence, and *intānetto sanpai* ("online worship") became a buzzword in popular media, as well as academic publications, as the possible future of religion (Reader and Tanabe 1998: 217–22). Numerous controversies within religious traditions concerning use of the internet emerged, highlighting key issues relating to innovation, authority, community, and identity (Dawson and Cowan 2004). For example, Mark MacWilliams has documented the intense debate within Nichiren Buddhist organizations around the online viewing and sharing of *gohonzon*, calligraphic mandala scrolls that serve as the "object of fundamental respect or devotion" (2006: 91).

The third wave of research, which pioneer of digital religion studies Heidi Campbell (2017) identifies as the "theoretical turn," saw scholars reflect on the earlier and somewhat premature predictions of the field and seek new methods and theories to explain the relationships between religion and new media. The fourth wave continued this critical, reflexive mode. As smartphones, wearable tech, and internet access proliferated—becoming ubiquitous for some, though not all—scholars questioned the relationship between "offline" and "online."

Study on religion and the internet in Japan started in the late 1990s, corresponding to the first wave of research mentioned above. Studies, including Ikegami and Nakamaki (1996); Tamura (1998); Tosa (1998); Kurosaki (2000); and Inoue ed. (2003), mapped the presence of websites run by religious organizations and how search engines categorized religion. In 1998, a research project named the Archive for Religion Information was set up at the Institute for Japanese Culture and Classics at Kokugakuin University. In the following years, other projects were supported by the Japanese Association for the Study of Religion and Society, such as "Jōhō Jidai to Shūkyō" (Information Age and Religion, 1996–8, led by Nakamaki Hirochika) and "Intānetto to Shūkyō" (Internet and Religion, 1998–2001, led by Tamura Takanori). These were followed by the project on "Shūkyō Comyunikēshon" (Religious Communication) in 2001, renamed "Shūkyō to Jōhō Gijutsu" (Religion and Information Technology) in 2011. In 1999, the project "Cyber Religion Self-Representation and Self-Understanding of Religious Communities on the Japanese Internet—The WWW as a Source for Japanese Studies" was established at Tübingen University (Germany) and led by Klaus Antoni, Birgit Staemmler, and Petra Kienle.

The first edited volume on digital religion in Japan to be published in English, edited by Erica Baffelli, Ian Reader, and Birgit Staemmler (2011), sits between these two later waves. The volume surveys a range of religious traditions—from Shinto shrines and Shin Buddhism to Kōfuku no Kagaku and Soka Gakkai—and digital media, including bulletin board systems (BBS), blogs, social networking services (SNS), and Wikipedia. The contributors find that the internet has predominantly reproduced and expanded religious institutions' and individuals' media strategies rather than totally transforming "the way people *do* religion" (MacWilliams 2006: 91, emphasis in original). In other words, in the first decade of the internet as we know it today, religion online won out over online religion.

As the internet becomes increasingly integrated into our everyday lives, our research should reflect this reality. Research on religion mediated by the internet must interrogate digital *and* material dimensions, as both are a part of human experience (Latour 2005;

Verbeek 2005). How do our physical and sociocultural contexts constrain or depend upon our use of various technologies? How, in turn, does the digital inform our bodily sensibilities and social relations? This co-constitutive, co-agentive relationship between the human body and technology is exemplified through what is now commonly referred to as the "Internet of Things" (IoT), a network of physical objects integrated into the Internet and are active participants in people's lives (Carretero and García 2013). Recent studies of Japanese religion on the internet have begun to explore the digital more broadly and deeply in response to these new theories, methods, and media, a trend that we hope will continue. Gould, Kohn, and Gibbs (2019) examine electronic and digital transformations of Japanese death rituals in the material culture of the *butsudan*, the domestic Buddhist altar, and how these innovations mediate relations with the dead. One of this chapter's authors, Kaitlyn Ugoretz, is conducting doctoral research that explores how Facebook's software plays a role in shaping digital Shinto communities' online practices and relationships with ritual objects and their digital representations.

Much of the internet in its current form remains unexplored by scholars of Japanese religion, and new dynamics, platforms, and practices are sure to emerge. Researchers have the practically impossible, but necessary, task of capturing snapshots (or screenshots) of the networks at the present moment for analysis, theorizing based upon an understanding of these networks over the *longue durée*, and staying up to date on new developments in the contemporary media landscape. At the moment, there is very little scholarship focusing on global social media platforms, including, but not limited to, Facebook, Twitter, Reddit, and Instagram, as well as Japanese language sites such as MIXI and 2ch/5ch.

FUTURE DIRECTIONS

As illustrated by surveying the state of the field and emerging trends in the study of the relationship between media and religion in the Japanese context, certain kinds of print and digital media are privileged while others, just as popular and complex, are heavily understudied. Religion and video game studies is an excellent example of a subject to which scholars of Japanese religion and media are well positioned to contribute. Video game studies is a growing subfield of digital religion, pioneered by the work of Heidi Campbell and Gregory Grieve (2014), Christopher Helland, Kerstin Radde-Antweiler, Xenia Zeiler (2018), and Rachel Wagner (2012), among others. The field currently has two dedicated academic journals: *Online—Heidelberg Journal of Religions on the Internet*, edited by Gregor Ahn and Tobias Knoll, and *gamevironments*, edited by Radde-Antweiler and Zeiler (Bosman 2019). Grieve, Helland, Radde-Antweiler, and Zeiler are spearheading the "Video Game Development in Asia" research project hosted by the University of Helsinki (Grieve et al. 2018).

Although Japan is known for consistently leading the video game industry, relatively little research has focused on Japanese religion in digital games. Jason Anthony (2014) and Rachael Hutchinson (2019) have notably examined Clover Studio and Capcom's popular 2006 game, *Okami*. Hirafuji Kikuko's work on Japanese mythology in popular culture, particularly video games, demonstrates that religious content and religious engagement with games is a promising direction for future research (2006, 2007, 2010).

There are several other academic lacunae we would like to see filled. More ethnographic study of the reception and impact of media is needed, particularly that which explores transnational engagements with Japanese religion and media. For example, Marie Kondo's popular resurgence in the West thanks to the translation of her books, *The Life-Changing*

Magic of Tidying Up (2014) and *Spark Joy* (2016), into English and her 2019 Netflix series has sparked global interest in her brand of "Japanese" spirituality (Thomas 2019a; Fickle, Leong, and Ting 2019).

There is also ample room for further exploration regarding creative interactions with media content on social media platforms, such as the use of videos created by religious organizations or religious topics and images in video-sharing websites like Niko Niko Dōga. Paul Levinson refers to these media platforms as "new new media" (2014). However, as many other new media theorists have critiqued, the distinctions between "new" and "old" media have broken down: when juxtaposed with Instagram and Quibi, are email and blogs still qualitatively new (Lunenfeld 1999; Herbig, Herrmann, and Tyma 2014)? If there is something beyond today's "new media," then it will be the new "new media." The horizon is ever beyond our reach even as new waves crest and fall. As Herbig, Herrmann, and Tyma suggest, perhaps we need new words to describe media (2014). With such a rich history of interactions between religion and media in Japan to draw upon, scholars of Japanese religion have the potential to contribute to this discussion.

Finally, we must note that this chapter was written in the midst of the global Covid-19 ("novel coronavirus") pandemic, which has precipitated severe restrictions on face-to-face interactions and an unprecedented shift toward digital media. In a matter of weeks in the winter and spring of 2020, national and local governments ordered the indefinite closing of schools, businesses, restaurants, and even religious organizations, as well as the social distancing of citizens. Creative use of the internet has become critical to the continuation of services and social interaction.

While temples and shrines have remained largely ambivalent to using the internet, many are innovating as demand for spiritual services increases. For example, several Shinto shrines in Japan and the United States have begun live-streaming purificatory rituals and composing prayers for a swift end to the epidemic. The Japanese internet has plucked the *amabie*—a scaled, three-legged *yōkai* (supernatural creature) with long hair and a beak—from obscurity, as it is said that seeing and reproducing its image ensures an abundant harvest and protects against epidemics (Hayashi 2020). People from all around the world are participating in the #AMABIEchallenge on Twitter, sharing their own apotropaic creations (Saunders 2020). Scholarship is needed to document current changes and determine how great and lasting of an impact the pandemic will have on Japanese religious organizations' and communities' relationships with media going forward.

See also Chapter 4, "Disasters," Chapter 5, "Economy and Spirituality," Chapter 15, "Materiality," Chapter 19, "'New Religions'," and Chapter 27, "Spirituality."

CASE STUDY

World-Wide Shinto: The Globalization of "Japanese" Religion

Kaitlyn UGORETZ

Brian[1] logged into Facebook one morning and checked the recent activity in the three Shinto interest groups in which he serves as an admin (short for "administrator"). The online Shinto communities (OSCs) had been busy: a handful of posts prompted hundreds of comments from both regularly active stakeholders and typically nonresponsive "lurkers." Usually an amiable admin who favors a light touch when moderating, Brian was so frustrated by what he saw that he posted a public announcement:

> Suddenly many people are asking: "Can non-Japanese practice Shinto?" There are ordained non-Japanese priests, shrines outside of Japan, and you would be hard-pressed to find Japanese opposed to non-Japanese practicing Shinto. There do exist legitimate concerns about people approaching Shinto disrespectfully or "mixing" it with other faiths. However, the simple question, "Is it okay for non-Japanese to practice Shinto (respectfully)" has a simple answer of "yes," and it's frankly bloody obvious if you just run a Google search. Please stop asking.

One member replied: "If a lot of people are asking, then the answer is not as obvious as you think it is."

Such exchanges between online Shinto community members, the majority of whom are not ethnically Japanese and live outside Japan, illustrate the complex and contested nature of contemporary Shinto. Scholars of Japanese religion are likely all too familiar with the definition of Shinto reinforced institutionally by the shrine umbrella organization Jinja Honchō, as well as conventionally in popular discourse: *Shinto is the indigenous faith of the people and land of Japan, an ancient tradition without founder, doctrine, or sacred texts.* While scholars have demonstrated that the construction of Shinto has been historically linked to transregional flows of knowledge, material, and power, essentialist interpretations of the tradition continue to hold currency among a wide range of audiences (Como 2009; Nakajima 2010; Suga 2010; Scheid and Nakai 2013; Dessì 2017; Hardacre 2017). In fact, while the recent growth of global Shinto communities speaks to the appeal

---

[1] The name has been changed to preserve anonymity.

of the tradition's ostensible ancient and foreign origins, their development calls such claims into question on a number of levels (Rots 2017b).

STUDYING ONLINE RELIGIOUS COMMUNITIES

Campbell and Lövheim (2011) identify four stages in the development of digital religion studies. Following descriptive, taxonomical, and theoretical turns, current scholarship is particularly concerned with the co-constitution of actors' online and offline social worlds. My research methodology is primarily based upon *netnography*, a specific set of research practices, orientations, and ethics related to the ethnographic study of the internet and social media networks (Kozinets 2015). Netnography incorporates the adaptation of traditional ethnographic methods, while emphasizing the use of "digitally native" methods for the collection, analysis, and presentation of digital data.

Acknowledging the co-determinative and co-constructive relationship between human and technological agents, I am interested in not only how people creatively mobilize digital technologies but also the ways in which technologies shape people's perceptions and practices. As such, I consider how the internet structures interactions within online religious communities. In order to examine the crucial offline experiences that ground individuals' identities as Shinto practitioners, I combine visual anthropology, text analysis, and participant observation to trace OSC members' material practices and encounters in the "real world," which include posting images of shrine visits, conducting rituals at domestic altars, and attending lectures on Shinto at Japanese cultural events. In this way, my research demonstrates that online and offline social networks work together to enable and augment a global Shinto subjectivity.

GENEALOGY OF ONLINE SHINTO COMMUNITIES

In the early 2000s, a software revolution transformed the character of the internet from a static archive to the dynamic social media environment known as Web 2.0. Online groups explicitly interested in Shinto can be traced back to the advent of Web 2.0, with the creation of the Shinto Mailing List (ShintoML) on Yahoo! Groups in 2000. ShintoML was extremely active for ten years, though activity began to taper off in 2010 as ShintoML members migrated to Facebook following the platform's upgrading of group features.

Today, as many as ten thousand people are members of an active Facebook OSC. These members tend to be non-Japanese with general knowledge of Japanese history and culture gleaned from popular Japanese media, the internet, and brief trips to Japan. However, the most active members have extensive knowledge of Shinto gained through personal study, several years of membership in OSCs, and ritual practice. A 2019 survey of fifty OSC members and *kamidana* ownership indicates that the majority live in the United States and the UK, although membership truly spans the globe. Most were raised in nominally Christian households, though others grew up in atheist and Buddhist families. Official group leadership, on the other hand, is populated by a mix of Japanese, part-Japanese, and Caucasian admins with varying levels of institutional involvement, ranging from lay shrine caretaker to senior priest.

KEY QUESTIONS IN GLOBAL SHINTO STUDIES

Several themes significant for the study of Japanese religions emerge from serious engagement with online Shinto communities. With such a diverse and dispersed collection of Shinto clergy and lay practitioners, compounded by a lack of access to Shinto shrines and materials, OSCs must creatively mobilize the sources and platforms available to them to establish a practical canon of shared knowledge, beliefs, and practices. Issues of authority are raised as OSC members seek, construct, and contest the legitimization of personal approaches to Shinto within a polyvocal network of shrines from various traditions within Shinto, academic and popular publications, online forums, blogs, wikis, and popular culture products. Notions of race, culture, and authenticity are complicated as self-identified non-Japanese Shinto practitioners reflexively question the boundaries of their participation in an avowedly indigenous tradition. Moreover, Shinto ontologies of the sacred are reconfigured as OSC members theorize and manage their relationships with kami, their local environment, and everyday and existential crises. Finally, situating these communities within discussions of Western and global religious movements, as well as historical Japanese ones, begs the complementary questions: What is "Japanese" about this emerging Shinto, and what about it is "global"?

CASE STUDY

Robots

KIMURA Takeshi

In March 2019, the Android Kannon "Mindar" (pronounced as *Maindar*, マインダー) at the Kōdaiji Zen Temple in Kyoto was unveiled to the public. To grasp its significance, it is necessary to locate it in its religious, cultural, and technological contexts. This entry thus is divided into three parts: the planning and creating process; the performance of the Android Kannon Mindar; and perceptions of and reactions to this phenomenon.

THE PLANNING AND CREATING PROCESS

A Rinzai Zen monk Gotō Tenshō at Kodai-ji Zen Temple had been wondering for a long time how one might utilize a computer to promoting the teaching of Buddhism. In July 2017, Ishiguro Hiroshi, a well-known robotics scholar at Osaka University, visited Kōdaiji, bringing several small robots with him. He had a conversation with Gotō, who suggested to Ishiguro that it might be an interesting idea to create a robot Śākyamuni.

In September 2017 was the first meeting to discuss what precisely to create, with Gotō, Ishiguro, several Zen monks, and others in attendance. The tentative original idea was that several robots would converse together on the teachings of Buddha. However, for technical reasons, a robot engaged in a monologue was adopted instead. After they chose the *Heart Sutra* to be narrated, they discussed which Buddha the robots would represent, and finally they decided on the Bodhisattva Kannon (Avalokiteśvara). Ishiguro proposed using the "Alter" robot, which he created with Ikegami Takashi of Tokyo University in 2016, as a prototype for the Android Kannon.

Ogawa Hiroshi, a robotics scholar at Osaka University, was actually responsible for the engineering part. For him, the appearance of the Android Kannon was a matter of design. He participated in the project as a sort of research experiment. Zen monks Sakaida Taisen (Kenninji Temple), Unrin'in Sōseki (Reigenin Temple), and Honda Dōryū (Baishōin Temple) were assigned to generate the narrative scenario based on books by Yamada Mumon, Nakamura Hajime, and others. They created a narration in which the Android Kannon Mindar begins to explain two key Buddhist concepts: *kū* (空, Emptiness) first and *jihi* (慈悲, Compassion) next. The other group was responsible for making a projection mapping.

Looking back at the historical development of Buddhist images from the earliest ones to various recent statues of buddhas and bodhisattvas, Gotō emphasized that the Android Kannon forms the point of contact between two backgrounds. Buddhist temples have always been the location of cutting-edge culture and technology as well as teaching, and the Bodhisattva Kannon traditionally manifests herself in thirty-three different forms; this time, as an android.

Mindar's Actual Performance

In order to understand how Mindar functions as a teaching tool, it is important to learn to see how Mindar performs within the context of Zen teaching. Mindar is programmed to deliver a sermon at a rather high vocal pitch on the teachings of the *Heart Sutra* for about thirty minutes. It stands still, changing facial expressions and moving its arms in the Kyōka Hall of the temple. On the front wall, English and Chinese translations of the sermons appear. On the 360-degree walls, changing pictures and scenery are programmed to be projected as the narration progresses. At the same time, prerecorded videos of the people sitting and listening to Mindar's sermon are projected on the wall. When an image of a person in the prerecorded video asks a question, it becomes clearly recognizable temporarily.

Mindar draws attention to its own metallic body and says it gives a hint for an understanding of the teaching of Buddha. Then, the android begins to address people's problems and sufferings, then explains the teaching of the *Heart Sutra*, especially the notion of emptiness: as everything changes and even the meaning of "I" or oneself changes, nothing is permanent. Then, Mindar asks what difference lies between humans and an android robot. The projected audience answers that a robot does not feel worries and troubles while humans do. Through the teaching of emptiness, humans learn to feel emphatic sympathy, and eventually, compassion emerges in their mind. Mindar's sermon ends with the words of the *Heart Sutra* projected on the wall soaring up into the screen of the ceiling.

Both Japanese and foreigners came to listen to the sermon of Mindar, and gave various responses to the unveiling event. Isobe Yumi, a staff member from Kōdaiji who was involved in Mindar project from the beginning, told me about a few interesting responses. Several members in the audience noted that the shadow of Mindar, with wires coming out of the head, appears to be more like the "real" Kannon. Several people wept during Mindar's sermon, something the monks did not expect.

In the Kōdaiji visitor comment book, responses by Japanese audience members are a mixture of positive and negative. One says that at the beginning, he felt awkward with the Android Kannon, but by the end, he was surprised to find that he accepted it. One says that the Android Kannon's sermon on the *Heart Sutra* was as moving as if possessed by the real Kannon. In contrast, one says that it just seems like a cold machine.

Responses by foreigners (mostly from Western countries) were sometimes negative, reflecting Western views of robots. One wrote that it is not right to build and showcase a machine priest at a religious institution. From the Buddhist world, Kōdaiji has received relatively positive responses. Monks of other Buddhist sects have come to see the android individually or as a group. The Zen monks who were responsible for the scenario regard the Android Kannon as a successful starting point to the teaching of Buddhism.

The Android Kannon Mindar is the product of various factors: negotiated ideas and plans among monks and robotics scholars, what type of robotics technology Ishiguro and Ogawa could offer, a limited budget, and limited time. Reflecting on future technological developments, Gotō says that artificial intelligence could be employed so that the Android Kannon would be able to converse with participants about the Buddhist teachings. This might be the next plan.

CHAPTER 17

Medicine

Katja TRIPLETT

Medicine and religion, with their respective ideas and practices concerned with healing, have long been connected in Japan. From the incorporation of Buddhism into Japanese culture from the sixth century CE, until Buddhist and medical practice were officially separated in the Meiji period, Buddhism and medicine were deeply intertwined.

The history of medicine and healing culture prior to the sixth century is as difficult to assess as prehistoric religion in Japan. Archaeological finds that include paleopathological data (data on ancient diseases) are relatively scarce. Relying on early textual sources from periods after the incorporation of Buddhism and Chinese-style medicine into Japanese culture distorts perspectives on ancient Japanese medicine, which appears to have been dominated by the idea of diseases caused by divine wrath or curses (*tatari*) and divine punishment for moral misdeeds. According to the *Nihon shoki* (720), two deities are responsible for creating the available methods for healing both humans and animals: Ōnamuchi no mikoto 大汝命 and Sukunabikona no mikoto 少彦名命. For most of Japanese history, however, the Chinese founding figure of medical healing, Shennong (Japanese: Shinnō) 神農, was the central focus of the doctors' reverence. Early texts such as the local gazetteers (*fudoki*) mention the use of prayer, exorcisms (*majinai*), and apotropaic methods, as well as bathing in hot springs—the latter a practice popular to this day. While there were no Daoist institutions in Nara period Japan, Daoist exorcisms, a tradition imported from China, were practiced. The inclusion of certain Daoist ritual forms and techniques added not only to the plurality of religion (Como 2015) but also to the plurality of curative techniques.

In Mahāyāna Buddhism, the form of Buddhism that came to Japan from China and Korea, devotion can be expressed through work to heal those afflicted with disease. While ordained Buddhists provide rituals for well-being and health, some Mahāyāna Buddhist texts state that it is also their duty to provide medical services to heal the physical body of those that are in pain. The popular epithet of the Buddha as the King of Doctors or the Supreme Healer has also encouraged monks and nuns to train in medicine to fulfill their duty of compassionate action. Famously, the Four Noble Truths, the foundation for all of the Buddha's teachings, are often related in the language of medicine: the Buddha identifies the symptoms of suffering (diagnosis), reveals the causes for suffering (etiology), states that there is a way to heal the disease (recovery), and finally prescribes a treatment, the path to liberation from suffering (Kleine and Triplett 2012: 1–2). Additionally, while sickness (*byō* 病) is one of the four sufferings (birth, old age, sickness, and death), in many texts it is used to denote all forms of suffering. The eradication of sickness is thus considered the ultimate liberation from suffering.

While Buddhism is concerned with healing as salvation, medicine is generally focused on healing the physical bodies of humans and animals by alleviating pain, ensuring well-being, and securing medical knowledge such as records of *materia medica*, medical formulae, and therapies. In Japan, where Buddhist monastics cared for people's physical well-being, religious and medical practice overlapped significantly for centuries. This does not mean, however, that all monastics were medical doctors or that there were no doctors outside Buddhist institutions. Japan's ruling elites were treated by both medically trained Buddhist monastics (*sōi* 僧医) and secular court doctors. Monastics and healers from the religious tradition of Shugendō treated other members of society. The practice of medicine followed particular monastic lineages as well as family genealogies. Religious and secular medical practitioners were thus in competition in ancient and medieval times.

This competition continued into the early modern period, which saw the rise of doctors trained at Neo-Confucian institutions and therefore outside of monastic circles. Access to such coveted knowledge as Chinese *materia medica* (*honzō* 本草), formulae and therapies (*hō* 方) including needling and moxibustion (*shinkyū* 鍼灸), and Indian-style eye surgery appears to have been restricted—or rather, attempts were made to restrict it—to initiates. However, as both monastic and Neo-Confucian doctors often shared close family ties, healing methods appear to have been shared despite initiatory vows to keep them secret. Nonetheless, the tradition of secrecy in the field of medicine poses a major challenge to the academic study of the history of medicine and religion in Japan. It was only in the early modern period, for instance, that medical lore was increasingly written down instead of merely passed down orally, and it is only in recent decades that the private archives of medical family clans have made previously secret records (*hiden* 秘伝, *kuden* 口伝) available for research (Okuzawa 1997).

From the sixth century onward, Buddhist texts, statues, images, and other expressions of material culture, as well as the practice of Chinese-style medicine, entered Japan in several waves. The new knowledge, tools, and materials were circulated, reproduced, and further developed by different actors in various social fields, including state-sponsored educational institutions, the imperial court, religious sanctuaries, and hospitals. The trend of following the Chinese model slowly changed during the late sixteenth century, when traders and Catholic missionaries from Europe started introducing new knowledge to Japan. Doctors and scholars adopted early modern and modern European medical ideas and further added to an already hybrid and highly dynamic medical culture in Japan. The close ties between Buddhist and medical practice produced a variety of healers, including non-ordained itinerant ritualists who provided services in Japan for many centuries. These healers, who were not part of the literati culture, have not received the attention they deserve. This is partly due to the lack of sources that would allow the activities of these important social actors to be highlighted.

After the official separation of religion and medicine in 1874, formerly Buddhist doctors either changed to a secular status and obtained a state medical license or gave up medicine altogether and devoted themselves to what was officially described as "religious" Buddhist practice. Monastics who had been doctors were thus limited to providing pastoral care and facilitating fundraising for the former temple hospitals, while the hospitals themselves changed ownership.

The connections between medicine and Buddhism in Japan are various. Buddhist rituals that pertain to healing the physical body and removing disease are referred to as *kaji* 加持 (Sanskrit: *adhiṣṭhāna*, "assistance") rituals. *Kaji* has remained the prevalent paradigm of Esoteric Buddhist healing since the Heian period. Pure Land Buddhist references to medicine link it to the practice of chanting Buddha Amida's name (*nenbutsu*) and directing one's thoughts to being born in his Pure Land—a realm featuring beings freed from sickness. Temples in the Zen Buddhist tradition offered medicines to cure all illnesses, drive out poison and bestow everlasting health (Williams 2005: 86–116). Today, pilgrimage sanctuaries may serve teas made from medicinal substances or provide healing water. Age-old cults of Buddhist deities with curative powers, especially Yakushi Nyorai (Sanskrit: *Bhaiṣajyaguru*), the "Medicine Buddha," and Kannon Bosatsu, are popular throughout Japan.

STATE OF THE FIELD

The field of the study of medicine and religion in Japan includes works of various disciplines and studies such as the history of medicine, philological studies of medical sources, cultural history of medicine, folk medicine, Buddhist folklore studies, biographical studies of historical figures, history of Buddhism, Buddhist studies, religious studies, and, finally, works on Buddhism and medicine (cf. Triplett 2019a: 6–16).

Fujikawa Yū (1865–1940) and Hattori Toshirō (also: Toshiyoshi, 1906–1992) address the topic of religion in their volumes on the history of medicine in Japan. Fujikawa's work includes the 1934 (revised edition 1978) summary of Japanese medical history in English, a translation from his German book on the topic (1911, reprinted 1976). Fujikawa collected Japanese medical sources to preserve them after the radical shift to European medicine. He appreciated premodern Japanese medicine but was an advocate for the shift to modern biomedicine. Hattori Toshirō, doctor and historian of medicine, shared this viewpoint. His history of medicine appeared between 1945 and 1978 covering the Nara to the Edo periods. Hattori emphasized the Indian and Chinese influences on early Japanese medicine. In a special volume (Hattori 1968), he explored Indian Buddhist sources to present what he called "Śākyamuni's medicine" (*Shaka no igaku*). Finally, Sakai Shizu published a now standard work on the history of Japanese medicine and healing in 1982.

In European languages, we encounter some aspects of religious history in Erhard Rosner's *Medizingeschichte Japans* (1989), an outline of the history of medicine in Japan in handbook format, and in the richly illustrated outline of Japanese traditional medicine by Wolfgang Michel-Zaitsu (2017). A German translation, published in 1999, of Ishihara Akira's (1924–1980) seminal book of 1959 relays important intellectual developments in the field of Japanese medicine. French-language volumes on the history of medicine in Japan were published by Pierre Huard et al. (1974) and Mieko Macé (2013). Those interested in the history of Japanese medicine in the English language, therefore, still have to rely on Fujikawa's work from the early twentieth century. However, Japan is well referenced in the volume entitled *Asian Medical Systems: A Comparative Study*, edited by Charles Leslie (1976) (Otsuka 1976).

Text editions of major medical sources include the 1993–2012 complete edition and translation into modern Japanese of the tenth-century compilation of medical texts from the Sui and Tang period China, the *Ishinpō* 医心方 (Essentials of Medicine). The editor Maki Sachiko, a historian and literary author, depicts premodern Japanese as "primitive." This evolutionist way of relating the history of medicine as the history of an increasing progression is shared by other authors. Studies on the Dutch School (*rangaku*) of science, technology, and medicine of the late Muromachi and the Edo periods focus exclusively on the impact of European medicine on healing in Japan (see, e.g., Beukers et al. 1991). However, the medical culture in these periods was highly eclectic, a point rarely mentioned in such studies.

Studies on traditional Chinese-style medicine (*kanpō* 漢方) as practiced in Japan, in contrast, tend to depict traditional medicine as superior to the Western models (e.g., Kosoto 1999). Cultural history writing with a focus on medicine characteristically includes so-called folk medicine in particular places or periods (Jannetta 1987). Other works looking at healing and therapies from ethnographical and folkloristic perspectives concentrate on *materia medica* and the production of healing remedies in Japanese culture (Miura 1980). Social, scientific, and anthropological studies centering on early modern or contemporary phenomena underscore the eclectic nature of Japanese medical culture but tend to ignore the historical perspective (these include, among others, Lock 1980; Ohnuki-Tierney 1984; Norbeck and Lock 1987; Sonoda 1988, 2010; and Powell and Anesaki 1990).

In addition, the subjects of healing and medicine in Japanese Buddhism feature prominently in Buddhist folklore studies (*bukkyō minzokugaku* 仏教民俗学), a field pioneered by historian Gorai Shigeru 五来重 (1908–1993). A volume edited by Gorai (1986) on different facets of devotional practices to Yakushi Nyorai is a key publication on this subject. Biographical studies of historical figures in Japan include publications on the Buddhist priest and physician Kajiwara Shōzen 梶原性全 (1265–1337) and his two influential medical works, the *Ton'ishō* 頓医抄 (Book of the Simple Doctor, 1303) and the *Man'anpō* 万安方 (Myriad Relief Formulas, 1315) (Goble 2009, 2011). The charismatic monk and Buddhist reformer Eison (or Eizon, 1201–1290) famously established bathhouses and other facilities to provide relief for outcasts, including those afflicted by leprosy (Quinter 2015: 105). The Neo-Confucian physician Kaibara Ekiken (or Ekken) (1630–1714) has received much attention for his ideas on medicine and other fields (Asuka 2003).

Unsurprisingly, works on Japanese Buddhist medicine reveal apologetic tendencies when the author is both a doctor and a Buddhist teacher (see, e.g., Obinata 1965; Kawada 1976, 2013). They focus on compassion, caring for suffering beings, and the social dimension of medical practice in Buddhism from a normative standpoint. Publications on "Buddhist medicine" (*bukkyō igaku* 仏教医学), a modern term, usually refer to medical ideas and practices from the Indian cultural sphere as contained in Buddhist texts known in East Asia (Fukunaga 1990).

Studies on early ideas of healing and medicine base their findings on Buddhist legends (*setsuwa*), especially those that report miracle healings and examples from Heian court literature. Some picture scrolls (*emakimono*) include images of the sick and medical treatments, providing insights into the medical culture of the past; particularly interesting in this respect is the twelfth-century picture scroll "Stories of the Hungry Ghosts" (*Gaki zōshi* 餓鬼草紙). Myths and legends from both Shintō and Buddhist traditions that describe physical disorders and their treatment in the context of religious ideas and rituals are also valuable sources.

In terms of works in the field of history of Buddhism in general, Paul Demiéville's encyclopedia entry on "sickness" (*byō*) (1937, 1985) laid the groundwork for the study of Buddhism and medicine in Western languages. Another classic study on the topic of Buddhism and healing is Raoul Birnbaum's book on the devotional cult of Bhaiṣajyaguru first published in 1979. On Esoteric Buddhism and medicine in Japan more specifically, there are two essays by the historian Nihon'yanagi Kenji on the use of ritual substances in Japanese Buddhist tradition (1994, 1997). Michel Strickmann explored "magical medicine" (e.g., spirit possession, demonology, exorcism) in East Asian Buddhism and Daoism with references to Japan (2002). Finally, a volume on the history of medical therapeutics (*iryō*) in ancient and medieval Japanese Buddhism was published by Shinmura Taku in 2013, directed to a general (Japanese) audience.

NEW APPROACHES

Addressing the challenges outlined above and avoiding the pitfalls of studying premodern medical systems in connection with religion requires—from a study of religions perspective— new approaches in methodology and theoretical considerations.

The basic theoretical problem relates to categorization. In order to study medicine and religion, sources such as medical compilations can be scanned for expressions of religion. In addition, religious sources can be examined to locate content referring to medicine. This seems to be a straightforward approach when a source has been categorized as either medicine or religion. But what about sources that have not been assigned to either category? What about sources that are considered to be related to "secular medicine" and devoid of religious connotations? A further complication that often arises when it comes to categorization is the notion of "magic." Some of the academic studies referred to above depict premodern medicine as a form of belief system: in the premodern period, the Japanese still believed in supernatural causes of disease and the corresponding healing methods are depicted as "magical" or "superstitious."

The first step to overcoming these obstacles may be to reread the textual materials and to reconsider religion, for example, Buddhism, and medicine as one connected field (see, e.g., Triplett 2019a on premodern Japan). It is also necessary to look for neglected or newly discovered sources (Dolce 2015). Research based merely on written text further limits our view of both medicine and religion. Recent studies have therefore paid increasingly more attention to material culture beyond the content of written text and picture scrolls. An example from such research includes academic studies of talismans and effigies and enquiries into the use of such objects (Lomi 2014; Andreeva 2018).

Publications such as the recent multiauthored anthology of English translations of written source materials, edited by Pierce Salguero (2017, 2019), point to new directions in the study of Buddhism and medicine in premodern and modern Asia. The anthology, which includes source materials from Japan, showcases the connections between Buddhism and medicine in East Asia and Tibet. As the regions covered in the anthology all share aspects of both Buddhist and medical culture, the anthology allows for a comparative study in this largely compartmentalized field.

FUTURE STUDY

The history of science has largely focused on contributions to science made by men. The history of medicine is no exception in this regard. Future studies must pay more attention to the contributions made by women. The study of religions has recently devoted more attention to the role of women in religion, but the field remains underdeveloped in this respect. In turn, the field of medicine and religion in Japan should also be studied beyond the framework of assumed male authority.

Because social actors in the field of veterinary medicine in pre- and early modern Japan were from the military or agricultural spheres, and owing to the fact that their textual material is largely preserved in agricultural departments, scholars of the history of medicine have not paid enough attention to the healing of animals. Animal studies is currently a popular field within the study of religions in Japan (Ambros 2012), so veterinary medicine and religion will be another fascinating field of future study (Triplett 2019b: 163–188).

New areas of study also include the healing provided by contemporary Buddhists in Japan. This is often couched in the language of psychotherapy in the wake of a global trend that views Buddhist practices as a form of (nonreligious) therapy, and in line with earlier trends, as the ultimate cure (Schrimpf 2018). Winston Davis (1980) and others have addressed the relationship between the activities and healing as well as psychotherapeutic practices of Japanese new religions. Because the field is continually evolving, the study of new religions and medicine remains a desideratum. The field of "new new religions" (*shinshin shūkyō* 新新宗教) (e.g., Shimazono 1992 for an early study) is especially dynamic and also requires constant updating.

See also Chapter 22, "Premodern Traditions."

CHAPTER 18

Minorities

TAKAHASHI Norihito

The increasing number of foreign residents in Japan since the late twentieth century has led to the multiculturalization of Japanese society. It has also caused diversification of Japanese religious culture. However, since multicultural policies of the government are not yet well established, many foreign residents face difficulties of various kinds in their daily lives. In this chapter, I consider the problems of ethnic minorities and the support activities for such minorities as conducted by religious organizations, especially Catholic churches and Islamic groups, in an attempt to create a harmonious multicultural society. In addition, the problems faced by these religious organizations due to the lack of mature immigration policies by the government are also discussed.

Japan's major religious tradition is based on the coexistence and amalgamation of Shinto and Mahāyāna Buddhism. These large religious traditions have had considerable influence on the lives of Japanese people. "Religious minorities" are thus people belonging to other, smaller religious groups and include Christians, Muslims, Theravāda Buddhists, and followers of new religions such as Soka Gakkai International (SGI). Religious minorities form a significant part of the population in Japan.

Two types of "religious minorities" exist in contemporary Japan: (1) members of small religious groups in general, and (2) ethnic and religious minorities who have foreign roots. Most foreign residents are classified under type (2), namely, "ethnic/religious minority." As a group, they tend to be excluded from standard public support. Religious organizations serve an important function in their daily lives, in addition to being pillars of their faith, because of the inadequate immigration policies for their social integration, coupled with insufficient social work undertaken for their benefit in Japan.

GROWTH OF FOREIGN RESIDENT POPULATION AFTER THE SECOND WORLD WAR

According to official statistics, in 2015, the total population of Japan was approximately 127,000,000, of which about 2,200,000 were foreign residents. Before and after the Second World War, several Koreans and Chinese settled in Japan, and they are often referred to as "oldcomers" or sometimes "old-timers." Oldcomers either immigrated or were forcibly displaced from other parts of East Asia, such as the Korean Peninsula, Taiwan (Formosa), and China, most of which were former Japanese colonies. Until the 1970s, these oldcomers constituted nearly the entire ethnic minority population. However, racial or ethnic prejudice and discrimination against oldcomers, especially Koreans, has been a serious problem since the Second World War. In recent years, there has been a considerable amount of hate speech and hate crime against Koreans.

TABLE 18.1 Changes in populations of major foreign residents in Japan (1980–2015)

	Total	Korea	China	The Philippines	Thailand	Indonesia	Vietnam	Brazil	Peru
1980	782,910	664,536	52,896	5,547	1,276	1,448	2,742	1,492	348
1985	850,612	683,313	74,924	12,261	2,642	1,704	4,126	1,955	480
1990	1,075,317	687,940	150,339	49,092	6,724	3,623	6,233	56,429	10,279
1995	1,362,371	666,376	222,991	74,297	16,035	6,956	9,099	176,440	36,269
2000	1,686,444	635,269	335,575	144,871	29,289	19,346	16,908	254,394	46,171
2005	2,011,555	598,687	519,561	187,261	37,703	25,097	28,932	302,080	57,728
2010	2,134,151	565,989	687,156	210,181	41,279	24,895	41,781	230,552	54,636
2015	2,232,189	491,711	714,570	229,595	45,379	35,910	146,956	173,473	47,721
2018	2,731,093	449,634	764,720	271,289	52,323	56,346	330,835	201,865	48,362

Source: Statistical Survey of Foreign Residents—Immigration Bureau of Japan (the Ministry of Justice).

On the contrary, "newcomers" are those who arrived in Japan mainly from Southeast Asia and South America, that is, "the Global South." Since the 1980s, there has been a marked increase in newcomers in Japan. This is due to the serious labour shortage resulting from the decreasing birth rate and aging population in Japan. Newcomers are largely from Vietnam, Philippines, Brazil, Peru, Indonesia, Thailand, and so on (see Table 18.1). Their arrival in Japan is via international marriages, education, blue-collar jobs in the manufacturing sector, or employment in sex work. Most of the newcomers are unskilled workers, who tend to face several difficulties in their daily lives. In addition, a significant number of them are illegal residents. The history of newcomers in Japan has also been that of their struggle against control and deportation.

ETHNIC/RELIGIOUS MINORITIES AND THEIR SOCIAL ENGAGEMENT

Chinese and Korean residents have long enriched Japanese religious culture. Chinese immigrants have built Taoist temples since the late nineteenth century. They also have continued to practice their religious rituals or festivals in Chinatowns in Nagasaki, Kobe, and Yokohama (Wang 2003). However, many Korean oldcomers (Zainichi Koreans) have been connected with not only traditional Korean religions, such as Confucian ancestor worship, Buddhism, and folk religion (Shamanism), but also with Christianity. Korean Christians established the Korean Christian Church in Japan (KCCJ) in the early twentieth century. These religions constitute the basis not only for practicing their faith but also for the formation of Korean ethnic communities and networks (Shūkyō shakaigaku no kai ed. 1986; Iida 2002; Visiočnik 2016). Furthermore, the number of Korean newcomer migrant workers and international students has increased since the 1990s. As many of them are Christians, mostly Protestants, they have built Korean Protestant churches all over Japan (Mullins 1998; Lee 2012).

Many religious organizations and communities, especially Christians, have participated in movements against racial or ethnic prejudice and discrimination. Korean Protestant churches have also played an important role in these movements. KCCJ, in particular, has been involved in human rights activities since the late twentieth century, for example, in tackling discrimination against Korean oldcomers. It has participated in various other issues, including the fingerprinting refusal movement, the social movement to protest the legally forced fingerprinting for foreign residents by Koreans and leftists in the 1980s; the petition for the "Basic Law for Foreign Residents of Japan," the ecumenical movement to legislate a basic law guaranteeing the rights of foreign residents since the late 1990s; and in the protest against hate speech in recent years.

Responding to their influential anti-racism appeal, Japan passed its first anti-hate speech bill in May 2016. There are several defects in this law, however. For instance, it limits its scope to covering racial discrimination against people of overseas origin and their descendants "who live legally in Japan." Nevertheless, these Christian groups have played an important role toward building a multicultural society in contemporary Japan.

However, since the 1980s, newcomers also have diversified the religious landscape in Japan. Some specific examples are as follows: (1) Christianity saw the multi-nationalization of Catholic churches and an increase in the number of Protestant churches established by people from foreign countries (especially Korea and Brazil); (2) Buddhism saw an increase in the number of Theravāda followers from Southeast Asia; (3) Islam saw immigrants from Islamic countries founding mosques throughout the nation; and (4) other religions such as Hinduism, Sikhism, and new religions became more established. However, since these religious groups are both minorities and operate on a small scale, most Japanese have not taken much interest in this trend, and many are not even aware of it (Pae 2007; Miki and Sakurai 2012; Miki 2017; Takahashi, Shirahase, and Hoshino 2018).

SUPPORT ACTIVITIES BY THE CATHOLIC CHURCH FOR ETHNIC MINORITIES

The Catholic Church in Japan has always had a strong relationship with foreign residents.

The number of foreign residents from Catholic countries such as the Philippines, Brazil, and Peru accounts for a large portion of Catholics. A significant number of devout members exist in each parish church.

Since the Second Vatican Council (1962–5), Catholic organizations in Japan have initiated various social activities, offering a wide range of support for foreign residents. Some of them include providing guidance for acquiring visas, aiding with interactions with government officials or police officers, resolving labor problems, supporting children's education, offering assistance in learning Japanese, and providing intervention for family problems such as divorce or domestic violence. In particular, human rights advocacy activities, undertaken by the Catholic Church for foreign residents, are prominent among nongovernmental organizations (NGOs).

The leading organizations providing support are the Catholic Commission of Japan for Migrants, Refugees, and People on the Move, otherwise known as J-CaRM, and the Japan Catholic Council for Justice and Peace. J-CaRM describes the aim of its activities as follows:

> Based on the Gospel, we are working to realize a multi-ethnic and multicultural society where not only are all people equal and their fundamental human rights respected, but where we also value each culture and ethnicity and can live together as brothers and sisters.
>
> In order to protect human rights and the dignity of the lives of refugees, migrants, and people on the move, we are conducting activities for networking, education, and advocacy, cooperating with pastoral and support activities inside and outside of churches.[1]

Besides being a national organization that supports migrants, refugees, and people on the move in Japan, J-CaRM also acts as a liaison and coordination structure for support staff belonging to each diocese, parish, and monastic order.

In Japan, the Catholic support structure for foreign residents is organized into three major divisions. First, parish church members and volunteers from the neighborhood carry out various activities in cooperation with other regional actors (government offices, related NGOs, medical institutions, lawyers, etc.). Second, support centers deal with problems within each diocese. Third, some monastic orders, for instance, the Society of Jesus and the Society of the Divine Word, organize support activities for foreign residents in collaboration with other Catholic and non-Catholic entities (Shirahase 2016).

---

[1]Source: the official website of Catholic Commission of Japan for Migrants, Refugees and People on the Move at https://www.jcarm.com/about/ (accessed October 31, 2019).

I introduce here two specific cases of support offered in the local communities. The first case is from Hamamatsu City (Shizuoka Prefecture). Many Brazilians and Peruvians, mostly workers in the manufacturing industries and their families, live in Hamamatsu. The Lehman Brothers' scandal of 2008 resulted in many of these workers becoming unemployed. The Catholic Hamamatsu Church then became a refuge or asylum for these needy foreign residents: it provided food assistance, support for regaining their livelihoods (including finding employment), and educational support for these foreign residents and their children. Because the local government and other NGOs did not initially have an adequate support system for these foreign residents, the Catholic Church organized these support measures in their place. There were similar instances in other areas of Japan as well at that time (Shirahase and Takahashi 2012).

The second case is about the disaster-stricken area of the Tohoku Region in the aftermath of the Great East Japan Earthquake (March 11, 2011). The population of foreign residents in the area is tiny. Among the residents there were some Filipina women married to Japanese men. However, most of them lived as wives of traditional Buddhist families, and consequently they did not go to the Catholic churches in the area. After the earthquake in Ōfunato City in Iwate Prefecture, three things changed. First, Catholic volunteers from other regions found the devastated Filipinas and offered them support. Second, priests and nuns have since cared for the Filipina believers. Third, Filipinas gradually gathered and constructed their own community hub at a local Catholic church. The church is now a base for their faith and for undertaking mutual aid activities in the local community.[2]

In Japan, the Catholic Church has approximately 440,000 members. Although it is only one of the minority religious groups, it is an established body that has a relatively long history and a substantial number of middle-class Japanese followers. In addition, the Catholic Church contacts foreign residents on a daily basis more often than other major religious groups (traditional Buddhist temples, Shinto shrines, new religions, etc.). Therefore, not only has multicultural coexistence (symbiosis) between foreign residents and Japanese people developed strongly in many parish churches, but these churches have also played a comparatively significant role in support activities in many local communities.

Furthermore, a distinctive feature of the Catholic Church is that most believers from foreign countries take part in the church's activities as "supporters." As the Catholic Church has a large network extending beyond regions and religions and ethnicities, it cooperates with various actors related to promoting multiculturalism.

MULTICULTURAL ENGAGEMENT OF MUSLIMS IN JAPAN

The history of Islam in Japan is comparatively relatively short. The relationship between Japanese people and Muslims began in the late nineteenth century. Moreover, some Muslim groups, such as the Tatars, came to Japan after the Japan-Russia War and the Russian Revolution. After that, the Japanese government aimed to establish connections with the Islamic world in order to expand its political and economic interests in the Asian region against Western countries, and therefore funded a few mosques, for instance, in

---

[2]This fieldwork visit was conducted at Ōfunato Catholic Church on March 10, 2016, with Tatsuya Shirahase and So Hoshino.

Kobe, Nagoya, and Tokyo. After the Second World War, the small community of Muslims continued their religious activities (Okai 2016).

Since the 1980s, there has been an increase in the number of Muslim newcomers from Pakistan, Bangladesh, Iran, Malaysia, Indonesia, and so on. Most of them carry out ethnic businesses such as working as used car dealers or in the Halāl business; some take up jobs and study in Japanese universities. In 2010, the Muslim population in Japan was estimated to be just over 100,000. This number could be broken down as follows: 20,000 Indonesians, 10,000 Pakistanis, 9,000 Bangladeshis, 5,000 Malaysians, 5,000 Iranians, 4,000 from Arab countries, 2,500 Turks, and 10,000 Japanese. As most of the Muslim newcomers were male, they often married Japanese women, who then converted to Islam. The second-generation population of Muslims has gradually increased in recent times. These Muslim newcomers have built mosques all over Japan, numbering around eighty as of 2014 (Tanada 2015).

First, mosques serve a social function for Muslims in Japan because they are spaces for professing their faith, worship, rituals, and Islamic education. Second, mosques play a central role in the social activities of Muslims, which are (1) mutual aid activities among Muslims, such as employment and livelihood support, and (2) activities for disaster-recovery assistance or educational aid in the national/transnational public sphere. Moreover, the Muslim community participates in various activities of the local communities and are committed to intercultural communication more actively than other newcomers do (Okai 2016).

As an example of the social activities conducted by one of the Islamic groups in Japan, let us consider the mosque Masjid Otsuka (Japan Islamic Trust), founded in Toshima Ward, Tokyo, in 1999 by Muslims from Pakistan and various other countries. It has an *imam* and is an important place of worship (*salat*) for Muslims living in its neighborhood. Masjid Otsuka offers Islamic education for children, Muslim certificates, marriage ceremonies, burial assistance, and so on. In addition, it also conducts various social activities, such as support for refugees (Rohingya people in Myanmar, Syrians, Pakistanis, and Afghans), assistance in the disaster-stricken area after the Great East Japan Earthquake in 2011, and other community activities in the neighborhood (Nejima 2014).[3]

Islamophobia and hate crimes against Muslims are serious problems in contemporary Western countries that have a large number of immigrants and refugees from Islamic countries; as a consequence, Muslim radicalism and extremism in the West are on the rise. Compared to the West, Japanese society has not experienced such incidents, although some anti-Islamic incidents occurred in recent years, such as the tearing and discarding of the Quran by a Japanese woman in Toyama Prefecture (2001),[4] a disclosure of surveillance over Muslims by the police (2010),[5] and movements against constructions of mosques in some cities.[6]

Nevertheless, Islamophobia and hate crimes are much lesser in Japan than in Western societies, not only because the number of Muslims is small but also because Muslims have engaged in social activities in many local communities. However, this situation may change if the number of Muslims rapidly increases.

---

[3]See the official website of Masjid Otsuka (Japan Islamic Trust) at http://www.islam.or.jp/support/ (accessed October 31, 2019).
[4]*Asahishinbun* (Toyama, morning edition), October 14, 2001, 33.
[5]*Asahishinbun* (National, morning edition), November 11, 2010, 1.
[6]*Asahishinbun* (Ishikawa, morning edition), September 26, 2011, 31.

CONCLUSION

Although earlier oldcomers, mainly from East Asia, have settled into the local communities, the number of foreign residents in contemporary Japan has rapidly increased because of the arrival of newcomers from "the Global South." This has led to a diversification of the Japanese religious culture. As mentioned earlier, ethnic minorities who have foreign roots overlap with part of the religious minorities in the existing Japanese context. For ethnic minorities facing various problems, their religion is often an essential aspect of their daily lives.

However, few religious groups provide support activities for such foreign residents from the standpoint of multiculturalism. Therefore, the activities pioneered by the Catholic Church and some of the Islamic groups are valuable for Japan, whose immigration policies for social integration and the prevalence of multiculturalism have been immature.

Nevertheless, I must point out the peculiar limitations of such religious groups in the Japanese context. Because of the constitutional separation of religion and the state, and the ordinary Japanese citizen's indifference to the social activities of religious groups, it is challenging to develop direct collaborations between governmental or secular institutions and religious organizations. Moreover, Christianity, including the Catholic Church, and Islam are just two among the small religious groups in Japan. The number of Japanese Christians is quite small, and their number is dwindling.

However, the number of foreign residents is on the increase because of Japan's severe labor shortage, resulting from both the decreasing birth rate and the aging population. Therefore, it is certain that the Catholic Church and Islamic groups have set an important precedent for other religious groups.

See also Chapter 7, "Empire and Colonialism," Chapter 12, "Globalization," Chapter 13, "Islam," and Chapter 19, "'New Religions'."

CASE STUDY

Daijō Islam (Mahayāna Islam)

KOMURA Akiko

Daijō Islam (Mahayāna Islam) is a Japanese Islamic thought conceived and developed by Abe Haruo (1920–1999). Abe was a follower of Jōdo Shinshū, the largest sect of Japanese Buddhism, founded by the monk Shinran in 1175. Abe converted to Islam because he came to believe that Islamic thought represented the essence of Shinran's teachings, namely *zettai-tariki* (salvation by the absolute power of Amitābha). Abe was an executive director of the Japan Islamic Congress (Nihon Isuramu Kyōdan) established in 1974. This Islamic group was active from the mid-1970s through the mid-1980s and developed the idea of "Mahayāna Islam," which adopted a mission approach similar to Mahayāna Buddhism.

The founder of the Japan Islamic Congress was Futaki Hideo (1908–1992), a Japanese Muslim doctor and a rather controversial figure. During the Second World War he belonged to the infamous Unit 731, a unit of the Imperial Japanese Army that conducted biological warfare research and chemical experiments on civilians. After the war, Futaki established a publishing company. He became involved in a case of blackmail and was arrested. After serving time in prison, he converted to Islam and worked as a Muslim doctor at a pain clinic in Shinjuku, Tokyo. Futaki was a charismatic person; his patients converted to Islam after being treated by him. At the peak of its expansion, the Japan Islamic Congress is said to have had about fifty thousand members. However, in the mid-1980s, Futaki's activities began to decrease probably because of his declining health, and the group gradually disintegrated. Futaki and his close associates tended to have a conflictual relationship with other Japanese members, for example, by converting without going through the standard procedure of having a testimony. He was also criticized for his inappropriate fundraising through Islamic organizations in other countries.

One of Futaki's most used expressions in his teaching was "O (Zero) is existence." These words probably mean that Islamic teachings begin when we realize the fact that our existence is like particles close to zero. Futaki mentioned:

> Actually, Islam is the same as the lifestyle or the mentality of the Japanese, which they have maintained for more than 2,600 years. Therefore, I believe that those hardworking 120 million Japanese, the Japanese race (*Yamato minzoku*) are all potential Muslims. It's not too much to say that our policy of Islamic mission lies there. (Futaki 1981: 65; translated by the author)

Futaki probably found some kind of human universality in Islamic teachings. Interestingly, he never insisted that his converts should strictly follow Islamic tenets. He often said to them: "Let Japanese Islam follow the Japanese way." This was the policy adopted by the Japan Islamic Congress and later described by Abe (1986:160) as a Mahayāna Buddhism-like (Daijo-teki) approach to Islamic mission. Futaki also said that in Islamic conversion, belief in Allah is the most, if not the only, important thing.

Although some Japanese Muslims tended to strictly follow Islamic tenets, members of Futaki's group were concerned that these tenets could easily turn into meaningless formalism (*keishikishugi*), far from the essential expression of Islamic religion. Also, strict adherence to Islamic tenets might lead to isolation from Japanese society.

Abe mentioned in his writings that Islam itself has only one right way, which is neither Mahāyāna nor Hīnayāna (Abe 1986: 148). However, among various Islamic sects, we see a self-evident trend of Hīnayāna Islam.

The system of thought of Mahāyāna Islam grew out of the practical Islamic activities carried out by the Japan Islamic Congress. Abe illustrates the characteristics of Mahāyāna Islam in comparison with those of Hīnayāna Islam, as shown below (see Table 18.2).

When the Japan Islamic Congress was active, the total Muslim population in Japan was only about thirty thousand. Islam was still seen as something new and unfamiliar, and Muslims in Japan were attempting to adapt to the Japanese context. Mahāyāna Islam should be understood as an attempt to ease strict Islamic principles for Japanese Muslim converts.

TABLE 18.2 Mahāyāna Islam versus Hīnayāna Islam by Abe Haruo

	Mahāyāna Islam	*Hīnayāna Islam*
実質性 Essentiality	形式よりも実質（精神）を重んじ、戒律の末節にとらわれない。 Emphasis on essence (spirit), rather than form. Freedom from detailed religious rules.	実質（精神）よりも形式を重んじ戒律や礼拝などに固執する。 Form is considered more important than essence (spirit). Adherence to religious rules and modes of worship.
思索性 Thinking	思索によって道を極めようとする。 Attempting to perfect the way [of Islam] through thought.	日常的実践によって正邪をわける。 Distinguishing between right and wrong through daily practice.
普遍性 Universality	個より一般を重んじ習俗にとらわれない。 Custom is not valued above the individual.	一般化を好まず習俗にとわれる。 Dislike of generalization, emphasis on Islamic custom.
流動性 Flexibility	固定を好まない。 Dislike of fixed forms and attitudes.	古いものにとらわれる。 Preoccupation with old things.
宗派性 Religious sectionalism	宗派にとらわれない。 Unimportance of differences in religious sects.	宗派の別にとらわれる。 Differences among religious sects are deemed important.
性差性 Gender Difference	性差別にとらわれず女性を対等に扱う。 Freedom from gender discrimination.	女性を低いものと見る。 Women are seen as inferior.

Source: Abe (1986): 149.

CHAPTER 19

"New Religions"

KATO Masato

The study of "new religions" (*shinshūkyō*) is one of the areas of research that has received much attention from scholars of religions in Japan starting from the latter half of the twentieth century. The relatively high level of interest in this particular field is in part attested to by the existence of a large edited volume titled *Shinshūkyō jiten* (Encyclopedia of New Religions), which was published in 1990 as the result of collective work conducted over several years. This chapter will outline key issues regarding these religious groups, including definitions and terminologies concerning the category "new religion," their characteristics, and other important aspects that previous works have illuminated. This outline will be followed by a discussion of potential directions of the field in the future by taking into account new and previously unaddressed questions.

DEFINITIONS AND TERMINOLOGIES

As a concept that is used to refer to various social groups and phenomena in many different historical and cultural contexts, the scope of the term "new religion," as used in the study of religions in Japan, first needs to be clarified. It is generally accepted that new religions refer to religious groups that originated and/or developed from around the beginning of Japan's modern period (1868–) until today. Included within this broad definition are a wide range of groups with various historical origins, from early new religions including Kurozumikyō, Tenrikyō, and Konkōkyō to the more recent ones such as Agonshū, Shinnyo-en, and Kōfuku no Kagaku (also known as Happy Science). Scholars have differently tried to divide these groups by the time periods in which they emerged or developed (see Astley 2006 for a summary of these discussions).

The term "new religion" began to be used among scholars of religions in Japan as an overarching category to make sense of the multifaceted reality concerning these religious groups within the history of religions in Japan. The category came to be used from around the 1970s in place of the more value-laden term *shinkō shūkyō* ("newly arisen religions"), which had been more commonly used by mass media and scholars in previous decades (Shimazono 2006 [1992]: 31–4). Some of the religious groups included under the rubric of new religions are also known with different names, such as *minshū shūkyō* ("popular religions"), which is often used to refer to those groups that came into being from toward the end of the early modern period through around the 1920s, and *shin shinshūkyō* ("new new religions"), which indicates new groups that developed after 1973, especially from the 1980s onward (Astley 2006: 103; Shimazono 2006 [1992]: 31–4). It must be noted, however, that the term "new religion" is a scholarly category that is rarely used by these organizations and their members to refer to themselves, a point that needs to be taken into account when, for instance, interacting with members of these religious groups (cf. Dolce 2012: xxxix–xl; Staemmler and Dehn 2011: 4).

Regarding the category "new religion," it must also be clarified as to what the word "new" indicates in the study of Japanese new religions. As Ian Reader points out, the notion of "new" in Japanese "new religions" does not indicate chronological newness per se but rather pertains to these groups' (1) "historical development in conjunction with the continuing processes of modernity," (2) "public perception as 'alternative' and 'outsider' movements," and (3) "contradistinction to established mainstream traditions" (Reader 2005: 93). Put simply, the meaning of the word "new" is understood in relation to not only the specific time period in which these groups developed but also how they are viewed by the general public in Japan and how they are distinguished from religious traditions that existed prior to the emergence of these new groups. It is precisely for this reason that early new religions such as Tenrikyō and Konkōkyō are also called "new" religions despite the fact that they are now nearly two centuries old.

The specific meaning attached to the word "new" in the study of Japanese "new religions" also relates to the distinctive place of these groups in Japanese society. Unlike other sociocultural contexts, in which "new religions" constitute a very small portion of the population, new religions in Japan are by no means a small minority in terms of the total number of people who are in one way or another involved in them. Staemmler and Dehn (2011: 5–6) estimate based on major extant literature that there are about three hundred to four hundred new religions in Japan, with 10–30 percent of the population being actively or passively involved in a new religion.

However, the relatively large number of people associated with these groups does not necessarily translate into a public perception that identifies new religions as part of the religious mainstream in Japan. The stigma and prejudice against new religions has existed for a very long time, but has become particularly acute in the wake of the 1995 Tokyo subway attack by the new religion Aum Shinrikyō, which disrupted the public order by killing thirteen people and injuring thousands with sarin nerve gas. The incident resulted in increased hysteria against new religions, reinforcing the public image of new religions as dangerous groups outside of society. As Levi McLaughlin notes in his article on Soka Gakkai, which is one of the largest Buddhist-derived Japanese new religions, the stigma of "otherness" that new religions in general carry in Japanese society cannot be easily removed and may continue to manifest in different forms (McLaughlin 2012a: 72). The newness of Japanese new religions is thus multilayered and needs to be understood in light of the specific historical, social, and academic contexts in which this term has come to be used.

MAJOR CHARACTERISTICS OF "NEW RELIGIONS"

The foregoing discussion suggests that religious groups included in the academic category of "new religion" are by no means monolithic and must be understood by taking into account their distinctive histories and traditions. At the same time, however, students of Japanese new religions have identified various characteristics that these religious groups have in common. Noting that these include both structural and conceptual characteristics, Ian Reader (2005: 88–91) identifies a set of nine common elements.

First, Japanese new religions are often lay-oriented movements, with non-ordained, ordinary members playing central roles in the process of propagation. Second, these religious movements usually begin with charismatic founders whose ability to provide spiritual healing and guidance through their connection with divine or spiritual realms attract followers. The charismatic authority of the founders is often retained after their passing through such ways as formulating a doctrine that ensures the continued presence of the founders, systematization of the founders' teachings, and transmission of charisma through familial succession. Third, many new religions place emphasis on sacred geographies built around holy centers that have cosmological significance in relation to the doctrine of the traditions.

Fourth, one of the most defining conceptual characteristics is a vitalistic worldview, a notion that was first developed by Tsushima et al. (1979) as a "vitalistic conception of salvation." This worldview centers on the idea of the cosmos as a living or a divine being that gives rise to and supports humans and other living beings in ways that guide them toward spiritual enhancement, leading to a perfect harmony with the divine being. Fifth, this idea of salvation is closely connected to the idea of self-cultivation as a method to control or improve one's course of life though spiritual training or practices. Sixth, the close connection between physical and spiritual realms relates to an emphasis on this-worldly salvation, which assumes the influence of spiritual forces on the physical world proportionate to the levels or qualities of one's morality or karmic status cultivated through spiritual practices.

Seventh, new religions also employ various spiritual techniques as a way to ensure individual salvation, which works in tandem with the aforementioned practice of self-cultivation. Eighth, new religions hold various forms of millennial orientations that stress the need for an imminent transformation of the world order based on their spiritual teachings. The degree to which new religions hold this worldview varies, and in many cases, these orientations come to be downplayed in the course of the groups' development. Finally, many Japanese new religions claim that their religious message concerns the restoration of original truths rather than the proclamation of completely new teachings.

Religious groups that fall into the category of "new new religions" also share some of the above-mentioned characteristics, such as the presence of charismatic founders, but they tend to emphasize ideas and practices that were not present or deemed significant in their older counterparts. These include appeal to mystical practices, other-worldly orientation of salvation, and apocalyptic consciousness coupled with increased emphasis on the arrival of a messianic figure, among others (Shimazono 2001; Astley 2006: 103–4). The motives for joining these groups are thus different. While older new religions have often appealed to relatively lower-class people seeking to be alleviated from poverty, illnesses, or other types of strife, new new religions have attracted relatively more well-off and highly educated individuals who hope to find spiritual meanings for their lives, as they live in a society primarily driven by the pursuit of economic growth through materialistic means (Astley 2006: 103–4; Watanabe 2011: 69–70).

New new religions are also said to show a renewed form of nationalistic attitudes in their teachings. Shimazono observes that nationalistic discourses identified in some of the new new religions, if not all, reflect, on the one hand, "a sense of ethnocentrism forged by [Japan's] economic superiority" and, on the other hand, "a perception that relations with foreign nations are becoming increasingly difficult in the ongoing process of internationalization and globalization" (2001: 132–3). According to Shimazono, this tendency is informed by a strand of discourse of cultural nationalism that postulates the superiority of Japan, especially in relation to its unique religious traditions and cultures (2001: 132–6) (see Tsukada 2012 for further discussion on this theme).

It is important to balance these observations about common characteristics of new religious movements with the historical continuities and connections that many of these groups maintain with or built upon more traditional organizations. For instance, Shimazono (1979) has demonstrated how early new religions such as Tenrikyō and Konkōkyō developed some of the elements of contemporaneous *minzoku shūkyō* (folk religions) in new ways, such as the idea of the Parent God, salvific rituals, and the idea of a living kami or deity. In terms of doctrinal foundations, Hubbard (1998) explained how a Buddhist-oriented new religion known as Shinnyo-en engages with the doctrinal tradition of its more traditional counterpart, namely, Shingon Buddhism, as well as how some of the group's beliefs that are often considered to originate in the folk tradition are in fact grounded in authoritative Buddhist doctrinal tradition. Moreover, Reader and Tanabe (1998) argue that the inclination toward this-worldly salvation plays a central role not only in new religions but also in established religions. In understanding the characteristic of new religions, it is therefore indispensable to be aware of both the historical connections with older counterparts and the common ground that contemporaneous religious groups share and emphasize.

MAJOR AREAS OF RESEARCH IN THE STUDY OF JAPANESE "NEW RELIGIONS"

Apart from the structural and conceptual characteristics that new religions share, scholars have highlighted various other themes central to the understanding of Japanese new religions. Numerous monographs on specific new religions exist, and one of the areas of inquiry that has attracted most attention, especially in the early stages of the development of the field, is the study of the founders, particularly those of early new religions. These works have, for instance, provided very detailed accounts of founders' biographies with a focus on significant events that contributed to the formation of their new identities, major teachings, rituals, and other practices that founders formulated during the course of their lives, and how their movements were received (or dismissed) by the authorities, local communities, and other members of the wider society.

Prominent works of this kind include Murakami Shigeyoshi's groundbreaking work on popular religions (*minshū shūkyō*) (1958); Shimazono Susumu's series of studies on Nakayama Miki (1798–1887), the founder of Tenrikyō (1977, 1978, 1980); Yasumaru Yoshio's monograph on Deguchi Nao (1837–1918), Ōmoto's founder (1977); and Helen Hardacre's study of Kurozumikyō (1986), among others. Works on more recent groups include Winston Davis's study on Sūkyō Mahikari (1980), Levi McLaughlin's monograph on Soka Gakkai (2019), and Erica Baffelli and Ian Reader's coauthored work on Agonshū (2019). Apart from the focus on founders, these and other monographs have shed light on the distinctive history and characteristics of various other groups by situating their analyses within the broader historical background of Japanese religions.

Sociological analyses of new religions' teaching and practices, organizations, and activities have also attracted much attention from various scholars. Some of the common characteristics of new religions discussed earlier, such as the focus on laity and the central role of charismatic founders, are indeed insights primarily drawn from a sociological approach. Another significant social aspect is the structure of organizations. Scholars such as Morioka Kiyomi (1989) and Shimazono (1996) have shed light on these structures in different ways by categorizing various groups according to different models, such as, for instance, Morioka's ideas of the "parent-child model" and the "fellows connected through a bureaucracy model." These organizational structures, which define the different ways in which members are connected with the organization itself as well as other members, are said to reflect the social structure of the broader society at the time of the group's founding and development (Watanabe 2011: 70–2).

These different organizational structures are in turn closely connected to how new religions are financed (Sakurai 2011). Based on their organizational structures, new religions conduct various activities, including rituals, proselytization, coaching and training of new members, events of mass participation and of small-group activities, and so forth. Many of these activities are intended to allow followers to cultivate their inner qualities based on ethical principles, which will in turn affect their life conditions pertaining to the attainment of happiness (Watanabe 2011: 79–81). Other important activities with social implications are conducted by new religions to express their religious ideals and reach out to society at large. These include the establishment of educational institutions including universities, medical institutions such as hospitals, cultural institutions such as libraries and museums, as well as various social service initiatives involving various types of subgroups or affiliated organizations, including NGOs involved with, for instance, disaster relief work, peace movements, and interreligious dialogue. Apart from social outreach programs organized by a specific group, large-scale initiatives, such as the World Conference of Religions for Peace (WCRP) and the Federation of New Religious Organizations of Japan (Shinshūkyō Dantai Rengōkai), are organized based on the participation of multiple new religions. Last but not least, some of the new religions' political involvement has caught much scholarly attention, with Soka Gakkai and its affiliated political party Kōmeitō often being seen as the most salient case (Watanabe 2011: 81–6; see Fisker-Nielsen 2012 and McLaughlin 2019 for the most recent English-language monographs).

Another area of inquiry worth mentioning is research on new religions' overseas expansion. This area of study began to develop around the 1980s, first through the work of scholars based in Japan and later followed by those based in the West from around the 1990s. Many of these works have focused on Japanese religions that were transmitted to countries and regions with substantial numbers of Japanese immigrants and their communities, such as Hawai'i (Yanagawa and Morioka 1979, 1981; Takahashi 2014), the West Coast of the United States (Yanagawa 1983), Brazil (Maeyama 1997; Watanabe 2001; Yamada 2018), and other South American countries (Inoue 1985; Nakamaki 1989, 2003). Other works have illuminated insights pertaining to groups operating in Japan's former colonial territories, including Taiwan (Fujii 1992, 1993, 1996, 1997, 2006, 2007; Terada 2009; Huang 2016, 2017a, 2017b) and South Korea (Lee and Sakurai 2011; Jin 2015, 2016, 2018). Scholars based in the West have studied the expansion of Japanese new religions in their own societies (Clarke and Somers 1994; Wilson and Dobbelaere 1994; Hammond and Machacek 1999; Clarke 2000).

Some of these works, particularly those focusing on the time periods before the 1950s, reveal how new religions played a key role in preserving and reconstructing migrants' sense of identity in the face of the need for social order as well as the desire to maintain cultural identity. Other works have discussed how some of the Japanese new religions attracted non-Japanese converts in Western cultural contexts and other places. In terms of Japan's former colonial territories, scholars have addressed the variety of ways in which locals engage with new religions' teachings and practices that can at times create either affinity or tension, based on general perceptions of Japan and Japanese religions in society at large.

NEW AND PREVIOUSLY UNADDRESSED QUESTIONS

The study of Japanese new religions over the past several decades has clarified many of the common themes and put forth detailed histories and characteristics of individual groups/organizations. In recent years, scholars with a variety of disciplinary backgrounds have begun to address new questions as informed by the development of conterminous fields of study. One of them relates to the fundamental ways in which the development of new religions has been narrated in academic discourse. In his monograph on Tenrikyō, Nagaoka Takashi (2015) highlighted the process by which the history of new religions after the death of the founders and the ensuing institutionalization has often been described as the aging of the group or the deviation from what they truly are. By employing a deconstructionist approach, together with an awareness of new research on the history of new religions, Nagaoka effectively nuances these unspoken assumptions in extant literature to propose instead a perspective that focuses on how followers of new religions have gone through the "dynamic process of collaborative interpretation" (*yomi no undō*) as they lived with the ever-changing tradition.

Worth mentioning also is the question surrounding the very notion of "new religion," whose conceptual limitation has already been briefly touched upon. As pointed out by Baffelli and Reader (2019), the notion of "new religion" as a discrete analytical category for studying religions in Japan has been questioned by various scholars such as Nancy Stalker and Byron Earhart in light of the continuities and common religious traits (such as founder veneration) that new religions share with established religious traditions. The problematic nature of the concept of "new religion" has also been critiqued by scholars concerned with the historical construction of the concept of "religion" as well as the category of "popular religions" (*minshū shūkyō*). An ongoing research project known as "Reconstruction of the Representation of the History of Japanese New Religions" (*Nihon shinshūkyō shi zō no saikōchiku*), which is a four-year research project sponsored by a Grants-in-Aid for Scientific Research Program (*Kagaku kenkyūhi josei jigyō*) and is based at Kyoto University, will certainly broaden the horizon of this field of inquiry.

Another important area that has attracted interest in the study of new religions is the question of gender. The focus on women has been one of the central themes in the study of new religions, especially when it concerns groups whose founders are female figures, notably Tenrikyō and Ōmoto. Many of the early works tended to present relatively positive appraisals of the liberating roles that these founders played in proclaiming new teachings, but more recent studies informed by research on gender and religions have provided more nuanced pictures of these women's views on gender roles (see, e.g., Kaneko 2003; Ambros 2013). Inose Yuri's (2017) recent survey article on gender and Japanese new religions, which introduces important frameworks to understand various conceptualization of gender in different groups, serves as an important point of reference to identify subareas and particular groups that may deserve further attention.

Recent developments in the field thus suggest the need to critically assess the very concept of "new religions" and various other subareas by drawing on insights from conterminous fields of study within the study of Japanese religions in particular and of religions in general. It remains to be seen how much longer the category of "new religion" will continue to be analytically useful, but the academic conversations about religious organizations and traditions that are grouped under this category are likely to continue to develop in ways that illuminate the wider study of Japanese religions and religion in general.

See also Chapter 5, "Economy and Spirituality," Chapter 11, "Gender," Chapter 16, "Media and Technology," Chapter 21, "Politics," Chapter 27, "Spirituality," and Chapter 29, "Women."

CHAPTER 20

Pilgrimages and "Sacred" Geography

Ian READER

Pilgrimage, as Shinno Toshikazu (1991:19) has noted, is one of the pillars of Japanese religious structure. From the development of legends and miracle tales about Buddhist figures such as Kōbō Daishi (Shingon school founder Kūkai) and Kannon, which have been central development of pilgrimage routes throughout Japan and have been used to spread popular forms of Buddhism, to mass pilgrimage cultic events centered on prominent Shinto shrines (e.g., *Ise mairi*), the practice of pilgrimage has rightly been viewed as of major importance across the Japanese religious spectrum (Shinno 1980, 1991, 1996; Hoshino 1981,1997; Shinjō 1982; Reader and Swanson 1997).

It is thus unsurprising that a rich academic literature has developed on the subject, notably in Japanese (see Reader 2015a) but also in Western languages (Ambros 2014). This literature has discussed pilgrimage historically and in the contemporary era, focusing on such topics as cults of devotion and the development of sacred geographies centered on Buddhist temples, Shinto shrines, and Japanese regional landscapes; themes of asceticism, entertainment, and the intersecting dynamics of pilgrimage, travel, tourism, and economics; and their intrinsic relationship to the older established religious traditions. Recently, too, studies have examined how religious institutions (most notably Buddhist temples) have continually used pilgrimages to increase their stature and have developed new pilgrimage routes as a means of encouraging and spurring popular devotion (Reader 2014).

However, this academic literature has concentrated almost wholly on established historic religious traditions—Shinto, Buddhism, and Shugendō—and the shrines, temples, mountains, and pilgrimages associated with them. It also has some significant gaps, and in this chapter I will draw attention to two of them, both of which contain major implications not just for the wider study of pilgrimage in Japan but also for understandings of the country's changing religious dynamics. While both relate to the recurrent Japanese religious tendency of developing sacred places and constructing new pilgrimages, they also signify departures from its normative patterns, in that these areas of pilgrimage involve the development of new modes of sacred geography that are not just distinct from the older religions but also signify challenges to them.

The first gap lies in the development, by "new religions" (*shin shūkyō*),[1] of new sacred centers, geographies, and pilgrimage sites that, while specific to individual movements,

---

[1] On this term, see Reader (2015b) and also Baffelli and Reader (2019), which raises questions about its continuing viability.

contain messages of universalism and posit new ways of viewing the world in contrast to the older traditions. The second is the recent phenomenon of *seichi junrei* ("sacred place pilgrimages"), a term that in contemporary Japan refers to sites that need not have any connection to formal religious structures or institutions and that are grounded in popular culture, notably associated with manga, anime, and related media. Thus far, the first of these has hardly featured in the study of pilgrimage in Japan while the second—*seichi junrei*—is now starting to be addressed by scholars because it raises critical questions about conceptualizations not just of pilgrimage but also of the term "religion" (*shūkyō*) in the contemporary era. Both are also indicative of the changing dynamics of religion in the modern era, as they offer alternatives and pose challenges to areas once dominated by the older traditions.

NEW RELIGIONS AND PILGRIMAGE

The development of new religions has been one of the most significant themes in modern Japanese organizational and religious history. Emerging in Japan since the early nineteenth century and offering people new ways of engaging with their religious needs as well as alternatives to the older traditions, they have challenged the existing traditions in terms of belonging, belief, practice, and meaning, and drawn large numbers of people away from them. Especially in the postwar era, in which the older traditions have been shown to be increasingly moribund and (especially for Shinto) troubling ties with nationalist and revisionist politics, new religions collectively may now constitute the mainstream in Japan in terms of active religious organizational adherence. They have offered what to many are inspirational teachings and charismatic leadership that provide individual hope and meaning, in contrast to the socially embedded and customary nature of the older traditions.

New religions also pose significant challenges in terms of how the world is spatially conceptualized. This is evident in the uses made in many new religions of the practice of pilgrimage and in their concepts of sacred geography, areas that are perhaps the least discussed aspects of new religions even as they are critical manifestations of their teachings. Their use of pilgrimage and sacred geography indicates how new religions have bypassed the world of Buddhas, kami, temples, and shrines and (in their own terms) made them irrelevant. They have also subverted the themes of localized and particularized sacrality that these stood for, while replacing them with a new universalized sacred geography that transcends the Japanese landscape while remaining imbued with undercurrents of Japanese nationalism and identity.

New religions have characteristically developed around charismatic founders who claim to have discovered new truths and to be conduits mediating transcendental spiritual forces. Frequently, such charismatic founder figures (especially after death) become venerated as deities and in effect become the main focus of worship in their movements. The sacred centers of worship such movements build—not infrequently where their founders received their initial revelations or where they were born, and frequently within the lifetime of their founders—are commonly proclaimed as key pilgrimage sites for their movements and as transcendent spiritual foci for the world at large. When founders die, their mausoleums often become key features of the centers they have constructed, thus adding a new dimension to pilgrimage there, while the spirit of the founder may be believed to still be present at the sacred center, thereby empowering it further.

Through constructing sacred centers that form the key focal point of their movements, new religions thus simultaneously enhance the charismatic standing of their founders and create new geographies within their codes of belief. This construction of new geographies and pilgrimages is commonly underpinned by concepts of universalism, in which the sacred center is portrayed not just as a place of special significance for believers but also as a locus for the symbolic and spiritual reorientation of the world. They may also serve, both for Japanese devotees and any overseas members, as signifiers of Japanese centrality in the world, and of the idea that Japan is a special, chosen country from which truth will spread to and transform the wider world.

Given the vast numbers of new religions that have emerged in Japan, it would be impossible to touch on more than a few examples here, and I will limit my comments to two movements, one of which is among the earliest new religions, and the other one of the most recent to have emerged in Japan. Tenrikyō, which developed in the first half of the nineteenth century, has its sacred center at Tenri in Nara Prefecture. This is where its founder, Nakayama Miki (1798–1887), was born, where she raised her family, received revelations from God the Parent that indicated she was the spiritual vehicle through which the world was to be transformed, and where she performed acts of spiritual healing and developed her teachings. Tenrikyō grew into one of Japan's largest religious organizations, with churches (*kyōkai*) all over Japan and with an overseas mission and members in several countries around the world.

Its headquarters remain at Tenri, which is dominated by its vast sacred center of worship. According to Tenri theology, Miki's spirit is still present there. It is also the place of origin of humanity according to Tenrikyō; it was in Tenri, within the precincts of her home, that Nakayama Miki, in 1875, identified the *jiba*, the place where humanity created by God the Parent first emerged into this world. The *jiba* is also the source of humanity's salvation and is marked by a wooden pillar—the *kanrōdai*—that according to Tenrikyō is where spiritual nectar comes to earth to sustain and transform humanity.

Tenri is thus the locus of humanity's origin, its prime point of connection with God the Parent and—since her demise—with the spirit of Nakayama. It is a cosmic center, where the physical and spiritual realms are conjoined and from which the truth will spread to the world. It is the sacred home to which all devotees should return, and as such, Tenrikyō emphasizes pilgrimage as a core practice.[2] Pilgrimage is a practice in Tenrikyō that reaffirms the doctrines of the movement, which are expressed in physical and spiritual forms in the shape of the *kanrōdai* and the *jiba*. Thus, going to Tenri is a return home, a pilgrimage to the original center of faith and of all humanity. Pilgrimage thus expresses a universal message while affirming that the physical center and spiritual home of humanity is in Japan.

The Tenrikyō message of universalism contains—certainly for Japanese adherents—a message about Japan's position in the world. This is also reinforced in the eyes of overseas members, for whom Tenri is the gateway through which they know, see, and conceptualize Japan. As Huang Yueh-Po (2017b) has shown, for example, for Taiwanese Tenrikyō

---

[2]Here one should note that an early English study of Tenrikyō (Ellwood 1982) described it as a "pilgrimage faith," while pilgrimage features widely in Tenrikyō publications and in the calendar and activities of its branch churches, which organize various pilgrimages to Tenri on special occasions (notably January 26, the anniversary of Nakayama's death). I have been invited and have gone on pilgrimages with different local churches and Tenrikyō priests on two occasions, in 1986 and 2006. Information on Tenri and the movement is based on my visits there and on Kato (2017).

devotees, Tenri represents their understanding of Japan; Japan, for them, is a sacred land because it is the fount of universal truth as expressed by Nakayama Miki and her religion, and Tenri, as the source of humanity and the point of union between this realm and that of the gods, is the world's sacred epicenter. This indicates not simply a sacralization of the world via Japan but a reorientation of overseas visions of Japan. Unlike the envisioned Japan of most foreign visitors (and of Japan's national tourist agencies) in which Kyoto, Nara, and historic monuments, temples, and shrines (along with affirmations of Japanese modernity such as Akihabara) are the symbols of "real" Japan, for overseas followers of new religions, it is places such as Tenri that signify the true Japan.

In Tenrikyō we can see one example of the development of a new mode of sacred geography that reorients the world away from the traditional sacred sites of Buddhism and Shinto and centers it on a religious founder, on the faith she has developed, and the concept of a universal center associated with that founder.

This can also be seen in Kōfuku no Kagaku, founded in 1986 by Ōkawa Ryūhō, whose birthplace along with other sites associated with his life prior to setting up his religious movement have been sacralized as sites of pilgrimage for followers. Ōkawa initially developed his movement around spiritual messages claimed to be transmitted to him from other realms, claiming to be a spiritual teacher and prophet with a mission to transform the world. Subsequently he has declared himself to be the manifestation of El Cantare, the supreme deity, as well as the reincarnation of the historical Buddha.

Kōfuku no Kagaku members are encouraged to make pilgrimages to its four head temples around Japan (the last stage of which, the Sōhonzan Nasu-Shoja in Tochigi Prefecture, is designated as the movement's inner sanctuary and Ōkawa's "final resting place"[3]) and Ōkawa's birthplace in Tokushima Prefecture in Shikoku. The movement has produced a pilgrimage guidebook for those who visit his place of birth (Akiya 2015: 18–19), where Ōkawa's father, who was involved in establishing the movement, is also memorialized, and it runs organized pilgrimage visits there.[4] Other places related to Ōkawa's life prior to founding his religion also have become pilgrimage sites, such as the company lodgings where he lived while working in Nagoya. Kōfuku no Kagaku has acquired the building concerned and transformed it into a place of pilgrimage where disciples can see aspects of his earlier life, from a reconstruction of his bedroom to the founder's shoebox (Baffelli and Reader 2019: 161).

The transformation of Ōkawa from teacher and prophet to supreme spiritual master and deity is one of many examples of how Japanese new religions elevate their founders into figures with a universal message of salvation and into sacred beings around whom pilgrimages may be constructed. Kōfuku no Kagaku's pilgrimages, focused on their sacred centers and the birthplace of their founder who (in the movement's eyes) is the universal creator deity, also, like pilgrimage in Tenrikyō, create a new sacred geography framed around concepts of universalism while being physically grounded in Japan, which serves as the sacred cosmic center of the world, the place where the Buddha and universal creator have chosen to reincarnate and manifest themselves in the person of Ōkawa.

In such cases—and these are representative rather than strikingly special examples in the new religions—sacred geography is being reoriented around human figures and founders and the movements they construct. It is also being universalized. While these are

---

[3] http://www.happyscience.org.my/images/retreat2015_2.pdf (accessed December 1, 2020).
[4] http://info.happy-science.org/2015/70/ (accessed December 1, 2020).

Japanese places, they are posited as central foci for all humanity. Of course, there is also a strong strand of Japanese specificity about new religions as many commentators have noted (Baffelli and Reader 2019), and for new religions in general, their membership is overwhelmingly Japanese. The identification of the sacred center for humanity within the Japanese landscape is in itself something that enhances the appeal of such movements in Japan and provides a sense of cultural identity. Yet it also enables such movements to transcend any sense of localism and of *just* being Japanese religions, and places them in a wider, universal context while also serving as the expression of authentic Japan for devotees from abroad.

The new religions have drawn followers away from the older traditions while their construction of new sacred centers presents a challenge to the one-time hegemony of the Buddhist-Shinto-folk axis. The locus of the sacred in Japan, in terms of modern Japanese movements, lies not in ancient temples and shrines and centered on figures from mythical and legendary pasts such as kami or Buddhist figures of worship, but in real people who manifested in this world—specifically, in Japan—with universalizing messages of revelation and insight. These speak to truths that go beyond the localized sacrality of the kami and Buddhas and represent a fundamental religious reordering of the world for followers. This reordering of sacred geography is also, of course, a concentration of it, focused on a single place or complex of places associated with specific founder figures. It is another example of how the new religions as a collective phenomenon present a reshaping of the religious environment.

SEICHI JUNREI

While the new religions represent challenges to mainstream orthodoxy and concepts of sacred geography, and present a new setting for pilgrimage, they remain, at least in terms of pilgrimage, understudied and an area to which the academic field needs to pay more attention. This is not quite with same with the idea of *seichi junrei*, which is beginning to attract some academic attention and also presents challenges for the older traditions. The term *seichi junrei* draws on the concept of pilgrimage; *junrei* is one of the most common Japanese terms for visits to sacred sites and is commonly translated as (and widely seen as) the most representative Japanese term for the English "pilgrimage." *Seichi* translates directly as "sacred place." Yet such "sacred place pilgrimages" that are designated by the term *seichi junrei* often have little or nothing to do with what have normally been identified under the two terms *seichi* and *junrei*. Rather than signifying temples, shrines and pilgrimage circuits associated with figures such as Kannon and Kōbō Daishi, *seichi junrei* are visits (pilgrimages) to places associated with popular culture, and particularly with locations depicted in media forms such as anime, manga, films, and television dramas.

Indeed, *Seichi junrei* is term developed by anime and manga fans (Imai 2012:170) who have taken terms with religious connotations and applied them to an area commonly understood as being in the secular realm. As Imai notes, any place that features in an anime—a park, a block of apartments, the forecourts of stations—and leaves an impression on fans can be a "sacred place" (*seichi*). What they do at such places resembles actions people undertake at shrines and temples. For example, fans may write and leave messages at a *seichi* and engage in various ritual processes there, notably scene reenactments, often dressed in the costumes of figures in the manga or anime concerned, in the locations in which they occurred on screen. Imai indicates that the term *seichi junrei* first appeared around 2000 and that its use, along with the sites being visited, has grown exponentially since (2012: 175). At the same time, devotees of anime and manga have developed social networks both on- and offline that bring them together in an "imagined society" (*kasō shakai*) in which the ordinary and everyday world is sacralized (2012: 186).

Imai draws attention to one example where the focus of fan visits is a religious institution: Washinomiya Shrine in Saitama Prefecture, which features in the anime *Raki★Suta* (Lucky Star) and which has attracted large numbers of anime fans in its wake. Shrine attendance has been boosted by anime fans, who write messages on *ema* (which now have depictions of Lucky Star characters on them) and participate in shrine festivals. They have, for instance, constructed a Lucky Star *mikoshi* (portable shrine) that they carry while wearing Lucky Star costumes during shrine festivals and have become prominent agents in the public face of the shrine. Indeed, people now visit Washinomiya Shrine to see the anime fans and their costumes, *mikoshi*, and festival participation. It is not just the shrine that is incorporated into the anime fans "pilgrimage," however, for the streets around it that feature in the anime also have become the focus of their visits, while local commercial agencies and tourist offices have encouraged the development of this practice (Imai 2012).

Another prominent *seichi junrei* site is in Chichibu, where anime fans have flocked to visit sites associated with, and enact scenes from, *Ano hi mita hana no namae wo bokutachi wa mada shiranai* (lit. "We Still Don't Know the Name of the Flower We Saw That Day") called *Ano hana* for short, which is set there. Initially a television series, this became a popular film in 2013. The film depicts the actions of a group of friends who reconvene after one of their number dies and then reappears in one of the friends' dreams, asking them to help her move on to the next life. Strikingly, her spirit seeks out her friends—not a Buddhist priest—for this, and their quest is largely confined to places and activities associated with the secular world and with their activities together as friends. What is striking about the location of *Ano Hana* is that Chichibu has long been known as the setting for one of Japan's most prominent Buddhist pilgrimages, the 34 temple Chichibu Kannon pilgrimage that since the Tokugawa period has attracted many pilgrims, notably from the Tokyo region. However, in recent years—certainly since the last decade of the previous century—pilgrim numbers to the Chichibu Kannon temples have declined significantly (Satō 2004: 154–60; Reader 2014: 6).

By contrast, the number of fans doing the *Ano Hana seichi junrei* have grown rapidly, and local and regional agencies, from transport firms servicing the area to town and regional tourist offices, have focused their promotional energies and publicity increasingly on the anime pilgrimage (Macwilliams 2015; Kawasaki 2015). They have produced an *Ano Hana* pilgrimage map and set up an *"Ano Hana* stamp rally" that involves getting a stamp book inscribed at various sites associated with the *Ano Hana seichi junrei*, an activity that mirrors and appropriates the traditional pilgrimage practice of *nōkyō* in which pilgrims carry special books and scrolls that are inscribed at each temple on a pilgrimage route such as the Chichibu Kannon route (Reader 2014: 151–8). Anime fans can also make use of the *Junrei basu* ("pilgrimage bus'") decorated with Ano Hana signs and on which the stops are announced with the voice of the deceased friend (Macwilliams 2015).

In these cases, such *seichi junrei* have either become a dominant aspect in the workings of a traditional shrine, as at Washinomiya, or, as at Chichibu, have begun to displace (certainly in the eyes of local commercial agencies) the more traditional pilgrimage that had long been a primary element in attracting visitors to the area. In the *Ano Hana seichi junrei*, the focus is on the everyday world of streets, bridges, and places, where the friends whose activities are central to the spiritual comfort of their departed friend gather. The

Ano Hana seichi junrei touches on just one of the Chichibu Kannon pilgrimage temples, and even then not on its main hall of worship but on locations in the temple precincts (Kawasaki 2015). As observers have noted, anime pilgrims pay little attempt to engage in normative practices such as praying at the temple (Macwilliams 2015). While the traditional pilgrimage continues to exist, albeit with a decreasing clientele, it is clearly being displaced in many respects by the anime pilgrimage, which basically eschews associations with traditional religious structures and which could be subliminally read as expressing alienation from traditional religion, given that the deceased spirit's solace is sought via friends and their activities in everyday places rather than via the traditional means of Buddhist temples, priests, and rituals.

While there are various *seichi junrei* that incorporate shrines and temples (such as at Washinomiya and the presence of one area within the temple precinct in Chichibu), they need not have any formalized religious sites involved at all. In these latter cases, pilgrimage has been taken wholly out of the precincts of shrines and temples; something that is found in *seichi junrei* sites such as the Yuri on Ice *seichi junrei* in Karatsu in Saga prefecture, which involves visits to places depicted in a popular television anime series about a young Japanese ice skater and his struggles to balance his love for pork cutlets and rice with the need to keep his weight suitable for Olympic level figure skating. The anime is set against the landscape of Karatsu and depicts its castle, shopping streets, a restaurant, even a veterinary hospital, and other such places, although religious institutions barely appear.[5] One can now take official Yuri on Ice *seichi junrei* pilgrimage tours[6] and get pilgrimage maps produced by local authorities and handed out at the station to visitors. At Karatsu, as in other *seichi junrei* locations, one can observe fans dressed in various costumes associated with the anime series; at times, as I have seen on occasion, with their own photographer taking pictures as they reenacted scenes.

The development of such new modes of pilgrimage has also been advanced by the Anime Tourism Association, an industry group including publishers and others, which has created an *Anime seichi 88* ("Anime Tourism 88 stop pilgrimage" in English)[7] of eighty-eight anime sites in a linked nationwide *seichi junrei*. The number of sites involved is striking, as this is the number of temple sites on Japan's best-known Buddhist pilgrimage, the 88 stage Shikoku pilgrimage. Anime pilgrimages are thus now not just focusing on specific areas associated with a particular anime or manga but are also extending their reach to form extended routes in the manner of traditional pilgrimages whose frameworks they are appropriating.

CONCLUDING THOUGHTS

These two areas—the creation of new cosmic sacred centers that form the focus of pilgrimage devotion for members of new religious movements, and the development of activities that appropriate religious terms and the idea of pilgrimage to sacred places—indicate that notions of pilgrimage are in continuing flux in Japan. It also indicates that any conceptualization and study of pilgrimage in Japan needs to extend beyond the standard focus on the established traditions that has been dominant thus far. The concept

---

[5]There is one scene that involves the steps of a shrine but nothing related to visiting or praying there.
[6]http://yurionice.com/news/detail.php?id=1055177 (accessed December 1, 2020).
[7]https://animetourism88.com/ja/sanctuary (accessed December 1, 2020).

and practice of pilgrimage in the new religions and their framing of their specific sacred sites as manifestations and centers of a universal cosmological order must be given more voice in the future study of pilgrimage in Japan.

In addition, more thought needs to be given to the importance of the new religions as agencies creating and reshaping notions of sacred geography in Japan—a sacred geography that is not limited to or centered on the temples and shrines of the older traditions. Another significant dimension in the framework of pilgrimage in the new religions is that it is essentially human-focused. While the founders who are memorialized at their centers may be regarded within these movements as akin to deities, they are also human in nature and thus represent a shift in focus away from that of the older traditions and their pilgrimage sites, related as they are to mythical or legendary figures, whether the kami of Shinto or figures such as Kannon or Kōbō Daishi[8] in Buddhism.

Of course, such centers are highly specific to particular movements: Kōfuku no Kagaku's pilgrimages centered on Ōkawa have a meaning and indicate a sacralization process specific to its own members. Certainly, Kōfuku no Kagaku, like other new religions with their messages of universal truth, ideally believes that everyone should accept their message and that their pilgrimage centers are not thereby specific to the movement but to all humanity, but the reality is different. Nonetheless, the new sacred geographies being constructed in this way represent, as do the new religions in general, a challenge to and a reorienting of the religious world and to the ways that subjects such as pilgrimage are conceptualized and discussed within that world.

In the development of *seichi junrei*, the appropriation of religious terminology by agencies such as anime fans and commercial agencies helps affirm the validity of their activities and affords them with the same status as "traditional" pilgrimages. It also validates the sites that are visited and transforms seemingly mundane aspects of the everyday world into places imbued with spiritual meanings. This sacralization of the ordinary also, as Okamoto Ryōsuke (2015) has argued, raises questions about contemporary conceptualizations of religion. Okamoto discusses within the criteria of *seichi junrei* not just anime and manga-related pilgrimages but also other sites of significance within Japanese popular culture that have come to be seen as *seichi* by fans, such as the stadium where the annual High School baseball tournament is held and which is viewed as sacred turf by players and fans alike. In examining these examples Okamoto draws attention to what he sees as to the secularization of society, which he associates with the weakening of established religions and institutional religious affiliations.

While it is evident that organized religions in general but especially the older established traditions and notably Buddhism are experiencing declining levels of adherence (Reader 2012), Okamoto does not see this as indicating the disappearance of religion but instead a recalibration of what it means. As society becomes increasingly secularized, traditional religions wane, but this opens up space for new modes of activity that can expand what falls under the rubric of religion (2015: 207). Okamoto is agnostic about whether phenomena such as *seichi junrei* will be sustainable in the long run, but he views their manifestation as evidence of a shift in thinking about the nature of religion rather than its disappearance.

While the idea of expanding concepts of religion as Okamoto does require further discussion,[9] his arguments—along with the use of religious terminologies by secular

---

[8] While Kōbō Daishi is portrayed as a posthumous incarnation in this world of the Shingon founder Kūkai, he is to all intents and purposes a legendary figure.
[9] This is an issue I intend to take up in a longer study in due course.

agencies such as Karatsu's tourist office and by anime fan groups—reflect notions that have been discussed in Western academic studies of pilgrimage in recent decades. These studies have discussed pilgrimage not simply as something associated with formal religious traditions and institutions, or even with figures such as saints and local deities, but as located also in contexts normally devoid of religious connotations. Concepts such as "secular pilgrimages" that focus on such places as the homes and graves of deceased rock stars, the sites of fan conventions, the graves of literary and political figures, and so on have been discussed widely in such terms, and scholars have also challenged ideas of what is deemed "sacred" (Reader and Walter 1993; Margry 2008). The study of *seichi junrei* indicates that such theoretical discussions are also relevant in Japan and thus, they should be part of any continuing discourse on pilgrimage there.

The creation of new sacred geographies that reorient the religious world around the person and teachings of specific charismatic figures, along with the development of new notions of pilgrimage revolving around aspects of popular secular culture, are not just indications of the fluid and evolving nature of pilgrimage culture in Japan but are also indicators of gravitational shifts in the structures of religion there. The rise of "new religions" and their development of new sacred centers offered people a path of religious faith not associated with established religious traditions. The new religions, especially in the second half of the last century, became de facto the most prominent religious organizations in Japan in terms of active religious membership and affiliation, and while they have more recently experienced problems of declining and aging memberships, they remain comparatively vibrant in institutional terms in comparison to the established traditions, to which they continue to represent, in organizational and membership-related terms, a significant challenge. Their development of new centers of religious gravity via the construction of new pilgrimage geographies is a symbolic manifestation of this wider challenge.

The development of *seichi junrei* represents another way in which the established religions are being challenged not just in terms of pilgrimage but also in terms of what is seen as "religious" and "sacred." It raises also questions about whether areas once dominated by the established and organizational religions structures are now being challenged and even taken over by new non-institutionalized forms that raise questions about traditional notions of what is secular and what is religious. As such, the fluctuating world of pilgrimage in Japan offers insights into the changing dynamics of religious structure as well as indicating the need to think beyond the frameworks that have thus far dominated the study of pilgrimage in Japan.

See also Chapter 3, "Cultural Heritage," Chapter 5, "Economy and Spirituality," Chapter 19, "'New Religions'," Chapter 25, "Space," and Chapter 28, "Tourism."

CHAPTER 21

Politics

ŌMI Toshihiro

The modern period (1868–1945) in Japan was a period that raised a number of important questions about the political nature of religion and the religious nature of politics. After numerous twists and turns, the Meiji government adopted the principle of freedom of belief (*shinkyō no jiyū*) in the constitution, which was ratified in 1889. However, this freedom was guaranteed only so far as it did not infringe upon the divine nature of the emperor (*tennō no shinseisei*). In other words, Japanese people could be Buddhists, Christians, or believe in other religions or in nothing at all and this did not constitute a problem. Nevertheless, to revere the emperor was considered a duty for the entire population. Thereby, Japanese religious professionals and lay devotees continued to question the compatibility of individual faith and the veneration of the emperor.

Before the war, many religious professionals thought that supporting the state was a positive activity. Therefore, they actively encouraged the protection of individual religious convictions and, at the same time, the maintenance of the state, which was centered on a divine emperor. This situation is described through the phrase "the Japanese model for the separation between politics and religion" (*Nihon-gata seikyō bunri*) (Yasumaru 1979). State and religion were technically separate, but the presence of the emperor, who was connected with specific religious discourses (based on Shinto), constituted the axis of the state authority. In spite of the inherent conflict with their beliefs, other religions continually tried to secure their endorsement within the national political structure.

During the war, this ambiguous separation between politics and religion tended to be dismantled, opening the way for a period in which the uniformity of the people's mindscape was considered essential. The necessity for every citizen to show respect for the divine nature of the emperor was increasingly stressed in the attempt to strengthen the unity of the national population. At the same time, religious professionals began to show a stronger awareness of this conflict with the state's mandated belief. The deification of the emperor and of Japan itself was inextricably intertwined with the upsurge of nationalism, while the political nature of religion and the religious nature of politics ended up reinforcing each other. In this chapter, I analyze the case of Buddhism, Christianity, new religions, and Shinto in relation to the above-mentioned facts, taking into account some of the most recent and relevant research results in this field.

Terms such as "pacification and protection of the states [through Buddhist rituals]" (*chingo kokka*) and "mutual dependence between imperial and Buddhist law" (*ōbō buppō sōi* 王法仏法相依) indicate that even in premodern Japan, it was normal for Buddhism to maintain ties with the state, thereby creating conditions for reciprocal support. Nevertheless, in the modern period, the relationship between Buddhism and the state was reorganized and the position of the emperor was at the center of various debates. A relevant example is given by the theoretical productions of movements of Nichirenism (*Nichiren-shugi*), that is, a nationalistic reframing of Nichiren's (1222–1282) teachings (Ōtani 2001).

Tanaka Chigaku (1861–1939), an advocate of Nichirenism, theorized the spiritual unification of Japan beginning from the emperor and including all Japanese subjects, who were supposed to base their ways of life on the teachings of the Lotus Sutra. Tanaka thought that the type of Buddhism introduced by Nichiren, and a model of the state centered on the emperor, were neither too close nor too distant. Nichirenism clearly aimed at a unification between politics and religion, fostering movements that pushed toward an intensification of the political nature of religion. Under the influence of Tanaka Chigaku, the Buddhist preacher Inoue Nisshō (1886–1967) argued for the use of terrorism to promote structural reforms, and the general Ishihara Kanji (1889–1949) provoked the Manchurian incident (1931) in order to hasten the "ultimate world war." These figures engaged in extremist political movements, substantiating them with both religious theories and religious experiences (Nakajima 2013).

In addition, among the monks of the True Pure Land School (Jōdo shinshū), there were some who tried to create strong connections between individual faith and either the emperor or the state. Akegarasu Haya 暁烏敏 (1877–1954), a True Pure Land monk of the Ōtani branch, is an emblematic case. During the Second World War, Akegarasu produced an unusual theory about the unity of politics and religion according to which the emperor was to be considered, at the same time, as a "living god" (*ikigami*) and a "living Buddha" (*ikibotoke*) (Niino 2014). It is likely that the True Pure Land School tradition of worshiping branch leaders as Buddhas provided the background for Akegarasu's exaltation of the divine nature of the human emperor. Since the premodern period, the True Pure Land School has venerated the successors of Shinran (1173–1262), who became leaders of other Jōdo shinhū congregations, as living Buddhas who transcended the human condition. In the modern period, Akegarasu's religious theories conflated the traditional faith in the congregation leaders and the representation of the emperor as a deified living Buddha (Ōmi 2016).

Such support for the emperor and the state, as provided by Akegarasu and other True Pure Land School thinkers, has also been explained in relation to the doctrines of national polity (*kokutai ron*) (Nakajima 2017). The National Learning (*Kokugaku*) of Motoori Norinaga (1730–1801) exerted a considerable influence on the premise of the national polity discourse, which was based on the sacralization of the imperial line. Norinaga's theories on taking refuge in the gods (kami) and criticizing human agency were strongly inspired by his True Pure Land beliefs, which gave absolute priority to the beneficent power (*tariki*) of the Buddha Amida, disregarding the value of human action. In other words, the doctrines of national polity, highly influential until the end of the Second World War, were at least in part conceptions adapted from True Pure Land discourses. Therefore, the True Pure Land School thinkers felt the logical and perhaps political necessity to link their theories of the self to the discourses about the emperor and the state.

Although the relationship between Buddhism and the state was reorganized in the modern period, the knot of this new interaction was actually an evolution of premodern theories and religious discourses. Since the ancient period, Buddhism constituted the base of Japanese society; even when we consider its political nature in the modern period, it is always important to take implicit traditional elements into account (Karatani 2012).

Unlike Buddhism, which was deeply rooted in Japanese society, Christianity was banned during the Edo period and began to propagate again in the modern period. Because of its Western origins and its conception of a god that transcends the state, Christianity was often attacked by ultranationalists. The famous "disrespect incident" (1890) in which the Christian and founder of the Nonchurch Movement Uchimura Kanzō (1861–1930) was criticized because he refused to bow deeply in front of the portrait of Emperor Meiji is well known. However, there were numerous other obstacles to the diffusion of Christianity within Japanese society (Suzuki 2010).

On the one hand, Christian missionaries and lay believers occasionally distanced themselves from Japanese religious culture. An emblematic example is the visits to Shinto shrines. Although the custom to worship at Shinto shrines was made compulsory by the state for students as part of the population's duties during the Meiji period, Sophia University and other Christian schools obstinately refused to pay homage to Shinto shrines, considering this a violation of their freedom of belief. Nevertheless, during the war it became problematic to carry on this kind of opposition and the obligatory visits to Shinto shrines became unavoidable for professors and students. Faith in the Christian god had to surrender to the realities of political power, which used a godlike emperor as its flag (Nakai 2017).

The theories of Yanaihara Tadao (1893–1961) show how Christians confronted the state during the war (Akae 2017). Yanaihara criticized the war from the perspective of the Christian ideal of "kingdom of God." Because of this, he was attacked by ultranationalists and forced to resign from his position at Tokyo Imperial University. Subsequently, Yanaihara went through a period of individual repentance, at the end of which he started talking about the salvation of the Japanese population based on the harmonization of nationalism and Christianity, which he defined as "Japanese-style Christianity." This theory basically shared the same contents of the national polity discourses, which were produced by right-wing groups in the same period. Nevertheless, Yanaihara maintained an original position because he never abandoned the Christian paradigm of the "kingdom of God" and did not replicate that rhetoric in relation to the power of a single country, even when exalting Japan.

Like all other religions, Christianity chose a path that was largely subservient to the state system of modern Japan. Nevertheless, the origins and history of Christianity demonstrate that it has always been difficult for this religion to spread widely in Japan; even now the percentage of Christians on the entire population is about 1 percent. For this reason, it is possible to interpret a part of the theoretical discourses produced by the Christians as attempts to obtain a certain degree of freedom from the authority of the state.

The new religions that developed in modern Japan brought with them many peculiarities. Because these new movements had been recently created relatively recently and catered to people who did not seek salvation in traditional religions such as Buddhism, they often suffered from a lack of social consensus, which often left them vulnerable to persecution. Kōdō Ōmoto, which was led by Deguchi Onisaburō (1871–1948), is a paradigmatic example (Kawamura 2017). This new religion quickly expanded its power in the first half of the twentieth century thanks to continuous propagation activities, but was stigmatized as a threat by the state and repeatedly suppressed.

Such issues created situations of significant instability for the new religions and their followers. During the war, therefore, many committed themselves to sustaining the state in order to be considered meritorious members of society. The case of Tenrikyō, in particular, has been studied in depth (Nagaoka 2015). Tenrikyō followers call all the services, from cleaning the headquarters to voluntary activities for the association, "daily donations" (*hinokishin*), which are considered expressions of gratitude for the kindness of their god. During the war, this concept of *hinokishin* was exploited quite practically in order to sustain the state on the home front. Tenrikyō followers interpreted this wartime collaboration as a viable way to present themselves as Japanese citizens who demonstrate gratitude to the emperor. In this way, the faith toward, on the one hand, the god of Tenrikyō and, on the other, the determination to be identified as part of the state was indissolubly tied together.

Like Christianity, new religions were religious minorities in modern Japan. Nevertheless, Christianity had an enormous power on the international level, and even in Japan it could count on followers who belonged primarily to the elite of society. The majority of the followers of the new religions, on the other hand, came from the subaltern strata of society and were occasionally marginalized. For this reason, these followers tried to overcome their sense of alienation, which derived in part from their exclusion from the wartime narrative of the unity of the Japanese population, by developing strong nationalistic feelings.

THE RELIGIOUS NATURE OF SHINTO

As we have seen, Buddhism, Christianity, and new religions all altered or suppressed their religious nature on behalf of the emperor and the state. Now, it may be illustrative to focus on Shinto, which provided the basis for the deification of the emperor and its developing modalities in modern Japan (Shimazono 2010). Shinto was considered a "non-religion" (*hi-shūkyō* 非宗教) and was treated as a sort of moral discourse for the public rites of the state. In spite of this definition, when professors and students of Christian universities tried to refuse paying homage to Shinto shrines, they actually demonstrated that Shinto and Shinto shrines did have religious associations.

The religious nature of Shinto can be clearly understood if we think about the vigorous participation of the population in worshiping the deified Emperor Meiji (1852–1912) at Meiji Shrine in Tokyo (Hirayama 2015). Built during the Taishō period, Meiji Shrine was considered a "sacred land" (*seichi*), which attracted both commoners, who liked visiting shrines and temples, and the elites, who controlled the country and society. Even today, and especially at the beginning of the new year, innumerable visitors flock to Meiji Shrine to enjoy the experience of being a part of a community of citizens and, at the same time, sharing a common religious milieu.

Until a few years ago, the indoctrination of the people about the divine nature of the emperor, which was based on Shinto, was often interpreted as a unilateral imposition of the state's authority over the population, using both the moral teachings reported in the Imperial Edict on Education and the compulsory visits to the Shinto shrines. Nevertheless, recent studies reveal that in many ways, the population itself voluntarily pushed toward a divinization of the emperor and the state according to a shared religious will. An example of this situation is the popular support for Meiji Shrine, but—as we have seen in this entry—even religious professionals and followers of Buddhism and new religions were active agents in reinforcing the veneration of the emperor. Future research should consider the various instances of and perspectives on the active politicization processes that derived from these religions in their efforts to contend with the state's mandatory acknowledgment of the divinity of the emperor.

See also Chapter 7, "Empire and Colonialism," Chapter 14, "Law," and Chapter 19, " 'New Religions'."

CASE STUDY

Religion, Socialism, and Secularization

James Mark SHIELDS

The New Buddhist Fellowship (*Shin Bukkyō Dōshikai*; hereafter, NBF) consisted of roughly a dozen young scholars and activists, many of whom had studied under prominent mid-Meiji Buddhist scholars Murakami Senshō (1851–1929) and Inoue Enryō (1858–1919). Principal among them were Sakaino Kōyō (1871–1933), Watanabe Kaikyoku (1872–1933), Sugimura Sojinkan (1872–1945), Katō Genchi (1873–1965), and Takashima Beihō (1875–1949). This group of seven would be joined in the following years by a number of others, including Suzuki Teitarō (Daisetsu) (1870–1966), a.k.a. D. T. Suzuki. While the NBF was overtly lay-oriented—in fact, strongly critical of traditional monastic or institutional Buddhism—several of the New Buddhists had been ordained as Buddhist priests, and most had some sort of Buddhist educational background, especially within the Nishi Honganji branch of the Shin sect.

In July 1900, a magazine called *Shin Bukkyō* (New Buddhism; hereafter, SB) was launched as the new movement's mouthpiece. The first edition begins with the group's "manifesto" (*sengen*), which opens with an apocalyptic call to arms. Here, as elsewhere, the New Buddhists borrow from the discourse of Buddhist decadence (*daraku Bukkyō*) that first arose with Neo-Confucians of the Edo period and was adopted by a number of secularists and Shinto nativists in the early years of Meiji, before being internalized by early Buddhist modernists such as Inoue Enryō and Nakanishi Ushirō (1859–1930). And yet, as I have argued elsewhere, the New Buddhists occasionally pushed the envelope further, beyond the rather straightforward ("Protestant") critique of Buddhist ritualism, monastic corruption, and materialist hypocrisy. In so doing, they veered into more explicitly political—even radical—forms of critique.

"Faith" (*shinkō*) was a matter of particular concern for the New Buddhists (SB 2, 13: 398–404). Indeed, the very first and arguably most significant of their six General Principles (*kōryō*) states: "We regard a sound Buddhist faith as our foundational principle." In the third article in the inaugural issue of the journal, Katō Genchi takes up the theme, by first denouncing the "worldliness" and "degeneration" of the Buddhist monks and temples of his day, and then going on to argue, somewhat unexpectedly, that far from being a matter of individual will or agency, "faith" is a product of religious and social evolution (SB 1, 1: 8–9). On the whole, while the New Buddhists insisted that "faith" must remain the foundation for New Buddhism, they were not calling for a return to the "stabilities" of traditional belief.

> While the root and foundation of religion is certainly faith, the contents on this faith will depend on the particular period and circumstances. Thus, over time, religions have no choice but to gradually develop and evolve ... As such, when we see people trying to bring back the old faith of Śākyamuni, Shinran, or Nichiren today in the Meiji period, all we can do is laugh at such a stupid and worthless idea. (SB 1, 1: 9)

As Katō goes on to explain, while the contents of faith today cannot be fully specified, it is also not quite true that "anything goes." Any faith suitable to the modern period must pass the test of reason and "natural, experiential knowledge" (*shizenteki keiken no chishiki*). Thus, "reliance on supernatural beings" is ruled out, as is anything that cannot be verified on the basis of information gleaned from our "ordinary, daily experience" (*hibi heijō no keiken*) (SB 1,1: 9). Moreover, Katō insists that faith must be directly applicable to "practice" or "projects" (*katsudō* or *jigyō*), thus moving toward the Marxist concept of praxis—or at least away from the "Protestant" separation between faith and works. Here as elsewhere, "faith" seems to act as an umbrella term denoting a sincere and enthusiastic commitment to the rational, ethical, and social aspects of New Buddhism, that is, practical wisdom, personal moral cultivation, and social reform (Yoshinaga 2011: 30). A closer examination of New Buddhist "sound faith" reveals that it comprises the following elements: (1) knowledge; (2) respect for emotions, including poetic feelings; (3) a focus on this world, that is, setting aside transcendence and concerns about the afterlife; (4) proactive engagement; (5) ethics; and (6) a positive or optimistic outlook (see, e.g., SB 1, 3: 82–9). It is, in short, the name for a particular, Buddhist, style of living; a commitment to fully investing in the practice (or "game") of living a flourishing life according to generic Buddhist principles.

A characteristic feature of the work of the New Buddhists is an unabashed affirmation of "this world" (*genseshugi* or *genseishugi*). While the modernistic emphasis on free inquiry and a rational, ethical, and scientific outlook were also in evidence among the figures representing the earlier Japanese Buddhist Enlightenment, the New Buddhists—some of them—took things much further in this direction, to the point where it could be legitimately asked what was left of "religion" (or "Buddhism") as normally understood. For instance, earlier Buddhist Enlightenment figure Nakanishi Ushirō had contrasted the "materialism" of the "old" Buddhism with the "spiritualism" of the new and, in similar fashion, the "scholarship" of traditional monastic Buddhism with the "faith" orientation of the new lay Buddhism. In contrast, the New Buddhists reverse these positions, so that it is the "old" Buddhism that focuses on "spiritual" matters, while New Buddhism is content with addressing "real" or "practical" issues of this life: poverty, hunger, and so on. Here again, the New Buddhists move away from a Protestant/liberal focus on individual belief toward something more akin to modern progressivism.

Moreover, while the New Buddhists attempted to clarify a new form of "faith," in doing so they radically transformed the ordinary sense of the term so that it became, as noted above, a synonym for "moral commitment" or "sincere engagement" (to use traditional Buddhist terms, "right intention"). Although they began their movement as self-identified "puritans," some, including Sugimura Jūō, were hesitant to push this idea too far, lest it begin to sound overly "renunciative," "severe," or "pessimistic." Here again, their "puritanism" was of a different sort than the "passive" and "world-denying" asceticism (*kin'yokushugi*) of monks and priests; rather, it denoted a sincere, focused and "pro-active engagement" with the world (*sekkyokutekina katsudō*), one that was also not averse to seeking "pleasure" (*tanoshimi mo motomu*) (SB 1, 5: 159). This creates a fascinating tension played out in the pages of New Buddhism, between, on the one hand, a renunciatory impulse inherited not only from classical Buddhist monasticism but also from nineteenth-century liberal Protestantism, and, on the other, an optimistic and this-worldly outlook emerging from Unitarianism, New Thought, Transcendentalism, and nineteenth-century progressivism.

Peter Nosco has argued that the Edo shogunate engaged in "pragmatic" efforts to bring about something like a separation of religion and politics—which is of course a key feature of concepts of modern secularism (or "secularization"). And yet, the New Buddhists were in the main resistant to that separation, at least if it implied that religion must or should remain confined to the realm of the "private" and the "individual" (Teeuwen 2013: 5). In *A Secular Age*, philosopher Charles Taylor makes the case for immanence as a crucial foundation of secular modernity, invoking the "immanent frame" as an understanding of the universe that constitutes a "natural" as opposed to "supernatural" order. Yet, the "immanent frame" of the New Buddhists was both a natural and a social frame. Indeed, in their version of secular Buddhism, the most significant appeal of Buddhism was in fact its promise to address social, economic, and arguably political problems. That is to say, while the NBF rejected state-sponsored religion, they did not envision a privatization of Buddhist faith and practice. Quite the contrary, I suggest, they argued for the socialization of such—in line, perhaps, with alternative conceptions of modernity more familiar to radical than liberal (or conservative) social and political theory.

CHAPTER 22

Premodern Traditions

HAYASHI Makoto

There is a broad agreement on the fact that no conceptualization has been as influential in the study of the history of Japanese religion as Kuroda Toshio's (1926–1993) *kenmitsu taisei ron* 顕密体制論 (exoteric-esoteric system theory). Scholars' views of Japanese religious history changed greatly after its appearance (See Dobbins 1996). In this chapter, I will approach the history of the field with an eye on its "post-Kuroda" developments, by focusing not on medieval Buddhism—Kuroda's own specialization—but on Shinto, Shugendō, and Onmyōdō, as there are already many studies dedicated to the history of research on Japanese Buddhism (especially Taira 1992).

SHINTO

While Kuroda was not a Shinto history specialist per se, he actively discussed it, exerting a considerable influence on this field. Kuroda boldly challenged the generally held image of Shinto as an ethnic religion that has existed without interruption since ancient times. Rather, he emphasized, based on his *kenmitsu taisei* theory, that Shinto was part of exo-esoteric (*kenmitsu*) Buddhism.

> Today we usually use "Shinto" to refer to a separate religion existing alongside Buddhism and Christianity, and there are many people who incorrectly believe that it has existed as such since the beginning of history. "Shinto" is also presently treated this way on a legal and institutional level. However, before *shinbutsu bunri* [separation of kami and buddhas] during the Meiji period [1868–1912], for at least one thousand years "Shinto" was part of the structure of a religious world (including various reformist and dissident schools) centered on *kenmitsu* Buddhism—originally an inferior, marginal part. It did not have an independent nature as an individual religion. (Kuroda 1990: 153)

Kuroda's view of Shinto was based on Tsuda Sōkichi's 1949 *Nihon no Shintō* (Japan's Shinto). He viewed Shinto in ancient and medieval times as what Tsuda called "the authority, power, functions, and activities of the gods," which was not an independent religion existing alongside Buddhism. Kuroda located Shinto within *kenmitsu* Buddhism, making clear that it was one secular form of the Buddha-Dharma rather than a religion independent from Buddhism.

Subsequently, Kuroda's theory was challenged by Takatori Masao, who, like Kuroda, had graduated from Kyoto University's Department of History. Takatori presented his *Shintō no seiritsu* (The Formation of Shinto, 1979) as the antithesis of Kuroda's view of Shinto. This book drew from Hori Ichirō's idea of Shinto as "latent intention." According to Hori, in Japan *shinbutsu shūgō* 神仏習合 (the amalgamation of kami and the buddhas) was only carried out in a loose form; only rarely did it develop into a systematic combinatory system (Hori 1975). Instead, there was a strongly rooted perception that the buddhas and the kami were different. Hori referred to this as *shunbetsu ishiki* 峻別意識 (awareness of distinctness), which Takatori rephrased as *shinbutsu kakuri* 神仏隔離 (separation of kami and buddhas). According to Takatori, a tendency to reject Buddhism emerged at the end of the Nara period (710–794) in reaction to the political activities and attempted coup of the monk Dōkyō (700–772), with aristocrats becoming hesitant to use Buddhist monks and ceremonies for imperial court rites. Along with *shinbutsu kakuri*, taboos, such as those surrounding death, emerged, and customs that avoided Buddhism spread from the imperial court to shrines, eventually influencing the lives of commoners. Engaging in meticulous argumentation while pointing to *shinbutsu kakuri* and this awareness of taboos, Takatori asserted that Shinto came into existence between the end of the Nara period and the early Heian period (794–1185), causing a stir in research on the history of Japanese religions.

Taking in Takatori's ideas, Satō Masato and Mitsuhashi Tadashi further advanced research on *shinbutsu kakuri*. These two scholars used *shinbutsu kakuri* to try to present an overall picture of religious beliefs and practices related to the kami during the Heian period. They saw the mid-Heian period—thus, a later age than Takatori had envisioned—as a watershed moment in Shinto history (Mitsuhashi 2007; Satō 2007). Satō introduced an institutional history perspective, which had been lacking in Takatori's work, and Mitsuhashi, inspired by Takatori, discussed not only the establishment of Shinto but also that of Japanese Buddhism and Onmyōdō during the Heian period. Mitsuhashi argued that the Heian aristocracy involved themselves in Shinto, Buddhism, and Onmyōdō, using each as needed without feeling that this was inconsistent. He also claimed that Japanese people's present-day use of various religious beliefs and practices as circumstances require has its roots in such behavioral patterns of the Heian aristocracy (Dolce and Mitsuhashi 2013; see also Teeuwen and Rambelli 2003).

Next, let us turn to Mark Teeuwen and Inoue Hiroshi, two scholars who have inherited Kuroda's view of Shinto. Teeuwen posed an important question that no one had yet raised: how to pronounce the two characters normally read today as *shintō* 神道. According to him, in the past they had been read as *jindō*, referring to native gods tamed by Buddhism (Teeuwen 2007). During the fifteenth century Ryōhen used *shintō*, the voiceless pronunciation of these characters, to refer to a specific school, an understanding that was later inherited by Yoshida Kanetomo (1435–1511). Teeuwen describes the significance of Yoshida Shinto as follows:

> Yoshida Kanetomo rewrote the view of Shinto that had emerged at Ise, cutting it off from Buddhism and re-fusing it with rites for the gods. Yoshida Shinto has many elements that connect to contemporary Shinto thought, particularly the fundamental understanding … that in Japan primitive Shinto—different from Buddhism and Confucianism—survives, having existed continually since the beginning of history. (Teeuwen 2017: 13)

The difference between *jindō* and *shintō* proposed by Teeuwen had an impact on many scholars and came to be frequently mentioned. Kuroda's conjecture that there was a fundamental change during the latter half of the medieval period in the concept was shown to be true and strengthened by Teeuwen (2010).

Inoue Hiroshi, on the other hand, has written a diachronic history of Shinto based on the *kenmitsu taisei* theory. Inoue, who had carried out research on provincial *ichinomiya* 一宮 shrines, considered Shinto history in terms of shrines, while flexibly incorporating research results from Takatori, Mitsuhashi, and Teeuwen. Inoue proposes the following four historical markers (Inoue 2006: 358–60). First, formal shrines were established during the latter half of the seventh century, along with the ancient *ritsuryō* state. Second, accompanying the establishment of the *kenmitsu* system, "Japan's religion" took form in the eleventh and twelfth centuries, conceptualizing kami and buddhas as forming one whole, and kami-related matters were referred to as *jindō*. Third, the disintegration of the *kenmitsu* system, the establishment of Yoshida Shinto, and the term *shintō* took root from the fifteenth to seventeenth centuries. Fourth, the establishment of "State Shinto" (*kokka shintō*) along with the formation of a modern nation-state occurred in the nineteenth century. Inoue insightfully linked the formation of the *kenmitsu* system during the second period to *jindō* and its disintegration during the third period to *shintō*.

As we can see, the scholars who carried on the *kenmitsu taisei* theory that began with Kuroda and the *shinbutsu kakuri* academic school that began with Takatori have engaged in Shinto research while rivaling and countering each other's scholarship. (In English, see Teeuwen and Rambelli 2003.)

SHUGENDŌ

The publication of the series of volumes entitled *Sangaku shūkyō-shi kenkyū sōsho* (Mountain Religion History Research Series; 18 vols., 1975–84) played a major role in the flourishing of research on Shugendō. Before its appearance, there were individual articles on sacred mountains in various localities, but many of them had been published in regional journals and were not easy to obtain. This landmark series made widely available a general overview of research on sacred mountains that exist throughout Japan. At the same time, it also led to the formation of connections among scholars. In 1980 the Sangaku Shugen Gakkai (English name: The Association for the Study of Japanese Mountain Religion) was formed, giving scholars in the field a place to gather, exchange information, and further their research by learning from others. Starting in 1985, the association began publishing the journal *Sangaku shugen* (English title: Japanese Mountain Religion), which released a considerable amount of scholarship every year, facilitating the sharing of even more information among scholars.

There have been two particularly influential leaders in Shugendō studies: Gorai Shigeru (1908–1993) and Miyake Hitoshi. Gorai understood Shugendō as an extension of itinerant folk religious practitioners called *hijiri* 聖 and emphasized its primitive religious nature (Gorai 1995a). According to him, Shugendō is at its core an "untamed" religion whose practitioners, the *yamabushi*, engage in ascetic practices to erase the karmic seeds of their transgressions. Gorai saw original Shugendō as carried out by *yamabushi* who were aloof from the world, and therefore thought that organized, institutionalized Shugendō had lost its vitality (Gorai 1995b). At a time when many scholars had explored and clarified the historical development of the Tōzan 当山 and Honzan 本山 schools by uncovering historical materials from local sacred mountains, Gorai continued to talk about the likes of itinerant ascetics such as Enkū (1632–1695) and Mokujiki (1718–1810). However, Gorai did not present an adequate explanation of how *yamabushi* who had rejected the secular world had been able to meet the needs of commoners living in it.

On the other hand, Miyake Hitoshi has contributed to Shugendō studies more than anyone else. He has carried out research for a considerable period of time and written a remarkable number of works from a wide perspective. Here, let us narrow our focus to consider Miyake's understanding of when Shugendō came into existence. In *Shugendō soshiki no kenkyū* (Study on Shugendō Organizations, 1999), he explains: "Japan's ancient mountain beliefs and practices came to acquire a religious form during the latter half of the Heian period under the influence of shamanism, Buddhism, and Shinto" (5). However, in *Shugendō no chiikiteki tenkai* (Shugendō's Regional Developments, 2012), Miyake attributes major importance to *Shosan engi* (Mountains' Origin Narratives), a collection of oral traditions regarding sacred mountains, and revises the time of the initial development of Shugendō to the first half of the medieval period. Thus, Miyake's understanding of the formative period of Shugendō has changed over the course of his research.

In recent years, important works of empirical research have been published, such as Suzuki Shōei's *Shugendō rekishi minzoku ronshū* (Essays on Shugendō History and Folklore: 3 vols., 2003–4) and Sekiguchi Machiko's *Shugendō kyōdan seiritsu-shi: Tōzanha o tsūjite* (History of the Formation of Shugendō Religious Organizations: The Tōzan School; 2009). Another influential recent scholar is Hasegawa Kenji, who argues that while *yamabushi* groups were part of organizations based on individual mountains in the Muromachi period (1336–1573), they then formed regional bonds that transcended these affiliations and were organized under the Shōgoin temple (Hasegawa 2016). Drawing from Hasegawa's research, Tokunaga Seiko wrote the following regarding the formation of Shugendō:

> The establishment of "Shugendō" can be traced back to the end of the thirteenth century into the fourteenth century. Generally, it was mentioned alongside exoteric (*ken* 顕) and esoteric (*mitsu* 密) forms of Buddhism. The "Onjōji Chapter" (*Onjōji no maki*) in the *Tengu zōshi* [Book of Tengu, end of the thirteenth century] states that the combination of "the single path of Shugen" with exoteric and esoteric Buddhism is "only practiced at our temple Onjōji" … At this time "Shugen" or "Shugendō" was what can be considered a component of *kenmitsu* Buddhism. Thus, it appears that Shugen was a category employed to emphasize the uniqueness of Onjōji's Buddhism. (Tokunaga 2015: 86–7)

Hasegawa and Tokunaga focused their research on when the terms "Shugen" and "Shugendō" appear in historical materials and their meaning, and their findings were valuable. Shugendō, until then approached either within folklore studies (Gorai) or within religious studies (Miyake), gradually became the object of empirical research by scholars of Japanese history. Hasegawa and Tokunaga, actively applying Kuroda's *kenmitsu taisei* theory to Shugendō history, made clear the process by which Shugendō grew independent from *kenmitsu* Buddhism (Tokieda, Hasegawa, and Hayashi 2015).

Another post-Miyake influential scholar is Suzuki Masataka. It is important to consider the fact that Suzuki prefers relying on the term "mountain beliefs" (*sangaku shinkō*) rather than "Shugendō" (Suzuki 2015b). Following the research of Tokunaga and Hasegawa, Suzuki became aware of the difficulties deriving from a loose application of the term "Shugendō" and decided to prioritize the concept of mountain beliefs, the flexibility of which allows for the explanation of various complex phenomena also associated to contemporary Japan. Suzuki defines Shugendō as a part of the mountain beliefs in which "mountain ascetic practices are informed and systematized according to Buddhist and Daoist theories in order to provide an embodiment of the power of the mountain" (Suzuki 2018a: 103–4). Using the term "mountain beliefs," it is possible to take into account various types of worship activities envisioning the mountain as a sacred space, or the ritual performing arts for venerating the mountain without worrying about the presence or the absence of a Shugendō influence. Although the concept of Shugendō has been increasingly circumscribed and fragmented in historical research, Suzuki's scholarship, which is grounded in extensive fieldwork, is extremely significant for highlighting the existence of a broad context defined as "mountain beliefs." (For a general review of new scholarship on Shugendō, see Castiglioni, Rambelli, and Roth 2020.)

ONMYŌDŌ

For a long time, Saitō Rei's *Ōchō jidai no onmyōdō* (Onmyōdō in the Classical Era; 1915) was the only study of Onmyōdō available. This changed in 1981 with the publication of Murayama Shūichi's *Nihon onmyōdō-shi sōsetsu* (A General History of Japanese Onmyōdō), which aroused scholars' interest in Onmyōdō. With Murayama taking the editorial lead, *Onmyōdō sōsho* (Onmyōdō Book Series, 4 vols.) was published between 1991 and 1993, and the subject finally came to be seen as a legitimate field of study. This series was compiled with the cooperation of senior scholars such as Murayama, as well as emerging new researchers such as Yamashita Katsuaki. While its significance in the history of Onmyōdō studies can be described in a variety of ways, I would like to focus on two points.

First, there was tension between these two generations of scholars concerning the definition of Onymōdō. Whereas Murayama defined it as a set of folk religious beliefs and practices from ancient China, Yamashita argued that the term did not appear in Chinese sources but came into existence in Japan, entering general use around the tenth century (Yamashita 1996: 22–5). At that time, terms such as Myōbōdō 明法道, Myōgyōdō 明経道, and Kidendō 紀伝道 also appeared. All these terms include the suffix "path" or "way" (*dō* 道) and refer to a specialized science/technology monopolized and transmitted by specific aristocratic families. Onmyōdō was one of these "paths." Yamashita's view that Onmyōdō actually emerged in Japan subsequently received support from many scholars and became commonly accepted (Yamashita 2010).

The second point about this series is that it began to explore Onmyōdō in other historical eras besides the Heian period. Yanagihara Toshiaki did so in the series' medieval volume and Kiba Akeshi and Takano Toshihiko in its early modern volume. Their chapters study how Onmyōdō was used politically during those periods by the state.

Onymōdō no kōgi (Lectures on Onmyōdō; 2002), edited by Koike Jun'ichi and myself, included articles by early career scholars, some of which covered Onmyōdō as it appeared in the likes of novels and manga. This was because Onmyōdō and the Heian period specialist Abe no Seimei (921–1005) have been popular for quite some time in such genres: notably, Yumemakura Baku's novel *Onmyōji* (The Onmyōdō Master), Okano Reiko's manga of the same title, and, based on these, the movie *Abe no Seimei*, which featured the well-known Kyogen and film actor Nomura Mansai II (1966–) in the leading role. In the manga and the movie, Abe no Seimei appears as a cool and shady Adonis who can defeat enemies with his mysterious techniques. While these representations of him completely differed from academic interpretations, Koike and I proposed that this contemporary image of *onmyōji* found in the media should also be an object of study.

Subsequently, new research on various aspects of Onmyōdō has been forthcoming. In addition to Yamashita Katsuaki's aforementioned scholarship, research on Onmyōdō in ancient times includes Suzuki Ikkei's *Onmyōdō* (2002), which covers yin-yang and five elements theory as well as geomancy, and Shigeta Shin'ichi's *Onmyōji to kizoku shakai* (Onmyōji Masters and the Aristocratic Society, 2004), which goes beyond the Kamo and Abe families to analyze lower-rank Onmyōdō state officers. Work on medieval Onmyōdō includes Akazawa Haruhiko's *Kamakura-ki kannin onmyōji no kenkyū* (Study on Kamakura Period Bureaucrat Onmyōji, 2011) and Kimura Junko's *Muromachi jidai no Onmyōdō to jisha shakai* (Muromachi Period Onmyōdō and Temple Society, 2012).

Akazawa criticizes Murakami Shūichi's view that a "samurai Onmyōdō" was established during the Kamakura period and makes clear that regardless of whether it was samurai or nobles, the number of *onmyōji* increased even more than during the Heian period; furthermore, their activities also diversified. Kimura, on the other hand, examines in detail the activities of the Kamo and Abe families during the middle and latter half of the Muromachi period. Research on early modern Onmyōdō includes my own *Kinsei onmyōdō no kenkyū* (Study on Early Modern Onmyōdō, 2005) and Umeda Chihiro's *Kinsei onmyōdō soshiki no kenkyū* (Study on Early Modern Onmyōdō Organizations, 2009). In my book, I showed the gradual development of early modern Onmyōdō and discussed how *onmyōji* started debates with religious specialists from other groups, such as *yamabushi*. Umeda focused on historical materials from the Kinai region around Kyoto and Osaka to elucidate the organization of the Tsuchimikado 土御門 honjo 本所 (the structure of the Tsuchimikado court family in charge of Onmyōji), examining the relationship between the early modern and medieval periods.

As we have briefly seen, Onmyōdō research situated within specific historical periods is steadily accumulating (Saitō 2014). It is my hope that new comprehensive histories of Onymōdō that draw from these findings will also appear soon. (In English, see Faure and Iyanaga, 2012.)

SHINTO, SHUGENDŌ, AND ONMYŌDŌ: A COMPARISON

While Kuroda's *kenmitsu taisei* theory exerted a decisive influence on Shinto and Shugendō research, there are no traces of it having done so in the case of Onmyōdō. What does this mean? In the case of Shinto and Shugendō, there were major turning points during the latter half of the medieval period. Shinto schools, such as Yoshida Shinto, emerged. Yoshida Kanetomo, a Jingikan 神祇官 (Department of Divinities) bureaucrat, rejected what he called Ryōbu Shūgō Shinto—essentially, Ise Shinto with deep influences from Esoteric Buddhism—and Honjaku Engi Shinto, which espoused the general idea that kami are avatars of buddhas and bodhisattvas. Similarly, in Shugendō history, the Honzan and Tōzan sects came into existence. The process of formation of these schools and Shugendō development as a fully organized sectarian movement was also related to the decline of *kenmitsu* Buddhism. On the other hand, the Tsuchimikado family, who had been court bureaucrats in charge of Onmyōdō, would decline throughout the Sengoku period (1467–1568), without producing any innovating thinker comparable to Kanetomo. We should note, however, that Onmyōdō did not have facilities like shrines, and nothing in terms of discursive apparatus that corresponded to *jindō*.

Looking back at the history of these subject areas, one notices that terminology emerged as a central issue in all of them. Mark Teeuwen made clear the different time periods in which *jindō* and *shintō* were used. In Shugendō studies, Hasegawa Kenji showed that

"Shugendō" first appeared in texts between the end of the thirteenth and the beginning of the fourteenth century. In Onmyōdō studies, it became clear that "Onmyōdō" was a Japanese term that did not exist in China and began to be used from around the eleventh century as one of multiple "paths" regarding divination, calendrical sciences, geomancy, and astronomy alongside Myōbōdō, Myōgyōdō, and Kidendō. In these three fields, the terms "Shinto," "Shugendō," and "Onmyōdō" can no longer be used in a generic or supra-historical fashion, and this has become one of the major characteristics of research on the history of Japanese religion in recent years.

See also Chapter 25, "Space."

CHAPTER 23

Sexuality

Or PORATH

Discussions on sexuality in Japanese religion were generally peripheral in nature until the publication of James Sanford's article on the so-called Tachikawa-ryū school (Sanford 1991). Sanford revealed to Western scholarship that there was a heterodoxical school in medieval Japan, with "some odd ideas" and "abominable" rituals, which could very well be regarded as the East Asian counterpart of the sexual practices in Hindu and Buddhist Tantra.

Ever since the publication of this article, discussions on sexuality and religion in Japan have generally attempted to either locate the phenomenon called "Tachikawa-ryū" or downplay the significance of this movement. While Japanese scholars in the last two decades have pointed out that the medieval period saw the emergence of a broad cross-sectarian discourse on sexuality, this realization has hardly been the norm in Western scholarship. Simply put, to automatically and uncritically assume that any sexual idea is a remnant of the Tachikawa movement is outdated and misinformed. I will outline the ways in which scholars have articulated their views on sexuality, beginning with the Tachikawa-ryū and then turning to broader matters, while offering some insights for moving research on sexuality in new directions.

THE TACHIKAWA PROBLEM

Sanford's work was groundbreaking for his time. Yet, Sanford mistakenly attributes any work that contains sexual elements as part of the "Tachikawa" lineage. For example, Sanford asserts that Dairyū's *Sangai isshinki* (Dairyū 1317 [1977]) is a "Tachikawa ritual manual." He also claims that Aizen myōō rites are influenced by the "Tachikawa" school, even though they can be traced to oral teachings centered on commentaries to the *Yugikyō* and *Rishukyō*, which are important to the spectrum of Esoteric Buddhism (Tendai Taimitsu, Shingon lineages, and other schools). In fact, sexual discourse was rather pervasive throughout all Esoteric schools (and even beyond, such as in Shinran's thought) from the latter half of the twelfth century until the first half of the fourteenth century. Scholars of sexuality and religion must acknowledge that many of the sexual developments in Japanese religions are reflective of a broader interest in sexuality, rather than originating in a single cult.

Fleshing out information about the practices and ideas of the "Tachikawa school" remains highly problematic, as most of the information comes from critiques against this movement, some of which do not even refer to said school. For example, the Shingon monk Shinjō (1215–?) authored *Juhō yōjinshū*, an attack on a "Skull Ritual." According to this text, Esoteric Buddhist monks who follow a particular teaching (transmitted in a set of scriptures entitled "Three Inner Sūtras") held a ritual that involves male and female practitioners purportedly having sexual intercourse 120 times. As the man ejaculates and the woman emits vaginal discharge, the male and female fluids are combined and smeared on a skull. After having prepared the skull with multiple layers of mandalas and sexual fluids, one must "brood" the skull for seven years until it begins to speak. When the process is completed in the eighth year, the skull transforms into an oracular deity that communicates events from the past, present, and future that are beneficial to the practitioner. This particular religious group is not named "Tachikawa-ryū"; it is simply designated as "this teaching" or "that teaching" (*kono hō, kano hō*). Yet, Sanford interprets that the skull ritual thus described was performed by the Tachikawa-ryū.

An important aspect of this ritual practice is that it incorporates the Esoteric Buddhist concept of *sokushin jōbutsu*, "realizing Buddhahood in one's own body." Here, the attainment of awakening in the present body, as the final goal, takes place through coitus with a partner. This is unusual in Japanese Esoteric Buddhism, since unlike Tibetan Buddhism, the union with a cosmic Buddha does not take place through the mediation of a consort. Shinjō vehemently criticizes these teachings and claims they are forgeries that should be considered "heterodoxical" and do not belong to the Shingon canon. Another text, *Hōkyōshō* (1375) by Yūkai (1345–1416), an authoritative figure within the Shingon establishment, engages in similar attacks and associates the name of "Tachikawa-ryū," which was a minor but orthodox branch of the Sanbō'in lineage, with the marginal movement described in the *Juhō yōjinshū*; he then correctly traces the Tachikawa-ryū's origins to a Ninkan *ajari* or senior monk (Van Den Broucke 1992).

Following in Sanford's footsteps, Susan Klein traces the *waka kanjō*, a consecration rite based on the Buddhist *abhiṣeka* to appoint masters, which introduces an initiand into the Esoteric Buddhist interpretation of Japanese vernacular poetry (*waka*). Klein explores one of the initiatory texts of the tradition, the *Ise monogatari zuinō* (ca. 1320), a commentary on the "Tale of Ise" (*Ise monogatari*) largely influenced by the work of Fujiwara no Tameaki (*c.* 1320–1390) (Klein 1998, 2002). Klein's study is innovative and one of the earliest to tackle sources outside the "Tachikawa" sphere of influence that similarly claim an equation between sexual congress and awakening, specifically, that "the Path of Poetry and the Path of Eroticism are a single path to enlightenment" (1998: 448). Klein is also the first to discuss that such "radical non-dualism" has been ordained by kami rather than Buddhas, specifically, Sumiyoshi Daimyōjin. Indeed, the sexual intercourse conceptualized in these texts was modeled after the conjugal act by the primordial gods Izanami and Izanagi. Thus, Klein was instrumental in bringing to our attention that a religious practice of sexuality was not exclusive to Buddhism but was also part of kami worship, and even to secular disciplines such as poetry.

In a similar vein, Fabio Rambelli points out that a group of medieval followers of Pure Land Buddhism, whom he calls "radical Amidists," advocated a novel interpretation of Shinran's doctrine. They believed in the power of Amida's vow to grant them the legitimacy to partake in sexual acts, among other deviant actions such as the consumption of meat and liquor. Rambelli demonstrates that outside of "Tachikawa," there were other Buddhist groups that articulated creative interpretations of sexual praxis and made heterodoxical actions as potentially subversive in political terms (Rambelli 2004).

Recent studies on the Tachikawa-ryū generally draw on the works of Iyanaga Nobumi, who, in a series of articles in Japanese and English, discusses long-held misunderstandings (Iyanaga 2002, 2004, 2006, 2010, 2011, 2018). Influenced by Stephen Köck, the first to critique Japanese scholarship concerning Tachikawa (Köck 2000), Iyanaga explains that "almost all of what has ever been written on this topic is based on a preconceived image and is in need of profound revision" (Iyanaga 2011: 803). Iyanaga argues that the texts mentioning the Tachikawa-ryū are heresiological and therefore biased in their interpretation, motivated as they are by sectarian and political motives surrounding the last years of the struggle between Southern and Northern courts and the latter's ultimate victory.

Iyanaga distinguishes between three different key conceptions of Tachikawa-ryū. First, the real Tachikawa-ryū, which existed as a sub-lineage of Shingon's Sanbōin-ryū from the twelfth century. The second, a specific current of religion that espoused aberrant teachings as its doctrine and practice, which existed from the mid-thirteenth century and was almost extinguished a century later. The only historical document which describes its contents, the *Juhō yōjinshū*, mentions no particular name for it. The third type of Tachikawa signifies "a vague set of Shingon lineages and currents of thought that were condemned as non-orthodox by certain Shingon monks," especially by Yūkai, because they would have been advocating teachings related to sexuality as a religious path (Iyanaga 2011: 804). Iyanaga claims that the study of Tachikawa-ryū suffers primarily because what is called "Tachikawa-ryū" most often refers to the third type, which was a label for a nebulous and possibly nonexistent set of phenomena. In sum, Iyanaga challenges the common narrative pervasive in Japanese scholarship (Mizuhara 1923; Moriyama 1965; Manabe 1999), which Sanford perpetuated in the West, namely, that the Tachikawa movement refers to a specific and constant historical phenomenon. The implication of Iyanaga's work, taken together with the work of other Japanese scholars (Sueki 2019: 22–8), is that there were in fact legitimate lineages that deployed sexual knowledge to inform their practices and doctrines beginning from the mid-twelfth century, and that the disparaging image of the Tachikawa-ryū should be refuted.

Gaétan Rappo builds on this scholarly legacy by thoroughly examining Yūkai's arguments via comparison with contemporaneous sources. He explains that Monkan, a Daigoji monk who has been largely seen as an adherent of Tachikawa and was often tied to peripheral heretical movements, became a target for criticism only because he was allied with the Southern Court. In contrast, monks who were affiliated with the Northern Court such as Yūkai sought to undermine Monkan's position. Thus, Rappo problematizes the notion that Monkan practiced "deviant" rituals at all, and argues that he was only constructed as a "heretic" following his death (Rappo 2014, 2017). Rappo finds no conspicuous sexual elements whatsoever in Monkan's work.

SEXUAL DISCOURSE AND HETERONORMATIVITY

Scholarship on the Tachikawa-ryū seems to largely ignore the question of male-male sexuality, despite the wide diffusion of literary and religious texts about youthful acolytes (*chigo* or *dōji*) and their romantic exploits with adult monks. Literature scholar Margaret Childs was the first to discuss the *chigo monogatari* corpus of monastic tales in English (Childs 1980). These tales, written during the Muromachi period (1336–1573), concern monks and their rapture with young boys, and the revelation that these boys are avatars of a bodhisattva (Childs 1991, 1996; Schmidt-Hori 2009). Some scholars have emphasized the religious nature of these stories: for example, art historian Melissa McCormick highlighted one tale's pronounced Shugendō components (McCormick 2012), while others have pointed to literary tropes of the *chigo*'s suffering (Abe 1998; Faure 1998b; Atkins 2008).

Religious studies scholar Bernard Faure has discussed the *chigo*'s role as the youthful deity Jūzenji, a manifestation of the Tendai god Sannō. Or Porath's work on *chigo kanjō* (the ritual consecration of acolytes) demonstrates that Tendai monks developed an institutionally sanctioned sexual initiation for *chigo*, wherein they empowered the novices as divine beings (Porath 2019). That *chigo* themselves were seen as incarnate gods, and not solely objects of sexual attraction, merits further attention, especially in relation to the pervasive sacrality of children in medieval Japan.

I would like to highlight potentially advantageous directions for future scholarship on the study of sexuality in medieval Japanese religion more generally. One crucial change in the field is that scholars have broadened the scope of research by recognizing that the religious context extends beyond the so-called "Tachikawa-ryū."

Japanese scholarship accepted the prevalence of sexual ideas in religion a long time ago, and many authors continue to express interest in this matter. In particular, Sueki Fumihiko has recently raised the possibility of "a sexual discourse" (*seiteki gensetsu*) in medieval Japanese religion (Sueki 2019). This is by no means a new claim; Iyanaga has pointed this out before, and Bernard Faure has discussed "fragments of a discours amoureux" (Faure 1998b). Faure conducted a thorough study of Buddhist sexuality, with particular attention to the broader East Asian cultural sphere. Faure examines the *vinaya* monastic codes, the issue of transgression, the connection between madness and sexuality, and homosexuality in Buddhism.

Many other scholars have discussed sexual ideas, elements, and myths in multiple Buddho-Shinto texts, traditions, and lineages.[1] Lucia Dolce uncovered a wealth of documents that are rich with sexual overtones, some of which contain pictorial depictions of the sexual positions used in ritual settings (Dolce 2015). In addition, Anna Andreeva looks at how the embryological dualist concepts of red/white or father/mother may allow one to interpret womanhood as sacred (Andreeva 2015). Despite the expanding scope of recent research on sexuality and reproduction in Japanese religions, there remains a need to move beyond heteronormative readings of sexual sources and thus to focus on broader discussions of medieval sexuality more generally. I mentioned above the *chigo kanjō* ritual, but even the so-called Tachikawa-ryū Skull Ritual, which espouses male-female sexual union as a practice that subsequently leads to spiritual attainment, hints at some connection to male-male sexual longing.

For example, the skull that is used in the ritual to deposit semen and vaginal discharge is decorated to look like a woman, mainly because the female deity Dakiniten inhabits the skull, but it is said that it can also be made to resemble a youth (*dōji*) (Sanford 1991: 12; Iyanaga 2015: 407). In patting the skull with white and rouge, the skull is meant to embody the gender characteristics of what would be an idealized object of sexual attraction for men. The skull and its encoded symbolism of the union of red and white (*shakubyaku nitai*) may not only be assigned to females but also to young boys. Even from short passages like this, we learn about the gender expectations and distinctive gender roles ascribed to boys in Buddhist monasticism, and how they might be connected to male-male erotic desire.

In fact, the role of boys as objects of sexual attention may have been greater than previously imagined in texts associated with the Skull Ritual. The *Juhō yōjinshū* mentions

---

[1] Yamamoto (1984, 1998); Abe (1998); Faure (1998b); Tanaka (1993, 1997); Yamashita (1993, 2005); Dolce (2010, 2015); Shibata (2010: 119–26, 290–2); Itō (2011); Eubanks (2012); Ogawa (2014); Andreeva (2015); Mizukami (2017); and Kameyama (2018, 2019).

the existence of "The Oral Teachings on the Chrysanthemum and Orchid" (*Kikuran no kuden*) that were lumped together with the Tachikawa lineage scriptures. As Iyanaga points out, the term *kikuran* might be an allusion to "homosexuality" (Iyanaga 2006). It is possible the two terms *kiku* and ran signify binary gendered pairs, and it is my belief that this encoding was employed to create a gender dichotomy replicating a heterosexual union and superimposing it on two males in order to sanction male-male ritualized sex. The evidence, while scarce, provides an interesting perspective on the possibility of a Buddhist tradition, perhaps even a school, that followed teachings of a male-male sexual nature.

SHINTO AND SEXUALITY

This discussion so far has focused primarily on Buddhism, and that is not a coincidence. First, there was no clear delineation between Buddhism and Shinto in premodern Japan, especially in the medieval period. Second, scholarship on Shinto and sexuality is scarce, and further research could reveal new perspectives on this issue. The postwar interpretation is that Buddhism rejects sexuality, while Shinto affirms it. Indeed, Buddhist views can present sexual desire and sexual practices as obstacles to enlightenment, while Shinto rituals are often associated with fertility, reproduction, and the agricultural cycle.

Sex was an important element of cosmogony and was harnessed to sustain political legitimacy in the *Nihon shoki* myth, in which the kami progeny is born through the hierogamy of Izanagi and Izanami. These sexual relations were incestuous (Murakami 1988); furthermore, the creation of the Japanese pantheon can be interpreted as a result of sexual transgression, while the creation of the Japanese islands resulted from Izanagi's masturbation (Screech 2009: 270–2). Sexual energy also possesses a redeeming power in the myths; it is the sexual "striptease" of Ame no Uzume that vanquishes darkness and summons the Sun's light into the world. The ancient mytho-histories include many additional references to sexual practices of the gods, including the coitus between the Miwa god, Ōmononushi no mikoto, who appeared as a snake and had sex with Yamato-totohi-momoso-hime, and Tamayori-hime's impregnation by a phallic arrow. Shinto often presents positive views on sexuality when confined to procreative acts.

But what happens in the medieval period? As mentioned earlier, it is well known that Buddhist consecration rituals (*kanjō*), such as the *waka kanjō* and *chigo kanjō* (Sexual Consecration of Acolytes), made elaborate use of sexual imagery and even accommodated sexual practices as part of their procedures, but sexuality also formed part of the Shinto ritual repertoire. Itō Satoshi has written extensively on concepts in Ise Shinto that appropriate non-dualistic notions of sex as part of the Shinto rites (Itō 2011). Other sexually related rituals dedicated to kami include the *Genshi kimyōdan* consecration of the Tendai Danna lineage, in which the kami Matara-jin was worshipped as the god of song and dance (Suzuki 2001: 263–316; Faure 2016). The ritual began around the medieval era and became in the early modern period a target of criticism for its sexual language, leading eventually to its demise. Included in its ritual procedures are cryptic vocabulary that signifies sexual ideas: for instance, the two boys Chōreita Dōji and Nishita Dōji who dance in the ritual are referred to as "penis" and "vagina." Of course, the ritual also intersects with local practices that transcended sectarian affiliation.

In addition, we must also pay attention to folk religion (*minzoku shūkyō*) or popular religion (*minkan shūkyō*), those practices that were carried out in shrine-temple complexes but did not enjoy the same sustained theorization as institutional religions. There is very little research on the sexual understandings of popular cults in Western scholarship. Hank Glassman highlights the role of *dōsōjin* or *sae no kami* (road-ancestor-god) as "gods of sexuality and fertility" and how the image of the bodhisattva Jizō gradually replaced these wayside gods in a process of assimilation that aided the incorporation of local cults into Buddhism (Glassman 2012). Stephen Turnbull has published an extensive monograph on the topic of sexual gods and recently looked at temples and shrines of an earthly nature that promote cults of fecundity and sexuality (2015). Indeed, in addition to an intriguing rethinking of premodern constructs of the body through the grotesque and artistic representations of sexuality (Tinsley 2017), this is one of the very few studies about sexuality in contemporary Japanese religion, and it goes without saying that further research is needed on this period.

Nevertheless, in all of the above research, the absence of discussions on nonreproductive sexuality in matters of Shinto is conspicuous. Did Shinto ever produce a discourse of male-male sexuality, given its focus on sexual procreation? Ogawa Toyoo has recently uncovered a text dated to 1301 from the Ise Jingū library that is called "Procedures for Daily Ritual Practices" (*Nichigyō shidai*). The last stage includes the "visualization of the primary object of worship" (*honzon kan*). According to the text, the practitioner is asked to visualize two kami, "the Chrysanthemum-Sun Youth and the Orchid-Moon Youth," as the father and mother of all sentient beings. The text adds: "if you pay them respect and worship them, there is no doubt that you will be loved by all beings above and below, mother and father, and child, and that you will gain love and blessings." The text also argues that deluded thoughts give rise to the Buddha. Such claims, together with the mention of receiving love in return, and the Tantric alignment of the Moon (white) and the Sun (red) evoking the respective duality of the semen and blood effluvia, makes the sexual context clear.

It is important to note that these explorations of male-male sexuality in Shinto are not anecdotal but rather understudied. In the *Honchō kotohajime*, by Fujiwara no Michinori (1106–1159), a medieval book that traces the primordial beginnings of various phenomena in kami lore, there is an entry on the origins of *nanshoku*, that is, male-male eros (Ogawa 2014: 625). It begs the question of why a Shinto text would even dedicate attention to this matter. The answer, I suspect, has to do with the previous evidence that certain medieval constellations of kami worship were also concerned with male-male sexuality. Thus, the subject is ripe for further study.

Moreover, considering that one can locate male-male sexual elements even in texts associated with the so-called heteronormative Tachikawa-ryū, we should reexamine Buddho-Shinto documents that were once said to belong to the "Tachikawa" repertoire, such as the *Sangai isshinki* by Dairyū, the *Jōge mibun no wa* by Jun'en (Yamashita 1993), and compare them to newly discovered texts such as Eisai's (1141–1251) *Ingonshū* from Shinpukuji's archives (Sueki 2019). Further inquiry into these documents may cast new light on our received notions of orthodox Buddhist teachings. We must strive to map out the cross-sectarian interpretation of sexuality by reexamining some of the so-called Tachikawa material.

CONCLUSION

For scholars of Japanese religion, the end of medieval sexuality occurred in the Edo period (1603–1868), when Buddhist authors co-opted tantric rituals and kami-worship knowledge and emptied their transgressive content. It is also the time in which Buddho-Shinto consecration rituals like the *genshi kimyōdan* and the *chigo kanjō* disappear. Buddhist archivists and compilers label certain documents of sexual nature with the words *jagi* (perverse ideas) and *fushin* (dubious), placing them in the category of history, no longer to be replicated.

Instead, a new type of commodified and commercial sexuality is born, associated with the red-light districts and the theater of all-male kabuki. The rise of the publishing industry in the 1600s, and the emergence of the urban-merchant class (*chōnin*), gave way to "secular" pursuits of sensual pleasure practiced outside the precincts of Buddhist monasticism, such as the disciplinary tradition of male-male sexuality or *shūdō* (Pflugfelder 1999), and the widespread consumption of erotic prints or *shunga* (Screech 2009). Even though male-male love (or any love) is commonly depicted in sources of the seventeenth and eighteenth centuries, it does not enjoy the same status in religious circles. Also, while an interest in sexing things still persists, such engendering of the sexes is relegated to nonhuman agents such as rice (Robertson 1984). This transition in the historiography of sexuality from a religious studies' lens is perhaps too neat, though it should be noted that my analysis of the Edo period here is an artifact of specific patterns of research interests, rather than a faithful representation of historical change.

It is necessary that scholars of religious studies continue to devote their attention and provide the most detailed account of eros in the middle ages, given its distinctiveness as a period that marks the production of sexual doxa and praxis under the auspices of religion.

See also Chapter 11, "Gender," and Chapter 22, "Premodern Traditions."

CHAPTER 24

Sound

ŌUCHI Fumi

Like many other religious traditions throughout the world, rituals and practices in the Japanese religious context have used different types of acoustic events and vocalization or utterances. When visiting a shrine, one should clap their hands before making a prayer to the deities. A Shinto priest invites deities to descend to the shrine by making a special vocalization called *keihitsu* 警蹕, then recites a prayer in the *norito* 祝詞 form. In Buddhist rituals, priests recite sutras, mantras, or *dhāraṇī*, chant a Buddha's name (particularly that of Amida), and give sermons, which often include musical aspects. Many ancient rituals as well as premodern and modern folkloric rituals were led by mediums, variously called *miko* 巫女 or 神子, *genza* 験者, *itako*, and *tayū* 太夫, who entered a state of possession by chanting magical formulas accompanied by musical instruments such as the drum, the *koto* 琴 (a type of long zither), or the *azusayumi* 梓弓 (catalpa bow). Shugendō, a combinatory tradition based on mountain retreat practices and systematized with ideas and practices derived from Esoteric Buddhism, the Yin-Yang tradition, and Daoism, also shows us clear examples of ritual sounds as in the case of the *horagai* 法螺貝 (shell conch).

All this suggests that acoustic events are a rich research subject from which to gain a new understanding of the performative, sensory, and material nature of religious traditions in Japan. Yet, little research on this theme has been attempted thus far, mainly because of the division between the study of music and other fields in the academia. Scholars in religious studies tend to think that music-related subjects have little to do with their own field of inquiry, while most musicologists consider religious studies as something out of reach, consisting in abstruse doctrinal ideas. Such estrangement between the two fields is unfortunate for both, since one of the crucial features of most, if not all, Japanese religious traditions is their close connection with entertainment and artistic performing arts (see Chapter 10 in this volume). Traditionally, there is no clear division between religious rituals and performing arts enacted for aesthetic or sensory pleasure. Aesthetic pleasure is, in fact, indispensable in many cases for activating ritual efficacy. The rich results of historical, theoretical, and ethnographical studies on performing arts such as *kagura*, *bugaku*, *dengaku* and different types of performance developed from the *nenbutsu* tradition and even artistically refined Noh theater can provide many possible subjects for further inquiry along these lines.

OVERVIEW OF PREVIOUS RESEARCH

Studies of various types of Buddhist vocal music have accumulated since the mid-ninth century. The earliest and perhaps most remarkable work is the theoretical discussion on musical scales included in the second chapter of the *Shittanzō*, written by the Tendai priest Annen (841–889/898). Annen explained the pentatonic system utilized by Buddhist vocal music, and this became the authoritative interpretation of the musical scale for all Buddhist traditions. Recent research shows that Annen did not merely theorize a system of musical tones but rather established a comprehensive system that incorporated different types of vocalization, including languages such as Chinese and Sanskrit, along with musical tones, locating them within a cosmological framework. Importantly, his theory seems to be based on the actual musical performance at his time. This suggests that, despite its abstract appearance, his musical theory was grounded in the performative effects of sound composition (Ōuchi 2016:134–40).

From the late Heian period to the Kamakura period, a number of theoretical and practical writings on Buddhist vocal presentations, such as *shōmyō* 声明 (Buddhist chant), *kōshiki* 講式 (Buddhist ceremonial lectures), and *shōdō* 唱導 (sermons), were produced, although they still had to be learned largely through oral transmission. This may be connected with the trend of transcribing secret teachings, developed by the medieval Esoteric Buddhist traditions under the partial influence of original enlightenment thought (*hongaku shisō*) (Hazama 1974: 267–74; Stone 1999: 129–30). These writings demonstrate that the authors developed refined aesthetic principles with the intention that they be actually performed, fully aware of the musical and sensory effects of performance. Analysis of some of these texts has begun to unveil how the performances were carried out at the time, in *shōmyō* (Iwahara 1997; Iwata 1999; Amano 2000; Ushio 2017), *dokyōdō* 読経道 (sutra chanting) (Shiba 2004), *kōshiki* (Sugano 1987; Nelson 2001; Mross 2016), *shōdō* (Komine 2009), and artistic Buddhist songs written in Japanese (*kyōke* 教化) (Kojima 2004).

These different types of vocal presentations are typical examples of the dual nature of Japanese ritual performance. On the one hand, each of them was performed in expectation of some religious efficacy, such as expressing repentance, achieving rebirth in the Pure Land, attaining enlightenment, and securing different types of worldly benefits. On the other hand, the performance had to meet certain aesthetic norms in order to attract audiences and involve them in the enactment of performance in order to accomplish its ritual purpose. Recent innovative studies on *shōmyō* in the Tendai tradition demonstrate that the dynamic correlation between the dual dimensions of vocal presentations was supported by theoretical ideas. For example, the profound contemplation system devised within Chinese Tiantai, systematized in the form of four types of *samādhi* (*shishu-zanmai* 四種三昧), took root in Japanese Tendai as musical liturgies. It should be emphasized here that a beautiful vocal presentation of the liturgies was considered to be equal in terms of religious efficacy to the deepest methods of contemplation for realizing enlightenment.

Importantly, the evolution of *shōmyō* was closely connected with the development of original understandings of Buddhist ideas on the somatic nature of human beings (Ōuchi 2016). This suggests that a multidisciplinary approach, utilizing doctrinal, historical, performative, and musicological lenses, can produce new research directions on this theme. Fortunately, the recent discovery of new materials on Buddhist rituals from temples like Shinpukuji has shed new light on the actual performance of rituals carried out in the twelfth century (Ninnaji konbyōshi kozōshi kenkyūkai, 1995). Comprehensive research on these rituals has just begun. A multidisciplinary approach to this precious finding could bring about exciting results.

Important research on the relationship between enlightenment and embodiment have been carried out in related subjects within the history of Japanese music. A number of theoretical and historical works written by medieval Gagaku musicians provide us with sophisticated notions of sounds and music. Among them, the *Kangen ongi* 管絃音義 (The Meaning of Instrumental Sounds, in *Gunsho ruijū*, 341) has attracted the attention of scholars in religious studies and in musicology because of its detailed description of a tonal system situated within a cosmological context (Abe 2016; Tashiro 2006; Shindō 2017).

Musical instruments themselves are another important source of information. The magical or divine power of musical instruments has interested scholars working on ancient and medieval myths and literature. This power was connected to religio-political authority, as seen, for example, in several instances in the eighth-century chronicles, the *Kojiki* and *Nihon shoki*, in which the *koto* was used for shamanistic purposes. The story of the precious *biwa* (a type of lute) named Genjō 玄象 in the late Heian anthology of tales *Konjaku monogatarishū* 今昔物語集 shows how an instrument's power may be linked to imperial authority. In the Buddhist context, Pure Land teachings give an especially prominent role to musical instruments in visual and literary representations of Amida's visit to dying people, as shown by medieval collections of tales on the rebirth in the Pure Land demonstrate (Ogi 1997; Ōuchi 2016). This is another subject that is still awaiting closer investigation.

TO BE EXPLORED IN FUTURE RESEARCH

As previously mentioned, one central reason for the stagnation in scholarly interest in the relations between sound and religion lies in the fragmentation and separation of academic fields. This in turn suggests that multidisciplinary approaches could open up new directions for potential research.

Scholars of literature have already attempted such new endeavors. Analyzing what type of power the voice or utterance was expected to have in the religious context of medieval tales and ballads, several multifaceted studies have unveiled the performative power of vocalization to link people in this world with the divine and with the other world, as well as examining its socio-political function (Abe 2001; Komine 2009; Inose 2018). The power of ritual vocalization in the medieval religious tradition culminated with the development of the concept of "attaining Buddhahood through the performance of *shōmyō*" (*shōmyō jōbutsu*), which was supported doctrinally by the idea that "the voice performs or accomplishes Buddhist practices" (*koe butsuji o nasu*). The distinctive development of this concept originated in the *Vimalakīrti-nirdeśa sutra*, which is an important clue for exploring the meaning and function of sound in religious traditions in Japan. In the original, the phrase simply means that in this world, Śākyamuni Buddha's teachings are conveyed verbally, not through other sensory sign systems (smells, flavors, light, figures, etc.) as happens in other Buddhist worlds. In medieval Japan, this resulted in the new idea that artistic expressions could equal Buddhist practices in work (Kojima 1999: 89–92; Ōuchi 2016: 100–3).

This innovative understanding offered a theoretical basis for the development of different types of Buddhist literature and vocal expressions. This theory emerged in parallel with a drastic change in the interpretation of Chinese poet Bo Juyi's (772–846) earnest desire that sinful karma caused by the bad deed of making up a fictional world in literature would turn into an opportunity for praising the Buddha's teaching. From the late Heian period onward, this new understanding that literature can function as Buddhist practice came to pervade society. The reason for these changes in interpretation should be investigated within the sociocultural context of the time, with attention to the spiritual and religio-political power of *waka* poetry as shown in myths and in the preface to the early Heian poetry anthology *Kokin wakashū*.

Different types of vocalization other than those that are explicitly musical should also be explored. The practice of chanting *mantra* and *dhāraṇī* in Esoteric Buddhist rituals and the practice of vocalizing the Sanskrit letter *A*, devised in Esoteric Pure Land teachings (*himitsu nenbutsu*), are particularly remarkable for their function as ritual climax. Despite the Esoteric Buddhist concept of the "three mysteries" (*sanmitsu*: being one with divinities through the ritual use of body, mouth/voice, and mind), and the theoretical emphasis on meditation (mystery of mind) on each of the three, ethnographical and performative analysis of Esoteric practices demonstrates that mantra ritual recitation, in which a practitioner repeatedly recites designated mantras for a long time, performs a critical function by generating a physical or sensorial experience in the practitioner of becoming one with the deity during the ritual process (Ōuchi 2016: 125–56). Another notable subject is the practice of intoning the sound *A*, which was performed for the sake of realizing Amida's salvation, particularly at one's deathbed (Sanford 2006; Stone 2007). The combination of Esoteric Buddhism and Pure Land teachings, which contributed to the development of deathbed rituals as a medieval Buddhist trend, is an important topic to look into in order to gain a deeper understanding of how Buddhism was adapted to Japanese culture.

Unlike Japanese Buddhist musical traditions, the sound culture in Shinto is more difficult to grasp. That is primarily due to the vagueness of the definition of Shinto itself. Modern ideas of Shinto include different types of cults to particular deities and ritual practices for them, which are carried out without specific doctrinal elaborations and canonical works. In this sense, Shinto may be understood as a system of methods for worshipping deities or offering prayers to them, or even "a system of signifiers" (Rambelli 2017). Therefore, the study of actual ritual performances, focusing on the sounds they involve, is one of the most promising subjects for exploring the nature of Shinto in its variety. Researches on ritual songs called *kagura uta* maintained in the Imperial traditions have been instigated recently (Urita 2015).

There are several other possible ways of exploring this theme. First, one might attempt a reconsideration of the historical developments of kami-cults, by addressing the role of sounds and music as they are depicted in written texts on myths from the ancient to the medieval periods, including theoretical and ritual writings of medieval kami-Buddha combinatory traditions, Yoshida Shinto, and philosophical texts of the early modern Kokugaku (National Learning) movement. This could result in a new understanding of how the various kami-cult traditions envisioned the physical and sensory nature of human beings, and how or how much this changed in the encounter with other religious traditions such as Buddhism, Yin-Yang thought, Daoism, Confucianism, and Christianity. The works of Hirata Atsutane (1776–1843) should be particularly fruitful in this regard, as suggested by his acute interest in stone flutes (*ame no iwabue*) and in the dances supposedly performed in the other world, as shown in his *Senkyō ibun* 仙境異聞 (*Hirata Atsutane zenshū*, 9).

Many of the religious sects newly established between the end of the Edo period and the Meiji period, commonly known as Sect Shinto (*kyōha shintō*), such as Ōmotokyō, Izumo Taishakyō, Konkōkyō, and Tenrikyō, have placed particular importance on music and performing arts. How each of them uses music in its rituals has been only partly investigated, but this subject could be explored as a whole alongside Atsutane's special attention to music-related phenomena in religious contexts.

Another subject worth pursuing is the investigation of the functions of acoustic events in accomplishing ritual purposes through a performative approach. Very few studies on the music created within individual traditions have been carried out, which demonstrates the lack of academic interest in this topic. Thus, it is remarkable that an anthology of the different types of ritual music connected to the kami-cults, the *Kamigami no ongaku: Shinto ongaku shūsei* (Kikkawa 2013), was even published. It collects examples of music from various genres of kami-cults under such classifications as Ceremonies of Shrine Shinto (including Imperial Court ceremonies), Ritual Music in Sect Shinto, and Shinto Folk Music—which is in turn divided into three subdivisions, that is, *kagura*-type, *dengaku*-type, and *furyū*-type. Noticeably, this collection contains the entire performance of a liturgy systematized in the Shrine Shinto tradition, including ritual sounds used for specific ritual purposes, such as beginning the ritual, inviting deities, and opening the doors of the kami altar, and the recitation of *norito* and purification invocations (*ōharae no kotoba* and *tokusa no haraekotoba*). Close investigation of the acoustic characteristics of these sounds and vocalizations, as well as their ritual effects, could shed new light on the issue of how the performativity of the ritual is appreciated in the tradition systematized as Shrine Shinto.

Yet, looking at the variety of styles of performance and the complicated combination of ritual content and purposes, the classification above does not always work. Rather, the analysis of acoustic events (the ritual sounds and music) in kami-cult traditions, focusing on the characterization of sound (including silence), the position and ritual role of the performer who is to produce the sound, and the type of sound instrument employed, in relation to the effect or function expected by the ritual, could be very productive. This type of research has been successfully applied to Shugendō rituals. A study of the ritual sounds and vocalizations used during the mountain retreat for attaining Buddhahood has revealed that the performative power of acoustic events contributes crucially to the achievement of the ritual purpose (Ōuchi 2005, 2009).

Despite the little attention paid so far to Confucianism as a soteriological way, the idea of sounds and music as developed in Confucian philosophies, particularly in Neo-Confucianism, is an important subject for investigating the spirituality of the Edo period, where secularism is thought to have dominated. Confucian ideas emphasized the importance of musical performances for spiritual cultivation, which led to the formation of detailed theoretical discourses on musical scales for its basis. Neo-Confucian scholars such as Ogyū Sorai (1666–1728), Hayashi Gahō (林鵞峰, 1618–1680), Nakamura Tekisai (中村惕斎, 1629–1702), and Uchibori Hidenaga (内堀英長, 1774–1832) devoted themselves to this theme. Some of their studies encouraged a movement towards refining Gagaku (Kayaki 2019). Research on this topic could shed new light on the understanding of religiosity or spirituality at the time and its relationship with the development of the intellectual and political interests on ancient culture that led to the Kokugaku movement.

In addition, material and physical dimensions of the different religious traditions are also a potential subject of interest. Two directions should be highlighted in particular: the importance of physical practice for realizing spiritual and religious achievements, and the sacred power of musical instruments.

Practitioners of different traditions have attempted to experience the essential change in mental or spiritual condition through ascetic practices. Many of them use sounds and vocalization as important agencies for accomplishing this process. For example, at the initiation training in Esoteric Buddhism, a practitioner performs the mantra recitation for hours as an essential component. Different types of ritual sounds and vocalization are required for the practice of mountain retreats in Shugendō, as mentioned above. Some practices systematized in modern Shinto sects have also employed utterance and ritual incantation as a part of bodily activities aiming at the mental cultivation. An example is Dewa Sanzan Shrine, which developed specialized training prior to adopting the *chinkon* 鎮魂 (pacifying the soul) practice transmitted at Isonokami Shrine, and the *misogi* 禊 (purification with water) practice systematized by the Association of Shinto Shrines (Jinja Honchō) (Ōuchi 1996). These practices using ritual vocalization are related to how our bodily nature is involved in achieving ritual purposes and how somaticity has been incorporated into religious traditions as a whole.

Despite their frequent appearance in legends and actual performances, the ritual significance of musical instruments has not been fully investigated. Several projects are being planned in this area. Instruments such as *koto* and drums were used for leading the possession by deities, as ancient myths and medieval *engi* (stories on the origin of deities, shrines, and temples) describe. The sacred image of the *koto* was replaced by the distinctive position of the *wagon* in the Shrine Shinto rituals and may have inspired the invention of the *yakumo-koto* 八雲琴 and the new music genre it spawned at the end of the Edo period, connected in part to the Kokugaku movement. Different types of drums have also been used in shamanistic rituals, transcending the times and differences in religious traditions. Examples can still be found today in many of the folkloric rituals and performing arts influenced by Shugendō practitioners (Averbuch 1995; Sangaku shugen gakkai 2003). The issue of how the performative power that comes from these (and other) instruments produces ritual efficacy also requires a multidisciplinary approach.

The *koto*, *sō* 箏, *ryūteki* 龍笛 (a type of flute used in *gagaku*), *biwa*, and occasionally the *shō* 笙 (Japanese mouth organ) were closely connected with the Imperial court (Toyonaga 2006; Inose 2018). Among them, the *biwa* has the most complex features within the religious context. The *Konjaku monogatari-shū* includes a story about the precious *biwa* called Genjō 玄象, one of the Imperial treasures, which was stolen by a demon and recovered by the famous aristocrat and musician Minamoto no Hiromasa 源博雅 (918–980). The play *Genjō* in Noh theater depicts the story of another precious *biwa*, named Shishimaru 獅子丸, which was rescued from the sea bed by a dragon god by order of Emperor Murakami and then given to the most talented medieval musician, Fujiwara no Moronaga 藤原師長 (1138–1192). Transmission of the most treasured pieces of the *biwa* repertoire took place in the form of Esoteric Buddhist consecration rituals (Inose 2018: 242–63). *Biwa* was also the instrument used by blind musicians called *biwa hōshi* 琵琶法師, who produced and performed the Tale of the Heike (*Heike monogatari*) and other warrior stories (Hyōdō 2000; Sunakawa 2001). Furthermore, another type of *biwa* performance dedicated to *kōjin* 荒神 (the deity of ground and fire) was transmitted in Kyushu and was later adopted within the Tendai school (Nakano 1994, Hyōdō 2009). Thus, *biwa* functioned as a nucleus connecting imperial authority, divine power, musicians, and ritual performers. How this position emerged must be explored through a comparative approach, perhaps expanding to other Asian cultures that also employ the *biwa*.

Unlike string instruments and drums, instruments made of metal like the gong and bell were not connected to the Imperial authority but had ritual power to ensure the passage from this world to the other world. They were used at the funerals, other ceremonies for the dead, and, interestingly, at the time of oath-making for the purpose of inviting deities as witnesses (Sasamoto 1990). Such differences in the ritual purposes of the strings and the metal instruments may be due to differences in their acoustic characteristics.

Therefore, collaborative research with experts in acoustic psychology could produce new understandings of this theme.

From another point of view, studies on musical culture may contribute to a general reformulation of the history of Japanese religions. For example, recent studies on Gagaku suggest that the performative power of the genre's sophisticated enactment worked as a powerful agency for promoting the kami-Buddha combinatory tradition (Ono 2019). The deep relationship between the dragon as a sea god or water god and musical instruments like the bell and the *biwa*, as seen above, suggests another important subject of study. There are several other examples related to the motif of a dragon attached to music in medieval tales and folkloric traditions (Abe 1986). This may provide an innovative perspective for investigating the maritime religious tradition of Japan, as suggested in a study of musical instruments dedicated to the sea god Ebisu (Ōuchi 2018).

Finally, the complex and ambivalent status of the manufacturers of musical instruments must be mentioned. Like some other specific professions, including those dedicated to religious performing arts, the makers of drums and bamboo instruments have a history of being discriminated against (Okiura 1990; Kyoto burakushi kenkyūjo 1986, 1989). The complex and dynamic relationship between discriminated people and imperial or religious authority is an important topic that calls into question the nature of religiosity in Japan.

See also Chapter 3, "Cultural Heritage," Chapter 10, "Folk Performing Arts," Chapter 15, "Materiality," and Chapter 22, "Premodern Traditions."

CASE STUDY

The *Matsuri* as Sonic Event

Andrea GIOLAI

Local *matsuri* are ubiquitous and diverse. Despite differences in size and duration, they tend to be rich in experience, in part because they represent increasingly rare moments in which communities can gather and celebrate. Numerous visual features set shrine festivals apart from everyday life, including the presence of children dressed in ceremonial costumes, colorful processions with banners and golden portable shrines (*mikoshi*), and the temporary repurposing of portions of public space. Just as different combinations of visual elements distinguish a *matsuri* from other gatherings, unique sonic practices participate in the articulation of its religious contents. For this reason, lending an ear to the aural dimension of a shrine festival can help us understand not only how ritual participation unfolds across multiple sensory modes but also how ritual actors conceptualize sound and hearing in relation to the immersive experience of being in the *matsuri*. With ethnographic examples from a section of Nara's Kasuga Wakamiya Onmatsuri 春日若宮おん祭 (hereafter, Onmatsuri), what follows is a brief "acoustemological" exploration of a Japanese local festival (Feld 2015), in line with recent attempts to establish a "sound-based approach" to the study of religion (Hackett 2016).

The rituals that make up Onmatsuri begin in July and gradually become more frequent, reaching a peak in the twenty-four hours between December 16 and December 17 (Ishii 1987; Amino and Niunoya 1991; Hatakama and Tsuguo 2016). At noon, a colorful procession in period attire unfolds throughout the streets of Nara, reaching a temporary shrine (*otabisho* お旅所) in the forest between Kasuga Grand Shrine and Kōfukuji temple two hours later. Here, sacred food and drinks are presented to Wakamiya jinja's kami, identified as the child of two of the kami enshrined at Kasuga. Between 2:30 p.m. and midnight, traditional performing arts are offered on a simple lawn stage in front of the temporary shrine, following the common three-part structure of many *matsuri*: "welcoming the gods, entertaining them, then seeing them off" (Terauchi 2016: 18). This exceptional display of medieval performing arts—some rarely performed elsewhere in Japan—is the hallmark of the Onmatsuri. The performances include reconstructed shrine dances and songs by female priestesses (*miko kagura*), as well as agrarian performances (*dengaku*) and local dances (*azuma asobi, yamato mai*), a mysteriously simple act with (now mostly ornamental) flutes and drums (*seinō*), a reconstructed example of early Nō theater (*sarugaku Nō*) and numerous items from the "elegant" or "courtly" repertoires (*gagaku* and *bugaku*). This portion of the *matsuri* is known as the Otabishosai お旅所祭.

Onmatsuri's size and complexity defy attempts to isolate basic units of analysis. Even a single section, such as the Otabishosai, offers a dazzling amount of auditory information, given the internal diversity of each performance, the sheer duration of the event, and the composite nature of the overall auditory field. Thus, conceiving the "soundscape" of the *matsuri* as an independent phenomenological aspect of a person's participation in the event would inevitably lead to a form of the so-called audiovisual litany, "a set of reductive binary oppositions between the visual and the auditory, positing the former as analytical and the latter as emotional" (Eisenberg 2015: 195; see Sterne 2003). Rather than treating Onmatsuri's music and sound individually, therefore, it is more productive to show how selected sonic practices fulfill specific functions within the phenomenological totality of ritual experience.

First and foremost, Onmatsuri's sonic practices exhibit a remarkable degree of "affective capacity" (Slaby and Mühlhoff 2019: 30–3): establishing vibrational relations, they connect representational and nonrepresentational elements of the *matsuri*, anchoring sensory perceptions in shared religious-semiotic meanings. At the most immediate level, sounds contribute to the transformation of bare spaces into sacralized places. When the body of the kami is brought down from the forest to Wakamiya jinja, for example, the crowd gathered in front of the *otabisho* intones a low, droning sound called *keihitsu* 警蹕, operating on the surrounding atmosphere by marking the space as sacred. In this instance, "sonic practices territorialize by virtue of combining physical vibration with bodily sensation and culturally conditioned meaning" (Eisenberg 2015: 199). Belief in the power of sound to draw away evil spirits is perhaps less important than the creation of a shared quality of perception. Thus, the grounds of the *matsuri* constitute "simultaneously a physical environment and a way of perceiving that environment" (Thompson 2002: 1, quoted in Eisenberg 2015: 198).

Nature is a central component of Onmatsuri, ostensibly because an important portion of the ritual takes place in the middle of an ancient forest. Consequently, Onmatsuri's "sonic environment" (*otokankyō*) (Terauchi 2011: 90) is characterized by the integration of voices, instrumental music, and the sounds/noises of the surroundings: the low hum of conversations, wind between the trees, birds' calls, the sound of streaming water, and the crackling of fire. In this peculiar sonic ambiance, the sound of footsteps on the gravel is a particularly important acoustic marker, because it signals the arrival of the procession carrying the body of the kami (*senkō no gi* 遷幸の儀).

Conversely, shortly after the last *bugaku* performance, the *shintai*, the object considered to house the kami, is carefully removed from the temporary shrine and the surrounding priests quickly form a new procession (*kankō no gi* 還幸の儀). As the procession disappears into the forest, leaving the human world behind, the sounds of the accompanying *gagaku* music gradually fade out. The process of seeing off the deity (*kamiagari*) is experienced not as a visual spectacle but by hearing it unfold (Terauchi 2011: 95). The intensity of these processions to and from the Wakamiya jinja cannot be overemphasized: because all of the lights are out, hearing becomes the preferred sensory channel. In this way, "experience through hearing" is indirectly acknowledged as a fundamental aspect of ritual participation (Terauchi 2011: 94).

However, attention to Onmatsuri's sonic environment should not be limited to natural sounds: immediately available to auditory awareness are also more deliberately "humanly organized sounds" (Blacking 1974) such as prayers (*norito*), brief explanations of each phase of the ritual broadcasted over loudspeakers, noise from the dining hall backstage, and above all, the music and singing performed onstage—all elements that do not require attentive listening but nonetheless convey relevant information about their sources.

In these examples, the distinction between musical and nonmusical sounds is far from self-evident. When asked to comment upon the artistic value of *gagaku* and *bugaku* in

Onmatsuri, members of the amateur group Nanto Gakuso 南都楽所 often downplay, contest, or even refute the idea that what they do should be considered "music." Instead, they emphasize the material effect of their sonic contributions, insisting that *gagaku* simply helps "support the *matsuri*" (*matsuri o sasaeru*). Another view shared by many members of the group is that the primary function of *gagaku* and *bugaku* is to "adorn and exalt" (*shōgon suru*) the kami—a concept with deep Buddhist roots. As these examples demonstrate, even when it is clearly distinct from other kinds of sonic experience, the "music" we encounter during a *matsuri* can have more complex functions than being aesthetically pleasing.

From the point of view of the participants in a *matsuri*, sonic practices "charge an entire place or situation with sonorous intensity" (Riedel 2019: 91), conjuring up an almost tangible "atmosphere of the past" defined in opposition to the contemporary urban soundscape. These evocations of the sonic past often bring about politically charged feelings of nostalgia. Therefore, any study of religious sonic practices should also consider the ideological discourses conveyed or enabled by sound. At the same time, because they are complex auditory experiences, *matsuri* can stimulate contrasting "ways of hearing" (*oto o kikoekata*) (Terauchi 2011: 94): at times, these "listening practices" (Sterne 2003: 90–5) can even challenge the centrality of human actors. During the Otabishosai, for example, all of the performances take place facing the temporary shrine, not the audience: this suggests that the kami themselves might be listening, with their own idiosyncratic preferences and dispositions toward sound. Indeed, how the kami's agency is construed and to what extent it is perceived by the performers and the audience are ideal subjects of careful ethnographic investigations.

As these short examples from Nara's Onmatsuri demonstrate, the study of *matsuri* as multilayered sonic events is a promising research area of immediate interest not only to ethnomusicologists and anthropologists but also to specialists of Japanese religions. The centrality of sonic practices in most, if not all, Japanese religious experiences invites us to lend an ear: what will be heard might surprise us.

CHAPTER 25

Space

Tatsuma PADOAN

Investigation of space as social category provides essential insights into religious practice, as it opens up fundamental questions about how to situate ritual action, when places start to be considered as sacred and why, and what kind of role environment plays in the religious construction of cultural life. Some scholars have even talked about a "spatial turn" in religious studies and Japanese religions more specifically (Tweed 2006; Knott 2010; Blair 2015; Rots 2017b; see also Smith 1987; Kawano 2005; Moerman 2005; Thal 2005; Ambros 2008; Grapard 2016;). In particular, the work of Henri Lefebvre, *The Production of Space* (1991), has played an influential role in reassessing social studies of space, as it is evident in many of these publications and in those scholars who have been associated with the aforementioned "spatial turn" in cultural theory and study of religions (Soja 1996; Knott 2005; Warf and Arias 2009).

Lefebvre provided a formidable critical analysis of space in late capitalist societies by looking at its construction through the creation and preservation of social relations and ideological values. Through the way we *perceive*, *conceive*, and *live* space, he says, we tend to reproduce hegemonic assumptions about political power and a modern Cartesian division between human subjects and reality. However, the approach here presented will tend to diverge from Lefebvre's (1991: 45) *representational view* of reality, which—despite his attempts to show interrelation between physical, mental and social fields (11, 29–31, 38–9, 73–4)—still betrays a strong divide between "language" and "real nature" (29–31, 70–1). Our main point of departure will be the fact that, from a *material semiotic perspective*, space is not only constructed, but also endowed with agency.

By adopting such perspective, in the first part of this chapter, I explore the possibility to investigate space from a semiotic point of view, examining the theoretical potentials of this approach, and the methodological issues involved. After a discussion of different theoretical scenarios, in the second part I move to a specific case study, namely, a contemporary Shugen community of ascetic practice. The Tsukasa-kō lay group affiliated with the Tenpōrinji temple on Mount Kongō is related to the revival of the pilgrimage to the "sutra mounds of the twenty-eight lodges of Katsuragi" (*Katsuragi no nijūhasshuku kyōzuka*). Through both theoretical discussion of spatial semiotics and the analysis of this case study, using both historical and ethnographic sources, I attempt to challenge the still too common view of semiotics as a theory of timeless symbols and representation. On the contrary, following the work of Paris School semioticians like Algirdas Julien Greimas, Paolo Fabbri, Manar Hammad, Jacques Fontanille, and Eric Landowski, and the material semiotic trend developed from their ideas by Bruno Latour, semiotics will here emerge as a theory of actions, passions, body and materiality.

THE SEMIOTICS OF SPACE

Yuri Lotman (1990: 271–2) has poignantly remarked that history has often been referred to as the memory of humankind. But if history is cultural memory, this means that "it is not only a relic of the past, but also an active mechanism of the present." He adds: "Memory is more like a generator, reproducing the past again; it is the ability, given certain impulses, to switch on the process of generating a conceptualized reality which the mind transfers into the past" (1990: 272). In other words, if history is a form of collective memory, it is based on a cultural reconstruction of the past from the point of view of the present, or of future expectations, hopes, and purposes. Such dialogue between memory and history is fundamental for the construction of social identities and, interestingly enough, proceeds through the introduction of cultural texts from the past. Texts and fragments from previous societies work as both condensers and generators of cultural memory (Lotman 1990: 18) and are then integrated into the space of the *semiosphere*, interacting with the mechanisms of contemporary world.

The "semiosphere," according to Lotman (1990: 123–42), is thus the internal sphere of culture in constant dialogue with its borders, a semiotic field of translations between different languages, texts, and discourses circulating at different levels, through which new meanings are produced. We will see in our case study how all these considerations about history, memory, and cultural spaces well apply to the important place of mountain asceticism called Katsuragi. Here, different semiotic texts were introduced and produced over the centuries; they were circulated and translated one into the other; and they were integrated into a semiosphere, where *different languages coexisted in a multilayered space*.

I thus argue that history is constantly included, integrated into a spatial semiotics. Here, I define *spatial semiotics* in three ways: (1) a space conceived as "semiosphere" or field of translation, constituted by multiple layers of cultural texts originating in the past and present time; (2) a space considered as "language" or a signifying set, which not only communicates social relations, but may also be manipulated to stipulate different subjectivities and forms of life; and most importantly, (3) a space understood as "actant" or by its syntactic character, in other words, either as an *object of value* constructed and negotiated by human and nonhuman actors, or as an *interacting subject* who can actively perform actions. Here, I try to explore both the theoretical scenarios and the methodological challenges offered by this approach to sacred space and history.

Along these lines, the natural world—or even "reality" itself—may be analyzed as a particular cluster of nonverbal languages or semiotic systems (Greimas and Courtés 1982: 374–5), while subjects are shaped and defined by the communicative processes they themselves manipulate, circulate, and interpret. Greimas and other semioticians of the Paris School studied the role of subjects by introducing the concept of "actant," which eventually led to the idea of *material semiotics* (Latour 2005: 54–5; see also Latour and Fabbri 1977). *Actants* are defined as syntactic positions occupied by every human or nonhuman *actor* that can perform an action or be acted upon (Greimas and Courtés 1982: 5–8). Actants are characterized by different *modalities*, like volition (as "wanting to"), obligation (as "having to"), ability (as "being able to"), knowledge (as "knowing how to"), and belief (as an oscillation between "accepting-doubting-refusing and admitting") (1982: 193–5), which in turn provide the ground for a semiotic investigation of *affects* and *passions* (Greimas and Fontanille 1993; Fontanille 2007). Actants are thus narrative and communicative roles (Subject, Object, Sender, Helper, Anti-Subject, etc.) that can be played out by concrete human and nonhuman actors, sometimes with the same actor playing several roles, or sometimes the same role played by several actors, at different times or even at the same time (in which case it will be called the "collective actant") (Padoan 2019: 88–9, 94–5).

With regards to spatial semiotics, the idea, following the approach of Paris School of semiotics, is to analyze space in terms of actions performed in and through it, by considering the role of nonhuman actors such as architectural elements, infrastructures, features of the landscape, parts of the urban environment, and so forth. I now consider what kind of implications these perspectives may have for the study of religious space in Japan.

INSIGHTS FROM THE FIELD OF JAPANESE RELIGIONS

Semiotic perspectives on Japanese religions have been offered by a number of scholars, most notably in the study of Buddhist cultural history (Faure 1991, 1998a; Grapard 1994, 2016; Abe 1999; Sharf 1999, 2005; Rambelli 2007, 2013). Even without systematically applying a semiotic methodology, Allan Grapard (2016) in his recent work *Mountain Mandalas* has proficiently used notions of sign and text to describe the construction and interpretation of sacred space by Shugen ascetics in Kyushu. Along the lines of our first and second definitions of spatial semiotics shortly outlined above, and in close connection to our case study, Grapard explains how:

> From a semiological perspective, it may already be advanced that mountains were treated by the *yamabushi* who resided there as signs to be deciphered and forming some sort of "natural text" from which a type of wisdom deemed necessary to salvation might be extracted. ... Mountains were thus covered, layer upon layer, by a number of texts, of which the *yamabushi* and others provided different meanings. (Grapard 2016: 5–6)

Although related more to religious materiality than sacred space, Fabio Rambelli's work *Buddhist Materiality* (2007) is to date one of the very few studies in Japanese religions to extensively apply semiotic models to themes closely related to our present discussion. By unfolding a vast array of semiotic instruments—from Baudrillard's *The System of Objects* (1996) and his typology of values (1981) to understand the role of materials in the construction of Buddhists' identity, to Eco's (1976) definition of ostensive signs applied to Buddhist icons and Genette's notion of transtextuality (1997)—Rambelli shows how materiality has been used to mediate and control the intersections between abstract and concrete, sacred and profane, culture and nature.

Examples of semiotic reflections on space in Japanese religions may also include Yamaguchi Masao (1988), who analyzed the concepts of center and periphery in Japan using Tartu School semiotics, as well as Hammad's work (2006) on religious aspects of Tea Ceremony (*Cha no yu*) and Jane Bachnik's research (1995) on indexical meanings in ritual.

SPATIAL SEMIOTICS IN KATSURAGI SHUGEN: SACRED SPACE IN KATSURAGI

Katsuragi is a remarkable mountain area, stretching for more than 100 km from Wakayama City on the west coast to Kame no se, where the River Yamato narrows between the ancient provinces of Yamato and Kawachi (Miyake 2001: 162–5). The main peak of this area is Mount Kongō (1125 m, literally "Mount Vajra"), located some 30 km south from modern Osaka (Kongōsan sōgō bunka gakujutsu chōsa iinkai 1988: 3).

One of the first written sources documenting ascetic activity in Katsuragi is the *Shoku Nihongi* (797), which recorded some events concerning the life of En no kimi Ozunu (entry 699) (*KT* 2: 4; Gorai 1980: 22). The figure of En no Ozunu (also En no Ubasoku, En no Gyōja) underwent different narrative transformations and embellishments, starting from the *Nihon ryōiki* (823), acquiring then a special role in the *Shozan engi* (late twelfth century), which we will soon examine. On the other hand, we know about a shrine dedicated to the god Hitokotonushi of Katsuragi, which was sponsored by the court at the time of the *Engishiki* (927), and which was given a number of offerings during the *ainamesai* (Bock 1970: 90–2). However, at least since the twelfth century, Katsuragi area has been crossed by a pilgrimage route, which connects together twenty-eight spots. Starting with the *Shozan engi*, these twenty-eight stations were associated by specific narratives with the twenty-eight chapters of the prominent Mahāyāna Buddhist scripture *Lotus Sutra*, which were said to be buried in sutra mounds (*kyōzuka*), one chapter for each spot, and venerated as the Word and Body of the Buddha inscribed into the land itself (Kashiba-shi Nijōsan Hakubutsukan 1999: 10; Padoan and Sedda 2018: 55–7).

The lay ascetic group I have been studying—called Tsukasa-kō and affiliated with the Shingonshū Daigoha Tenpōrinji temple on top of Mount Kongō—was founded by the *bettō* Rev. Katsuragi Kōryū (b. 1972) in 2005 and is part of a larger Shugendō revivalist trend that started after the Second World War. Shugendō, literally meaning "the way to master/acquire ascetic powers," may be described as a Japanese form of mountain asceticism that, according to current views, emerged around the late thirteenth century in major sacred mountain areas (Blair 2015: 272), combining together Buddhist Esoteric, Daoist, and shamanic elements with the worship of kami, the local deities. Having first met this group in 2008, I have studied their activities from an ethnographic perspective over the years, conducting interviews and participant observation during ritual performances, pilgrimages, communal gatherings, celebratory events, business meetings, as well as cleaning activities at their main temple.

The modern history of this temple is closely related to the 1868 edicts *shinbutsu bunri rei* ("Kami-Buddha Separation Edicts"), which dramatically reconfigured the role of Shugendō in Katsuragi and across Japan (Tamamuro 1977; Sekimori 2005). In 1871, three years after the promulgation of the edicts, the temple Tenpōrinji with its Ōshukubō (Great Temple Lodgings) on top of Mount Kongō was dismantled by the supporters of the new regime, who tried to separate a supposedly "pure" Shinto from its "foreign" Buddhist influences. This amounted to the laicization of the abbot of Tenpōrinji Katsuragi Shinjun (1842–1905) and his conversion to the position of head priest of the Shinto shrine Katsuragi jinja (Katsuragi and Ōya 1988: 183). The pilgrimage to the twenty-eight sutra mounds was no longer undertaken. This changed in the second half of the twentieth century, when a group of Buddhist temples connected with Shugendō—first Inunakisan in 1953, then Miidera in 1958 and Shōgoin the following year—started to retrace the ancient pilgrimage spots and paths (Nakano 2002: 280).[1]

---

[1] See Padoan (forthcoming), for a more comprehensive analysis of this case study.

A SEMIOTICS OF THE NATURAL WORLD

One of the narratives contemporary ascetics often refer to when discussing the origin of the pilgrimage route is the aforementioned *Shozan engi* (Grapard 1982; Kawasaki 2005; Roth Al Eid 2014), which states: "Ritual procedure of the mansions: under the steps walked by En no Gyōja, there are 69,384 characters" (*NST* 20: 117, translation by the author). This passage establishes an exact correspondence between the number of Chinese characters contained in the *Lotus Sutra* (69,384) and the number of steps that En no Gyōja undertook to complete the pilgrimage. In other words, the written text becomes the mountain and the mountain becomes a spatial text not to be *read*, but rather *walked*, by the ascetics, following the steps of the legendary founder. Moreover, this may be an example of *inter-semiotic translation*—a translation from one semiotic system to another—from the written language of the sutra to a *semiotics of the natural world* (Greimas and Courtés 1982: 374–5), namely, the spatial landscape of the mountains. Using the term *translation*, we wish to emphasize that the content of the verbal text is not *read* in the mountain but is rather *perceived* through the landscape's phenomenological and "sensible qualities" (375), that is, experienced through the *mediation* of the mountain's natural elements and of the perceiving body of the practitioner who walks throughout the pilgrimage route.

Therefore, the figure of En no Gyōja plays here the role of *mediator* (Latour 2005: 39) between the practitioner and the Katsuragi territory, in which the teachings of the Buddha are inscribed word by word, character by character. These narratives are continuously brought back to memory today, both orally and through a reenactment of the founder's ritual actions, as we can see from the following ethnosemiotic analysis.

TEXTS, BODIES, PLACES

During the ritual performed nowadays at the twenty-eight sutra mounds, Katsuragi ascetics chant a series of mantras and sutras, accompanied by the rhythmic shaking of *shakujō* (short Buddhist staff provided with six metal rings on top). The whole ceremony is temporally demarcated by the sound of *horagai* conch shells at the beginning and at the end, and lasts for about eight minutes. The main prayer offered is the *Heart Wisdom Sutra* (*Hannya shingyō*).

Moreover, rhythmic intensification, use of tools, and positions in space play a crucial role during the ritual, with the practitioners *facing the mound* where the *Lotus Sutra* chapter is venerated. The act of praying in front of sacred scriptures containing the Word of the Buddha, considering them as main icons of worship, has been considered standard Buddhist practice in Japan for a long time (Moerman 2007: 252). For the Shugen practitioners in particular, the sutra mound may be considered as an *object of value*, a term used in semiotics to indicate specific targets of action—human or nonhuman actors, namely, people, deities, animals, things, or portions of space playing the actantial role of "object"—which are phenomenologically invested with values by the acting subjects (Greimas 1987: 84–105). Portions of space where sacred scriptures have been buried are in fact invested with religious meanings by the ascetics, becoming objects of worship, that is, objects of value actively constructed by the practitioners. However, the values invested in the sutra chapters enable the semiotic construction of sutra mounds not as inert things but as *bodies*.

The *Lotus Sutra* itself provides justification for this practice *at the level of enunciation* or metacommunication—namely, that level of communication whose aim is to create and modify the relations between the parties inscribed in the communicative process—by clarifying to the readers, as a sort of manual of instructions, the way the scripture itself should be venerated. The sutra itself states: "Whatever place a roll of this scripture may occupy, in all those places one is to erect a stupa of seven jewels … There is no need to even lodge a *śarīra* [corporal relic of the Buddha] in it. What is the reason? Within it there is already a whole body of the Thus Come One [i.e., the Buddha himself]" (*T* 9.262.31b; Hurvitz 1976: 178). In this and other passages, the *Lotus Sutra* presents itself as corporal relic of the Buddha.

It is striking that in well-documented Buddhist practices across Asia, relics and religious icons have been envisaged for centuries, in a clear *nonrepresentational* and immanentist move, as the concrete material presence of the body of the Buddha on earth, rather than as symbols or representations of the sacred (Faure 1998a; Sharf 1999; Sharf and Sharf 2001).[2] The same devotional attitude is shared by ascetic practitioners in Katsuragi, who ritually engage with the sutra mounds, in the same way in which they perform prayers, chants, and mantric powerful ritual formulas in front of other Buddhist icons.

RITUAL ENUNCIATION OF SPACE

The practitioners and the sutra mound face one another in a ritual situation—using a term of Landowski (1989), in the "semiotic context"—establishing a *relation of copresence*. Both are characterized by what Hammad (2006: 75–115) calls "immanent referential" (*référentiel immanent*). These are centers of reference inscribed in humans, things, architectural elements, and other nonhuman actors, orienting spatial directions around them according to topological schemes and axial systems (e.g., front/back, up/down, right/left, etc.). Positions of people and things in space can be related to the mutual intersection of their immanent referential, according to the form of interaction prescribed, or the course of action followed (Hammad 2006: 82–3). In other words, when people approach a material object or a particularly marked place, especially in ritual situations (but often in other circumstances too), they need to be aware of the immanent referential inscribed in it, as when for example a pot or tray in a *cha no yu* tea ceremony should be handled from a particular side (2006: 84–5).

If we apply this to the ritual stage performed in Katsuragi, we can see how practitioners, icons, and mounds have all their centers of reference in the space, and how places inscribed with the *Lotus Sutra* are worshipped from a particular spatial position, as they have to be oriented towards the Shugen ascetics. Such referential embedded in the sutra mounds makes them the "zero point," the *topos* around which space and ritual action are deictically and indexically structured, as an immanent "I" according to which a copresent "you" (the ascetics) and a lateral "them" (human bystanders or deities evoked through mantras) are spatially rearranged. Ritual thus works as a *concerted conversation*, in which different nonhuman actors are *brought together* and *put into motion* by the enunciation of space.[3] Space is here not only produced by actions, but it can actually become a producer

---

[2] See Henare, Holbraad and Wastell (2007) for other examples of nonrepresentational approaches to materiality, coming from ethnographic research.
[3] Some of the Buddhist deities evoked through mantras are Hōki Bosatsu, Zaō Gongen, Fudō Myōō, the Seven Great Womb Divine Children of Katsuragi, and the Eight Great Vajra Divine Children of Ōmine.

of actions itself, an acting subject or *topos* (a "spatial actant," following Hammad 2002 [1989]) eliciting a response from the practitioners, prompting their *volitions* and *obligations* to perform the ritual.

If *in presentia*, as immanent referentials, we can observe ascetics and mound in mutual relation, *in absentia,* we instead have a second couple of elements, consisting in the figure of the founder En no Gyōja, and in the *Lotus Sutra* considered as relic and Body of the Buddha, according to the following homologation:

Ascetics: Mound:: En no Gyōja: Body of the Buddha

However, what occurs through this ritual is actually a *presentification* of the second couple of terms within the first one. Practitioners, in fact, constantly stress the idea that En no Gyōja and the Buddha left their concrete *traces* on those mountains. Moreover, En no Gyōja often emerges as a strong simulacrum of identification for them, not only as a devotional figure, but also as *exemplar* to be embodied while praying and walking. What they describe in the interviews in terms of an *immediate* religious experience is expressed in ritual through the *mediation* of these two simulacra of identification, En no Gyōja and the Buddha's Body:

Ascetics : Mound :: En no Gyōja : Body of the Buddha

We could consider this as an *apparatus of enunciation*, namely, a way of constructing subjectivities in ritual discourse. We might more precisely define this operation, in semiotic terms, as a "shifting in" or *engagement* (Greimas and Courtés 1982: 100–2) corresponding, on one hand, to the embodiment of the founder's identity by the practitioners and, on the other hand, to the identification of the Buddha's Body with the landscape (the sutra mound or *topos*, which is the *actor* to whom the prayers are offered). Such operation is realized *through* the ritual activation and *presentification* of the traces left by the two virtual terms *in absentia*. Also, this *presentification* is achieved through *rhythm*, through voice, prosodic elements, and tools, all activated by the body.

From a semiotic point of view, *ritual becomes a way to mobilize space* through a specific form of interaction, connected to a particular manipulation of time: namely, a ritual interaction between human and nonhuman bodies (*topoi*) facing each other, bringing the past into the present, through an operation of presentification and synchronisation.

CONCLUSION

Either considering the sutra mound as *object of value*—the target of ritual action—or as *acting subject*—a topological body prescribing ritual acts—the *Lotus Sutra* is materially buried and inscribed in the mountains. It is not just the representation of a transcendent or remote reality these practitioners think about or imagine. The *Sutra*, considered as Body of the Buddha, is embedded in the natural landscape of the mountain and can only be grasped through the experience of the ascetic practice.

This claim is supported not only by the fact that the revivalist ascetics themselves were always very keen to stress the importance of experiencing the practice and the mountain through their body and affectivity (often using expressions like *ogamu kimochi*, or "mood to pray," and *mi ni tsukeru*, or "learning through the body") but also by the idea that gods and Buddhas live in the landscape, an idea that I found was not commonly shared by tourists or hikers. The body of the practitioners plays the role of *great translator* in the

Katsuragi pilgrimage, creating a specific *semiotics of the natural world* by realizing—as we have seen in the analysis of the ritual—the presence of the Buddha. And yet, such ritual activities produce *spaces* and *times*, which overlap with other spaces and times, including the premodern mythological narratives, the mountain trails as differently practiced by hikers and tourists, and different pilgrimages made by ascetic groups in competition with each other.

To conclude, we have seen that history, from a semiotic perspective, is not to be considered as a hard timeline of reality, running below signs, meanings, texts, and discourses. History, especially in the case of religious revivalist movements, is instead understood as a strategy of memory. But as we have seen, history is also constantly included and integrated into a spatial semiotics, into a semiosphere constituted by multiple layers of cultural texts originated in the past. All these modes of experience compose a multiple, multifaceted landscape, which we may end up calling the "mountains of Katsuragi."

See also Chapter 8, "Environmentalism," Chapter 15, "Materiality," Chapter 20, "Pilgrimages and 'Sacred' Geography," and Chapter 24, "Sound."

CHAPTER 26

Spiritualism and Occultism

YOSHINAGA Shin'ichi

New religions have been studied since the Second World War in Japan, including by scholars such as Oguchi Iichi, Murakami Shigeyoshi, Yasumaru Yoshio, Shimazono Susumu, Inoue Nobutaka, and many others. However, the history of spiritualism and occultism has not been paid the attention it deserves. The difficulty in describing occult phenomena is not a valid reason for this academic indifference because such difficulties also occur when studying, for example, the lives of founders of new religious movements. Rather, one of the main reasons for this indifference lies in the relatively short life of most occult organizations. From the 1910s to 1920s, Spiritualism in Japan spread mainly through books and periodicals; a few groups centered around the practice of spirit mediumship also appeared. Spiritual-psychic healing (*seishin ryōhō*) groups, which appeared in large numbers, contributed to the vogue of Western occultism, but most of them disappeared in the 1930s and were forgotten, often leaving no trace behind. It is thus not surprising that the vogue of spiritualism before the Second World War remained largely unnoticed by scholars before the 1980s.

This academic atmosphere changed in the 1980s. Japan saw a popular boom of the occult (*okaruto būmu*) in the 1970s, which led to the rise of the concept of the "spiritual world" (*seishin sekai*), an equivalent term for New Age, and of so-called new new religions (*shin shin shūkyō*) in the 1980s. This turned the attention of some researchers to the historical background of such developments. For example, an independent researcher, Imura Kōji, published a breakthrough work, *Reijutsuka no kyōen* (The Banquet of Spiritual/Psychical Healers, 1984), which described the activities of famous *reijutsuka* from the late Meiji period up to the early Showa. Inspired by this work, Nishiyama Shigeru, a sociologist of religion, advocated the new term *reijutsu shūkyō* (literally, "spiritual power religions") to historically connect the contemporary spiritual trends of the eighties with the occult boom in the Taishō era (e.g., Nishiyama 1988).

Besides his monumental works, Shimazono also wrote articles in which he proposed the term *shin reisei undō* ("new spirituality movement") to cover phenomena ranging from the New Age of the 1980s to the spiritual boom after 1990 (e.g., Shimazono 1992). Tsushima Michihito, another sociologist, wrote about the political aspects of spiritual movements in 1920s and 1930s, such as Ōmotokyō and Shinsei Ryūjin-kai (e.g., Tsushima 1989). Tsushiro Hirofumi wrote about the ritual elements of modern Esoteric Shintoism; his

---

I would like to express my gratitude to Dylan Luers Toda (Academic Translator) for editing my English draft and Ioannis Gaitanidis (Chiba University) for adding bibliographical information. Without them, this chapter would not have been written.

book, *Chinkon gyōhō ron* (1990), is still a classic study on this subject. Ichiyanagi Hirotaka wrote pioneering works on hypnotism (1997) and psychic research (1994) in modern Japan from the viewpoint of literary studies. A few more scholars have been following in their footsteps recently, such as Horie Norichika (see Chapter 27 in this volume) or Yoshinaga Shin'ichi (e.g., 2004, 2015). However, studies on the history of spiritualism and occultism in Japan are still scarce (see also Kurita, Tsukada, and Yoshinaga 2019).

A larger problem may be whether the categories of spiritualism or occultism can actually be applied to Japanese religious history, and if so, how far back in history (see, e.g., Morrow 2018). As is well known, Spiritualism was born out of Western religious culture of the nineteenth century (see, e.g., Josephson-Storm 2017). It is usually described as religious practices centered around the belief in the possibility of communicating with the spirits of the dead through the intervention of mediums. It grew out of mesmerism and Swedenborgianism, both of which had been exported from Europe to the Americas, and spread rapidly after the famous Rochester rapping in 1848.[1] Later, American spiritualism was exported to Europe, where it led to two other movements, namely, occultism in France and psychical research in Great Britain. Occultism, with its basic ideas, was founded by Eliphas Levi (1810–1875) in the mid-nineteenth century. It was constructed around a practice and belief in the magical power of the living person's will, as opposed to spiritualism's focus on the belief in and powers of the departed souls. Levi's psychologized system of magic and his encyclopedic books of esoteric legacies influenced the movement's successor, Theosophy. Though occultism, strictly defined, and spiritualism differ in their object of attention, namely, the living or the dead, both of them are situated between Christianity and natural sciences, and shared the same premise that supernatural phenomena are controlled by human beings, living or dead, not by the seemingly arbitrary will of God, as envisioned for instance by Calvinist Protestants.

The traces of Western occultism in its broader sense can also be found in modern Japan. Very roughly, its history could be divided into four phases, namely, the periods from 1880 to 1929, 1930 to 1945, 1945 to 1969, and the 1970s to today. In the first period, mesmerism was imported and developed into a Japanese style of mind cure called *seishin ryōhō*, and the esoteric Shinto practice called *chinkon kishin hō*, which I discuss later on, spread during the Taishō era (1912–26). During the second period, spiritual seekers turned to the history of an often imagined "ancient Japan" from which "undiscovered" Shinto classics were allegedly "found" and deciphered according to Japanese ultranationalist interpretations; a small nationalistic new religious movement, Shinsei Ryūjin Kai, was a typical example of this phase. The third phase saw the decrease of interest in the occult

---

[1] Mesmerism refers to a cluster of cultural movements inspired by the German Franz Anton Mesmer (1734–1815), who allegedly discovered "animal magnetism," namely, a procedure by which magnets can be used to amplify and channel a "fluid" that he believed accumulated within bodies, with therapeutic effects. Swedenborgianism refers to the thought (and latter interpretations of it) of the Swede Emanuel Swedenborg (1688–1772), who wrote extensively on the spiritual structure of the universe, claimed to be in possession of clairvoyant powers, and advanced the idea that humans choose their own heaven or hell after death. The origins of another movement that had significant influence during the nineteenth century, namely, Spiritualism, are usually associated with the experiences in 1848 of the three daughters of John D. Fox, in a farm near Hydesville, New York, in the vicinity of Rochester. The Fox sisters claimed that mysterious knockings heard about the house were efforts to communicate with them by the spirit of a peddler who had died in the house. For explanations of these and other movements and names usually associated with Western esotericism and occultism, see the Dictionary of Gnosis & Western Esotericism (Hanegraaff et al. 2006).

as a consequence of the backlash against the Second World War Japanese regime and the primacy of technology during the Cold War. Nonetheless, Seichō no ie, a Japanese "new thought"-type of religion, which professed that healing depends on one's own mind, was one of the few channels through which translations of new thought, spiritualism, yoga, and Theosophy were published in Japan. The fourth period, briefly discussed above, centers on the growth of New Age thought, the spiritual boom, and other more recent developments.

This chapter focuses on the first period because it covers the beginning of Japanese occultism and Shinto esotericism and their transformations. Three streams of occultism ran through this period. The first stream is comprised of Western works on spiritualism and occultism translated into Japanese; not only Theosophy but also Steiner's anthropology was introduced to Japan before the Second World War. The second stream concerns the re-enchantment and indigenization of hypnotism. Hypnotism was introduced as a psychological method and was transformed into a magical or psychical technique, which was influenced by traditional Esoteric Buddhism and mountain worship (Shugendō). The third stream is the diffusion of a controlled possession called *chinkon kishin hō*. It became popular through Ōmotokyō, which rapidly grew in the Taisho era. In the remaining part of this chapter, I trace the history of "imported" and "homegrown" occultism in Japan and the transformations of its interpretations from the 1880s to the 1920s.

HYPNOTISM

The exact year when hypnotism was first introduced to Japan is not clear, but it began to be known to intellectuals around 1885, when the first book on hypnotism entitled *Dōbutsu denki gairon* (An Outline of Animal Electricity) was published. Although Mesmer is credited as the original author, this is in fact a Japanese translation of writings by the American mesmerist John Bovee Dods (1795–1872).[2] This small book explains hypnotic phenomena by positing the existence of electricity in fluid form within the human body. At that time, hypnotism was explained theoretically either as a psychological phenomenon or a physical phenomenon based on some kind of fluid.

The fluid theory of electricity was criticized by Inoue Enryō (1858–1919), the most influential proponent of hypnotism in the late nineteenth century. Inoue was a Buddhist philosopher and the founder of Toyo University. He became famous as the author of an anti-Christian philosophical work, *Shinri no konjin* (The Golden Compass of Truth, 3 vols.), published in 1886/7. This book attacked the irrationality of Christianity and praised Buddhism for its understanding of philosophy and natural science. Inoue then turned his attention to psychology. For him, the supernatural aspects of religions should be explained mainly by psychology, without resorting to unnecessary hypotheses of supernatural beings like animal spirits, souls of the dead, or gods. For him, hypnotism could also be explained as a psychological process of suggestion and belief. Inoue did not admit the possibility of a telepathic relationship between the hypnotist and the subject and denied the existence of fluids like electricity.

---

[2] More specifically, pp. 1–11 are a translation of pp. 8–17 of *Six Lectures on the Philosophy of Mesmerism* (Boston: William A. Hall, 1843); pp. 11–15, 17–21, 21–32 and 32–42 are from pp. 18–23, 51–7, 205–24 and 216–24, respectively, of *The Philosophy of Electrical Psychology* (New York: Fowler and Wells, 1852). The provenance of the content of pp. 15–17 is unknown.

Although hypnotism was explained rationally by authoritative scholars, the theory of subtle fluids survived in popular books on hypnotism. Kondō Yoshizō wrote *Majutsu to saiminjutsu* (Magic and Hypnotism) in 1892. He distinguished *saiminjutsu* (hypnotism) from *majutsu* (magic), because the latter could directly influence other persons at a distance, while the former needs hypnotic trance and verbal suggestions. Kondō posited the existence of a gaseous fluid emitted by the nervous system as a medium connecting the brain activity of one person to that of another. His book also debunked the existence of spiritual entities in the same way as Inoue Enryō but did admit the possibility of magical deeds based on the human will. His book was republished several times and became a longtime bestseller.

In 1903 Takeuchi Nanzō (or Kusuzō) translated Albert Moll's book *Der Hypnotismus* (1889) into Japanese as *Saiminjutsu jizai* (Mastering the Way of Hypnotism). This book became a bestseller and influenced many later books and therapists of hypnotism. It could be said that Japan was "hypnotized." However, just before this book was published, a more sensational and more unorthodox theory of hypnotism came out. Kuwabara Toshirō (1873–1906), instructor of Chinese literature at Shizuoka School of Education (now Shizuoka University), had begun a series of articles on hypnotism in a prestigious journal of education in 1903. According to his articles, he first became interested in hypnotism after reading Kondō's *Majutsu to saiminjutsu* and began to make experiments on it. After success in inducing clairvoyance in his subjects, his hypnotic experiments took on psychic or magical colors. At last, he came to believe in the miraculous power of human will, which could make various miraculous deeds possible, including healing physical diseases and moving inorganic objects by mere will power. He called this phenomenon *seishin reidō* (excellent movement of mind) to distinguish it from usual term for hypnotism (*saiminjutsu*). His articles, full of miraculous wonders, were enthusiastically received by readers, and were republished in three volumes from 1903 to 1904, which also sold well.

Kuwabara's three volumes, *Seishin reidō*, were welcomed by well-educated people because he narrated his experiences in the first person and built an original system of pan-psychic cosmology without using traditional Buddhist terms. According to his theory, mind (*seishin*) is itself energy, which every moving thing possesses, so that a human mind can influence another human mind or even an inanimate object at a distance without the need for the medium of a subtle fluid. The universe is the supreme self, consisting of myriad minds (all made of energy), so when the mind of an individual self becomes united with the supreme self of the universe, it can do what the universe can. Kuwabara seems to have borrowed these ideas from the Eastern philosophies of Buddhism, Confucianism, and also Indian philosophy, but they are also related to German Romanticism, and, as he himself admitted, his theory of the mind resembles Frederic W. H. Myers's (1843–1901) idea of subliminal self.

Setting aside the source of his pan-psychical cosmology, Kuwabara inherited Kondō Yoshizō's distinction between magic and hypnotism, and admitted the possibility of the power of mind having a direct effect on distant phenomena, just as Kondō did; in this regard, Kuwabara disagreed with Inoue and other academic psychologists. But Kuwabara did not employ a physical medium in his cosmology, like Dods's "electricity" or Kondō's "gas." By positing the mind as being itself fluid energy, Kuwabara tried to find a compromise between Inoue's psychological explanation and Kondō's physical one. In this way, Kuwabara tried to preserve the magical phenomena of both folk beliefs and traditional religions, and judging by the popularity his book enjoyed, he seems to have been successful.

As a result, around 1904–5, those who were interested in hypnotism could be classified into three groups. The first consisted of medical professionals, who tried to control or ban the use of hypnotism by nonmedical people. The second was the group of psychologists and hypnotists who claimed that practitioners should learn psychology. The third group was composed of healers who followed Kuwabara's system and who protested against the controls advocated by the first two groups. Such differences were reflected in their titles; therapists of the second group were called *saiminjutsu-shi* (hypnotists), while the healers of the last group were called *seishin ryōhō-ka* (mind curers) or *reijutsu-ka* (psycho-spiritual healers), although the distinction between them was vague at best. The term *seishin ryōhō-ka* derived from their belief that one's mind can directly cure the mind and body of others; *reijutsu* from the belief that it was a mysteriously excellent (*rei*) technique (*jutsu*). Later, in the Taishō era, *reijutsu* would come to mean "spiritual technique" because *rei* also has the meaning of "spiritual," but at first it had no mystical connotation. A heated controversy emerged among the three factions, and in 1908 (Meiji 41) a law controlling the use of hypnotism was issued. This law forbade the "abuse" of hypnotism but left untouched its "appropriate use," leaving the criteria to distinguish between them unclear. After this law was issued, most medical doctors stopped using hypnotism, which left the entire field of hypnotism to unorthodox healers. Those healers using *seishin ryōhō* or *reijutsu* would increase dramatically during the Taishō era (1912–26).

From the viewpoint of religious history, anomalous or supernatural phenomena were traditionally explained as the intervention of an animistic pantheon of gods and spirits. Inoue tried to replace such explanations with a rationalistic system of psychology, by using hypnotism, and by making Buddhism itself rationalistic. Ironically, however, hypnotism was re-enchanted by Kuwabara Toshirō, himself a pious believer in spiritual cultivation (*seishinshugi*), a form of modernized Buddhism advocated by Kiyozawa Manshi (1863–1903).

Overall, there were three main options to explain supernatural phenomena at the beginning of the twentieth century. The traditional option, the most popular, involved supernatural beings or animal spirits. As will be discussed later, this animistic system of Shinto had already been modernized by Honda Chikaatsu. The second option was to relate supernatural beings to subjective or psychological phenomena, as illusions caused by hypnotic trances. Inoue took this option and it became a scientifically authoritative explanation. The third option was offered by Kuwabara, which posited the power of mind based on a vitalistic view of the universe, without resorting to the existence of spirits.

PSYCHICAL RESEARCH AND "SHINREI"

Following the boom of hypnotism, Japanese society saw the rise of psychic research toward the end of the Meiji era (1912), first introduced to Japan by Hirai Kinza (1859–1916), a professor of English at Tokyo School of Foreign Languages (now Tokyo University of Foreign Studies). When he was young, he organized a committee to invite Henry Olcott (1832–1907), president of the Theosophical Society, to Japan. In 1889 his plan was realized and Olcott's lectures in Japan put a final touch to the Buddhist revival that had been going on since Inoue's time. After that, Hirai traveled around the United States from 1892 to 1894 to propagate Buddhism, during which time he attended and read a paper at the World Parliament of Religions. From 1892 to 1893, he stayed at the house of William Atwell Cheney, a famous lawyer, in Los Angeles. The Cheneys were Unitarians who were also interested in psychic research, spiritualism, and Eastern religions. Hirai did some psychic experiments with William and his wife, Annie Elizabeth, at their house. Hirai's own success of psychometry convinced him of the existence of psychic abilities. After coming back to Japan, Hirai became a Unitarian and started teaching at Tokyo School of Foreign Languages, but kept silent about his experiences of psychic research while a Unitarian. He began to write about psychic research again in 1905 after leaving Unitarianism.

Hirai helped Matsumura Kaiseki (1859–1939), a former Christian pastor, form a syncretic religious organization in 1907 called Dō-kai (Society of the Way) that mixed Confucianism, Christianity, and Buddhism. Hirai himself had considered the merits of a "synthetic religion"—an ideal new religion that should be formed by mixing the better part of various religious traditions. In addition, both Hirai and Matsumura shared an interest in psychic research and formed a group called Shinshō-kai (Society for Psychic Phenomena). Through this group, Hirai repeated some of the psychic experiments he had done during his stay in Los Angeles.

Though the group itself was small and short-lived, it attracted both intellectuals and journalists, and thus its influence was far-reaching. One of its members was Fukurai Tomokichi (1869–1952), an associate professor of psychology at Tokyo Imperial University. He was the first scholar to write a doctoral thesis on hypnotism. At first, he was rather critical of psychic phenomena associated with hypnotic trance, but around 1908 he began to take a favorable attitude toward them. Fukurai seems to have learned about psychic research through Shinshō-kai and became famous for his own experiments with two female psychics, Mifune Chizuko and Nagao Ikuko, from 1910 to 1911. Though it is still unclear whether those two women used a trick or not in their experiments of clairvoyance and thoughtography, Fukurai's experiments provoked sensational reactions in the media, which led to a major scandal in which Fukurai's findings were utterly discredited. As a consequence, Fukurai had to resign his professorship in 1914. His resignation closed the door of Japanese universities to academic research on not only psychic research but also psychotherapy. Fukurai himself turned to traditional Esoteric Buddhism for his personal spiritual search.

The media coverage of Fukurai's experiments led to his resignation from the University of Tokyo but also to the publication of books on psychic research and spiritualism, which reflected the revival of interest in spiritualism happening simultaneously in the Western world. Interestingly, many of those Japanese books had *shinrei* in their titles, the first being Hirai Kinza's *Shinrei no gensho* (Psychic phenomena), published in 1909, which offered a report of his experiments and an introduction to the field. *Shinrei* was originally used to mean "mind" or "soul" of living persons, first in Christian contexts and then in Buddhist books, but Hirai added psychic dimensions to this term. For instance, in 1917, Oliver Lodge's *Survival of Man* (1909) was translated as *Shinrei seikatsu* (literally meaning "spiritual life"). As this book was written by a famous physicist, it sold very well. In addition, as this book was originally written for the cause of spiritualism rather than psychic research, the connotation of spirits existing after the end of life was added to *shinrei*. As a result, *shinreishugi* is now used to mean spiritualism while *shinrei kenkyū* means psychic research. This has often caused confusion, requiring the meaning of *shinrei* to be deliberately contextualized.

Two prolific authors are worth mentioning here. Shibue Tamotsu (or Shibue Ekiken, 1857–1930) was one of the pioneering intellectuals who taught and translated English books on various subjects after the Meiji Restoration. From 1909 to 1910, he published eleven books related to mesmerism, spiritualism, and psychic research, according to the catalogue of the National Diet Library. He usually translated and condensed English, German, and French books into one. For example, his first book on this topic, titled *Shinshō oyobi sono jikken* (Psychic Phenomena and Their Experiments), was actually a combination of books by Frank Podmore (1856–1910), Pierre Janet (1859–1947), Myers, Maximilian Dessoir (1867–1947), and others. *Kaseikai no jikkyō* (The Reality of Mars) was a translation of Théodore Flournoy's (1854–1920) *From India to Planet Mars* (1900). Another author, Takahashi Gorō (1856–1935), was more of a psychic thinker compared to Shibue, who was a professional writer. Takahashi was also a teacher of English and a translator of various books. He was first known as a scholar of English and a militant defender of Christian causes, but during the first decade of the twentieth century, he came to be interested in psychic research through Western writings. His first book on that topic was *Shinpi tetsugaku* (Mystical Philosophy) in 1903. After some years of silence, Takahashi began writing on spiritualism again, seemingly stimulated by Hirai and Fukurai. He wrote six books from *Shin tetsugaku no shokō* (Dawn of New Philosophy, 1910) to *Yūmei no reiteki kōtsū* (Spiritual Interaction between the Seen and the Unseen, 1921). These books contained a blend of various Western occult thought. Takahashi also translated four books of spiritualism including *Psychic Philosophy as the Foundation of a Religion of Natural Law* (1896) by V.C. Desertis, the pseudonym of the British psychic researcher and spiritualist Stanley De Brath (1854–1937). This book was published under the title of *Shinreigaku kōwa* (Lecture on Spiritualism, 1915).

Some mention should also be given to Theosophical publications. After an initial boom of Theosophical articles in Buddhist journals around 1889, when Henry Steel Olcott made a lecture tour of Japan, few, if any, were published until the translation of H. P. Blavatsky's *Key to Theosophy* (1889) as *Reichigaku kaisetsu* (Introduction to Theosophy) in 1912. Its translators were Edward Stanley Stephenson and Udaka Heisaku. Stephenson was the grandson of Lord Edward Stanley, Earl of Derby, and came to Japan in 1898. Later, he taught English at the Imperial Naval Engineering College, Yokosuka, from 1902 to 1922, while presiding at a Theosophical lodge in Zushi, Kanagawa. He was a member of the Theosophical Society (T.S.) in Point Loma, led by Katherine Tingley (1849–1929), a prominent Theosophist. It seems this publication was financially supported by the Kanagawa lodge.

Another Theosophical group in Japan was related to the T.S. in Adyar, India. In 1920, the Tokyo International Lodge was founded by an Irish poet, James H. Cousins, with Kon Buhei, and Beatrice and Daisetsu Suzuki as its members. Kon was famous as a vegetarian and captain of an ocean-going ship and a firm believer in the world teacher. He translated Jiddu Krishnamurti's *At the Feet of the Master* (1910) into Japanese as *Arakandō* in 1925. However, these two books on Theosophy seem to have sold less than the books of spiritualism, and Theosophy had important but limited influence on some intellectuals (see Yoshinaga 2009, 2012).

SPIRITUAL HEALING

Just as interest in psychic research grew around 1910, mental-physical practices came into vogue among students and middle-class people. The most famous method was the *Okada-shiki seiza hō* (Okada method of calm sitting), which was invented by Okada Torajirō in the early 1900s (see Kurita 2014). In addition to this, the traditional ways of breathing in Zen Buddhism were revived and adopted, and the way of breathing and concept of prana presented by Yogi Ramacharaka, the pseudonym of William Walter Atkinson (1862–1932), were imported from America. These breathing practices themselves were not esoteric and spread as ways to improve one's physical and mental health. But soon abdominal breathing became the way to develop psychic power. For example, Mifune Chizuko, who had participated in Fukurai's experiments, came to employ these techniques for developing her clairvoyant abilities. *Seishin ryōhō* healers also employed abdominal breathing in order to improve their healing power. Kihara Kibutsu and Hiyama Tesshin were the earliest healers that used such physical methods. Gradually, the main objects of *seishin ryōhō* shifted from healing patients to developing the healing power, or the magical power, of the healers.

The largest organization of *seishin ryōhō* was Taireidō (The Way of Great Spirit, see Yoshinaga 2008). It offered ten-day programs for training psychic abilities, which included telepathy and clairvoyance as well as healing. Those who completed this course were given a diploma—it was not a public document but Taireidō's private degree—that allowed them to begin "medical" practice, which required a rather large sum of money. Taireidō trained thousands of healers, who in turn started their own brands of healing methods all over the country. Many psychic/mental healers appeared throughout Japan owing to Taireidō and other *seishin ryōhō* schools.

Taireidō's theory posits the existence of *reishi* (spirit-particles) in each individual and a *tairei* (great spirit) in the universe. A *reishi* is an entity beyond mental and physical phenomena, so being able to control it would allow one to carry out physical and mental healing. Worshiping *tairei* was also necessary for acquiring such power. In practice, however, the system combining *reishi* and *tairei* was not consistent, so Taireidō drifted from pseudo-medical healing by *reishi* to a religious cult of *tairei* toward the end of the 1920s. What is important to note here is that Taireidō did not rely on the concept of individual souls or spiritual beings, as the term *rei* normally suggests.

ŌMOTOKYŌ AND SPIRITUALISM

The rapid expansion of Ōmotokyō was another characteristic of the Taishō era. Ōmotokyō's *chinkon kishin hō* promised its adherents an instant and easy acquisition of psychic power. At the beginning, the members of this religious organization were mostly from its original neighborhood in a rural area of Kyoto Prefecture, but in the Taishō period, middle-class people living in urban areas began to join it; interestingly, many officers of the Navy also became followers.

The history of *chinkon kishin hō* (see also Staemmler 2009) can be summarized as follows. In premodern Japan, possession by spirits, far from being an unusual phenomenon, was used in a variety of religious contexts, such as Esoteric Buddhism (*Mikkyō*), Shugendō (mountain religion), and other mountain cults like Ontakekyō. However, one of the most influential mediumships was born outside of such religious organizations. It was systematized by Honda Chikaatsu (1822–1890), a scholar of national classics (*Kokugaku*). He was born in Satsuma (now Kagoshima Prefecture) and studied under Aizawa Seishisai (1782–1863), a nationalist thinker of the Mito school. Honda became interested in spiritual possession when he saw a girl possessed by an animal spirit and carried out research on these phenomena. He came to the conclusion that the authentic spiritual possession is found in the ancient ages of Japan, when Empress Jingū was possessed by gods and was thus able to know the divine will. Honda tried to "revive"—or, rather, recreate—the "authentic" method of spiritual possession based on the national myths of *Kojiki* and *Nihon shoki* (see also Namiki 2019).

The method he came up with is the *chinkon kishin hō*. It consists of two distinct parts: the *chinkon-hō* (literally, the method to stabilize one's soul) and the *kishin-hō* (method to become possessed). The former is a kind of mental concentration to develop one's psychic power; this is necessary for one to become a *saniwa* (controller and judge of spirits possessed). The ritual of *kishin-hō* involves a medium (*kannushi*) and a controller (*saniwa*). The latter blows a stone whistle to tranquilize the medium and make him or her ready for possession. Once the medium is taken over by a spiritual entity, the controller begins questioning the medium to find out what god or spirit has come. Often the spiritual beings turn out to be inferior animal spirits, but sometimes the "authentic" high-ranking gods mentioned in *Kojiki* or *Nihon shoki* also appear.

After the Meiji restoration, the government created a sort of state religion, generally known as State Shinto, based on the national myths of *Kojiki* and *Nihon shoki* in order, on the one hand, to unite the formerly feudal domains into one unified state, and, on the other, to ban such religious practices as mediumship and magical rituals in an effort to make Japan civilized. Partly owing to Inoue, who decried these very practices, possession by animal spirits was despised as superstition (*meishin*) by intellectuals. Its practitioners, if possessed by fox spirits or goblins (*tengu*), were sometimes arrested by the police. But if the gods of the *Kojiki* and *Nihon shoki* possessed the medium, the situation was not as easy for the police to handle. The gods of the classics were part of the belief that constructed State Shinto and thus supported national unification ideologies. In other words, Honda's strategies struck a sensitive point in State Shinto.

One "modern" characteristic of *chinkon kishin-hō* is in the use of experiments for showing the existence of gods and supernatural worlds, which was of course a premise of modern spiritualism. Nagasawa Katsutate, one of Honda's disciples, was a Shinto priest in Shizuoka. He had been arrested for performing the healing prayers traditionally held at his shrine, Kasamori Inari, since the premodern period, as Inari was the fox god and thus an animal spirit. This incident might be the reason he started to learn the *chinkon kishin-hō* from Honda, when the latter resided in Shizuoka. Nagasawa began spiritual experiments with mediums at Miho Shrine in Shimizu (Shizuoka Prefecture). It is said that gods showed miraculous deeds through a boy medium, Miyagishima Kinsaku. Kinsaku is said, for example, to have correctly predicted the occurrence of the First Sino-Japan War (1894–5). Such miracles induced Nagasawa to start a small new religious movement, Inari Kōsha (Group for Worshiping Fox Spirits).

In 1898 (Meiji 31), Ueda Kisaburō (later Deguchi Onisaburō, 1871–1948), originally from Kameoka near Kyoto, joined Nagasawa's group and returned with knowledge of the *chinkon kishin-hō*. He did experiments with mediums and became famous as a *saniwa* in the Tanba area (the northwest part of Kyoto prefecture). The following year, Ueda was invited to divine the god who possessed an old woman, Deguchi Nao, who lived in Ayabe near Kyoto. She said that the god possessing her was Ushitora-no-Konjin (golden god of the northeast). Her possession was spontaneous, and the gods in her pantheon had little relation to those found in the national classics. Although the theologies of Deguchi and Ueda were different, they began to cooperate with each other. Ueda married Deguchi's youngest daughter and had to change his name to Deguchi Onisaburō by a divine order conveyed through Nao. Onisaburō's theology was more nationalistic and more sophisticated than Nao's, but Onisaburō did not disavow her divine messages.

One of her prophecies was about the upcoming *tatekae tatenaoshi* (reconstruction of the world).

In the Taishō era, Ōmotokyō claimed that Nao's prophecy would be realized in the near future, which was rumored to be the year Taishō 10 (1921). Onisaburō's *chinkon kishin-hō* and Nao's millenarian prophecy attracted adherents among navy officers and intellectuals, and Ōmotokyō grew rapidly from a local religious group in the rural area of Tanba to a nationally recognized new religious movement based in the urban areas.

CONCLUSION: THE TAISHŌ ERA AS A "SPIRITUAL" AGE

An important characteristic of the Taishō era was the "cross-pollination" of the various streams of occultism discussed in this entry. Within those crossing streams, Ōmotokyō seems to have become a locus of such spiritual activity.

First, some joined Ōmotokyō through Theosophy. An ex-naval officer, Iimori Masayoshi, became interested in theosophy through E. S. Stephenson. Iimori initially decided to move to Point Loma in California with his daughter but changed his mind at the last moment and instead went to the headquarters of Ōmotokyō. He soon became an ardent proselytizer for Ōmoto teachings and converted one of Stephenson's colleagues, Asano Wasaburō, to Ōmotokyō. Asano then became a master of *chinkon kishin hō* and one of the leading figures in the group. Among the many intellectuals in his circle was Taniguchi Masaharu (1893–1985). Taniguchi would go on to build a new religious movement, Seichō no ie, which was influenced by *seishin ryōhō*, new thought, spiritualism, and Shinto.

Second, *seishin ryōhō* movements absorbed influences from abroad. For example, Taireidō translated and published articles on psychic research and Theosophy in their journal. It also published an article on Kandinsky, whose paintings are said to be influenced by theosophical representations of the aura. But the most important influence from abroad was that of an American yogi, Ramacharaka (see Atkinson 2011); his methods of breathing and controlling *prana* became popular among *seishin ryōhō* healers, and its legacy would later flow into Usui Mikao's Reiki healing (see Hirano 2010; Stein 2017).

Third, Nagasawa Katsutate and Deguchi Onisaburō were both interested in Western esotericism. Nagasawa read translations of books on spiritualism, including such books as psychic researcher and spiritualist V. C. Desertis's *Shinreigaku kōwa*, and Deguchi absorbed the worldview of Swedenborg. For instance, Deguchi's doctrinal collection of texts, *Reikai monogatari*, borrowed descriptions of the spiritual world from Swedenborg's *Heaven and Hell* (1758, later translated by D.T. Suzuki in 1910, as *Tenkai to jigoku*). Asano Wasaburō, who must have read books in English about spiritualism and theosophy before joining Ōmotokyō, created a group called "Shinrei Kagaku Kenkyūkai" (Research Association on Psychical Science) in 1923 after he left Ōmotokyō in 1921. Despite its name, this society was actually engaged in spiritualist activities. It was one of the few Japanese organizations that adopted a Western-style spiritualism, albeit mixed with Shintoism.

Fourth, there were not only friendly encounters but also antagonisms. For example, Taireidō lost many of its members to Ōmotokyō. On one occasion, Tanaka Morihei, the founder of Taireidō, met Asano, then the second-highest officer of Ōmotokyō, to discuss which group was superior theoretically or practically. At the end of their discussion,

Tanaka and Asano had a kind of duel over their psychic powers. It is uncertain who was the winner, but as this duel clearly shows, there were two general directions of interpreting supernatural phenomena. According to one, supernatural beings have personalities that possess mediums, whereas for the other, supernatural phenomena are controlled by the willpower of practitioners. These antagonistic theories correspond fairly closely to the distinction between spiritualism and occultism in the Western world.

I have here provided only a brief synopsis of the fertile history of Western esotericism in Japan. There remain quite a number of stories left untold. As I wrote in the beginning, the difficult question is the precise degree of similarity between "esotericism" in America or Europe and in Japan. But it will take more research and writing to clarify this complicated history.

See also Chapter 19, "'New Relgions'," and Chapter 27, "Spirituality."

CHAPTER 27

Spirituality

HORIE Norichika

The English word "spirituality" is currently translated in Japanese publications as *reisei* 霊性 or transcribed as *supirichuariti* スピリチュアリティ. The latter is more often used than the former, especially in the academic fields of religious studies, psychology, and nursing science.[1] Many Japanese authors who use the word *supirichuariti* often assume that it has the same pronunciation and implication as the original English word "spirituality." However, one cannot say there is no difference between the two. The Japanese words *reisei* and *supirichuariti* are both polysemous, as is the English "spirituality." The terms owe their rich meanings to actual use in specific sociohistorical contexts.

In the academic fields of religious studies and psychology, scholars have elaborated on spirituality as a technical term and understand its meaning. Researchers articulate spirituality as a multidimensional concept or scale based on surveys, which sometimes makes it difficult to understand what they exactly mean by "spirituality." Yet, their use of the word does not deviate from the basic English meanings of spirituality, such as "the quality or condition of being spiritual" or "an immaterial or incorporeal thing or substance" (cf. *OED*). In the sociology of religion, the term "spirituality" is also used as a sociocultural category to refer to personalized beliefs and practices concerning the spiritual—spirits or spiritual energy—outside organized religion (Horie 2011). In a previous publication, the present author defined spirituality as follows:

> Spirituality refers to both (1) belief in what cannot usually be perceived but can be felt internally, and (2) practices to experience [this feeling] and bring about changes, accompanied more or less by (3) selective assimilation of religious cultural resources, and (4) attitudes of individualism or anti-authoritarianism. (Horie 2019: 15)

Among the Japanese general public, this category of "spiritual but not religious" (SBNR) is commonly called *supirichuaru* (Arimoto 2011). Originally, this word transcribed to the English adjective "spiritual," but it has now become a noun for this particular cultural genre. However, compared with the use of the term "SBNR" in literature in English, *supirichuaru* in Japanese has a stronger relationship with belief in deceased spirits as supernatural beings and a tendency to emphasize *genze riyaku*, worldly benefit (Horie 2009:11).

---

[1] In the National Diet Library Online Database, 2,657 records contain *reisei*, and 1,872 records contain *supirichuariti*. When limited to the period of the 2010s, more records exist for *supirichuariti*, 836, than for *reisei*, 630 (last searched on January 31, 2020). Most publications containing *reisei* concern Christianity and the history of Japanese thought. Those containing *supirichuariti* span the fields of religious studies, psychology, and nursing science.

DAISETSU SUZUKI'S JAPANESE SPIRITUALITY

Before the year 2000, "spirituality" was often translated into Japanese as *reisei*. *Rei* means "spirit," and *sei* is a suffix that corresponds to "-ity" and originally means "nature." This word was circulated by a book, titled *Nihonteki reisei* (Japanese Spirituality) (1944), written by Suzuki Daisetsu (D. T.) (1870–1966), a prominent Buddhist thinker particularly influential in spreading Zen and Buddhist belief outside Japan. He defined *reisei* as "religious consciousness" and differentiated it from "religion."

According to Suzuki, *reisei* implies experiences from within, that is, awareness of what comes from the supra-individual self (*chōkoko* 超個己), which transcends the individual self (*koko* 個己). The phrase "supra-individual self" seems similar to "higher self" or "the transpersonal" in the vocabulary of contemporary Western spirituality. However, Suzuki seemingly considered it more broadly as "what is beyond oneself" in general.

Suzuki gave an example: the judgment that flowers are beautiful. In this case, it is the "individual self" that seeks to obtain the object of "beautiful flowers." On the other hand, it is the effect of spirituality to recognize that the value of beauty derives from the "supra-individual self," when one reflects on one's feeling that "flowers are beautiful."

This supra-individual self is not the Other, which is absolutely different from the self, because the supra-individual self is the source of the individual self and the authentic form of the "self." According to Suzuki, the individual self is a reflection of the supra-individual self, the great cosmic spirit. Therefore, the supra-individual self may be close to the Indian concept of Brahman, since Brahman is considered to be the ultimate principle of the universe and, at the same time, to be consistent with the individual self (Ātman). Moreover, Suzuki links the work of the supra-individual self with the Pure Land school and Amida Buddha's original vow and Other Power (*tariki*), suggesting that Shinran (1173–1263), the founder of True Pure Land Buddhism (Jōdo shinshū) who realized that his Own Power (*jiriki*) was also due to Other Power, opened the door to Japanese spirituality. Suzuki acknowledges that Christian theology presents a similar idea that humans live by the power of God. However, he believes that Catholics regard God as the ultimate agent and give less importance to the self-awareness of spirituality than Buddhists.

According to Suzuki, "religion" should essentially encourage awareness of *reisei*, but it easily turns into a tool for magical and political purposes. Suzuki believes that *reisei* appears in human relationships with the Great Earth (*daichi*), such as in agricultural work. Therefore, *reisei* is to be found in the lives of ordinary people, as well as in the lives of the clergy. Suzuki also described some actual cases of common people's spiritual lives.

Suzuki's theory of *reisei* could be considered an antecedent of today's theory of spirituality. It is possible that Suzuki may have been aware of Western mysticism when he developed his theory because he had translated Swedenborg's writings and was familiar with the theosophy of the period. However, he did not accept Swedenborg's overly realistic descriptions of heaven or the spiritual world. According to Yoshinaga Shin'ichi, Suzuki thought that one could only perceive something like the world of spirits beyond the five senses in a certain psychological state (Yoshinaga 2014: 131). Thus, Suzuki anticipated the psychological understanding of spirituality grounded in everyday life, which differed from the literalistic view of the "other world" developed by spiritualism at that time.

The word *reisei* was seldom used for decades after Suzuki, but it appears in Christian writings as a translation of the English word "spirituality." Since the 1980s, many books on the New Age Movement have been translated into Japanese, and the word *reisei* has been used again in terms of New Age spirituality.

OCCULT BOOM, SPIRITUAL WORLD (*SEISHIN SEKAI*), NEW AGE, AND NEW SPIRITUALITY

Spirituality, as a sociocultural category, has emerged in popular Japanese culture and has consequently appeared in different forms in mass media. These representations have the following features. First, the people concerned—including not only the committed participants/practitioners but also the light users or customers and the audience—dislike being called "religious." Second, these people also show an aversion to fixed dogmas, binding structures of organizations, and the worship of leaders. Third, although they are individualists, it seems that sudden fads (often called "booms" by the Japanese mass media) appear around their shared interests and consumption behaviors. Finally, however, when controversial issues emerge, the people concerned no longer want to be identified with the "boom."

Since approximately 1967, people influenced by American Beatnik poets and Indian religions began to live in communes and wandered in and outside Japan (Yamada 2013). Their groups became known as *Hippī zoku* ("Hippie Tribes"). In addition to this phenomenon, after the first oil crisis of 1973, television and publications featured ghosts, psychics, psychic photography, supernatural powers (like spoon-bending), Nostradamus's prophecies about the end of the world, and so on, leading to the so-called Occult Boom (Maeda 2016).

In 1978, the Kinokuniya Bookstore held a book fair called "Books on the Spiritual World in India and Nepal," and, thereafter, *Seishin Sekai* ("Spiritual World") was established as the name of a section in the bookstore (Prohl 2007: 360). According to Shimazono Susumu, a booklist on the "Spiritual World" published by a magazine at that time featured books from "Oriental" religions; books on meditation, fantastic or religious literature; and classical books on philosophy in both the East and West (Shimazono 2007a: 169). These kinds of books may have attracted hippies who were interested in mystical thoughts and practices around the world but did not fall under the category of the occult boom aforementioned. Thus, the "Spiritual World" was initially unrelated to the occult boom.

Marilyn Ferguson's *Aquarian Conspiracy* was published in the United States in 1980 and was translated into Japanese just a year later. It claimed that the "New Age" would come when people's consciousnesses evolved from old civilizations and religions, which are oriented toward violence and power, into a spirituality aimed at love and peace (Ferguson 1980). This idea has also been widely accepted through other American New Age books, translated into Japanese shortly after their original publication. These include many books on *Nyū Saiensu* ("New Science," referring to various kinds of New Age "science"), which advocated for the unity of religion and science, as well as books on transpersonal psychology, which explored altered states of consciousness that transcend ego consciousness. The catalog of the "Spiritual World" books from the 1990s listed fewer entries concerning literature and philosophy and more entries concerning psychology, physical and mental health, nature and ecology, and mysticism and the occult (Shimazono 2007a: 169).

Shimazono considered both New Age and *Seishin Sekai* to be local or emic concepts and proposed instead an analytical concept, the Shin Reisei Undō or "New Spirituality Movement", to comparatively describe these global phenomena. After 2000, Shimazono began using the broader concept of Shin Reisei Bunka or "New Spirituality Culture" (Shimazono 2004: ch. 15), and eventually he has come to use the term *atarashī supirichuariti* or "new spirituality" (Shimazono 2007: v). According to his understanding, this new spirituality served to replace organized religion and encourage the awakening of individual consciousnesses. This concept could encompass various movements and cultural phenomena, such as hippies, the Occult Boom, the Spiritual World, and the New Age.

However, the word "new" does not adequately cover the phenomena I will describe later, that is, spiritual care by religious specialists, the individualistic return to traditional religions, and esotericism in established religions, the importance of which is increasingly recognized in the West. Therefore, the present author has adopted the term "spirituality" without "new" as a comprehensive concept, attempting to classify its subcategories based on comparative research of various spirituality forms in the United States, the UK, and Japan, including spirituality in foreign religions, spirituality in established religions, folk spirituality, systematic spirituality (Horie 2013b: 113), and pop spirituality (Horie 2019).

SPIRITUALITY AND SPIRITUAL CARE IN PSYCHOLOGY AND MEDICINE

Many studies on spirituality in Japan are published in the fields of psychology, medicine, and nursing, as is equally true in English-speaking countries. From the viewpoints of humanistic psychology and transpersonal psychology, individuals seek spirituality in the wake of the self-transcendent experiences they have had in the process of their own personal growth (Nihon Toransupāsonaru Shinrigaku Seishin Igakukai, Andō, and Yuasa 2007). Buddhist psychology, which linked mindfulness meditation with cognitive behavioral therapy, developed in the late 2000s and also maintains this perspective (Inoue, Kato, and Kasai 2012).

On the other hand, some researchers have conducted questionnaire and interview surveys to identify how Japanese people perceive spirituality. Such studies were stimulated by the debate about whether to include "spiritual health" in the World Health Organization's definition of health (Tazaki, Matuda, and Nakane 2001; Higa 2002). Takeda and Futoyu (2006), who reviewed studies on spirituality among elderly Japanese, classified the dimensions of spirituality into "meaning and purpose of life," "attitude toward death and dying," "self-transcendence," "harmony with others," "resources for support," and "harmony with nature." They also identified the category of "support by the deceased" under the dimension of "resources for support." Ancestors and ancestral memorial tablets are listed as examples of this category, but this would likely not appear in the list of factors constituting Westerners' spirituality.

Awareness of death, dying, and the deceased (relatives and/or ancestors) seems to play an important role in spirituality among Japanese people. Spirituality has also been discussed in the field of *shiseigaku* ("death and life studies"), which corresponds to thanatology and death studies in Western countries. Two types of practitioners are particularly interested in spirituality: (1) those who are concerned with spiritual care in order to support the meaning of life and perceptions of the afterlife in dying persons, and (2) those who are concerned with grief care to help the bereaved maintain their bonds with loved ones who have passed away. Grief care is sometimes included within spiritual care when broadly defined (see, e.g., the activities of the Japan Society of Spiritual Care).

"Spiritual care" was introduced as part of Cicely Saunders' hospice care, or palliative care. Nevertheless, in Japan, this phrase is used as a proper noun, referring to a unique technique, rather than as a common noun, referring to one aspect of hospice care. Japanese scholars also tend to emphasize that spiritual care is not necessarily linked to a particular religion (Kubodera 2000), while Saunders linked spiritual care more or less to religious beliefs. However, "continuing bonds" with the deceased have been emphasized in religious specialists' practices of grief care since the Great East Japan Earthquake (Horie 2016).

KATAKANA "*SUPIRICHUARITI*": THE TRANSFORMATION OF *REI* (SPIRITS)

After 2000, scholars in the fields of transpersonal psychology and sociology of religion began to use *supirichuariti* スピリチュアリティ in *katakana* (the phonetic syllabary used today for most non-Japanese words) to transcribe the English word "spirituality" instead of *reisei* 霊性 in *kanji* (Chinese characters). According to these scholars, *katakana* is better than *kanji* because the word *rei* 霊 in *reisei* reminds readers of "ghosts" (Nishihira 2003). Some of their definitions of spirituality often stress a connection with what transcends the ego in general (Itō, Kashio, and Yumiyama 2004: i). These scholars also prefer not to use *rei* because they believe the word would remind Japanese people of organized "religion." At the same time, they attempted to broadly encompass "the religious" in the concept of spirituality. The underlying factor might be that "religion" has developed extremely bad connotations among the Japanese since the Tokyo subway sarin gas attack, which was perpetrated in 1995 by members of the religious organization Aum Shinrikyō.

After 2000, Ehara Hiroyuki (1964–), a spiritualist medium, appeared in magazines and on television programs, leading to the "Spiritual Boom." Ehara emphasized spirits' watching over beloved persons rather than seeking vengeful punishment and more often referred to people's connections to close relatives' spirits rather than to ancestral spirits. He did not limit his conception of spirits to the spirits of the dead. He supported the idea of reincarnation, which assumed partial rebirth from group souls rather than total reincarnation of individual's soul as a whole, and did not adhere to ancestor worship. According to his understanding, spirits of deceased family members only watch over the bereaved, and a person's self from a previous life is believed to be a guardian spirit in the present life, who is more influential than the spirits of the deceased. He also stressed that those living in this world are also spiritual beings, who keep on reincarnating.

While Ehara apparently assumed the reality of *rei* in terms of spiritualism, he also often uses the *katakana* word *supirichuaru*. He presented himself as a "spiritual counselor," encouraging readers and viewers to become independent—unlike conventional *reinōsha* (spiritual or psychic mediums), who often make clients rely on them authoritatively. Ehara did not accept clients directly but only demonstrated spiritual counseling on television and in magazines. The structure of his spiritual counseling was first to practice clairvoyance about clients' auras and/or previous lives, then interpret their problems and worries psychologically, and, finally, empower them by persuading them that their guardian spirits and deceased relatives were watching over them.

Ehara encouraged individuals to reflect on themselves according to spiritual truths and to live independently as responsible agents without relying on others. However, the spiritual counselors who adopted his teachings and imitated his way of counseling won many customers in the spiritual market (Hashisako 2008; Gaitanidis 2011). Unprecedented, large-scale trade fairs specializing in pop spirituality, such as the *Iyashi*

Feā (Healing Fair) and *Supikon* (Spiritual Convention), emerged and presented various types of spiritual counseling, aura photography, divination and fortune-telling, reiki and similar healing, power stone sales, and other related services.

Ehara's popularity peaked around 2007, but criticism of the Spiritual Boom also arose because of his increasing exposure in the mass media. Lawyers involved in anti-cult movements and some sociologists of religion (Ishii 2008) argued that spiritual claims should not be made assertively in the public media. They expressed paternalistic concerns that women and younger people, lacking social experiences and the ability to foresee the risks involved, would easily believe in spiritual matters and could become victims of *reikan shōhō* (spiritual-pressure sales methods) (Zenkoku Reikan Shōhō Taisaku Bengoshi Renrakukai 2007; Sakurai 2009).

The anti-spiritual discourse became even stronger during the 2010s, with the rise of social media, making particular practitioners more prone to criticism on the internet. According to the author's previous research, the word "spiritual" among online users has negative implications, such as falsehood, credulity, and fraud (Horie 2018: 134). As a result, spiritual practitioners gave up using the word "spiritual" and began using the word *kaiun* (fortune-bringing). However, lawyers came to criticize the "*kaiun* sales promotion methods" as being fraudulent, thus creating a spiral.[2]

SPIRITUALITY AFTER THE GREAT EAST JAPAN EARTHQUAKE

Rehabilitation of Rei

After the Great East Japan Earthquake in 2011, some intellectuals and the media resumed using *reisei* in Chinese characters as the word for "spirituality" (Uchida and Shaku 2014; Wakamatsu 2015; Kanabishi 2016). In 2013, an NHK (Japan's public broadcasting organization) documentary program[3] featured experiences in which survivors felt the presence of the deceased through dreams, sensations, and material evidence (for details of these experiences, see Parry 2017). The audience's response to the program was largely sympathetic (Horie 2016: 200–1; Horie 2018: 158–62), probably against the background of a long-term rise in spiritual belief. Opinion polls confirm that belief in spirits and/or the afterlife is low among the elderly but high among the young. Spiritual belief has been evidently rising for approximately half a century, since the Occult Boom of the 1970s (Horie 2018: 147–50).

Individualistic Return to Tradition

Research concerning publications and social networking service (SNS) users' profiles, focusing on spirituality, has shown that the Great East Japan Earthquake heightened an overall societal yearning for spirituality (see Figures 1.2 and 9.2 in Horie 2019). This yearning has taken the form not only of the consumption of goods and services sold in

---

[2] For an example of this criticism, see "Kaiun Shōhō, Shinkoku na Higai: Muryō to Kōkoku, Kitōryō nisen man en" (Fortune-Bringing Sales Methods, Serious Casualties: Free Service on Advertisement, but Twenty Billion Yen for Prayers), *Asahi Shinbun*, August 28, 2014, p. 36.

[3] "Naki hito tono 'Saikai': Hisaichi, Sandomeno Natsu ni ("Reunion" with Deceased Persons: From Disaster Areas in the Third Summer)," NHK, August 23, 2013. Available online: http://www6.nhk.or.jp/special/detail/index.html?aid=20130823 (accessed December 7, 2020).

the spiritual market but also of an individualistic return to traditional religions. In my fieldwork, I have often heard stories about young women appealing to Buddhist priests for help with their anxiety—about their lives, the future, and loneliness—at events hosted by temples, even in Tokyo, relatively far from the disaster areas (cf. Horie et al. 2013: 28).

As early as around 2009, certain shrines and temples all over Japan were already believed to be "power spots"—places where one can feel spiritual energy—and many people visited them. After the earthquake, the word *seichi* (sacred place) came into use. In 2013 Ise Jingū Shrine was visited by the largest number of worshipers ever (14.2 million to the Inner and Outer Shrines). This year was associated with the ceremonies for the *shikinen sengū* (regular shrine removal), which are performed only once every twenty years.[4] Since around 2014, the pilgrims' practice of obtaining the *goshuin* (red stamps) of shrines and temples in their red stamp booklets has become increasingly popular (Horie 2018: 26).

Since the 2000s, Buddhism or Shugendō practices have been attracting more newcomers, who participate briefly and individually, without permanent membership in the group, after accessing information on the internet. Among these practices are not only Zen meditation, which has been popular for generations, but also *takigyō* (ritual devotion under a waterfall) or mountain asceticism, in which participants walk around a mountain area and offer prayers to Buddhas and Deities for a few days. These are often called *puchi shugyō* (brief practices), and a popular manga artist has compiled her experiences of them (Oguri 2007). In addition, wealthy temples in metropolitan areas offer unique workshops, which differ from normal practices, as well as yoga, vegetarian cuisine for ascetics, music concerts, and so on. For example, religious specialists in Tokyo, who supported the victims of the Great East Japan Earthquake, have been holding *Kōgen* 向源, an event combining these contents into a structure similar to a rock festival, since 2011. Thus, interest in spiritual issues has resulted in an individualistic participation in traditional religions such as Shinto and Buddhism, including Shugendō (Horie 2018: 25–34).

Political Polarization

Prior to the Great East Japan Earthquake, Japanese pop spirituality centered on the individualistic consumption of spiritual goods and services through the market. Carrette and King's argument, that today's spirituality is the neoliberal commercialization of religious resources, seems also to be true regarding Japanese spirituality (Carrette and King 2004).

However, the Fukushima Daiichi Nuclear Power Plant Accident, which followed the Great East Japan Earthquake in March 2011, awakened the post-materialist and postcapitalist aspects of Japanese spirituality. The first antinuclear demonstration in Kōenji, Tokyo, a month after the accident, was launched by a group promoting a new social movement, partially continuing the hippies' counterculture lineage discussed above. The demonstration adopted the style of a parade, with dance music and protesters dressed in a style reminiscent of the "Anti-Nuclear Movement New Wave" after the Chernobyl nuclear accident. Antinuclear demonstrations peaked in 2012, linked to global trends in which social media became an important vehicle for social movements. In the process,

---

[4] "Ise Jingū Sanpai, Sakunen wa 973man nin: Kaigen de Chūmoku, Kako 3banme no Ōsa" (Visitors to Ise Jingu Shrine, 9.37 Million Last Year: Attracted Due to the Imperial Succession, Marked the 3rd Highest Number in the Past), *Asahi Shinbun*, January 9, 2020: 19.

many social media users rediscovered the hippies' postcapitalist, earth-based spirituality, represented by the "Festival of Life" held in 1988 (after the Chernobyl nuclear accident), 2000, and 2012 (after the Fukushima nuclear accident) (Horie 2013a). This tendency of disaster-inspired spirituality goes along with the "engaged spirituality" advocated by Carrette and King, since it aims at social justice and sustainable lifestyles which move beyond neoliberal consumerism (Carrette and King 2004: 182).

However, the Liberal Democratic Party (LDP), with a platform promoting nuclear energy, came back to power in December 2012, and Japan entered the era of prime minister Abe Shinzō's administration, the longest-lasting government in constitutional history. As mentioned previously, it is also during this period that the popularity of Shinto shrines has increased in the realm of individualistic spirituality. Abe has organized his cabinets with members strongly connected to the Nippon Kaigi (Japan Conference), a conservative political group that includes leaders from Jinja Honchō (the Association of Shinto Shrines) and the Shintō Seiji Renmei (Shinto Association of Spiritual Leadership). On the other hand, Abe's wife, Akie, who has an ecological view against nuclear power plants, has expressed her sympathy toward earth-based spirituality and has also interacted with anti-government movement leaders. However, her relationship with a kindergarten that provided extremely nationalistic education was regarded as a controversial issue. As a result, some intellectuals expressed concern that spiritual naturalism might come close to prewar ultranationalism (Nakajima 2017a).

In recent years, Shinto has developed a political side aimed at returning to the prewar militaristic regime, and a cultural side, which promotes both ecological and pacifist discourses. The ecological discourse states that Japanese animism worships nature as deities and is appropriate for environmental protection, and the pacifist discourse emphasizes that Japanese polytheism is more tolerant of different kinds of belief than monotheism. The political side is essential to the activity of Jinja Honchō as a religious organization, but the spiritual pilgrims favor the cultural side and are likely not interested in politics and only sympathetic to Shinto ecology and pacifism (Horie 2017a; Rots 2017b). Apparently, those values conflict with the LDP's policies of exercising the right to collective self-defense abroad and of promoting nuclear power and exporting coal-fired energy.

Discourses combining harmony with nature and religious peace are, in fact, very similar to New Agers' attacks on Christianity in the United States since the 1970s. Additionally, they are more systematically practiced by Buddhist institutions than by Shinto organizations through anti-nuclear statements and trans-sectarian support for disaster victims (Shimazono 2012: ch. 5). The popularity of Shinto spirituality should be understood as an attempt to rediscover and reorganize traditional religions via spiritual values that are developing globally, rather than as an expression of nationalism. Japanese spirituality differs from Western spirituality, especially in post-Protestant countries, in that its criticism of monotheistic religions and its naturalist claims are more easily understood to come from conservatism rather than radicalism (Horie 2013b).

The space of political discourses in Japan is becoming polarized between right and left due to the rise of social media. As spiritual people dislike binding organizations, most of them are, in reality, nonpartisan. However, their behaviors have been subject to sociohistorical contexts and politico-economic conditions. When a picture of political polarization is projected onto such behaviors, it appears that both spiritual leftists and spiritual rightists exist. One may want to ask in which direction Japanese spiritual people are going. Polarization is one possible answer. In the online discursive space, such division may actually be advancing, and this situation is, perhaps, not peculiar to Japan.

See also Chapter 4, "Disasters," Chapter 5, "Economy and Spirituality," Chapter 20, "Pilgrimages and 'Sacred' Geography," Chapter 21, "Politics," and Chapter 26, "Spiritualism and Occultism."

CHAPTER 28

Tourism

YAMANAKA Hiroshi

Japan's cultural heritage tourism has become an important market in recent years and is continuing to expand, in part because of the usage of UNESCO World Heritage designations to stimulate tourism. This chapter aims to provide an overview of research on Japanese religion related to tourism and cultural heritage. Religious cultural heritage generally refers to temples, shrines, churches, pilgrimage sites, routes taken to visit temples and shrines, sacred mountains, festivals, and so on. However, it also covers "living religious culture" that is so intertwined into everyday life that it is not readily recognized as a cultural heritage.

The relationship between religion and tourism began to receive attention in the study of Japanese religion in the first decade of 2000. Of course, using religious heritage as a tourist attraction is not new: this has been the practice in Nara and Kyoto for quite some time. However, these cases are typically discussed only in the context of tourism studies, not by scholars of Japanese religion. This does not mean that no scholarship on religion in the past has paid attention to the tourism perspective, however; a primary example is research on temple and shrine pilgrimages in the early modern period. Since the publication of the groundbreaking work of Shinjō Tsunezō (Shinjō 1964), many studies have been conducted on well-known pilgrimages, such as Ise, Saikoku, and Shikoku (e.g., Iwahana 2003; Satō 2004; Tanaka 2004; Thal 2005; Ambros 2008). Ian Reader's recent work on the Shikoku pilgrimage in terms of markets may also be included in this category (Reader 2014).

In this overview of studies on Japanese religion related to tourism and cultural heritage, I adopt a sociological perspective, which analyzes religion not as an ahistorical, eternally static entity but as something continually and dynamically reconstructed. I divide this subject into three areas: (1) the commodification of UNESCO World Heritage sites and related changes in religious practices; (2) how religious practices, including pilgrimage, are represented and modified by the mass media (newspapers, television, etc.); and (3) the influence of means of transportation (such as railroads) on cultural heritage.

WORLD HERITAGE SITES AND CHANGES IN RELIGION

Much research on tourism and cultural heritage considers the commodification of the sacred places designated as World Heritage sites and related changes in religious practices. While famous temples and shrines in places like Nara and Kyoto (such as Hōryūji) have been favorite tourist spots for the Japanese for a long time, and therefore did not experience major religious changes after designation as World Heritage sites, circumstances differ when minority religions, local sacred sites, or religious practices are designated. Designation as a World Heritage site gives a "universal value" to religious traditions embedded in local society. Tourism-related developments that try to use this newly acquired prestige to commodify these religious traditions bring about changes and conflicts in the understanding and definition of both "religion" and "'tradition."

For instance, the designation of a group of Christian sites in Nagasaki as a World Heritage site is an interesting example (Matsui 2013). Unlike other World Heritage sites in Japan, these represent a minority religion that was harshly oppressed and discriminated against. With the cooperation of the Nagasaki archdiocese, the tourism industry made use of the World Heritage site brand and promoted the idea of a "pilgrimage" (*junrei*) there in order to sell "Nagasaki Pilgrimage" travel packages that included visits to churches and martyr sites. Thus, many tourists began to visit small, depopulated churches. However, the priests and believers of some churches on remote islands (as in the Gotō archipelago) strongly rejected exposure to the gaze of tourists. There are also developments that contrast with these reactions. Even after religious freedom was recognized during the Meiji period (1868–1912), some hidden Christians did not convert to Catholicism but maintained their beliefs that mixed Christianity with Buddhism, Shintoism, and folk religion. Now, some individuals are actively working to use their connection to this history as a tourist resource. Their efforts are driven by a desire to promote their community and to strengthen their own collective memories, which include lore about martyrs. In this sense, issues emerge in both cultural heritage and tourism relating to commodification as well as the identity politics of hidden Christians, who had largely sunk into historical oblivion (Yamanaka 2012b).

It has been pointed out that at the sacred site of Sefa utaki, located in the southern part of Okinawa's main island, religion split into two types upon World Heritage site designation (Kadota 2013). On the one hand, we find "orthodox" religion, believed to go back directly to the rites of the Ryukyu Kingdom's royal family, the eastern pilgrimage (*agariumai*) of the patriarchal family unit (*monchū*). On the other hand, we have religious practices that involve worship mediated by folk religious specialists such as *yuta*. The former is flourishing while strengthening its tourist elements, whereas the latter has been excluded from the *utaki*, for the reason that the fires employed in their rituals pose a hazard. The designation of Sefa utaki as a World Heritage site can thus be considered a process of "making valuable" a local sacred site as a piece of heritage common to humanity. The process may be considered as a form of "discursive secularization" as defined by Aike P. Rots. He uses the term to refer to "the process by which belief, practices and institutions previously classified as 'religion' are redefined and reconfigured ... as 'culture,' 'tradition,' 'heritage'" (Rots 2017b: 13–14). Therein, various religious practices split into two conflicting categories: "desirable religion" and "undesirable religion."

At Kumano (Wakayama Prefecture), designated as a World Heritage site in 2004, a conflict has emerged surrounding the desirable and undesirable form of the Otō Festival at Hayatama Taisha's Sessha-Kamikura shrine (Amada 2012). The Otō Festival is a fire festival held in winter during which men with torches run down the 538 stone steps from the peak of Mt. Kamikura. On the day of the festival, women are not allowed on the premises, and people fight and collapse after too much drinking. It has become renowned as a boisterous men's festival at which, even today, blood is shed. However, after designation as a World Heritage site, the shrine called for people to restrain from such behavior, with the argument that such a violent festival involving bloodshed is not appropriate for a World Heritage site. However, the locals reacted strongly against what they saw as an inappropriate intervention in their festival. Such dis-embedding of a local festival from its context because of World Heritage site designation is increasingly bringing about changes to local traditions and giving rise to conflicts between UNESCO standards and traditional actors.

REPRESENTATIONS OF CULTURAL HERITAGE IN THE MEDIA

The activity of walking has seen an increase in popularity as more and more people become interested in caring for their health and enjoying nature. This means that pilgrimage routes are becoming important tourist destinations, as indicated by the growing popularity of the Camino de Santiago (the Way of St. James) in Spain. In Japan, this trend is also affecting the pilgrimage trail known as the Kumano Kodō. Prior to the restoration that returned it to its original purpose, the trail had been abandoned by pilgrims for a very long time. The geographer Kanda Kōji investigated the process by which Kumano has developed into a tourist destination. His method was to track the way in which Kumano's image has shifted since the years before the Second World War through an examination of changes in national and local governments' promotional strategies (Kanda 2010). Originally, Doro Gorge and Nachi Falls were renowned destinations in Kumano. With the designation of Yoshino-Kumano National Park in 1936, however, it was not Nachi Falls but the Kumano coastline that received attention alongside Doro Gorge. The Kumano trail also became the focus of nationalistic discourse during the war years due to its association with the mythical expedition of Emperor Jinmu. The conclusion we may draw here is that, up until the prewar years, pilgrimage routes did not function as tourist attractions in the way they do now.

After the war, progress was finally made with the improvement of the Kumano Kodō, due to development projects and surveys of historic roads conducted by the Agency for Cultural Affairs in the 1970s and the "Hundred Greatest Historical Roads" project of the 1990s. Subsequently, in 1999, Wakayama Prefecture held the "Nanki Kumano Exhibition" over a period of four months. Kumano Kodō was presented there as a place of rest and relaxation, an escape from the bustle of modern life. As a result of this event, the movement to have Kumano Kodō recognized as a world heritage site began at the level of local government; this plan eventually came to fruition when the designation was granted in 2004. Kumano Kodō is a pilgrimage trail that appears to be very old and rich in architectural history, but in fact, it has been intentionally constructed and is now enthusiastically utilized for tourist purposes. The Kumano Hongū Grand Shrine, located at the center of the old trail, and the Tourism Association for Wakayama Prefecture's Tanabe City have formed a partnership with the city of Santiago de Compostela in printing a "Dual Pilgrim Credential." Individuals who walk both pilgrimage routes can be recognized as "Dual Pilgrims." As of 2018, it was reported that the number of dual pilgrims had reached one thousand.

In comparison to the architecturally distinct Kumano Kodō, there is the pilgrimage route of Shikoku Island, which has attracted devout pilgrims for centuries. The Shikoku pilgrimage has also developed deep ties with the tourism industry. The geographer Mori Masato has studied the pilgrimage from a multidisciplinary approach involving historiography, anthropology, and sociology. He has demonstrated how the Shikoku pilgrimage has functioned as a constructed space from the Meiji period to the present day and is the product of reciprocal interactions between various social structures, including temples, the state, the media, and railway companies. According to Mori, since the 1920s, the Shikoku pilgrimage has come to occupy a position within the context of tourism as well as religious practice. During this period, Mori writes, "people using various means of transportation in order to travel the pilgrimage efficiently as a leisure activity were called 'modern pilgrims.'" In the 1930s, hiking outside the city was recommended as a healthy pastime, with the Shikoku pilgrimage being viewed as "religious hiking" (Mori 2005: 139–40).

A particularly interesting finding in Mori's research is that the focus on simply walking the Shikoku pilgrimage is actually a new phenomenon. The idea that walking is itself an aesthetic training and the correct way to conduct the pilgrimage, Mori notes, was mainly emphasized by monks of the Shingon sect as the tide of the war turned increasingly dire. They tried to change diverse Shikoku pilgrimages, which had been carried out separately without a standardized meaning, practice, and organization until then, into an authentic pilgrimage with unified meaning and rules. Considering that there was no rule regarding what color pilgrims should wear in the Edo period, a discourse that Shikoku pilgrims must wear white clothing was taken up as a kind of antithesis to modern pilgrims. In other words, the idea of the authentic pilgrim, who walks the Shikoku trail dressed in white garments, was actually born within the context of modernization, with the antecedent emergence of elements such as transportation networks, leisure classes that arose alongside the expansion of cities, and mass media such as newspapers and magazines.

After the war, the relationship between the Shikoku pilgrimage and tourism became incomparably closer than it had been during the 1930s. From the 1970s onward in particular, the Shikoku pilgrimage's ties to tourism grew ever deeper as a result of initiatives such as the Shikoku prefectural and local government's drive toward the development of tourism. From the 1990s onward, there was a new pilgrimage boom, triggered largely by exposure through the media, including NHK (Japan's national broadcasting organization) and various travel magazines. Interaction with locals and nostalgia for the lost rural landscapes of Japan occupied the foreground of the media depiction of the Shikoku pilgrimage, with religious narratives left concealed in the shadows. The term "walking pilgrim," which appeared in the 1990s, was unconnected with the prewar search for religious authenticity. Rather, its discursive use was tied to the functions or goals of "relaxation" or "self-discovery."

It is therefore not only pilgrimage trails and religious sites that have been altered and reconstructed as a result of tourism, but also religion itself and its practices. For example, it is surprising to see the extent of the changes in the image of *itako*, mediums said to summon the dead at Mt. Osore and the Sōtō sect temple Entsūji's Taisai (Grand Festival), in magazine and newspaper reports from the prewar period to today (Ōmichi 2017). The Tōhoku region guidebook published by Kōtsūsha in 1953 states that one can meet the deceased on Mt. Osore, but it does not mention the *itako*, who only appear in tourist guidebooks beginning in the 1960s. *Itako* came to Entsūji around the end of the Taishō period (1912–26) and the early Shōwa period (1926–89). Even though they did not suddenly appear on the mountain, they became objects of popular attention after media coverage began in the 1960s. Articles about the Taisai festival in local newspapers published between 1946 and 1979 indicate that people actually went there to see the *itako* only from the 1960s onwards, thus approaching the mountain as tourists first and foremost. Thus, the media's focus on *itako* brought about major changes in Mt. Osore as a sacred site. For example, while *itako* séances were traditionally part of private Buddhist rituals for the dead at Entsūji, in the media, they were represented as central.

Similarly, the gap between the media's representations of festivals and the actual festivals has been problematized also in folklore studies. Kawamura Kiyoshi has discussed this problem in relation to the Sannō Festival held in Monzenmachi Minazuki, Ishikawa Prefecture (Kawamura 2003). The Sannō Festival is a traditional summer festival held at Hiyoshi Shrine in the Sea of Japan facing Minazuki, which dates back to the early modern period. During the festival, floats and portable shrines proceed through the rural community. A 1995 episode of the NHK show *Furusato no denshō* (Lore of the Villages) depicts it as an expression of the folk religious beliefs of rural fishing people that have been transmitted for generations on the Oku-Noto peninsula. The show emphasized its portable shrines and Shinto rituals, and treated the floats—which have strong entertainment value—as secondary elements.

However, Kawamura contends that this depiction is far from the actual situation in the village. Many of the people who pull the floats do not live in the community, and most participants in the festival are city residents without any relationship to the fishing industry. In other words, unlike the show's depiction, Minazuki is not a rural community that transmits simple religious beliefs. Furthermore, it is not the portable shrines or the Shinto rites but the floats that are most important to those who run the festival. Regarding this gap between the self-understanding of the people that run the festival and the representations of people from the outside that depict these "others," Kawamura holds that the meaning of "folklore" (folk cultural heritage) as researched by folklore studies is continually reconstructed and changed by the media.

MEANS OF TRANSPORTATION AND SACRED SITES

The development of tourism cannot be separated from the rapid advancement of transportation methods since the beginning of modernity. Their development made it more convenient to get to a destination and changed which temples and shrines people chose to visit. It even changed the content of religious practice. The *hatsumōde*, or first shrine visit of the New Year that forms part of *Shōgatsu sanganichi*, now a major annual event in Japan, is deeply related to the development of railroads from the Meiji period onwards (Hirayama 2015).

While *hatsumōde* did exist during the Edo period (1603–1868), its form differed considerably. At that time, the event took place on the first shrine/temple festival day (*ennichi*) in January and was based on *ehō mairi* religious beliefs, which hold that visiting a shrine in the direction of the Toshigami (the god of the New Year) brings about good fortune. However, in the modern period the number of shrine visitors who emphasized entertainment more than *ehō* increased, and railway companies with lines extending from downtown Tokyo to the suburbs actively sought to lure visitors to the temples and shrines along those lines. Consequently, *hatsumōde* became unrelated to *ehō* and festival days. In this way, traditional temple visits related to *ehō* radically decreased, and the temples and shrines easily accessible from the railways (Naritasan, Meiji Jingū, Kawasaki Daishi, etc.) became the main destinations for visitors. Furthermore, while throughout the early modern period *oshi* (low-ranking Shinto priests) and *yamabushi* (mountain ascetics) played the role of connecting people to sacred mountains, modern railway companies became secular "coordinators of religion" (Tsushima 2012).

However, it was not only railway companies brought people to the sacred sites; sacred mountains also actively worked to acquire modern means of transportation to attract visitors (Uda 2015). For example, Enryakuji on Mt. Hiei has a strong identity as a religious training mountain and at first did not have much desire to bring in visitors. However, upon the memorial service marking 1,100 years since Saichō's death held in 1921, the temple considered building a railway to make it easier for people to visit. Anticipating that the temple grounds would turn into a tourist spot after improved access, it decided to preserve its sacred nature by dividing the grounds into sacred and secular spaces, which included the relocation of multiple buildings. Enryakuji deserves our recognition for its well-constructed strategy to increase the number of visitors and avoid secularization as much as possible, while making skillful use of railway companies and other actors planning to engage in the development of tourism at Mt. Hiei.

Mt. Takao (on the outskirts of Tokyo), which built a cable car around the same time, is also an interesting example. Half of the religious groups (*kōsha*) related to Mt. Takao were established between 1946 and 1985; most were established in 1965 (Inui 2005). According to Inui Kentarō, *kōsha* suddenly increased as a consequence of the temple's cooperation with a tourist company, as part of the head priest's development plan. This company established many *kōsha* in Gunma and Saitama, where it is based. Members used buses provided by the company to visit Mt. Takao for religious and sightseeing purposes. In sum, the active use of railways and buses by sacred sites has increased the number of visitors, both believers and tourists.

CONCLUSION

Above, I briefly discussed several topics covered in studies on cultural heritage and tourism. This area of research is still undeveloped and lacks a large body of scholarship. However, as the growing popularity of collecting stamps (*goshuin*) at religious sites among young people, who hardly care about the religious meaning of such stamps, illustrates, today's Japanese religious landscapes are undeniably changing. Kanda Myōjin, a famous shrine in Tokyo, for example, sells a special stamp book (*goshuin-chō*) in collaboration with popular anime *Love Live!* to appeal to young people and foreign tourists. In other words, today we can see more religious consumers than devoted believers at a sacred place like a shrine. While quite a few scholars of Japanese religion are uncomfortable discussing tourism because of its connection to consumption, it is necessary for us to pay more attention to such rapidly changing aspects of the current Japanese religious situation.

See also Chapter 3, "Cultural Heritage," Chapter 8, "Environmentalism," Chapter 20, "Pilgrimages and 'Sacred' Geography," and Chapter 25, "Space."

CHAPTER 29

Women

Emily B. SIMPSON

The study of women in Japanese religions, like the study of gender more generally, has gone through a series of trends. From case studies of extraordinary women and merely adding women to the historical record, academic studies on the role of women in societies past and present have come to critically consider the gender order, a network of systems that not only reinforced gender norms but also defined gender itself. Indeed, the use of "women" and "gender" as almost interchangeable terms in both academic literature and university departments demonstrates both a continuing need to address gaps in the study of women and an ambivalence about how best to do so.

While gender theory is ably addressed in another chapter in this handbook, I merely note here that "gender," drawing from Joan Scott's seminal work on gender as a category of analysis, is used to denote "a social category imposed on a sexed body" and "the social creation of ideas about appropriate roles for women and men" (Scott 1988: 1056). As such, gender allows a consideration of the societal constructs applied to all genders, including those outside of the traditional binary. However, the vast majority of studies on gender, especially in premodern times, still center on women's experiences, actions, and subordinate roles, as the various works I explore here show. Even those with "gender" in the title tend to focus almost exclusively on women, though also attending to the gender order in which they operate. Nonetheless, we must be careful to distinguish between "women" and "gender" as categories of analysis, particularly in religious studies. The role of religions in considering gender from ontological and soteriological perspectives was and remains vitally important in framing and shaping gender ideas in society more broadly.

In the case of Japan, the role of women in religious traditions has a long and vibrant history, but key trends within Japanese religious studies itself have complicated the study of women and gender. Writing on the contemporary Zen movement Sanbōkyōdan, Robert Sharf posits the existence of a division of labor within the field: Buddhologists, trained in philology and textual analysis, work primarily with texts and are interested in doctrinal sophistication rather than popular or contemporary developments, while the study of modern religious traditions, notably new religions, is largely conducted by scholars trained in social science methodology, with a greater focus on how external forces such as socioeconomic change influence the development of new religious trends. Sharf sees this as detrimental to both groups, in that studies of Buddhism lack the benefits of ethnographic observation, while studies of new religions often lack "theologically nuanced" approaches or contextualization in history prior to the Meiji period (Sharf 1995: 452–3). To this, I would add that the majority of Buddhologists in Japanese studies work on the medieval period, within the rich landscape of Buddhist sectarian development, rather than the contemporary, modern, or even early modern period.

Sharf's division of labor is directed primarily toward the study of Buddhism, but he highlights divisions in the field equally relevant for the consideration of gender, particularly in premodern times. Women were generally not involved in the major doctrinal developments of the Kamakura period, though notable exceptions include the revival of female monasticism at Hokkeji (Meeks 2010) and the crucial role of Shinran's wife Eshinni (1182–1268; Dobbins 2004). In "The Disappearing Medium," Lori Meeks, drawing on Sharf's observations, rightly notes that religious studies is far more apt to exclude figures and traditions that do not neatly fit into particular schools and categories. While this bias may be attributed in part to sources—in Japan, monks at large temple complexes left far more documentation behind than itinerant religious specialists—it is also due to the tendency of religious studies to favor doctrinal debates and innovations rather than unaffiliated, itinerant, and/or lower-class religious figures. The gender implications are legion: with fewer opportunities to engage in monastic or priestly life, women were far more often to be found in these latter categories. Furthermore, as Meeks shows, terms such as *miko* encompassed women of considerable wealth and connection as well as itinerant *arukimiko* (Meeks 2011). In addition, though premodern Japanese women wrote an impressive number of texts, most are not specifically religious in nature and thus are usually considered from a literary rather than religious studies perspective.

Both Sharf and Meeks indicate the spheres of interest that have long dominated Japanese religious studies: study of doctrine and theology in clearly organized religious groups, and contemporary ethnographies of living religious traditions. Fortunately, the field has shifted in important ways over the past few decades, allowing further consideration of many marginalized groups, including women. In order to more fully capture the religious landscape of Japan, and the role of women within it, scholars have approached the study of women and religion in new ways, from edited volumes dedicated to the consideration of women in Japanese history and in specific religious traditions, to reconsiderations of androcentric discourses and interrogations of the gender paradigms proposed by religious groups today.

WOMEN AND RELIGIONS IN (MOSTLY) PREMODERN JAPAN: THE EDITED VOLUMES APPROACH

Considerations of gender in premodern Japan in the West first blossomed in the 1990s among historians. Three edited volumes can attest to this development: the earliest, *Recreating Japanese Women*, edited by Gail Bernstein (1991), is perhaps the most famous, but no chapter focuses predominantly on religion. In contrast, *Gender and Japanese History*, edited by Wakita Haruko, Anne Bouchy, and Chizuko Ueno (1999), is a two-volume set consisting largely of translations of Japanese scholarship, divided into four categories. The "Religion and Customs" section includes discussions of nunhood in the Heian and Kamakura periods, constructions of gender in early new religions and contemporary shamanism, and the religious consciousness of contemporary Japanese women. Though the project was criticized for lacking an overall discussion of methodology or the broader implications of gender (Hastings 2001), it demonstrated the importance of religion in creating gender roles. In a similar vein, *Women and Class in Japanese History*, edited by Hitomi Tonomura, Anne Walthall, and Wakita (1999), considers how both gender and class shaped women's experience throughout Japanese history. Yet again, chapters dealing specifically with religion were sparse, covering female sovereignty in ancient Japan, medieval nunhood, and medieval women's associations.

Notable in all three of these compilations of essays is the predominance of historians rather than religious studies scholars. While scholars of religion such as Helen Hardacre and Kawamura Kunimitsu contributed to *Gender and Japanese History*, for example, many of those writing on religion were historians. For instance, Wakita, editor of two of these compilations, was a historian of medieval Japan and an expert on Noh. In "The Formation of the Ie and Medieval Myth," Wakita analyzed deities in Noh theatre, the *Shintōshū* (c. 1350), and picture scrolls of origin stories (*engi emaki*) to show how the medieval *ie* household was reflected in representations of the divine in theatre, mythology, and popular stories. Thus, the impetus to "include" women came first from the field of history before being fully embraced by religious studies scholars.

However, by the early 2000s, focus on women within philosophical and religious systems within East Asia began to emerge. *Women and Confucian Cultures in Premodern China, Korea and Japan*, edited by Dorothy Ko, Jahyun Kim Haboush, and Joan R. Piggott (2003), considers the role of Confucianism in premodern East Asia. Though the authors were primarily historians, their focus on Confucianism required them to consider other philosophical discourses as well. In the case of Japan, Piggott's chapter on "The Last Classical Female Sovereign" considers how Empress Kōken-Shōtoku (713–770, reigned 749–58 as Kōken and 765–700 as Shōtoku) creatively employed Shinto and Buddhist ideas to support her reign as well as the Confucian patriarchal concepts that ultimately ended the ascension of female monarchs. For the Edo period (1600–1868), Noriko Sugano and Martha C. Tocco examine how state indoctrination of filial piety and women's education respectively facilitated the spread of Neo-Confucian ideas regarding women's roles.

More clearly focused on religion, specifically Buddhism, is the monumental compilation *Engendering Faith: Women and Buddhism in Premodern Japan*, edited by Barbara Ruch (2002). *Engendering Faith* is a collection of twenty essays, many by Japanese scholars, presenting relevant insights on the role of women and gender in Buddhism in Japan and also in China. Topics range from nuns to female deities, divorce temples to burial practices, and from women's salvation to misogynistic attitudes toward women (the five "obstructions" and male-only sacred spaces).[1] This large collection presents many important insights into specific figures, movements, and trends in premodern Japanese Buddhism, and is organized in both thematic and chronological progression. As such, *Engendering Faith* presents a more cohesive treatment of the larger picture of women and women's roles in premodern Buddhism than can often be found in such compilations.

A year later, Bernard Faure published *The Power of Denial: Buddhism, Purity and Gender* (2003). This massive work continues the analytical work Faure initially performed in *The Red Thread: Buddhist Approaches to Sexuality* (1998b), addressing the treatment of sexuality in Buddhist philosophy and texts from India, China, and especially Japan; in *The Power of Denial*, Faure turns to the question of gender. Faure begins with "Buddhism and Women" by considering the female *sangha* and the three rhetorics of subordination, salvation, and equality before examining the different categories of women highlighted in Buddhist texts in Part 2: "Imagining Buddhist Women." His final section, "Women Against Buddhism," considers how women have challenged Buddhism's misogynistic discourses

---

[1] The five obstructions are the five Buddhist figures that women cannot become, including Indra, Mara, Brahma, a *cakravartin* or ethical ruler, or a Buddha. The practice of forbidding women access to sacred spaces, notably temples and mountains, is called *nyonin kinsei* and will be discussed later in this chapter.

and created their own roles within the sangha, such as the *kumano bikuni*. This systematic approach allows one to consider the assimilation and development of Buddhism in Japan and how Buddhist and native ideas of gender clashed, commingled, and created new paradigms. Throughout, Faure weaves between precedents set in India and China and developments in Japan, drawing not only from sutras and the writings of key priests but also from folklore, art, and other culturally embedded sources (Faure 2003).

Both *Engendering Faith* and *The Power of Denial* are invaluable contributions to our knowledge of women and gender in Buddhism, and there are advantages to having both an edited volume with multiple authors and diverse research, on the one hand, and a systematic consideration by one author, on the other. Both approaches are needed, for instance, in the consideration of women and Shinto, in which there is as yet no full-length study, though both edited volumes and monographs on Shinto have proliferated in recent years (Breen and Teeuwen 2010, 2013; Hardacre 2017). Similarly, a comprehensive consideration of Confucianism's lasting legacy in Japan that considers both gender and religion as key categories would also be welcome. The presence of Daoism in Japan is particularly understudied, but from the little that has been published, it is clear that female deities and gendered practices play a particularly important role (Como 2009), which merits further examination. The case of women in early Christianity is a notable exception to this dearth of gender treatment, as the role of early women martyrs is well documented (Ward 2009, 2010, 2012).

It is no accident that the most targeted work on women and religion in premodern Japan thus far focuses on Buddhism, given the field's enduring tendency to prioritize Buddhism and the relative predominance of Buddhist sources, especially before the early modern period. Most recently, Karen Gerhart's edited volume *Women, Rites and Ritual Objects in Premodern Japan* (2018) offers examinations of moving house and fertility rituals, female deities, death practices for women, and women's patronage, the vast majority of which are Buddhist. While there is certainly more work to be done on women and Buddhism, scholars must increasingly consider the role of other religious traditions in shaping gender, womanhood, and women's roles.

CRITICAL EVALUATIONS OF ANDROCENTRISM IN JAPANESE RELIGIONS

In 2015, Barbara Ambros published *Women in Japanese Religions*, a book that provides an overview of key roles that women played in the development of Buddhism, Shinto, and other religious traditions across Japanese history. Ambros's central argument is that the ambivalent or even misogynistic religious discourses surrounding gender both subordinated women and offered opportunities for them to engage in religious activities creatively and sometimes independently of their male counterparts. This accessible text, covering both historical developments and roles as well as important debates within the scholarship, can easily be used as a textbook for undergraduate classes.

Some have criticized Ambros's approach as insufficiently critical of the unequal systems behind religious discourses and their concepts of gender, and thus inadvertently justifying androcentric interpretations (see Chapter 11 in this volume). The criticism merits our attention because the question of how we reconcile virulently androcentric discourses with women who participated in their perpetuation is vitally important to the field of gender studies. If we explore how women accepted, evaded, or ignored —but did not oppose—misogynistic religious concepts, does that signal tacit approval of these concepts and the unequal society that generated them? On the other hand, if we analyze and condemn the gender order but do not discuss women's interactions and appropriations of it, don't we neglect women's agency and creativity?

Recent scholarship has shown that this need not be a binary choice. In emphasizing what women did with the androcentric views of religious traditions rather than focusing solely on the views themselves, Ambros joins feminist scholars who have reevaluated the role of women in premodern societies with the actions, written records, and potential agency of women in mind. Ambros herself cites Dorothy Ko, a historian of China, who has examined women's participation and perpetuation of misogynistic ideology, most notably in her history of foot-binding (1994, 2007). In the study of premodern Japan, Anne Walthall (1990, 1991, 1998), Nomura Ikuyo (1996, 2004), and Hitomi Tonomura (1994, 2006, 2007) have all shown that by focusing exclusively on the misogyny of religious discourse, we neglect the ways in which women embraced, circumvented, and rejected the hierarchies and exclusions of diverse societal beliefs.

The work of Lori Meeks perhaps best exemplifies the difficulty and necessity of this balancing act in the religiosity of premodern Japan. Her first book, *Hokkeji and the Reemergence of Female Monastic Orders in Premodern Japan* (2010), focused on the revitalization of the convent Hokkeji in Nara, restored under the auspices of the Shingon Ritsu monk Eison (1201–1290). Through careful study of the documents written by Eison and key nuns at Hokkeji, Meeks shows that female monastics did not overtly challenge such misogynistic ideas as *henjo nanshi*, the notion that women must first be reincarnated as a man before achieving Buddhahood or enlightenment, derived from the Devadatta chapter in the *Lotus Sutra*. Instead, Hokkeji nuns focused on the veneration of relics, practical rituals such as memorial rites, and the valorization of the mother figure. Nor did they credit Eison as a founding figure, since nuns were already living at Hokkeji before his ordination of them in 1249. Instead, they looked to Empress Kōmyō (701–760) as their original founder and as an example of female morality and monasticism.

The Blood Bowl Sutra is another example of a particularly misogynistic discourse that was used to denigrate women, but was also used by women for their own ends. This sutra, originating in China in the tenth or eleventh centuries and entering Japan in the fifteenth, suggests that women are condemned to the Blood Bowl hell, in which they stand in a pool of uterine blood, because of the polluted nature of their menstrual and parturient blood. Scholars have written about the sutra's history, treatment of women, and practical worship in the medieval period (Glassman 2008) and in the Sōtō Zen tradition (Williams 2005). However, Meeks has recently published a comprehensive treatment of the sutra and its commentaries as well as the ways in which women, their families, and sororities interpreted its teachings. For instance, women used talismans, rites, and other strategies associated with the Blood Bowl cult in order to protect themselves during childbirth and circumvent menstrual taboos. The ways in which "women were able to use discourses derived from the Blood Bowl Sutra to seek practical solutions to the very real obstacles they faced in daily life," Meeks argues, also demonstrates how nuanced and multidisciplinary studies of religious concepts give us a far broader understanding of how these ideas were actually interpreted and utilized (Meeks 2020: 13).

The question of how best to balance diverse androcentric strategies rooted in religious traditions with the strategies of women themselves, who find meaning or vocation in supporting, eliding, or occasionally rejecting the former, will continue to dominate questions of women and gender within religious traditions, whether premodern, modern, or contemporary. Accordingly, it is a debate we should consider with care but also embrace as studies of women and religion continue to emerge.

WOMEN AND RELIGION IN MODERN AND CONTEMPORARY JAPAN

One bridge between the premodern and the present day is that the omission of women's labor from religious spheres remains a problem in contemporary Japan, as recent scholarship on women's roles in religious institutions has shown. In the past five years, two major English-language journals on Japanese religion have produced special issues specifically dealing with this question across religious traditions, identifying common threads across Buddhist, Christian, Shinto, and new religious groups.

In 2015, the *Journal of Religion in Japan* devoted a special section of issues 2–3 to "Gender Issues in Modern and Contemporary Japanese Religions," edited by Monika Schrimpf and Mira Sontag. In the introduction, the editors ask two questions: "How are gender codes applied to justify discrimination, or conversely, to support women's (self-)empowerment in th e Japanese context? How do they affect religious identities, and how are they consolidated, deconstructed or changed in religious discourses?" (Schrimpf and Sontag 2015: 95). The 2015 special section considers these questions through fieldwork conducted among Christian feminists (Sonntag), Shin Buddhist women (Heidegger), and ordained Buddhist priests (Schrimpf), as well as Mika Odaira's article on Miyamoto Shigetane, a Meiji-era Shinto priest who focused on the education and, as Odaira argues, the proselytization of women. Yet the other three pieces are in closer conversation, as they all consider gender within the context of reform movements within religious groups as well as the multiplicity of views among believers. While there is evidence of empowerment in Schrimpf's examination of ordained Buddhist women, all three speak to enduring discrimination within their sect, and in the case of Christian women, marginalization (Schrimpf and Sontag 2015).

Though similarly focused on contemporary women in religious sects, the "Gendering Religious Practices in Japan: Multiple Voices, Multiple Strategies" issue of the *Japanese Journal of Religious Studies* is not only larger but more engaged in critical analysis and gender theory (Kawahashi and Kobayashi 2017). Though this was not the first time that the *Japanese Journal of Religious Studies* featured gender in a special issue (see Nakamura 1983 and Kawahashi and Kuroki 2003), I will focus on the most recent special issue here. Editors Kawahashi Noriko and Kobayashi Naoko, in the introduction, raise several issues for the reader's consideration: the romanticizing of women's agency in the face of androcentrism; the false equation of gender and women in scholarly studies; the need to situate the study of gender and religion in contemporary Japan within the context of the feminist movement and the current backlash against it; and the continuing effects of androcentric views within the scholarly community of religionists, particularly but not solely in Japan. The depth and complexity of these issues is reflected in the articles themselves, from the ordination of women in the Anglican-Episcopal Church of Japan (Miki); the ambiguous role of temple wives within the Sōtō Zen sect (Kawahashi); the experience of three women Buddhist priests (Rowe); interrogating stereotypes of female ascetic practitioners and their access (or lack thereof) to specific sites (Kobayashi); and women who practice forms of spirituality outside of formal religion, allowing them to ignore or transcend androcentric social expectations (Komatsu).

Of particular note is Inose Yuri's examination of gender in Japanese new religions. Following Susan Palmer's typology of gender formation in North American new religions, Inose divides these religions into categories of "Sex Complementarity," in which men and women are perceived as different but complementary; "Sex Polarity," in which men and women are entirely different, and men superior; and "Sex Unity," in which the distinction of sex is seen as superficial and irrelevant (Palmer 1994: 9–12; Inose 2017: 18–19). Though the use of "sex" in place of "gender" does not reflect our current understanding of these terms, the typology is useful for considering the gender attitudes of diverse religions. While Inose focuses on Soka Gakkai (sex complementarity, which she also identifies as the predominant pattern in Japan), Reiyūkai (sex polarity), and the political interest group Nippon Kaigi, she also highlights how these gender views mirror those of contemporary Japanese society and that despite these androcentric views, many women participate avidly in religious activities and find validation in them.

Indeed, notions of gender falling somewhere on the spectrum between complementarity and polarity have become key concepts and discussions not only within the new religions (see Ambros 2015: 158–66 for a succinct overview) but also within Shinto. The Association of Shinto Shrines has cited changing gender roles as a source of moral decline in current Japanese society and called for female priests to set examples as good wives and wise mothers, rhetoric that Japanese feminists have vigorously criticized (Hardacre 2005: 239–40). In addition, rhetoric concerning the "innate" differences between men and women—embodied, social, and familial—continues to define the often subordinate roles that women priests fulfill within the shrine hierarchy, even while the presence of active gender discrimination is denied (Ochi 2010, 2015). Complementarity may be the new terminology for enduring androcentric notions from earlier times, not only the "good wife, wise mother" of the Meiji period, which has continued to function as a catchphrase today (Koyama 2013), but also earlier concepts, such as Confucian familial roles.

RECOMMENDATIONS FOR FURTHER INQUIRY

Scholarship over the past few decades has greatly added to our understanding of women's roles, experience, and ideas within religious traditions of Japan. While I have highlighted some key approaches and areas in need of further inquiry, I would like to indicate a number of topics in which scholarship is either overdue or in need of reconsideration.

Perhaps most needed is a broad examination of women in Shinto. While the diverse roles and concepts of women in Buddhism is now well documented, there is not yet a systematic and critical consideration of women in Shinto. Ambros's general treatment of women and religion provides short but important coverage of certain figures, concepts, and categories: female deities and rulers, *miko* and priestesses, nativist women, and the systematic masculinization of the Shinto priesthood (2015). However, the careful reader will soon find that much of the research in these areas focuses on individual women, like the Kamo priestess Seishi (Kamens 1990) or the nativists Tadano Makuzu (1763–1825; Gramlich-Oka 2006), or on the developments in Shinto as a whole, with gender issues an afterthought.

The deliberate removal of women priests from Shinto shrines in the Edo and Meiji periods, for instance, is often mentioned in the context of Shinto in general (Hardacre 2017) or in specific sects like Awashima (Ariyasu 2015; Simpson 2018: 77) but has rarely become the focus of inquiry. As of 2018, women constituted a mere 16 percent of the

Shinto priesthood, with some regional variation (Bunkachō 2019). While Odaira Mika has evaluated the role of women in Shinto up until 1871 (2003, 2009) and Ochi Mika has written on contemporary women shrine priests (2010, 2015), there is no study combining the two, considering the postwar period, examining regional differences, or anything yet written in English on this subject. In addition, the rules surrounding taboos against blood pollution at Shinto shrines and their shifts in different periods, especially the medieval, has been inadequately explored.

Similarly, while there is growing interest in the study of *matsuri* both past and present, the topic of gender representation in *matsuri* has not been explored. It is well known that many *matsuri* limit the participation in certain key activities, such as carrying the *mikoshi* (portable shrine), pulling the float, or attempting a central task, to men. Women may play key roles in the festival's planning and execution but rarely on the center stage. Yet, this is changing in some places. For example, the Dontosai, carried out all over Miyagi but most famously in Sendai at Osaki Hachimangū, involves *hadaka mairi* or a "naked procession" to the shrine. As with most "naked" festivals, the participants are not actually nude— they wear short linen trousers—but modesty is one reason often given for *matsuri* being limited to men. In Sendai, women were permitted to participate (wearing white jackets as well) in the early 2000s, while participation by non-Japanese was permitted after the Triple Disaster of March 11, 2011. The reasoning behind both enduring bans on women and cases where women's participation has been allowed, as well as any regional trends or differentiation, not only merits further scrutiny but also provides an opportunity to consider gendered participation rather than women alone.

Regarding gendered participation in religious activities, there is a distinct lack of scholarship that crosses the premodern and modern divide. Scholars considering case studies of discrete *matsuri* today, for instance, often provide a short historical survey and question notions of *matsuri* as unchanged performative relics of the past but delve no deeper, while scholars of the premodern touch on lingering vestiges of historical tradition but focus primarily on their period of specialization. A notable exception is Lindsey DeWitt's work on *nyonin kinsei*, the prohibition of women from sacred mountains, islands, and other ritual spaces. Though her early work centered on female exclusion at Mt. Ōmine, recently she has examined Okinoshima and its designation as a World Heritage Site despite its continuing prohibition of women visitors. In both sites, DeWitt has provided an in-depth deconstruction of both the history of these bans and the current narratives concerning their so-called timeless nature, the latter of which are often used to justify the continued exclusion of women (DeWitt 2015, 2018a). By considering the actual and imagined history of so-called traditional gender practices, DeWitt is able to offer a new way to consider gender concepts from Japanese religions, and this methodology could be utilized for a variety of topics in gender and religious studies.

In addition, I would like to suggest a reconsideration of the earlier trend in feminist studies to "add in the women." We know that simply adding in women's stories to the historical record is not enough, and that careful analysis of societal structures and gender norms must be an integral part of any scholarship on individual women, women's groups, or gender issues. However, there are many topics in religious studies that do not take women fully into account, even when the topic or practice unquestionably centers on women. For instance, in the *Nanzan Guide to Japanese Religions*, Kawahashi Noriko discussed how English monographs on *mizuko kuyō*, memorial rites for unborn children, have been treated, notably in two books by Western scholars, with little discussion of how women themselves view and accept this practice (Kawahashi 2006). In her work on clerical marriage and the role of *jizoku* or priests' wives, Kawahashi offers compelling approaches with which to analyze how religious discourse, societal norms, and misogyny affect conceptualizations and practices of both men and women (Kawahashi 2012).

This refocus on women themselves in key religious concepts related to female bodies or womanhood can also be extended to the premodern period. For example, scholars have devoted considerable attention to theories of embryology within Esoteric Buddhism, such as the "five stages of the embryo within the womb" (*tainai goi*) and "ten months in the womb" (*tainai totsuki zu*). These adaptations of Chinese medicine and Buddhist texts on the body became key visualizations and meditation rituals within the Tendai and Shingon sects (Itō 1996a; Abe 1998; Dolce 2015). However, until recently, little attention has been paid to the wombs in which these embryological developments were thought to occur, nor to how these concepts influenced fertility and childbirth practices. A growing interest in premodern medical practices and their close relationship with religious notions of health and body has helped address this disconnect, and the recent work of scholars such as Anna Andreeva and Benedetta Lomi on Esoteric rituals for women, Heian and Kamakura period childbirth practices, and other practical adaptations of esoteric gestational theories has richly illuminated the connection between religious theory and women's lives (Andreeva 2017a, 2018; Lomi 2018). But the fact that so much work on embryology was undertaken with so little connection to actual women points, if not directly to lingering androcentrism, at least to the persistence of a paradigm in the field in which theological constructs are given precedence over practical religiosity.

See also Chapter 11, "Gender," Chapter 17, "Medicine," and Chapter 23, "Sexuality."

CASE STUDY

Mountain Worship and Women

KOBAYASHI Naoko

On September 27, 2014, a large volcanic eruption occurred on Mt. Kiso Ontake. Fifty-eight people died and five people went missing. This was the worst volcanic disaster in the area since the Second World War. The news of the eruption was immediately reported on the news website Yahoo!News, and one reader commented: "That's why women should not enter the mountain!" This comment received more "likes" (*ii ne*) than all the other comments on the same news. The comment referred to the popular belief that when women enter the mountain, the mountain god gets angry and bring disasters. This belief is based on the idea that women are essentially unclean, due to their monthly menstrual cycle. This example shows that a discriminatory tradition toward women is still alive and well in Japan.

The first written source that defines childbirth and menstrual blood as polluting is the Ritsuryō legal code, which was introduced in Japan during the ninth century under the influence of the Chinese legislative system of the Tang period (Katsuura 1995). Buddhist teachings were also used to reinforce this idea. In particular, the Buddhist notion of the five hindrances (*goshō* 五障) limits the spiritual attainment of possible rebirths of women, and thus comes the supposed necessity for women to transform their female bodies into male ones (*henjō nanshi* 変成男子) in order to attain buddhahood. Therefore, temporary uncleanliness, which occurs only for the limited periods of childbirth and menstrual cycle, turned into a permanent exclusion of women from sacred sites (*nyonin kekkai* 女人結界) because the five hindrances stigmatized women as essentially unclean beings (Taira 1992). In addition, the prohibition of women from entering and staying at Buddhist temples, which was based on the monastic regulations prohibiting sexual acts with women (*fujainkai* 不邪淫戒), led to the establishment of permanent female exclusion from key sacred areas (Ushiyama 1996).

The banning of women from sacred sites was publicly lifted according to the legal act no. 98 of Dajōkan Fukoku (Council of State Proclamation) promulgated by the Meiji government in 1872. Since then, women have been legally allowed to enter sacred areas, including sacred mountains on the Japanese archipelago. However, even after the lifting of such bans against women, there are certain sites where the system of female exclusion is still maintained for religious reasons, regardless of the government's decree. Sanjōgatake of Mt. Ōmine (Nara prefecture) is a typical example. Moreover, even though the exclusion of women from sacred sites was eliminated by law, taboos and restrictions against women in mountain worship are still deeply rooted in folk customs.

For example, several Kiso Ontake religious confraternities still consider menstruation as "unclean" and each confraternity has a specific ritual protocol to purify such "uncleanness." In some confraternities, menstruating women cannot climb Mt. Kiso Ontake or participate in rituals and training sessions without performing purification practices (*fujō barai* 不浄祓いの法). Furthermore, in general, there is a tendency to look down upon women during their menstrual periods as essentially "unclean" beings. Therefore, during the Kiso Ontake divine possession ritual (*oza* 御座), fewer female practitioners of the confraternity play the role of the medium whose body is possessed by the god in comparison to their fellow male practitioners.

In recent years, however, it has become more controversial to regard menstruation as "impure" and use it as a reason to exclude a woman from sacred areas. Consequently, there are cases in which entirely different explanations are used to place restrictions on menstruating women. For example, a certain Kiso Ontake group in the Kinki area refuses to admit menstruating women to steep areas on the mountain, claiming that a supposed lack of blood supply to the brain of a menstruating woman increases the danger that she might stagger and fall. A male practitioner in his forties who is a member of this group emphasized that they were not placing restrictions on women because of any impurity due to menstruation, and explained—with seeming confidence—the adequacy of their logic according to which "women will understand, if this is the reason."

In other words, preaching restraints on women because of the uncleanliness of menstruation is admitted to be an anachronism. Therefore, contemporary explanations of certain ascetic groups are justified on medical grounds and are based on the speculation that a menstruating woman may become anemic due to blood loss and easily stumble or fall down. Because these reasons are presented as logical and scientific, women are supposed to accept them without complaining. Moreover, another male ascetic practitioner from a Kiso Ontake confraternity in Aichi Prefecture explained that the reason to exclude women from the mountains during the menstrual cycle is based on "scientific theories" according to which bears are attracted to the smell of blood. These discourses mirror a recent backlash against gender studies and feminist researchers who dismiss these discriminatory logics as a blatant misuse of "scientific grounds" to justify arbitrary arguments (Seguchi 2006).

In contrast with Kiso Ontake confraternities, present-day Shugendō religious groups avoid preaching that women cannot enter sacred mountains and perform ascetic practices due to their menstrual uncleanliness. However, there still remains in mountain asceticism (Shugendō) a sense that mountains are essentially places for male practitioners, and most Shugendō groups are still male-centric. A woman who became the first scholar priest (*gakusō*) of a Shugendō group in Kyoto in 2001 told me that during the training, she was requested to make ascetic practices without any consideration for her being a woman, including during the menstrual cycle. She always changed clothes and slept in the same room as the other male scholar priests and there was a tacit understanding that she had to do everything exactly in the same way as in the standard training of male priests. She continued her ascetic training even during menstruation without any special consideration, desperately attempting to be just like the other male priests.

As mentioned above, the idea of women's uncleanliness, and thus female discrimination, and male-centrism still exit in mountain asceticism in Japan. Certainly, in recent years, it is increasingly difficult for male practitioners to exclude women from sacred mountains due to a supposed impurity of menstrual blood. Nevertheless, certain male practitioners tend to offer different rationalizations to explain and normalize the bans against women's participation in ascetic practices. In other words, the exclusion of women still continues but is articulated in different terms. Furthermore, the people who teach women these norms continue to be men, who are invariably in leading positions in mountain worship confraternities (Kobayashi 2017). Thus, woman's nature is still often interpreted as an ascribed objective value, and her actions are regulated by men. This is a typical attitude that patriarchal societies have taken toward women. Moreover, men who hold vested rights at in sacred mountains often have little awareness of these problems.

BIBLIOGRAPHY

"Yu-ri!!! on ICE seichi junrei ofisharu tsuā hatsubai kettei!!!" yurionice.com, October 31, 2017. Available online: http://yurionice.com/news/detail.php?id=1055177 (accessed December 15, 2020).

125 Years Memory (2015), [Film] Dir. Tanaka Mitsutoshi, Japan: Toei Company and Turkey: Böcek Yapım.

Abe H. (1986), *Isuramukyō* (Islam) (For Beginners Series), 10th ed., Tokyo: Gendai Shokan.

Abe R. (1999), *The Weaving of Mantra: Kūkai and the Construction of Esoteric Buddhist Discourse*, New York: Columbia University Press.

Abe Y. (1968) "Religious Freedom under the Meiji Constitution (Part 1)," *Contemporary Religions in Japan*, 9 (4): 268–338.

Abe Y. (1986), "Taishokan no seiritsu," in Agō T. and Fukuda A. (eds.), *Kōwaka bukyoku kenkyū*, vol. 4, 80–195, Tokyo: Miyai Shoten.

Abe Y. (1998), *Yuya no kōgō: Chūsei no sei to seinaru mono*, Nagoya: Nagoya Daigaku Shuppankai.

Abe Y. (2001), *Seija no suisan: Chūsei no koe to woko-naru mono*, Nagoya: Nagoya Daigaku Shuppankai.

Abe Y. (2016), "Gogyō saimon to gogyō mandara: Chūsei Nihon no shūkyōteki shintairon no keifu," in Saitō H. and Inoue T. (eds.), *Kagura to saimon no chūsei: hen'yō suru shinkō no katachi*, 70–92, Kyoto: Shibunkaku Shuppan.

Act on Penal Detention Facilities and the Treatment of Inmates and Detainees (2005). Available online: https://elaws.e-gov.go.jp/document?lawid=417AC0000000050 (accessed December 4, 2020).

Adachi I. et al., eds. (1999, or. ed. 1942) *Nihon shokumotsushi*, 4 vols., Tokyo: Yūzankaku.

Ahlin, L. (2013), "Mutual Interests? Neoliberalism and New Age during the 1980s," in F. Gauthier and T. Martikainen (eds.), *Religion in Consumer Society: Brands, Consumers and Markets*, 175–88, London: Routledge.

Akae T. (2017), *Yanaihara Tadao: sensō to chishikijin no shimei*, Tokyo: Iwanami Shoten.

Akagawa N. (2014), *Heritage Conservation and Japan's Cultural Diplomacy: Heritage, National Identity and National Interest*, Abingdon: Routledge.

Akagawa N. (2015), "Intangible Heritage and Embodiment: Japan's Influence on Global Heritage Discourse," in W. Logan, M. Nic Craith, and U. Kockel (eds.), *A Companion to Heritage Studies*, 69–86, Chichester, UK: Wiley-Blackwell.

Akagawa N. (2016a), "Japan and the Rise of Heritage in Cultural Diplomacy: Where Are We Heading?," *Future Anterior: Journal of Historic Preservation, History, Theory, and Criticism*, 13 (1): 125–39.

Akagawa N. (2016b), "Rethinking the Global Heritage Discourse – Overcoming 'East' and 'West'?," *International Journal of Heritage Studies*, 22 (1): 14–25. https://doi.org/10.1080/13527258.2015.1068213.

Akamatsu T., and Fukushima H., eds. (1982), *Shin Bukkyō*, 4 vols., Kyoto: Nagata Bunshōdō.

Akasaka N., ed. (1992), *Kugi no shinsō*. Tokyo: Shin'yōsha.

Akashi H., and Matsuura S., eds. (1975), *Shōwa tokkō dan'atsushi: Shūkyōjin ni taisuru dan'atsu*, vol. 3, 1935–41; vol. 4, 1942–5, Tokyo: Taihei Shuppansha.

Akazawa H. (2011), *Kamakura-ki kannin onmyōji no kenkyū*, Tokyo: Yoshikawa Kōbunkan.

Akiya K. (2015), *Kōfuku no Kagaku*, Tokyo: Taibundō.

Allison, A. (2006), *Millennial Monsters: Japanese Toys and the Global Imagination*, Berkeley: University of California Press.

Altglas, V. (2016), "Spirituality, the Opiate of Scholars of Religion?," *Religion*, 46 (3): 420–8.

Ama M. (2015), "'First White Buddhist Priestess': A Case Study of Sunya Gladys Pratt at the Tacoma Buddhist Temple," in S. A. Mitchell and Quli N. E. F. (eds.), *Buddhism beyond Borders: New Perspectives on Buddhism in the United States*, 59–74, Albany: State University of New York Press.

Amada A. (2012), "Honrai no matsuri no yukue: Wakayama Shingū-shi Otō Matsuri ni kansuru gensetsu wo megutte," in Yoshitani H. (ed.), *Kyōdo saikō: Aratana kyōdo kenkyū wo mezashite*, 223–42, Tokyo: Kadokawa Gakugei Shuppan.

Amano D. (2000), *Tendai shōmyō no kenkyū*, Kyoto: Hōzōkan.

Ambros, B. (2008), *Emplacing a Pilgrimage: The Ōyama Cult and Regional Religion in Early Modern Japan*, Cambridge, MA: Harvard University Asia Center.

Ambros, B. (2012), *Bones of Contention: Animals and Religion in Contemporary Japan*, Honolulu: University of Hawai'i Press.

Ambros, B. (2013), "Nakayama Miki's View of Women and Their Bodies in the Context of Nineteenth Century Japanese Religions," *Tenri Journal of Religion*, 41: 85–116.

Ambros, B. (2014), "Pilgrimage in Japan," *Oxford Bibliographies: Buddhism*. Available online: https://www.oxfordbibliographies.com/view/document/obo-9780195393521/obo-9780195393521-0195.xml (accessed December 15, 2020).

Ambros, B. (2015), *Women in Japanese Religions*, New York: New York University Press.

Amino Y., and Niunoya T. (eds.) (1991), "Chūsei no sairei: chūō kara chihō e" (VHS and commentary), in *Taikei Nihon rekishi to geinō: oto to eizō to moji ni yoru* Vol. 4, Tokyo: Heibonsha.

Amino Y. (1986), *Igyō no ōken*, Tokyo: Heibonsha.

Amino Y. (1994), *Chūsei no hinin to yūjo*, Tokyo: Akashi Shoten.

Anderson, B. (1983), *Imagined Communities: Reflections on the Origin and Spread of Nationalism*, London: Verso Editions and NLB.

Anderson, E. (2014), *Christianity and Imperialism in Modern Japan: Empire for God*, London: Bloomsbury.

Andreeva, A. (2015), "'Lost in the Womb': Conception, Reproductive Imagery, and Gender in the Writings and Rituals of Japan's Medieval Holy Men," in A. Andreeva and D. Steavu (eds.), *Transforming the Void: Embryological Discourse and Reproductive Imagery in East Asian Religions*, 420–78, Leiden: Brill.

Andreeva, A. (2017a), "Explaining Conception to Women? Buddhist Embryological Knowledge in the *Sanshō ruijūshō* (Encyclopedia of Childbirth, ca. 1318)," *Asian Medicine*, 12 (1–2): 170–202.

Andreeva, A. (2017b), *Assembling Shinto: Buddhist Approaches to Kami Worship in Medieval Japan*, Cambridge: Harvard University Press.

Andreeva, A. (2018), "Devising the Esoteric Rituals for Women: Fertility and the Demon Mother in the *Gushi nintai sanshō himitsu hōshū*," in K. M. Gerhart (ed.), *Women, Rites, and Ritual Objects in Premodern Japan*, 53–88, Leiden: Brill.

Andrews, D. K. (2014), "Genesis at the Shrine: The Votive Art of an Anime Pilgrimage," *Mechademia*, 9 ("Origins"): 217–33.

Anime seichi: Otozurete mitai Nihon no anime seichi 88 (2019). *Anime Tourism 88*. Available online: https://animetourism88.com/ja/88AnimeSpot (accessed December 15, 2020).

Anthony, J. (2014), "Dreidels to Dante's Inferno: Toward a Typology of Religious Games," in H. Campbell and G. Grieve (eds.), *Playing with Religion in Digital Games*, 25–46, Bloomington: Indiana University Press.

Arai, P. (1999), *Women Living Zen: Japanese Sōtō Buddhist Nuns*, Oxford: Oxford University.

ARC (n.d.-a), "About ARC." Available online: http://www.arcworld.org/about_ARC.asp (accessed December 15, 2020).

ARC (n.d.-b), "JAPAN: Shintos Commit to Sustainable Management of Sacred Forests." Available online: http://www.arcworld.org/projects.asp?projectID=161 (accessed December 15, 2020).

Arimoto Y. (2011), *Supirichuaru shijō no kenkyū: Dēta de yomu kyū-kakudai māketto no shinjitsu*, Tokyo: Tōyō Keizai Shinpōsha.

Ariyasu M. (2015), *Awashima shinkō: nyonin kyūsai to umi no Shugendō*, Tokyo: Iwata Shoin.

Astley, T. (2006), "New Religions," in P. L. Swanson and C. Chilson (eds.), *Nanzan Guide to Japanese Religions*, 91–114, Honolulu: University of Hawai'i Press.

Asuka Heritage Promotion Committee (Nihon isan "Asuka" miryoku hasshin jigyō seishin kyōgikai) (2016), "'Asuka joshi kikō.' Nihon isan 'Asuka' miryoku hasshin jigyō seishin kyōgikai."

Asuka, R. (2003), *La médecine traditionnelle japonaise*, Paris: L'Harmattan.

Atkins, P. S. (2008), "*Chigo* in the Medieval Japanese Imagination," *The Journal of Asian Studies*, 67 (3): 947–70.

Atkinson, W. W. (2011), *The Kybalion: The Definitive Edition*, ed. with introduction by P. Deslippe, New York: Tarcher/Penguin.

Aupers, S., and D. Houtman (2006), "Beyond the Spiritual Supermarket: The Social and Public Significance of New Age Spirituality," *Journal of Contemporary Religion*, 21 (2): 201–22.

Aupers, S. and D. Houtman, eds. (2010), *Religions of Modernity: Relocating the Sacred to the Self and the Digital*, Leiden: Brill.

Averbuch, I. (1995), *The Gods Come Dancing: A Study of the Japanese Ritual Dance of Yamabushi Kagura*, New York: Cornell University East Asia Program.

Bachnik, J. (1995), "Orchestrated Reciprocity: Belief versus Practice in Japanese Funeral Ritual," in J. van Bremen and D. Martinez (eds.), *Ceremony and Ritual in Japan*, 108–45, London: Routledge.

Baffelli, E. (2016), *Media and New Religions in Japan*, London: Routledge.

Baffelli, E. (forthcoming 2022), "Living Aum: Austerities, Emotion, and the Feeling Community of Female Ex-Aum Members," *Nova Religio*, 25 (3).

Baffelli, E., and I. Reader (2012), "Editors' Introduction: Impact and Ramifications: The Aftermath of the Aum Affair in the Jpanese Religious Context," *Japanese Journal of Religious Studies*, 39 (1): 1–28.

Baffelli, E., and I. Reader, (2019), *Dynamism and the Ageing of a Japanese 'New' Religion: Transformations and the Founder*, London: Bloomsbury.

Baffelli, E., and J. Caple, eds. (2019), "Religious Authority in East Asia: Materiality, Media and Aesthetics" (special issue), *Asian Ethnology*, 78 (1).

Baffelli, E., I. Reader, and B. Staemmler, eds. (2011), *Japanese Religions on the Internet: Innovation, Representation, and Authority*, London: Routledge.

Baffelli, E., J. Caple, L. McLaughlin, and F. Schröer, eds. (forthcoming), "The Aesthetics and Emotions of Religious Belonging: Examples from the Modern Buddhist World," unpublished manuscript.

Baker, D., and F. Rausch (2017), *Catholics and Anti-Catholicism in Chosŏn Korea*, Honolulu: University of Hawai'i Press.

Bartel, R. C., and L. Hulsether (2019), "Classifying Capital: A Roundtable Introduction," *Journal of the American Academy of Religion*, 87 (3): 581–95.

Barthes, R. (1982), *The Empire of Signs*, London: Jonathan Cape.

Baudrillard, J. (1981), *For a Critique of the Political Economy of the Sign*, St Louis, MO: Telos.

Baudrillard, J. (1996), *The System of Objects*, London: Verso.

Baumann, M. (2001), "Global Buddhism: Developmental Periods, Regional Histories, and a New Analytic Perspective," *Journal of Global Buddhism*, 2: 1–43.

Beckwith, C. I. (2009), *Empires of the Silk Road: A History of Central Eurasia from the Bronze Age to the Present*, Princeton, NJ: Princeton University Press.

Bellah, R. (1957), *Tokugawa Religion: The Values of Pre-Industrial Japan*, Glencoe, IL: The Free Press.

Benedict, T. O. (2018), "Practicing Spiritual Care in the Japanese Hospice," *Japanese Journal of Religious Studies*, 45 (1): 175–99.

Benjamin, W. (2001), "Strada a senso unico," in R. Tiedemann, H. Schweppenhäuser, and E. Ganni (eds.), *Opere Complete di Walter Benjamin*, vol. 2, 409–63, Turin: Einaudi.

Bennett, J. (2010), *Vibrant Matter: A Political Ecology of Things*, Durham: Duke University Press.

Benvenuto, S. (2020), "Benvenuto in clausura," *Antinomie scritture e immagini*, March 5. Available online: https://antinomie.it/index.php/2020/03/05/benvenuto-in-clausura/ (accessed December 15, 2020).

Berman, M. (2018), "Religion Overcoming Religion: Suffering, Secularism, and the Training of Interfaith Chaplains in Japan," *American Ethnologist*, 34 (2): 228–40.

Beukers, H., A. M. Luyendijk-Elshout, M. E. van Opstall, and F. Vos., eds. (1991), *Red-hair Medicine: Dutch-Japanese Medical Relations*, Nieuwe Nederlandse Bijdragen tot de Geschiedenis der Geneeskunde en der Natuurwetenschappen, 36, Amsterdam: Atlanta.

Blacking, J. (1974), *How Musical Is Man?* Seattle: University of Washington Press.

Blair, H. (2011), "Zaō Gongen: From Mountain Icon to National Treasure," *Monumenta Nipponica*, 66 (1): 1–47.

Blair, H. (2015), *Real and Imagined: The Peak of Gold in Heian Japan*, Cambridge, MA: Harvard University Press.

Blavatsky, H. P., E. S. Stephenson, and Utaka H. (alt. Udaka), trans. (1910), *Reichigaku kaisetsu*, Tokyo: Hakubunkan.

Bock, F., trans. (1970), *Engi shiki: Procedures of the Engi Era*, 2 vols., Tokyo: Sophia University Press.

Boden, A. L. (2007), *Women's Rights and Religious Practice*, London: Palgrave Macmillan.

Boret, S. P. (2014), *Japanese Tree Burial: Ecology, Kinship and the Culture of Death*, Abingdon: Routledge.

Borup, J. (2004), "Zen and the Art of Inverting Orientalism: Buddhism, Religious Studies and Interrelated Networks," in P. Antes, A. W. Geertz, and R. R. Warne (eds.), *New Approaches to the Study of Religion. Volume 1: Regional, Critical, and Historical Approaches*, 451–87, Berlin: Walter de Gruyter.

Borup, J. (2013), "Aloha Buddha—the Secularization of Ethnic Japanese-American Buddhism," *Journal of Global Buddhism*, 14: 23–43.

Borup, J. (2016), "Propagation, Accommodation and Negotiating Social Capital: Jōdo Shinshū Responses to Contemporary Crises," *Japanese Religions*, 40 (1 & 2): 85–107.

Borup, J. 2018. "Prosperous Buddhism, Prosperity Buddhism, and Religious Capital," *Numen*, 65 (2–3): 256–88.

Borup, J., and F. Rambelli, eds. (2019), "The Materiality of Japanese Religions," *Japanese Religions*, 43 (1-2): 1–16.

Bosman, F. (2019), "The Sacred and the Digital: Critical Depictions of Religion in Digital Games," *Religion*, 10 (2): 1–5.
Bowring, R. (2005), *The Religious Traditions of Japan 500–1600*, Cambridge: Cambridge University Press.
Bowring, R. (2017), *In the Search of the Way: Thought and Religion in Early-Modern Japan, 1582–1860*, Oxford: Oxford University Press.
Boxer, C. R. (1951), *The Christian Century in Japan, 1549–1650*, Berkeley: University of California Press.
Boyd, J., and Nishimura T. (2004), "Shinto Perspectives in Miyazaki's Anime Film *Spirited Away*," *Journal of Religion and Film*, 8 (3): Article 4. Available online: https://digitalcommons.unomaha.edu/jrf/vol8/iss3/4/ (accessed April 11, 2020).
Breen, J. (2019), "Abdication, Succession and Japan's Imperial Future: An Emperor's Dilemma," *The Asia-Pacific Journal*, 17 (9). Available online: https://apjjf.org/2019/09/Breen.html (accessed December 15, 2020).
Breen, J., and M. Teeuwen, eds. (2000), *Shinto in History: Ways of the Kami*, London: Routledge.
Breen, J., and M. Teeuwen, (2010), *A New History of Shinto*, West Sussex, UK: Wiley-Blackwell.
Brown, B. (2001), "Thing Theory," *Critical Inquiry*, 28 (1): 1–22.
Brox, T., and E. Williams-Oerberg (2017), "Buddhism, Business, and Economics," in M. Jerryson (ed.), *The Oxford Handbook of Contemporary Buddhism*, 504–17, New York: Oxford University Press.
Brumann, C. (2012), "Multilateral Ethnography: Entering the World Heritage Arena," Max Planck Institute for Social Anthropology Working Paper 136. Available online: http://www.eth.mpg.de/cms/en/publications/working_papers/pdf/mpi-ethworking-paper-0136.pdf (accessed December 15, 2020).
Brumann, C. (2014a), "Shifting Tides of World-Making in the UNESCO World Heritage Convention: Cosmopolitanisms Colliding," *Ethnic and Racial Studies*, 37 (12): 2176–92.
Brumann, C. (2014b), "Heritage Agnosticism: A Third Path for the Study of Cultural Heritage," *Social Anthropology: The Journal of the European Association of Social Anthropologists*, 22 (2): 173–88.
Brumann, C., and R. A. Cox, eds. (2010), *Making Japanese Heritage*, London: Routledge.
Brumann, C., and D. Berliner, eds. (2016), *World Heritage on the Ground. Ethnographic Perspectives*, New York: Berghahn.
Buljan, K., and C. M. Cusack (2015), *Anime, Religion and Spirituality: Profane and Sacred Worlds in Contemporary Japan*, Sheffield: Equinox.
Bunkachō (2018), *Policy of Cultural Affairs in Japan*. Available online: http://www.bunka.go.jp/english/report/annual/pdf/r1394357_01.pdf (accessed December 15, 2020).
Burity, J. A. (2013), "Enterpreunerial Spirituality and Ecumenical Alterglobalism: Two Religious Responses to Global Neoliberalism," in T. Martikainen and F. Gauthier (eds.), *Religion in the Neoliberal Age: Political Economy and Modes of Governance*, 21–36, London: Routledge.
Burns, S. L. (2002), "The Body as Text: Confucianism, Reproduction, and Gender in Early Modern Japan," in B. Elman, H. Ooms, and J. Duncan (eds.), *Rethinking Confucianism: Past and Present in China, Japan, Korea and Vietnam*, 178–219, Los Angeles: UCLA Asia Pacific Monograph Series.
"Butsuzen Kekkonshiki. Tsukiji Honganji" (2010), *Rekishi Tokuhon*, 55 (10): 142–7.
Campbell, H. (2017), "Surveying Theoretical Approaches within Digital Religion Studies," *New Media & Society*, 19 (1): 15–24.

Campbell, H., and G. Grieve, eds. (2014), *Playing with Religion in Digital Games*, Bloomington: Indiana University Press.

Campbell, H., and M. Lövheim (2011), "Introduction: Rethinking the Online-Offline Connection in the Study of Religion Online," *Information, Communication & Society*, 14 (8): 1083–96.

Carretero, J., and J. D. García (2013), "The Internet of Things: Connecting the World," *Personal and Ubiquitous Computing*, 18 (2): 445–7.

Carrette, J., and R. King (2005), *Selling Spirituality: The Silent Takeover of Religion*, Oxon: Routledge.

Carter, C. (2018), "Power Spots and the Charged Landscape of Shinto," *Japanese Journal of Religious Studies*, 45 (1): 145–73.

Castiglioni, A., (2019) "From *Your Name.* To *Shin-Gojira*: Spiritual Crisscrossing, Spatial Soteriology, and Catastrophic Identity in Contemporary Japanese Visual Culture," in F. Rambelli (ed.), *Spirits and Animism in Modern Japan*, 171–86, London: Bloomsbury.

Castiglioni, A., F. Rambelli, and C. Roth, eds. (2020), *Defining Shugendō: Critical Studies on Japanese Mountain Religion*, London: Bloomsbury.

Chamberlain, B. H. (1912), *The Invention of a New Religion*, London: Watts.

Chiba J. (2001), *Chiiki shakai to Shinshū*, Kyoto: Hōzōkan.

Childs, M. H. (1980), "*Chigo Monogatari*: Love Stories or Buddhist Sermons?," *Monumenta Nipponica*, 35 (2): 127–51.

Childs, M. H. (1991), "*The Tale of Genmu*," in M. H. Childs (ed.), *Rethinking Sorrow: Revelatory Tales of Late Medieval Japan*, 31–52, Ann Arbor: University of Michigan Center for Japanese Studies..

Childs, M. H., trans. (1996), "The Story of Kannon's Manifestation as a Youth (*Chigo Kannon Engi*)," in S. D. Miller and P. G. Schalow (eds.), *Partings at Dawn: An Anthology of Japanese Gay Literature*, 33–5, San Francisco: Gay Sunshine Press.

Chilson, C. (2017), "The Meaning of Life in Medicine: Nonreligious Spiritual Care in Japan," *European Journal for Person Centered Healthcare*, 5: 527–33.

Choi H. (2009), *Gender and Mission Encounters in Korea: New Women, Old Ways*, Berkeley: University of California Press.

Clarke, P. B., ed. (2000), *Japanese New Religions in Global Perspective*, Surrey: Curzon Press.

Clarke, P. B., and J. Somers, eds. (1994), *Japanese New Religions in the West*, Folkestone, Kent: Curzon Press/Japan Library.

Cleere, H. (2001), "The Uneasy Bedfellows: Universality and Cultural Heritage," in R. Layton, P. G. Stone, and J. Thomas (eds.), *Destruction and Conservation of Cultural Property*, 22–9, London: Routledge.

Collcutt, M. (1981), *Five Mountains: The Rinzai Zen Monastic Institution in Medieval Japan*, Cambridge, MA: Harvard University Press.

Collins, R. (1997), "An Asian Route to Capitalism: Religious Economy and the Origins of Self-Transforming Growth in Japan," *American Sociological Review*, 62 (6): 843–65.

Como, M. (2009), *Weaving and Binding: Immigrant Gods and Female Immortals in Ancient Japan*, Honolulu: University of Hawai'i Press.

Como, M. (2015), "Daoist Deities in Ancient Japan: Household Deities, Jade Women and Popular Religious Practice," in J. L. Richey (ed.), *Daoism in Japan: Chinese Traditions and their Influence on Japanese Religious Culture*, 24–36, London: Routledge.

Counihan, C., and P. van Esterik, eds. (1997), *Food and Culture: A Reader*, New York: Routledge.

Covell, S. G. (2005), *Japanese Temple Buddhism: Worldliness in a Religion of Renunciation*, Honolulu: University of Hawai'i Press.

Covell, S. G. (2012a), "The Temple / Juridical Person: Law and the Temple in Japan," in L. Dolce (ed.), *Japanese Religions Vol. II: The Practice of Religion*, 3–21, London: Sage.

Covell, S. G. (2012b), "Money and the Temple: Law, Taxes and the Image of Buddhism," in I. Prohl and J. K. Nelson (eds.), *Handbook on Contemporary Religion*, 159–76, Leiden: Brill.

Cowan, D. E., and J. K. Hadden, eds. (2000), *Religion on the Internet: Research Prospects and Promises*, New York: JAI Press.

Cox, R. A., and C. Brumann (2010), "Introduction," in C. Brumann and R. A. Cox (eds.), *Making Japanese Heritage*, 1–17, London: Routledge.

Corrywright, D., and B. Schmidt, eds. (2018), *Essays in Honor of Ursula King*, Bristol: University of Bristol Press.

Cwiertka, K. J. (1998), *The Making of Modern Culinary Tradition in Japan*, Leiden University.

Dairyū (1977 [1317]), *Sangai Isshinki: Sanken Itchi Sho* 三界一心記: 三賢一致書, Tokyo: Rittaisha.

Daly, Patrick, and Tim Winter, eds. (2012), *Routledge Handbook of Heritage in Asia*, Abingdon: Routledge.

Darlington, S. M. (2012), *The Ordination of a Tree: The Thai Buddhist Environmental Movement*, Albany: State University of New York Press.

Dauvergne, P. (1997), *Shadows in the Forest: Japan and the Politics of Timber in Southeast Asia*, Cambridge, MA: MIT Press.

Davis, W. (1980), *Dōjō: Magic and Exorcism in Modern Japan*, Stanford, CA: Stanford University Press.

Davis, W. (1992), *Japanese Religion and Society: Paradigms of Structure and Change*, Albany: State University of New York Press.

Dawson, A. (2013), "Entangled Modernity and Commodified Religion: Alternative Spirituality and the 'New Middle Class'," in F. Gauthier and T. Martikainen (eds.), *Religion in Consumer Society: Brands, Consumers and Markets*, 127–42, London: Routledge.

Dawson, L. L., and D. E. Cowan, eds. (2004), *Religion Online: Finding Faith on the Internet*, London: Routledge.

De Vries, H. (2001), "In Media Res. Global Religion, Public Spheres, and the Task of Contemporary Comparative Religious Studies," in H. de Vries and S. Weber, (eds.), *Religion and Media*, 3–42, Stanford, CA: Stanford University Press.

Deal, W. E. (1999), "Nichiren's *Risshō ankoku ron* and Canon Formation," *Japanese Journal of Religious Studies*, 26 (3–4): 325–48.

Demiéville, P. (1937), "Byō," in P. Demiéville et al. (eds.), *Hōbōgirin: dictionnaire encyclopédique du bouddhisme d'après les sources chinoises et japonaises* (reprint in Siary and Benhamou 1994: 349–412), 224–65, Tokyo: Maison franco-japonaise.

Demiéville, P. (1985), *Buddhism and Healing* (= Hōbōgirin entry on "Byō," trans. Mark Tatz), Lanham, MD: University Press of America.

Desertis, V.C., Takahashi G., trans. (1915), *Shinreigaku kōwa*, Tokyo: Genkōsha.

Dessì, U. (2014), "Risshō Kōseikai within Globalization," *Journal of Religion in Japan*, 3 (2–3): 121–40.

Dessì, U. (2017), *The Global Repositioning of Japanese Religions: An Integrated Approach*, Abingdon: Routledge.

DeWitt, L. E. (2015), "A Mountain Set Apart: Female Exclusion, Buddhism, and Tradition at Modern Ōminesan, Japan," PhD dissertation, University of California, Los Angeles.

DeWitt, L. E. (2018), "Island of Many Names, Island of No Name," in F. Rambelli (ed.), *The Sea and the Sacred in Japan: Aspects of Maritime Religion*, 39–52, London: Bloomsbury.

DeWitt, L. E. (2020), "World Cultural Heritage and Women's Exclusion from Sacred Sites in Japan," in P. Rots and M. Teeuwen (eds.), *Sacred Heritage in Japan*, 65–86, Abdingdon: Routledge.

Dobbins, J. (2004), *Letters of the Nun Eshinni: Images of Pure Land Buddhism in Medieval Japan*, Honolulu: University of Hawai'i Press.

Dobbins, J. C. ed. (1996), "The Legacy of Kuroda Toshio," special issue of *Japanese Journal of Religious Studies*, 23 (3 –4).

Doblmeier, M. (2015), *Chaplains: on the Front Lines of Faith*, Alexandria: Journey Films.

Dolce, L. (2010), "Nigenteki genri no gireika: Fudō, Aizen to chikara no hizō." In L. Dolce and Matsumoto I. (eds.), *Girei no chikara: Chūsei shūkyō no jissen sekai*, 159–208. Kyoto: Hōzōkan.

Dolce, L., ed. (2011), *Japanese Religions*, 4 vols., London: Sage.

Dolce, L. (2012), "The Practice of Religion in Japan: An Exploration of the State of the Field," in L. Dolce (ed.), *The Critical Discourse on Japanese Religions*, xix–lvii, London: Sage.

Dolce, L. (2015), "The Embryonic Generation of the Perfect Body: Ritual Embryology from Japanese Tantric Sources," in A. Andreeva and D. Steavu (eds.), *Transforming the Void: Embryological Discourse and Reproductive Imagery in East Asian Religions*, 253–310, Leiden: Brill.

Dolce, L., and Mitsuhashi T., eds. (2013), *Shinbutsu shūgō saikō*, Tokyo: Benseisha.

Domenig, G. (1997), "Sacred Groves in Modern Japan: Notes on the Variety and History of Shintō Shrine Forests," *Asiatische Studien: Zeitschrift der Schweizerischen Asiengesellschaft*, 51: 91–121.

Dorman, B. (2005), "Mixed Blessings Reactions of Two Japanese NRMs to Postwar Media Portrayals," *Nova Religio: The Journal of Alternative and Emergent Religions*, 9 (2): 7–32.

Dorman, B. (2012a), "Scholarly Reactions to the Aum and Waco Incidents," *Japanese Journal of Religious Studies*, 39 (1): 153–77.

Dorman, B. (2012b), *Celebrity Gods: New Religions, Media, and Authority in Occupied Japan*, Honolulu: University of Hawai'i Press.

Dorman, B., and I. Reader (2007), "Projections and Representations of Religion in Japanese Media," *Nova Religio*, 10 (3): 5–12.

Doy, G. (1998), *Materializing Art History*, Oxford: Berg.

Duara, P. (2015), *The Crisis of Global Modernity: Asian Traditions and a Sustainable Future*, Cambridge: Cambridge University Press.

DuBois, T. D. (2016), *Empire and the Meaning of Religion in Northeastern Asia: Manchuria 1900–1945*, Cambridge: Cambridge University Press.

Dwivedi, D., and S. Mohan (2020), "La comunità degli abbandonati," *Antinomie scritture e immagini*, March 8. Available online: https://antinomie.it/index.php/2020/03/12/la-comunita-degli-abbandonati/ (accessed December 15, 2020).

Earhart, H. B. (1970), "The Ideal of Nature in Japanese Religion and Its Possible Significance for Environmental Concerns," *Contemporary Religions in Japan*, 11 (1–2): 1–26.

Eco, U. (1976), *A Theory of Semiotics*, Bloomington: Indiana University Press.

Eisenberg, A. J. (2015), "Space," in D. Novak and M. Sakakeeny (eds.), *Keywords in Sound*, 193–207, Durham: Duke University Press.

Eisenstadt, S. N. (1996), *Japanese Civilization: A Comparative View*, Chicago: University of Chicago Press.

Ekuan K. (1998 [1980]), *The Aesthetics of the Japanese Lunchbox*, ed. David Stewart, Cambridge, MA: Massachussetts Institute of Technology Press.

Ellwood, R. (2008), *Introducing Japanese Religion*, New York: Routledge.

Ellwood, S. R. (1982), *Tenrikyo: A Pilgrimage Faith – The Structure and Meanings of A Modern Japanese Religion*, Tenri: Tenri University Press.

Eubanks, C. (2012), "Sympathetic Response: Verbal Arts and the Erotics of Persuasion in the Buddhist Literature of Medieval Japan," *Harvard Journal of Asiatic Studies*, 72 (1): 43–70.

Faure, B. (1991), *The Rhetoric of Immediacy*, Princeton, NJ: Princeton University Press.

Faure, B. (1998a), "The Buddhist Icon and the Modern Gaze," *Critical Inquiry*, 24 (3): 768–813.

Faure, B. (1998b), *The Red Thread: Buddhist Approaches to Sexuality*, Princeton, NJ: Princeton University Press.

Faure, B. (2003), *The Power of Denial: Buddhism, Purity and Gender*, Princeton, NJ: Princeton University Press.

Faure, B. (2016), *Gods of Medieval Japan: Volume 2, Protectors and Predators*, Honolulu: University of Hawai'i Press.

Faure, B., and Iyanaga N., eds. (2012), "The Way of Yin and Yang. Divinatory Techniques and Religious Practices," special issue of *Cahiers d'Extrême-Asie*, 21.

Feld, S. (2015), "Acoustemology," in D. Novak and M. Sakakeeny (eds.), *Keywords in Sound*, 12–21. Durham: Duke University Press.

Fenollosa, E. (1912), *Epochs of Chinese and Japanese Art*, New Hampshire: William Heinemann.

Ferguson, M. (1980), *The Aquarian Conspiracy: Personal and Social Transformation*, Los Angeles: J. P. Tarcher.

Fickle, T., A. W. Leong, and G. Ting (2019), "Sparking Joy: Religion, Representation & Marie Kondo," *The Revealer*, February 20. Available online: https://therevealer.org/sparking-joy-religion-representation-marie-kondo/ (accessed December 15, 2020).

Fisker-Nielsen, A. M. (2012), *Religion and Politics in Contemporary Japan: Soka Gakkai Youth and Komeito*, London: Routledge.

Fitzgerald, T. (2000), *The Ideology of Religious Studies*, Oxford: Oxford University Press.

Fitzgerald, T. (2007), *Religion and the Secular: Historical and Colonial Formations*, Sheffield, UK: Equinox.

Fontanille, J. (2007), *Semiotics of Discourse*, New York: Peter Lang.

Foster, M. D. (2011), "The UNESCO Effect: Confidence, Defamiliarization, and a New Element in the Discourse on a Japanese Island," *Journal of Folklore Research*, 48 (1): 63–107.

Foster, M. D. (2015), "UNESCO on the Ground: Local Perspectives on Global Policy for Intangible Cultural Heritage," *Journal of Folklore Research*, 52 (2-3): 143–56.

Fountain, P., and L. McLaughlin (2016), "Salvage and Salvation: An Introduction," *Asian Ethnology*, 75 (1): 1–28.

Four Head Temples Sacred Pilgrimage (2015), happyscience.org, April. Available online: http://www.happyscience.org.my/images/retreat2015_2.pdf (accessed December 15, 2020).

Fowler, C. (2019), "Technical Art History as Method," *Art Bulletin*, 101 (4): 8–17.

Fujii T. (1992), "Taiwan ni okeru nikkei shinshūkyō no tenkai (1)," *Tōkyō Gakugei Daigaku kiyō dai 2 bumon jinbun kagaku*, 43: 41–51.

Fujii T. (1993), "Taiwan ni okeru nikkei shinshūkyō no tenkai (2)," *Tōkyō Gakugei Daigaku kiyō dai 2 bumon jinbun kagaku*, 44: 13–22.

Fujii T. (1996), "Taiwan ni okeru nikkei shinshūkyō no tenkai (3)," *Tōkyō Gakugei Daigaku kiyō dai 2 bumon jinbun kagaku*, 47: 11–18.

Fujii T. (1997), "Taiwan ni okeru nikkei shinshūkyō no tenkai (4)," *Tōkyō Gakugei Daigaku kiyō dai 2 bumon jinbun kagaku*, 48: 47–53.

Fujii T. (2006), "Sengo Taiwan ni okeru Tenrikyō no tenkai," *Tenri Taiwan gakuhō*, 15: 63–75.

Fujii T. (2007), "Sengo Taiwan ni okeru Nihon shūkyō no tenkai," *Shūkyō to shakai*, 13: 105–27.

Fujikawa Y. (1911), *Geschichte der Medizin in Japan. Kurzgefaßte Darstellung der Entwicklung der japanischen Medizin mit besonderer Berücksichtigung der europäischen Heilkunde in Japan*, Tokyo: Kaiserlich Japanisches Unterrichtsministerium.

Fujikawa Y. (1978), *Japanese Medicine*, New York: AMS Press.

Fujikawa Y., J. Ruhräh, and Amano K. (1934), *Japanese Medicine*, New York: P.B. Hoeber.

Fujimura K. (2019), "Sekai isan kōho 'Mozu furuichi kofungun' no tennōryō kofun no imi wo meguru kattō," paper presented at the Nihon Chiri Gakkai shunki gakujutsu taikai, Tokyo. https://doi.org/10.14866/ajg.2019s.0_146 (accessed December 15, 2020).

Fujioka M. (2015), *Shōhi shakai no hen'yō to kenkō shikō: Datsubusshitsu-shugi to aimaisa taisei*, Tokyo: Harvest.

Fujita S. (2016 [1996]), "Tokenai reikan/reishi shōhō no nazo: Azamuku gawa no rinri / Azamukareru gawa no shinri", in Inoue N. (ed.), *Shakai no hen'yō to shūkyō no shosō*, 232–42, Tokyo: Iwanami Shoten.

Fujiyama M. (2011a), "Shūkyōkai no shinsai shien ga hōdō sarenai riyū 1: Hanshin / Higashi Nihon Daishinsai no hikaku yori," Tokyo: Shūkyō Jōhō Sentā (Center for Information on Religion), August 22. Available online: http://www.circam.jp/reports/02/detail/id=2007 (accessed December 5, 2020).

Fujiyama M. (2011b), "Shūkyōkai no shinsai shien ga hōdō sarenai riyū 2: Hanshin / Higashi Nihon Daishinsai no hikaku yori," Tokyo: Shūkyō Jōhō Sentā (Center for Information on Religion), August 22. Available online: http://www.circam.jp/reports/02/detail/id=2008 (accessed December 5, 2020).

Fukuhara T. (1995), *Sairei bunkashi no kenkyū*, Tokyo: Hōsei Daigaku Shuppankyoku.

Fukunaga K. (1990), *Bukkyō igaku jiten: ho, Yōga*, Tokyo: Yūzankaku Shuppan.

Fukuyama Y. (2010), "Japanese Encounters with Ajanta," in *Indo-Japanese Joint Project for the Conservation of Cultural Heritage, Archeological Survey of India*, 13–32, Tokyo: National Research Institute of Cultural Properties.

Futaki H. (1981), "'Isuramu Fukken' e no shiken: Nihonjin musurimu to shite kangaeru," *Jiyū*, 258: 61–8.

Gaitanidis, I. (2010), "Socio-Economic Aspects of the 'Spiritual Business' in Japan: A Survey among Professional Spiritual Therapists," *Religion & Society (Shūkyō to shakai)*, 16: 143–60.

Gaitanidis, I. (2011), "At the Forefront of a 'Spiritual Business': Independent Professional Spiritual Therapists of Japan," *Japan Forum*, 23 (2): 185–206.

Gaitanidis, I. (2019), "More Than Just a Photo? Aura Photography in Digital Japan," *Asian Ethnology*, 78 (1): 101–25.

Gardner, R. A. (2001), "Aum and the Media: Lost in the Cosmos and the Need to Know," in R. J. Kisala and M. R. Mullins (eds.), *Religion and Social Crisis in Japan: Understanding Japanese Society through the Aum Affair*, 133–62, New York: Palgrave.

Gardner, R. A. (2005), "Collective Memory, National Identity: Victims and Victimizers in Japan," in C. H. Badaracco (ed.), *Quoting God: How Media Shape Ideas about Religion and Culture*, 153–72, Waco: Baylor University Press.

Garrett, P. (2018), "Bad Neighbors and Monastic Influence: Border Disputes in Medieval Kii," in J. R. Goodwin and J. R. Piggott (eds.), *Land, Power, and the Sacred. The Estate System in Medieval Japan*, 377–402, Honolulu: University of Hawai'i Press.

Gauthier, F., T. Martikainen, and L. Woodhead (2013), "Introduction: Religion in Market Society," in T. Martikainen and F. Gauthier (eds.), *Religion in the Neoliberal Age: Political Economy and Modes of Governance*, 1–18, London: Routledge.

Gay, S. (2001), *The Moneylenders of Late Medieval Kyoto*, Honolulu: University of Hawai'i Press.

Gekkan Jūshoku (February 2017), *Shūkyō yosan to wakaru dentō*.

Gell, A. (1996), "Vogel's Net: Traps as Artworks and Artworks as Traps," *Journal of Material Studies*, 1 (1): 15–38.

Gell, A. (1998), *Art and Agency: An Anthropological Theory*, Oxford: Clarendon Press.

Genette, G. (1997), *Palimpsests*, Lincoln: University of Nebraska Press.

Gerhart, K., ed. (2018), *Women, Rites, and Ritual Objects in Premodern Japan*, Leiden: Brill.
Glassman, H. (2008). "At the Crossroads of Birth and Death: The Blood-Pool Hell and Postmortem Fetal Extraction," in J. I. Stone and M. N. Walter (eds.), *Death and the Afterlife in Japanese Buddhism*, Honolulu: University of Hawai'i Press.
Glassman, H. (2012), *The Face of Jizō: Image and Cult in Medieval Japanese Buddhism*, Honolulu: University of Hawai'i Press.
Gluck, C. (1985), *Japan's Modern Myths*, Princeton, NJ: Princeton University Press.
Goa, D. J., and H. G. Coward (1983), "Sacred Ritual, Sacred Language: Jōdo Shinshū Religious Forms in Transition," *Studies in Religion/Sciences Religieuses*, 12 (4): 363–79.
Goble, A. E. (2009), "Kajiwara Shōzen (1265–1337) and the Medical Silk Road: Chinese and Arabic Influences on Medieval Japanese Medicine," in A. E. Goble, K. R. Robinson, and Wakabayashi H. (eds.), *Tools of Culture: Japan's Cultural, Intellectual, Medical and Technological Contacts in East Asia, 1000–1500s*, 231–57, Ann Arbor, MI: Association for Asian Studies.
Goble, A. E. (2011), *Confluences of Medicine in Medieval Japan: Buddhist Healing, Chinese Knowledge, Islamic Formulas, and Wounds of War*, Honolulu: University of Hawai'i Press.
Godelier, M. (1999), *The Enigma of the Gift*, Chicago: University of Chicago Press.
Gorai S. (1980), *Shugendō nyūmon*, Tokyo: Kadokawa Shoten.
Gorai S., ed. (1986), *Yakushi shinkō (Minshū shūkyō-shi sōsho)*, Tokyo: Yūzankaku Shuppan.
Gorai S. (1995a), *Sabutsu hijiri: Enku to Mokujiki*, Tokyo: Kadokawa Shoten.
Gorai S. (1995b), *Shugendō no rekishi to tabi*, Tokyo: Kadokawa Shoten.
Gosden, C., and Y. Marshall (1999), "The Cultural Biography of Objects," *World Archaeology*, 31 (2): 169–78.
Gotō T., Sakaida T., Unrin'in S., and Honda D., eds. (2019), *Manga Andoroido Kannon ga Hannya Shingyō wo katarihajimeta*, Kyoto, Kamogawa.
Gould, H., T. Kohn, and M. Gibbs (2019), "Uploading the Ancestors: Experiments with Digital Buddhist Altars in Contemporary Japan," *Death Studies*, 43 (7): 456–65.
Graburn, N. (2004), "The Kyoto Tax Strike: Buddhism, Shinto, and Tourism in Japan," in E. Badone and S. R. Roseman (eds.), *Intersecting Journeys: The Anthropology of Pilgrimage and Tourism*, 125–39, Urbana: University of Illinois Press.
Graf, T. (2016), "Documenting Religious Responses to 3.11 on Film," *Asian Ethnology*, 75 (1): 203–19.
Gramlich-Oka, B. (2006), *Thinking like a Man: Tadano Makuzu (1763–1825)*, Leiden: Brill.
Grapard, A. G. (1982), "Flying Mountains and Walkers of Emptiness: Toward a Definition of Sacred Space in Japanese Religions," *History of Religions*, 21 (3): 195–221.
Grapard, A. G. (1984), "Japan's Ignored Cultural Revolution: The Separation of Shinto and Buddhist Divinities in Meiji ("Shimbutsu Bunri") and a Case Study: Tōnomine," *History of Religions*, 23 (3): 240–65.
Grapard, A. G. (1994), "Geosophia, Geognosis, and Geopiety: Orders of Significance in Japanese Representations of Space," in R. Friedland and D. Boden (eds.), *NowHere: Space, Time, and Modernity*, 372–401, Berkeley: University of California Press.
Grapard, A. G. (2000), "The Economics of Ritual Power," in J. Breen and M. Teeuwen (eds.), *Shinto in History: Ways of the Kami*, 68–94, Richmond, Surrey: Curzon.
Grapard, A. G. (2016), *Mountain Mandalas: Shugendō in Kyushu*, London: Bloomsbury.
Greimas, A. J. (1987), *On Meaning: Selected Writings in Semiotic Theory*, London: Frances Pinter.
Greimas, A. J., and J. Courtés (1982), *Semiotics and Language*, Bloomington: Indiana University Press.

Greimas, A. J., and J. Fontanille (1993), *The Semiotics of Passions*, Minneapolis: University of Minnesota Press.

Grieve, G., K. Radde-Antweiler, X. Zeiler, and C. Helland, (2018), "Editors' Introduction: Video Game Development In Asia: Voices From The Field," *gamevironments*, 8: 1–9.

Guth, C. M. E. (1996), "Kokuhō: From Dynastic to Artistic Treasure," *Cahiers d'Extrême-Asie*, 9: 313–22.

Guth, C. M. E. (2004), "Takamura Kōun and Takamura Kōtarō: On Being a Sculptor," in Takeuchi M. (ed.), *The Artist as Professional in Japan*, 152–79, Stanford, CA: Stanford University Press.

Guthmann, T. (2017), "Nationalist Circles in Japan Today: The Impossibility of Secularization," *Japan Review*, 30: 207–25.

Habito, R. L. F. (1997), "Mountains and Rivers and the Great Earth: Zen and Ecology," in M. E. Tucker and D. R. William (eds.), *Buddhism and Ecology: The Interconnection of Dharma and Deeds*, 165–75, Cambridge, MA: Harvard University Press.

Hackett, R. I. J. (2016), "Sound," in M. Stausberg and S. Engler (eds.), *The Oxford Handbook of the Study of Religion*, 316–28, Oxford: Oxford University Press.

Haga M. (1995), "Self-Development Seminars in Japan," *Japanese Journal of Religious Studies*, 22 (3–4): 283–99.

Haga M., and R. Kisala (1995), "Editor's Introduction: The New Age in Japan," *Japanese Journal of Religious Studies*, 22 (3–4): 235–47.

Hall, M., ed. (2011), *Towards World Heritage: International Origins of the Preservation Movement*, Farnham: Ashgate.

Hammad, M. (2002 [1989]), *The Privatisation of Space*, Lund: Lund University Press.

Hammad, M. (2006), *Lire l'espace, comprendre l'architecture*, Limoges: PULIM.

Hammond, P. E., and D. W. Machacek (1999), *Soka Gakkai in America: Accommodation and Conversion*, New York: Oxford University Press.

Hanegraaff, W. J., A. Faivre, R. van de Broek, and J. P. Bach (2006), *Dictionary of Gnosis & Western Esotericism*, Leiden: Brill.

Hanley, S. B. (1997), *Everyday Things in Premodern Japan: The Hidden Legacy of Material Culture*, Berkeley: University of California Press.

Happy Science, "International Retreat: Great Holy Land Pilgrimage, Japan, July 7–12, 2015," happy-science.org. Available online: http://info.happy-science.org/2015/70/ (accessed December 15, 2020).

Hara J. (2009), "Kinsei jisha kenkyū wo megutte," in Hara J., Nakayama K., Tsutsui H., and Nishigai K. (eds.), *Jisha sankei to shomin bunka*, 5–8, Tokyo: Iwata Shoin.

Harada T., Tachikawa T., and Nishida S., eds. (2017), *Supirichuariti ni yoru chiiki kachi hatsugen senryaku*, Tokyo: Gakubunsha.

Hardacre, H. (1986), *Kurozumikyō and the New Religions of Japan*, Princeton, NJ: Princeton University Press.

Hardacre, H. (2003), "After Aum: Religion and Civil Society in Japan," in F. J. Schwartz and S. J. Pharr (eds.), *The State of Civil Society in Japan*, 135–53, Cambridge: Cambridge University Press.

Hardacre, H. (2005), "Constitutional Revision and Japanese Religions," *Japanese Studies*, 25 (3): 235–47.

Hardacre, H. (2007), "Aum Shinrikyō and the Japanese Media: The Pied Piper Meets the Lamb of God," *History of Religions*, 47 (2): 171–204.

Hardacre, H. (2017), *Shinto: A History*, New York: Oxford University Press.

Harootunian, H. (2019), *Uneven Moments: Reflections of Japan's Modern History*, New York: Columbia University Press.

Harvey, D. C. (2001), "Heritage Pasts and Heritage Presents: Temporality, Meaning and the Scope of Heritage Studies," *International Journal of Heritage Studies*, 7 (4): 319–38.

Hasegawa K. (2016), *Shugendō soshiki no keisei to chiiki shakai*, Tokyo: Iwata Shoin.

Hashimoto H. (2006), *Minzoku geinō no kenkyū to iu shinwa*, Tokyo: Shinwasha.

Hashisako M. (2008), "'Sei naru mono' no anzen sōchi: 'Supikon' no Jirei kara,", *Nenpō shakaigaku ronshū*, 21: 25–36.

Hashisako M. (2014), "'Uranai, omajinai' to shōjo: Zasshi 'Mai Bāsudei' no bunseki kara," *Shūkyō kenkyū*, 88 (3): 597–619.

Hastings, S. (2001), "Review of Gender and Japanese History," *Monumenta Nipponica*, 56 (1): 102–4.

Hatakama K., and Tsuguo Y. (2016), *Sairei de yomitoku rekishi to shakai: Kasuga Wakamiya Onmatsuri no 900 nen*, Tokyo: Yamakawa Shuppansha.

Hattori T. (1955), *Heian jidai igaku no kenkyū*, Tokyo: Kuwana Bunseidō.

Hattori T. (1971), *Muromachi Azuchi Momoyama jidai igaku-shi no kenkyū*, Tokyo: Yoshikawa Kōbunkan.

Hattori T. (1978), *Edo jidai igakushi no kenkyū*, Tokyo: Yoshikawa Kōbunkan.

Hattori T. (1982 [1968]), *Bukkyō kyōten wo chūshin to shita Shaka no igaku*, Nagoya: Reimei Shobō.

Hattori T. (1988 [1945]), *Nara jidai igaku no kenkyū*, Tokyo: Yoshikawa Kōbunkan.

Hayakawa K. (1971), *Hayakawa Kōtarō zenshū*, 2 vols., Tokyo: Miraisha.

Hayashi M. (2005), *Kinsei Onmyōdō no kenkyū*, Tokyo: Yoshikawa Kōbunkan.

Hayashi M., and Koike J., eds. (2002), *Onmyōdō no kōgi*, Kyoto: Sagano Shoin.

Hayashi S. (2020), "Yōkai ni takusu 'ekibyō taisan' hannin-hangyo 'amabie' dōga ya rateāto, SNS de hirogaru neri-kiri mo tōjō," *Asahi Shinbun*, April 9. Available online: https://digital.asahi.com/articles/DA3S14436272.html?_requesturl=articles/DA3S14436272.html (accessed December 15, 2020).

Hazama J. (1974), *Nihon bukkyō no kaiten to sono kichō 2: Chūko Nihon bukkyō no kenkyū* (reprint), Tokyo: Sanseidō.

Heelas, P. (2008), *Spiritualities of Life: New Age Romanticism and Consumptive Capitalism*, Oxford: Blackwell.

Heidegger, S. (2015), "Shin Buddhism and Gender: The Discourse on Gender Discrimination and Related Reforms," *Journal of Religion in Japan*, 4 (2–3): 133–83.

Helland, C. (2000), "Online-Religion/Religion-Online and Virtual Communitas," in D. E. Cowan and J. K. Hadden (eds.), *Religion on the Internet: Research Prospects and Promises*, New York: JAI Press.

Henare, A., M. Holbraad, and S. Wastell, eds. (2007), *Thinking through Things: Theorising Artefacts Ethnographically*, London: Routledge.

Henry, T. (2014), *Assimilating Seoul: Japanese Rule and the Politics of Public Space in Colonial Korea, 1910–1945*, Berkeley: University of California Press.

Herbig, A., A. Herrmann, and A. Tyma, eds. (2014), *Beyond New Media: Discourse and Critique in a Polymediated Age*, Lanham: Lexington Books.

Hewison, R. (1989), "Heritage: An Interpretation," In D. L. Uzzell (ed.), *Heritage Interpretation. Vol. 1: The Natural and Built Environment*, 15–23, London: Belhaven Press.

Hickey, W. S. (2015), "Two Buddhisms, Three Buddhisms, and Racism," in S. A. Mitchell and Quli N. E. F. (eds.), *Buddhism beyond Borders: New Perspectives on Buddhism in the United States*, 35–56, Albany: State University of New York Press.

Higa H. (2002), "Supirichuariti hyōtei shakudo no kaihatsu to sono shinraisei datōsei no kentō," *Nihon kango kagaku kaishi*, 22 (3): 29–38.

Higuchi K. (1960), *Nihon shokumotsu-shi*, Tokyo: Shibata Shoten.

Hirafuji K. (2006), "Contemporary Mythology in Japan," International Conference on Comparative Mythology, Harvard & Peking University, Beijing, May 11–13.

Hirafuji K. (2007), "Gurōbaru-ka shakai to haipā shinwa: Konpyūtā RPG ni yoru shinwa no kaitai to saisei," in Matsumura K. and Yamanaka H. (eds.), *Gendai to shinwa*, 31–48, Tokyo: LITHON.

Hirafuji K. (2010), "A New Perspective on Japanese Myth Education," *Kokugakuin Daigaku kenkyū kaihatsu suishin kikō kiyō*, 2: 65–77.

Hirai K. (1909), *Shinrei no genshō*, Tokyo: Keiseisha.

Hirano N. (2010), "'Kindai' to iu kategorī ni okeru 'fuhen' to 'kobetsu': teate ryōhō no 80nen-shi wo jirei to shite," *Waseda Daigaku Daigakuin Bungaku Kenkyū-ka kiyō*, 56: 47–61.

Hirasawa, C., and B. Lomi, eds. (2018), "Modest Materialities: The Social Lives and Afterlives of Sacred Things in Japan" (special issue), *Japanese Journal of Religious Studies*, 45 (2): 217–26.

Hirayama N. (2015), *Hatsumōde no shakaishi: tetsudō ga unda goraku to nashonarizumu*, Tokyo: Tōkyō Daigaku Shuppankai.

Hishiki M. (2007), *Shiminteki jiyū no kiki to shūkyō: kenpō, Yasukuni Jinja, seikyō bunri*, Tokyo: Hakutakusha.

Hjarvard, S. (2008), "The Mediatization of Society: A Theory of the Media as Agents of Social and Cultural Change," *Nordicom Review*, 29 (2): 105–34.

Hobsbawm, E. J., and T. O. Ranger, eds. (1983), *The Invention of Tradition*, Cambridge: Cambridge University Press.

Honda Y. (1960), *Zuroku Nihon no minzoku geinō*, Tokyo: Mainichi Shinbunsha.

Hoover, S. (2009), "Complexities: The Case of Religious Cultures," in K. Lundby (ed.), *Mediatization: Concept, Changes, Consequences*, 123–38, New York: Peter Lang.

Hori I. (1975), *Sei to zoku no kattō*, Tokyo: Heibonsha.

Horie N. (2009), "Spirituality and the Spiritual in Japan: Translation and Transformation," *Journal of Alternative Spiritualities and New Age Studies*, 5.

Horie N. (2011), *Supirichuariti no yukue*, Tokyo: Iwanami Shoten.

Horie N. (2013a), "Datsu/han genpatsu undō no supirichuariti: ankēto to intabyū kara ukabiagaru seimeishugi," in Kokusai Shūkyō Kenkyūjo (ed.), *Gendai shūkyō 2013* 78–112, Tokyo: Akiyama Shoten.

Horie N. (2013b), "Narrow New Age and Broad Spirituality: A Comprehensive Schema and a Comparative Analysis," in S. J. Sutcliffe and I. Saelid Gilhus (eds.), *New Age Spirituality: Rethinking Religion*, 99–116, Durham: Acumen.

Horie N. (2016), "Continuing Bonds in the Tōhoku Disaster Area: Locating the Destination of Spirits," *Journal of Religion in Japan*, 5: 199–226.

Horie N. (2017a), "The Making of Power Spots: From New Age Spirituality to Shinto Spirituality," in J. Borup and M. Qvortrup Fibiger (eds.), *Eastspirit: Transnational Spirituality and Religious Circulation in East and West*, 192–217, Leiden: Brill.

Horie N. (2017b), "Shokuba supirichuariti to wa nanika," *Shūkyō kenkyū*, 91 (2): 229–54.

Horie N. (2018), *Gendai Nihon no shūkyō jijō*, Tokyo: Iwanami Shoten.

Horie N. (2019), *Poppu Supirichuariti*, Tokyo: Iwanami Shoten.

Horie N. et al. (2013), "Bukkyō būmu ni tsuite: sōryo ni yoru ippan-muke no torikumi ibento ni kansuru 2012 nen no chōsa kara," *Seishin Joshi Daigaku Gakujutsu Repository*, http://id.nii.ac.jp/1045/00000046.

Hoshino E. (1981), *Junrei: sei to zoku no genshōgaku*, Tokyo: Kōdansha Gendai shinsho.
Hoshino E. (1997), "Pilgrimage and Peregrination: Contextualizing the Saikoku Junrei and the Shikoku Henro," *Japanese Journal of Religious Studies*, 24 (3–4): 271–300.
Hosking, R. (1996), *A Dictionary of Japanese Food: Ingredients and Culture*, Rutland: Tuttle.
Hoskins, J. (1998), *Biographical Objects: How Things Tell the Stories of Peoples' Lives*, New York: Routledge.
Hospice Palliative Care Japan (2019), *Kanwa kea byōtō nyūinryō todokede juri shisetsu-sū byōshō-sū no nendo suii*. Available online: https://www.hpcj.org/what/pcu_sii.html (accessed December 4, 2020).
Hsiao H. M., Yew-Foong H., and P. Peycam, eds. (2017), *Citizens, Civil Society and Heritage-Making in Asia*, Singapore: ISEAS Publishing.
Huang Y. (2016), "Colonial Encounter and Inculturation: The Birth and Development of Tenrikyo in Taiwan," *Nova Religio: The Journal of Alternative and Emergent Religions*, 19: 78–103.
Huang Y. (2017a), "Embracing Ritual Healing: The Case of Sazuke in Tenrikyo in Contemporary Taiwan," *Journal of Religion and Health*, 56 (4): 1317–34.
Huang Y. (2017b), "Pilgrimage, Modernity, Tourism, and Nostalgia: Tenrikyō's Ojibagaeri in Post-colonial Taiwan," *Japanese Journal of Religious Studies*, 44 (2): 281–307.
Huard, P., Oya Z., and Wang M., eds. (1974), *La médecine japonaise des origines à nos jours*, Paris: Dacosta.
Hubbard, J. (1998), "Embarrassing Superstition, Doctrine, and the Study of New Religious Movements," *Journal of the American Academy of Religion*, 66 (1): 59–92.
Hur, N. (2007), *Death and Social Order in Tokugawa Japan: Buddhism, Anti-Christianity and the Danka System*, Cambridge, MA: Harvard University Asia Center.
Hurvitz, L., trans. (1976), *Scripture of the Lotus Blossom of the Fine Dharma*, New York: Columbia University Press.
Hutchinson, R., (2019), *Japanese Culture through Videogames*, New York: Routledge.
Hyōdō H. (2000), *Heike monogatari no rekishi to geinō*, Tokyo: Yoshikawa Kōbunkan.
Hyōdō H. (2009), *Biwa hōshi: 'ikai' wo kataru hitobito*, Tokyo: Iwanami Shoten.
Ichiyanagi H. (1994), "*Kokkurisan*" *to Senrigan: Nihon kindai to shinreigaku*, Tokyo: Kōdansha.
Ichiyanagi H. (1997), *Saiminjutsu no Nihon kindai*, Tokyo: Seikyūsha.
Ide E. (2017), "'Anshin no otera shindan' no tanjō hiwa (zenpen)," *Otera no mirai*, August 31, 2017. Available online: http://www.oteranomirai.or.jp/diag/ (accessed December 15, 2020).
Iida T. (2002), *Zainichi Korian no shūkyō to matsuri: Minzoku to shūkyō no shakaigaku*, Kyoto: Sekai Shisōsha.
Ikegami Y., and Nakamaki H., eds. (1996), *Jōhō jidai wa shūkyō wo kaeru ka*, Tokyo: Kōbundō.
Illouz, E. (2008), *Saving the Modern Soul: Therapy, Emotions, and the Culture of Self-Help*, Berkeley: University of California Press.
Imai N. (2009), "Anime 'Sacred Pilgrimages': The Potential for Bridging Traditional Pilgrimage and Tourism Activities through the Behavior of Visitors to Anime 'Sacred Place'—An Analysis of 'Votive Tablets' (ema) at Washinomiya Shrine, Saitama Prefecture—," trans. I. Gagne, *University of Hokkaido Cultural Resources Management Annals*, 11 (3): 1–22.
Imai N. (2012), "Fan ga nichijō wo 'seika' suru: Ema ni kakerareta negai," in Yamanaka H. (ed.), *Shūkyō to tsūrizumu: Sei naru mono no hen'yō to jizoku*, 170–89, Kyoto: Seikai Shisōsha.
Imai S. (2018), *Otaku bunka to shūkyō no rinkai*, Kyoto: Akihiro Shobō.
Imao F., and Takagi H., eds. (2017), *Sekai isan to tennōryō kofun wo tou*, Kyoto: Shibunkaku Shuppan.
Imon F. (1972), *Sezoku shakai no shūkyō*, Tokyo: Nihon Kirisutokyōdan Shuppankyoku.

Inaga S. (2009), "The Interaction of Bengali and Japanese Artistic Milieus in the First Half of the Twentieth Century (1901–1945): Rabindranath Tagore, Arai Kanpō, and Nadalal Bose," *Japan Review*, 21: 149–81.

Inose Y. (2017), "Gender and New Religions in Modern Japan," *Japanese Journal of Religious Studies*, 44 (1): 15–35.

Inose C. (2018), *Chūsei ōken no ongaku to girei*, Tokyo: Kasama Shoin.

Inoue W., Kato H., and Kasai K., eds. (2012), *Bukkyō shinrigaku kīwādo jiten*, Tokyo: Shunjūsha.

Inoue E. (1886/87), *Shinri kinshin*, Kyoto: Hōzōkan.

Inoue H. (2006), *Nihon no jinja to Shintō*, Tokyo: Azekura Shobō.

Inoue K. (1937), *Monkan Shōnin*, Kyoto: Jinbun Shoin.

Inoue N. (1985), *Umi wo watatta Nihon shūkyō: Imin shakai no uchi to soto*, Tokyo: Kōbundō.

Inoue N. (1992), "Recent Trends in the Study of Japanese New Religions," *New Religions: Contemporary Papers on Japanese Religions*, 2: 4–24.

Inoue N. (1994), "Masukomi to shinshūkyō," in Inoue N., Tsushima M., Nishiyama S., Kōmoto M., and Nakamaki H. (eds.), *Shinshūkyō jiten*, 516–19, Tokyo: Kōbundō.

Inoue N. et al., eds. (1990), *Shinshūkyō jiten*, Tokyo: Kōbundō.

Inoue N., ed. (2003), *IT jidai no shūkyō wo kangaeru*, Kyoto: Chūnichi Shinbunsha and Hōzōkan.

Inui K. (2005), "Kōsoshiki no kessoku to hatten," *Sangaku shugen*, 35: 81–98.

Ishiguro H. (2009), *Robotto to wa nani ka: hito no kokoro wo utsusu kagami*, Tokyo: Kōdansha.

Ishihara A. (1959), *Nihon no igaku: sono nagare to hatten*, Tokyo: Shibundō.

Ishihara A., and M. Blümmel, trans. (1999), *Medizinwissenschaft in Japan: Strömungen und Entwicklungen*, Düsseldorf: Triltsch.

Ishii K. (2008), *Terebi to shūkyō: Ōmu igo wo toinaosu*, Tokyo: Chūō Kōron Shinsha.

Ishii T. (1987), "The Festival of the Kasuga Wakamiya Shrine," *Theatre Research International*, 12 (2): 134–47.

Isnart, C., and N. Cerezales, eds. (2020), *The Religious Heritage Complex: Legacy, Conservation, and Christianity*, London: Bloomsbury.

Isomae J. (2014), *Religious Discourse in Modern Japan: Religion, State, and Shinto*, trans. G. Amstutz and L. E. Riggs, Leiden: Brill.

Isomae J. (2015), "Epilogue: Reimagining Early Modern Japan—Beyond the Imagined/Invented Modern Nation," in P. Nosco, J. E. Ketelaar, and Kojima Y. (eds.), *Values, Identity, and Equality in Eighteenth- and Nineteenth-Century Japan*, 323–47, Leiden: Brill.

Itō M. (2003), *Gendai shakai to supirichuariti: Gendaijin no shūkyō ishiki no shakaigakuteki tankyū*, Hiroshima: Keisuisha.

Itō M., Kashio N., and Yumiyama T., eds. (2004), *Supirichuariti no shakaigaku: gendai sekai no shūkyōsei no tankyū*, Kyoto: Sekai Shisōsha.

Itō S. (1996a), "Ise niji wo megutte: Kokinchū, Isechū to Mikkyō setsu, Shintō setsu," in Sugahara S. (ed.), *Shinbutsu shūgō shisō no tenkai*, 77–122, Tokyo: Kyūko Shoin.

Itō S. (1996b), "Tainai totsuki setsu no keisei," *Nihon bungaku*, 45 (6): 65.

Itō S. (2011), *Chūsei Tenshō Daijin shinkō no kenkyū*, Kyoto: Hōzōkan.

Ivy, M. (1995), *Discourses of the Vanishing: Modernity, Phantasm, Japan*, Chicago: University of Chicago Press.

Iwahana M. (2003), *Dewa sanzan shinkōken no kenkōzō*, Tokyo: Iwata Shoin.

Iwahara T. (1997), *Zōho kōtei Shōmyō no kenkyū*, Osaka: Tōhō Shuppan.

Iwai H., and Hiwa H. (1981), *Shinsen*, Tokyo: Hōsei Daigaku Shuppankyoku.

Iwamoto M., ed. (2013), *Sekai isan jidai no minzokugaku: gurōbaru sutandādo no juyō wo meguru Nikkan hikaku*, Tokyo: Fūkyōsha.

Iwata M. (1983), *Kagura genryū-kō*, Tokyo: Meichō Shuppan.
Iwata S. (1999), *Shōmyō no kenkyū*, Kyoto: Hōzōkan.
Iyanaga N. (2002), "Tantrism and Reactionary Ideologies in Eastern Asia: Some Hypothesis and Questions," *Cahiers d'Extrême-Asie*, 13: 1–33.
Iyanaga N. (2004), "Tachikawa-ryū to Shinjō *Juhō yōjin-shū*," *Nihon Bukkyō sōgō kenkyū*, 2: 13–31.
Iyanaga N. (2006), "Secrecy, Sex and Apocrypha: Remarks on some Paradoxical Phenomena," in B. Scheid and M. Teeuwen (eds.), *The Culture of Secrecy in Japanese Religion*, 204–28, London: Routledge.
Iyanaga N. (2010), "Mikkyō girei to 'nenzuru chikara': *Hōkyōshō* no hihanteki kentō oyobi *Juhō yōjinshū* no 'dokuro honzon girei' wo chūshin ni shite," in L. Dolce and Matsumoto I. (eds.), *Girei no chikara: chūsei shūkyō no jissen sekai*, 127–58, Tokyo: Hōzōkan.
Iyanaga N. (2011), "Tachikawa-ryū," in C. Orzech, H. Sørensen, and R K. Payne, (eds.), *Esoteric Buddhism and the Tantras in East Asia*, Handbook of Oriental Studies, Section 4, China 24, 803–15, Leiden: Brill.
Iyanaga N. (2015), "'Human Yellow' and Magical Power in Japanese Medieval Tantrism and Culture," in A. Andreeva and D. Steavu (eds.), *Transforming the Void: Embryological Discourse and Reproductive Imagery in East Asian Religions*, 344–419, Leiden: Brill.
Iyanaga N. (2018), "Iwayuru 'Tachikawa-ryū' oyobi dokuro honzon girei wo megutte," *Chisan gakuhō*, 67: 1–96.
Jaffe, R. M. (2004), "Seeking Śākyamuni: Travel and the Reconstruction of Japanese Buddhism," *Journal of Japanese Studies*, 30 (1): 65–96.
Jaffe, R. M. (2006), "Buddhist Material Culture, 'Indianism', and the Construction of Pan-Asian Buddhism in Prewar Japan," *Material Religion*, 2 (3): 266–92.
Jaffe, R. M., ed. (2010), "Editor's Introduction: Religion and the Japanese Empire," *Japanese Journal of Religious Studies*, 37 (1): 1–7.
Jaffe, R. M. (2015), *Selected Works of D.T. Suzuki, Volume I: Zen*, Berkeley: University of California Press.
Jaffe, R. M., (2019), *Seeking Śākyamuni: South Asia in the Formation of Modern Japanese Buddhism*, Chicago: University of Chicago Press.
James, S. P. (2004), *Zen Buddhism and Environmental Ethics*, Aldershot: Ashgate.
Janku, A. (2009) "'Heaven-Sent Disasters' in Late Imperial China," in C. Mauch and C. Pfister (eds.), *Natural Disasters, Cultural Responses: Case Studies toward Global Environmental History*, 233–64, Lanham, MD: Lexington Books.
Jannetta, A. B. (1987), *Epidemics and Mortality in Early Modern Japan*, Princeton, NJ: Princeton University Press.
Jin J. (2015), "Sengo no Kankoku ni okeru Nikkei shinshūkyō no tenkai: Tenrikyō no genchika wo megutte," *Kankokugaku no furontia*, 1: 42–59.
Jin J. (2016), "Kankoku ni okeru Tenrikyō no tenkai: Sengo no kattō to henbō wo megutte," *Jisedai jinbun shakai kenkyū*, 12: 181–97.
Jin J. (2018), "Kankoku ni okeru Tenrikyō no juyō: Kindaika to no kanren wo megutte," *'Reisei' to 'heiwa'*, 3: 100–12.
Jinja Honchō, ed. (2000), *'Shintō to ekoroji' shinpojiumu hōkokusho: Hābādo Daigaku Sekai Shūkyō Kenkyūjo shusai*, Tokyo: Jinja Honchō.
Jinja Shinpō (2019), "Ronsetsu," August 12.
JNEB (n.d.), "The Religious and Scholarly Eco Initiative (RSE) and the Religious Based Solar Power Generators Association." Available online: https://jneb.net/activities/buddhistenergy/rse/ (accessed December 15, 2020).

Jōdo Shinshū Honganji-ha dai 9 kai shūsei kihon chōsa jissen senta (2011), *Dai 9 kai shūsei kihon chōsa johōsho*, Kyoto: Jōdo Shinshū Honganji-ha shūmu kikakushitsu.

Joint Commission International (2020), "JCI Accredited Organizations." Available online: http://www.jointcommissioninternational.org/about-jci/jci-accredited-organizations/#q=Japan (accessed December 4, 2020).

Jokilehto, J. (2006), "World Heritage: Defining the Outstanding Universal Value," *City & Time*, 2 (2): 1–10.

Joo, R. B. (2011), "Countercurrents from the West: 'Blue-Eyed' Zen Masters, Vipassanā Meditation, and Buddhist Psychotherapy in Contemporary Korea," *Journal of the American Academy of Religion*, 79 (3): 614–38.

Jorgensen, J. (2017), "Poch'ŏn'gyo and the Imperial State: Negotiations between the Spiritual and Secular Governments," in E. Anderson (ed.), *Belief and Practice in Imperial Japan and Colonial Korea*, 177–204, Singapore: Palgrave Macmillan.

Josephson, J. Ā. (2011), "The Invention of Japanese Religions," *Religion Compass*, 5 (10): 589–97.

Josephson, J. Ā. (2012), *The Invention of Religion in Japan*, Chicago: University of Chicago Press.

Josephson-Storm, J. (2017), *The Myth of Disenchantment: Magic, Modernity, and the Birth of the Human Sciences*, Chicago: University of Chicago Press.

Joy, M. (2008), "Women's Rights in the Context of Religion," *Svensk religionshistorisk arsskrift (Swedish Yearbook of the History of Religions)* (April): 181–200.

Juergensmeyer, M. (2006), "Thinking Globally about Religion," in M. Juergensmeyer (ed.), *Oxford Handbook of Global Religions*, Oxford: Oxford University Press. Available online: https://www.oxfordhandbooks.com/view/10.1093/oxfordhb/9780195137989.001.0001/oxfordhb-9780195137989-e-1?print=pdf (accessed December 15, 2020).

Kadota T. (2013), *Junrei tsūrizumu no minzokushi: Shōhi sareru shūkyō keiken*, Tokyo: Shinwasha.

Kadota T. (2017), "Okinawa no seichi to shūkyōtekina mono no kankōteki saihakken," in Kim S., Okamoto R., and Zhou Q. (eds.), *Higashi Ajia kankōgaku: manazashi, basho, shūdan*, 127–60, Tokyo: Aki Shobō.

Kakiuchi E. (2014), "Cultural Heritage Protection System in Japan: Current Issues and Prospects for the Future," *GRIPS Discussion Paper* 14–10: 1–12.

Kalland, A. (2002), "Holism and Sustainability: Lessons from Japan," *Worldviews*, 6 (2): 145–58.

Kalland, A., and P. J. Asquith (1997), "Japanese Perceptions of Nature: Ideals and Illusions," in P. J. Asquith and A. Kalland (eds.), *Japanese Images of Nature: Cultural Perspectives*, 1–35, Surrey: Curzon Press.

Kamens, E. (1990), *The Buddhist Poetry of the Great Kamo Priestess: Daisaiin Senshi and Hosshin Wakashū*, Ann Arbor: University of Michigan Press.

Kameyama T. (2018), "Chikotsu Daie's View on the 'Inherent Existence' (*honnu*): An Analysis of Its Relationship with the 'Sangen menju'," *Journal of Indian and Buddhist Studies*, 66 (3): 1169–74.

Kameyama T. (2019), "Sangen menju to *Kanjō hikuketsu*: Nihon mikkyō-shi ni okeru Chikotsu Daie no ichi," *Shinshū bunka: Shinshū bunka kenkyūjo nenpō*, 28: 1–20.

Kanabishi K., ed. (2016), *Yobisamasareru reisei no shinsaigaku*, Tokyo: Shin'yōsha.

Kanazawa Y. and Manako A. (2013), "Kyōkaishi to kōsei katsudō," in Kasai K. and Itai M. (eds.), *Kea to shite no shūkyō*, 42–73, Tokyo: Akashi Shoten.

Kanda K. (2010), "Kumano no kankōchika no katei to sono hyōshō," *Kokuritsu minzokugaku hakubutsukan kenkyū hōkoku*, 156: 137–61.

Kaneko J. (2003), "Can Tenrikyō Transcend the Modern Family? From a Humanistic Understanding of Hinagata and Narratives of Foster Care Activities," *Japanese Journal of Religious Studies*, 30 (3–4): 243–58.

Kanzaki N. (1990), *Kankō minzokugaku e no tabi*, Tokyo: Kawade Shobō Shinsha.

Karatani K. (2012), "Buddhism and Fascism," in S. M. Lippit (ed.), *History and Repetition*, 170–209, New York: Columbia University Press.

Kasahara K. (2001), *A History of Japanese Religion*, trans. Gaynor Sekimori, Tokyo: Kosei.

Kasai K. (2016), "Introducing Chaplaincy to Japanese Society: A Religious Practice in Public Space," *Journal of Religion in Japan*, 5 (2–3): 246–62.

Kashiba-shi Nijōsan Hakubutsukan, ed. (1999), *En no Gyōja to Katsuragi shugen*, Kashiba: Kashiba-shi Nijōsan Hakubutsukan.

Kashio N., ed. (2002), *Supirichuariti wo ikiru*, Tokyo: Serika Shobō.

Katō Y. (2015), *Karā serapī to kōdō shōhi shakai no shinkō: Nyū eiji, supirichuaru, jiko keihatsu to wa nani ka?*, Tokyo: Sanga.

Katō G. (1921), *Shūkyōgaku gaisetsu*, ed. Amako T., Tokyo: Ryūbunkan.

Kato M. (2017), "Tenrikyō," *World Religions and Spirituality Project: Japanese New Religions and Minority Traditions*. Available online: https://wrldrels.org/2015/03/22/tenrikyo/ (accessed December 15, 2020).

Katsuragi M., and Ōya Y. (1988), "Kongōsan kindaishi nenpyō," in Kongōsan sōgō bunka gakujutsu chōsa iinkai (ed.), *Kongōsanki*, 181–93, Gose: Katsuragi jinja shamusho shiseki Kongōsan hōsankai.

Katsuura N. (1995), *Onna no shinjin: Tsuma ga shukke shita jidai*, Tokyo: Heibonsha.

Kawada Y., ed. (1976), *Bukkyō shisō to igaku*, Tokyo: Tōyō Tetsugaku Kenkyūjo.

Kawada Y., ed. (2013), *Bukkyō kango to kanwa kea, Seimei tetsugaku nyūmon*, Tokyo: Daisan Bunmeisha.

Kawahashi N. (2005). "Folk Religion and Its Contemporary Issues," in J. Robertson (ed.), *A Companion to the Anthropology of Japan*, 452–66, Oxford: Blackwell.

Kawahashi N. (2006), "Gender Issues in Japanese Religions," in P. L. Swanson and C. Chilson (eds.), *Nanzan Guide to Japanese religions*, 323–35, Honolulu: University of Hawai'i Press.

Kawahashi N. (2012), *Saitai Bukkyō no minzokushi: Jendā shūkyōgaku kara no apurōchi*, Kyoto: Jinbun Shoin.

Kawahashi N. (2016a), "Shinto," in N. A. Naples et al., (eds.), *The Wiley Blackwell Encyclopedia of Gender and Sexuality Studies*, vol. v, 2239–41, Hoboken, NJ: Wiley Blackwell.

Kawahashi N. (2016b), "Book Review: Barbara Ambros," *Reading Religion*, May 22, 2016. Available online: http://readingreligion.org/books/women-japanese-religions (accessed December 15, 2020).

Kawahashi N. (2017), "Women Challenging the 'Celibate' Buddhist Order: Recent Cases of Progress and Regress in the Sōtō School," *Japanese Journal of Religious Studies*, 44 (1): 55–74.

Kawahashi N., and Kuroki M. (2003), "Editor's Introduction: Feminism and Religion in Modern Japan," *Japanese Journal of Religious Studies*, 30 (3–4): 207–16.

Kawahashi N., and Kobayashi N. (2017), "Editors' Introduction: Gendering Religious Practices in Japan Multiple Voices, Multiple Strategies" (special issue), *Japanese Journal of Religious Studies*, 44 (1): 1–13.

Kawahashi N., Komatsu K., and Kuroki M. (2013), "Gendering Religious Studies: Reconstructing Religion and Gender Studies in Japan," in Z. Gross, L. Davies, and A. Diab (eds.), *Gender, Religion and Education in a Chaotic Postmodern World*, 111–23, New York: Springer.

Kawamura K. (2017), *Deguchi Nao, Onisaburō: sekai wo sushō no yō ni itasuzoyo*, Kyoto: Mineruva Shobō.

Kawamura T. (2003), "Fōkurorizumu to media hyōshō: Ishikawa-ken Monzenmachi Minazuki no Sannō matsuri wo jirei to shite," *Nihon minzokugaku*, 236: 155–71.

Kawanami H. (2013), "Implications of International Relief Work and Civil Society for Japanese Buddhists Affiliated with Traditional Denominations," in Kawanami H. and G. Samuel (eds.), *Buddhism, International Relief Work, and Civil Society*, 101–21, London: Palgrave Macmillan.

Kawano S. (2005), *Ritual Practice in Modern Japan*, Honolulu: University of Hawai'i Press.

Kawasaki N. (2015), "Chichibu sanjūyonkasho Jōrinji: anime ga egaku 'himitsu bochi' to iu seichi," in Hoshino E., Yamanaka H. and Okamoto R. (eds.), *Seichi junrei tsūrizumu*, 150–3, Tokyo: Kōbundō.

Kawasaki T., ed. (2005), *Ōmine no kuden, engi keisei ni kan suru bunkengakuteki kenkyū*, Kagaku kenkyūhi hojokin kiban kenkyū n. 14510477.

Kawase T. (2017), "State Shinto Policy in Colonial Korea," in E. Anderson (ed.), *Belief and Practice in Imperial Japan and Colonial Korea*, 19–37, Singapore: Palgrave Macmillan.

Kayaki T. (2019), *Nihon kinsei-ki ni okeru gakuritsu kenkyū: Ritsuryo shinsho wo chūshin to shite*, Tokyo: Tōhō Shoten.

Kent, E. F. (2013), *Sacred Groves and Local Gods: Religion and Environmentalism in South India*, Oxford: Oxford University Press.

Kern, M. (2000), "Religious Anxiety and Political Interest in Western Han Omen Interpretation: The Case of the Han Wudi Period (141–87 B.C.)," *Studies in Chinese History*, 10: 1–31.

Ketelaar, J. (1990), *Of Heretics and Martyrs in Meiji Japan: Buddhism and Its Persecution*, Princeton, NJ: Princeton University Press.

Kikkawa E., ed. (2013), *Kamigami no ongaku: Shintō ongaku shūsei*, Tokyo: Nihon Dentō bunka shinkō zaidan. (CD book)

Kikuchi A. (2020), "What Does It Mean to Become UNESCO Intangible Cultural Heritage? The Case of Aenokoto," in A. P. Rots and M. Teeuwen (eds.), *Sacred Heritage in Japan*, 113–33, Abingdon: Routledge.

Kim H. (2010), "A Buddhist Colonization?: A New Perspective on the Attempted Alliance of 1910 Between the Japanese Sōtōshū and the Korean Wŏnjong," *Religion Compass*, 4 (5): 287–99.

Kim H. I. (2012), *Empire of the Dharma: Korean and Japanese Buddhism, 1877–1912*, Cambridge, MA: Harvard University Asia Center.

Kim H. I. (2018), *The Korean Buddhist Empire: A Transnational History, 1910–1945*, Cambridge, MA: Harvard University Asia Center.

Kimura J. (2012), *Muromachi jidai no Onmyōdō to jisha shakai*, Tokyo: Benseisha.

Kimura T. (2018), "Masahiro Mori's Buddhist philosophy of robot." *Paladyn, Journal of Behavioral Robot* 9 (1): 72–81.

King, U. (2004), "General Introduction," in U. King and T. Beattie (eds.), *Gender, Religion and Diversity: Cross-Cultural Perspectives*, 1–10, New York: Continuum.

Kirshenblatt-Gimblett, B. (1998), *Destination Culture: Tourism, Museums, and Heritage*, Berkeley: University of California Press.

Kirshenblatt-Gimblett, B. (2006), "World Heritage and Cultural Economics," in I. Karp, C. Kratz, L. Szwaja, and T. Ybarra-Frausto (eds.), *Museum Frictions: Public Cultures/Global Transformations*, 161–202, Durham: Duke University Press.

Kisala, R. (1999), *Prophets of Peace: Pacifism and Cultural Identity in Japan's New Religions*, Honolulu: University of Hawai'i Press.

Kisala, R., and M. R. Mullins, eds. (2001), *Religion and Social Crisis in Japan: Understanding Japanese Society through the Aum Affair*, New York: Palgrave.

Kiso I. (2015), *Sekai isan bijinesu*, Tokyo: Shōgakukan.

Kitagawa, J. (1966), *Religion in Japanese History*, New York: Columbia University Press.

Klautau, O. (2012), *Kindai Nihon shisō to shite no bukkyō shigaku*, Kyoto: Hōzōkan.

Klautau, O., ed. (2014), "The Politics of Buddhist Studies in Early Twentieth-Century Japan," *Japanese Religions*, 39 (1–2): 53–70.

Klein, S. B. (1998), "*Ise Monogatari Zuinō*: An Annotated Translation," *Monumenta Nipponica*, 53 (1): 13–43.

Klein, S. B. (2002), *Allegories of Desire: Esoteric Literary Commentaries of Medieval Japan*, Cambridge, MA: Harvard University Press.

Kleine, C., and K. Triplett (2012), "Introduction to 'Religion and Healing in Japan'," *Japanese Religions* (special issue: Religion and Healing in Japan, ed. C. Kleine and K. Triplett), 37 (1–2): 1–12.

Knott, K. (2005), *The Location of Religion: A Spatial Analysis*, London: Equinox.

Knott, K. (2010), "Religion, Space, and Place: The Spatial Turn in Research on Religion," *Religion and Society: Advances in Research*, 1: 29–43.

Ko, D. (1994), *Teachers of the Inner Chambers: Women and Culture in Seventeenth-Century China*, Stanford, CA: Stanford University Press.

Ko, D. (2007), *Cinderella's Sisters: A Revisionist History of Footbinding*, Berkeley: University of California Press.

Ko, D., J. K. Haboush, and J. Piggott, eds. (2003), *Women and Confucian Cultures in Premodern China, Korea, and Japan*, Berkeley: University of California Press.

Kobayashi N. (2017), "Sacred Mountains and Women in Japan: Fighting a Romanticized Image of Female Ascetic Practitioners," *Japanese Journal of Religious Studies*, 44 (1): 103–22.

Köck, S. (2000), "The Dissemination of the Tachikawa-ryū and the Problem of Orthodox and Heretic Teachings in Shingon Buddhism," *Indo tetsugaku bukkyōgaku*, 7: 69–83.

Kodera Y. (1929), *Geijutsu to shite no kagura no kenkyū*, Minzoku geijutsu sōsho series, Tokyo: Chiheisha Shobō.

Koga, Y. (2016), *Inheritance of Loss: China, Japan, and the Political Economy of Redemption After Empire*, Chicago: University of Chicago Press.

Koike Y. (2013), "Gurōbarizēshon to serufu-supirichuariti," in Kubota H. (ed.), *Bunka sesshoku no sōzōryoku*, 207–20, Tokyo: Lithon.

Kojima Y. (1999), "'Isshin keirei koe sumite' kō: Hōmon no uta ga umidasareruba," *Kikan Bungaku*, 10 (2): 81–93.

Kojima Y. (2004), "Kyōke to iu hōe no kayō: kyōkeshi no yamanami," in Nihon kayō gakkai (ed.), *Kayō no jikū*, 275–94, Osaka: Izumi Shoin.

Kokushi Suda Masatsugu sensei henshū iinkai, ed. (1979), *Kokushi Suda Masatsugu sensei*, Tokyo: Geijutsu Seikatsusha.

Komatsu K. (2017), "Spirituality and Women in Japan," *Japanese Journal of Religious Studies*, 44 (1): 123–38.

Komine K. (2009), *Chūsei hōe bungeiron*, Tokyo: Kasama Shoin.

Komura A. (2015), *Nihon to Isuramu ga deau toki: Sono rekishi to kanōsei*, Tokyo: Gendai Shokan.

Komura A. (2016), "Nihon to Isuramu to no kankei kara miru Nihonjin no shūkyōsei ni tsuite no ichikōsatsu: Nihon no Musurimu shakai ni okeru shomondai wo tōshite miru Nihon bunka," *Journal of International Behavioral Studies*, 11: 1–19.

Komura A. (2019), *Nihon no Isuramu: Rekishi, shūkyō, bunka wo yomitoku*, Tokyo: Asahi Shinbun Shuppansha.

Kondo M. (2014), *The Life-Changing Magic of Tidying Up: The Japanese Art of Decluttering and Organizing*, New York: Ten Speed Press.

Kondo M. (2016), *Spark Joy: An Illustrated Masterclass on the Art of Organizing and Tidying Up*, New York: Ten Speed Press.

Kondō Y. (1892), *Majutsu to saiminjutsu*, Tokyo: Eisaishinshisha.

Kongōsan sōgō bunka gakujutsu chōsa iinkai, ed. (1988), *Kongōsanki*, Gose: Katsuragi jinja shamusho shiseki Kongōsan hōsankai.

Kopytoff, I. (1986), "The Cultural Biography of Things: Commoditization as Process," in A. Appadurai (ed.), *The Social Life of Things: Commodities in Cultural Perspective*, 64–91, Cambridge: Cambridge University Press.

Korsmeyer, C. (1999), *Making Sense of Taste: Food and Philosophy*, Ithaca: Cornell University Press.

Kōshitsu henshūbu, ed. (2014), *'Chinju no mori' ga sekai wo sukuu*, Tokyo: Fusōsha.

Kosoto H. (1999), *Kanpō no rekishi: Chūgoku, Nihon no dentō igaku*, Tōkyō: Taishūkan Shoten.

Koyama S. (2013), *Ryōsai Kenbo: The Educational Ideal of 'Good Wife, Wise Mother' in Modern Japan*, Leiden: Brill.

Kozinets, R. (2015), *Netnography: Redefined*, London: SAGE.

Krishnamurti, J., and B. Kon, trans. (1925), *Arakandō*, Tokyo: Buntōsha.

Kubodera T. (2000), *Supirichuaru kea nyūmon*, Tokyo: Miwa Shoten.

Kumakura I. (2002), *Nihon ryōri bunkashi*, Kyoto: Jinbun Shoin.

Kumakura I., and Ishige N. (1991), *Shoku no bigaku*, Tokyo: Domesu.

Kurita H. (2014), "Shinshū sōryo to Okada-shiki seizahō," *Kindai Bukkyō*, 21: 116–44.

Kurita H., Tsukada H., and Yoshinaga S. (2019), *Kin-gendai Nihon no minkan seishin ryōhō: fukashina/okaruto enerugī no shosō*, Tokyo: Kokusho Kankōkai.

Kuroda T. (1990), "Chinkon no keifu," in Kuroda T. (ed.), *Nihon chūsei no shakai to shūkyō*, 127–56, Tokyo: Iwanami Shoten. (English translation by A. Grapard (1996), "The World of Spirit Pacification: Issues of State and Religion," *Japanese Journal of Religious Studies*, 23 (3–4): 321–51)

Kurosaki H., ed. (2000), *Denshi nettowākingu no fukyū to shūkyō no hen'yō*, Tokyo: Kokugakuin Daigaku.

Kuwabara T. (1904), *Seishin reidō*, 3 vols., Tokyo: Kaihatsusha.

Kyōichi S. (2010), *Shakaiteki kenkō-ron*, Tokyo: Tōshindō.

Kyoto burakushi kenkyūjo, ed. (1986), *Chūsei minshū to geinō*, Kyoto: Aunsha.

Kyoto burakushi kenkyūjo, ed. (1989), *Kinsei minshū to geinō*, Kyoto: Aunsha.

Labadi, S. (2013), *UNESCO, Cultural Heritage, and Outstanding Universal Value: Value-Based Analyses of the World Heritage and Intangible Cultural Heritage Conventions*, Lanham, MD: AltaMira Press.

Laffin, C. (2013), *Rewriting Medieval Japanese Women: Politics, Personality, and Literary Production in the Life of Nun Abutsu*, Honolulu: University of Hawai'i Press.

Lancashire, A. T. (2011), *An Introduction to Japanese Folk Performing Arts*, SOAS Musicology Series, Burlington: Ashgate.

Landowski, E. (1989), "Pragmatics and Semiotics," in P. Perron and F. Collins (eds.), *Paris School Semiotics, Vol. I: Theory*, 95–103, Amsterdam: John Benjamins.

Latour, B. (1993), *We Have Never Been Modern*, Cambridge, MA: Harvard University Press.

Latour, B. (2005), *Reassembling the Social: An Introduction to Actor-Network-Theory*, New York: Oxford University Press.

Latour, B., and P. Fabbri (1977), "Pouvoir et devoir dans un article de science exacte," *Actes de la recherche en sciences sociales*, 13: 81–95.

Lau, K. (2000), *New Age Capitalism: Making Money East of Eden*, Philadelphia: University of Pennsylvania Press.

Law, J. M. (2010), "A Heady Heritage: The Shifting Biography of Kashira (Puppet Heads) as Cultural Heritage Objects in the Awaji Tradition," in C. Brumann and R. A. Cox (eds.), *Making Japanese Heritage*, 111–23, London: Routledge.
Lee D.D., ed. (2019), *Eco-Art History in East and Southeast Asia*, Newcastle upon Tyne: Cambridge Scholars.
Lee H. (2012), "Kankokujin nyūkamā no Kirisutokyōkai," in Miki H. and Sakurai Y. (eds.), *Nihon ni ikiru imintachi no shūkyō seikatsu: Nyūkamā no motarasu shūkyō tagenka*, 193–224, Kyoto: Mineruva Shobō.
Lee T. (2000), "A Political Factor in the Rise of Protestantism in Korea: Protestantism and the 1919 March First Movement," *Church History*, 69 (1): 116–42.
Lee W. B., and Sakurai Y., eds. (2011), *Ekkyō suru Nikkan shūkyō bunka: Kankoku no Nikkei shinshūkyō, Nihon no Kanryū kirisutokyō*, Sapporo: Hokkaidō Daigaku Shuppankai.
Lefebvre, H. (1991), *The Production of Space*, Oxford: Blackwell.
Leslie, C., ed. (1976), *Asian Medical Systems: A Comparative Study*, Berkeley: University of California Press.
Levinson, P. (2014), *New New Media*, 2nd ed., London: Pearson.
Lévi-Strauss, C. (1983), *Le regard éloigné*, Paris: Plon.
Lewin, B., (1994), "Activity of the Aya and Hata in the Domain of the Sacred," trans. R. K. Payne and E. Rozett, *Pacific World: Journal of the Institute of Buddhist Studies*, new series, 10 (Fall): 219–30.
Lian, M. (2019), "Religious Innovation for Sustainability: Greening God in the Japanese New Religious Movement Seichō no Ie," MA thesis, University of Oslo.
Licha, K. (2015), "Embryology in Early Modern Sōtō Zen Buddhism," in A. Andreeva and D. Steavu (eds.), *Transforming the Void: Embryological Discourse and Reproductive Imagery in East Asian Religions*, 479–521, Leiden: Brill.
Lock, M. M. (1980), *East Asian Medicine in Urban Japan: Varieties of Medical Experience*, Berkeley: University of California Press.
Lodge, O., and Fujii H., trans. (1917), *Shinrei seikatsu*, Tokyo: Dainihon Bunmei Kyōkai Jimusho.
Lofton, K. (2017), *Consuming Religion*, Chicago: University of Chicago Press.
Lomi, B. (2014), "Dharanis, Talismans, and Straw-Dolls Ritual Choreographies and Healing: Strategies of the *Rokujikyōhō* in Medieval Japan," *Japanese Journal of Religious Studies*, 41 (2): 255–304.
Lomi, B. (2018), "Ox Bezoars and the Materiality of Heian-period Therapeutics," *Japanese Journal of Religious Studies*, 45 (2): 227–68.
Long, H. (2012), *On Uneven Ground: Miyazawa Kenji and the Making of Place in Modern Japan*, Stanford, CA: Stanford University Press.
Longman, C., and T. Bradley, eds. (2015), *Interrogating Harmful Cultural Practices*, Farnham, UK: Ashgate.
Loo, T. (2020), "The Politics of Japan's Use of World Heritage: From Ratifying the World Heritage Convention to the Mozu-Furuichi Tumulus Clusters," in A. P. Rots and M. Teeuwen (eds.), *Sacred Heritage in Japan*, 18–43, Abingdon: Routledge.
Lotman, Y. M. (1990), *Universe of the Mind*, Bloomington: Indiana University Press.
Lowe, B. D. (2014), "States of 'State Buddhism': History, Religion, and Politics in Late Nineteenth- and Twentieth Century Scholarship," *Japanese Religions*, 39 (1–2): 71–93.
Lowenthal, D. (1985), *The Past Is a Foreign Country*, Cambridge: Cambridge University Press.
Lowenthal, D. (1998), *The Heritage Crusade and the Spoils of History*, London: Viking.
Lunenfeld, P., ed. (1999), *The Digital Dialectic: New Essays on New Media*, Cambridge: Massachusetts Institute of Technology Press.

Lynch, G. (2007), *The New Spirituality: An Introduction to Progressive Belief in the Twenty-First Century*, London: I.B. Tauris.

Lynch, G., J. Mitchell, and A. Strhan, eds. (2011), *Religion, Media and Culture: A Reader*, London: Routledge.

Macé, M. (2013), *Médecins et médecine dans l'histoire du Japon: aventures intellectuelles entre la Chine et l'Occident*, Collection Japon, Paris: Les Belles Lettres.

MacWilliams, M. (2006), "Techno-Ritualization: The Gohonzon Controversy on the Internet," *Heidelberg Journal of Religions on the Internet*, 2 (1): 91–122.

MacWilliams, M. (2015, August), "Rethinking Sacred Discourse in the Japanese Pilgrimage Tradition: 'Ano Hana,' Anime Pilgrimage, and the Chichibu Thirty-Four Temple Circuit" (conference paper), International Association for the History of Religions conference, Erfurt, Germany.

Madhok, S., A. Phillips, and K. Wilson, eds. (2013), *Gender, Agency and Coercion*, London: Palgrave Macmillan.

Maeda R. (2016), *Ima wo ikinuku tame no 70 nendai okaruto*, Tokyo: Kōbunsha.

Maeyama T. (1997), *Ihō ni Nihon wo matsuru: Burajiru Nikkeijin no shūkyō to esunishiti*, Tokyo: Ochanomizu Shobō.

Makdisi, U. (2008), *Artillery of Heaven: American Missionaries and the Failed Conversion of the Middle East*, Ithaca: Cornell University Press.

Maki S. (1993–2012), *Ishinpō: Maki Sachiko zenshaku seikai*, 30 vols., Tokyo: Chikuma Shobō.

Manabe S. (1999), *Jakyō Tachikawa-ryū*, Tokyo: Chikuma Shobō.

Margry, P. J. (2008), "Secular Pilgrimage: A Contradiction in Terms?," in P. J. Margry (ed.), *Shrines and Pilgrimage in the Modern World: New Itineraries into the Sacred*, 11–46, Amsterdam: Amsterdam University Press.

Marra, M. (1991), *The Aesthetics of Discontent: Politics and Reclusion in Medieval Japanese Literature*, Honolulu: University of Hawai'i Press.

Marra, M. (2002), *Japanese Hermeneutics: Current Debates on Aesthetics and Interpretation*, Honolulu: University of Hawai'i Press.

Martin, C. (2014), *Capitalizing Religion Ideology and the Opiate of the Bourgeoisie*, London: Bloomsbury.

Masuzawa, T. (2005), *The Invention of World Religions: Or, How European Universalism was Preserved in the Language of Pluralism*, Chicago: University of Chicago Press.

Matsubara M. (2010), "Maintaining a Zen Tradition in Japan: The Concrete Problem of Priest Succession," in C. Brumann and R. A. Cox (eds.), *Making Japanese Heritage*, 189–201, London: Routledge.

Matsuda A., and L. E. Mengoni, eds. (2016), *Reconsidering Heritage in East Asia*, London: Ubiquity Press.

Matsui K. (2013), *Kankō senryaku to shite no shūkyō*, Tsukuba: Tsukuba Daigaku Shuppankai.

Matsui K. (2018), "Sekai isan no sōzō to basho no shōhinka," *Chiri kūkan*, 11 (3): 177–8.

Matsui T. (2013), *Kotoba to māketingu: "Iyashi" būmu no shōhi shakaishi* (Marketing and Words: The "Healing" Boom in the History of Consumer Society), Tokyo: Sekigakusha.

Matsushita S. (1991), *Iwai no shoku bunka*, Tokyo: Tōkyō Bijutsu.

Matsutani M. (2012), *Church over Nation: Christian Missionaries and Korean Christians in Colonial Korea*, PhD dissertation, Harvard University.

Matsuzaki K. (1996), "Kibutsu no kuyō kenkyū josetsu: Kutsu no kuyō wo chūshin ni," *Mingu kenkyū*, 112: 23–32.

Mauss, M. (1990 [1950]), *The Gift*, London: Routledge.

Maxey, T. (2014), *The "Greatest Problem": Religion and State Formation in Meiji Japan*, Cambridge, MA: Harvard University Asia Center.

McCormick, M. (2012), "Mountains, Magic, and Mothers: Envisioning the Female Ascetic in a Medieval *Chigo* Tale," in G. P. A. Levine, A. Watsky, and G. Weisenfeld (eds.), *Crossing the Sea: Essays on East Asian Art in Honor of Professor Yoshiaki Shimizu*, 107–33, Princeton, NJ: P.Y. and Kinmay W. Tang Center for East Asian Art, Princeton University.

McDermott, H. T. (2006), "The Hōryūji Treasures and Early Meiji Cultural Policy," *Monumenta Nipponica*, 61 (3): 339–74.

McGuire, M. (2013), "What's at Stake in Designating Japan's Sacred Mountains as UNESCO World Heritage Sites? Shugendō Practices in the Kii Peninsula," *Japanese Journal of Religious Studies*, 40 (2): 323–54.

McLaughlin, L. (2012a), "Did Aum Change Everything? What Soka Gakkai Before, During, and After the Aum Shinrikyō Affair Tells Us About the Persistent 'Otherness' of New Religions in Japan," *Japanese Journal of Religious Studies*, 39 (1): 51–75.

McLaughlin, L. (2012b), "Sōka Gakkai in Japan," in J. Nelson and I. Prohl (eds.) *Handbook of Contemporary Japanese Religion*, 269–308, Leiden: Brill.

McLaughlin, L. (2013), "What Have Religious Groups Done After 3.11? Part 2: From Religious Mobilization to 'Spiritual Care'," *Religious Compass*, 8: 309–25.

McLaughlin, L. (2016a), "Hard Lessons Learned: Tracking Changes in Media Presentations of Religion and Religious Aid Mobilization after the 1995 and 2011 Disasters in Japan," *Asian Ethnology*, 75 (1): 105–38.

McLaughlin, L. (2016b), "Religious Responses to the 2011 Tsunami in Japan," *Oxford Handbooks Online*. Available online: https://www.oxfordhandbooks.com/view/10.1093/oxfordhb/9780199935420.001.0001/oxfordhb-9780199935420-e-29?rskey=uVMIW0&result=1 (accessed December 15, 2020).

McLaughlin, L. (2019a), "Utilizing Buddhist Resources in Post-Disaster Japan: Taniyama Yōzō, 'Vihāra Priests and Interfaith Chaplains' (2014)," in P. Salguero (ed.), *Buddhism and Medicine: An Anthology of Modern and Contemporary Sources*, 164–76, New York: Columbia University Press.

McLaughlin, L. (2019b), *Soka Gakkai's Human Revolution: The Rise of a Mimetic Nation in Modern Japan*, Honolulu: University of Hawai'i Press.

McLaughlin, L. (2020), "Japanese Religious Responses to COVID-19: A Preliminary Report," *The Asia-Pacific Journal*, 18 (9): 1–23.

McLaughlin, L., A. P. Rots, J. Thomas, and Watanabe C. (2020), "Why Scholars of Religion Must Study the Corporate Form," *Journal of the American Academy of Religion* 88 (3): 693–725.

McMullin, N. (1984), *Buddhism and the State in Sixteenth-Century Japan*, Princeton, NJ: Princeton University Press.

McMullin, N. (1988), "On Placating the Gods and Pacifying the Populace: The Case of the Gion 'Goryō' Cult," *History of Religions*, 27 (3): 270–93.

Meeks, L. (2010), *Hokkeji and the Reemergence of Female Monastic Orders in Premodern Japan*, Honolulu: University of Hawai'i Press.

Meeks, L. (2011), "The Disappearing Medium: Reassessing the Place of Miko in the Religious Landscape of Premodern Japan," *History of Religions*, 50 (3): 208–60.

Meeks, L. (2020), "Women and Buddhism in East Asian History: The Case of the Blood Bowl Sutra, Part II: Japan," *Religion Compass*, 14 (4): e12335.

Meskell, L., ed. (2015), *Global Heritage: A Reader*, Chichester, Wiley Blackwell.

Mesmer, F. A., and Suzuki M., trans. (1885), *Dōbutsu denki gairon*, Tokyo: Iwafuji Jōtarō.

Métraux, D. (2013), "Soka Gakkai International: The Global Expansion of a Japanese Buddhist Movement," *Religion Compass*, 7 (10): 423–32.
Meyer, B., and A. Moors. (2005), *Religion, Media, and the Public Sphere*, Bloomington: Indiana University Press.
Meyer, B., and M. de Witte (2013), "Heritage and the Sacred: Introduction" (special issue), *Material Religion*, 9 (3): 274–81.
Michel-Zaitsu, W. (2017), *Traditionelle Medizin in Japan von der Frühzeit bis zur Gegenwart*, München: Kiener Verlag.
Miki H., and Sakurai Y., eds. (2012) *Nihon ni ikiru imintachi no shūkyō seikatsu: Nyūkamā no motarasu shūkyō tagenka*, Kyoto: Mineruva Shobō.
Miki H., ed. (2017), *Ikyō no Nyūkamātachi: Nihon ni okeru imin to shūkyō*, Tokyo: Shinwasha.
Miki M. (2017), "A Church with Newly-Opened Doors: The Ordination of Women Priests in the Anglican-Episcopal Church of Japan," *Japanese Journal of Religious Studies*, 44 (1): 37–54.
Min K. (2005), *A History of Christian Churches in Korea*, Seoul: Yonsei University Press.
Minamoto J. (1993), "Buddhism and the Historical Construction of Sexuality in Japan," *U.S.-Japan Women's Journal*, 5: 87–115.
Misaki G. (1999), *Shikanteki bi ishiki no kenkyū*, Tokyo: Perikansha.
Mitchell, R. H. (1976), *Thought Control in Prewar Japan*, Ithaca: Cornell University Press.
Mitchell, S. A. (2016), *Buddhism in America: Global Religion, Local Contexts*, London: Bloomsbury.
Mitsuhashi T. (2007), "Bukkyō juyō to jingi shinkō no keisei: shinbutsu shūgō no genryū," *Shūkyō kenkyū*, 81 (2): 123–48.
Miura S. (1980), *Kusuri no minzokugaku: Edo jidai senryū ni miru*, Tokyo: Ken'yūkan.
Miura T. (2019), *Agents of World Renewal: The Rise of Yonaoshi Gods in Japan*, Honolulu: University of Hawai'i Press.
Miyake H. (1999), *Shugendō soshiki no kenkyū*, Tokyo: Shunjūsha.
Miyake H. (2001), *Shugendō: sono rekishi to shugyō*, Tokyo: Kōdansha.
Miyake H. (2012), *Shugendō no chiikiteki tenkai*, Tokyo: Shunjūsha.
Mizohata S. (2016), "Nippon Kaigi: Empire, Contradiction, and Japan's Future," *The Asia-Pacific Journal: Japan Focus*, 14 (21): 4.
Mizuhara G. (1923), *Jakyō Tachikawaryū no kenkyū*, Kyoto: Zenseisha Shosekibu.
Mizukami F. (2008), *Taimitsu shisō keisei no kenkyū*, Tokyo: Shunjūsha.
Mizukami F. (2017), *Nihon Tendai kyōgakuron: Taimitsu, jingi, kokatsuji*, Tokyo: Shunjūsha.
Moerman, D. M. (2005), *Localizing Paradise*, Cambridge, MA: Harvard University Press.
Moerman, D. M. (2007), "The Archeology of Anxiety," in M. Adolphson, E. Kamens, and Matsumoto S. (eds.), *Heian Japan, Centers and Peripheries*, 245–71, Honolulu: University of Hawai'i Press.
Moore, R. A. (2011), *Soldier of God: MacArthur's Attempt to Christianize Japan*, Portland, ME: MerwinAsia.
Morgan, D. (2011), "Mediation or Mediatisation: The History of Media in the Study of Religion," *Culture and Religion*, 12 (2): 137–52.
Mori M. (2005), *Shikoku henro no kingendai*, Osaka: Sōgensha.
Morioka K. (1989), *Shinshūkyō undō no tenkai katei: Kyōdan raifu saikuru ron no shiten kara*, Tokyo: Sōbunsha.
Morioka K. (1994), "Attacks on the New Religions. Risshō Kōseikai and the 'Yomiuri affair'," *Japanese Journal of Religious Studies*, 21 (2–3): 281–310.
Morita S. (2003), "Fōkurorizumu to tsūrizumu: Minzokugaku ni okeru kankō kenkyū," *Nihon minzokugaku*, 236: 92–102.
Morita T. (1925), *Gendai jiin keiei hō*, Tokyo: Nihon Shūkyō Gakkai.

Moriya T. (2000), *Yemyo Imamura: Pioneer American Buddhist*, Honolulu: Buddhist Study Center Press.

Moriyama S. (1965), *Tachikawa jakyō to sono shakaiteki haikei no kenkyū*, Tokyo: Rokuyaon.

Morris-Suzuki, T. (1998), *Reinventing Japan: Time, Space, and the Nation*, Armonk, NY: M.E. Sharpe.

Morrow, A. (2018), "Boundary Work in Japanese Religious Studies: Anesaki Masaharu on Religious Freedom and Academic Concealment," *Correspondences*, 6 (2): 117–43.

Mrazek, J., and M. Pitelka, eds. (2008), *What's the Use of Art? Asian Visual and Material Culture in Context*, Honolulu: University of Hawai'i Press.

Mross, M. (2016), "Vocalizing the Lament over the Buddha's Passing: A Study of Myōe's *Shiza kōshiki*," *Japanese Journal of Religious Studies*, 43 (1): 89–130.

Mullins, M. R. (1998), *Christianity Made in Japan: A Study of Indigenous Movements*, Honolulu: University of Hawai'i Press.

Mullins, M. R. (2001), "The Legal and Political Fallout of the Aum Affair," in R. J. Kisala and M. R. Mullins (eds.), *Religion and Social Crisis in Japan: Understanding Japanese Through the Aum Affair*, 71–86, Basingstoke: Palgrave Macmillan.

Mullins, M. R. (2017), "Religion in Occupied Japan: The Impact of SCAP's Policies on Shinto," in E. Anderson (ed.), *Belief and Practice in Imperial Japan and Colonial Korea*, 229–48, Singapore: Palgrave Macmillan.

Murakami F. (1988), "Incest and Rebirth in *Kojiki*," *Monumenta Nipponica*, 43 (4): 455–63.

Murakami S. (1958), *Kindai minshū shūkyōshi no kenkyū*, Kyoto: Hōzōkan.

Murata H. (2003). "Spiritual Pain and Its Care in Patients with Terminal Cancer: Construction of a Conceptual Framework by Philosophical Approach," *Palliative and Supportive Care*, 1: 15–21.

Murayama S. (1981), *Nihon Onmyōdō-shi sōsetsu*, Tokyo: Hanawa Shobō.

Murayama S. et al., eds. (1991–3), *Onmyōdō sōsho*, 4 vols. Tokyo: Meicho Shuppan.

Mytera (n.d.). Available online: http://mytera.jp/ (accessed December 15, 2020).

Nagamura M. (2018), "*Hijiri* and Temple Monks: Contrasting Styles of Estate Management," trans. J. R. Goodwin, in J. R. Goodwin and J. R. Piggott (eds.), *Land, Power, and the Sacred: The Estate System in Medieval Japan*, 197–210, Honolulu: University of Hawai'i Press.

Nagaoka T. (2015), *Shinshūkyō to sōryokusen: Kyōso ikō wo ikiru*, Nagoya: Nagoya Daigaku Shuppankai.

Nakai, K. (2017), "Senjika no Jōchi Daigaku: Katorikku-kei daigaku wa ikani 'Nihon seishin' to torikonda ka," in Ejima N. et al., (eds.), *Senji Nihon no daigaku to shūkyō*, 83–130, Kyoto: Hōzōkan.

Nakajima M. (2010), "Shinto Deities that Crossed the Sea: Japan's 'Overseas Shrines', 1868–1945," *Japanese Journal of Religious Studies*, 37 (1): 21–46.

Nakajima S. (2008), *Okonai: Kokoku matsuri no katachi*, Tokyo: INAX.

Nakajima S., and Uno H. (1999), *Kamigami no shukō: Kokoku no shinsen*, Kyoto: Shibunkaku.

Nakajima T. (2005), *Otera no keizaigaku*, Tokyo: Tōyō Keizai Shinpōsha.

Nakajima T. (2013), *Ketsumeidan jiken*, Tokyo: Bungei Shunjū.

Nakajima T. (2017a), "Nachuraru to nashonaru: Nipponshugi ni katamuku ayausa," *Chūnichi shinbun*, March 28. Available online: https://www.chunichi.co.jp/article/feature/rondan/list/CK2017032802000265.html (accessed May 11, 2020).

Nakajima T. (2017b), *Shinran to Nihonshugi*, Tokyo: Shinchōsha.

Nakamaki H. (1989), *Nihon shūkyō to Nikkei shūkyō no kenkyū*, Tokyo: Tōsui Shōbō.

Nakamaki H. (2003), *Japanese Religions at Home and Abroad: Anthropological Perspectives*, London: Routledge.

Nakamura H. (1975), *Oshakasama*, Tokyo: Tamagawa Daigaku Shuppanbu.

Nakamura I. (2001), *Saishi to kugi*, Kyoto: Hōzōkan.

Nakamura K. (1983), "Women and Religion in Japan: Introductory Remarks," *Japanese Journal of Religious Studies*, 10 (2–3): 115–21.

Nakamura K. (1990), "Tainai totsuki no zu no shisōshi," *Iwate Daigaku kyōiku gakubu nenpō*, 50 (1): 23–36.

Nakano E. (2002), *Katsuragi no mine to shugen no michi*, Kyoto: Nakanishiya Shuppan.

Nakano H. (1994), *Mōsō*, Tokyo: Meicho Shuppan.

Nakayama K. (2009), "Minzokugaku kara mita Nihon no jisha sankei bunka,' in Hara J., Nakayama K., Tsutsui H., and Nishigai K. (eds.), *Jisha sankei to shomin bunka*, 37–64, Tokyo: Iwata Shoin.

Namiki E. (2019), "Honda Chikaatsu's Spiritual Learning as a Means of Bringing Blessings and Guiding the Nation," *Journal of Religion in Japan*, 7 (3): 276–305.

Nejima S. (2014), *Musurimu NGO: Shinkō to shakai hōshi katsudō*, Tokyo: Yamakawa Shuppansha.

Nelson, J. (2013), *Experimental Buddhism: Innovation and Activism in Contemporary Japan*, Honolulu: University of Hawai'i Press.

Nelson, J. (2017), "Diasporic Buddhisms and Convert Communities," in M. Jerryson (ed.), *The Oxford Handbook of Contemporary Buddhism*, Oxford: Oxford University Press. Available online: https://www.oxfordhandbooks.com/view/10.1093/oxfordhb/9780199362387.001.0001/oxfordhb-9780199362387-e-21 (accessed December 15, 2020).

Nelson, S. (2001), "Fujiwara no Takamichi sōshiki hossoku yōi jōjō ni okeru kōshiki no ongakuteki kōsei," in Fukushima K. (ed.), *Chūsei ongakushi ronsō*, 215–77, Osaka: Izumi Shoin.

Nihon Hosupisu Kanwa Kea Kyōkai (2016), "Kanwa kea byōto nyūin-ryō todokede juri shisetsusū, byōshōsū no nendo suii." Available online: http://www.hpcj.org/what/pcu_sii.html (accessed December 15, 2020).

Nihon Seisansei Honbu Yoka Sōken (2017), *Rejā hakusho 2016*, Tokyo: Japan Productivity Center.

Nihon shisō taikei (NST) (1970–82), 67 vols., Tokyo: Iwanami Shoten.

Nihon Toransupāsonaru Shinrigaku Seishin Igakukai, Andō O., and Yuasa Y., eds. (2007), *Supirichuariti no shinrigaku: Kokoro no jidai no gakumon wo motomete*, Osaka: Seseragi Shuppan.

Nihon'yanagi K. (1994), *Bukkyō igaku gaiyō*, Kyoto: Hōzōkan.

Nihon'yanagi K. (1997), "Nihon mikkyō igaku to yakubutsugaku," in Yamada K. and Kuriyama S. (eds.), *Rekishi no naka no yamai to igaku*, 545–66, Kyoto: Kokusai Nihon Bunka Kenkyū Sentā; Shibundō.

Niino K. (2014), *Kōdō Bukkyō to tairiku fukyō: jūgonen sensō-ki no shūkyō to kokka*, Tokyo: Shakai Hyōronsha.

Ninnaji konbyōshi kozōshi kenkyūkai, ed. (1995), *Shukaku hosshinnō no girei sekai: Ninnaji-zō konbyōshi kozōshi no kenkyū*, Tokyo: Benseisha.

Nishiguchi J. (1987), *Onna no chikara: kodai no josei to Bukkyō*, Tokyo: Heibonsha.

Nishihira T. (2003), "Supirichuariti saikō: rubi to shite no supirichuariti," *Japanese Journal of Transpersonal Psychology/Psychiatry*, 4 (1): 8–16.

Nishiyama S. (1988), "Gendai no shūkyō undō: 'Rei=jutsu' kei shinshūkyō no ryūkō to 'futatsu no kindaika'," in Ōmura E. and Nishiyama S. (eds.), *Gendaijin no shūkyō*, 169–210, Tokyo: Yūhikaku.

Niwano N. (1976), *Buddhism for Today: A Modern Interpretation of the Threefold Lotus Sutra*, Tokyo: Kōsei.

Noguchi K. (2014), *Sekai isan ni sarete Fujisan wa naite iru*, Tokyo: PHP Kenkyūjo.
Nomura F., and Usui A., eds. (1996), *Josei to kyōdan: Nihon shūkyō no omote to ura*, Tokyo: Hābesutosha.
Nomura I. (1996), "Kamakura jidai no komonjo ni miru josei no bukkyō ninshiki-shinsei," *Bukkyōshi kenkyū*, 39: 1–30.
Nomura I. (2004), *Bukkyō to onna no seishinshi*, Tokyo: Yoshikawa Kōbunkan.
Norbeck, E., and M. Lock, eds. (1987), *Health, Illness, and Medical Care in Japan: Cultural and Social Dimensions*, Honolulu: University of Hawaiʻi Press.
Nosu K. (1939), *Life of Buddha in Frescoes: Mulagandhakuti vihara*, Sarnath, Benares: The Maha Bodhi Society.
O'Brien, D. M. (with Yasuo Ohkoshi) (1996), *To Dream of Dreams: Religious Freedom and Constitutional Politics in Postwar Japan*, Honolulu: University of Hawaiʻi Press.
Oak, S. (2015), *The Making of Korean Christianity: Protestant Encounters with Korean Religions, 1876–1915*, Waco: Baylor University Press.
Obadia, L., and D. C. Wood (2011), "Economics and Religion, Economics in Religion, Economics of Religion: Reopening the Grounds for Anthropology?," *Research in Economic Anthropology*, 31 (1): xiii–xxxvii.
Obeysekere, G. (2006), "Thinking Globally about Buddhism," in M. Juergensmeyer (ed.), *The Oxford Handbook of Global Religions*, Oxford: Oxford University Press.
Obinata D. (1965), *Bukkyō igaku no kenkyū*, Tokyo: Kasama Shobō.
Ochi M. (2010), "Joshi shinshoku: josei no shinshutsu wa aru no ka," in Ishii K. (ed.), *Shintō wa doko e iku ka*, 93–112, Tokyo: Perikansha.
Ochi M. (2015), "Shinshoku kōkeisha mondai ni okeru josei no yakuwari ni tsuite no ichikōsatsu," *Jinja Honchō sōgō kenkyūjo kiyō*, 20: 45–79.
Odaira M. (2003), "Jingi saishi ni okeru josei shinshoku no hataraki: kodai jingū-kyūchū no saishi kara," *Gakushūin Daigaku jinbun kagaku ronshū*, 12: 41–67.
Odaira M. (2009), *Josei shinshoku no kindai: jingi girei, gyōsei ni okeru saishisha no kenkyū*, Tokyo: Perikansha.
Odaira M. (2015), "Modern Women's Education and Religion in Yamaguchi Prefecture: The Publication of *Joshidō*," *Journal of Religion in Japan*, 4 (2–3): 212–39.
Odo F. (2004), *No Sword to Bury: Japanese Americans in Hawaiʻi During World War II*, Asian American History and Culture, Philadelphia: Temple University Press.
Ogawa T. (2014), *Chūsei Nihon no shinwa, moji, shintai*, Tokyo: Shinwasha.
Ogawara M., ed. (2010), *Kindai Nihon no bukkyōsha: Ajia taiken to shisō no hen'yō*, Tokyo: Keiō Gijuku Daigaku Shuppankai.
Ogi M. (1997), *Nihon kodai ongakushi ron*, Tokyo: Yoshikawa Kōbunkan.
Ogihara-Schuck, E. (2014), *Miyazaki's Animism Abroad: The Reception of Japanese Religious Themes by American and German Audiences*, Jefferson: McFarland.
Oguri S. (2007), *Puchi shugyō*, Tokyo: Gentōsha.
Ohnuki-Tierney, E. (1984), *Illness and Culture in Contemporary Japan*, Cambridge: Cambridge University Press.
Okabe T. (2012), "Kōza kaisetsu e no omoi: Rinshō shūkyōshi kōsō ni tsuite (1)," *Jissen shūkyōgaku kifu kōza nyūsuretā*, 1: 2–4.
Okai H. (2016), "Isurāmu sekai to Zainichi Musurimu," in Nishihara K. and Tarumoto H. (eds.), *Gendaijin no kokusai shakaigaku nyūmon: Toransunashonarizumu to iu shiten*, 146–63, Tokyo: Yūhikaku.
Okamoto R. (2015), *Seichi tsūrizumu: sekai isan kara anime no butai made*, Tokyo: Chūkō Shinsho.

Okamoto T. (2015), "Otaku Tourism and the Anime Pilgrimage Phenomenon in Japan," *Japan Forum*, 27 (1): 12–36.

Okamoto T. (2018), *Anime seichi junrei no kankō shakaigaku: Kontentsu tsūrizumu no media komyunikēshon bunseki*, Tokyo: Hōritsu Bunkasha.

Okazaki M. (2010), "Chrysanthemum and Christianity: Education and Religion in Occupied Japan, 1945–1952," *Pacific Historical Review*, 79 (3): 393–417.

Okazaki M. (2012), *Nihon senryō to shūkyō kaikaku*, Tokyo: Gakujutsu Shuppankai.

Okiura K. (1991), *Take no minzokushi: Nippon bunka no shinsō wo saguru*, Tokyo: Iwanami Shoten.

Okiura K. (2016), *Okiura Kazumitsu chosakushū: Yūgei hyōhaku ni ikiru hitobito*, Tokyo: Gendai Shokan.

Okuyama N. (2016), "Meiji Indo ryūgakusei: Sono Minami Ajia taiken o megutte," *Indogaku Bukkyōgaku Kenkyū*, 64 (2): 1042–1035.

Okuzawa Y. (1997), "Me'ishi-tachi no hidensho to ryūha," in Yamada K. and Kuriyama S. (eds.), *Rekishi no naka no yamai to igaku*, 195–228, Kyoto: Kokusai Nihon Bunka Kenkyū Sentā.

Ono S. (2019), *Gagaku no kosumorojī: Nihon shūkyō shikigaku no seishinshi*, Kyoto: Hōzōkan.

Orikuchi S. (1995), *Orikuchi Shinobu zenshū*, 3 vols., Tokyo: Chūō Koronsha.

Otera Oyatsu Club (n.d.) "Otera oyatsu kurabu to ha." Available online: https://otera-oyatsu.club/ (accessed December 15, 2020).

Otsuka Y. (1976), "Chinese Traditional Medicine in Japan," in C. Leslie (ed.), *Asian Medical Systems*, 322–40, Berkeley: University of California Press.

Ōkawa S. (1942), *Kaikyō gairon*, Tokyo: Keiō Shobō.

Ōkubo M. (1991), "The Acceptance of Nichiren Shōshū Sōka Gakkai in Mexico," *Japanese Journal of Religious Studies*, 18 (2–3): 189–211.

Ōmi T. (2016), "Kindai Bukkyō to Shintō," *Gendai shisō*, 45 (2): 282–9.

Ōmichi H. (2017), *Itako no tanjō: masumedia to shūkyō bunka*, Tokyo: Kōbundo.

Ōshima A. (2007), *Mukei minzoku bunkazai no hogo: Mukei bunka isan hogo jōyaku ni mukete*, Tokyo: Iwata Shoin.

Ōtani E. (2001), *Kindai Nihon no Nichirenshugi undō*, Kyoto: Hōzōkan.

Ōtani E., Kikuchi A. and Nagaoka T. (2018), *Nihon shūkyō no kīwādo: kindaishugi wo koete*, Tokyo: Keiō Gijuku Daigaku Shuppankai.

Ōuchi F. (1996), "Shintō gyōhō ni okeru koe no gihō: 'Dewa Sanzan jinja rensei shugyō dōjō' no baai," *Gunma kenritsu joshidaigaku kiyō*, 17: 35–46.

Ōuchi F. (2005), "'Koe' to 'oto' ga tsukuru girei: Shugendō girei no oto kūkan," in Shimazu K. and Kitamura M. (eds.), *Sennen no shugen: Haguro yamabushi no sekai*, 128–53, Tokyo: Shinjuku Shobō.

Ōuchi F. (2009), "The Lotus Repentance Liturgy of Shugendō: Identification from Vocal Arts," *Cahiers d'Extrême-Asie*, 18: 169–93.

Ōuchi F. (2016), *Bukkyō no koe no waza: satori no shintaisei*, Kyoto: Hōzōkan.

Ōuchi F. (2018), "Musical Instruments for the Sea-God Ebisu: The Mythological System of Miho Shrine and Its Performative Power," in F. Rambelli (ed.), *The Sea and the Sacred in Japan: Aspects of Maritime Religion*, 53–63, London: Bloomsbury.

Padoan, T. (2019), "Reassembling the Lucky Gods: Pilgrim Economies, Tourists, and Local Communities in Global Tokyo," special issue on "Pilgrimages, Ontologies, and Subjectivities," *Journeys (Berghahn Books)*, 20 (1): 75–97.

Padoan, T. (forthcoming), "On the Semiotics of Space in the Study of Religions: Theoretical Perspectives and Methodological Challenges," in T. Poder and J. Van Boom (eds.), *Sign,

Method, and the Sacred: New Directions in Semiotic Methodologies for the Study of Religion, Berlin: De Gruyter.

Padoan, T., and F. Sedda (2018), "Sémiotique et anthropologie," in A. Biglari and N. Roelens (eds.), *Sémiotique en interface*, 37–68, Paris: Kimé.

Pae S. (2007), *Tonari no kamisama*, Tokyo: Fusōsha.

Pai, H. I. (2013), *Heritage Management in Korea and Japan: The Politics of Antiquity and Identity*, Seattle: University of Washington Press.

Palmer, S. J. (1994), *Moon Sisters, Krishna Mothers, Rajneesh Lovers: Women's Roles in New Religions*, Syracuse: Syracuse University Press.

Pandey, R. (1998), *Writing and Renunciation in Medieval Japan: The Works of Poet-Priest Kamo no Chōmei*, Ann Arbor: University of Michigan Press.

Park, A. (2015), *Building a Heaven on Earth: Religion, Activism, and Protest in Japanese Occupied Korea*, Honolulu: University of Hawai'i Press.

Park, C. (2003), *Protestantism and Politics in Korea*, Seattle: University of Washington Press.

Parkes, G. (2010), "Body-Mind and Buddha-Nature: Dōgen's Deeper Ecology," in J. W. Heisig and R. Raud (eds.), *Frontiers of Japanese Philosophy 7: Classical Japanese Philosophy*, 122–47, Nagoya: Nanzan Institute for Religion and Culture.

Parry, R. L. (2017), *Ghosts of the Tsunami: Death and Life in Japan's Disaster Zone*, New York: Farrar, Straus & Giroux.

Pedersen, P. (1995), "Nature, Religion and Cultural Identity: The Religious Environmentalist Paradigm," in O. Bruun and A. Kalland (eds.), *Asian Perceptions of Nature: A Critical Approach*, 258–76, Surrey: Curzon Press.

Pereira, R. A. (2008), "The Transplantation of Sōka Gakkai to Brazil: Building 'the Closest Organization to the Heart of Ikeda-Sensei'," *Japanese Journal of Religious Studies*, 35 (1): 95–113.

Pew Research Center (2009), *Mapping the Global Muslim Population: A Report on the Size and Distribution of the World's Muslim Population*, October. Available online: http://www.npdata.be/Data/Godsdienst/PEW/Pew-Muslimpopulation-2009.pdf#search=%27Mapping+the+Global+Muslims+Population%27 (accessed December 15, 2020).

Pfister, U. (2008), "Origins and Principles of World Art History," in K. Zijlmans and W. van Damme (eds.), *World Art Studies: Exploring Concepts and Approaches*, 69–89, London: Valiz.

Pflugfelder, G. M. (1999), *Cartographies of Desire: Male-Male Sexuality in Japanese Discourse, 1600–1950*, Berkeley: University of California Press.

Plate, B. S. (2003), *Representing Religion in World Cinema: Film Making, Myth Making, Culture Making*, New York: Palgrave Macmillan.

Poggendorf, L. (2019), "Nihon no shinseina kankō supotto: futatsu no chomeina jinja to sono chihō kankō seisaku no hikaku," *Gendai shakai kenkyū*, 16: 111–21.

Porath, O. (2019), "The Flower of Dharma Nature: Sexual Consecration and Amalgamation in Medieval Japanese Buddhism," PhD dissertation, University of California, Santa Barbara.

Porcu, E. (2014), "Pop Religion in Japan: Buddhist Temples, Icons, and Branding," *Journal of Religion and Popular Culture*, 26 (2): 157–72.

Porcu, E. (2018), "Japanese Buddhisms in Diaspora," in *Oxford Research Encyclopedia, Religion*, Oxford: Oxford University Press.

Powell, M., and Anesaki M. (1990), *Health Care in Japan*, London: Routledge.

Prison Reformation Conference (2003), "The Statement of Prison Reformation Conference, Ministry of Justice." Available online: http://www.moj.go.jp/content/000001612.pdf (accessed December 15, 2020).

Prohl, I. (2007), "The Spiritual World: Aspects of New Age in Japan," in J. Lewis and D. Kemp (eds.), *Handbook of New Age*, 359–74, Leiden: Brill.

Prohl, I., and J. Nelson (2012), *Handbook of Contemporary Japanese Religions*, Leiden: Brill.

Pye, M., ed. (2013), *Interactions with Japanese Buddhism: Explorations and Viewpoints in Twentieth-Century Kyōto*, Sheffield, UK: Equinox.

Quinter, D. (2015), *From Outcasts to Emperors: Shingon Ritsu and the Mañjuśrī Cult in Medieval Japan*, Leiden: Brill.

Quli N. (2008), "Multiple Buddhist Modernisms: *Jhāna* in Convert Theravāda," *Pacific World: Journal of the Institute of Buddhist Studies*, third series, 10: 225–49.

Rambelli, F. (2001), *Vegetal Buddhas: Ideological Effects of Japanese Buddhist Doctrines on the Salvation of Inanimate Beings*, Kyoto: Italian School of East Asian Studies.

Rambelli, F. (2004), "'Just Behave as You Like': Radical Amida Cults and Popular Religiosity in Premodern Japan," in R. K. Payne and K. K. Tanaka (eds.), *Approaching the Land of Bliss: Religious Praxis in the Cult of Amitabha*, 169–201, Honolulu: University of Hawai'i Press.

Rambelli, F. (2007), *Buddhist Materiality: A Cultural History of Objects in Japanese Buddhism*, Stanford, CA: Stanford University Press.

Rambelli, F. (2013), *A Buddhist Theory of Semiotics*, London: Bloomsbury.

Rambelli, F. (2014), "Gods, Dragons, Catfish, and Godzilla: Fragments for a History of Religious Views on Natural Disasters in Japan," in R. Starrs (ed.), *When the Tsunami Came to Shore: Culture and Disaster in Japan*, 50–69, Leiden: Brill.

Rambelli, F. (2017), "Shintō aruiwa shinifian no shūkyō," *Gendai shisō*, 45 (2): 230–9.

Rambelli, F., ed. (2018), *The Sea and the Sacred in Japan: Aspects of Maritime Religion*, London: Bloomsbury.

Rambelli, F., ed. (2019), *Spirits and Animism in Contemporary Japan: The Invisible Empire*, London: Bloomsbury.

Rappo, G. (2014), "Un Ritualiste à la Cour Impériale: Itinéraire et Ouvre du Moine Monkan (1278–1357)," PhD dissertation, Université de Genève.

Rappo, G. (2017), *Rhétoriques de L'hérésie dans le Japon médiéval et moderne: Le moine Monkan (1278–1357) et sa réputation posthume*, Paris: L'Harmattan.

Rappo, G. (2020), "'Deviant Teachings': The Tachikawa Lineage as a Moving Concept in Japanese Buddhism," *Japanese Journal of Religious Studies*, 47 (1): 103–33.

Rath, E., and S. Assmann, eds. (2010), *Japanese Foodways: Past and Present*, Champaign: University of Illinois Press.

Rath, E. (2010), *Food and Fantasy in Early Modern Japan*, Berkeley: University of California Press.

Rausch, F. (2014), "Dying for Heaven: Persecution, Martyrdom, and Family in the Early Korean Catholic Church," in C. Horlyck and M. Pettid (eds.), *Death, Mourning, and the Afterlife in Korea: Ancient to Modern Times*, 213–36, Honolulu: University of Hawai'i Press.

Ravitch, F. S. (2013), "The Shinto Shrine Cases, Religion Culture or Both—The Japanese Supreme Court and One Hundred Years of Establishment of Religion Cases," *Brigham Young University Law Review*, 505: 505–20.

Ravitch, F. S. (2014), "The Japanese Prime Minister's Visits to the Yasukuni Shrine Analyzed under Articles 20 and 89 of the Japanese Constitution," *Michigan State International Law Review*, 22 (3): 713–30.

Reader, I. (1990), "The Animism Renaissance Reconsidered: An Urgent Response to Dr. Yasuda," *Nichibunken Newsletter*, 6: 14–6.

Reader, I. (1991), *Religion in Contemporary Japan*, Basingstoke: Macmillan.

Reader, I. (2000), *Religious Violence in Contemporary Japan: the Case of Aum Shinrikyō*, Honolulu: University of Hawai'i Press.

Reader, I. (2005), "Chronologies, Commonalities and Alternative Status in Japanese New Religious Movements," *Nova Religio: The Journal of Alternative and Emergent Religions*, 9 (2): 84–96.

Reader, I. (2006), "Positively Promoting Pilgrimage: Media Representations of Pilgrimage in Japan," *Nova Religio: The Journal of Alternative and Emergent Religions*, 10 (3): 13–31.

Reader, I. (2011), "Buddhism in Crisis? Institutional Decline in Modern Japan, " *Buddhist Studies Review*, 28 (2): 233–63.

Reader, I. (2012), "Secularisation R.I.P? Nonsense! The 'Rush Hour Away from the Gods' and the Decline of Religion in Contemporary Japan," *Journal of Religion in Japan*, 1 (1): 7–36.

Reader, I. (2014), *Pilgrimage in the Marketplace*, New York: Routledge.

Reader, I. (2015a), "Japanese Studies of Pilgrimage," in D. Albera and J. Eade (eds.), *International Perspectives on Pilgrimage: Itineraries, Gaps and Obstacles*, 23–46, New York: Routledge.

Reader, I. (2015b), "Japanese New Religions: An Overview," *World Religions and Spirituality Project: Japanese New Religions and Minority Traditions*. Available online: https://wrldrels.org/wp-content/uploads/2017/03/Japenese-New-Religions.WRSP_.pdf (accessed December 15, 2020).

Reader, I., and G. J. Tanabe (1998), *Practically Religious: Worldly Benefits and the Common Religion of Japan*, Honolulu: University of Hawai'i Press.

Reader, I., and P. L. Swanson (1997), "Editors' Introduction: Pilgrimage in the Japanese Religious Tradition," *Japanese Journal of Religious Studies*, 24 (3–4): 225–70.

Reader, I., and T. Walter, eds. (1993), *Pilgrimage in Popular Culture*, Basingstoke, UK: Macmillan.

Reid, D. (1991), "Religion and State in Japan, 1965–1990," in D. Reid (ed.), *New Wine: The Cultural Shaping of Japanese Christianity*, 33–58, Berkeley: Asian Humanities Press.

Reinders, E. (2016), *The Moral Narratives of Hayao Miyazaki*, Jefferson: McFarland.

Richey, J. L. (2015), *Daoism in Japan: Chinese Traditions and Their Influence on Japanese Religious Culture*, London: Routledge.

Richie, D. (1985), *A Taste of Japan*, Tokyo: Kodansha International.

Riedel, F. (2019), "Atmosphere," in J. Slaby and C. von Scheve (eds.), *Affective Societies: Key Concepts*, 85–95, London: Routledge.

Robertson, J. (1984), "Sexy Rice. Plant Gender, Farm Manuals, and Grass-Roots Nativism," *Monumenta Nipponica*, 39 (3): 233–260.

Robertson, J. (2007), "Robo Sapiens Japanicus: Humanoid Robots and the Posthuman Family," *Critical Asian Studies*, 39 (3): 369–98.

Rocha, C. (2000), "Zen Buddhism in Brazil: Japanese or Brazilian?," *Journal of Global Buddhism*, 1: 31–55.

Rocha, C. (2004), "Zazen or Not Zazen?: The Predicament of Sōtōshū's *Kaikyōshi* in Brazil," *Japanese Journal of Religious Studies*, 31 (1): 163–84.

Rocha, C. (2008), "All Roads Come from Zen: Busshinji as a Reference to Buddhism," *Japanese Journal of Religious Studies*, 35 (1): 81–94.

Roof, W. C. (2001), *Spiritual Marketplace: Baby Boomers and the Remaking of American Religion*, Princeton, NJ: Princeton University Press.

Rosler, M., C. W. Bynum, N. Eaton, M. A. Holly, A. Jones, M. Kelly, R. Kelsey, A. LaGamma, M. Wagner, O. Watson, and T. Weddigen (2013), "Notes from the Field: Materiality," *Art Bulletin*, 95 (1): 10–37.

Rosner, E. (1989), *Medizingeschichte Japans*, Leiden: Brill.

Roth Al Eid, C. (2014), "Au-delà des montagnes: une étude de l'imaginaire religieux dans le Japon médiéval à travers le Shozan engi (fin XII siécle)," PhD dissertation no. L. 814, Geneva: Université de Genève.

Rots, A. P. (2015), "Sacred Forests, Sacred Nation: The Shinto Environmentalist Paradigm and the Rediscovery of *Chinju no Mori*," *Japanese Journal of Religious Studies*, 42 (2): 205–33.

Rots, A. P. (2017a), "Public Shrine Forests? Shinto, Immanence, and Discursive Secularization," *Japan Review*, 30: 179–205.

Rots, A. P. (2017b), *Shinto, Nature and Ideology in Contemporary Japan: Making Sacred Forests*, London: Bloomsbury.

Rots, A. P. (2019a), "'This Is Not a Powerspot': Heritage Tourism, Sacred Space, and Conflicts of Authority at Sēfa Utaki," *Asian Ethnology*, 78 (1): 155–80.

Rots, A. P. (2019b), 'Trees of Tension: Re-Making Nature in Post-Disaster Tohoku', *Japan Forum*, https://doi.org/10.1080/09555803.2019.1628087.

Rots, A. P., and M. Teeuwen, eds. (2017), "Formations of the Secular in Japan," special issue, *Japan Review*, 30.

Rots, A. P., and M. Teeuwen, eds. (2020), *Sacred Heritage in Japan*, Abingdon: Routledge.

Rowe, M. M. (2011), *Bonds of the Dead: Temples, Burial, and the Transformation of Contemporary Japanese Buddhism*, Chicago: University of Chicago Press.

Rowe, M. M (2017), "Charting Known Territory: Female Buddhist Priests," *Japanese Journal of Religious Studies*, 44 (1): 75–101.

Ruch, B. ed. (2002), *Engendering Faith: Women and Buddhism in Premodern Japan*, Ann Arbor: University of Michigan Center for Japanese Studies.

Russell, J. E. (2011), "Cultural Property and Heritage in Japan," PhD thesis, SOAS, University of London.

Saitō H. (2014), *Onmyōjitachi no Nihon-shi*, Tokyo: Kadokawa Shuppansha.

Saitō R. (1915), *Ōcho jidai no Onmyōdō*, Tokyo: Kōin Sōsho Kankōsho.

Sakai S. (1982), *Nihon no iryō-shi*, Tokyo: Tōkyō Shoseki.

Sakurai Y. (2009), *Rei to kane: Supirichuaru bijinesu no kōzō*, Tokyo: Shinchōsha.

Sakurai Y. (2011), "Economic Aspects," in B. Staemmler and U. Dehn (eds.), *Establishing the Revolutionary: An Introduction to New Religions in Japan*, 89–118, Zurich: LIT.

Salguero, C. P., ed. (2017), *Buddhism and Medicine: An Anthology of Premodern Sources*, New York: Columbia University Press.

Salguero, C. P., ed. (2019), *Buddhism and Medicine: An Anthology of Modern and Contemporary Voices*, New York: Columbia University Press.

Sanford, J. H. (1991), "The Abominable Tachikawa Skull Ritual," *Monumenta Nipponica*, 46 (1): 1–20.

Sanford, J. H. (2006), "Breath of Life: The Esoteric Nembutsu," in R. K. Payne (ed.), *Tantric Buddhism in East Asia*: 161–89, Boston: Wisdom Publications.

Sangaku shugen gakkai, ed. (2003), *Sangaku shugen, 32: Shugen to geinō tokushū*, Tokyo: Sangaku shugen gakkai.

Sasamoto M. (1990), *Chūsei no oto, kinsei no oto: kane no oto no musubu sekai*, Tokyo: Meicho Shuppan.

Sassen, S. (2001), "Spatialities and Temporalities of the Global: Elements for a Theorization," in A. Appadurai (ed.), *Globalization*, 260–78, Durham: Duke University Press.

Sataki Y. (2009), *"Sekai isan" no shinjitsu: kajōna kitai, ōinaru gokai*, Tokyo: Shōdensha.

Satō H. (2004), *Henro to junrei no shakaigaku*, Kyoto: Jinbun Shoin.

Satō M. (2007), "Shinbutsu kakuri no yōin wo meguru kōsatsu," *Shūkyō kenkyū*, 81 (2):149–73.

Saunders, R. (2019), "Secrets of the Sedgwick Shōtoku," *Impressions*, 40: 83–98.

Saunders, R. (2020), "Amabie: The Japanese Monster Going Viral," *BBC*, April 23. Available online: http://www.bbc.com/travel/story/20200422-amabie-the-japanese-monster-going-viral (accessed December 15, 2020).

Sawada, J. T. (2004), *Practical Pursuits: Religion, Politics, and Personal Cultivation in Nineteenth-Century Japan*, Honolulu: University of Hawai'i Press.

Sawada, J. T. (2006), "Sexual Relations as Religious Practice in the Late Tokugawa Period: Fujidō," *Journal of Japanese Studies*, 32 (2): 341–66.

Scheid, B., and K. Nakai, eds. (2013), *Kami Ways in Nationalist Territory: Shinto Studies in Prewar Japan and the West*, Vienna: Austrian Academy of Sciences.

Schmid, A. (2000), "Colonialism and the 'Korea Problem' in the Historiography of Modern Japan: A Review Article," *Journal of Asian Studies*, 59 (4): 951–76.

Schmidt-Hori, S. (2009), "The New Lady-in-Waiting Is a *Chigo*: Sexual Fluidity and Dual Transvestism in a Medieval Buddhist Acolyte Tale," *Japanese Language and Literature*, 43 (2): 383–423.

Schopen, G. (1997), *Bones, Stones, and Buddhist Monks: Collected Papers on the Archaeology, Epigraphy, and Texts of Monastic Buddhism in India*, Honolulu: University of Hawai'i Press.

Schrimpf, M. (2015), "Children of Buddha, or Caretakers of Women? Self-Understandings of Ordained Buddhist Women in Contemporary Japan," *Journal of Religion in Japan*, 4 (2–3): 184–211.

Schrimpf, M. (2018), "Medical Discourses and Practices in Contemporary Japanese Religions," in D. Lüddeckens and M. Schrimpf (eds.), *Medicine – Religion – Spirituality: Global Perspectives on Traditional, Complementary, and Alternative Healing*, 57–90, Bielefeld: transcript Verlag.

Schrimpf, M., and M. Sonntag (2015), "Introduction," *Journal of Religion in Japan*, 4 (2–3): 95–104.

Scott, J. W. (1986), "Gender: A Useful Category of Historical Analysis," *The American Historical Review*, 91 (5): 1053–75.

Screech, T. (2009 [1999]), *Sex and the Floating World: Erotic Images in Japan, 1700–1820*, London: Reaktion.

Sedgwick, E. K. (2003), *Touching Feeling: Affect, Pedagogy, and Performativity*, Durham: Duke University Press.

Segawa H. (1918), *Kaikyō*, Tokyo: Keiseisha.

Seguchi N. (2006), "'Kagakuteki' hoshu-ha gensetsu wo kiru! Seibutsu jinruigaku no shiten kara mita seisa ronsō," in Ueno C. et. al. (eds.), *Bakkurasshu!: naze jendā furī wa tatakareta no ka*, 310–39, Tokyo: Sōfūsha.

Seikyō Kankei wo Tadasu Kai, ed. (2001), *Zoku jitsurei ni manabu: Seikyō bunri—Konna koto made kenpō ihan?* Tokyo: Tendensha.

Seikyō Kankei wo Tadasu Kai, ed. (2013), *Shin jitsurei ni manabu: Seikyō bunri—Konna koto made kenpō ihan?* Tokyo: Tendensha.

Sekai Kyūseikyō Izunome (2008), "Ecology Movement." Available online: http://www.izunome.jp/en/action/envi/ (accessed December 15, 2020).

Sekiguchi M. (2009), *Shugendō kyōdan seiritsu-shi: Tōzanha wo tsūjite*, Tokyo: Bensei shuppan.

Sekimori, G. (2005), "Paper Fowl and Wooden Fish: The Separation of Kami and Buddha Worship in Haguro Shugendō, 1869–1875," *Japanese Journal of Religious Studies*, 32 (2): 197–234.

Sekimori, G. (2015), "Foetal Buddhahood: From Theory to Practice – Embryological Symbolism in the Autumn Peak Ritual of Haguro Shugendō," in A. Andreeva and D. Steavu (eds.), *Transforming the Void: Embryological Discourse and Reproductive Imagery in East Asian Religions*, 522–58, Leiden: Brill.

Sen S., Kidosaka I., and Miyata N. (1993), *Gyōji to shikitari no ryōri*, Tokyo: Fujin Gahōsha.

Shaner, D. E. (1989), "The Japanese Experience of Nature," in J. B. Callicott and R. T. Ames (eds.), *Nature in Asian Traditions of Thought: Essays in Environmental Philosophy*, 163–82, Albany: State University of New York Press.

Sharf, R. (1995), "Sanbōkyōdan: Zen and the Way of the New Religions," *Japanese Journal of Religious Studies*, 22 (3–4): 417–58.

Sharf, R. (1999), "On the Allure of Buddhist Relics," *Representations*, 66: 75–99.

Sharf, R. (2001), "Introduction: Prolegomenon to the Study of Japanese Buddhist Icons," in R. Sharf and E. H. Sharf (eds.), *Living Images: Japanese Buddhist Icons in Context*, 1–18, Stanford, CA: Stanford University Press.

Sharf, R. (2005), "Ritual," in D. Lopez (ed.), *Critical Terms for Buddhist Studies*, 245–70, Chicago: University of Chicago Press.

Sharf, R., and E. Sharf, eds. (2001), *Living Images: Japanese Buddhist Images in Context*, Stanford, CA: Stanford University Press.

Sheldrake, P. (2012), *Spirituality: A Very Short Introduction*, Oxford: Oxford University Press.

Shiba K. (2004), *Dokyōdō no kenkyū*, Tokyo: Kazama Shobō.

Shibata K. (2010), *Nihon mikkyō jinbutsu jiten: Daigo sōden tanbo*, Tokyo: Kokusho Kankōkai.

Shibue E. (1910), *Kaseikai no jikkyō: Kōshinjutsu kikō*, Tokyo: Daigakukan.

Shibue T. (1909), *Shinshō oyobi sono jikken*, Tokyo: Naigai Shuppan Kyōkai.

Shigeta S. (2004), *Onmyōji to kizoku shakai*, Tokyo: Yoshikawa Kōbunkan.

Shimazono S. (1977), "Kamigakari kara tasuke made: Tenrikyō no hassei josetsu," *Komazawa Daigaku Bukkyō gakubu ronshū*, 8: 209–26.

Shimazono S. (1978), "Utagai to shinkō no aida: Nakayama Miki no tasuke no shinkō no kigen," *Tsukuba Daigaku tetsugaku shisō gaku kei ronshū*, 3: 117–45.

Shimazono S. (1979), "The Living Kami Idea in the New Religions of Japan," *Japanese Journal of Religious Studies*, 6 (3): 389–412.

Shimazono S. (1980), "Tenrikyō kenkyūshi shiron: Hassei katei ni tsuite," *Nihon shūkyōshi kenkyū nenpō*, 3: 70–103.

Shimazono S. (1991), "The Expansion of Japan's New Religions into Foreign Cultures," *Japanese Journal of Religious Studies*, 18 (2–3):105–32.

Shimazono S. (1992), *Shinshin shūkyō to shūkyō būmu* (series Iwanami Bukkuretto 237), Tokyo: Iwanami Shoten.

Shimazono S. (1996), "Sei no shōgyōka: Shūkyōteki hōshi to zōyo no hen'yō," in Ishii K. and Shimazono S. (eds.), *Shōhi sareru 'shūkyō'*, Tokyo: Shunjūsha.

Shimazono S. (1998), "The Commercialization of the Sacred: The Structural Evolution of Religious Communities in Japan," *Social Science Japan Journal*, 1 (2): 181–98.

Shimazono S. (2001), *Posuto modan no shinshūkyō: Gendai Nihon no seishin jōkyō no teiryū*, Tokyo: Tōkyōdō.

Shimazono S. (2004), *From Salvation to Spirituality: Popular Religious Movements in Modern Japan*, Melbourne: Trans Pacific Press.

Shimazono S. (2006 [1992]), *Gendai kyūsai shūkyō-ron*, Tokyo: Seikyūsha.

Shimazono S. (2007a [1996]), *Seishin sekai no yukue: Shūkyō, kindai, supirichuariti*, Tokyo: Akiyama Shoten.

Shimazono S. (2007b), *Supirichuaritī no kōryū: shin reisei bunka to sono shūhen*, Tokyo: Iwanami Shoten.

Shimazono S. (2010), *Kokka Shintō to Nihonjin*, Tokyo: Iwanami Shoten.

Shimazono S. (2012), *Gendai shūkyō to supirichuariti*, Tokyo: Kōbundō.

Shimazono S., and Tsuruoka Y., eds. (2004), *"Shūkyō" saikō*, Tokyo: Perikansha.

Shimizu M. (1998), *Dokyō no sekai; nōdoku no tanjō*, Tokyo: Yoshikawa Kōbunkan.

Shindō K. (2017), "Kangen ongi no Tendai shisō," *Tendai gakuhō*, 60: 183–91.

Shinjō T. (1982), *Shaji sankei no shakai keizaishiteki kenkyū*, Tokyo: Hanawa Shobō.

Shinmura T. (2013), *Nihon bukkyō no iryōshi*, Tokyo: Hōsei Daigaku Shuppankyoku.

Shinno T. (1980), *Tabi no naka no shūkyō*, Tokyo: NHK Books.
Shinno T. (1991), *Nihon yugyō shūkyōron*, Tokyo: Yoshikawa Kōbunkan.
Shinno T., ed. (1996), *Nihon no junrei: junrei no kōzō to chihō junrei*, Tokyo: Yūzankaku.
Shintei zōho kokushi taikei (KT) (1964–7), 66 vols., Tokyo : Yoshikawa Kōbunkan.
Shirahase T. (2016), "Tabunka kyōsei no ninaite to shite no Katorikku," in Research Center for Christianity and Culture (ed.), *Gendai bunka to Kirisutokyō*, 99–133, Tokyo: Kirisuto Shinbunsha.
Shirahase T., and Takahashi N. (2012), "Nihon ni okeru Katorikku kyōkai to nyūkamā," in Miki H. and Sakurai Y. (eds.), *Nihon ni ikiru imintachi no shūkyō seikatsu: Nyukamā no motarasu shūkyō tagenka*, 55–86, Kyoto: Mineruva shobō.
Shoji, R. (2003), "'Buddhism in Syncretic Shape': Lessons of Shingon in Brazil," *Journal of Global Buddhism*, 4: 70–107.
Shūkyō shakaigaku no kai, ed. (1986), *Ikoma no kamigami: Gendai toshi no minzoku shūkyō* , Tokyo: Sōgensha.
Silva, K. D., and N. Kamal Chapagain, eds. (2013), *Asian Heritage Management: Contexts, Concerns, and Prospects*, Abingdon: Routledge.
Silverman, H., ed. (2011), *Contested Cultural Heritage: Religion, Nationalism, Erasure, and Exclusion in a Global World*, New York: Springer.
Simpson, E. B. (2018), "An Empress at Sea: Sea Deities and Divine Union in the Legend of Empress Jingū," in F. Rambelli (ed.), *The Sea and the Sacred in Japan: Aspects of Maritime Religion*, 65–78, London: Bloomsbury.
Singer, J. (2012), "Head Monk of Kyoto Temple Takes Buddhism into the Community," *The Japan Times*, May 26. Available online: https://www.japantimes.co.jp/community/2012/05/26/general/head-monk-of-kyoto-temple-takes-buddhism-into-the-community/#.Wczv9VtL9aQ (accessed December 15, 2020).
Slaby, J., and R. Mühlhoff (2019), "Affect," in J. Slaby and C. von Scheve (eds.), *Affective Societies: Key Concepts*, 27–41, London: Routledge.
Smith, H. (1972), "Tao Now: An Ecological Testament," in I. G. Barbour (ed.), *Earth Might be Fair: Reflections on Ethics, Religion, and Ecology*, 62–82, Englewood Cliffs: Prentice-Hall.
Smith, J. Z. (1987), *To Take Place: Toward Theory in Ritual*, Chicago: University of Chicago Press.
Smith, L. (2006), *Uses of Heritage*, London: Routledge.
Smith, L. (2011), *All Heritage is Intangible: Critical Heritage Studies and Museums*, Amsterdam: Reinwardt Academie, Amsterdamse Hogeschool voor de Kunsten.
Smits, G. (2012), "Conduits of Power: What the Origins of Japan's Earthquake Catfish Reveal about Religious Geography," *Japan Review*, 24: 41–65.
Soja, E. W. (1996), *Thirdspace: Journeys to Los Angeles and Other Real-and-Imagined Places*, Malden: Blackwell.
Sonntag, M. (2015), "Christian Feminism in Japan: 'Minoritarian' and 'Majoritarian' Tendencies, Struggles for Self-Assertion, and Multiple 'Lines of Flight'," *Journal of Religion in Japan*, 4 (2–3): 105–32.
Sonoda K. (1988), *Health and Illness in Changing Japanese Society*, Tokyo: Tokyo University Press.
Sonoda K. (2010), *Shakaiteki kenkō-ron*, Tokyo: Tōshindō.
Sonoda M. (2000), "Shinto and the Natural Environment," in J. Breen and M. Teeuwen (eds.), *Shinto in History: Ways of the Kami*, 32–46, Richmond: Curzon Press.
Sonoda M. (2020), "Our Way of Shrines and Shinto: Asking about What Shrine Shinto Will Look Like in the Future, the Local Shrine Grove – a Shinto Model of One's Home, and Shrines and Shinto," in M. MacWilliams and Okuyama M. (eds.), *Defining Shinto: A Reader*, 323–34, New York: Routledge.

Sōyō (2001), *Shintō wo shiru hon: chinju no mori no kamigami e no shinkō no sho*, Tokyo: Ōfū.
Staemmler, B. (2009), *Chinkon kishin: Mediated Spirit Possession in Japanese New Religions*, Münster: LIT Verlag.
Staemmler B., and U. Dehn (2011), "Introduction," in B. Staemmler and U. Dehn (eds.), *Establishing the Revolutionary: An Introduction to New Religions in Japan*, 1–9, Zurich: LIT.
Stalker, N. (2008), *Prophet Motive: Deguchi Onisaburō, Oomoto and the Rise of New Religions in Imperial Japan*, Honolulu: University of Hawai'i Press.
Statistics Bureau, Ministry of Internal Affairs and Communications, Japan (2018), *Japan Statistical Yearbook*. Available online: https://www.stat.go.jp/english/data/nenkan/67nenkan/index.html (accessed December 15, 2020)
Steenstrup, C. (1996), *A History of Law in Japan Until 1868*, Leiden: E.J. Brill.
Stein, J. (2017), "Hawayo Takata and the Circulatory Development of Reiki in the Twentieth Century North Pacific," PhD dissertation, University of Toronto, Canada.
Sterne, J. (2003), *The Audible Past: Cultural Origins of Sound Reproduction*, Durham: Duke University Press.
Stolow, J. (2005), "Religion and/as Media," *Theory, Culture & Society*, 22 (4): 119–45.
Stolz, R. (2014), *Bad Water: Nature, Pollution, and Politics in Japan, 1870–1950*, Durham: Duke University Press.
Stone, J. (2014), "A Vast and Grave Task: Interwar Buddhist Studies as an Expression of Japan's Envisioned Global Role," in J. T. Riner (ed.), *Culture and Identity: Japanese Intellectuals during the Interwar Years*, 217–33, Princeton, NJ: Princeton University Press.
Stone, J. I. (1999), *Original Enlightenment and the Transformation of Medieval Japanese Buddhism*, Honolulu: University of Hawai'i Press.
Stone, J. I. (2007), "The Secret Art of Dying: Exoteric Deathbed Practices in Heian Japan," in B. J. Cuevas and J. I. Stone (eds.), *The Buddhist Dead: Practices, Discourses, Representations*, 134–74, Honolulu: University of Hawai'i Press.
Strickmann, M. (2002), *Chinese Magical Medicine*, Stanford, CA: Stanford University Press.
Suda M. (1936), "Kaikyō mondai (Kan)," *Dai-Asia*, 4 (3): 56–60.
Sueki F. (2019), "Kōzanji-bon *Juhō yōjinshū* to Tachikawa-ryū," *Kōzanji tenseki monjo sōgō chōsadan kenkyū hōkoku ronshū*, 39: 22–8.
Suga N., (2010), "Pawāsupotto to shite no jinja," in Ishii K. (ed.), *Shintō wa doko e ikuka*, 232–52, Tokyo: Perikansha.
Suga K. (2010), "A Concept of 'Overseas Shinto Shrines': A Pantheistic Attempt by Ogasawara Shōzō and Its Limitations," *Japanese Journal of Religious Studies*, 37 (1): 47–74.
Sugahara, S. (ed.) (1994), *Chūsei shintō shisō keisei katei no kenkyū* (Kenkyū seika hōkokusho). Tokyo: Waseda Daigaku.
Sugano F. (1987), "'Ongaku kōshiki' no rōei: sho rōeifu to no kanren ni oite," *Nihon kayō kenkyū*, 26: 75–83.
Sugano F. (1990), "*Ongaku kōshiki* to seigaku," *Nihon kayō kenkyū*, 30: 56–63.
Sunakawa H. (2001), *Heike monogatari no keisei to biwa hōshi*, Tokyo: Ōfūsha.
Suzuki D. T. (1959), *Zen and Japanese Culture*, Princeton, NJ: Princeton University Press.
Suzuki D. T. (trans. N. Waddell) (1988), *Japanese Spirituality*, Santa Barbara, CA: Greenwood.
Suzuki I. (2002), *Onmyōdō: jujutsu to kijin no sekai*, Tokyo: Kōdansha.
Suzuki M. (2001), *Kami to hotoke no minzoku*, Tokyo: Yoshikawa Kōbunkan.
Suzuki M. (2014), "Denshō wo jizoku saseru mono to wa nani ka: Hiba Kōjin kagura no baai," *Kokuritsu rekishi minzoku hakubutsukan kenkyū hōkoku*, 186: 1–29.
Suzuki M. (2015a), "Minzoku geijutsu no hakken: Kodera Yūkichi no gakumon to sono igi," *Meiji seitoku kinen gakkai kiyō*, 52: 24–43.

Suzuki M. (2015b), *Sangaku shinkō: Nihon bunka no kontei wo saguru*, Tokyo: Chūō Kōron Shinsha.
Suzuki M. (2018a), "Sangaku shinkō," in Ōtani E., Kikuchi A., and Nagaoka T. (eds.), *Nihon shūkyōshi no kīwādo: kindaishugi wo koete*, 100–6, Tokyo: Keiō Gijuku Daigaku Shuppankai.
Suzuki M. (2018b), *Kumano to kagura: Seichi no kongenteki chikara wo motomete*, Tokyo: Heibonsha.
Suzuki N. (2010), *Shinkyō jiyū no jiken shi: Nihon no kirisutokyō wo megutte*, Tokyo: Oriensu shūkyō kenkyūjo.
Suzuki R., and Takagi H., eds. (2002), *Bunkazai to kindai Nihon*, Tokyo: Yamakawa Shuppansha.
Suzuki, S. (2003–4), *Shugendō rekishi minzoku ronshū*, 3 vols., Kyoto: Hōzōkan.
Swanson, P. L. and C. Chilson, eds. (2006), *Nanzan Guide to Japanese Religions* (Nanzan Library of Asian Religion and Culture), Honolulu: University of Hawai'i Press.
Swedenborg, E. and Suzuki D.T., trans. (1910), *Tenkai to jigoku*, Tokyo: Eikoku Rondon Swedenborg Kyōkai.
Taira M. (1992), *Nihon chūsei no shakai to Bukkyō*, Tokyo: Hanawa Shobō.
Taira T. (2009), "The Problem of Capitalism in the Scholarship on Contemporary Spirituality," in T. Ahlbäck (ed.), *Postmodern Spirituality*, 230–44, Turku: Donner Institute.
Taishō shinshū daizōkyō (T) (1924–32), 100 vols. Tōkyō: Issaikyō kankōkai and Daizō Shuppan.
Takahashi G. (1903), *Shinpi tetsugaku*, Tokyo: Shōbundō.
Takahashi G. (1910), *Shin tetsugaku no shokō*, Tokyo: Maekawa Bun'eikaku.
Takahashi G. (1921), *Yūmei no reiteki kōtsū*, Tokyo: Kōbundō Shoten.
Takahashi N. (2014), *Imin, shūkyō, kokoku: Kingendai Hawai ni okeru Nikkei shūkyō no keiken*, Tokyo: Hābesutosha.
Takahashi N., Shirahase T., and Hoshino S. eds. (2018), *Gendai Nihon no shūkyō to tabunka kyōsei*, Tokyo: Akashi Shoten.
Takahashi R. (1960), *Oshakasama*, Tokyo: Daidōsha.
Takahashi T. (2005), *Yasukuni mondai*, Tokyo: Chikuma Shinsho.
Takaki Y. (2013), "Gurīfu kea kenkyūjo no sōsetsu keii to ayumi," *Gurīfu kea*, 1: 3–13.
Takano T., ed. (2000), *Minkan ni ikiru shūkyōsha*, Tokyo: Yoshikawa Kōbunkan.
Takatori M. (1979), *Shintō no seiritsu*, Tokyo: Heibonsha.
Takeda D. (1991), "The Fall of Renmonkyō, and Its Place in the History of Meiji-Period Religions," trans. Norman Havens, in Inoue N. (ed.), *New Religions: Contemporary Papers in Japanese Religion*, vol. 2, 25–57, Tokyo: Kokugakuin University.
Takeda K., and Futoyu Y. (2006), "Conceptual Structure of Spirituality in Elderly Japanese," *Kawasaki iryō fukushi gakkai-shi*, 16 (1): 53–66.
Takeuchi N. (1903), *Saiminjutsu jizai*, Tokyo: Daigakukan.
Tamamuro F. (1977), *Shinbutsu bunri*, Tokyo: Kyoikusha.
Tamamuro F. (1999), *Sōshiki to danka*, Tokyo: Yoshikawa Kōbunkan.
Tamura T. (1998), "How Does the Internet Work for Religions Based in Japan?," *Nenpō Tsukuba Shakaigaku*, 10: 21–38.
Tanabe, G. J. (2005), "Grafting Identity: The Hawaiian Branches of the Bodhi Tree," in L. Learman (ed.), *Buddhist Missionaries in the Era of Globalization*, 77–100, Honolulu: University of Hawai'i Press.
Tanabe, G., ed. (1999), *Religions of Japan in Practice*, Princeton, NJ: Princeton University Press.
Tanabe, G. J., and W. J. Tanabe (2012), *Japanese Buddhist Temples in Hawai'i: An Illustrated Guide*, Honolulu: University of Hawai'i Press.
Tanada H. (2015), *Nihon no mosuku: Zainichi Musurimu no shakai katsudō*, Tokyo: Yamakawa Shuppansha.
Tanaka T. (1993), *Gehō to aihō no chūsei*, Tokyo: Sunagoya Shobō.
Tanaka T. (1997), *Seiai no chūsei*, Kyoto: Yōsensha.

Tanaka T. (2004), *Seichi wo meguru hito to michi*, Tokyo: Iwata Shoin.

Tanaka T. (2011), *Shintō no chikara*, Tokyo: Gakken.

Tani D. (2007), "Jimintō shinkenpō sōan wo kenshō suru," in Katorikku Chūō Kyōgikai (ed.), *Shinkyō no jiyū to seikyō bunri*, 17–44, Tokyo: Katorikku Chūō Kyōgikai.

Taniguchi M., and Taniguchi J. (2010), '*Mori no naka' e iku: Hito to shizen no chōwa no tame ni Seichō no Ie ga kangaeta koto*, Tokyo: Nihon Kyōbunsha.

Taniyama Y. (2012), "The Vihāra Movement: Buddhist Chaplaincy and Social Welfare," in J. S. Watts and Tomatsu Y. (eds.), *Buddhist Care for the Dying and Bereaved*, 75–94, Somerville: Wisdom Publications.

Tankha, B. (2017), "Exploring Asia, Reforming Japan: Ōtani Kōzui and Itō Chūta," in S. Esenbel (ed.), *Japan on the Silk Road: Encounters and Perspectives of Politics and Culture in Eurasia*, 155–80, Leiden: Brill.

Tashiro S. (2006), "*Kangen ongi* no oto sekai: gakuri ga tsukuru oto no kosumorojī," *Nihon bungaku*, 55 (6): 25–36.

Taylor, C. (2007), *A Secular Age*, Cambridge, MA: Harvard University Press.

Tazaki M., Matsuda M., and Nakane Y., eds. (2001), "Supirichuariti ni kansuru shitsuteki chōsa no kokoromi: kenkō oyobi QOL no gainen no karami no naka de," *Nihon iji shinpō*, 4036: 24–32.

Teeuwen, M. (2007), "Comparative Perspectives on the Emergence of *Jindō* and *Shintō*," *Bulletin of the School of Oriental and African Studies*, 70 (2): 373–402.

Teeuwen, M. (2010), "Jindō to Shintō no seiritsu ni tsuite no hikaku kōsastu," *Nihon shisōshi kenkyū*, 42: 1–34.

Teeuwen, M. (2013), "Early Modern Secularism? Views of Religion in *Seji kenbunroku* (1816)," *Japan Review*, 25: 3–19.

Teeuwen, M. (2017), "Shintō no gainenka to yūtopia," *Gendai shisō*, 45 (2): 8–14.

Teeuwen, M. (2020), "Kyoto's Gion Float Parade as Intangible Heritage: Between Culture, Religion, and Faith," in A. P. Rots and M. Teeuwen (eds.), *Sacred Heritage in Japan*, 134–58, Abingdon: Routledge.

Teeuwen, M., and A. P. Rots (2020), "Heritage-Making and the Transformation of Religion in Modern Japan," in A. P. Rots and M. Teeuwen (eds.), *Sacred Heritage in Japan*, 1–17, Abingdon: Routledge.

Teeuwen, M., and F. Rambelli (2003), "Introduction: Combinatory Religion and the *Honji Suijaku* Paradigm in Pre-Modern Japan," in M. Teeuwen and F. Rambelli (eds.), *Buddhas and Kami in Japan: Honji Suijaku as a Combinatory Paradigm*, 1–53, London: Routledge/Curzon.

Terada Y. (2009), *Kyū shokuminchi ni okeru Nikkei shinshūkyō no juyō: Taiwan Seichō-no-Ie no monogurafu*, Tokyo: Hābesutosha.

Terauchi N. (2011), *Gagaku wo kiku: hibiki no niwa e no izanai*, Tokyo: Iwanami Shoten.

Terauchi N. (2016), "Ancient and Early Medieval Performing Arts," in J. Salz (ed.), *A History of Japanese Theatre*, 4–19, New York: Cambridge University Press.

Terumoto Y. (1932), *Shinsen no tsukurikata*, Tokyo: Usui Shoten.

Thal, S. (2005), *Rearranging the Landscape of the Gods: The Politics of a Pilgrimage Site in Japan, 1573–1912*, Chicago: University of Chicago Press.

Thomas, J. B. (2012), *Drawing on Tradition: Manga, Anime, and Religion in Contemporary Japan*, Honolulu: University of Hawai'i Press.

Thomas, J. B. (2013), "The Concept of Religion in Modern Japan: Imposition, Invention, or Innovation?" *Religious Studies in Japan*, 2: 3–21.

Thomas, J. B. (2015), "The Buddhist Virtues of Raging Lust and Crass Materialism in Contemporary Japan," *Material Religion*, 11 (4): 485–506.

Thomas, J. B. (2019a), "Domesticity & Spirituality: Kondo is Not an Animist," *Marginalia*, February 8. Available online: https://marginalia.lareviewofbooks.org/domesticity-spirituality-kondo-not-animist/ (accessed December 15, 2020).

Thomas, J. B. (2019b), *Faking Liberties: Religious Freedom in American-Occupied Japan*, Chicago: University of Chicago Press.

Thomas, J. B. (2019c), "Spirit/Medium: Critically Examining the Relationship between Animism and Animation," in F. Rambelli (ed.), *Spirits and Animism in Modern Japan*, 157–70, London: Bloomsbury.

Thornbury, E. B. (1997), *The Folk Performing Arts: Traditional Culture in Contemporary Japan*, Albany: State University of New York Press.

Thornton, S. (2015), "Buddhist Chaplains in the Field of Battle," in D. S. Lopez Jr. (ed.), *Buddhism in Practice*, 441–6, Princeton, NJ: Princeton University Press.

Tinsley, E. (2017), "The Composition of Decomposition: The *Kusōzu* Images of Matsui Fuyuko and Itō Seiu and Buddhism in Erotic Grotesque Modernity," *Journal of Asian Humanities at Kyushu University*, 2:15–45.

Tokieda T., Hasegawa K., and Hayashi M., eds. (2015), *Shugendō-shi nyūmon*, Tokyo: Iwata Shoin.

Tokunaga S. (2015), "Shugendō no seiritsu," in Tokieda T., Hasegawa K., and Hayashi M. (eds.), *Shugendō-shi nyūmon*, 77–92, Tokyo: Iwata Shoin.

Tonomura H. (1994), "Black Hair and Red Trousers: Gendering the Flesh in Medieval Japan," *American Historical Review*, 99 (1): 129–54.

Tonomura H. (1997), "Re-envisioning Women in the Post-Kamakura Age," in J. Mass (ed.), *The Origins of Japan's Medieval World: Courtiers, Clerics, Warriors, and Peasants in the Fourteenth Century*, 138–69, Stanford, CA: Stanford University Press.

Tonomura H. (2006), "Coercive Sex in the Medieval Japanese Court: Lady Nijō's Memoir," *Monumenta Nipponica*, 61 (3): 283–338.

Tonomura H. (2007), "Birth-giving and Avoidance Taboo: Women's Body versus the Historiography of 'Ubuya'," *Japan Review*, 19: 3–45.

Tonomura H., A. Walthall, and Wakita H., eds. (1999), *Women and Class in Japanese History* (no. 25), Ann Arbor: University of Michigan Center for Japanese Studies.

Tosa M. (1998), *Intānetto to shūkyō*, Tokyo: Iwanami Shoten.

Totman, C. (1989), *The Green Archipelago: Forestry in Pre-Industrial Japan*, Berkeley: University of California Press.

Toyonaga S. (2006), *Chūsei no tennō to ongaku*, Tokyo: Yoshikawa Kōbunkan.

Triplett, K. (2019a), *Buddhism and Medicine in Japan: A Topical Survey (500–1600 CE) of a Complex Relationship*, Berlin: De Gruyter.

Triplett, K. (2019b), "Potency by Name? 'Medicine Buddha Plant' and Other Herbs in the Japanese *Scroll of Equine Medicine* (*Ba'i sōshi emaki*, 1267)," *Himalaya* (special issue, "Approaching Potent Substances in Medicine and Ritual across Asia," ed. B. Gerke and J. van der Valk), 39 (1): 189–207.

Tsuchiya Y. (2002), *The Fine Art of Japanese Food Arrangement*, Tokyo: Kodansha International.

Tsuda S. (1949), *Nihon no Shintō*, Tokyo: Iwanami Shoten.

Tsuji K., and Takahashi T. (1985), *Kamigami no ae*, Tokyo: Shibata Shoten.

Tsukada H. (2012), "Cultural Nationalism in Japanese Neo-New Religions: A Comparative Study of Mahikari and Kōfuku no Kagaku," *Monumenta Nipponica*, 67 (1): 133–57.

Tsushima M. (1989), "Emperor and World Renewal in the New Religions: The Case of Shinseiryûjinkai," trans. N. Havens, *Transactions of the Institute of Japanese Culture and Classics, Kokugakuin University*, 63: 266–31.

Tsushima M. (2012), "Tetsudō to reijō: Shūkyō kōdinētā to shite no Kansai Shitetsu," in Yamanaka H. (ed.), *Shūkyō to tsūrizumu: Sei naru mono no jizoku to hen'yō*, 37–57, Kyoto: Sekai Shisōsha.

Tsushima M., Nishiyama S., Shimazono S., and Shiramizu H. (1979), "The Vitalistic Concept of Salvation in Japanese New Religions: An Aspect of Modern Religious Consciousness," *Japanese Journal of Religious Studies*, 6 (1–2): 139–61.

Tsushiro H. (1990), *Chinkon gyōhō ron: Kindai Shintō sekai no reikonron to shintairon*, Tokyo: Shunjūsha.

Tucker, M. E., and J. H. Berthrong, eds. (1998), *Confucianism and Ecology: The Interrelation of Heaven, Earth, and Humans*, Cambridge, MA: Harvard University Press.

Tucker, M. E., and D. R. Williams, eds. (1997), *Buddhism and Ecology: The Interconnection of Dharma and Deeds*, Cambridge, MA: Harvard University Press.

Turnbull, S. R. (2015), *Japan's Sexual Gods: Shrines, Roles, and Rituals of Procreation and Protection*, Leiden: Brill.

Tweed, T. A. (2006), *Crossing and Dwelling: A Theory of Religion*, Cambridge, MA: Harvard University Press.

Uchida K. (2006), *Monkan-bō Kōshin to bijutsu*, Kyoto: Hōzōkan.

Uchida K. (2010), *Go-Daigo Tennō to mikkyō*, Kyoto: Hōzōkan.

Uchida K. (2012) "Shinshutsu no Tachikawa-ryū shōgyō ni tsuite: honkoku to kaidai," *Mikkyō zuzō* 31: 1–18.

Uchida T. and Shaku T. (2014), *Nihon reisei ron*, Tokyo: Nihon Hōsō Shuppan Kyōkai.

Uda T. (2014), "Kankōchi to shite no toshi kinkō reizan no keisei to tenkai: Kaihatsu shihon no dōkō wo chūshin to shite," *Tabi no bunka kenkyūjo hōkoku*, 24.

Uda T. (2015), "Hieizan ni okeru tetsudō fusetsu to Enryakuji," *Rekishi chirigaku*, 57 (3): 20–35.

Ueda M., ed. (2004), *Tankyū 'chinju no mori': Shasōgaku e no shōtai*, Tokyo: Heibonsha.

Ueda M. (2013), *Mori to kami to Nihonjin*, Tokyo: Fujiwara Shoten.

Ueda N. (2004), *Ganbare Bukkyō: otera runesansu no jidai*, Tokyo: Nihon Hōsō Shuppan Kyōkai.

Ueki Y. (2001), *Yama, hoko, yatai no matsuri: fūryū no kaika*, Tokyo: Hakusuisha.

Ugoretz, K. (2019a), "As the Spirit Moves You: How Studio Ghibli Films Leave Room for A Range of Religious Interpretations," *Beneath the Tangles*, September 23. Available online: https://beneaththetangles.com/2019/09/23/studio-ghibli-films-leave-room-for-a-range-of-religious-interpretations/ (accessed December 15, 2020).

Ugoretz, K. (2019b), "Drawing on Shinto? Online Shinto Communities' Religious Responses to Miyazaki Hayao's Anime," paper presented at the Annual American Academy of Religion, San Diego, November 24.

Ukai H. (2015a), *Jiin shōmetsu*, Tokyo: Nikkei BPsha.

Ukai H. (2015b), *Ushinawareru "chiiki" to "shūkyō": jiin shōmetsu*, Tokyo: Nikkei BPsha.

Umeda C. (2009), *Kinsei Onmyōdō soshiki no kenkyū*, Tokyo: Yoshikawa Kōbunkan.

Umehara T. (1995 [1991]), *Mori no shisō ga jinrui wo sukuu*, Tokyo: Shōgakukan.

Urita M. (2015), "Kagura hikyoku no tokuchō: Jingū shikinen sengū no gi to sokuirei go-kashikodokoro mikagura no gi wo hikaku shite," *Nihon kayō kenkyū*, 55: 63–72.

Ushio K. (2017), *Nanzan shinryū shōmyō taikei*, Kyoto: Hōzōkan.

Ushio M. (1985), *Kagura to kamigakari*, Tokyo: Meicho Shuppan.

Ushiyama Y. (1996), "'Nyonin kinsei' sairon," *Sangaku shugen*, 17: 1–11.

Van den Broucke, P. (1992), *Hōkyōshō: "The Compendium of the Precious Mirror" of the Monk Yūkai*, Ghent, Belgium: Rijksuniversiteit Ghent.

Van der Beer, P. (2001), *Imperial Encounters: Religion and Modernity in India and Britain*, Princeton, NJ: Princeton University Press.

Veidlinger, D., ed. (2019), *Digital Humanities and Buddhism: An Introduction*, Berlin: De Gruyter.
Verbeek, P. (2005), *What Things Do: Philosophical Reflections on Technology, Agency, and Design*, trans. R. P. Crease, University Park: Pennsylvania State University Press.
Vilhar, G., and C. Anderson (1999), *Gracious Gifts: Japan's Sacred Offerings*, Tokyo: Shufu-no-tomo-sha.
Vincentelli, E. (1999), "Bittersweet Sympathies: For a Japanese Animator, Grown-up Messages are Kid Stuff," *Village Voice*, October 26. Available online: https://www.villagevoice.com/1999/10/26/bittersweet-sympathies/ (accessed December 15, 2020).
Visiočnik, N. (2016), "The Role of Religion in the Life of Zainichi Koreans in Japan," *Asian Studies*, 4 (1): 229–43.
Viswanathan, G. (1998), *Outside the Fold: Conversion, Modernity, and Belief*, Princeton, NJ: Princeton University Press.
Vlastos, S., ed. (1998), *Mirror of Modernity: Invented Traditions of Modern Japan*, Berkeley: University of California Press.
Wagner, R. (2012), *Godwired: Religion, Ritual, and Virtual Reality*, New York: Routledge.
Wakabayashi H. (2015), "Disaster in the Making: Taira no Kiyomori's Move of the Capital to Fukuhara," *Monumenta Nipponica*, 70 (1): 1–38.
Wakamatsu E. (2015), *Reisei no tetsugaku*, Tokyo: Kadokawa Gakugei Shuppan.
Wakamori T. et al., eds. (1975–84), *Sangaku shūkyōshi kenkyū sōsho*, 18 vols., Tokyo: Meicho S huppan.
Wakita H. (1992), *Nihon chūsei joseishi no kenkyū*, Tokyo: Tōkyō Daigaku Shuppankai.
Wakita H., A. Bouchy, and. Ueno C., eds. (1999), *Gender and Japanese History: Religion and Customs, the Body and Sexuality*, vol. 1, Osaka: Osaka University Press.
Walker, B. L. (2010), *Toxic Archipelago: A History of Industrial Disease in Japan*, Seattle: University of Washington Press.
Walthall, A. (1990), "The Family Ideology of the Rural Entrepreneurs in Nineteenth Century Japan," *Journal of Social History*, 23 (3): 463–83.
Walthall, A. (1991), "The Life Cycle of Farm Women in Tokugawa Japan," in G. L. Bernstein (ed.), *Recreating Japanese Women, 1600–1945*, Berkeley: University of California Press.
Walthall, A. (1998), *The Weak Body of a Useless Woman: Matsuo Taseko and the Meiji Restoration*, Chicago: University of Chicago Press.
Wang Y. (2003), *Sugao no chūkagai*, Tokyo: Yōsensha.
Ward, H. N. (2009), *Women Religious Leaders in Japan's Christian Century, 1549–1650*, Farnham, UK: Ashgate.
Ward, H. N. (2010), "Women Martyrs in Passion and Paradise," *Journal of World Christianity*, 3 (1): 47–66.
Ward, H. N. (2012), "Women and Kirishitanban Literature: Translation, Gender, and Theology in Early Modern Japan," *Early Modern Women*, 7: 271–81.
Warf, B., and S. Arias, eds. (2009), *The Spatial Turn: Interdisciplinary Perspectives*, London: Routledge.
Watanabe C. (2019), *Becoming One: Religion, Development, and Environmentalism in a Japanese NGO in Myanmar*, Honolulu: University of Hawai'i Press.
Watanabe M. (1974), "The Conception of Nature in Japanese Culture," *Science*, 183 (4122): 279–82.
Watanabe M. (2001), *Burajiru Nikkei shinshūkyō no tenkai: Ibunka fukyō no kadai to jissen*, Tokyo: Tōshindō.

Watanabe M. (2011), "New Religions: A Sociological Approach," in B. Staemmler and U. Dehn (eds.), *Establishing the Revolutionary: An Introduction to New Religions in Japan*, 69–88, Zurich: LIT.

Watson, B., trans. (2013), *Record of Miraculous Events in Japan: The Nihon ryōiki*, New York: Columbia University Press.

Wattles, M. (1996), "The 1909 Ryūtō and the Aesthetics of Affectivity," *Art Journal*, 55 (3): 48–56.

Watts, J., and Tomatsu Y. (2012), *Buddhist Care for the Dying and Bereaved*, New York: Simon and Schuster.

Watts, J. S., ed. (2013), *Lotus in the Nuclear Sea: Fukushima and the Promise of Buddhism in the Nuclear Age*, Yokohama: International Buddhist Exchange Center.

Weisenfeld, G. (2012), *Imaging Disaster: Tokyo and the Visual Culture of Japan's Great Earthquake of 1923*, Berkeley: University of California Press.

Weiss, L. (2007), "Heritage-Making and Political Identity," *Journal of Social Archaeology*, 7 (3): 413–31.

Wendelken, C. (2000), "Pan-Asianism and the Pure Japanese Thing: Japanese Identity and Architecture in the Late 1930s," *Positions*, 8 (3): 819–28.

Wetterberg, O. and E. Löfgren, eds. (2019), "Religious Spaces as Cultural Heritage," special issue, *Religions*. Available online: https://www.mdpi.com/journal/religions/special_issues/religious_heritage (accessed December 15, 2020).

White, L., Jr. (1967), "The Historical Roots of Our Ecologic Crisis," *Science*, 155 (3767): 1203–7.

Wilkinson, D. (2017), "Is There Such a Thing as Animism?," *Journal of the American Academy of Religion*, 85 (2): 289–311.

Williams, D. R. (2002), "Camp Dharma: Japanese-American Buddhist Identity and the Internment Experience of World War II," in C. Prebish and M. Baumann (eds.), *Westward Dharma: Buddhism beyond Asia*, 191–200, Berkeley: University of California Press.

Williams, D. R. (2005), *The Other Side of Zen: A Social History of Sōtō Zen: Buddhism in Tokugawa Japan*, Princeton, NJ: Princeton University Press.

Williams, D. R. (2012), "Buddhist Environmentalism in Contemporary Japan," in J. K. Nelson and I. Prohl (eds.), *Handbook of Contemporary Japanese Religions*, 373–92, Leiden: Brill.

Williams, D. R. (2019), *American Sutra: A Story of Faith and Freedom in the Second World War*, Cambridge, MA: Harvard University Press.

Williams, D. R., and Moriya T., eds. (2010), *Issei Buddhism in the Americas*, Urbana: University of Illinois Press.

Wilson, B., and K. Dobbelaere (1994), *A Time to Chant: The Sōka Gakkai Buddhists in Britain*, New York: Oxford University Press.

Wilson, J., and Moriya T., eds. (2016), *Selected Works of D. T. Suzuki, volume III: Comparative Religion*, Berkeley: University of California Press.

Winter, T. (2014), "Heritage Studies and the Privileging of Theory," *International Journal of Heritage Studies*, 20 (4): 556–72.

Wittner, L. S. (1971), "MacArthur and the Missionaries: God and Man in Occupied Japan," *Pacific Historical Review*, 40: 77–98.

Woodard, W. P. (1972), *The Allied Occupation of Japan 1945–1952 and Japanese Religions*, Leiden: E. J. Brill.

World Health Organization (2002), "WHO Definition of Palliative Care." Available online: http://www.who.int/cancer/palliative/definition/en/ (accessed December 15, 2020).

Wright, L., and J. Clode (2005), "The Animated Worlds of Hayao Miyazaki: Filmic Representations of Shinto," *Metro*, 143: 46–51.

Yamada K. (2013), *Ai amu Hippī: Nihon no Hippī Mūbumento shi '60-'90*, Tokyo: Mori to Shuppan.

Yamada M. (2018), *Shinshūkyō no Burajiru dendō*, Tenri: Tenri Daigaku Oyasato Kenkyūjo.

Yamada N. (2010), *Shinshūkyō to manē. Kazeisarenai 'kyōdai saisen bako' no himitsu*, Tokyo: Takarajimasha.

Yamada N. (2012), *Kane to shūkyō*, Tokyo: Tetsujinsha.

Yamagishi K. (2008), "Freedom of Religion, Religious Political Participation, and Separation of Religion and State: Legal Considerations from Japan," BYU L. Rev. 919. Available online: https://digitalcommons.law.byu.edu/lawreview/vol2008/iss3/7 (accessed December 4, 2020).

Yamaguchi M. (1988), "'Center' and 'Periphery' in Japanese Culture – in Light of Tartu Semiotics," in H. Broms and R. Kaufmann (eds.), *Semiotics of Culture. Proceedings of the 25th Symposium of the Tartu-Moskow School of Semiotics, Imatra, Finland, 27th-29th July 1987*, 199–291, Helsinki: Arator.

Yamakura A. (2017), "Transnational Contexts of Tenrikyo Mission in Korea: Korea, Manchuria, and the United States," in E. Anderson (ed.), *Belief and Practice in Imperial Japan and Colonial Korea*, 153–76, Singapore: Palgrave Macmillan.

Yamamoto H. (1984), "Chūsei Hie-sha no Jūzenji shinkō to ninaite shudan: Eizan, reidō, fugeki no sansō kōzō wo megutte," *Terakoya gogaku bunka kenkyū ronsō*, 3: 25–64.

Yamamoto H. (1993), *Henjōfu: Chūsei shinbutsu shūgō no sekai*, Tokyo: Shunjūsha.

Yamamoto H. (1998), *Ijin: Chūsei Nihon no hikyōteki sekai*, Tokyo: Heibonsha.

Yamamoto Y., and Imano T. (1973), *Kindai kyōiku no tennōsei ideorogi: Meijiki gakkō gyōji no kōsatsu*, Tokyo: Shinsensha.

Yamamoto Y., and Imano T. (1976), *Taishō・Shōwa kyōiku no tennōsei ideorogi 1 Gakkō gyōji no shūkyōteki seikaku*, Tokyo: Shinsensha.

Yamanaka H. (1996), "Manga bunka no naka no shūkyō," in Shimazono S. and Ishii K. (eds.), *Shōhi sareru "shūkyō"*, 158–84, Tokyo: Shunjūysha.

Yamanaka H. (2007), "Nagasaki kyōkaigun to tsūrizumu," *Tetsugaku shisō ronshū*, 33: 156–75.

Yamanaka H. (2008), "The Utopian 'Power to Live': The Significance of the Miyazaki Phenomenon," in M. W. MacWilliams (ed.), *Japanese Visual Culture: Explorations in the World of Manga and Anime*, 237–55, Armonk: M. E. Sharpe.

Yamanaka H. (2012a), *Shūkyō to tsūrizumu: Sei naru mono no jizoku to hen'yō*, Kyoto: Sekai Shisōsha.

Yamanaka H. (2012b), "Nagasaki no kyōkaigun to Kakure kirishitan," in Hoshino E. and Yamanaka H. (eds.), *Seichi junrei tsūrizumu*, Tokyo: Kōbundō.

Yamashita K. (1996), *Heian jidai no shūkyō bunka to Onmyōdō*, Tokyo: Iwata Shoin.

Yamashita K. (2010), *Onmyōdō no hakken*, Tokyo: Nihon Hōsō Shuppankai.

Yamashita T. (1993), "Tainai totsuki no yūrai: Bussho 'Jōge mibun no wa' 'Jōge mibun go' wo megutte," *Tōkyō Seitoku Tanki Daigaku kiyō*, 26: 93–110.

Yamashita T. (2005), "Shūgendō Gotai honnu honrai busshin setsu: Sono kyōri to shite no tainai goi to sono tenkai," *Tōkyō Seitoku Tanki Daigaku kiyō*, 38: 21–32.

Yamauchi H. (1994), *Shoku no rekishi jinruigaku*, Kyoto: Jinbun Shoin.

Yanagawa K., ed. (1983), *Japanese Religions in California: A Report on Research within and without the Japanese-American Community*, Tokyo: Department of Religious Studies, University of Tokyo.

Yanagawa K., and D. Reid (1979), "Between Unity and Separation: Religion and Politics in Japan, 1965-1977," *Japanese Journal of Religious Studies*, 6 (4): 500–21.

Yanagawa K. and Morioka K., eds. (1979), *Hawai Nikkei shūkyō no tenkai to genkyō: Hawai Nikkei-jin shūkyō chōsa chūkan hōkoku*, Tokyo: Tōkyō Daigaku Shūkyōgaku kenkyūshitsu.

Yanagawa K. and Morioka K., eds. (1981), *Hawai Nikkeijin shakai to Nihon shūkyō: Hawai Nikkei-jin shūkyō chōsa hōkokusho*, Tokyo: Tōkyō Daigaku Shūkyōgaku kenkyūshitsu.

Yanagihara T. (1977), *Denshō Nihon ryōri*, Tokyo: Nihon Hōsō Shuppan kyōkai.

Yanagita K. (1998), *Yanagita Kunio zenshū*, vol. 19, Tokyo: Chikuma Shobō.

Yasuda H. (2010), "World Heritage and Cultural Tourism in Japan," *International Journal of Culture, Tourism and Hospitality Research*, 4 (4): 1–10.

Yasumaru Y. (1977), *Deguchi Nao*, Tokyo: Asahi Shinbunsha.

Yasumaru Y. (1979), *Kamigami no Meiji ishin: Shinbutsu bunri to haibutsu kishaku*, Tokyo: Iwanami Shoten.

Yonan, M. (2011), "Toward a Fusion of Art History and Material Culture Studies," *West 86th: A Journal of Decorative Arts, Design History, and Material Culture*, 18 (2): 232–48.

Yoshida M., and Tsune S., eds. (1989), *Naorai: Communion of the Table*, Hiroshima: Mazda Motor Corporation.

Yoshikawa S., ed. (1995), *Shoku bunkaron*, Tokyo: Kenpakusha.

Yoshinaga S., ed. (2004), *Nihonjin no shin, shin, rei: Kindai minkan seishin ryōhō sōsho*, Part I (8 vols.) and Part II (7 vols.), Tokyo: Kuresu Shuppan.

Yoshinaga S. (2008), "Tairei to kokka: Taireidō ni okeru kokkakan no imi," *Jintai Kagaku*, 17 (1): 35–51.

Yoshinaga S. (2009), "Theosophy and Buddhist Reformers in the Middle of the Meiji Period," *Japanese Religions*, 34 (2): 119–130.

Yoshinaga S. (2011), "Shin bukkyō to wa nani mono ka? 'jiyū tōkyū' to 'kenzen naru shinkō'," in Yoshinaga S. (ed.), *Kindai ni okeru chishikijin shūkyō undō no gensetsu kūkan: 'Shin Bukkyō' no shisōshi, bunkashiteki kenkyū*, 27–43, Tokyo: Grants-in-Aid for Scientific Research, no. 20320016.

Yoshinaga S. (2012), "After Olcott Left: Theosophy and 'New Buddhists' at the Turn of the Century," *Eastern Buddhist*, 43 (1–2): 103–32.

Yoshinaga S. (2014), "Suzuki Daisetsu and Swedenborg: A Historical Background," in Hayashi M., Ōtani E., and P. L. Swanson (eds.), *Modern Buddhism in Japan*, 112–43, Nagoya: Nanzan Institute for Religion and Culture.

Yoshinaga S. (2015), "The Birth of Japanese Mind Cure Methods," in C. Harding, Iwata F., and Yoshinaga S. (eds.), *Religion and Psychotherapy in Modern Japan*, 76–102, New York: Routledge.

Young, C. (2014), *Eastern Learning and the Heavenly Way: The Tonghak and Ch'ŏndogyo Movements and the Twilight of Korean Independence*, Honolulu: University of Hawai'i Press.

Yumiyama T. (1995), "Varieties of Healing in Present-Day Japan," *Japanese Journal of Religious Studies*, 22 (3–4): 267–82.

Yumiyama T. (2004), "Kachi sōtaishugi e no taiō: Aum Shinrikyō to Nyūeiji undō," in Itō M., Kashio N. and Yumiyama T. (eds.), *Supirichuariti no shakaigaku: Gendai sekai no shūkyōsei no tankyū*, 249–68, Tokyo: Sekai Shisōsha.

Zachmann, U. M. (2012), "The Postwar Constitution and Religion," in I. Prohl and J. Nelson (eds.), *Handbook of Contemporary Japanese Religions*, 215–40, Leiden: Brill.

Zenkoku kyōkaishi renmei (2017), "Katsudō suru kyōkaishi no ninzū ." Available online: http://kyoukaishi.server-shared.com/index.html (accessed December 15, 2020).

Zenkoku Reikan Shōhō Taisaku Bengoshi Renrakukai (2007), "Yōbōsho, Nihon Minkan Hōsō Renmei, Nihon Hōsō Kyōkai e." Available online: https://www.stopreikan.com/kogi_moshiire/shiryo_20070221.htm (accessed May 11, 2020).

WEBSITES

http://ceremonyjapan.jp/en/
http://obousan.jp/price.html
http://www.bloomberg.com/news/articles/2015-12-15/try-a-coffin-for-size-the-death-business-is-thriving-in-japan
http://www.funeral.co.jp
http://www.ipss.go.jp/pp-newest/e/ppfj02/ppfj02.pdf
https://www.irhpress.co.jp/products/list.php?category_id=94
https://www.nippon-foundation.or.jp/en/what/projects/culture_support/iroha-nihon/
https://www.yano.co.jp/press-release/show/press_id/1765

CONTRIBUTORS

Emily Anderson is an independent researcher and curator. Having received her PhD in modern Japanese history from UCLA in 2010, she was Assistant Professor of Japanese History at Washington State University (Pullman, Washington) from 2010 to 2014 and postdoctoral fellow at University of Auckland in 2014. She is the author of *Christianity in Modern Japan: Empire for God* (Bloomsbury, 2014) and the editor of *Belief and Practice in Imperial Japan and Colonial Korea* (2017) as well as a number of articles and book chapters on religion and imperialism in Japan and the Pacific. She also has extensive experience developing museum exhibits, including *Cannibals: Myth and Reality* (San Diego Museum of Man, 2015–ongoing), and cocurated with Duncan Williams, *Sutra and the Bible: Faith and Japanese American World War II Incarceration* (Japanese American National Museum, opening fall 2021).

Erica Baffelli is currently Senior Lecturer in Japanese Studies at the University of Manchester (UK). Before arriving at Manchester in 2013, she was visiting researcher at Hosei University (Tokyo) and postdoctoral research fellow of the Japan Society for the Promotion of Science (2005–7), and Lecturer/Senior Lecturer in Asian Religions at the University of Otago (New Zealand, 2007–13). She is interested in religion in contemporary Japan, with a focus on groups founded from the 1970s onwards. Her publications include: Baffelli and Caple, eds. (2019), "Religious Authority in East Asia: Materiality, Media and Aesthetics," special issue of *Asian Ethnology*, 78 (1); *Dynamism and the Ageing of a Japanese 'New' Religion: Transformations and the Founder* (with Ian Reader; Bloomsbury, 2018); *Media and New Religions in Japan* (2016); Baffelli and Reader, eds. (2012), "Aftermath: the Impact and Ramifications of the Aum Affair," special issue of the *Japanese Journal of Religious Studies*, 39 (1); and Baffelli, Reader, and Staemmler (eds.), *Japanese Religions on the Internet: Innovation, Representation and Authority* (2011).

Jørn Borup is an associate professor at the Department of the Study of Religion at Aarhus University. His research areas include Japanese Buddhism, Buddhism in the West, religious diversity, spirituality, and religion and migration. Besides articles for journals and publications in Danish, he is the author of *Japanese Rinzai Zen Buddhism: Myōshinji, a Living Religion* (2008); *Eastspirit: Transnational Spirituality and Religious Circulation in East and West* (coedited with M. Q. Fibiger; 2017); *The Critical Analysis of Religious Diversity* (coedited with L. Kühle and W. Hoverd; 2018); and *Religious Diversity in Asia* (coedited with L. Kühle and M. Q. Fibiger; 2019). For the journal *Japanese Religions,* he coedited with Fabio Rambelli a special issue on "The Materiality of Japanese Religions" (2019) and he was a guest editor for *Journal of Religion in Japan* on a special issue on Japanese Buddhism in Europe (forthcoming). He has been director of the Center for Contemporary Religion and chair of the Department of the Study of Religion (Aarhus University), and is the chair of the Danish Association for the Study of Religion. He has for a period been a travel writer, being the author of the Danish travel guide to Japan.

Andrea Castiglioni is a senior lecturer at Nagoya City University, specializing in early modern Shugendō history and ascetic movements. Recent publications include *Defining Shugendō: Critical Studies on Japanese Mountain Religion* (with Fabio Rambelli and Carina Roth, Bloomsbury, 2020); Castiglioni (2019), "Devotion in Flesh and Bone: The Mummified Corpses of Mount Yudono Ascetics in the Edo Period," *Asian Ethnology*, 78 (1); "From Your Name. to Shin-Gojira: Spiritual Crisscrossing, Spatial Soteriology, and Catastrophic Identity in Contemporary Japanese Visual Culture," in F. Rambelli (ed.), *Spirits and Animism in Contemporary Japan* (Bloomsbury, 2019); and "Shika, sekibutsu, engi ga kataru Yudonosan shinkō: Muromachi makki kara Edo shoki made" (The Faith in Mount Yudono through Poems, Stone-Buddhas, and Engi from the End of the Muromachi Period to the Early Edo Period), *Nihon bungaku no tenbō hiraku* (2017).

Lindsey E. DeWitt is a Flanders Research Foundation (FWO) postdoctoral fellow at the Centre for Buddhist Studies, Ghent University. Before her current post, DeWitt held a two-year Japan Society for the Promotion of Sciences (JSPS) postdoctoral fellowship affiliated with Kyushu University (2016–18) and a one-year appointment as Assistant Professor of Japanese Religions at Kyushu University (2015–16). She received her PhD in Asian Languages and Cultures (Buddhist Studies) from UCLA in 2015. DeWitt's research aims to articulate the social and historical dimensions of Japanese religions, with a focus on women's exclusion (*nyonin kinsei*, *nyonin kekkai*), sacred space (especially mountains and Shugendō), and the modern discourses of tradition and cultural heritage. She is currently preparing a monograph on religious World Heritage Sites in Japan that uphold, or once did, male-only access policies.

Aura Di Febo (PhD in Japanese Studies, University of Manchester, 2019), is currently a lecturer in Japanese at the University of Leeds. Her doctoral research focused on the social care activities promoted by the lay Buddhist organization Risshō Kōseikai. She used social welfare as a lens to investigate the ways religious actors negotiated religious meanings and the public presence of religion within contemporary Japanese society. More recently, she was awarded a postdoctoral fellowship within the UKRI project "Religion and Minority: Lived Religion, Migration and Marginalities in Secular Societies." Her research explores the intersection of youth religiosity and social inclusion by looking at two dimensions of marginality experienced by second-generation members of Japanese new religious groups.

Ioannis Gaitanidis is Assistant Professor at the Graduate School of Global and Transdisciplinary Studies, Chiba University (Japan). His doctoral thesis and subsequent publications have centered on the activities of individuals who offer therapeutic treatments that they present as alternative or complementary to modern medicine, and which often include references to the katakana word, *supirichuaru*. More recently, he has been interested in the analysis of discourse that is critical of these activities, coming both from within and from outside the so-called spiritual business. Preliminary results of this recent project were published in "'Spiritual Apostasy' in Contemporary Japan: Religion, Taboos and The Ethics of Capitalism," *Silva Iaponicarum* (60/61). Thanks to Professor Yoshinaga Shin'ichi, Ioannis has also had the chance to look at the global histories of ideologies and practice of these contemporary "spiritual therapies." A special issue of *Japanese Religions*, 44, on "Japanese Religions and the Global Occult," coedited with Justin Stein, is due for publication in early 2021. Finally, he has also published on teaching methodologies in

Japanese Studies and coedited a textbook written in Japanese and titled *Critical Japanese Studies* (2020), which targets university teachers and students interested in combining Japanese Studies research with collaborative learning to unpack stereotypical images of Japan.

Andrea Giolai is a lecturer at Leiden University's Institute for Area Studies. He holds an MA in Japanese studies (Ca' Foscari University) and a PhD in Area Studies (Ca' Foscari University and Leiden University), and he is a classically trained flutist. He has been a Japan Foundation fellow at the Research Institute for Japanese Traditional Music at Kyoto City University of Arts (2015–16) and a JSPS postdoctoral fellow at the International Research Center for Japanese Studies (2017–19). In his research, he focuses on Japanese traditional music and dance, the auditory dimension of religious rituals, and the reconstruction of ancient performing arts. Focusing on local traditions of "courtly" music and dances (gagaku, bugaku) from the point of view of historical (ethno)musicology and apprenticeship-based ethnography, his studies analyze how notions of authenticity and claims to the sonic past emerge out of a network of materials, political actors, performers, and listeners. His publications include: Giolai (2020), "Encounters with the Past: Fractals and Atmospheres at Kasuga Wakamiya Onmatsuri," *Journal of Religion in Japan* 9 (1–3), on the relationship between local gagaku practitioners and the matsuri of Nara; and Giolai (2019), "Sensing the Music: Oral Mnemonics as a 'Technique of Affective Sensitization' in Japanese Court Music," *Asian Anthropology* 18 (3), on the bodily processes at the core of gagaku pedagogy.

Allan G. Grapard is Professor Emeritus of Japanese Religions at the University of California, Santa Barbara. He is the author of many publications on sacred space and Shinto-Buddhist combinatory systems in Japan; the complete list would be too long for the present purpose. His books include *The Protocol of the Gods* (1992) and *Mountain Mandalas* (Bloomsbury, 2016).

Hayashi Makoto is a professor in the Department of Religious Studies at Aichi Gakuin University. His research primarily concerns Onmyōdō in the Edo period and modern Buddhism. His publications include *Kinsei Onmyōdō no kenkyū* (2005), *Tenmonkata to Onmyōdō* (2006), and *Shibukawa Harumi* (2018). He coedited *Buddha no henbō* (2014) and the book series *Nihonjin to shūkyō* (2014–15) and *Shin Onmyōdō sōsho* (2020–21).

Horie Norichika (PhD in Religious Studies, University of Tokyo, 2008) is a professor at the Center for Death and Life Studies and Practical Ethics at the University of Tokyo. He is the author of *Rekishi no naka no shūkyō shinrigaku* (Psychology of Religion in History, 2009), *Supirichuariti no yukue* (The Future of Spirituality, 2011), and *Poppu supirichuariti* (Pop Spirituality, 2019); and the editor of *Gendai Nihon no shūkyō jijō* (The Religious Situation in Contemporary Japan, 2018) and *Shūkyō to shakai no sengoshi* (Postwar History of Religion and Society, 2019). He has also written many articles in English: "Spirituality and the Spiritual in Japan: Translation and Transformation" (2012), "Narrow New Age and Broad Spirituality: A Comprehensive Schema and a Comparative Analysis" (2013), "The Contemporary View of Reincarnation in Japan: Narratives of the Reincarnating Self" (2014), "Continuing Bonds in the Tōhoku Disaster Area: Locating the Destination of Spirits" (2016), and "The Making of Power Spots: From New Age Spirituality to Shinto Spirituality" (2017). His research focuses on broad areas of religious studies and death and life studies, such as contemporary Japanese religions, spiritual but not religious (SBNR), views on the afterlife, psychology of religion, environmental ethics, and risk theories.

Kasai Kenta works for the Institute of Grief Care at Sophia University (Tokyo) to develop Japanese nondenominational chaplaincy training as a supervisor. His research has been focused on the study of secular mutual support association/networks of religious origin, including history and organization of Alcoholics Anonymous, and a contextual study of meditation as a therapeutic method through self-monitoring and reflection. His Japanese translation of Ernest Kurtz's classic study *Not-god: A History of Alcoholics Anonymous* (1979) was published in 2020. He has been making an effort to describe the methods and thought of grief/bereavement care at Sophia University and the experience of the trainee as an attentive clinical listener. His publications include: "Introducing Chaplaincy to Japanese Society" (*Journal of Religion in Japan*, 2016), *Modernity and Meditation: Altered States of Consciousness* (2010, in Japanese), and *Sobriety in Communality: People who believe in their Recovery from Alcoholism* (2007, in Japanese). He also coedited *Religion as Care* (2013, in Japanese), *Keywords for Buddhism and Psychology* (2012, in Japanese), and *Keywords for Religious Studies* (2006, in Japanese).

Kato Masato is currently a part-time lecturer at Tenri University. He earned his first MA in Ethics and Social Theory / Religion and Society at Graduate Theological Union in Berkeley, CA, in 2009 and his second MA in Religions of Asia and Africa at SOAS University of London in 2013. He received his doctorate in the Study of Religions from SOAS in 2018. His doctoral research focused on how social actors of Japanese new religions negotiate the cultural identity relating to Japan in overseas contexts through the case of the expansion of Tenrikyō in France. After obtaining his PhD, he was affiliated with the Centre for the Study of Japanese Religions, SOAS University of London, as a postdoctoral research associate from June 2018 to May 2020. His research interests include Japanese new religions and their overseas expansion, religions in contemporary Japan, and the construction of "religion" and its conterminous categories in the Japanese context. His article, "Legitimating a Religion through Culture: Revisiting Peter Clarke's Discussion on the Globalisation of Japanese New Religions," is forthcoming in *Journal of Contemporary Religion*.

Kawahashi Noriko is Visiting Professor at International Research Center for Japanese Studies (Nichibunken) and visiting research fellow at the Nanzan Institute for Religion and Culture. She obtained a doctorate in Religious Studies from Princeton University in 1992. She has published extensively on gender and religion in Japan and Okinawa, both in English and Japanese. She has coedited with Kuroki Masako a special issue of the *Japanese Journal of Religious Studies* on "Feminism and Religion in Contemporary Japan," 30 (3–4). She has also coedited with Kobayashi Naoko a special issue of the *Japanese Journal of Religious Studies* on "Gendering Religious Practices in Japan," 44 (1). Her recent articles include "Gender Issues in Japanese Religions" (in *Nanzan Guide to Japanese Religions*, 2006), "Folk Religions and its Contemporary Issues" (in *A Companion to the Anthropology of Japan*, 2005), "Re-Imagining Buddhist Women in Contemporary Japan" (in *Handbook of Contemporary Japanese Religions*, 2012), and "Embodied Divinity and the Gift: The Case of Okinawan Kaminchu" (in *Women, Religion, and the Gift*, 2017). She has been engaged in feminist ethnographic research on contemporary Buddhist women in Japan and has published *Saitai bukkyo no minzokushi* (2012).

Kimura Takeshi (PhD, University of Chicago) is a professor at the Faculty of Humanities and Social Sciences at the University of Tsukuba, Japan. While his main research area is on Indigenous religions of North America and Japan and American Studies, he also deals with contemporary social issues such as sustainability and robotics / AI. His publications include: "Hopi konchū shinwa" (On Hopi Insect Myths), *Tetsugaku shisō ronshū* (45); "Andoroido kenkyūsha ga shūkyō ni tsuite kataru koto no igi" (On the Significance of Android Scholars Talking about Religion), *Shūkyō kenkyū* (93); "Robotto-AI to shūkyō ni tsuite no joronteki kōsatsu" (Preliminary Study on Robot-AI and Religion), in Tsumagari and Hosoda (eds.), *Baikaibutsu no shūkyōshi* (2019); "The Beginning of a Long Journey: Maintaining and Reviving the Ancestral Religion among the Ainu in Japan," in Greg Johnson and Siv Ellen Kraft (eds.), *Handbook of Indigenous Religion(s)* (2017); "Masahiro Mori's Buddhist Philosophy of Robot," *Paladyne. Journal of Behavioral Robotics*, 2018; "Windigo: shinwa to jinkaku hen'yō on aida" (Windigo: Between Myth and Personal Transformation), *Tsukuba Area Studies* (39); "Robotics and AI in the Sociology of Religion: A Human in *Imago Roboticae*," *Social Compass*, 2017; and "James H. Cone's Black Theology of Liberation as Post-Modern Public Philosophy," *The Journal of American and Canadian Studies* (33). Currently he is working on a book on Native American myths and religion.

Kobayashi Naoko is Associate Professor of Religion at Aichi Gakuin University. She is also Research Associate at Nanzan Institute for Religion and Culture and visiting researcher at the Gender and Religions Research Center at Ryūkoku University. She has surveyed women ascetic practitioners on Mt. Kiso Ontake and Mt. Ōmine while participating in ascetic training with them. She obtained a doctoral degree from Nagoya University in 2010 with a dissertation on "Analytical Study of Various Aspects of Religious Texts in Ontake Fraternities." She has presented papers on women ascetic practitioners at several international conferences, including the IAHR World Congress in Toronto (2010) and in Erfurt (2015). She is the author of several articles on this topic, including "Gendering the Study of Shugendō: Reconsidering Female Shugenja and the Exclusion of Women from Sacred Mountains," *Japanese Review of Cultural Anthropology*, 12. With Kawahashi Noriko she coedited the special issue of the *Japanese Journal of Religious Studies* on "Gendering Religious Practices in Japan" (44 (1)). Her article "The Necessity of Gender Perspective in Folk Religious Studies" appeared in the *Journal of Religious Studies* Special Issue on *Gender and Sexuality* (93 (2)).

Paulina K. Kolata is a lecturer in Religious Studies within the Department of Theology and Religious Studies at the University of Chester and an Early Career Research Fellow at the University of Manchester with the "Religion and Minority: Lived Religion, Migration and Marginalities in Secular Societies" project supported by the UKRI ESRC-AHRC UK-Japan SSH Connections Grant Scheme and based at the University of Manchester (UK) and Toyo University (Japan). In 2019, she completed her PhD in Japanese Studies at the University of Manchester with her doctoral work interrogating the impact of demographic changes and regional economic decline on Buddhist temple communities in contemporary Japan. Her main research areas focus on Buddhism, economy, disruptive demographics, and Buddhist materiality, networks, and aesthetics explored through ethnographic research methods, and visual and participatory action research methodologies. She has recently published a chapter on "The Story beyond UNESCO: Local Buddhist Temples and the Heritage of Survival in Regional Japan" (*Sacred Heritage in Japan*, 2020) and is currently working on a book manuscript based on her doctoral research titled *Doing Belonging in Troubled Times: Buddhist Temple Communities in Contemporary Japan*.

Komura Akiko (PhD in Area Studies, Sophia University, Tokyo) is a lecturer in the College of Sociology at Rikkyo University; she teaches cultural and religious anthropology both in English and Japanese. She specializes in Islam and has conducted extensive anthropological research about Islam and the way of life of Japanese Muslims. She has published two books: *When Japan Meets Islam: Its History and Possibility* (2015) and *Islam in Japan: Analyzing Its History, Religion and Culture* (2019), and many articles about intercultural understanding between Islam and Japan. She is currently conducting research about recent topics in Japanese culture, religion, and society, such as anime and Japanese religion, anime used in regional revitalization, intercultural problems in international tourism, and cross-cultural interaction between Japanese and foreign workers.

Levi McLaughlin is Associate Professor at the Department of Philosophy and Religious Studies at North Carolina State University. He received his PhD from Princeton University after previous study at the University of Tokyo, and he holds a BA and MA in East Asian Studies from the University of Toronto. Levi is coauthor and coeditor of *Kōmeitō: Politics and Religion in Japan* (2014) and coeditor of the special issue "Salvage and Salvation: Religion and Disaster Relief in Asia" (*Asian Ethnology*, June 2016). He is author of *Soka Gakkai's Human Revolution: The Rise of a Mimetic Nation in Modern Japan* (2019), and numerous articles and book chapters on intersections of religion, politics, disaster, and related topics.

Mark R. Mullins is currently Professor of Japanese Studies and Religious Studies, and Director of the Japan Studies Centre, at the University of Auckland. Prior to this appointment in 2013, he was engaged in academic work in Japan for twenty-seven years and taught at Shikoku Gakuin University, Meiji Gakuin University, and Sophia University, where he also served a three-year term as editor of *Monumenta Nipponica*. He completed his postgraduate studies in the sociology of religion and East Asian traditions at McMaster University (PhD 1985). He is the author, editor, and coeditor of a number of works, including *Religion and Society in Modern Japan*, coedited with Shimazono Susumu and Paul Swanson (1993); *Christianity Made in Japan* (1998); *Religion and Social Crisis in Japan*, coedited with Robert Kisala (2001); *Critical Readings on Christianity in Japan* (2015); and *Disasters and Social Crisis in Contemporary Japan*, coedited with Kōichi Nakano (2016). In recent years his research has focused on neo-nationalism, which is addressed in his forthcoming book, *Yasukuni Fundamentalism: Japanese Religions and the Politics of Restoration* (2021).

Ōmi Toshihiro is Associate Professor in the Department of Literature, Musashino University, Japan, and the author of *Kindai bukkyō no naka no Shinshū* (2014), *Butsuzō to Nihonjin* (2018), and *Kagakuka suru bukkyō* (2020).

Halle O'Neal is Reader in Japanese Buddhist art and Co-Director of Edinburgh Buddhist Studies at the University of Edinburgh. Previously she held a postdoctoral fellowship at the Edwin O. Reischauer Institute of Japanese Studies, Harvard University, and a Mellon Assistant Professorship at Vanderbilt University. O'Neal's recent book, *Word Embodied: The Jeweled Pagoda Mandalas in Japanese Buddhist Art*, was published in 2018 and explored the intersections of word and image, relics, and reliquaries, as well as the performativity and objecthood of Buddhist texts. Her current monograph project, "Writing against Death: Buddhist Palimpsests of Medieval Japan," examines the materiality of death and mourning and the visualization of memory and embodiment in Japanese letter sutras using the lens of reuse and recycling. She has published articles in journals such as *Art Bulletin*, *Artibus Asiae*, and *Journal of Oriental Studies*. She is the guest editor of a forthcoming special issue on reuse and recycling in Japanese material culture with *Ars Orientalis*. She sits on the editorial boards of *Art Bulletin* and *Art in Translation* and is Associate in Research at the Reischauer Institute of Japanese Studies. O'Neal is the recipient of the American Council of Learned Societies (ACLS) Robert H. N. Ho Family Foundation Research Fellowship in Buddhist Studies for 2020–1 and a Leverhulme Trust Research Fellowship for 2021–2.

Ōuchi Fumi is a professor of musicology at Miyagi Gakuin Women's University (Sendai), where she directs the Music Liaison Center. She specializes in musicology and Japanese religions. She holds a BA in Music from Miyagigakuin Women's University, a master's degree in Musicology from Kunitachi College of Music, and a PhD in Religious Studies from SOAS, University of London. Her book *Bukkyō no koe no waza: Satori no shintaisei* (2016) received the 2017 Tanabe Hisao Prize. She is now working on her new project on the relations between music (musical instruments), maritime divinity, and political authority. She published among others: "Musical Toys Offered to Gods at Miho Shrine: Instruments for Renewing Ritual Communication," *Japanese Journal of Religious Studies*, 45 (2); "Shinshin wo hiraku koe: Bukkyō no koewaza," *Shinshin hen'yō kenkyū*, 8; "Musical Instruments for the Sea-God Ebisu: The Mythological System of Miho Shrine and Its Performative Power," in F. Rambelli (ed.), *The Sea and the Sacred in Japan: Aspects of Maritime Religion* (Bloomsbury, 2018); "Shōmyō ni miru koe no chikara," *Bungaku/Gogaku*, 199; "Buddhist Liturgical Chanting in Japan: Vocalisation and the Practice of Attaining Buddhahood," in A. Michaels et al. (eds.), *Grammars and Morphologies of Ritual Practices in Asia* (2010); and "The Lotus Repentance Liturgy of Shugendō: Identification from Vocal Arts," *Cahiers d'Extrême-Asie*, 18.

Tatsuma Padoan (PhD, Venice) is Lecturer in East Asian Religions (Assistant Professor) at University College Cork, and a research associate at SOAS, University of London. As an anthropologist and a semiotician, he has worked on ritual in Japan—including pilgrimage, asceticism, ritual apprenticeship, religious materiality, and spirit possession—as well as on the study of design practices and the politics of urban space. His monograph *Towards a Semiotics of Pilgrimage: Ritual Space, Memory and Narration in Japan and Elsewhere* is forthcoming.

Richard K. Payne (PhD in the History and Phenomenology of Religion, Graduate Theological Union, Berkeley, 1985) is the Yehan Numata Professor of Japanese Buddhist Studies, Institute of Buddhist Studies, Berkeley, and member of the Graduate Theological Union's Core Doctoral Faculty. He is the author of *Language in the Buddhist Tantra of Japan: Indic Roots of Mantra* (Bloomsbury, 2018), and editor or coeditor of several works: *Tantric Buddhism in East Asia* (2005), *Esoteric Buddhism and the Tantras in East Asia* (the Japan section; 2011), *Homa Variations: The Study of Ritual Change across the Longue Durée* (2016), *Pure Land Buddhism in China: A Doctrinal History* (2 vols., 2017), *Scripture:Canon::Text:Context: Essays in Honor of Lewis Lancaster* (2015), and several other works. In addition, his work with online publications includes: Editor-in-Chief of Oxford Bibliographies/Buddhism, and Coeditor-in-Chief of Oxford Research

Encyclopedia of Religion/Buddhism. He chairs the Editorial Committees of Pure Land Buddhist Studies series, University of Hawai'i Press; Contemporary Issues in Buddhist Studies Series, Institute of Buddhist Studies; and is Senior Editor for *Pacific World: Journal of the Institute of Buddhist Studies*. His continuing research is on *homa*, specifically, and tantric Buddhist ritual more generally.

Or Porath is a postdoctoral researcher and instructor in the Department of East Asian Languages and Civilizations at the University of Chicago. Porath is a scholar of Buddhist studies with broad interests in East Asian religions, the history of gender and sexuality, and monasticism. He studies the religions of Japan, specifically the influential school of Tendai Buddhism, its doctrines and practices, and the intersection between Buddhist worldviews and issues of gender and sexuality. His current book project, *The Dharma of Sex: Initiation and Deification in Buddhist Consecration Rituals*, examines the "consecration of acolytes" (*chigo kanjō*), a sexual initiation that was doctrinally sanctioned in orthodox Buddhist teachings. In this work, Porath investigates how male-male sexual acts were sanctified and given official legitimation in Tendai doctrinal concepts, and the manner in which they shed light on the Buddhist assimilation of local forms of worship including Shinto. He is the author of "The Cosmology of Male-Male Love in Medieval Japan: *Nyakudō no Kanjinchō* and the Way of Youths," *Journal of Religion in Japan*, 4 (2); and "Nasty Boys or Obedient Children? Childhood and Relative Autonomy in Medieval Japanese Pedagogical Texts," in Sabine Frühstück and Anne Walthall (eds.), *Child's Play: Multi-sensory Histories of Children and Childhood in Japan* (2017). Porath is currently coediting with Fabio Rambelli a volume about consecration rituals (*kanjō*) in East Asia.

Fabio Rambelli (PhD in East Asian Studies, University of Venice and Oriental Institute of Naples, 1992) is a professor of Japanese religions and cultural history and International Shinto Foundation endowed chair in Shinto Studies at the University of California, Santa Barbara. He is the author of *Vegetal Buddhas* (2001), *Buddhist Materiality* (2007), *Buddhism and Iconoclasm in East Asia: A History* (with Eric Reinders; Bloomsbury, 2012), *A Buddhist Theory of Semiotics* (Bloomsbury, 2013), *Zen Anarchism* (2013), and editor or coeditor of *Buddhas and Kami in Japan* (with Mark Teeuwen; 2003), *The Sea and the Sacred in Japan: Aspects of Maritime Religion* (Bloomsbury, 2018), *Spirits and Animism in Contemporary Japan: The Invisible Empire* (Bloomsbury, 2019), and *Defining Shugendō: Critical Studies on Japanese Mountain Religion* (with Andrea Castiglioni and Carina Roth; Bloomsbury, 2020). He works at the intersection of philosophical discourses, material practices, and everyday life in premodern Japan. He is currently writing a monograph on the imagination of India in premodern Japan and another on the cultural history of the *shō*, an ancient instrument still used in the classical music and dance repertory (Gagaku and Bugaku) at the Imperial Court of Japan. He also plays music: the *shō*, the saxophone, and the flute.

Ian Reader is Professor Emeritus at the University of Manchester, where he was previously Professor of Japanese Studies. He has also held academic positions in Scotland, Hawai'i, Denmark, and Japan. His recent books include *Dynamism and the Ageing of a Japanese "New" Religion* (with Erica Baffelli; Bloomsbury, 2019), *Health-Related Votive Tablets from Japan: Ema for Healing and Well-Being* (with Peter de Smet; 2017), *Pilgrimage: A Very Short Introduction* (2015), and *Pilgrimage in the Marketplace* (2014). His latest book,

Pilgrims until We Die: Unending Pilgrimage in Shikoku, coauthored with John Shultz, is being published in 2021.

Aike P. Rots is Associate Professor of Asian Studies at the University of Oslo. He holds a PhD from the University of Oslo, an MA degree from SOAS, and BA degrees from Leiden University. He is the author of the monograph *Shinto, Nature and Ideology in Contemporary Japan: Making Sacred Forests* (Bloomsbury, 2017) and the coeditor of *Sacred Heritage in Japan* (2020) and *Formations of the Secular in Japan* (special issue of *Japan Review*, 2017), both with Mark Teeuwen. Other recent publications include: McLaughlin, Rots, Thomas, and Watanabe (2020), "Why Scholars of Religion Must Investigate the Corporate Form," *Journal of the American Academy of Religion, Religion,* 88 (3); Rots (2019), "World Heritage, Secularisation, and the New 'Public Sacred' in East Asia," *Journal of Religion in Japan,* 8 (1–3); and Rots (2019), "'This Is Not a Powerspot': Heritage Tourism, Sacred Space, and Conflicts of Authority at Sēfa Utaki," *Asian Ethnology* 78 (1). In addition, he has written articles and book chapters on reforestation projects, modern Shinto, secularization and sacralization theory, religion in Vietnam, and Japanese Christianity. He is currently leader of the ERC-funded project *Whales of Power: Aquatic Mammals, Devotional Practices, and Environmental Change in Maritime East Asia* (Starting Grant, 2019–23), a comparative study of changing human-nature relations and ritual practices in the Asia-Pacific region.

James Mark Shields is Professor of Comparative Humanities and Asian Thought and was Inaugural Director of the Humanities Center at Bucknell University (Lewisburg, PA). Educated at McGill University (Canada), the University of Cambridge (UK), and Kyoto University (Japan), he conducts research on modern Buddhist thought, Japanese philosophy, comparative ethics, and philosophy of religion. He is the author of *Critical Buddhism: Engaging with Modern Japanese Buddhist Thought* (2011), *Against Harmony: Progressive and Radical Buddhism in Modern Japan* (2017), and coeditor of *Teaching Buddhism in the West: From the Wheel to the Web* (2003), *Buddhist Responses to Globalization* (2014), and *The Oxford Handbook of Buddhist Ethics* (2018).

Emily B. Simpson is a lecturer in the Department of Religion at Dartmouth College. In 2019, she completed her PhD in East Asian Languages and Cultural Studies at the University of California, Santa Barbara. Her main research areas include Shinto and Buddhist combinatory systems, modes of divinization, vernacular texts such as *engi*, and gender and notions of womanhood in medieval Japan. She is the author of "Sacred Mother Bodhisattva, Buddha and Cakravartin: Recasting Empress Jingū as a Buddhist Figure in the *Hachiman gudōkun,*" *Journal of Religion in Japan,* 2017; and "An Empress at Sea: Sea Deities and Divine Union in the Legend of Empress Jingū," in Fabio Rambelli (ed.), *The Sea and the Sacred in Japan: Aspects of Maritime Religiosity* (Bloomsbury, 2018). Her book project *Crafting a Goddess: Divinization and Womanhood in Late Medieval and Early Modern Narratives of Empress Jingū* expands on her doctoral research into Empress Jingū, the Hachiman cult, and early modern women's cults centered on childbirth and fertility.

Paride Stortini is a PhD candidate in the History of Religions at the University of Chicago, Divinity School. He has a BA in East Asian studies from the University of Venice and an MA in religious studies from the University of Padua. His fields of research include modern intellectual history of Japanese Buddhism, transnational Buddhist modernisms, Orientalism in the study of Asian religions, reception of Buddhism in Europe, Buddhist visual and material culture, and heritage studies. He is particularly interested in how religious narratives, practices, and imagery of Buddhism are used in a transnational context to address challenges of modernity and of cultural encounter. His doctoral project investigates ideas and images on ancient India redeployed by late-nineteenth- and early-twentieth-century Japanese Buddhist priests, intellectuals, and artists when they redefined their identity and proposed different and often contrasting visions of modernity. A preliminary result of this research was published in the volume *Buddhism in the Global Eye* (Bloomsbury, 2020). In an additional project, he analyzes the concept of the Silk Road in post-Second World War Japanese religious and literary imaginaire, visual culture, and heritage preservation, and he demonstrates that this concept provides an intersection of religious and moral discourses with ideas of cosmopolitanism, pacifism and international collaboration. Part of this research appeared in the journal *Japanese Religions*, 43. Finally, in another article under publication in the *Journal of Religion in Japan*, he investigates deployments of Japanese Buddhism in contemporary political and social debate in Italy, with specific reference to Zen in Traditionalist culture and Soka Gakkai in the media.

Suzuki Masataka is a professor emeritus at Keiō University, Tokyo, and president of the Association for the Study of Japanese Mountain Religion. An anthropologist of religion, he specializes in Shugendō history and Japanese ethnology; he has carried out field work in Japan, Southwest China, South India, and Sri Lanka. His many books include *Kumano and Kagura: Seichi no kongenteki chikara wo motomete* (Kumano and Kagura: Exploring the Fundamental Power of Sacred Places; 2018), *Sangaku shinkō: Nihon bunka no kontei wo saguru* (Mountain worship: exploring the roots of Japanese culture; 2015), *Saishi to kūkan no kosumorojī: Tsushima to Okinawa* (The Cosmology of Ritual and Space: An Anthropological Study of Tsushima and Okinawa Islands in Japan; 2004), *Nyonin kinsei* (The Exclusion of Women from Sacred Spaces; 2002), *Kami to hotoke no minzoku* (The Folklore of Kami and Buddhas; 2001), and *Yama to kami to hito: Sangaku shinkō to Shugendō no sekai* (Mountains, Gods, and Humans: The World of Mountain Worship and Shugendō; 1991).

Takahashi Norihito is a professor at the Faculty of Sociology, Toyo University, Tokyo, Japan. He obtained a PhD from Hitotsubashi University, Tokyo, Japan. He served as a visiting academic from April 2018 to March 2019 at the Faculty of Humanities, the University of Manchester, UK. His research field is the sociology of religion. He is especially interested in overseas missionary works of Japanese religious groups and the development of religious groups of migrants in Japan. His current research focuses on religious groups of migrants and the social support offered by the Catholic Church and other faith-based organizations (FBOs) for immigrants facing difficulty, and the overseas missions of Japanese Buddhists and other new religions. He has authored and edited various publications, including *Gendai Nihon no Shūkyō to tabunka kyōsei* (Religion and Multicultural Coexistence in Contemporary Japan; 2018) and *Shūkyō to shakai no frontia* (The Frontiers of Religion and Society in Contemporary Japan; 2012).

Katja Triplett was Professor of the Study of East Asian Religions at Göttingen from 2012 to 2016 and is currently based at the Humanities Centre for Advanced Studies in the Humanities and Social Sciences "Multiple Secularities – Beyond the West, beyond Modernities" at Leipzig University. Her doctorate in the study of religions from Marburg

University, where she also studied Japanese linguistics and social and cultural anthropology, was published as *Menschenopfer und Selbstopfer in den japanischen Legenden* (Human Sacrifice and Self-sacrifice in the Japanese Legends, 2004) with a focus on the Buddhist legend "Matsura Sayohime." Katja Triplett held a postdoctoral research fellowship at the Centre for the Study of Japanese Religions, School of Oriental and African Studies (SOAS), University of London in 2004–5. From 2007 to 2012 she was Associate Professor at the Department of the Study of Religions and curator of the Museum of Religions (Religionskundliche Sammlung) at Marburg University. Her main fields of interest are East Asian Buddhism, religion and medicine, and visual and material culture. She has published widely on Japanese religions. Among her recent publications are *Buddhism and Medicine in Japan: A Topical Survey (500–1600 CE) of a Complex Relationship* (2019) and "Pediatric Care and Buddhism in Premodern Japan: A Case of Applied 'Demonology'?," *Asian Medicine*, 14 (2).

Kaitlyn Ugoretz is a PhD Candidate in East Asian Languages and Cultural Studies at the University of California, Santa Barbara. She holds BA and MA degrees in East Asian Languages and Civilizations from the University of Pennsylvania. Supported by the Social Science Research Council and Japan Foundation, her dissertation project, "World-Wide Shinto," explores the globalization of Shinto through a multi-sited ethnographic study of online communities of transnational Shinto practitioners. Ugoretz's research interests include media, technology, materiality, and digital humanities. Her work has appeared on public platforms such as the anime and religion blog *Beneath the Tangles* and the educational YouTube channel *Religion For Breakfast* and *Eat Pray Anime*.

Yamanaka Hiroshi is an emeritus professor in religious studies at the University of Tsukuba (Japan), where he completed his PhD in sociology of religion. He is former president of the Japanese Association for Religious Studies. He is also currently a visiting professor at Kokugakuin University, Tokyo. His original academic concern was the sociological analysis of a religious organization in modern Britain, but his interests gradually got wider and changed. Recently, he is studying the transformation of religion in modern society, focusing on consumption and popular culture. His publications include: *Shūkyō to tsūrizumu* (2012); "Shōhi shakai ni okeru gendai shūkyō no hen'yō," *Shūkyō kenkyū*, 389; *Gendai shūkyō to supirichuaru māketto* (2020); "The Utopian 'Power to live': The Significance of the Miyazaki Phenomenon," in Mark W. MacWilliams (ed.), *Japanese Visual Culture: Exploration in the World of Manga and Anime* (2008).

Yoshinaga Shin'ichi is a former professor of Maizuru National College of Technology and now a visiting research fellow at the Research Center for World Buddhist Cultures, Ryukoku University. He has been Editor of *Japanese Religions* (NCC Center for the Study of Japanese Religions) since 2014. He studied the religious philosophy of William James before turning to the history of modern Buddhism, new religions, and esoteric movements in Japan. He edited the fifteen volumes of the reprint series of Japanese mind cures, titled *Nihonjin no shin, shin, rei: Kindai minkan seishin ryōhō sōsho* (Japanese Body, Mind and Spirit: An Anthology of Modern Folk Spiritual/Psychical Therapies; 2004). He has also coedited *Religion and Psychotherapy in Modern Japan* (2014), for which he contributed the chapter "The Birth of Japanese Mind Cure Methods"; and *Kingendai Nihon no minkan seishin ryōhō* (Modern and Contemporary Spiritual/Psychical Therapies: Aspects of Occult Energy; 2019). His articles on modern Buddhism include: "After Olcott

Left: Theosophy and 'New Buddhists' at the Turn of the Century," *The Eastern Buddhist*, 43 (1/2); "Three Boys on a Great Vehicle: 'Mahayana Buddhism' and a Trans-National Network," *Contemporary Buddhism*, 14; "Suzuki Daisetsu and Swedenborg: A Historical Background," in *Modern Buddhism in Japan* (Nanzan Institute for Religion and Culture, 2014); and "The first Buddhist mission to the West: Charles Pfoundes and the London Buddhist mission of 1889 – 1892" (with Brian Bocking and Laurence Cox, *Diskus*, 16 (3).

INDEX

anime 139–40
animism 66, 68, 140, 248
animals 155–6
Aum Shinrikyō 29, 35, 36, 124–5, 245

Brazil, Japanese religion in, 103, 104. *See also* diaspora and Japanese religions
Buddhism 13, 15, 43–9, 50–4, 58–9, 61–3, 66–7, 87–88, 94–5, 102, 103, 105–6, 107–9, 118–19, 131, 149, 151–7, 182, 186–7, 189–91, 201–7, 209–12, 247, 257–8, 260, 261
Danka system 44, 118, 119–20
Buddhism in the West, 104
Buddhist Churches of America, 102–3, 105. *See also* diaspora and Japanese religions
Buddhist studies 2

chaplaincy, 12–18, 27, 28, 31, 32, 33. *See also* spiritual care
Christianity, 15, 17, 59, 60, 118, 120, 123, 124, 159–61, 187–8, 252
Kirishitan 118–19, 120
colonialism, 3, 55–60, 101, 135
Confucianism and Neo-Confucianism, 152, 213
crisis 10–11, 51, 54, 65, 66, 68, 71, 73 125, 135, 243
cultural heritage, 19–25, 79–80, 251–5. *See also* folklore and folk religion; pilgrimage
Tourism and UNESCO 19, 21, 79–80
and cultural properties (*bunkazai*) 21–2, 79

diaspora and Japanese religions 102, 107–9. *See also* Brazil, Japanese religion in; Hawai'i, Japanese religions in
disasters and religion, 16, 27–33, 71, 75, 80, 138, 143, 161

economy, 35–42, 43–9, 51–4, 91–92
environmentalism 65–72, 73–6, 248
Esoteric Buddhism (*mikkyō*) 201–3, 210–11, 212. *See also* Shugendō

food 85–92, 114, 115–16, 217
folklore and folk religion 29, 77–84, 154, 196, 209, 215, 254, 255. *See also* cultural heritage and religion
foreign residents 157–9, 163

gender 93–8, 257, 259–60. *See also* sexuality; women and religion
Genze riyaku. See worldly benefits
Gion festival 19, 20, 21, 29, 78
globalization 99–106, 107–10, 145–7

Hawai'i, Japanese religions in 102, 107–8. *See also* diaspora and Japanese religions
healing 36, 37, 38, 39, 40

Islam 111–16, 165–6
and Buddhism 111–12
Halāl, 114, 115, 116
Japanese Muslims 111, 115, 116, 161–2, 165–6

Jinja honchō (Association of Shinto Shrines) 4, 67, 70, 122, 70, 71, 72, 122, 145, 214, 248. *See also* Shinto
Jōdo Shinshū (True Pure Land Sect) 45–6, 61, 186

Kōbō Daishi 175, 179, 182
Kōfuku no kagaku 4, 138, 139, 141, 167, 178, 182

law and legal system 13–15, 32, 117–28. *See also Shūkyō hōjin*; politics and religion
"unity of rites and government" 118, 119, 122, 128

materiality 43–4, 46, 61–3, 129–35, 223
and Buddhist art 130, 131, 132
and Buddhist artifacts 129, 130, 131, 132, 133, 134, 226
Matsuri (religious festivals) 217–19, 252–3, 255, 264

media and technology 39–40, 133, 137–44, 142, 145–8,, 149–50, 253–5
medicine and religion, 151–6, 265
minorities 157–63, 165–6
Mindar 149–50, 130
music 209–15. *See also* sound studies

nature 29–30, 65, 71–2, 74–5
new age 36, 37, 38, 39, 243–4
new religions 27, 30, 36, 48, 59–60, 70–1, 73–5, 59–60, 94, 95, 103, 105, 120–2, 137–8, 156, 167–73, 176–9, 187–8, 229–39, 263
Nichiren Buddhism 29, 186

occultism 229–39, 243–4
Okinawa and Ryukyu islands 71, 90, 252
Ōmoto 121, 172, 187, 212, 229, 231, 236–7, 238
Onmyōdō 100, 197–8, 199

performing arts 77–84, 209–15, 217–19
pilgrimage 46, 140, 175–83, 252, 253–4
politics 101, 185–8, 189–92, 247–8. *See also* law and legal system
power spots 4, 39, 247

ritual 86, 90–92, 226–7

sacred sites. *See* pilgrimage
space 221–8. *See also* pilgrimage
secularization 21, 191
sexuality 201–7. *See also* gender, women
Shinto 55, 56, 57, 58, 61, 67–70, 85–87, 88–89, 94, 100, 101–2, 120–1, 122, 145–7, 151, 188, 193–5, 198, 205–6, 209, 212–13, 214, 217–19, 230, 236–7, 247, 252–3, 256, 263–4. *See also* Jinja Honchō
State Shinto 55, 57, 58, 120–1
Yasukuni Shrine 55, 121, 122, 124, 125–6
Shugendō 195–7, 198–9, 209, 223–7, 247, 267–9
Shūkyō hōjin (religious juridical persons) 44–5, 51. *See also* law and legal system
sound studies 209–15, 217–19. *See also* music
Soka Gakkai 48, 58, 70, 103, 157
spiritual care 12–18, 28, 30, 31, 35, 39, 75, 154, 156, 244–5
spiritual healing 40, 156, 229–39
spiritualism 229–39
  theosophy 230, 231, 233, 238, 242
spirituality 241–9
  and economy 35–42
  and ideology 36
  and new age 1, 15, 16, 36, 37, 39, 48, 108, 229, 231, 242, 243–4, 248
  and technology 39–40
Supirichuariti. *See* spirituality

Tenrikyō 27, 60, 137, 167, 168, 170, 172, 177–8, 187–8, 212
tourism 46–7, 251–6. *See also* cultural heritage; pilgrimage

women and religion 94–5, 257–65, 267–9. *See also* gender; sexuality
worldly benefits (*genze riyaku*) 2, 9, 47, 74, 169–70, 210, 241

Zen Buddhism 27, 46, 66–8, 103